T0338314

The Samuel Gompers Papers

THE
Samuel Gompers
PAPERS

VOLUME
4
A National Labor Movement
Takes Shape, 1895–98

Editors
Stuart B. Kaufman
Peter J. Albert
Grace Palladino

Assistant Editor
Edwin Gabler

Contributing Editors
Ileen A. DeVault
Elizabeth A. Fones-Wolf

UNIVERSITY OF ILLINOIS PRESS
Urbana and Chicago

This book is printed on acid-free paper.

Library of Congress Cataloging-in-Publication Data
(Revised for vol. 4)

The Samuel Gompers papers.

  Includes bibliographies and indexes.
  Contents: v. 1. The making of a union leader,
1850-86 — v. 2. The early years of the American Federation
of Labor, 1887-90. — v. 3. Unrest and depression, 1891-94 —
v. 4. A national labor movement takes shape, 1895-98.
  1. Trade-unions—United States—History—Sources.
2. Labor and laboring classes—United States—History—
Sources. 3. Gompers, Samuel, 1850-1924—Archives.
I. Gompers, Samuel, 1850-1924. II. Kaufman, Stuart Bruce.
HD6508.S218 1986   331.88′32′092   84-2469
ISBN 0-252-01138-4 (alk. paper : set)

CONTENTS

INTRODUCTION

"The near future, promises, no doubt, a revival in the organization of the workingmen of our country," Samuel Gompers predicted early in 1896. The AFL had successfully weathered the storm of economic depression, and now, with his reelection as president, Gompers stood ready to lead it, as he expressed it, toward the unification of "all classes of wage-workers under one head, through their several organizations . . . [so] that class, race, creed, political and trade prejudices may be abolished [and] that support, moral and financial, may be given to each other."[1]

Despite a small budget, which led the Federation to rely for the most part on the efforts of volunteer—as opposed to paid—organizers, the AFL continued to organize new unions and attract the affiliation of independent bodies in the period between 1895 and 1898, the years spanned by this volume. It appointed special organizers for such industries as mining and textiles and underwrote short-term campaigns to organize southern and western workers. Overall, it chartered thirty-six national and international unions, sixty-one central labor unions, and well over seven hundred local and federal labor unions during these four years,[2] an accomplishment that contrasted starkly with the continued decline of the KOL.

This fourth volume of the Samuel Gompers Papers begins just after the close of the AFL's 1894 Denver convention. There, after serving eight consecutive terms as president, Gompers was defeated for reelection by John McBride, and the Federation voted to move its headquarters from New York City to the more centrally located Indianapolis. During the coming months—his "sabbatical year"—when Gompers was no longer serving as an officer of the Federation, he remained active in the movement. He played an important role in the January convention of the New York State Workingmen's Assembly and, as second vice-president, in the affairs of his own union, the CMIU. His organizing trip on behalf of the United Garment Workers of America in the late spring and early summer gave him his first direct contact with the South and its deep racial divisions. He traveled some 5,000 miles and, despite a severe attack of gastritis, delivered addresses—extemporaneously, as was almost invariably his custom—at between sixty and seventy local meetings.[3]

In August and September Gompers went to Europe as an AFL delegate to the British Trades Union Congress in Cardiff and used the opportunity to confer with European labor leaders and to address meetings in Great Britain, Ireland, France, Holland, and Germany. This experience provided him with opportunities to develop his thinking on the nature and direction of the British and continental labor movements and strengthened his conviction that, for the most part, British trade unionists shared his opposition to partisan political action by labor organizations. During this trip Gompers also renewed family ties, visiting his birthplace in London and becoming acquainted with his European relatives.[4]

Following his reelection as AFL president in December 1895, Gompers left his family in New York City and moved to Indianapolis. His year there was a difficult one for him. In his official capacity, he felt cut off from the movement after the day-to-day interaction with other prominent trade unionists that he had been used to in New York. "It is very hard on us here," he wrote Henry White; "seldom seeing any one and still less often, having an opportunity for consultation."[5] These months were also a time of severe personal trial. A second and more serious bout of gastritis prostrated him for nearly a month and was, he wrote, nearly fatal.[6] He was able to visit his family in New York only twice during the course of the year, and the necessity of maintaining two households placed him in a financially difficult position, which was aggravated by his unwise decision to give an untrustworthy colleague access to his bank account. It was not until 1897, when the AFL moved its headquarters back east to Washington, D.C., that Gompers was able to resume family life and enjoy a measure of financial stability. An additional source of satisfaction, after a difficult year with AFL secretary August McCraith, was his excellent working relationship with McCraith's successor, Frank Morrison.[7]

As president of the AFL, Gompers worked at a backbreaking pace, devoting much of his time to the mundane but essential tasks that devolved upon the principal officer of the Federation. "I am at the office early in the morning," he wrote a friend, "and, with the exception of times for meals, I am usually . . . here until midnight."[8] He carried on a voluminous correspondence with local labor leaders, legislators, employers, social reformers, and European trade unionists, edited the *American Federationist* (which had an average monthly run of 10,000 or more copies during these years), mediated jurisdictional and factional conflicts, investigated and attempted to resolve strikes and boycotts, undertook frequent organizing and speaking trips, and expanded his network of trade unionists who would serve as organizers, lobbyists, or sources of information. As these multifaceted activities were the principal focus of Gompers' work, the documents that reflect them are the core of this volume.

Of all his activities as AFL president, Gompers thought his correspondence to be one of the most important, and it increasingly restricted the amount of time he could spend traveling, lecturing, and organizing. Dictated in what he termed his plain, blunt style, his letters, he believed, established "an Esprit de Corps . . . which cannot obtain in any other way." He counselled John Chorley of the Blacksmiths that "without an officer who can devote his entire time to the building up [of] the correspondence connected with the International Union, success and great growth is absolutely impossible. The few dollars which an organization pays an officer is [a] bagatelle when compared to the great good it does for the members in the shape of increased wages, less hours of labor, less burdensome conditions, [and] more manhood and independence instilled in the hearts and minds of workers."[9]

Throughout these years, Gompers continued his efforts to expand the AFL's influence among workers in the South and the West, two areas that had long posed significant organizational problems for the Federation. A lack of funds limited the dimensions of both campaigns, but the AFL nevertheless pledged $500 on behalf of southern workers in 1895 and sent two organizers to the region late in 1896. Particularly in relationship to the South, Gompers was forced to come to grips with widespread race prejudice. The International Association of Machinists, for example, which dropped the "color line" from its constitution in order to join the AFL in 1895, still retained it in its ritual; likewise, southern locals of the International Molders' Union refused to follow the national leadership's advice and admit black members. Although Gompers continued in his writings and speeches to emphasize the practical benefits of organizing all workers, he came to accept segregated unions as a local option.

Organizing in the West posed different, if equally difficult, problems. AFL affiliates had long agreed that organizing western workers must be given serious attention, but, as with the South, the Federation's meager resources limited its ability to wage an effective campaign in this vast, sparsely populated, and unevenly developed region. Although the AFL endorsed its western members' call for the government's free coinage of silver at a ratio of 16 to 1 and contributed funds for the defense of Utah's eight-hour law, western critics during the national political campaign of 1896 asserted that Gompers did not effectively support silver candidates or, worse, that he was a "gold-bug." The Federation's failure to appoint a special organizer for the West, after it voted to do so at its 1896 convention, was a source of further tension.[10]

Western dissatisfaction with the AFL crystallized in the hard-rock mining regions after the Western Federation of Miners (WFM) lost a hard-fought strike at Leadville, Colorado, in 1896-97. Edward Boyce, president of the WFM, criticized the AFL for what he considered its failure to support the strike—a charge Gompers vehemently denied. Boyce subsequently organized the Western Labor Union in 1898, an alternative, western-based federation that looked more favorably than the AFL on industrial unionism and independent labor party politics, thereby channeling long-term regional tensions into a full-blown secessionist movement.

Ideological differences within the labor movement compounded regional divisions. Supporters of the SLP, for example, expressed increasing dissatisfaction with the AFL's trade union program, particularly after the Federation's 1894 convention rejected the collectivist Plank Ten and resolved to avoid partisan political action—a decision reaffirmed by the AFL's 1895 meeting. Late in 1895 followers of Daniel DeLeon, a vocal critic of "pure and simpledom," organized the Socialist Trade and Labor Alliance (STLA) with a program advocating political action and industrial unionism. In practice, however, the STLA generally did not concentrate on unorganized workers in manufacturing or extractive industries but instead recruited its members along traditional craft and ethnic lines that directly competed with existing organizations—as exemplified by its attempt in 1897 to lure the National Union of Textile Workers and the Boot and Shoe Workers' International Union away from the AFL.[11] Gompers answered DeLeon's criticisms in a variety of forums, including correspondence, the labor press, workers' mass meetings, and conventions of both national unions and the Federation itself.

Gompers also confronted a challenge during these years from Eugene Debs. He ridiculed Debs's attempt, in June 1897, to launch the Social Democracy of America—a plan to usher in the socialist commonwealth by founding a utopian colony in the West and supporting socialist political campaigns. Debs, in turn, declared trade union tactics in general (and strikes in particular) to be futile, and he endorsed Edward Boyce's denunciation of the AFL after the loss of the Leadville strike. During the United Mine Workers' strike of 1897, when Debs joined KOL Grand Master Workman James Sovereign in the West Virginia coalfields, he publicly impugned Gompers' and the AFL's commitment to the strikers, and the socialist press subsequently repeated his charges. Finally, together with Boyce, Debs called for a reorganization of the labor movement along regional lines.[12]

Gompers forcefully articulated his own views in the face of such critics. He reiterated the basic tenets of trade unionism in the *American Federationist,* and used that journal as well to publish domestic and foreign labor news, develop a trade union analysis of political issues and current events, air criticism and complaints, and provide a forum for prominent labor leaders and reformers sympathetic to working people. He informed public opinion on the question of organized labor by participating in debates, delivering speeches, and corresponding with students, clergymen, and employers on the issues of the day. He was particularly visible in public discussions of American foreign policy during the course of the Spanish-American War, declaring his strong support for the "Cuba libre" movement and his belief that the United States should use its power for humanitarian, rather than imperialistic, ends. In the same vein, he contributed articles to the popular press discussing labor's opposition to large standing armies and the state's abuse of its judicial and police powers. The movement of the Federation's headquarters to Washington, D.C., afforded him an opportunity to expand the AFL's lobbying efforts and provided him with greater access to the president, members of Congress and congressional committees, and executive departments of the national government.

Covering a significant four-year period in the history of the United States—from the depths of economic depression to the Spanish-American War—this volume of the Samuel Gompers Papers explores the AFL's continued growth as an institution, illuminates the fierce struggle for power that accompanied that growth, and documents Samuel Gompers' role as leader of the Federation. By mid-1898, when the country emerged from its war with Spain as a major power on the world stage, the AFL was more broadly based, both industrially and geographically, than it had been at any previous time in its history. Despite its limited resources, it had made considerable strides toward creating a truly national labor organization.

A National Labor Movement Takes Shape maintains the editorial style outlined in our previous volumes.[13] We would like to remind the reader that we annotate individuals, organizations, events, and the like at their first mention in the text. If this first mention and annotation occurred in an earlier volume, an entry in the index of this one will direct the reader to it. We do not annotate again here except in two cases: first, the important labor figures or unions included in the glossary, and, second, the delegates to AFL conventions, who are annotated as to the union they represented.

ACKNOWLEDGMENTS

The Samuel Gompers Papers project could not continue its work without the ongoing assistance of many institutions and individuals. It is with pleasure and a deep sense of gratitude that we acknowledge the following, who contributed to the publication of the project's fourth volume.

We remain indebted to the labor movement for its continuing support. In an ongoing partnership with the University of Maryland and federal agencies, the AFL-CIO Executive Council and many national and international unions have granted us access to their records from the Gompers era and given us permission to copy and publish pertinent material, made generous donations to the project, and followed the progress of our work with keen interest. In addition to the grants from the Council, we are pleased to acknowledge contributions from the Joseph Anthony Beirne Memorial Foundation of the Communications Workers of America, the George Meany Memorial Archives, and the following unions: the Associated Actors and Artistes of America, the Bakery, Confectionery and Tobacco Workers' International Union, the International Brotherhood of Boilermakers, Iron Ship Builders, Blacksmiths, Forgers, and Helpers, the International Union of Bricklayers and Allied Craftsmen, the United Brotherhood of Carpenters and Joiners of America, the Amalgamated Clothing and Textile Workers' Union, the International Brotherhood of Electrical Workers, the International Union of Electronic, Electrical, Salaried, Machine, and Furniture Workers, the International Union of Operating Engineers, the Association of Flight Attendants, the United Food and Commercial Workers' International Union, the United Garment Workers of America, the International Ladies' Garment Workers' Union, the Glass, Molders', Pottery, Plastics, and Allied Workers' International Union, the American Flint Glass Workers' Union, the American Federation of Government Employees, the Laborers' International Union of North America, the National Association of Letter Carriers, the International Longshoremen's Association, the International Association of Machinists and Aerospace Workers, the Mechanics' Educational Society of America, the United Mine Workers of America, the Newspaper Guild, the Office and Professional Employees' International Union, the International Brotherhood of Painters and Allied Trades of the United States and Canada, the United Paperworkers' International Union, the United Association of Journeymen and Apprentices of the Plumbing and Pipe Fitting Industry of the United States and Canada, the American Postal Workers' Union, the International Federation of Professional and Technical Engineers, the Brotherhood of Railway Carmen of the United States and Canada, the Retail, Wholesale, and Department Store Union, the Seafarers' International Union of North America, the Service Employees' International Union, the International Alliance of Theatrical Stage Employes and Moving Picture Machine Operators of the United States and Canada, the American Federation of State, County, and Municipal Employees, the United Steelworkers of America, the International Brotherhood of Teamsters, Chauffeurs, Warehousemen, and Helpers of America, and the Amalgamated Transit Union.

In addition, we wish to acknowledge the vital and continuing assistance of two federal agencies, the National Historical Publications and Records Commission (NHPRC) and the National Endowment for the Humanities (NEH). The NHPRC and the NEH have provided the core of our funding, and the NHPRC has awarded subventions to the University of Illinois Press to defray some of the project's publication costs. A grant from the Stiftung Volkswagenwerk enabled us to search archives in Germany, Holland, France, and England for Gompers documents.

We also thank the University of Maryland at College Park, which has supported and housed the project from the beginning, our colleagues in the History Department, our chair, Richard Price, and our dean, Robert W. Griffith. The department and University facilitate our work in countless ways and, specifically, provide released time to Dr. Kaufman, office space and equipment, encouragement and financial support, and student assistance.

As was the case with previous volumes, we have continued to draw on the collections and staffs of area libraries and research institutions. These include the Catholic University of America, the George Meany Memorial Archives, the Library of Congress, the Library of the U.S. Department of Labor, the McKeldin Library at the University of Maryland, and the National Archives. In addition to these institutions, located in our immediate vicinity, we have received invaluable assistance for this volume from, among others, the Eisenhower Library at the Johns Hopkins University, the Massachusetts Historical Society, the Mikrofilmarchiv der deutschsprachigen Presse, the New York Public Library, Oberlin College, the State Historical Society of Wisconsin, the Toledo-Lucas County Public Library, the University of Chicago

Library, and the University of Michigan. We are most appreciative of the support given us by these institutions.

Among the many individuals who have assisted us with this volume are Earl W. Carroll, president of the United Garment Workers of America, Joyce M. Bellamy, Mary Ann Coyle, Robert L. Fraser, Gregory C. Harness, Walter V. Hickey, Dolores Janiewski, G. S. Kealey, George Kovtun, Vernon Lidtke, Patrick McGrath, Harold L. Miller, Janet Myder, Werner Pflug, Donald A. Ritchie, John Saville, Jonathan Schneer, Dorothee Schneider, Richard A. Storey, Marek Swiecicki, and Wojciech Zorniak.

In addition, non-editorial members of our staff have played key roles in producing *A National Labor Movement Takes Shape*. We are indebted to our research assistants, Katherine Morin and Michael Honey, who worked with us with care and diligence on a day-to-day basis, and to our two indefatigable typists, Vicky Comer and Megan Albert, who labored with unfailing accuracy and good humor. We owe a similar debt to the several graduate students who helped us: Marla J. Hughes, Mary Beth Corrigan, Cindy Bendroth, Gu Ning, Marie Schwartz, and Beverly Ann and Guenter Tlusty.

Finally, as was the case with our previous volumes, members of our board of editorial advisors were of invaluable assistance. David Brody, Melvyn Dubofsky, Louis Harlan, Walter Licht, Nick Salvatore, and Irwin Yellowitz took time from their busy schedules to review the book in manuscript form and to provide us with critical comments as well as specific suggestions for improvement. Their generous contributions of time and their careful judgment have improved this volume immeasurably.

Notes

1. "An Editorial by Samuel Gompers in the *American Federationist*," Feb. 1896; "A Circular," Feb. 12, 1896, both below.

2. Secretary's reports, AFL, *Proceedings*, 1895-98. SG estimated the membership of the AFL at 620,000 in 1897 and 1898; the AFL's *History, Encyclopedia [and] Reference Book*, published two decades later, put the figure at just over 250,000 (SG to F. M. Colby, Mar. 9, 1897, reel 11, vol. 19, p. 45, SG Letterbooks, DLC; "Excerpts from Samuel Gompers' Testimony before a Subcommittee of the Education and Labor Committee of the U.S. Senate," June 16, 1898, below; *American Federation of Labor: History, Encyclopedia [and] Reference Book* [Washington, D.C., 1919], p. 63). The discrepancy probably involves different methods of calculation for different purposes—for example, counting the total membership of a union as opposed to the number of members upon which dues were paid. Also, some workers may have been counted more than once because of membership in city central or state bodies, as well as in the union of their trade.

3. "An Article in the *Union Printer and American Craftsman*," Apr. 27, 1895, n. 1, below.

4. "To George McNeill," July 17, 1895, n. 2, below.

5. July 18, 1896, reel 9, vol. 15, p. 618, SG Letterbooks, DLC.

6. SG wrote William McKinstry on Jan. 24, 1896, that "this was the first day that I have been to the office in nearly three weeks. During that time I have been confined to my bed, suffering and almost tortured by illness and disease. Have been so sick that my life was often despaired of and it was the greatest struggle of both science on the part of my doctor and pluck on my own that carried me through. He has visited me over forty times since Jan. 7. I have a male nurse attending me day and night. You can judge, therefore, that I have had, by no means, either an easy or pleasant time of it" (reel 341, vol. 356, p. 53, ibid.).

7. "Morrison & I are getting along splendidly," SG wrote John O'Sullivan in the spring of 1897 (Apr. 3, 1897, reel 11, vol. 19, p. 382, ibid.). His views of McCraith, however, were decidedly negative: "He grew too fast in the movement for his own good; eaten up with his own conceit; . . . impulsive, not unkind, yet vindictive: strange combination. . . . Having worked with him for a year I tried to get along with him . . . but it is absolutely impossible for any one to work in traces with him . . . for McCraith will certainly endeavour to domineer and get his colleague 'in a hole'" (to Edward O'Donnell, Aug. 5, 1897, reel 12, vol. 20, p. 833, ibid.).

8. SG to P. J. Maas, Nov. 11, 1897, reel 13, vol. 21, p. 844, ibid.

9. SG to John Tobin, Apr. 1, 1897, reel 11, vol. 19, p. 337, ibid.; SG to John Chorley, Nov. 17, 1897, reel 13, vol. 21, p. 955, ibid.

10. SG reacted angrily to criticism of the AFL's lack of expenditures in the West. Writing George Whitaker, for example, he said, "I am fully aware as to the sentiment that has been created for the purpose of dividing the workingmen up into sectional lines, but this is no reason why the true trade unionists should allow themselves to be diverted from their true course or to expect unreasonable things, and, when I say 'unreasonable,' I mean that the A.F. of L. has no hidden treasure, nor magical fund from which to draw upon at will. That every cent contributed by our fellow unionists is utilized to the very best possible advantage in their interests, but, so long as these contributions are in the nature of one fourth of a cent per month, or, in other words, three cents a year, vast treasuries to expend large sums ad libitum cannot be accumulated. We are doing the very best we can and shall go on doing that, extending our operations and the field of our work in the same proportion as our opportunities afford" (June 10, 1897, reel 12, vol. 20, p. 174, ibid.).

11. L. Glen Seretan, *Daniel DeLeon: The Odyssey of an American Marxist* (Cambridge, Mass., 1979), p. 153.

12. Nick Salvatore, *Eugene Debs: Citizen and Socialist* (Urbana, Ill., 1982), pp. 172, 203.

13. See *The Making of a Union Leader*, pp. xxii–xxiv, and *Unrest and Depression*, p. xxii. In our endnotes following letters, we indicate if there were secretarial notations that a document was dictated by SG or was to be filed with his private papers.

SYMBOLS AND ABBREVIATIONS

A and P and TD	Autograph and printed and typed document
A and PD	Autograph and printed document
AFL	American Federation of Labor
ALpS	Autograph letter, letterpress copy, signed
ALS	Autograph letter, signed
AWpS	Autograph wire (telegram), letterpress copy, signed
CMIU	Cigar Makers' International Union
DLC	Library of Congress
DNA	National Archives of the United States, Washington, D.C.
FOTLU	Federation of Organized Trades and Labor Unions of the United States and Canada
KOL	Knights of Labor
MdU	University of Maryland, College Park
MiU	University of Michigan, Ann Arbor
PD	Printed document
PLSr	Printed letter, signature representation other than stamp
SG	Samuel Gompers
SLP	Socialist Labor party
T and ALpS	Typed and autograph letter, letterpress copy, signed or stamped with signature
T and ALS	Typed and autograph letter, signed or stamped with signature
T and PD	Typed and printed document
TLp	Typed letter, letterpress copy
TLpS	Typed letter, letterpress copy, signed or stamped with signature
TLpSr	Typed letter, letterpress copy, signature representation other than stamp
TLS	Typed letter, signed or stamped with signature
TLSr	Typed letter, signature representation other than stamp
TUC	Trades Union Congress of Great Britain
TWpSr	Typed wire (telegram), letterpress copy, signature representation other than stamp

SHORT TITLES

AFL, *Proceedings,*
1893
AFL, *Report of Proceedings of the Thirteenth Annual Convention of the American Federation of Labor, Held at Chicago, Ill., December 11th to 19th, Inclusive, 1893* (1893?; reprint ed., Bloomington, Ill., 1905)

AFL, *Proceedings,*
1894
AFL, *Report of Proceedings of the Fourteenth Annual Convention of the American Federation of Labor, Held at Denver, Colorado, December 10, 11, 12, 13, 14, 15, 16, 17, and 18, 1894* (1894?; reprint ed., Bloomington, Ill., 1905)

AFL, *Proceedings,*
1895
AFL, *Report of Proceedings of the Fifteenth Annual Convention of the American Federation of Labor, Held at New York, N.Y., December 9th to 17th, Inclusive, 1895* (1895?; reprint ed., Bloomington, Ill., 1905)

AFL, *Proceedings,*
1896
AFL, *Report of Proceedings of the Sixteenth Annual Convention of the American Federation of Labor, Held at Cincinnati, Ohio, December 14 to 21, Inclusive, 1896* (1896?; reprint ed., Bloomington, Ill., 1905)

AFL, *Proceedings,*
1897
AFL, *Report of Proceedings of the Seventeenth Annual Convention of the American Federation of Labor, Held at Nashville, Tennessee, December 13th to 21st, Inclusive, 1897* (1897?; reprint ed., Bloomington, Ill., 1905)

AFL Records
Peter J. Albert and Harold L. Miller, eds., *American Federation of Labor Records: The Samuel Gompers Era,* microfilm (Sanford, N.C., 1979)

The Early Years of the AFL
Stuart B. Kaufman et al., eds., *The Samuel Gompers Papers,* vol. 2, *The Early Years of the American Federation of Labor, 1887-90* (Urbana, Ill., 1987)

The Making of a Union Leader
Stuart B. Kaufman et al., eds., *The Samuel Gompers Papers,* vol. 1, *The Making of a Union Leader, 1850-86* (Urbana, Ill., 1986)

SG, *Seventy Years*
Samuel Gompers, *Seventy Years of Life and Labor: An Autobiography,* 2 vols. (New York, 1925)

Unrest and Depression
Stuart B. Kaufman and Peter J. Albert et al., eds., *The Samuel Gompers Papers,* vol. 3, *Unrest and Depression, 1891-94* (Urbana, Ill., 1989)

SG Letterbooks
The Letterbooks of the Presidents of the American Federation of Labor, 1883-1925, Library of Congress

CHRONOLOGY

1895	Jan. 1-Dec. 31	John McBride serves as AFL president
	Jan. 8-11	SG serves as delegate to the New York State Workingmen's Assembly convention, Albany, N.Y.
	Feb. 26	Erdman arbitration bill introduced in U.S. House of Representatives
	Apr.-July 4	SG tours South and Midwest as an organizer for the United Garment Workers of America
	June-Nov.	Eugene Debs jailed in Woodstock Prison, McHenry Co., Ill., for violating 1894 Pullman strike injunction
	Aug. 14-Sept. 28	SG and P. J. McGuire travel to Europe as fraternal delegates to the TUC meeting in Cardiff (Sept. 2-7); they visit London, Manchester, Liverpool, Dublin, Paris, Hamburg, and Amsterdam
	Dec. 9-17	AFL convention, New York City
	Dec. 13	Socialist Trade and Labor Alliance organized in New York City
	Dec. 14	SG elected AFL president; assumes office Jan. 1, 1896
1896	June 19	Miners' strike begins in Leadville, Colo.
	June 29-July 2	Socialist Trade and Labor Alliance convention, New York City
	July 4-10	SLP convention, New York City
	Sept. 7-12	TUC meets in Edinburgh
	Sept. 21	Strikers attack Coronado and Emmet mines at Leadville, Colo.
	Sept. 28-Oct. 15	SG serves as delegate from CMIU 144 to CMIU convention, Detroit
	Dec. 14-21	AFL convention, Cincinnati
	Dec. 18	Frank Morrison elected AFL secretary; assumes office Jan. 1, 1897
1897	Jan.	AFL headquarters moved from Indianapolis to Washington, D.C.
	Jan. 1	After serving as CMIU second vice-president since 1886, SG becomes the union's first vice-president
	Jan. 25	U.S. Supreme Court rules four seamen who left the *Arago* subject to arrest for violating their contract (*Robertson* v. *Baldwin*)
	June 15-17	Final convention of the American Railway Union, Chicago

	June 17	President McKinley sends Hawaiian annexation treaty to Senate
	June 17-21	Founding convention of the Social Democracy of America, Chicago
	July 4-Sept. 11	United Mine Workers of America strike in Pennsylvania, Ohio, Indiana, Illinois, West Virginia, Kentucky, and Tennessee
	July 9	SG and other labor leaders meet in Pittsburgh in support of striking coal miners
	July 26	Judge John W. Mason issues injunction against speaking or organizing among coal miners in Marion Co., W.Va.; it is followed in mid-August by broader injunctions from Judge John J. Jackson and others
	July 27	SG and other labor leaders meet in Wheeling, W.Va., in support of striking miners and to protest Judge Mason's injunction
	July 28	SG, James Sovereign, and M. D. Ratchford meet with Gov. George Atkinson of W.Va., to protest Judge Mason's injunction
	Aug. 30-31	Conference of labor and reform leaders, St. Louis
	Sept. 10	Striking miners in Luzerne Co., Pa., shot by Sheriff James Martin and deputies in the "Lattimer Massacre"
	Sept. 27-29	Conference of labor and reform leaders, Chicago
	Oct. 29	Henry George dies
	Dec. 13-21	AFL convention, Nashville
	Dec. 15-16	Associated Labor Press of America organized in Nashville
	Dec. 20-22	National Building Trades Council of America organized in St. Louis
1898	Jan. 17-May 20	New England textile workers' strike
	Feb. 15	U.S. battleship *Maine* explodes and sinks in Havana harbor
	Feb. 28	U.S. Supreme Court upholds constitutionality of Utah eight-hour law (*Holden* v. *Hardy*)
	Apr. 25	Joint congressional resolution declares war on Spain, effective Apr. 21
	May 10	Western Labor Union organized in Salt Lake City
	June 1	Erdman Act signed into law
	June 11	The Social Democratic party founded
	June 18	Act establishing U.S. Industrial Commission signed into law

Documents

John McBride's Presidency of the AFL

"The king is dead! Long live the king!" proclaimed the Boston *Labor Leader* in December 1894 when John McBride was elected AFL president. Praising McBride as "a man of ability and influence," the paper noted that his long service in the movement, his skillful leadership of the miners, and his impressive political record all boded well for Gompers' successor.[1] The *Cleveland Citizen* was equally optimistic, suggesting that McBride's experience with the KOL might even help him bring about the amalgamation of the labor movement as a whole. "Sixty percent of the Knights of Labor, including the mineworkers, glassworkers, shoeworkers and several large district assemblies, are preparing to wheel into line with the Federation," the paper reported, and Patrick Murphy, secretary of New York's KOL District Assembly 49, maintained that McBride's election "would bring about the mutual recognition of membership cards as between the Federation and the Knights of Labor."[2] Other observers were more hesitant about predicting such sweeping changes in Federation policy. "McBride is generally credited with being a radical," Joseph Buchanan cautioned early in 1895, "but I doubt if there will be any change in the policy of the Federation on that account."[3]

McBride's active participation in the 1894 national elections and his enthusiastic response to the AFL's political program encouraged speculation that, as president, he might endorse the formation of a labor party.[4] But in his first editorial in the *American Federationist*, McBride sought to "quiet the fears of honest but uninformed friends of the trade union movement, and to satisfy the doubting Thomases and a speculative press, as to whether I am, as they allege, too conservative or too radical; too much or too little of a trade unionist; too ultra or too indifferent as a political reformer. . . . In my official relations with affiliated unions," he announced, "I shall be guided by the constitutional provisions of the American Federation of Labor."[5] Similarly, he explained that "when I say that I am a limited socialist I only say what every citizen of the country must say, for we have now a limited socialism, and it is simply a question of opinion how far it should extend." He went on to qualify his endorsement of the socialist demand for government ownership of the means of produc-

3

tion. "I believe that the government should . . . take charge of such productions as the people may elect from time to time," he contended, but added that this position "leaves the opening broad enough to admit or exclude anything."[6]

In his conduct of the presidency, McBride found himself hampered by illness, charges of corruption, and the Federation's precarious financial position. No sooner had he taken office than he contracted influenza and then suffered a relapse from the nicotine poisoning that had afflicted him in 1894. Recuperating in Hot Springs, Ark., he did not resume his presidential duties until late April 1895. In the interim he appointed James Duncan, the AFL's second vice-president and the chief officer of the Granite Cutters' National Union, to serve as the Federation's acting president. McBride's failure to secure the Executive Council's approval, however, raised questions about the constitutionality of his action. "Prest. McBride has no power to do so [appoint an interim officer], any more than I would have to appoint a New Treas.," John Lennon complained. "I am not and never have been a kicker, but I will not consent to the establishment of a Precedent that an Officer has the right to assign his duties to any one without the consent of the proper authority of the Union."[7]

Lennon's protest notwithstanding, Duncan assumed authority in McBride's absence and took his appointment seriously, adjudicating local difficulties, handling correspondence, and overseeing publication of the *American Federationist.* He sought to organize tobacco workers, to amalgamate the brassworkers, metal polishers, and platers into a single union, and to form a national union of coremakers. He also involved himself in the brewers' controversies with the KOL in Pittsburgh, Boston, and Chicago, in jurisdictional fights involving stationary and marine engineers, musicians, and painters, and in factional struggles between rival central labor unions in Chicago, Milwaukee, St. Louis, and Louisville. And, in perhaps his most significant action, he proposed to the racially exclusive International Association of Machinists (IAM) that it could meet the AFL's conditions for affiliation without changing its racial structure. "I suggested the propriety of your convention changing your constitution on the point in question," he wrote IAM president James O'Connell, "so as to leave it optional with local unions as to the disposal of colored applicants instead of imperatively prohibiting them as at present. . . . [I]t seems to me that the Southern Lodges could act as they do now with a provision in your constitution leaving it a question of local option."[8]

Soon after returning to Indianapolis in April to reassume office, McBride was called upon to defend himself against charges that he had accepted a bribe in 1894 during an American Railway Union strike of the Columbus, Hocking Valley, and Toledo Railroad and had then given some of the money — $600 — to Mark Wild, an employee of the firm and chairman of the union's grievance committee. McBride countered that the money had been raised by an anonymous source to help Wild, who had worked to settle the strike despite the fact that he had been blacklisted for his participation in it.[9] Although McBride had successfully answered these charges at the United Mine Workers' convention earlier in 1895, Wild alleged that the convention had merely whitewashed the story to protect McBride's reputation. These accusations led McBride to ask the Columbus (Ohio) Trades and Labor Assembly to reinvestigate the matter, and in April the AFL's Executive Council appointed P. J. McGuire to go to Columbus and then report his findings to the Council.[10] McGuire subsequently indicated that Wild had failed to appear at the hearings that were held in May, and that no definitive evidence had been adduced against McBride.[11]

As president of the Federation during a year when both the nation and the labor movement were still recovering from the economic depression of the 1890s, McBride found his scope of action restricted by a lack of resources. When workers in Salt Lake City asked for the AFL's assistance in securing passage of Utah's eight-hour law, for example, he had to turn them down. "The hard times following the slump in silver . . . in 1893 has made every labor union in the Country feel its blighting effect," he pointed out, "and to day . . . nearly all are compelled to neglect, for the want of funds, things that should be attended to."[12] AFL Secretary August McCraith confirmed this assessment, noting in his financial reports that most unions were complaining of "dullness" in their trades and a corresponding decline in membership. "For the present," he continued, "we have no money for special appropriations or anything of a costly nature." McBride and McCraith responded to these financial difficulties by curtailing travel and other expenses, reducing office staff, and making a concerted effort to get affiliates and advertisers to settle their debts. They not only maintained the solvency of the Federation, but, by the fall, McBride saw his way clear to make an organizing trip through the East.[13]

Despite differences in personality and leadership styles, John McBride shared Samuel Gompers' faith in trade unionism and the primacy of economic, rather than political, struggle. Like his predecessor, McBride saw no easy solution to the labor question, and he refused to endorse "experimental schemes" that promised quick results.[14] Neither was he likely to rush into a strike unprepared, and he criticized "so-called leaders" who lacked the "business judgment" to recognize "the uselessness of making threats when powerless to execute them."[15] And, although he favored the unification of labor's forces, like Gompers he was unwilling to sacrifice trade autonomy or trade unionism in the process. When the Milwaukee Federated Trades Council endorsed the amalgamation of the AFL and the KOL, McBride refused to publish its resolution in the *American Federationist* since the document claimed that the two organizations were "continually making war upon each other, to the detriment of the labor movement." Arguing that the trade unions had "never made war on the K. of L." and had no controversy with the Knights "other than that which springs from our defense of trade union methods and principles against attacks made upon them" by the KOL, McBride made it clear that the "only tangible method for securing Unity" was to leave "trade matters to the trades."[16]

Similarly, his practical trade unionism governed his political stance. While he argued that "wage workers cannot hope to be free in the shops, mines and factories while trudging in party slavery to the polls," he also maintained that it would be useless for the Federation to focus its efforts on the creation of an independent labor party. Like Gompers, McBride believed that the AFL's best opportunity to influence politics lay in backing politicians—regardless of party—who were sympathetic to labor and in supporting legislation favorable to labor's interests. "By this method," he insisted, "the nationalizing of the means of transportation and communication could be accomplished and the municipal ownership of water, heat, light and power plants be assured."[17]

When John McBride addressed the AFL's 1895 convention, he congratulated delegates on the Federation's growth, both numerically and financially, over the previous twelve months. The AFL had granted 8 charters to national and international unions, 8 to central labor unions, and 141 to local and federal labor unions.[18] Although trade conditions had not improved materially and organized labor could not boast of any great achievements in 1895, the Federation had not suffered any great defeats and had held its own during a punishing nationwide depression.

When the ballots were cast to elect the AFL's president, however, Samuel Gompers was returned to office by a very narrow margin. The complex dynamics of the Federation's annual conventions—the interplay of regional, ideological, ethno-cultural, and personal rivalries—belie any simple explanation of the vote. No doubt Gompers benefited from the fact that the 1895 convention met in the East—in his hometown of New York City—just as McBride had been helped by the location of the 1894 meeting in Denver. Moreover, the illness and subsequent absence of James Gelson, a delegate whose vote was apparently pledged to McBride, may well have affected the outcome of this very close contest. Gompers himself thought McBride's defeat was caused by his endorsement of compulsory arbitration, "notwithstanding the decisive, positive declaration of the A.F. of L."[19]

McBride, on the other hand, considered the vote a result of his portrayal as a socialist. Nevertheless, he said, he felt no disappointment at the result of the election, telling one reporter he had been "anxious to get out of the harness for three years."[20] Thanking his supporters for their loyalty, McBride announced that while he had no intention of severing his connection to the labor movement, he would not, in the future, either seek or occupy any official position. Instead, he continued his work with the People's party and launched a career as a journalist.

Notes

1. *Labor Leader* (Boston), Dec. 22, 1894.
2. *Cleveland Citizen*, Dec. 22, 1894; *New York World*, Dec. 18, 1894.
3. *Cleveland Citizen*, Jan. 12, 1895. See also the *Chicago Inter Ocean*, Dec. 18, 1894.
4. In some early interviews, John McBride described himself as a socialist and speculated that the labor movement might field a presidential candidate as early as 1896 (*Minneapolis Tribune*, Jan. 13, 1895; *Chicago Tribune*, Jan. 2, 1895). The *New York Times*, Jan. 2, 1895, reported the story somewhat differently. "In the next national campaign," the paper quoted him as saying, "I hope to see labor organizations unite on a Presidential candidate." The SLP, however, dismissed McBride as a "pure and simpler" (*People*, July 1, 1894).
5. *American Federationist* 1 (Feb. 1895): 282.
6. *National Labor Tribune*, Dec. 27, 1894.
7. John Lennon to August McCraith, Feb. 27, 1895, and Mar. 4, 1895, reel 143, frames 13 and 17, *AFL Records*. Lennon also protested "emphatically" to McBride (Lennon to McBride, Feb. 27, 1895, frame 16, ibid.). According to Art. VI, sec. 2 of the AFL constitution, Secretary McCraith was empowered to perform the president's duties until the Executive Council elected a successor.
8. James Duncan to James O'Connell, Mar. 27, 1895, reel 9, vol. 13, p. 78, SG Letterbooks, DLC. Philip Taft argues, however, that this idea did not originate with Duncan, and that the method had apparently already been employed by a number of national and international unions (Philip Taft, *The A.F. of L. in the Time of Gompers* [New York, 1957], p. 310).
9. McBride's and Mark Wild's statements are included in the proceedings of the 1895 United Mine Workers' convention. Eventually it was revealed that local coal operators had raised the money "in consideration of the fact that Mr. Wild had advised a settlement without regard to himself and with the full knowledge that he would not be reinstated." Apparently the operators were grateful for Wild's "disinterested act" and they believed that

"it would be wrong to permit him and his family to suffer under the circumstances" (*United Mine Workers' Journal,* May 16, 1895. See also Chris Evans, *History of the United Mine Workers of America,* 2 vols. [Indianapolis, 1918-20], 2: 365-68).

10. AFL Executive Council Minutes, Apr. 24, 1895, reel 2, frame 1085, *AFL Records.* The International Furniture Workers' Union specifically asked the Council to investigate the charges. See also Duncan to Patrick McBryde, Apr. 12, 1895, reel 8, vol. 12, pp. 59-60, SG Letterbooks, DLC.

11. AFL Executive Council Minutes, Dec. 9, 1895, reel 2, frame 1092, *AFL Records.*

12. McBride to J. C. Morris, June 11, 1895, reel 8, vol. 12, pp. 184-85, SG Letterbooks, DLC; see also McBride to Edward Gaby, July 1, 1895, ibid., pp. 226-27.

13. Secretary's Report, AFL Executive Council Minutes, Apr. 22, 1895, reel 2, frame 1087, *AFL Records; United Mine Workers' Journal,* Oct. 10, 1895.

14. *American Federationist* 2 (Mar. 1895): 10.

15. United Mine Workers of America, *Proceedings,* 1895, p. 50.

16. McBride to H. J. Obrecht, Sept. 13, 1895, reel 8, vol. 12, pp. 398-99, SG Letterbooks, DLC.

17. President McBride's Report, AFL, *Proceedings,* 1895, pp. 15-16.

18. Ibid., p. 20.

19. SG to Daniel Harris, Feb. 8, 1899, reel 18, vol. 27, p. 172, SG Letterbooks, DLC; *Seventy Years,* 1: 370.

20. *Paterson Labor Standard,* Jan. 4, 1896.

An Article in the *Boston Herald*

[January 9, 1895]

EX-PRESIDENT GOMPERS DINED.

A banquet was tendered ex-President Gompers of the American Federation of Labor at the Quincy House yesterday afternoon by trade union leaders of Boston and personal friends. George E. McNeill[1] was toastmaster.

After the cigars had been lighted, Mr. McNeill paid a high tribute to Mr. Gompers' work in behalf of the trade union movement of America. Frank K. Foster[2] responded to the toast, "The Trade Union Standard Bearer," and at the conclusion of his remarks Mr. Gompers was presented, in behalf of his friends in Boston, with a complete set of Herbert Spencer's works.

All of the speakers paid warm tributes to the ex-president of the A.F.L., and stated that they were proud of the fact that Mr. Gompers was defeated in fighting for a principle; and also that no man could truthfully accuse him of dishonesty or of having sought to use the labor movement for his personal aggrandizement.

The prediction was made that the forces that compassed Mr. Gompers' defeat at Denver[3] would themselves be defeated at the New York convention of the A.F.L.,[4] and that the principles of trade unionism would dominate the labor people of this country.

Mr. Gompers assured his friends that he would continue to work energetically for trade unionism, notwithstanding his retirement from the office of president of the American Federation of Labor.

Boston Herald, Jan. 9, 1895.

1. George Edwin McNEILL was serving as general manager of the Massachusetts Mutual Accident Association.

2. Frank Keyes FOSTER, a Boston printer, served as secretary of the Massachusetts State Federation of Labor (1889-95) and edited the *Labor Leader* in Boston (1887-97).

3. The AFL held its 1894 convention in Denver, Dec. 10-18.

4. The 1895 AFL convention was held in New York City, Dec. 9-17.

An Excerpt from a News Account of the 1895 Convention[1] of the New York State Workingmen's Assembly

[January 27, 1895]

STATE BRANCH A.F. OF L.

. . .

Resolution that all organizations affiliated with S.B. A.F. of L.[2] go into independent political action, with a special view to the collective ownership by the people of all the means of production and distribution. This resolution was referred by the Resolution Committee to the Committee on Good of the Organization, and as the clerk started to read the first part of the preamble Delegate Gompers jumped to the floor and moved that the resolution be laid on the table without further reference. The motion was seconded, but Delegate Heimerdinger[3] of C.P.U. 251 demanded in the name of his organization that the resolution be read, and then, if Mr. Gompers had not the moral courage to fight the issue on the floor of the convention, and more especially so where his own international[4] as well as his local union[5] had voted in favor of a similar resolution, that he must be branded as a traitor to the very principles that he advocates, "I will follow where trade unions lead." Delegate Gompers thereupon stated that he made the motion only to expedite matters, as he did not think the convention should waste its time discussing such a resolution, but still, if it was the sense of the body and they would limit the time for discussion, he would withdraw his motion. A motion was made that one hour's time be given to discussing the resolution, which was amended to two hours. The amendment was carried. Delegate Katz[6] of Troy was the first speaker. He recapitulated the proceedings of the A.F. of L. at Denver, the tricks that Mr. Gompers and his friend Mr. Strasser[7] had resorted to to further their own ends, despite the wishes of the rank and file of their organization. He also stated that in spite of the opposition of Mr. Gompers and his accomplices, the new trade unionists would yet compel him to swallow the pill, no matter how bitter it was to him, and compel him to come out flat-footed for honest labor politics or be sunk into oblivion. Delegate Ihmsen[8] of Troy also spoke in favor of the resolution, but adhered strictly to the merits thereof. Mr. Gompers spoke against. He started right in to mislead the delegates by stating that the English trade unions had compelled the city council in London in giving out work to contractors to observe trade union principles in regard to hours of labor, rates of wages, etc., and were now substituting direct dealing by the city with its men, therefore doing away with the contractor and his profit, limiting exploitation of the laboring classes. The Socialist Labor party, the disrupter of trade unions, is endeavoring— and I see by the introduction of this measure, which calls for the "collective ownership by the people of all the means of production and distribution"—to make the A.F. of L. the tail to their kite. To prove this I will state what happened in New York city last Summer. A joint conference[9] had been called by the People's party. They met at 50 East 10th street. There were represented the People's party, the S.L.P., D.A. 49, K. of L. and the Central Labor Federation. After having referred a platform, which was, nominally speaking, entirely Socialistic in its origin, to a referendum vote, and which was adopted, they parted with the understanding that they would meet in joint convention for the purpose of making nominations. Instead of carrying out their promise the S.L.P. held their convention[10] by themselves, nominated their own candidates, and expected those that had been represented at the conference to support their ticket. This statement is true, and I stake my reputation thereon. The trade unions alone must emancipate labor, and I am willing to start life anew in the very slums to organize the laboring classes into trade unions, and once we reach the high water mark, we will make our demands, secure them peacefully if we can, forcibly if we must. We will not lie down, but stand up and be mowed down if our demands are not acceded to. The S.L.P. has for years been endeavoring to force this pill down our throats, but as long as I have a voice they will not succeed; they are the followers of a professor[11] without a title and without a chair, and I will meet any of the exponents of new trade unionism at any time before a representative body of men to debate the issue. The Socialists created disturbance at Denver, they are endeavoring to do the same here; do not allow it; vote against this measure to a man, and let us again renew our pledges to our trade unions. Delegate Heimerdinger then got the floor and started to dissect the argument brought forward by Mr. Gompers. It is true, he said, that the English unions were stronger and further advanced than ours, but Mr. Gompers failed to state that the English trade unionists had no other weapon with which to combat against concentrated capital than their organizations until a few short years ago, when they were granted the right of franchise, which they immediately took advantage of and elected men from their own rank and file, who knew their wants and conditions, to the city council, the House of Parliament and the magistrate's bench. These were the people that brought about the state of affairs that at the present time exists in the City Council of London, by and through the use of the ballot. In regard to the resolution, if Mr. Gompers does not understand the English language he should have the purport of the resolution explained. I stated distinctly that we invite the labor organizations affiliated with the S.B. A.F. of L., as well as other organizations in this State, to go into an independent political movement, with a special view toward the collective ownership by the people of all the means of production and distribution. The A.F. of L. had the opportunity of becoming the political party of the wage slaves at Denver, which would have made the S.L.P. a party of propaganda only, but the misleaders of labor, ably assisted by fake representatives from fake and defunct organizations, succeeded in defeating the will of the rank and file. I claim, and justly so, that Mr. Gompers having been instructed by his international union to vote in favor of the entire eleven planks, as presented, his own local, No. 144, having voted in favor thereof, he has proven himself a traitor to his own organization and was not fit to represent any body of men. In regard to the statement made by Mr. Gompers, and on which he staked his reputation, I would state that it is a deliberate falsehood. I was a delegate to that conference; he was not; the only understanding that was reached by the conference was in regard to having watchers at the polls to secure an honest count. Nothing outside of this was agreed upon. The S.L.P. was asked to postpone their convention, which they could not consistently do, and the conference adjourned sine die. At Denver, when Mr. John Burns[12] heard that the convention had rejected plank 10, he stated that the delegates were jackasses. I do not think Mr. Gompers exempted himself from the balance of the delegates. Mr. M. Raphael[13] spoke in favor of the resolution, and thought it wise to allow the affiliated unions to take a vote. Thereon Delegate John J. Junio,[14] while in favor of the resolution and stating that sooner or later we must adopt and pursue this course, did not think that the masses were ready for it; he therefore voted against it. The time for discussion having expired the vote was taken. The following votes were recorded in favor: Heimerdinger, Ball, Raphael, Ihmsen, Katz, Wehyle, Pratt[15] and Steer.[16]

The Committee on Officers' Report then reported that they did not coincide with the president in regard to his statement that the masses of the State of New York were not ripe to go into an independent political movement. They recommended that such a course should be pursued, but Mr. Gompers introduced a substitute reading about as follows: "We again pledge our fealty to the trade unions, and will, whenever the opportunity occurs, elect labor men to our Legislature." Comrade Steers got the floor and said that the two resolutions before the house involved principles that were of greater importance than any other principles [or] questions that had come before the convention during the entire session, and held that, this being true, the house could not consistently apply the gag rule and limit opportunity for a full and thorough discussion upon their merits, assuming the above to be acquiesced in from the attitude of interest manifested, and held that the resolution offered by the Committee on Good of the Organization involved the same principles underlying the resolution that had been defeated the day before, and that the argument upon it, in order to enlighten, must necessarily follow on the same or similar lines, and, inasmuch as Mr. Gompers' substitute was diametrically opposed to it in principle, that it was necessary that they be considered in comparison in order to facilitate a speedy conclusion as to their relative merits—that prejudice alone had dominated, and upon prejudice would the opposition to the committee's resolution rely to defeat it. Asserting that the committee's resolution, if passed with a full understanding of what it meant by the delegates, would result in positive benefit, inasmuch as its import would be imparted and be understood by the man at home, and when the workers once determined to accept those views they would consent to act upon those lines, and the best of results must surely follow. That on the other hand, Mr. Gompers' substitute meant positively nothing; that when he came to speak in support of his proposition he would be forced to rely upon the existing prejudice to find an argument at all. It was observable that he had the day before defeated a very important resolution by merely asserting that it committed the body to the S.L.P.; held that whether or not the resolution at hand did or did not read similarly, or even identically, with the propositions of the S.L.P., that it was the bounden duty of the delegate to consider it alone upon its merits, and charged that it was betrayal of their constituencies if they permitted themselves to be governed by any other consideration; it was the words in the bill that they were to deal with. Mr. Gompers had the day before grandiloquently portrayed the intolerance of the Socialists by their repeated demands that you must swallow our whole dose; it is our particular brand of reform that you must accept, and that alone. Well, what of it? Had not others the same criticism to fling at the trade unionists? Had we not, the country over, under the inspiring messages of Mr. Gompers and his fellow advisers, called loudly upon the workers to accept of none but our particular brand of labor organization? Rightly, too! We stood stoutly for our course, because we knew that it was in conformity with the necessities of the times, right in the economic field, and how could we consistently howl intolerance at the S.L.P. when they likewise held in the face of popular intolerance that their brand of organization in the political sense was precisely right, and by all that is great and good they are right. We Socialists are proud of our collective courage when we face the opposing world with our propositions, and we want everybody to know it. That Mr. Gompers realizes the imperative necessity for a forward political movement on behalf of labor is readily perceived when we recall his various arraignments of existing conditions. Indeed, we will here read from a city paper[17] what he said right here on this floor during the session upon the subject, and I presume Mr. Gompers will not dispute it:

"To-day there are a million and a half wage workers tramping through this country in idleness. We find our lawmakers trampling the rights of the people under foot. We find our representatives, or rather our misrepresentatives, dallying with questions to hoodwink or rob the people, instead of truthfully ascertaining what the cause of the evil is and finding a remedy for it.

"One year and half ago, when the industrial panic struck us, the corporations, the banks, the newspapers, all said that the cause was the Sherman silver law. The result was, the President called upon Congress to repeal that law. It was then confidently predicted that in a few days the wheels of industry would revolve. These men, finding no change for the better—but, on the contrary, finding the lack of employment more general—set about to find another reason. They then began tinkering with the tariff, but with no better result. To-day Congress is trying to find a means of stopping this depression. It is buying bonds or selling bonds, in order to secure gold. It is just stopping up the spigot and allowing the gold to run out at the bunghole.

"The same incompetency is to be found in our State Legislature. Our governor[18] seeks to stop day work on the capitol and let the contract to the sweaters of New York."[19]

Now, what more terrible arraignment of our condition as a people could be penned or worded in so brief a space as that? Yet Mr. Gompers seems to be wholly oblivious of the pressing necessity of a class consciousness on the part of the workers. Judging him by his substitute proposition, one would think and expect that one who has had the extended and varied experience, by virtue of his long-time service as the chief executive of so great an organization as the A.F. of L., and who is capable of uttering such a vivid description of our miserable situation as has Mr. Gompers, would propose some remedy that would appear at least plausible; but not so with Mr. Gompers. What do we find in his substitute to meet the crying needs of the times? Nothing— positively nothing. Here Mr. Gompers took the floor and consumed twenty minutes in saying nothing more than scoring the S.L.P. He could bring up no counter argument. Although both Heimerdinger and Katz had asked for the floor the gag law was applied by one of the delegates calling for the question and being followed by half a dozen more. The vote on Mr. G.'s substitute was as follows, the same eight having their votes recorded against. In the election for officers Delegate Heimerdinger nominated Delegate M. Raphael as the delegate to the A.F. of L., lauding him for his sterling qualities and the respect in which he is held by all who have come in contact with him, but probably Mr. Raphael is too progressive for Mr. Gompers, so he nominated Mr. John J. Junio of Auburn, who defeated Mr. Raphael by eleven votes. After an address by Miss Fairview[20] on woman suffrage the convention adjourned sine die. Mr. Harris[21] was an impartial chairman and deserves great credit for the able and efficient manner in which he presided.

People (New York), Jan. 27, 1895.

1. The 1895 New York State Workingmen's Assembly (NYSWA) convention met Jan. 8-11 in Albany, N.Y.

2. That is, the New York State Branch of the AFL, the NYSWA.

3. David Seymour Heimerdinger was a member of CMIU cigar packers 251 of New York City and was active in the New York City Central Labor Federation (CLF). He later became an organizer for the AFL.

4. The CIGAR Makers' International Union of America.

5. CMIU 144 of New York City.

6. Rudolph Katz, a Troy, N.Y., cigarmaker, was an SLP organizer.

7. Adolph STRASSER, former president of the CMIU, served the AFL as an arbitrator of jurisdictional disputes, a legislative representative in Washington, D.C., in 1895, and as an organizer and auditor for the CMIU.

8. Thomas H. Imerson, a Troy, N.Y., iron molder, was the SLP candidate for assemblyman for Rensselaer Co., N.Y., District 1 in 1894.

9. In April 1894 a delegation from the People's party met with representatives of the SLP, KOL District Assembly 49, the New York City CLF, the Prohibition party, and the Manhattan Single Tax Club to discuss united action. The AFL and the New York City Central Labor Union (CLU) were also invited but did not attend. In two sessions, on Apr. 2 and Apr. 16, the conference decided to submit to referendum vote a socialist declaration of political and economic principles and a plan for cooperation in elections.

10. The New York State SLP convention met in Syracuse, N.Y., on June 9, 1894.

11. Daniel DELEON was the editor of the SLP's official organ *People* from 1891 until 1914, and the SLP's leading figure during that period. In 1895 he organized the Socialist Trade and Labor Alliance and, as a member of its general executive board, functioned as the leader of that organization.

12. John Elliott BURNS, a member of the Amalgamated Society of Engineers, was a Member of Parliament from 1892 to 1918.

13. Michael Raphael.

14. John J. JUNIO was president of the Auburn, N.Y., CLU and of Auburn CMIU 311.

15. Probably Mervyn Pratt, a New York City ironworker who was a member of

the United Tin and Sheet Iron Workers' Benevolent and Protective Association and the secretary of the building trades section of the New York City CLU.

16. William Frank Steer (variously Steere), an Albany, N.Y., cigarmaker who ran for lieutenant-governor of New York in 1894 on the SLP ticket. The measure was defeated 42-8.

17. *Albany Evening Journal,* Jan. 10, 1895.

18. Levi Parsons Morton (1824-1920) served as a Republican governor of New York from 1895 to 1897.

19. In 1865 the New York legislature authorized the governor to appoint a New Capitol Commission to oversee work on the building of a new capitol in Albany; the building was finally completed in 1897. On Jan. 24, 1895, capitol commissioner Isaac G. Perry issued a statement to the New York senate recommending that work on the new capitol be completed by day work rather than by the contract system.

20. Florence Fairview, a suffragist and women's labor organizer who apparently went under several assumed names, adopted the name Fairview because, as she put it, "I take a fair view of things" (*New York Times,* Aug. 30, 1897). She addressed the 1895 AFL convention and was active in organizing women tobacco workers in St. Louis in 1896. She subsequently experienced difficulties in her relations with the labor movement, reflected in SG's rejection of her application for the chartering of a federal labor union in July 1896 and her brief appearance before the AFL's 1896 convention to refute charges—unspecified in the record—by the NYSWA.

21. Daniel HARRIS, a member of CMIU 144 of New York City, was president of the NYSWA from 1892 to 1897 and treasurer of the New York City CLU in 1895.

From Ernest Bohm[1]

New York, Jan. 29, 1895.

Mr. Samuel Gompers.

Sir:

Relative to several reports, one being published in The People of January 27, 1895, which quote you as being willing and anxious to debate the labor movement with a representative of "New Trades Unionism," I am instructed to notify you, and herewith do, that the the Central Labor Federation of New York accepts your challenge and awaits your further pleasure.

Respectfully yours,　Ernest Bohm,
Cor. Sec'y.　Central Labor Federation.

People (New York), Feb. 17, 1895.

1. Ernest BOHM was secretary of the New York City Central Labor Federation from 1889 to 1899. A member of the SLP, he served as secretary of the general executive board of the Socialist Trade and Labor Alliance (1896-98).

To Ernest Bohm

New York, Feb. 2, 1895.

Mr. Ernest Bohm,
Secretary Central Labor Federation,
64 Fourth street, New York City.
Sir:

I am in receipt of your letter of Jan. 29,[1] in which you say that I am quoted by that monumental libeler, that assassin of men's characters, one of your official organs, The People, as being "willing and anxious to debate the labor movement with a representative of New Trades Unionism," and that that challenge is accepted by your organization.

In reply I desire to say that I am always anxious and willing to discuss the labor movement, but I do not understand the attitude the representative of your organization would take upon the question. I have always taken the affirmative when discussing or debating the labor movement. I have always favored it. Will the representative of your organization take the negative? Will he oppose it? No other inference can be drawn from your letter.

Nor am I dependent alone upon your letter for justification for my inference. The chief characteristics of your organization since its existence have been to decry the work of the labor movement, to ridicule its accomplishments, to slander the men who have been the staunchest devotees, only measuring the venom by the degree of their devotion. It has wrecked unions where it could not control them. It has taken the weak-kneed out of existing unions and started rival organizations, thus making the efforts for improved conditions or the battle against worse conditions futile and impotent. It has split the labor movement of this city and elsewhere, where its contaminating influence has at all been felt. It has spread confusion and chaos in the labor movement when unity is essential to its success.

And in the face of these wonderful achievements of your misnamed Central Labor Federation, you expect me to debate the "Labor Movement" with one of your representatives.

Pshaw! You are not in earnest. Your organization is not only vicious, but in this instance at least it has become positively funny.

I have seen, heard and read of New Trade Unionists and New Trade Unionism, but they are not scabs, union wreckers or opponents of the labor movement. Your assumption that your organization is representative of New Trade Unionism is as unfounded as it was repudiated by the man who gave that term its origin and significance — John Burns.

Do you think I will be forgotten in the labor world, and for that reason create an opportunity for me to address the workers? Did you not gloat over my death? Did not your official organ print a nice epitaph upon my demise?[2] Why resuscitate or revive me? After killing me and nicely laying me away you find I still live, and you doubtless discovered that fact since the State Federation convention. Let me add I shall meet you and yours in the days to come and then and there when the labor movement is antagonized by your organization or any one else you will find me in evidence.

Yours hopefully,   Samuel Gompers.

People (New York), Feb. 17, 1895.

1. Above.
2. "Powderly — Gompers," *People*, Dec. 23, 1894.

An Article in the *New York World*

[March 4, 1895]

LABOR LEADER DAMPF BURIED.

The delegates to the Central Labor Union and a great crowd of workers met at Clarendon Hall at 9 A.M. yesterday to attend the funeral of Meyer Dampf, the dead labor leader, who killed himself a week ago while suffering from alleged temporary insanity brought on by the grippe.[1]

The body rested in state in the centre of the hall. The coffin was buried under flowers, topped by an immense wreath from Leader Dampf's friends in the Socialist Labor Party. The Progress Society sang a hymn. Samuel Gompers, Henry Weismann,[2] Delegate James P. Archibald[3] and Col. A. E. Seifert, of the Gilsa Post, G.A.R., of which Dampf was a member, spoke. The funeral party proceeded to the Cigarmakers' Union headquarters, where many joined the procession. The body was buried in Washington, L.I., Cemetery.

New York World, Mar. 4, 1895.

1. Meyer Dampf, financial secretary of CMIU 144, committed suicide shortly before Adolph Strasser was to have audited the local's books. The audit subsequently uncovered a substantial shortage. See "To Adolph Strasser," July 29, 1895, below.

2. Henry WEISMANN was editor of the *Bakers' Journal* and the *Deutsch-Amerikanische Bäcker-Zeitung*, the organs of the Journeymen Bakers' and Confectioners' International

Union of America (JBCIU), from 1891 to 1895, and was editor of the combined dual-language *Bakers' Journal and Deutsch-Amerikanische Bäcker-Zeitung* and international secretary of the JBCIU from 1895 to 1897.

3. James Patrick ARCHIBALD was an officer in the New York City Central Labor Union and its successor, the Central Federated Union, from 1882 to 1904, with the exception of one year. In 1895 he helped found the National Paper Hangers' Protective and Beneficial Association, serving as its president for seven years.

An Article in the *Union Printer and American Craftsman*

[April 27, 1895]

MR. GOMPERS'S TOUR.

Samuel Gompers has gone on a tour of the South and West[1] in the interest of the Garment Cutters' Union.[2] The first place he stopped in was Scranton, Pa., the home of T. V. Powderly.[3] Of course, Sam felt called upon to roast the Knights of Labor. He seems to work on the principle that "we rise by the things that are under our feet," and among other things which he seeks to set his feet upon is the order of the Knights. The Scranton K. of L. resented Mr. Gompers's attacks, and proceeded to make it hot for him. They succeeded. Scranton was treated to an exhibition "bear garden" labor demonstration that, while it doubtless attracted considerable attention, did very little good in the way of amalgamating the organizations and causing a spirit of unity to pervade the town.

The Industrial News, in an impartial account of the meeting, says:

["]Mr. Gompers will never forget his visit to Scranton. The memory of it will not be pleasant.

["]It was announced that Mr. Gompers had come to enthuse the members of the Trades Unions of the city. Whether his visit was a success in that respect or not is a subject for debate, but every one of the 250 persons assembled in the hall that evening will make sworn affidavit that excitement enough was created to satisfy the most critical.

["]The speaker then stated he had something to say, and any person not wishing to listen had the privilege of retiring from the hall. Of course no one left. It was, as the farmers' almanac says, 'time to prepare for a storm.' The storm came with a rush. The speaker started it by a recital of the difficulties and rivalry between the American Federation of Labor and the Knights of Labor. He then returned to the subject of 'sweatshops,' and said: 'In New-York there is a firm that antagonizes organized labor and particularly the garment-workers as does no other firm in the United States of America. The firm to which I refer is that of Hackett, Carhart & Co.'[4] Mr. Gompers then explained the lockout, and the action taken by the K. of L. in granting a charter to the men who took the places of the men locked out by the firm. 'The way to bring this firm to its sense of justice and strike a strong blow at it is to refuse to patronize the home merchants who handle their goods. In Scranton the representatives of that concern are Collins & Hackett.'

["]What a noise there was when this statement was made. Cheers and hisses came from all sides.

["]President Roach[5] jumped up and excitedly exclaimed that Mr. Gompers was in error; that the movement against Hackett, Carhart & Co. was an attempt to deny that firm the right to join the Knights of Labor, and that Mr. Gompers was deliberately misstating facts.

["]Mr. Gompers insisted he was correct, and said he expected he would be 'roasted' in the daily papers the next day, because Collins & Hackett advertised in those papers.

["]The excitement had been growing more and more intense, when the meeting was declared adjourned. Mr. Gompers was immediately surrounded by a large crowd. Two or three excited individuals attempted to speak all at once. One man was too heavy for the chair he was standing on and he came to the floor with a crash, thus giving the impression that preparations were being made for a scrap. Another person, for the sake of variety, turned out a light over the platform, and the audience hurriedly commenced to depart.

["]While the crowd was jammed about the door, J. J. Collins mounted a table and announced that there will be a meeting in the same hall next Tuesday evening, when ex-General Master Workman Powderly will speak.["]

We shall certainly watch the tour of Mr. Gompers with interest. It bids fair to be tempestuous, but withal worth keeping an eye on.

Union Printer and American Craftsman (New York), Apr. 27, 1895.

1. In April 1895 SG embarked on an extended trip through the South and Midwest for the United Garment Workers of America (UGWA) Trades Council of New York and Vicinity; his objectives were to promote the union label, agitate against the sweatshop system, and implement a boycott of Hackett, Carhart, and Co. At the direction of the UGWA, he visited cities where the firm "had its principal trade" (SG to August Todtenhausen, Mar. 18, 1896, reel 9, vol. 14, p. 405, SG Letterbooks, DLC). His stops included Pittsburgh and Scranton, Pa., Washington, D.C., Richmond and Norfolk, Va., Charleston, S.C., Savannah, Augusta, Macon, and Atlanta, Ga., Birmingham, Montgomery, and Mobile, Ala., New Orleans and Shreveport, La., Galveston and Houston, Tex., Little Rock and Hot Springs, Ark., Memphis and Nashville, Tenn., St. Louis, Louisville, Ky., Cincinnati, Oberlin, and Cleveland, Ohio, and Chi-

cago; he returned to New York City in July. The UGWA paid SG some $800—a salary of $30 a week plus expenses (hotel, railroad, doctor, etc.). The *New York Press* reported that SG's "journeys must have aggregated 5,000 miles or more. On an average he spoke on five days of every week, sometimes speaking two or three times in one day. All told, he must have delivered 60 or 70 addresses" (July 21, 1895). For versions of the speech—entitled "Organized Labor, the Republic's Savior"—that SG delivered during the tour, see "An Excerpt from a News Account of an Address in Mobile," May 18, 1895, and "Excerpts from a News Account of an Address in Galveston," May 27, 1895, below.

2. The United GARMENT Workers of America.

3. Terence Vincent POWDERLY, a machinist, had been grand master workman (1879-83) and general master workman (1883-93) of the KOL. He was admitted to the Pennsylvania bar in 1894.

4. The UGWA's dispute with Hackett, Carhart, and Co. during 1894 culminated in the AFL's 1894 convention approving a boycott. Charges against the firm included discrimination against union employees and refusal to honor the union's standards of wages and hours. The AFL's annual convention in December 1895 lifted the boycott after the firm agreed to abide by union conditions.

5. James Roach was the president of the Scranton Central Labor Union.

An Article in the *Savannah Morning News*

[May 6, 1895]

GOMPERS' TALK ON LABOR.

Samuel Gompers of New York, ex-president of the American Federation of Labor, delivered his lecture on Organized Labor, the Republic's Savior, at Masonic hall yesterday afternoon. Mr. Gompers is in the city in the interest of the labor organizations, and is being entertained by committees from the Knights of Labor and the Savannah Trades Assembly. He is a well known labor leader and is traveling through the south in the interest of the various organizations.

His address at Masonic hall was against capital and capitalists, and in behalf of the workingmen and their condition. In the course of his talk he asserted that the city was paying its laborers 60 cents a day, and went on to inveigh against this as a great crime against the workingmen.

Alderman Falligant,[1] who was in the audience, corrected the speaker. He informed Mr. Gompers that the city hired no labor at the price mentioned, and that he probably referred to the road work, which is being done by the county several miles from the city, for which negroes living in that locality are hired at 60 cents a day. This, Dr. Falligant said, is a fair return for the labor given and especially when it was considered that the men are paid to do work which, under the law, it was their business to do without pay.

Mr. Gompers did not agree with the alderman on this point, and asserted that it was a crime for men to be compelled to work for 60 cents a day under any conditions.

After the lecture Mr. Gompers had a conference with representatives of the labor organizations here. He is emphatic in his opposition to the "sweat shop" practices in the large cities, and his purpose is to enlist a sentiment against the purchase of goods manufactured in "sweat shops." His audience was largely of members of the various labor organizations in the city, although there was quite an attendance of others, who were anxious to hear the labor leader.

Savannah Morning News, May 6, 1895.

1. Louis A. Falligant, a Savannah, Ga., physician, served as a city alderman from 1895 to 1897.

An Excerpt from an Article in the
Atlanta Constitution

[May 11, 1895]

MR. GOMPERS IS HERE

. . .

MR. GOMPERS' VIEWS.

"Before I left home for this tour of the south," he said, "I was advised not to come and was told that I would not find any organized labor down here. It was said to me that the south would not permit organized labor and that any one who attempted to say a word in behalf of the cause would be ostracized and maybe maltreated.

"I have been in Washington, Norfolk, Richmond, Charleston, Augusta, Savannah, and Macon, and I am here now. I have never been in any section of the country where I found the laboring man more sincerely and honestly respected than right here in the south. To tell you the truth, I have been really surprised at what I have seen. To me it looks like the people down here, even the moneyed men, appear to realize that the workingmen are the backbone of the country and for the laboring men everyone seems to have a respect. I don't find them downtrodden like I find them in the east and worth to the merchants just what they have in their purse when they go to buy.

On the other hand, I find the great majority of them well dressed, more than ordinarily well educated and with credit at the stores. I find, too, that no few of them have bank accounts and deal with banks that don't cut off on a small overcheck. I discover, too, very much to my surprise, that the large majority of them are home-owners and that while they are the producers here, as they are everywhere, they are not given to consuming everything they make."[1]

. . .

Atlanta Constitution, May 11, 1895.

1. SG denied the accuracy of this story. See "To Henry Blount," May 12, 1895, below.

To Henry Blount[1]

[May 12, 1895]

MR. GOMPERS GOES TODAY.

. . .

. . . It seems that in the talk had with him Mr. Gompers claims he was misquoted[2] and some of the laboring men of the city have secured from him the following letter, which they ask to be printed. The letter reads:

"H. P. Blount, Secretary Atlanta Federation of Trades.[3] Dear Sir and Brother—I am quoted as saying many things which I never uttered—which I do not believe to exist and which are contrary to the facts.

"I did not say that the laboring men of the south are more sincerely respected in the south than the workmen in the east or any other part of the country. In truth, I do not believe that to be the case, for there is usually very little, if any, respect entertained by 'moneyed men' for skilled workmen who receive the munificent wage of 10 cents per hour.

"It is not true that the workmen of the south are 'well dressed,' certainly not as well dressed as they are entitled to be, and by all means not so well dressed as to cause comment from me.

"It is not true that I said that the workmen have 'credit at the stores.' In truth, I am not aware that they have credit at all at the stores. I know, however, that it would be better if the workmen earned sufficient wages, and received them weekly in ready cash, to save them the costly luxury of 'credit at the stores.'

"I did not find that the workmen have 'bank accounts,' neither did I say so. I have serious doubts (and these are confirmed by the representative labor men whom I have met in the south) that the workmen whose wages range all the way down to 60 cents a day are in a position to have 'bank accounts.'

"Nor am I aware, and did not say, that 'a large majority of them (workmen) are home-owners.' In fact, I am reliably informed that not three per cent of the workers are 'home-owners.'

"I am not unmindful of the many kind things said of me personally in The Atlanta Constitution, The Atlanta Journal and The Atlanta Commercial, but I care less for the pretty compliments paid me than my desire to be truthful and consistent, and to be so reported.

"Of course I recognize the right of a newspaper in not publishing such parts of my remarks or public speech as it may see fit to omit, but that does not imply that it has the right to so misrepresent my utterances as to be at variance with the truth and in conflict with my conscience and convictions.

"In order that those who were not present at the interview, or at the meeting may not be deceived as to my observations and remarks, I write this to you and through you to organized labor and the fair-minded public.

["]Fraternally yours,   Samuel Gompers."

Atlanta Constitution, May 12, 1895.

1. Henry Percy Blount was vice-president of International Typographical Union 48 of Atlanta.

2. See "An Excerpt from an Article in the *Atlanta Constitution*," May 11, 1895, above.

3. The Atlanta Federation of Trades was formed in 1891 and affiliated with the AFL during the same year.

An Excerpt from a News Account of an Address in Mobile

[May 18, 1895]

ORGANIZED LABOR.

Temperance Hall was filled last night with a representative audience of workingmen of the city, to listen to an address on the subject of "Organized Labor," by Mr. Samuel Gompers, ex-president of the Federation of Labor, who is at present travelling through the South in the interest of the garment workers of the city of New York, in their struggle against the iniquitous sweat shop system in operation in that city, and more particularly directed against the clothing manufacturing firm of Hackett, Carhart & Co. of that city.

Mr. Gompers is a man of small stature, being very little over five feet in height, but he is by no means a small man, for he has a rotundity of figure that will bring the scales down close to, if not over, the two hundred pound mark. He has coal black hair and mustache, his hair being flowing and his mustache well kept. He was attired last night in a close fitting Prince Albert coat, that accentuated the rotundity of his figure. His delivery is earnest, with no attempt at oratory, and his enunciation is distinct. His voice is deep and sonorous, and he speaks as a man thoroughly en rapport with the subject he discusses.

He was escorted to the stage by Messrs. Judge,[1] Jones[2] and Grove,[3] members of the Central Trades Council,[4] and was introduced to the audience by Mr. Mike Judge, the president of that organization, in a few well-chosen words.

Mr. Gompers said that he appreciated the opportunity of addressing the workingmen of Mobile, and then went right to the heart of his subject, by calling the attention of his audience to the problems that have confronted the laboring man during this, the last half of the nineteenth century, and stated that they were appalling enough to make even the dullest of the laborers stop and ask the question, whither are we drifting? There were over two million workingmen now walking the streets of our cities and the country roads, who were willing and anxious to work, but who were unable to get it; and we are told that the cause of this condition of affairs is overproduction. To my mind there is no excuse so flimsy as this cry of overproduction to cover the sins of the moneyed power against the laboring people. What does overproduction mean? Because we have too much meat the working people can have none to eat; because there is an overproduction of wheat and corn the working people can have no bread; because there is an overproduction of clothes the working people can have no clothes to wear; because there is an overproduction of houses the working people must go shelterless. Away with such an explanation.

I am not unmindful of the progress of this country, but to a hungry man that progress is a sham and civilization is a failure. So long as a man who wants work is without it to that man society and government do a wrong. The speaker then referred to the declaration of independence, which he said guarantees to every man certain inalienable rights, among them being the right of life, liberty and happiness; and there are some to-day who believe that this declaration of our fathers is one of glittering generalities only. The right to life is not only the right to breathe, but the right to maintain that life and the opportunity to work so that you can maintain that life. No man who is willing to work should be denied the opportunity, so that he may maintain his manhood and sustain his wife and little ones.

The speaker then related the history of the downfall of the Roman empire, and showed how when the people became divided into two classes they no longer stood together, but became an easy prey to the barbarians. He warned his hearers that the same cancer that caused the downfall of Rome is now preying at the vitals of this republic, and he called upon them to preserve its integrity, and to hand it down to their children unimpaired. He then turned his attention to the trusts and corporations and showed how they were banded together on one side and the people on the other, and said that if they could combine for their benefit, how much more necessary was it for the workingmen to organize themselves. He said that there was a federal law[5] against combinations and trusts, but that no officer of the government had been found fearless enough to enforce it. He stated that the interstate commerce law had lain dormant until it came in handy to use against the working people when they attempted to assert their rights and protect themselves. When questions of finance come up, it is the sound of the money that controls legislation, and not the voice of the people. There is an oligarchy of money growing up in this country in which dollars, not men, rule.

He paid his respects to the Astors, Vanderbilts and Rockefellers, who spend, he said, most of their time abroad, hobnobbing with lords and princes, and who would give millions of dollars if they could establish an oligarchy in this country, so that they could be the lords and princes of it.

He referred to the condition of the laborer in Alabama, and said that it was in no way creditable to the workingmen of the state. One of the bad features is the low wages paid to your lowest laborers. If the negro laborers are allowed to continue to receive these low wages they will inevitably drag you down to their level, and you cannot improve your own condition unless you help the negro to move up higher. Help him to organize. I do not want you to dance with him, or sleep with him, or kiss him, but I do want you to organize with him. Corporations care nothing for color or race, all they want to know is how cheap you will work. The question of wages is like water, in that it seeks its level. The higher level must come down to the lower level, or the lower level must be raised up to the higher.

The speaker then referred to the condition of the miners at Pratt City,[6] and said that it did not reflect much credit on the workingmen of the state. In this connection he jumped on the commissary stores, or, as he called them, the "Pluck me" establishments, and told how the laborers were paid in tickets, and that these tickets had to be taken to these commissaries, and there the miner or other workman bought his supplies at a profit to his employer of anywhere from 20 to 30 per cent.

He characterized as a crime against society the repeal by the last legislature of the statute prohibiting the employment by corporations of children for more than ten hours per day.[7] The plea made for its repeal was that it would bring into the state more manufacturers. God save us, said the speaker, from such defenders of the women and children of labor. He urged his hearers to have that law reenacted on the statute book at the earliest possible moment.

He told his hearers that the great trouble with many of them is that there are too many party men, and too few labor men. He is neither a Republican nor a Democrat, nor a Populist, but he is a union man, and that he views every question that is brought up from that standpoint, and not as to how it will affect the party. He referred to the sovereignty of the people, and what duties of citizenship they are expected to perform, and said that an overworked and underpaid people cannot exert that influence which is to be expected of a people who are prosperous and contented. A corporation who controls the stomachs of its workingmen comes mighty near to controlling their votes.

Low wages and long hours of labor are not conducive to commercial prosperity. You can compare the countries where the highest wages and the shortest hours prevail with those where the lowest wages and the longest hours prevail, and you will find the greatest commercial prosperity exists in those countries where the former state of affairs exists. If low wages and long hours were conducive to commercial prosperity, then China ought to head the list of the nations of the earth, but you are all aware that she does not.

The speaker then explained to his hearers the system of manufacturing known as the sweat shop system. He described in earnest, forcible language the homes of these people in the crowded tenement houses of New York, and stated that in one room from early morn till late at night, and in that room, reeking with filth, they perform all the functions of life that are possible. There the germs of disease lurk, and are disseminated broadcast through the land, wherever this sweat shop clothing goes. The garment workers of America, he said, are combatting this great evil, and they ask the support of the workingmen of Mobile in their fight against this system, which is fostered by the firm of Hackett, Carhart & Co., clothing manufacturers of New York.

Mr. Gompers announced himself as against strikes on general principles, but said that he would never take away from the workingman the right to strike whenever it was deemed to be necessary. The labor organization which resolved that it would not strike reminded him of the dude regiment of New York, that resolved to disband whenever war was proclaimed. He favored arbitration, but not the arbitration of the lion with the lamb, for that kind of arbitration generally wound up with the lion on the outside of the lamb. He favored the arbitration of two lions. When England has trouble with Egypt, the Boers or Nicaragua, she bombards, but if she has a difference with these United States, she says to this country: "Let's get together and talk this matter over"; or in other words, she is willing to arbitrate. Arbitration never comes when one party is all-powerful and the other is ground down, and if you want to be in a position to arbitrate, you must work and struggle for it, and strengthen yourselves for it. This is why I wish to impress upon you the importance of strong and thorough organization.

He urged upon his hearers the benefits of thorough organization, and said that they were making history, and that they will be cursed or blessed just as they perform or neglect their duties. He made an urgent plea for a better manhood, a nobler womanhood and a happier childhood.

The speaker was frequently applauded during his address, and at the close.

. . .[8]

Mobile Daily Register, May 18, 1895.

1. Michael T. Judge, a mason and builder, was president of the Mobile, Ala., Central Trades Council (CTC).

2. Samuel I. Jones, a printer, was vice-president of the Mobile CTC.

3. Ernest J. Grove, a dry goods salesman, was corresponding secretary of the Mobile CTC.

4. The Mobile CTC was founded in 1889, representing members of trades unions, the KOL, and the state Farmers' Alliance. It affiliated with the AFL in 1902.

5. The Sherman Antitrust Act, which was signed into law on July 2, 1890 (U.S. *Statutes at Large,* 26:209), made it a federal misdemeanor to promulgate contracts, combinations, or conspiracies that restrained interstate or foreign commerce.

6. Pratt City was one of several mining communities involved in a wave of strikes in the Alabama coalfields beginning Apr. 14, 1894, led by the independent United Mine Workers of Alabama. The union's settlement with the powerful Tennessee Coal, Iron, and Railroad Co. on Aug. 15 included some concessions to the miners, but the union failed to win its demand for a forty-cent per ton rate. The strike publicized the hazardous conditions in the industry and the deprivation of the miners.

7. In 1887 the Alabama legislature enacted a law imposing fines on manufacturers

who compelled children under eighteen or women to work more than eight hours a day, permitted children under fourteen to work more than eight hours, or employed children under fifteen in coal or iron mines (Laws of 1886-87, chap. 49). The law was repealed on Dec. 5, 1894.

8. The meeting adopted resolutions calling for the more thorough organization of workers, the abolition of tenement-house and sweatshop labor, the consumption of union-labelled goods, and support for the United Garment Workers of America's campaign against Hackett, Carhart, and Co.

To the Editor of the *Garment Worker*

New Orleans, May 21, 1895.

Editor of *Garment Worker:*

Being in the throes of hard and persistent work, it is sometimes impossible to write as often as I would like to, nor is it within my power to attempt to give you a description of what is being done. There is too much of it and to attempt to recall how my work is progressing, and how the workingmen are co-operating with me, would probably appear like conceit or vain glory. Suffice be it that in every place I have visited the workers when informed of the true state of affairs have pledged themselves to do all within their power to help the U.G.W. of A. in rooting out the sweat shop system, and to make the firm of Hackett, Carhart & Co. realize, that it is to their advantage to amicably adjust their differences with the organizations. Of course, in some instances the work devolved upon me is most difficult, especially in such places where labor is poorly organized, but that has only stirred me to redouble my activity in bringing organizations into being.

In Montgomery, Ala., for instance, I organized a mixed Federal Labor Union, and had them apply for a charter from the A.F. of L. A special committee was appointed by the trades unions to demand union labeled goods from the dealers, and Hackett, Carhart & Co. will no doubt hear from them. I forwarded you the resolutions adopted at a mass meeting held at Birmingham.[1] The dealers seem very favorably inclined, and pledged their support to the unions. The dealers in Montgomery gave me every assurance of support.

At Mobile a great mass meeting was held which I addressed, as well as the meeting of the Trades Council, and Cigarmakers' Union No. 219. The mass meeting adopted the following resolutions:

. . .[2]

I visited the dealers with the usual favorable results, and left Mobile on the 12.45 train for New Orleans, and should have arrived at 5 o'clock. A wreck on the road delayed us three hours, however; the Reception Committee of the unions waited until nearly 8 o'clock. They had arranged for a gathering of representative labor men, and hungry and travel worn I hurried to the meeting. There were about one hundred and fifty earnest men present. A speech of welcome and my response was gone through and it was heartily appreciated by all present, who represented unions of different affiliations. A great mass meeting was held Tuesday evening in one of the largest halls of the city, the Mayor[3] of the city being also present, and you can rest assured, that Mr. Leon Godchaux, the large retailer of Hackett, Carhart & Co. of this city, began to realize that we are not asleep, and that this concern as well as the tools Hackett, Carhart & Co. have been employing to blindfold the workers has been of no avail.

I had no intention of going to Texas, as this State is almost like a continent in itself, but such earnest invitations were sent to me by the unions of Galveston and Houston, that I have been compelled to make arrangements to visit said city. I will write you later. Don't forget to send me a large package of label circulars to every place I visit. Accept my congratulations because of the adoption of the union label by Cane, McCaffrey & Co.,[4] and I have no doubt that your organization and the firm will be greatly benefited by the same, and will reap the advantage of the agitation done.

Trusting that my efforts will prove of lasting benefit to all toilers, and particularly to the garment workers, and that I may aid in the emancipation of the abominable sweating system, I am

Fraternally yours,   Samuel Gompers.

Garment Worker 2 (June 1895): 8.

1. SG spoke at a mass meeting in Birmingham, Ala., on May 13, 1895. The resolutions pledged the support of Birmingham workers in the United Garment Workers of America's campaign against Hackett, Carhart, and Co. and for the abolition of the sweatshop system in the clothing trade.

2. See "An Excerpt from a News Account of an Address in Mobile," May 18, 1895, n. 8, above.

3. John Fitzpatrick was the Democratic mayor of New Orleans from 1892 to 1896.

4. Cane, McCaffrey, and Co. was a New York City clothing firm.

A News Account of an Address in New Orleans

[May 23, 1895]

WOMEN WAGE EARNERS.

Before a small attendance, ex-President Samuel H. Gompers delivered his third address since coming to New Orleans to the Portia

Club last evening. The heavy showers just at the time of beginning the address kept many away who otherwise would have been present to listen to the speaker.

Mr. Gompers was introduced by the president of the Portia Club, Miss Florence Huberwald,[1] in a few felicitous remarks. In beginning his address, he said that he had often spoken to smaller audiences than were then present, but he had always made it a point to keep his engagements and make his speech even if there was but one person besides himself to hear it. Mr. Gompers mentioned the fact that the first labor union he ever belonged to was composed of himself and one other man, and they attended all the meetings—and held all the offices.

Then turning to the subject of women in labor organizations, Mr. Gompers said that the watchword and motto was "Organization for Self-Protection." As with the men, without organization they could accomplish nothing. It would be a hard struggle at first, but final success was only a question of time. He had had many years' experience in labor troubles, but he had never witnessed such heroism anywhere as was shown by the women in the great strike of '77.[2] In fact, in troubles of all kinds, women show far more fortitude than men, and he had met very few women during his lifetime who, once having entered a conflict in which she felt she was on the right side, would ever give up the struggle.

One great handicap to women workers in the field of labor organizations was the mistaken idea that many of them had that the emancipation of women depended upon the good will and charity of humanity. The speaker mentioned a prominent lady of New York who delivered a course of lectures in New York which was patronized by "society." The lecturer soon discovered her mistake and found that she had been talking all theory. She later learned that [the] plain fact in regard to the labor question was that the laborer hirer strove to obtain the greatest amount of labor at the least possible wage. Mr. Gompers said that his experience of thirty years had taught him the power of wealth and he recognized the impending struggle by the working classes for better conditions. Working women were governed by an inexorable law—a law that confronted every wage earner—the greatest amount of work for the least pay.

Many labor unions had declared against this law by insisting upon "Equal pay for equal work," whether men or women. "Women are employed in the industries not because they do more work, do better work, or do it more cheerfully, but for the plain reason that they work for less wages than the men. The only remedy for this inequality in wages is the organization of the women. Men have shown what can be done by organization. All the improvement in hours of labor and in wages can be duplicated by the women if they will only organize.

"To-day Lady Wilke,[3] of England, Miss Frances E. Willard and many other prominent women are working in harmony to organize the working women in the various trades. . . .[4] Too many of our girls are taught from childhood not to look upon life as it really is, but to look upon it as a means toward one end—marriage.

"That education is not the wisest which teaches the girls that they deindividualize themselves by marriage; in fact, if girlhood and womanhood were more independent, there would be less work for the divorce courts."

Mr. Gompers said that, speaking as a man of family, he would have women thoroughly independent; that this condition was the best for the development of the family.

The speaker called attention to the hollow mockery surrounding the actions of what is termed "society." How many women of wealth and position are sick of frittering their lives away and are ready and anxious to reach out and help the women and girls who toil for their daily bread and render them self-supporting, self-asserting and self-governing.

There was no position too high for women to aspire to; none too menial not to warrant the careful consideration of any one. Women would never exercise their political rights until they organize. The corporations which control the stomachs of the working people also control their votes. It was the same way with the working women.

Mr. Gompers assured his small audience that he was greatly in favor of woman's suffrage, but he was confident that woman's emancipation without organization would be a mere matter of form; that all the voting would be done by a few of "the upper ten," while the corporations controlled the rest. Women of wealth should educate their working sisters that they must assert their rights. It was not always the most practical thing to do to form a political party, as the time to wait is too long, and often the real issue is lost sight of among conflicting party measures. What should be looked after was not party interests, but class interests; all measures were of value only in so far as they aided the wage earner; what helps these helps the great mass of the people. He would earnestly urge that working men and women pay less attention to parties and become more engaged in the interests of labor.

In fact, it made no especial difference in the condition of the laboring man whichever party was in power. The only question among the political parties was the spoils question. Those who were in wanted to stay in, and those who were out were fighting all the time to get in. These parties had no consideration for living issues. The working women should foster a spirit of independence against party domination. In regard to the money question, he himself was on the side of silver, but so far as the ordinary working man was concerned the money question cut no figure. He never saw any money paid, as it is the custom to pay with a system of checks.

At this juncture one of the ladies asked why the working men did not right their wrongs at the polls. Mr. Gompers said that it was on account of poor organization; that as they were now, most working men could not afford to vote the way they desired; they would lose their positions if they did.

The speaker then went on to describe the system of Miss Una Dodge's[5] work in New York. He said that she was doing a great work and had accomplished a great amount of good, but she did not recognize the trades union principle. The clubs were organized to help the working women to live in better circumstances, but no general organization for bettering their condition from a labor standpoint. He was afraid that later these clubs might interfere with the regular trades unions.

At this point the members of the club commenced to ask the speaker numerous questions about labor problems, and the address was turned into a general conversation which lasted for a few minutes, after which a vote of thanks was tendered Mr. Gompers for his interesting discourse.

New Orleans Times-Democrat, May 23, 1895.

1. Florence F. Huberwald was a music teacher and secretary at the New Orleans College of Music.
2. See "The New York City Cigarmakers' Strike of 1877-78 and Its Aftermath," in *The Making of a Union Leader,* pp. 95-96.
3. Lady Emilia Dilke was the leader in Great Britain of the Women's Protective and Provident League (after 1889 the Women's Trade Union and Provident League, and after 1891 the Women's Trade Union League) from 1886 until her death in 1904.
4. These ellipses are in the original.
5. Probably Grace Hoadley Dodge, a New York City philanthropist, who was founder and president of the Teachers' College of Columbia University. She began organizing working girls' clubs in 1884 and helped establish the Association for Working Girls' Societies the following year, serving as a director of the organization that by the 1890s was national in scope.

Excerpts from a News Account of an Address in Galveston

[May 27, 1895]

GOMPERS' LECTURE.

Last evening Samuel Gompers, ex-president of the American federation of labor, lectured at the Tremont opera house on "Organized Labor, the Republic's Saviour." The lower part of the house was well filled. On the stage were members of the Galveston labor legislative council,[1] under whose auspices the lecture was given. Mr. Gompers speaks clearly and slowly, but hesitates occasionally as though hunting for a word, but the right word always comes. He was applauded many times throughout his lecture.

. . .

Mr. Gompers spoke substantially as follows:

"I would indeed be wanting were I not to express my sense of gratification at this opportunity to be enabled to address an audience of workingmen, citizens of this beautiful island city. It is the first opportunity I have had of meeting face to face the people of Galveston, to come among you, friends and brothers and fellow-citizens, to preach the old gospel of labor and labor's rights, and to sing to you the same old song condemnatory of labor's wrongs. (Cheers.) My presence may be fraught with some good. Some may question the propriety of discussing material life on the Sabbath evening. To me the thought is, the holier the day the holier the deed; and when the thought is for man's benefit, materially and morally, Sunday is the best day— a day consecrated to the relief of our fellow men. (Applause.) Hear what I have to say, not for my sake, but for the great cause I represent. I ask you to examine carefully what I present and to accept what is good and right and reject what is bad.

"In this year 1895 we find our people and our country in a condition never paralleled in the history of man. Here we are living in a country grand and broad and fertile as any in the universe, with a providence as kind as the sun which shines resplendent upon sixty-five millions of people as thoughtful as any that ever graced the earth, yet we see signs that are calculated to make the wisest stop and ask, 'Whither are we drifting?' When we see two millions of our fellow men walk the streets and the highways of our country begging for the opportunity to earn bread by the sweat of their brow; when we see such conditions exist it is enough to cause us to inquire and see something wrong at the basis of society. We live in a republic and are supposed to be a self-governing people. When there are two millions of people without employment, I ask you to think whether there is danger to our country and to the well being of our people. (Applause.) A little more than a century ago there were men assembled in the colonial congress who declared that we of this country were free and independent and who gave us a new bill of rights, a new declaration that man was entitled to certain rights, to liberty and the pursuit of happiness. There are some who now say this declaration is a mere glittering generality. That declaration meant more than the simple right to breath, for all animals possess this. It carries with it the opportunity to live. (Cheers.) Shakespeare, the greatest poet of England, says you might as well take my life as to take away the means whereby I live. You might as well deny the right to live as to deny the opportunity to maintain life. (Cheers.)

"There is no instance that compares with our country's history so closely as does the Roman republic of 2000 years ago. There existed a people in that country that organized a republic on the consent of the governed. But with the growth of the republic there arose an ingenuity that filched certain rights, certain privileges and certain franchises. Soon there were two classes in that republic, the patrician and the plebian. There are a number of superficial observers who say that Rome perished in one night. The fact is that numbers filched the rights of others, dividing the people and lulling them into fancied security until the republic became a republic only in name. It is no wonder that Rome fell an easy prey to a band of barbarians. I ask you whether the same elements, the same conditions have not grown up in our republic. Is it not true that we have privileges granted, do we not see class legislation, trusts, corporations, growing up wealthy and powerful? Do we not see people on the other hand looking for their rights and to defend the republic? (Cheers.)

"A few years ago the people demanded the passage of the anti-trust law. We see to-day trusts—for example, beef that we need every day, oil for illuminating our houses, coal for warming our houses. Everything we need is a subject of speculation. I ask you, my friends, if you have seen the part of the governing officers in enforcing the law and protecting the people? We had a few years past a law known as the interstate commerce law. Have you seen the strong right arm of the government to defend the people? Has that law been used? The strong right arm is on the side of the corporations. (Cheers.) That law in the interest of the people lay dormant until little more than a year ago it was made an instrument of oppression. It was made a means of excuse to call out the federal troops to oppress the people for the corporations.

"Not more than a few months ago congress tried to do one act of justice, to enact an income tax law. That law declared in a measure that those who are receiving so much contribute a little toward governmental support. That law was declared by the higher courts holding views in consonance with capital to be unconstitutional.[2] Now the only people who can constitutionally pay taxes are those who work to produce wealth, and those who own it. It is tragically sad to see so many idle. Go into Pennsylvania; go to the New England factories; look into your own cotton and woolen mills here and observe the conditions prevailing. They are having men and women work twelve hours a day. Sometimes these employes are compelled to work an hour longer. The working people to-day can not read the Good Book in the old spirit. 'Thy people are not my people, nor thy God my God.'

"I ask you to consider life in the great tenement houses of New York, where twenty or thirty families live in one house, where families eat and drink and make factories out of the little rooms they live in, all for the great modern dollar. This clothing comes among you. Many a man goes to a store and buys a suit that looks well and is surprised that one of his children has consumption or fever; the little boy or girl has caught it because you are so negligent as to buy sweat made clothing of New York. There is one house that has made a point to disrupt organized labor, that has broken away from the sweat houses. Go to your clothing houses and ask them to help you to stamp out the sweat house system.

"When you see the great corporations on one hand and on the other the working men, lulled into fancied security that they enjoy liberty; when we see the millionaires free, they might as well locate in China and be free. We see that the workingmen must struggle for liberty, and if they have it they must struggle to maintain it. He who is free must himself strike the blow. No people maintain progress where the workingmen are on the down scale. Organized labor is the republic's saviour. (Cheers.) Is it not a fact that millionaires court honors of monarchs? Would it not be much to their ease if they could go to the courts of Europe as Duke Vanderbilt or Duke Astor? They would not then bother our ambassadors so much seeking introductions to his royal highness. (Laughter.) If this republic is to be safe it will come through the efforts of the working people, who made this government, but it has been controlled by trusts, and dominated by Wall street, New York, and Threadneedle street, England. Our financial policy is on the basis of what other countries say.

"There is only one enlightened, intelligent expression of labor, and that is expressed in organized labor. Show me manliness in a town and I will show you a town where labor is organized. The man outside of organized labor hides his light under a bushel. If you know better than we come in and teach us. Help us to raise the standard of manhood higher to prevent wrongs between man and man. You will find organizations among all classes of the community. Our state governments are organizations. Our city governments are organizations. Do we not see railroad corporations organize? Do we not see banking institutions having their organizations? Do we not see trusts? Do we not see all forms of organizations? If those people who own millions find it to their benefit to organize, how much more essential for you and me? (Cheers.) Professional men organize. The ministers of the cloth organize. The doctors have their medical associations. If a doctor violates the rules of the medical association he would be wrung down as a quack. Lawyers have their bar associations. They have their rules of ethics governing their profession. If a man with the eloquence of Demosthenes and not a lawyer should arise to plead in court the judge, in the capacity of walking delegate of workmen's union, would ask this man to show his working card. (Loud cheers and laughter.) They call it a diploma. If he did not have the card he would not be allowed to work in that law shop. (More laughter.) He would be termed a shyster. Can labor be blamed if we, too, organize, establish rules and create a system of honor, and have a pet name for one who will violate our ethics?

"The captains of industry are often wanting in their economic ideas. They cry overproduction, business dull and trade choked. What do they do? They say, if you will accept a reduction of 10 per cent or work one hour longer we will conduct the business. Don't be fooled. Times are bad because the people have not the wherewith to buy the things they need. The remedy for this is not to cut wages or work an hour longer. One need but state the proposition to the average school of political economy as a solution for the industrial crisis. We are not captains of industry, nor statesmen, but we have a degree of horse sense, and we say that no trade is so profitable as comes from those receiving high wages, who can cultivate tastes and special aptitudes. Some say American labor shall come down from its high pedestal. No doctrine is so false. Look at any country and you will find where the hours of labor are least wages are highest, and the greatest prosperity in commerce and industry prevails. Long hours and small pay prevail in China. China should therefore stand at the head of civilization, yet 400,000,000 of Chinamen went flying before 14,000,000 of pigmies.[3]

"I believe you will agree with me that the laboring men of Galveston, made intelligent by organization, will bear comparison with any in

America. I was glad to come among a people that are organized. The honorable manner in which they threw themselves around the locked out at the cotton mills is gratifying.[4] Eternal vigilance is the price of liberty and of wages. It is your duty to stand by your banner of labor as true as you stand by the banner of your country. (Cheers.)

"I have done as much as any man to prevent strikes. There is one thing I will not do. I will not join in any 'holler' against strikes. Let the workingmen once declare that they will not strike under any circumstances and corporations will do all the striking for us. Such organizations remind me of a dude regiment which resolved it would disband whenever a war breaks out. We don't want to strike, but we reserve the right to strike.

"Arbitration is all right, but you must not try to arbitrate between lions and lambs. When England has a dispute with Egypt, the Boers or with Nicaragua she threatens to bombard them at once. When she has a dispute with the United States she says: 'Come, let us talk the matter over.' I would be untrue to myself if I held up the false beacon light until workingmen became a prey to cupidity. If you are in favor of arbitration urge organization."

The speaker next advocated eight hours for work, eight hours for recreation and eight hours for rest. He urged the importance of laborers using their leisure time for their own self-improvement and for the improvement of their families.

. . .

Galveston Daily News, May 27, 1895.

1. The Galveston Labor Council was organized in 1894.

2. The U.S. Supreme Court declared the income tax provisions of the 1894 Wilson-Gorman Tariff Act unconstitutional in *Pollock* v. *Farmers' Loan and Trust Co.* (157 U.S. 429; 158 U.S. 601), which it decided in 1895.

3. Possibly a reference to the recent Chinese defeat in the Sino-Japanese War, although Japan's population was over 30 million.

4. Between four hundred and five hundred men, women, and children walked out of the Galveston Cotton Mills on Feb. 20, 1895, protesting the company's policy of requiring overtime beyond the customary sixty-six-hour week. The company claimed that the overtime was needed in order to test its new looms. When the workers returned the following day, the company locked them out. An arbitration committee of the city council proposed a settlement that would have excused from overtime those physically unable to work longer hours, but the company rejected the proposal as a bad precedent and was able to restore production by hiring new workers.

An Article in the *Garment Worker*

June 9th, 1895.

Press dispatches from Little Rock, Ark., state that Samuel Gompers has been prostrated with gastritis brought about by overwork, at his hotel at that place. This occurred just prior to a mass-meeting which he was to have addressed in the Tabernacle. The ambition of the unions of Little Rock, and the great tribute paid to Bro. Gompers is shown by the fact that the Tabernacle has a seating capacity of at least ten thousand.

A later telegram to the General Office reports that Bro. Gompers has somewhat recovered and intends to meet all engagements made.

Garment Worker 2 (June 1895): 8.

An Excerpt from a News Account of an Address in Memphis

[June 11, 1895]

HE FAVORS ORGANIZED LABOR

Samuel Gompers, one of the leaders of labor organizations in the United States and a fluent orator, last night at the Young Men's Hebrew Association Hall addressed an audience composed not only of the laboring element of the city, but representative business men, taking as his theme "Organized Labor," in whose behalf he has long been identified.

Previous to his remarks, Walter A. Brennan[1] was chosen chairman of the meeting and J. A. Orchid[2] secretary.

In beginning his speech Mr. Gompers stated that he had been seriously ill a few days ago, and only through his enthusiasm and interest he has on the subject was he able to acquire enough will power to address the people of this city.

. . .

"You hear on every hand calls for a larger army and navy. Does this country fear invasion from foreign powers? No. The fear is that a civil turbulence between two classes of people in this country is brewing. That is the subject that is just now agitating their minds, before a crisis is reached. Is that not an evidence which goes conclusively to show that such a crisis is expected to be precipitated sooner or later? Congress can, but will not alleviate this condition, and I will venture to assert that not one in this audience can enumerate six laws that were passed during the recent session that were beneficial to the laboring class.

"Memphis is the Mecca for those having something to say regarding progression, and I here take occasion to condemn and criticize one of the most prominent citizens of your town. That man is Capt. J. H. Martin,[3] who, at Atlanta, some days ago, at a public meeting, arose and endorsed the action of Grover Cleveland since he has been president, at the same time declaring that the latter's salary should be raised to $100,000 and given the office for life. This gentleman of your city should at once immigrate to Russia, where he can have his heart's desire regarding tyranny. I think it is bad enough to have him for four years, much less for life. This republic, if it continues in its present course, will finally be swept away; not by sudden violence, but by the gradual stealing away of our rights. Will the people not exert themselves to keep the United States from being destroyed by its own folly? There has never been a time when a tyrant could not get a judge to approve his acts under the disguise of the dignity of the law. Never before has this fact been so manifest as at present.

"In matters pertaining to this State I desire to mention the trouble that occurred at Coal Creek a few years ago,[4] when convict labor was given precedence over free men vainly trying to earn an honest living. In this case the State was partial to the convicts. The great lawyer, Blackstone, once said that there was no law unless justice was given. Do you call the case I cite justice? It is a funny state of affairs when a convict is taken care of better than an honorable man."

After denouncing the sweat shop system in New York and declaring himself for the free and unlimited coinage of silver at the ratio of 16 to 1, Mr. Gompers concluded his speech.

At the close of Mr. Gompers's address Gen. W. H. Sebring[5] arose in the audience and stated that a committee bore an invitation to Mr. Gompers from the Central Bimetallic League of Shelby county, and read the following communication:

Memphis, Tenn., June 10, 1895.

To Hon. Samuel Gompers:

The Bimetallic League of Shelby county has commissioned us to express to you its sympathies with the noble efforts of yourself and your co-laborers to better the condition of our toiling fellow-citizens, and to convey to you its earnest and cordial invitation to attend the great bimetallic convention in this city on the 12th and 13th instants, and take part in its deliberations. We are, very respectfully,

W. H. Sebring,
T. U. Sisson,[6]
John E. Bell.[7]

To this invitation Mr. Gompers responded as follows:

["]Gentlemen of the Bimetallic Committee:

["]I wish to say that I am deeply gratified for your courteous invitation, and I regret that I am forced by circumstances to decline it. My ticket is already purchased, and I must leave on this evening's train to fill my appointment in Nashville.[8] In the great battle of which your convention is but an opening skirmish, my sympathies and my prayers are with you.

["]I will add that, in my judgment, the laborers of our great country are a unit for the free and unlimited coinage of both gold and silver at the ratio of 16 to 1. In every convention they have so declared. I have probably seen and intimately associated with more laborers in their councils and work shops than any man present, but if I have ever met an intelligent laborer who was a goldbug I do not recall it. I have never met and hope I shall never meet such an anomalous creature.

["]Allow me to suggest that perhaps even you gentlemen of the Bimetallic League underestimate the foe with which you and I have to deal. Few men who have not had occasion to observe his methods realize the power of money. The goldbug is unscrupulous. He weighs hearts and human happiness in the same scales that he weighs a pound of pork. He is the lineal-descendent of the same old gang of Tories who during the revolutionary struggle of our forefathers for independence besought congress to make terms with the British king. He is stronger now than then, for at that time he had no American president to abet him.

["]He has followed his nefarious robbery of the American people so long that he has persuaded himself that his crimes are legitimate — like the gambler who has plied his trade undisturbed until he has grown rich, and thus characterizes as revolutionary any attempt to enforce the law, and insists that it is an infringement upon his vested rights.

["]My brothers, let me say to you that you have not only the goldbug of Wall street to fight, but wherever a gilded civilization exists, whether it be in autocratic Russia, in that libel upon a republic, France, in that constitutional monarchy, Germany, or in that land of gamblers and stock-jobbers, England, every Shylock clamoring for his pound of flesh will make the fight his own. His money will be used against us. To meet it we can only rely upon the patriotic resentment of a brave and intelligent people.

["]The financial question is a great one. It will never be settled till it is settled right. But the greatest of all questions which the American people have to grapple with is the overshadowing problem of labor.

["]Again I thank you for your cordial invitation.["]

After listening to a number of resolutions denouncing the sweat shop system, etc., which were read by N. O. Pinard,[9] Mr. Gompers at once drove to the Louisville & Nashville depot to depart for Nashville, where he lectures tonight.

Memphis Commercial Appeal, June 11, 1895.

1. Walter A. Brennan, a high school janitor and engineer, was president of the Memphis Trades Council (TC).

2. John A. Orchi was president of CMIU 266 of Memphis and secretary of the Memphis TC. He became an organizer for the AFL.

3. Probably J. Henry Martin, a Memphis businessman.

4. See *Unrest and Depression,* p. 215, n. 4.

5. William H. Sebring was a Memphis travel agent.

6. Thomas U. Sisson was a Memphis lawyer.

7. John E. Bell, a Memphis lawyer, lived in Idlewild, Tenn.

8. SG spoke in Nashville on June 11, 1895.

9. William O. Pinard was secretary of Journeymen Barbers' International Union of America (JBIUA) 36 of Memphis. He later became an organizer for the JBIUA and an AFL general organizer for the state of Tennessee.

To Samuel Mitchell[1]

June 18th 1895.

My Dear Son: —

Just a little respite from work, worry or pain and I take advantage of it to, first, acknowledge the receipt of your recent letter and second to say to you that I appreciated your kind words and earnest solicitude for me, more than I can find words to express.

I am doing the best I can to take care of myself. The work of nearly 25 years in the one constant, never ending struggle, the intensity and persistancy with which I have striven have at last told on me. They have made the inroads on my constitution, which I fear will never be as strong again as it was of yore. I think however that I am now on the road to recovery.

You can imagine how I suffered when I tell you that I lost 22 pounds in six days. In the past week I have again gained 12 pounds.

There are considerations, which I hope to explain on my return, which require my being at Oberlin O. on the 25th and Chicago July 4-5. If it were not for these two dates I would be home on the 24th. It would be useless however to come home and then in a few days after make a trip of 2.000 miles (there and back). Don't you agree with me on that point? Otherwise I would gladly come home. I long to be home and see all those who are so near and dear dear to my heart. I would answer the summons of my Darling Henrietta to come home from the Union.

In the turmoil of duties I omitted to send felicitation to you and my Dear Rose[2] on the anniversary of your and her marriage.[3] Dear Girl, she wrote me that never since her marriage has she been so happy as she is now, and I know that you are to be credited with her contented state of mind. You can appreciate how ardent is my wish that you may both live long in happiness and prosperity together and with the Darling Baby, a source of pleasure, more grand and beautiful than your fancies can picture.

Pardon, if I can write no more now, Kiss my Rose & Henrietta for me and give my love to Mother and the children. and for yourself accept the kindest feeling and best wishes of

Your Dear Father   Saml Gompers.

N.B. Please ask Rose to excuse my not writing to her direct.

SG

ALS, George Meany Memorial Archives, Silver Spring, Md.

1. Samuel MITCHELL, the husband of SG and Sophia Gompers' daughter Rose, was a letter carrier.
2. Rose Gompers MITCHELL, daughter of SG and Sophia Gompers.
3. Samuel Mitchell and Rose Gompers were married on May 3, 1891.

An Excerpt from an Article in the
Cleveland Plain Dealer

Oberlin, June 25. [1895]

GOMPERS ROILED[1]

. . .

Mr. Samuel J. Gompers, ex-president of the American Federation of Labor, spoke on trade unions. He blamed the economists in that they tried to defend existing conditions. The labor movement was born of hunger. The hungry man considers all progress a delusion and a snare. Socialists would defer the struggle, but labor faces boldly existing evils. We hear much of the risks of capital, but never of the dangers which labor undergoes. The capitalist at his worst is better [off?] than labor at its best. No country can become great over the poverty of its people. Wealth and combines have proved themselves superior to law and these labor must fight. The very laws, few as they are, which intended to help labor, have been turned against it by the courts and the influence of capital. Mistake of economic life is in attempting to adjust industrial conditions to civil law, while the reverse should be true. As long as man and man have the relations of buyer and seller the labor movement will be on.

To hear two prominent labor leaders debate is a privilege not often enjoyed in Oberlin. This afternoon Samuel Gompers, ex-president of the American Federation of Labor, and "Tommy" Morgan,[2] the Socialist, of Chicago, got into a warm discussion. Last evening Morgan, in his address said that in a convention held in Denver last December the officers of the Federation of Labor as delegates violated their instructions to vote for plank 10, which was offered by Morgan. In this plank collective ownership of all elements of production and distribution was advocated. This afternoon Gompers, early in his address, answered Morgan's charges. He denied Morgan's statement, assuring the audience that if such instructions had been given they would have been obeyed and furthermore claiming that plank 10 was warmly supported by the officers of the American Federation of Labor.

Gompers' slap at Morgan made the latter jump to his feet again.

This time the Chicago Socialist intimated that the officers of the American Federation of Labor have been and can be bribed.

This accusation aroused Gompers tremendously. He emphatically denied the hints at his dishonest actions and said that no men in the world are doing more to raise the condition of the workingman than the officers of the American Federation of Labor. He then proceeded to criticize the Socialists in their methods of pursuits. He said that the Socialist does not meet the questions of the day, but is constantly putting off present problems. Morgan again defended his position by denying Gompers' allegations. At this point Hon. James Monroe,[3] who was presiding, announced that the session would close. Apparently good feeling existed, but it is said that Gompers and Morgan have had trouble before.

. . .

Cleveland Plain Dealer, June 26, 1895.

1. SG was speaking at the Oberlin Summer School of Christian Sociology, a conference on the "Causes and Proposed Remedies for Poverty" that was held June 20-29, 1895. In addition to SG, the speakers included Jane Addams, Robert Bandlow, Clarence Darrow, Washington Gladden, Thomas Morgan, and Carroll Wright.

2. Thomas John MORGAN was a Chicago machinist, brass finisher, and, later, a lawyer, and was a prominent figure in the SLP. He served as general secretary of the International Machinists' Union in 1894 and 1895.

3. James Monroe (1821-98) held the chair of political science and modern history at Oberlin. He served as a Republican congressman from Ohio from 1871 to 1881.

A News Account of an Address in Chicago

[July 5, 1895]

GRAND FETE OF LABOR

. . .

ADDRESS OF SAMUEL GOMPERS.

Samuel Gompers, fraternal delegate to the British trades union congress, followed Gov. McKinley with an extemporaneous address on the "Logic of the Labor Movement." He said:

Mr. Chairman, Friends, Fellow Citizens, Fellow Working Men and Women: I have, with you, enjoyed a pleasurable afternoon listening to the able and eloquent speeches of the distinguished gentlemen who have addressed us. It is indeed inspiring to hear the history of the past recounted, to hear of the glorious achievements of the men who participated in the struggles for the liberty which we now enjoy. I stand here in full accord with every sentiment expressed of patriotism and of love for law and order, and am ready to sing loud and long the pean of praise and place the halo of loveliness, truthfulness and godliness upon the tomb and around the heads of the martyrs and chieftains and warriors and statesmen who fought so bravely and so nobly and devised everything so wisely and handed down to us this great document, the declaration of independence of these United States, and gave to mankind a declaration not only of the freedom and independence of our country from the domination of any other, but gave to the world a new meaning to the rights of man. But, my friends, in coming together as we do on each recurring anniversary of our national birthday it is not only wise to refer eloquently and display our knowledge of and faith in the traditions of the past, but it is also meet for us to consider the living questions that present themselves today. Not more than a few days ago, I am informed, one of the metropolitan papers said that when these labor men speak it is the same old talk. True it is, 'tis pity 'tis true. But 'tis true. It is the same old talk because the same old wrongs exist. Each age brings forth its new problems, and it is required that the men of each age shall endeavor to discover the solution for these problems. Today it is not the political government which is the problem to be solved; the industrial concerns of our people is the problem. I am not desirous at this gathering to interject one discordant note in the beautiful harmony and rhyme of language and oratory and eloquence. I won't mar the beauty and joy of this grand occasion, this great demonstration, but I think that it is wise, as men and women, that it is becoming as Americans and as patriots, that we should not close our eyes to existing conditions and imagine ourselves into a fool's paradise.

A little more than a year ago the convention[1] of the American Federation of Labor was being held here, and in the city hall of this, the great metropolis of our country, the men and women who were delegates to that convention were compelled to carefully thread and find their way on the stone floors of your municipal building lest they tread upon men who lay upon its cold stones. In this broad country of ours, with the land as rich as anywhere in the world, yielding up its treasures at the touch of man; with 70,000,000 of people as earnest, as energetic, as this world has ever produced; with the agencies of human ingenuity harnessing the forces of nature to man's needs; with inventions and discoveries, with the application of new forces to industry in commerce, we saw in the years 1893 and 1894 as many unemployed men in our country as the population embraced in the year 1776 when this country was declared free and independent. My friends, this is a condition of affairs which should make the foolish as well as the wise stop and ask themselves and to advise with each other as to whither we are drifting. In these United States, a government in theory by declaration, by constitutional enactments, resting upon the consent of the governed, where the people are supposed to be and are by law the sovereigns, a condition of affairs which thrusts three millions of people upon the streets into idleness bodes no good for the future. On every hand we see arising discontent among the masses, and on the other hand attempts at repression. In every one of our cities we see immense fortresses being built in our streets upon the most scientific principles of military strategy. Are they constructed with a view of repulsing a foreign foe? We hear the cry that the army of the country must be strengthened. Is there any danger of any country attacking these United States? Then why these great citadels in our cities and the demand for an increase in the army? Is it not in itself a confession that there are conditions arising continually in our country which are placing self-government in jeopardy?

The labor question stands as an interrogation point to all these explanations and apologies which are made for the maladministration of our industrial and commercial affairs. It punctures the assertions of political economists and questions those who speak by the card. The labor movement stands as a protest against the wrongs existing heretofore and as the manifest organization of the masses of the people, who have the most direct interest in seeing that the masses shall not go down in the social and economic scale. What is the logic of the labor movement? We see that the men intrusted with the commerce and the industry of the country, who, by chance or opportunity or special privilege or charter under the laws, are fostered, encouraged and supported, are popularly known as captains of industry. If the captains of any military organization were to have attempted to conduct a military struggle upon such false lines, upon such lines as lead to disaster and starvation of many of our people, they would have been deposed from their military commands. If these men are entitled to the name of captains of industry, they are also responsible for the failure of their maneuvers in their efforts to conduct industrial and commercial affairs. If ever men have demonstrated their incapacity, their impotence to conduct commerce and industry, the men in command of our economic and social conditions have certainly given plain proof of it. The sooner the organized labor movement gathers within its folds the earnest, sincere, active, energetic, intelligent and aggressive workers, the sooner will the wrongs inflicted be remedied, the sooner will the impotent be displaced by those competent to lead affairs economically, socially and industrially. Some speak of strikes in a denunciatory manner, and since Chicago has had some experience in the matter of strikes, it will not be amiss to at least say a few words upon this subject, for in it is concerned something of the logic of the labor movement.

What is a strike? It is a refusal on the part of the sellers of a certain article to continue to sell on the terms upon which they sold before. We hear of lockouts. A lockout is nothing more or less than a refusal on the part of a buyer to buy something on the terms that he bought before, and so long as the relations between the employer and employee shall continue to be of the buyer and of the seller the matter of withholding sale or withholding purchase will continue. We might as well look this question squarely in the face and discuss it as it is, not as we would like it to be. I wish the time were at hand on this one hundred and nineteenth anniversary of our nation's existence when we might proclaim the millennium to mankind and achieve it. But, alas, the millennium is not here.

I know that strikes are sometimes accompanied by acts of violence, and I think there are none who protest against this violence so much as do the organizations of labor and the men who are connected with the movement of labor. But serious as this is, wrongful as this is, it is one of the manifestations of the struggles of the human race. From time immemorial it has been a question of one man controlling the labor of another, and labor has always had the load upon its shoulders. It is the continual effort on the part of this Hercules, this modern Samson, who is bound hands and feet, to gradually strike one of the cords from off his limbs. I admit that it is wrong for this violence to take place at any time, but I want you to bear in mind, too, that the struggles in previous ages for the establishment of a greater degree or a fairer degree of justice among men have been accomplished with bloodshed, bushwhacking and sometimes murder and rapine. Strikes can be avoided to a very great extent provided that the toilers shall organize, for there is none who respect right so much as those who know that back of that right is the power and might to enforce it.

The movement of labor grows out of the necessities of the toilers. It grows from hunger in the first instance—hunger for bread. In the next, hunger for home and develops into hunger for knowledge, a hunger for a brighter day to come, hunger for more fraternal feeling, hunger for higher aspirations, a higher condition between the manhood and womanhood of our country. There are few who understand the sentiment underlying the organized labor movement. There are few who care to take the trouble to understand it. But beneath it all is the sentiment of the stout-hearted men and the strong willed men to go down into the factory and the mills and the workshops and take the child from out [of] their precincts and place it in the schoolroom or playground. Modern capitalism has in many instances run mad, so that even to-day in some of our southern states we see the government declaring to those who possess wealth: "Come to our state. We offer you our women, we offer you our children, no matter how young they may be, take them; do with them what you will; place your octopus upon them; drag them into the factory, into the mill or into the mine; grind their bones into dollars; we give you full privilege, only come."

No race of barbarians that ever existed yet offered up children for money. I take second position to no man in my devotion to the institutions of our country. I take second position to no man in my love of the emblem of our country that floats over us. But I am not unmindful of the evils which exist, and I adjure you and implore you to not only revere the past, but to look the present squarely in the face and organize and organize, and in organization seek the causes underlying the present evils which surround us and endeavor to emulate the good example, the humanity, the patriotism, the nobility of character and motive that prompted Jefferson and Washington and Paine to do their duty.

Chicago Chronicle, July 5, 1895; *National Labor Tribune*, Aug. 22, 1895.[2]

1. The AFL's 1893 convention met in Chicago, Dec. 11-19.

2. The text of this document was transcribed from two damaged and incomplete issues of the *Chicago Chronicle*—the only extant copies of the paper that could be located—and from the *National Labor Tribune*, which reprinted a portion of the *Chronicle*'s coverage of SG's address.

To George McNeill

July 17th, [189]5.

Dear friend McNeill,

Your favor of recent date to hand and contents noted. I have also read the constitution of the newly formed organization,[1] and I can only say that it meets my hearty approval. There are a number of men who cannot belong to the trade union movement proper, and it would be a most excellent thing if an institution could be formed wherein their attainments could be utilized toward furthering and co-operating with the trade union movement. Of course care must be exercised however in order to prevent many new converts and philanthropic persons from attempting to undertake to direct the labor movement, rather than be its advisors and conductors. We have had too much of this sort of thing to allow another to occur by our own device. We must not create another "Frankenstein." I believe that the provisions made in the temporary constitution were a sufficient guarantee against such a calamity. In line with what I have said you can readily understand I accept the honorary position, and will do all within my power to aid the new movement.

You may have heard that I have been seriously ill on my recent trip. News papers while speaking of its seriousness, never knew how critically ill I was. It was a long trip and my will power I am sure overcame the disease, and saved me for some years more, I hope, of good work.

I would be pleased to accept the invitation to come to Plymouth, at the summer school to deliver an address, but since my return I feel that it is necessary for me to take some little rest before my departure for Europe[2] to attend the British Trade Union Congress.[3] I would be delighted to come down to Boston to see you and our other friends, but under the circumstances I am sure you will appreciate the fact that I ought not to. I am also pleased to learn that our friend Lloyd's ability[4] is being taken advantage of to further the interest of our fellow workers.

I wish you could go with McGuire[5] and I to the other side. It would give me more pleasure than I can attempt to describe. Remember me kindly to Mrs. McNeill[6] and to my numerous friends, and accept for yourself the best wishes of

Yours sincerely   Saml Gompers

I never hear from [our friends. . . .]

T and ALpS, reel 341, vol. 356, p. 1, SG Letterbooks, DLC.

1. Probably a reference to the National Educational and Economic League, created in the spring of 1895 by the Boston Christian socialist William Dwight Porter Bliss and a number of like-minded reformers. George McNeill served as the League's president and Henry Lloyd as its secretary. The organization, whose existence was apparently very brief, was meant to propagate the tenets of Fabian socialism among workers, especially those in trade unions.

2. The AFL's 1894 convention elected SG and P. J. McGuire as fraternal delegates to the TUC meeting at Cardiff in September 1895; accompanied by SG's cousin Emanuel, they sailed for Europe on Aug. 14. In addition to attending the congress, SG and McGuire traveled to Manchester, Liverpool, Dublin, Paris, Hamburg, and Amsterdam, where they conferred with local labor leaders and addressed labor meetings, including sessions of the Dublin Trades Council (TC) and the Hamburg TC. SG visited relatives in London and Amsterdam. The three arrived back in New York on Sept. 28.

3. The 1895 meeting of the TUC was held in Cardiff, Wales, Sept. 2-7.

4. Henry LLOYD, a member of United Brotherhood of Carpenters and Joiners of America (UBCJA) 33 of Boston, was general president of the UBCJA from 1896 to 1898. He served as president of the Boston Central Labor Union in 1896.

5. Peter James McGUIRE was secretary of the Brotherhood of Carpenters and Joiners of America (after 1888 the UBCJA) from 1881 to 1901. He served as first vice-president of the AFL from 1890 to 1900.

6. Adeline J. Trefethen McNeill.

An Article in the *Labor Leader*[1]

[July 27, 1895]

HAVING FUN WITH SAM.

Samuel Gompers must bear a charmed life. At least, several of his friends in Chicago believe so. A year ago those three practical jokers,

Dick Powers,[2] J. J. Ryan[3] and Jim Linehan, attempted to bump the life out of the ex-president of the American Federation of Labor by giving him a front seat in the boat which shoots the chutes, a full account of which was published in the Eight Hour Herald at the time. Sam was in town last week to show his love for the stars and stripes. If Sam is anything he is truly a citizen, and does not believe in any of the peculiar "isms" whose only presence in the labor movement is for the purpose of disrupting it. After he had had his say at Sharpshooters' Park he was taken in hand by Linehan, G. W. Perkins,[4] and several other good citizens and given a good time. Friday, Linehan proposed a ride through the city on bicycles. No sooner proposed than accepted, as Gompers holds the record for speed on Manhattan Island, and he wanted to exhibit his proficiency on the wheel before his Chicago friends. The wheels were secured and the party started over on the West side. After riding along Lake street, under the elevated road and over the corduroy roadway, the conspirators branched off in other streets possessing more or less disreputable pavements. Whenever there was an unusually rocky piece of roadway, Perkins and Linehan would turn to Gompers and say: "Now, Sam, let us take advantage of this splendid track and speed our wheels." Their victim would pull his hat down over his eyes to hide the revengeful glitter therein and say: "I have heard of your streets before, but never thought they were as bad as this." "Why, this is the boulevard," said Linehan, "and you have nothing to equal it in New York." Gompers was sweating blood about this time. He did not like to show his feelings to the others, and kept manfully on. In this way, after several hours riding, about ten miles had been covered, but Gompers thought he had ridden one hundred. Not a sandy road nor a rocky street was forgotten by the men who were taking their guest out for a spin. Sometimes an unusually bad alley was spied by Linehan, and he would enter it. Gompers, of course, followed. It was about 8 P.M. when the party, all tired out by their extraordinary feat, stopped at a North side summer garden. Then Gompers took his friends into confidence and told them that he would never, no, never, take another bicycle ride in Chicago until the streets had been paved. He grew eloquent over the streets of New York. That he had been the victim of his friends he never suspected, and there is no telling what line of revenge he will work upon when he finds out he had simply fallen into a trap laid for him by his Chicago friends.

Labor Leader (Boston), July 27, 1895.

1. Reprinted from the *Eight-Hour Herald* (Chicago).
2. Richard POWERS, a Chicago sailor, served as president of the Lake Seamen's Union from its foundation in 1878 into the 1890s.

3. John J. Ryan was a member of the gas fitters' association of Chicago.
4. George William PERKINS was president of the CMIU from 1891 to 1926.

To Fusataro Takano[1]

July 28th, [189]5

Mr. F. Takano,
Hengo, Tokio, Japan
Dear Sir:—

I am in receipt of your favor of May 10th, but in as much as I have been on a three months trip in the interest of the trade union movement throughout the entire south, and south west, I have been unable to give either any attention or reply before my return. I write now in the hope that this may [reach] you, and that I may as soon as possible receive a reply.

It is unnecessary for me to say that I read your letter with not only pleasure but with a great deal of interest and have even wondered how you had fared after your arrival in Japan. I presume that your experience as a war correspondent must have been varied, interesting and exciting.

As a humanitarian as well as a man of affairs I am in some doubt as to whether the best results have been obtained by the termination of hostilities between your country and China.[2] At present, it is the same barbarous Chinese dynasty and corrupt institutions in power there, without the slightest hope coming for reformation of any kind to the people of China, and which has resulted in their suffering, sacrifice and death. Possibly had that Empire become dismembered, [and] the dynasty and the royal family dethroned, it might have resulted in the opening up of a new era for the people of that country, and help to push forward the people of the entire world in their struggles toward a civilization so much to be desired.

I am willing to confess that this criticism may be the result of misinformation, but from reading not only that which is published, but between the lines, it is the only conclusion to which I have arrived. Any information from you upon that or any other matter would be cheerfully and cordially received.

While the newspapers here gave quite extended accounts from the seat of war daily and several of them being rivals, taken in the aggregate, they were no doubt fairly accurate.

Before you receive this letter I shall leave for Europe. You may have read that I have been elected by the American Federation of Labor to attend the British Trade Union Congress which convenes in Cardiff, Wales Sept. 2nd. Of course, I shall return here about the middle of October and begin preparations for the next annual convention of the A.F. of L. which will be in session in New York City December 9th.

By the way, will you return to the United States by that time? If so it would give me pleasure to see that an invitation was extended you to read a paper before the convention.[3] Let me know in reply to this. If you could send your answer so that it could reach me in London by the end of September, then address it to me c/o Mr. Samuel Wood,[4] 19 Buckingham St. London. [. . . office.] Otherwise send your answer to 28 Lafayette Place, New York City.

As per your request I shall ask my successor[5] to send you the "Federationist" from the time you failed to receive them.

I am sure you use your best judgment to do what you can and began at the right time to disseminate a better knowledge and feeling among the wage workers of Japan for their organization and self-protection. The movement in Formosa Japan is somewhat incomprehensible to many here and a little explanation on that point if you could give it would be a pleasure to me and a number of friends.

Pardon me if I cannot discuss the change in the personal of the Executive head of the A.F. of L. You can readily understand that delicacy forbids me to more than refer to it. I thank you however for your very kind consideration of my devotion to the great cause of labor.

With kind wishes to you and hoping to hear from you at your earliest convenience, I am

Sincerely yours   Saml Gompers.

TLpS, reel 341, vol. 356, pp. 4-5, SG Letterbooks, DLC.

1. Fusataro TAKANO was a Japanese labor leader. In 1897 he reconstituted the Shokkō Giyū-kai (Fraternal Society of Workers) and was appointed secretary of the Rōdō Kumiai Kisei-kai (Society for the Promotion of Trade Unions).

2. The immediate cause of the Sino-Japanese War (July 1894-April 1895) was competition for control of Korea. The victorious Japanese forced territorial and other concessions from China, including the cession of Formosa, some of which they later relinquished under pressure from the European powers. The war marked Japan's emergence as a modern state with imperial ambitions.

3. There is no indication that Takano addressed the convention.

4. Samuel WOODS, secretary of the Parliamentary Committee of the TUC from 1894 to 1904, was a miners' leader and a Liberal/Labour Member of Parliament.

5. John McBRIDE was president of the United Mine Workers of America from 1892 to 1895. He was elected president of the AFL over SG in 1894, and was narrowly defeated for that office the next year.

To Adolph Strasser

28 Lafayette Pl. NY City. July 29th [189]5

Friend Strasser: —

I was in hopes to be able to stop over at Buffalo on my way East but owing to my severe illness on the trip, had to come on home as soon as possible. Then I learned that you were at Buffalo.

During my stay at Chicago I had a general talk with Mr Perkins and he stated that your first intimation to him was that Dampf's accounts were about $10.000. short but that from your later examinations you believed the shortage to be about $4.000.

Mr Perkins was doubtful as to the advisability of publishing the matter of this shortage owing to the injury, we both felt sure, it would do the good name of our organization. He said he would do whatever seemed best. For my part, it seems to me that the publication can do no good and only do injury. However if it is got to come let it come. I believe firmly if his accounts are a few hundred or even a thousand dollars short it was due to his weakness to help others, whose suffering and appeals he could not withstand; and if it [is] a much larger amount he was mentally unsound.

I had a number of talks with Mrs Dampf and she is the most disconsolate woman I ever met. She is constantly weeping; and then the fear that if the shortage is so large that she cannot cover it, possible exposure and then her children who look with reverence upon their Father's memory, they will have to blush for him and feel the sting of public scorn and the injury to their future, resulting therefrom. I myself feel this matter keenly since I counted myself his friend and he mine.

Mrs Dampf said that if it involved no more than about a thousand dollars she would take the last $500. she has (After paying debts this is all she has left from the Lodges he belonged to) and with the $500. due her by the Int Union, pay it off. She says, that if the amount is so much that she cant pay it and exposure is to follow, there would be neither comfort or consolation in making the sacrifice of taking the thousand dollars from her children.

I feel sure you could write freely to Mr Perkins and he would be largely governed by your judgement as to the best course to persue.

In all likelihood I shall leave here Aug. 14th for Cardiff and would be pleased to hear from you before then.

Hope you are in good health and doing well.

Sincerely yours,   Saml Gompers.

ALpS, reel 341, vol. 356, pp. 6-7, SG Letterbooks, DLC.

From John McBride

July 31 / 1895.

My Dear Sam:—

In reply to yours of the 27th inst.[1] permit me to say that at the last meeting of the Executive Council the question of expense in connection with yourself and P. J. M[cGu]ire's trip to the British Trade Union Congress was considered and 30 days time allowed for the trip, while wages and expenses will be allowed as per Section 6, Article 11[2] of our Constitution.

Having estimated the probable cost in wages and expenses, at $250.00 each, a check for the amount is enclosed.

I have also sent you the printed matter requested. If anything on file here will be of service to you let me know and it will be forwarded you.

I trust you may have a pleasant voyage going and coming, and that you will enjoy yourself while there.

Fraternally yours,   John McBride

TLpS, reel 8, vol. 12, p. 274, SG Letterbooks, DLC.

1. To John McBride, Aug. [July] 27, 1895, reel 341, vol. 356, pp. 2-3, SG Letterbooks, DLC.

2. Art. XI, sec. 6 of the AFL constitution provided that members of the Executive Council or speakers engaged by the Council would be remunerated at $3.50 per day for loss of time while involved in Federation activity, plus hotel and traveling expenses.

An Article in the *Union Printer and American Craftsman*

[Aug. 17, 1895]

GOMPERS AND MAGUIRE.

Samuel Gompers and P. J. Maguire sailed on the Berlin last Wednesday to represent the American Federation of Labor at the annual meeting of the British Trades Congress, which convenes at Cardiff, Wales, on September 2, and continues in operation for one week.

On Tuesday evening a farewell reception was tendered to Messrs. Gompers and Maguire at the rooms of the Social Reform Club,[1] at No. 88 Second-ave. Mr. Maguire did not attend this reception, although he had signified his intention to be present, and as a consequence Mr. Gompers was the lion of the evening.

A committee had previously been appointed to prepare a suitable demonstration in honor of the departure of the two delegates, and this committee, under the chairmanship of Organizer Derflinger,[2] of No. 6, had decided to charter a steamer and escort the Berlin, with Messrs. Gompers and Maguire on board, down the bay. This programme was carried out, and at 10 A.M. Wednesday about one hundred representative labor men, together with quite a number of ladies, including Mrs. Gompers[3] and daughter,[4] boarded the steamer Rosa at the Barge Office and proceeded to the American Line docks, where the Berlin, with Messrs. Gompers and Maguire on board, was preparing to sail.

The committee appointed for the purpose was unable to find Mr. Maguire, but Mr. Gompers was captured and taken over on board the Rosa, where he was presented with a beautiful floral horseshoe by a committee from the Hand in Hand Benevolent Society,[5] and also with a congratulatory testimonial from the members of the Central Labor Union. In both instances Mr. Gompers responded in a few well-chosen words, expressing his appreciation.

At 11 o'clock, after a hearty handshake all around, Mr. Gompers was hurried aboard the Berlin, while the smaller boat steamed slowly out into the bay to await the coming of the big liner which was bearing the American workingmen's friend to foreign shores. For about an hour the Rosa moved slowly around the bay, the waters of which were nearly as smooth as a mirror, while the passengers ate, drank, sang, smoked and danced, keeping, in the meantime, one eye on the American Line dock.

James P. Archibald, with a big pair of marine glasses, was on the lookout, and suddenly he shouted "Sail, Oh!" in true nautical style, and instantly hilarity ceased and every eye was fastened on a big black boat which was slowly backing out from shore. As the Berlin bore down upon the Rosa the boat struck up "Say au revoir, but not good bye," and as the the liner passed out to sea Mr. Gompers, with his handkerchief tied to a cane, stood on the sterndeck with Mr. Maguire by his side and waved his adieus. The Rosa puffed along beside the big boat for a few moments, but soon gave it up and returned her passengers to the Battery. All felt that they had done homage to a worthy cause in wishing "bon voyage" to the American delegates to the Trades Congress.

The music for the occasion was furnished gratuitously by members of the Manhattan Musical Union.[6]

A large portion of the credit for the success of the affair was due to the efforts of Immigration Inspector McSweeney, John Bogert,[7] secretary of the Social Reform Club, W. F. Derflinger, organizer for

Typographical Union No. 6, and Daniel Harris, of the Cigarmakers' Union. Prominent among others present were Messrs. Thomas Crowley,[8] of Cincinnati; Edward Feeney, of the Board of Arbitration; James Edwards,[9] of the C.L.U.; Secretary White,[10] of the Garment Makers; William Lester,[11] W. F. Speer,[12] Stephen Bell,[13] John Desmerais,[14] Martin Healey,[15] Fred M. Bushway, J. Boden, James McKim, Henry Blaete, J. E. Bousch,[16] Thos. Lennon, S. Collins, J. H. Williams,[17] Robert Watchorn,[18] M. Pratt and M. Brown.

Union Printer and American Craftsman (New York), Aug. 17, 1895.

1. The Social Reform Club of New York was formally organized Nov. 22, 1894, to promote public understanding and improvement of industrial and social conditions. SG, who was a member of its advisory committee, recalled that its regulations required that 50 percent of the members be wage earners; the club's annual report for 1898 indicated that of 310 members, wage earners accounted for over one third. The club engaged in non-partisan support of legislation and sponsored classes, lectures, and conferences. The 1894 AFL convention recommended the establishment of non-partisan social reform clubs in each community under charters issued by the Federation, in order to "bring together, for mutual aid and instruction, such persons of various vocations as entertain a serious interest in the social problem, and desire to influence public opinion in favor of union labels and of the trades union movement in general, and such economic reforms as will serve to leave to the worker the wealth which he produces" (AFL, *Proceedings*, 1894, p. 46).

2. William F. Derflinger, a Brooklyn printer, was an organizer for International Typographical Union (ITU) 6 of New York. He served as a mediator between the United Garment Workers of America (UGWA) and the firm of Hackett, Carhart, and Co. in 1895.

3. Sophia Julian GOMPERS.

4. Either Rose Gompers Mitchell or Sadie Julian GOMPERS.

5. The Hand-in-Hand Benevolent Society was a Jewish mutual benefit organization that provided its members with medical care and free burial in New York's Washington Cemetery. SG had joined the society when he was eighteen years old.

6. The Manhattan Musical Protective Union was organized in April 1894 and affiliated with the AFL as union 6352 in May of that year.

7. John N. Bogert, a delegate from ITU 6 to the New York City Central Labor Union (CLU) in 1895, later served as an organizer for the AFL.

8. Probably Thomas F. Crowley, a member of ITU 3 of Cincinnati.

9. James C. Edwards was a member of the Tile Layers' Helpers' Union of New York City, affiliated with the KOL as Local Assembly 7789—the Hexagon Labor Club—until 1895. Edwards was the Tile Layers' delegate to the New York City Board of Walking Delegates (BWD) in 1894.

10. Henry WHITE, a member of UGWA 4 (clothing cutters) of New York City, served as general secretary of the UGWA from 1895 until 1904.

11. William Lester was a member of ITU 6.

12. Wilbur F. Speer of Brooklyn was secretary-treasurer of ITU 6.

13. Stephen Bell was a member of ITU 6.

14. John S. Desmerais (variously Desmarais) was a Brooklyn proofreader.

15. Martin Healey (variously Healy) was a member of ITU 6.

16. Jacob E. Bausch was a member of the United Wood Carvers' Association of

New York. He served as that organization's delegate to the New York City BWD in 1894 and later became secretary of the New York City CLU.

17. Possibly James H. Williams, who was active in the New York City CLU.

18. Robert WATCHORN, a former miner, served as the first chief factory inspector of Pennsylvania from 1893 to 1895, when he became an inspector with the U.S. Bureau of Immigration.

An Excerpt from an Article in the *Sun*

[September 5, 1895]

CARDIFF CONGRESS

The Mayor of Cardiff[1] gave a reception to the delegates in the Park Hall last night, which a crowd of delegates and a large number of local celebrities attended. There is one matter which had been upon my mind for several days anent the American delegates. The subject is a somewhat delicate one, and I did not care to say anything which might reach their ears before their formal reception by the Congress, lest it should somewhat embarrass them. The truth is that the arrangements for the reception of those gentlemen have been anything but creditable to our national hospitality. I understand that when our delegates visited America they were treated right royally, and with painstaking as well as profuse hospitality. For the first day or two here Messrs. Gompertz and McGaire were left to rub along pretty much as they could; they were, indeed, treated with the utmost cordiality by every individual, but the hospitality was personal, and not collective.

THEY HAVE NOT COMPLAINED.

Let me make it quite clear that no complaint has reached me from the delegates, either directly or indirectly. My conclusions are the result of personal observations and of admissions made by members of the Reception Committee and the Parliamentary Committee. The explanation appears to be that the Parliamentary Committee left matters to the Reception Committee; whilst I am assured by a member of the latter committee that the American visitors were not so much as introduced to them in a formal way. I hope this somewhat broad hint will not be lost upon the Parliamentary Committee during the remainder of the delegates' stay.

. . .

Sun (London), Sept. 5, 1895.

1. Alderman P. W. Carey was Cardiff's mayor.

An Excerpt from a News Account of Addresses by Samuel Gompers and P. J. McGuire at the 1895 Trades Union Congress in Cardiff

[Sept. 6, 1895]

THE TRADES UNIONS CONGRESS.

. . .

Reception of American Delegates.

Messrs. S. Gompertz and P. J. M'Guire, of the American Federation of Labour, were at this stage introduced to the Congress by the President[1] who heartily welcomed them in the name of the trade unionists of Great Britain and Ireland.—(Applause.)

Mr. Gompertz said that whilst he fully appreciated the kindly feeling manifested he recognised that the compliment was meant for the great body of the working men of America.—(Applause.) He looked forward to the time when the solidarity of labour amongst all English-speaking races should be firmly established the world over. He and his colleague had not come to teach, and yet not altogether as learners, to England, but with a full sense of their equality with England. He had been asked to express his opinion of the Trades Congress. He should say that they were here much the same as the American Federation. They had their goodnesses and they had their failings.—("Hear, hear," and laughter.) The fact was that in both countries, owing to their environment, they had too much to do at Congress, and too little time to do it in. But when they considered all things he thought that both that Congress and the American Federation would bear favourable comparison with either the House of Commons in England or the Congress of America. He went through the history of the struggles of labour after freedom in America. Although in the great American War the moneyed classes of England stood on the side of slavery, the weavers and spinners of Lancashire, to their ever-lasting honour be it said, refused to recognise the belligerent South, and stood up for the freedom and rights of man.—(Applause.) He thanked those working men, as their great President, Abraham Lincoln, had thanked them before.—(Applause.) They had had their difficulties in America, owing partly to the size of their country and the splitting up of authoritative power amongst the different governing bodies in the States. Each State dealt very largely with its own labour laws. Then there were differences of language and of national association, and of character, amongst the many races which made up the great American people. The trade union movement, however, in

America, as well as in England, was the historical as well as the natural development which made for working-class freedom. They had done, then, with high-sounding phrases, and went for solid work. They believed in getting what they could in a reasonable and yet in a radical manner. They were reasonable in making radical demands, but they took care that those demands should be of a really radical kind. — (Applause.) He believed in labour men doing all that was possible to advance the cause, even if the step forward was a small one, so that less might remain for their children to do. — (["]Hear, hear.["]) Trade unionists should be trade unionists first and party men afterwards. They needed, too, a larger charity and a larger respect for each other's views. They needed to recognise the difficulties in front, the power that stood opposed to them, and he who did not recognise these things was not fit, in his opinion, to act as a leader of labour opinion. — (Applause.) He reminded the Congress that in America they had taken their children out of the factories and workshops and put them in the schools, and they had taken their women away from mining labour. — (Applause.) They were not content with that, but each gain they made gave them a greater zest for more. — (Applause.) By coming to that Congress they hoped to establish a bond of international good feeling, so that, in the good old Scriptural words, they might "beat their swords into ploughshares and their spears into pruning hooks," and, he might add, cease from making powder monkeys out of men. — (Applause.)

Mr. P. J. M'Guire also addressed the Congress. He said he and his colleague represented 681,000 men and women organized in 53 national and international trade unions, in eleven of their States. Forty-four trades councils from as many American cities were represented in the American Federation.

. . .

Manchester Guardian, Sept. 6, 1895.

1. John Hogan Jenkins, a Cardiff shipwright, was a delegate to the TUC from the Amalgamated Union of Operative Bakers and Confectioners, a union he had helped organize. He later served as mayor of Cardiff (1903-4) and as a Labour Member of Parliament (1906-10).

An Interview with Samuel Gompers and P. J. McGuire in the *Bakers' Journal and Deutsch-Amerikanische Bäcker-Zeitung*[1]

[October 2, 1895]

INTERESTING REPORT OF GOMPERS AND MCGUIRE.

Brothers Gompers and McGuire, the fraternal delegates of the A.F. of L. to the English Trade Union Congress, returned home last Saturday. They are both in good health and well supplied with a stock of information about labor abroad, which we are confident will be used to the advantage of organized labor in America.

We reproduce here a partial report made in an interview with a *Daily News* reporter, which will prove of more than common interest as an outline of the interesting information we may receive when the delegates make their full and detailed report.

In view of manifold misrepresentations of the transatlantic labor movement, largely due to a faction interested in duplicating the political movement of the workers of European countries in America, the information of our friends will prove the more timely.

"We had a fine voyage over and are glad to get back home.

"Our reception was very cordial and fraternal, and at some of the great industrial centers the trade councils met us and gave us a grand welcome. They also loaded us down with information.

"The American workman is far superior to his English cousin. Even the man who does the commonest kind of labor in the United States is higher than the best mechanic in Great Britain. There are more comforts for our workingmen, that is beyond question. Our home life is a great improvement over theirs. We would rather live on the top floor of a tall tenement in our big cities, than occupy the first floor of one of their houses.

"The social and economic side of the life of toilers in the Kingdom is very small compared to ours. About the only sociability they enjoy is the 'free and easies.' Then the public house life is largely confined to a section of the place in which they live.

"The most extravagant workingman in Great Britain does not spend as much as any one of our own mechanics.

"We did not find the workingmen on the other side at all ignorant. On the contrary we were surprised at their intelligence, and their desire for education and knowledge.

"There is no question that the organized labor of England is much further advanced than our own movement. They readily recognize the tangible benefits to be derived from organization, and that many of the results are immediate. There is also a better general appreciation on the part of the public as to the achievements and purposes of the labor organizations there. That, of course, is due to the fact that England has four generations of trade unions, and that she had been long an industrial country, when manufacturing was first developing in America. The labor members in England can point to their forefathers as union men, while we have difficulty in referring to our parents as members of labor organizations. This early commencement of their movement contributes largely to its permanency now.

"The British labor movement would have achieved greater results for the workers if there were a better practical labor movement in Continental Europe than there is. It would have afforded the English movement more room for development. English trade unions have held numerous congresses in trying to bring the unions of the other nations up to their standard, but only in the case of the miners have they succeeded. The miners now hold international congresses every year. The other trades have not been able to meet in congress for the second time.

"The failure of the union men of all countries in Europe to work together is due entirely to their political differences. Factions divide them everywhere.

"Except in England the workingmen have not secured the right of coalition. Many had that right, but lost it by going into politics, and now they are trying to regain this power.

"In England alone they have held it on account of their absolute independence of politics. The workingmen of England are neither partisan nor sectarian, yet they use all parties and churches for the purpose of advancing the interests of labor. Neither do they raise issues of a political or religious nature. Not eight-tenths of the workingmen of England exercise the right of suffrage. The English cannot understand the cosmopolitan character of the labor movement in the United States.

"The English papers print very little about this country. Anything that reflects upon the country and can be used to show, as they believe, the failure of republican government, is readily printed. Political corruption here is what they like to publish. Sporting matters and stories about big strikes are about the only news they care for from this country. In all other respects America is too remote for their notice.

"We discovered a growing sentiment in favor of the strict trade union movement in France and Germany. In the latter country we met representative trade unionists as well as the leaders of the Socialist movement. We demonstrated to the German Socialists that the trade union movement was eminently practical.

"We learned that our trade unions were misrepresented to the German workingmen through the medium of their correspondents here, men who claimed to be authorized to speak for us here when, as a matter of fact, they are wholly unknown to our union members.

"In France the trade union movement is typified by the miners. They had a big strike in France lately and collected 50,000 francs for the support of the strikers. As a rule, the French workers have no funds, and assist one another as necessity demands.

"We attended a Socialist meeting in France, and all that was raised for the striking miners was 85 cents which was thrown on the platform.

"We were astonished to see that the Socialists, where they were in power, could not and did not improve the conditions of the workers who elected them to office.

"We were told, also, that a Government labor exchange had to be closed because the workingmen made demands upon it beyond its purpose and capacity.

"We also visited a number of the cigar factories, which are part of the Government monopoly of tobacco industries, and were greatly disappointed. They are far behind us in the preparation and manufacture of tobacco leaf. The cigar trade is in a most primitive condition. If that is a type of Government control of industries we ought to try to steer our ship far from it."

Mr. Gompers promised the cigarmakers of Amsterdam to put their case before his union. They are in need of funds.

"The great question in England," said Mr. McGuire, "is the subject of the unemployed. Were it not that the labor organizations limit the operations of the machines, the question would be far more serious than it is. Besides the men in England do not care to work very fast. Thus a building which would be completed in this city in three months requires over one year for its construction there.

"The women are well organized in England and Ireland. They are not bent upon getting married too early."

The two delegates reserved their report of the British Trade Union Congress for the convention of the Federation of Labor, which will meet in this city in December. The Congress presented Mr. Gompers and Mr. McGuire with gold medals.

Bakers' Journal and Deutsch-Amerikanische Bäcker-Zeitung, Oct. 2, 1895.

1. This interview, which was widely reprinted, first appeared in the *New York Daily News.* SG disputed its accuracy (see "To the Editor of the *New Yorker Volkszeitung,*" Oct. 8, 1895, below).

An Article in the *United Mine Workers' Journal*

[Oct. 3, 1895]

If Samuel Gompers, fraternal delegate to the late British trade union congress, and who, with P. J. Maguire has just returned, has uttered half of the silly twaddle that the newspapers give him credit for, he has proven, more than by any other thing we know him guilty of, his unfitness to be considered a representative of labor. He has also proven how necessary it is for him to study a few volumes of statistics, and to get an analytic mind to apply them for him.

Among the things he is reported as saying is, that his impression is that the American workman ["]is better fed, better clothed, has more liberty and is thought to be a much bigger man in every way than the Englishman."

"I would rather live," said he, "on the seventh floor of an American tenement than in the first flat of an Englishman's house."

Now, we have always taken Mr. Gompers to be a very sensible man; and, as he, as a "cockney born" himself, can have no natural desire to gratify a morbid insular egotism, in what he has said we are at a loss to know why he should at once, as soon as he sniffs a New York reporter, sail in, a la Chauncey M. Depew, or Boss Croker,[1] to tell the American workingman how well he is off compared with other working people. We would like to ask Mr. Gompers whether he saw any Woodstocks[2] while he attended the conference, or whether in the whole island he met with any picture real or imaginary, or any dread of such to be to correspond with that of Eugene V. Debs,[3] one of the ablest and sincerest labor leaders of the world, who has been for the last four or five months incarcerated in an American prison, without having the privilege of a trial by a jury of his peers? If not, what comes then of the empty boast of being bigger? Besides, if the seventh [floor] flats of American tenements are such pleasant habitats, where on earth has your occupation gone to, Mr. Gompers? What need is there for you or any other agitator if things are so lovely?

The truth is, labor is in a deplorable condition the civilized world over, and, with the exception of a few favored and privileged industries in this country just about in the same condition, and it comes with poor grace from a man of Mr. Gompers's standing to use language which is not borne out by the facts and which tends to lull our people into sort of feeling of contentment-by-comparison.

The only conclusion we can arrive at is that Mr. Gompers was talking for effect or has been misquoted.

United Mine Workers' Journal, Oct. 3, 1895.

1. Richard Croker, an Irish-born politician active in the New York City Democratic party beginning in 1868, became boss of the Tammany machine in 1886.

2. Eugene V. Debs was incarcerated in Woodstock Prison, McHenry Co., Ill., in 1895, following his conviction for violating an injunction during the 1894 Pullman strike.

3. Eugene Victor DEBS founded the American Railway Union in 1893 and served as its president. In 1897 he organized the Social Democracy of America.

To the Editor of the *New Yorker Volkszeitung*

Oct. 8th [18]95.

Editor, New York Volkszeitung:—

In your issue of yesterday you publish a report[1] of a committee made to a meeting of the C.L.F. that I am induced to break the rule I usually observe of ignoring the false, ridiculous or malicious statements which you often publish in reference to my utterances upon or in connection with the labor movement.

The report I refer to is based upon words I never uttered and to which I would take exception. It is evident to even a casual reader of the report, as you published it, that the "committee" drew upon their imagination to falsely and maliciously malign me, to place me in a questionable position, before the workers of Germany, France and America.

It would be useless to particularize the incidents and mis-representations made in this "report". I deem it sufficient for all fair minded people, people who know me, or who know something of my true character (Not as I have been frequently painted in your paper) to say that the "report" is a mass of rubbish with no foundation of fact for a basis.

Will you have at least the fairness to publish this note?[2]

Samuel Gompers.

ALpS, reel 341, vol. 356, pp. 15-16, SG Letterbooks, DLC.

1. The *New Yorker Volkszeitung* of Oct. 7, 1895, in an article entitled "Antwort auf Gompers" ("Answer to Gompers"), published a summary of the report that appeared in full in the *People* of Oct. 13 (see "An Article in the *People*," Oct. 13, 1895, below).

2. A portion of SG's letter (the second paragraph and the first sentence of the third paragraph, slightly rewritten) was published in the *New Yorker Volkszeitung* on Oct. 9, 1895.

John McBride to the Executive Council of the AFL

Indianapolis, Ind.   Oct. 10 / 1895.

To The Executive Council.

Our delegates to the Cardiff Congress report that they "found it impossible to secure return passage before Sept. 21st and this prolonged their stay longer than prescribed by the resolution of the Executive Council," which you will remember was 30 days. They, therefore ask for an additional allowance of 12 days, making 42 days in all.

Please vote on this at once.[1]

Fraternally,   John McBride
President   A.F. of L.

P.S.—The total bill of each is $403.00.

TLS, AFL Executive Council Vote Books, reel 8, frame 122, *AFL Records*.

1. The majority of the AFL Executive Council voted to approve the request; August McCraith, who, along with James Duncan, had been "much opposed" to the trip, voted against it (James Duncan to August McCraith, July 25, 1895, Granite Cutters' National Union Records, reel 140, frame 667, *AFL Records*).

An Article in the *People*

[Oct. 13, 1895]

BARNUM SAMMY

Fellow Delegates: In justice to the international labor movement your committee on education and public affairs must call your attention to the latest display of "pure and simple" imbecility on this side of the Atlantic.

Mr. Sam Gompers and Mr. P. J. McGuire returned from Europe a week ago. As their mission to the British Trade Union Congress this year, like the corresponding mission of Burns and Holmes[1] to the convention of the American Federation of Labor last year, was to stem the advancing tide of Socialism with a "pure and simple" broomstick, the capitalistic press of this city not only made haste to interview them, but, as you may see from the annexed clipping, embellished its report of their story with a cut of the proud, martial and somewhat Barnum-like countenance of "our own and only Sammy."

The first utterance of Mr. Gompers may have been a joke. "The American workman," said he, "is far superior to his English cousin. Even the man who does the commonest kind of labor in the United States is *higher* than the best mechanic in Great Britain."

That it actually was a joke would appear from his next remark concerning the "high" and the "low," namely: "We would rather live on the *top floor* of a tall tenement house in our big cities than occupy the first floor of one of their houses."

Joke or no joke, let that pass. The old capitalistic sophism now revived by Gompers, that the American workman should be content to be less miserable than his foreign cousin, if it ever impressed any thoughtless person, has no longer a basis of fact to wriggle upon. In many trades the actual earnings of labor are now lower in this country than in Europe, and a few days ago it was shown that the average receipts of a Hocking Valley miner were at the rate of $18.26 per month, while in Belgium, the country of low wages, the average was $26.00.

Mr. Gompers did not find that the workingmen on the other side were "at all ignorant." On the contrary, he was "surprised at their intelligence." Aye, actually surprised when he looked at himself. "There is no question," he said, "that the organized labor of England is much further advanced than our own movement." This, however, he attributes to the fact that "England has four generations of trade unionism pure and simple," till lately undisturbed by independent labor politics, chiefly because, in his own words, "not eight-tenths of the workingmen of England can even now exercise the right of suffrage."

What a boon to the working class this wholesale disfranchisement of its members has been, and what sort of advance the pure and simple trade unionism so long promoted by such political disabilities was able to make, may be inferred from the following statement of P. J. McGuire in the same interview: "The great question in England is the subject of the unemployed. Were it not that the labor organizations limit the operations of the machines, the question would be far more serious than it is. Besides, the men do not care to work very fast. For instance, a building which in this city would be completed in three months requires over one year for its construction there. As to the women, they are not bent upon being married too early."

Slow machines, slow work and Malthusianism, such are, therefore, the practical results of four generations of that famous trade unionism which in England was best promoted by the disfranchisement of the working class. No machine, no work and no children would be its ideal. Not only, then, should the American workman esteem himself happy to be so much "higher" on the top floor of a tall rookery than the British cousin on the ground floor of a low shanty, but he should by all means give up his right of suffrage for fear of being tempted into independent political action (as those of his British cousins who exercise the franchise have lately begun to see) by the Socialistic prospect of enjoying at a comfortable hearth the full benefits of quick work on the rapid machines of the Co-operative Commonwealth.

Such is also, mark you, the sort of trade unionism, in favor of which Mr. Sam Gompers has discovered "a growing sentiment" in France and Germany. "In the latter country," he says, "we met representative trade unionists as well as the leaders of the Socialist movement. We demonstrated to the German Socialists that the trade-union movement ('pure and simple,' of course), was eminently practical." Let us, therefore, get ready for the news, that thanks to Gompers and McGuire, such as Liebknecht and Bebel have at last seen the error of their ways, surrendered Socialism, apologized to Bismarck,[2] determined to be "practical," embraced "schwanz" politics,[3] and become the German agents of "our own and only Sammy," once more enthroned in the presidential chair of the A.F. of L.

Poor, long-abused Sammy! Innocent victim of the perversity of American Socialists! He learned "that our trade unions were misrepresented to the German workingmen through the medium of their correspondents here; men who claimed to be better authorized to speak for us here, when, as a matter of fact, they are wholly unknown to our union members."

But the day of reckoning is in sight. Should the United Central Labor Federation and the Socialist Labor Party of America make bold to send delegates to the next International Labor Congress, they might find the door of that great body shut in their faces by order of Sam Gompers.

Leaving the ground of "pure and simple" imbecility for the broader domain of "pure and simple" mendacity, Gompers is further credited with the following statements:

"Wherever we found the Socialists in power in France, we also found that wages were lower, and that strikes were generally failures. We were astonished to see that the Socialists, where they were in power, could not and did not improve the conditions of the workers who elected them to office. We were told, also, that a Government labor exchange had to be closed because the workingmen made demands upon it beyond its purpose and capacity. Workingmen had secured the right of coalition, but lost it by going into politics."

To all of which the answer may be made, in the famous words of Horace Greely, "You lie, you villain, you lie!"

1. The Paris Labor Exchange (Bourse du Travail) was the direct

result of independent labor politics. It was instituted through the efforts of the Socialist representatives in the municipal council of the French capital, and it was finally suppressed by the higher national power (then and still now in the hands of the capitalist class), because the trade unions of the Exchange refused to give to the police the names and addresses of their members.

2. Thanks to Socialist officials in many municipal administrations and to the 58 Socialist representatives in the National Assembly, not only was the condition of labor improved to the full extent of such concessions as an aggressive and determined minority can exact from a capitalistic majority, but the murderous hand of the military power was paralyzed on several occasions, the right of coalition was maintained, and three prime ministers and one president of the Republic were driven out of office upon labor issues, while in this country Cleveland was allowed by trade unionism "pure and simple" to shoot workingmen to his heart's content and to establish a "government by injunction." Think of a Gompers spitting on a Jaurès![4]

3. Thanks to the councils of Prudhommes (or boards of arbitration, in which the employee has an equal voice and vote with the employer) the French workingmen waste but little efforts and means on that sort of strikes upon which "pure and simple" misleaders manage to live handsomely. For instance, of the 25,000 disputes between employers and employees during the year 1892, all but 267, involving about 400 establishments and 108,000 strikers were settled by these councils. Of these 267 strikes, 158, involving 76,000 men, were either entirely successful or finally compromised advantageously to the employees. Now compare these statistics with such as are available in this country. In the same year there were in the State of New York alone 2,398 strikes, and although we were told that 1,541 were successful, the all-important result is shown by the further statement of the New York Bureau of Labor Statistics, that "those who engaged in strikes in 1892 lost $815,000 in wages and $200,000 in disbursements by the unions for the support of strikers, to secure an eventual gain of $497,000, theoretically annual, but practically of short duration. Taking all the data into consideration, the New York State strikers in 1892 lost over $1,000,000 to secure an actual gain of less than $200,000.

While this man Gompers is in himself a person of very small caliber, the falsehoods which he is able to retail through a capitalist press naturally eager to publish them, should not be allowed to pass unchallenged. Your committee, therefore, suggests that measures be taken by this body to widely expose here and abroad these falsehoods and their obvious purpose.[5]

People (New York), Oct. 13, 1895.

1. David HOLMES was president of the Amalgamated Weavers' Association (1884-1906) and a member of the Parliamentary Committee of the TUC (1892-1900).

2. Otto von Bismarck (1815-98) was chancellor of the German Empire between 1871 and 1890. Under Bismarck's leadership the Reichstag passed laws restricting the meetings, publications, and finances of the growing Sozialistische Arbeiterpartei Deutschlands (Socialist Labor Party of Germany).

3. A derogatory term referring to the policy of promoting labor's interests through politicians of the existing political parties rather than endorsing an independent labor party. The phrase might be translated as "coattail politics."

4. Jean Jaurès (1859-1914), a philosopher and leading French socialist noted for his support of the Carmaux miners' strike in 1892 and of Alfred Dreyfus in his treason trial in 1898, was a moderate Republican in the Chamber of Deputies from 1885 to 1889, and returned to serve as a Socialist from 1893 to 1898 and from 1902 until his death.

5. The report was delivered by Lucien Sanial to a meeting of the New York City Central Labor Federation.

An Excerpt from an Interview in the *Minneapolis Tribune*

[October 27, 1895]

LABOR

. . .

Samuel Gompers is a small, dark man. He is decidedly below medium height. He has thick, curly hair, slightly graying. He wears a moustache, and is very soldierly in appearance. He is neither stout nor thin—rather the former, if anything. He is quiet and silent, rarely flashing into brilliant utterance. Indeed, he seems to be very cautious in all things. He was born in England half a century ago, and is of Jewish extraction. He first entered the labor movement through the cigarmakers' unions, and rose rapidly. He is a calm, safe, steady man. He dislikes what he calls "fads." He never takes up socialistic schemes, and the socialists and anarchists hotly oppose him. Indeed, it was owing to a combination of socialists that he was defeated for re-election.

"I don't think any man can compare American and European conditions," he said, when he was asked about the outlook for labor in the two continents, "without being impressed with the superiority of the workingmen's lot in this country. There is really no comparison between the two. In Europe, especially in London, the workrooms lie in the most awful slums. I myself have seen things in the London slums calculated to horrify the most callous observer. The degradation is so fearful that we wonder there is no social revolution immediately. I am no longer surprised that socialism is so strong in Europe. Over here the toilers are in a very bad way. I am not saying their lot is a happy one among ourselves. Far from that. But of the two, the American evil is infinitely the least."

"But is it not inevitable that this suffering should exist?"

"Inevitable under our present system, yes. Inevitable under equitable social conditions, no. I don't care how much wealth there is, and how few to share it, there will be suffering if its distribution be inequitable. The question of the distribution of wealth is, in my opinion, the key to the situation. There it is where so many sincere friends of mankind, I think, miss the point. We hear much about plenty for everyone in the future and how that result can be brought about. But there is plenty for everyone now if everyone could get his share. But if the Socialists occasionally overlook a point, so do their opponents. For instance, the anti-Socialists write long articles to demonstrate what they are pleased to term the fallacies of socialism. Very good. Now what does the Socialist do? Simply points out the fact upon which his argument is based — that fact being the great privation and misery of the working classes. There is no getting over that fact, and that fact counts in favor of the Socialist every time. You may contest the theory of socialism all you please, but you cannot contest the fact that [it is] human misery which gives the movement all its strength. But take away that misery and you take away the strength of socialism."

The next question put to Mr. Gompers had reference to the immediate future of labor.

"It is my belief," said he, "that the workingman is tired of mere rhetoric and theory. He is weary of connecting himself with movements that mean long agitation and a remote amelioration of his conditions. It is an old complaint that most social reforms will not come to pass until we are all dead. We want to do something here and now. That something, to appeal very strongly, should take the form of an increase of wages. That is my philosophy for the present. Increase the workingman's purchasing power."

"How about the money question? Do the workers favor silver or gold?"

"I do not see that that question means anything. Understand me, I am not hedging. But I have no authority to speak for the workingman on that point. As I told you before, the workingman wants more purchasing power. He wants wages that will buy him a lot of the things he needs. Whether these wages be gold or silver or paper is another question, and a question for each man to settle as he thinks best. But there must be something wrong with a social system that is unable to settle its own money matters. And when anything is wrong with the social system the workingman gets the worst of it."

Mr. Gompers could not be induced to say anything about the presidential campaign next year. Nor would he say much about strikes. He was very warm on the subject of Debs, however, and declared that that leader was a very much wronged man.

· · ·

Minneapolis Tribune, Oct. 27, 1895.

To the Editor of the *Cigar Makers' Official Journal*

New York, October 30, 1895.

In the last issue of the *Journal* there appears an article[1] signed by Messrs. Sinn,[2] Behnke[3] and Brinkman,[4] of Union 90 of New York, which, though it contained many inaccuracies of statement and which on the face of them, and from official reports, bear their own refutation, I shall not refer to them, but chiefly confine what I may have to say to those portions which are practically a covert attack upon the members of the International Union Executive Board.

In the first place the complaint is made that the Executive Board has voted against approving strikes for an increase of wages, and then the further charge that owing to the manner of the "wording" of the applications in other instances, they are approved. Of course the Executive Board can only be governed by how an application is "worded." It is not within the province of the Executive Board to attempt to obtain information outside of the applications submitted. I am free to say, however, that unless there were the best of grounds given in an application for an increase of wages, during the industrial crisis of the past two years, I have invariably voted against its approval.

I have believed, with the International President, that during such periods, if our organization can but maintain prevailing wages and conditions in the trade, it would be a great achievement, and that all attempts in other directions would prove abortive. Look at the Philadelphia strike[5] for instance. The fact is that there are many people who can not, while there are others who will not learn from experience.

Up to 1873 there was no fixed policy in matters of strikes in the International Union. Neither the Executive Board nor the members of the International Union had the power to disapprove a proposed strike. The exact system or lack of system advocated by these gentlemen prevailed during those years. The officers of the International Union were simply automatons or machines, with the ability to nod their heads in the affirmative, but deprived of the power to say no, even when the existence of the organization was at stake, and the interests of the cigar makers were imperilled. The result of that one-sided arrangement was the almost entire destruction of the International, so that the members of the craft were literally at the mercy of their employers, without power or influence to resist any encroachment, and the International Union reduced to 1,017 members, with not a dollar in its treasury.

If, as our friends propose, the local boards should have sole authority to declare whether the International Union shall approve and support a strike is the great end desired, then it seems to me that it would logically follow to abolish the Executive Board of the International Union entirely, and at least save them from becoming simple figureheads.

It is well known that local executive boards are frequently influenced by local conditions. They base their acts and expressions from the standpoint of local interests. If they had the authority to engage in strikes at any time their respective localities desired, and could draw upon the funds of the International Union *ad libitum,* we might witness the day when nearly all our members in the various localities would be out on strike, drawing upon the funds at one and the same time and leaving our International Union a wreck, to be buffeted and kicked by all, workingmen and employers alike.

What do our friends think the result of their policy would have been had it been in vogue up to this time? Do they for a moment imagine that our organization would have been so great and so steadfast a friend and defender during the crucial times of 1893-95? Certainly not, since it would have been an impossibility to create such a fund as we had at the beginning of the crisis; but even if we could have accumulated such a fund would it not have disappeared long before this time?

The International Union has a policy, and it has a certain degree of discipline. The members of the organization understand it. The employers understand it too, and these are the greatest safeguards which win the confidence of our fellow-workmen on the one side and the caution of the employers to attack our members on the other.

I am free to admit that we ought to endeavor to devise a means by which the approval or disapproval of a strike may be more quickly ascertained, but I deny that non-unionists would be gained to the organization if they knew that the local executive boards would have the absolute power to approve strikes. As a matter of fact, at least now, our members and non-unionists fully appreciate the fact that when the International Union approves an application to strike it does not simply mean a resolution of sympathy; it means financial support. While on the other hand, to go back to the planless method of the previous era of our organization, and which the committee of Union 90 practically proposes, would mean the approval of strikes with the following "bill of fare" for the men in the struggle:

"Sympathy without relief,
Mustard without beef."

The factor which prevents a better and more thorough organization of the cigar makers of New York is not due to the provisions of the International Union Constitution, nor to the votes of the Executive Board, but in truth to the divisions which are created by men who devote more of their time and activity to the enunciation of a theory than to the practical work of organizing our fellow craftsmen on essentials to attain tangible results.

I am confident that the members of the Executive Board are actuated by a single purpose in voting upon the various applications submitted to them, and that is to do that which is best for the members of our craft, and to see to it that the organization shall be the very best of protectors and defenders in the great struggle incident to their daily life and labor.

Perhaps I am as impatient as anyone may be at what may be termed the "slow progress" made, but I still recognize that it is progress, and the very fact that it is slow is the best evidence that it cannot be made to go at a greater ratio than the willingness of the members as well as industrial conditions will admit of.

Let me add that I have too great a faith in the members of the International Union to believe that they will ever attempt to engraft in our organization what once nearly proved its downfall.

Fraternally yours,   Samuel Gompers.

Cigar Makers' Official Journal, Nov. 1895.

1. The letter, dated Sept. 20, 1895, appeared in the *Cigar Makers' Official Journal* of October 1895.

2. Jacob Sinn of New York City was a member of CMIU 90.

3. Edward Behnke of New York City was a member of CMIU 90.

4. Probably Englebert Brückmann, a member of CMIU 90.

5. CMIU locals 100, 165, and 293 of Philadelphia were involved in a strike to equalize wages that began in June 1894 and apparently ended unsuccessfully in September of that year.

To the Editor of the *Cigar Makers' Official Journal*

New York, Nov. 6, 1895.

To the Editor of the Cigar Makers' Journal:

If the people who control the destinies of the socialist labor party of New York claim anything it is that they demand and accord others justice. How they belie that claim let this single incident tell. For years their principal paper has abused, maliciously maligned and misrepresented the active trade unionist; the more active they were the surer were they to come in for the fullest share of the paper's characteristic falsification.

A few weeks ago they published a venemous and false statement[1] concerning me. I allowed it to pass by, the same as many of their previous utterances, but a few personal friends, one of whom was an attache of the *Volkszeitung,* urged me to write to the paper repudiating or denying the statement. I confess that I was simple enough to do so, but instead of publishing the letter[2] they mutilated those portions which they printed and suppressed some of the most important features. A few days ago they again viciously slandered me,[3] when I wrote them the following letter:

New York, Oct. 28 [29], 1895.

Editor of New Yorker Volkszeitung:

There you are, at it again. To those who do not understand your motives, it would appear strange that you seem unable to refer to me in any way without misrepresenting me, but I doubt that you can impress your willful lying about me upon all your readers.

Your article on me, published today, is certainly baseless, for as a matter of fact there is no politician, not even of your stripe, who can "use" me. There may be exceptions, but the rule is that you politicians are all tarred with the same stick. You all see "party advantage," and the real interest of the workers may go to the dogs for all you care.

As a matter of fact, my name was put on the list of speakers by the Cigar Makers' Union for last Saturday's meeting[4] without my knowledge or consent, and when I went to the meeting it was for the purpose of finding out whether there was any political trick in it, and if there was to denounce it. In opening the meeting the chairman repudiated the insinuation, and asserted that since the International Organizer[5] was in the city the local union desired to take advantage of the opportunity to organize the cigar makers of the uptown district into the International Union.

After that statement, I addressed the assemblage with the same object in view, not even by indirect means mentioning party politics, or politics at all. I then left the meeting, when Mr. Woods, the International Organizer, began to address it. I know Mr. Woods well, and I am confident he spoke on the same lines. You see now upon what flimsy grounds you based your venomous editorial attack on me.

While writing I might as well correct one previous false statement attributed to me. I never said that the subscriptions in France to help the Carmaux strike[6] were small. As a matter of fact, I never referred to the subject at all.

Perhaps, as opportunity arises, I may recall one after another the many false and malicious statements you have published in reference to my actions and utterances.

Will you have the fairness to publish this letter?[7] (You remember I asked the same question in my last letter to you.) If you do, do so without mutilation.

Samuel Gompers.[8]

One would think that since they have the entire columns of the paper at their disposal, and that they could with greater vehemence make a fresh onslaught upon me, they would at least publish the letter, but to all who know the significance of my request to the editor to publish the letter without mutilation this will appeal with greater force. Every reference to them was suppressed, distorted and changed, so that the entire letter appeared unintelligible, and then renewed their attack in the same shamefaced manner.

The great body of workers cannot appreciate how unfair these men who mask behind the name "socialist" in New York City are toward any man who is an energetic and a true trade-unionist. It is essentially true that they exhibit more spleen and bitterness in their efforts to destroy the usefulness of any man in the active trade-union movement than in any to secure fair conditions or justice for the toilers from the capitalistic class.

I ask you to publish the above for the edification of our fellow workers here and elsewhere.

Fraternally yours, Samuel Gompers.

Cigar Makers' Official Journal, Dec. 1895.

1. See "An Article in the *People,*" Oct. 13, 1895, above; a shorter version of the piece was published in the *New Yorker Volkszeitung* on Oct. 7.

2. See "To the Editor of the *New Yorker Volkszeitung,*" Oct. 8, 1895, above.

3. "Die Parteilosigkeit von Gompers und Genossen" (Gompers and Friends' Non-alignment with Political Party), *New Yorker Volkszeitung,* Oct. 29, 1895.

4. The *New Yorker Volkszeitung* characterized the assembly as a workers' political mass meeting held in New York City under the auspices of a cigarmakers' local.

5. James WOOD, a vice-president (1893-1905) of the CMIU, was a member of CMIU 218 of Binghamton, N.Y.

6. Glassworkers at the Verrerie Ste. Clothilde in Carmaux, France, voted to strike on July 31, 1895. At issue was the dismissal on the previous day of Marien Baudot, one of their number who was a leader of the Chambre syndicale des verriers de Carmaux, the local glassworkers' union, which was affiliated with the Fédération du Verre (the national Federation of Glassworkers). The workers voted to return to work on Aug. 6, but their employers refused to reopen the factory, thereby turning the strike into a lockout. The union officially ended the strike on Nov. 22; few union members were rehired. An article in the *People* of Oct. 27, 1895, claimed that SG, in order to belittle the socialists, had said their appeal on behalf of the Carmaux glass workers had produced only 84¢ in contributions. The *People* reported that contributions through Oct. 5 had amounted to $10,430.

7. The *New Yorker Volkszeitung* published much of SG's letter on Oct. 30, 1895, under the headline "Billig und schlecht" (Cheap and Bad).

8. For a slightly different version of this letter see reel 341, vol. 356, pp. 19-20, SG Letterbooks, DLC.

To George Perkins

New York Nov. 9th [189]5.

Geo. W. Perkins.
Monon Bldg. Chicago, Ill.
Decline nomination president and if Neuroth[1] declines I accept first vice[2] you should announce declinations in circular

Saml Gompers.

AWpS, reel 341, vol. 356, p. 36, SG Letterbooks, DLC.

1. William B. NEUROTH was a member of CMIU 24 of Denver and a vice-president (1892-96) of the CMIU.

2. SG was serving as CMIU second vice-president in 1895 when he became a candidate for first vice-president. He was elected in early 1896 and took office Jan. 1, 1897.

To George Perkins

Nov. 16th [18]95.

Personal

Friend Perkins: —

Yours of the 18th to hand and contents noted & I assure you that I appreciate more than I can tell you the frank tone of your letter and kind words of commendation, as well as your offer to assist in my election to the presidency of the AF of L. or that of any staunch trade unionist. I am frank to say to you that I should esteem it a pleasure to be again the president of the Federation. It is not the question of honor to me for I have had a full share of that, but I feel that in that position I can do better work than in any other in the world, to advance the cause as dear to our hearts. Nor is it a question of the salary for as a matter of fact I am confident I could do much better financially outside the pale of the trade union movement. In truth an offer which I have rejected is still open to me, with a good salary, but I then must bid good bye to and part company with the cause, the movement and the old friends and associates of a life time. This is too much and I can't do it. The movement as I have often said has become part of my very self my yearnings, hopes — everything. Even in the past year organizing, lecturing, travelling and writing I have not done so much worse financially out of office than I formerly did in it. Hence you will see confirmed that which you already know, that it is not the money which prompts me to say that I should again like to fill the position I formerly held. Then again it has been generally recognized that the Denver convention hardly did me justice in approving and heartily commending my every act and then defeating me. (Do you know that it was the vote of my colleague Mr. Barnes[1] which defeated me, I am not speaking of its influence in getting delegates who would otherwise have voted for me, but his vote) I have been told that it is my duty to give the convention an opportunity of (what people say) repairing the injustice they did me. I am am sure that I [am] as fully, if not better, equipped to fill the position now as ever I was in my life and I am as confident that in it I could assume the aggressive against all anti-unionists, in whatever garb they may appear or under whichever mask they disguise. You will therefore [see that I?] fall entirely into your way of thinking on this matter. You say that Mr McBride has used his trip to make "combinations" to secure his re-election. That Sec'y. McCraith is sending out [. . .] letters as to the achievements of the present administration with the same object in view. I have heard the same thing.

Someone said to me that Mr McBride came East for the sole purpose of his announcing his candidacy and stopping at such places where "combinations" could be made. You say that it is my duty to do everything in my power to assure the election. Well I can not do anything. I cannot play the part of a hypocrite I never yet asked directly or indirectly any man to vote for me or made combinations to secure my advancement to any position. If any one believes that the interest of our movement would be furthered by my election they must of their own volition endeavor to bring about that result. If you can show to a number of the delegates that in the interest of our cause they ought to vote for me I am sure that you will do so and I shall appreciate your action beyond measure. Heretofore I even forbade that, but in so far I now can see my error, more especially in view of what I am reliably informed McB. is doing.

Mr Ashe[2] is an old and intimate friend of mine and if elected I think would vote for me. Mr Dawley[3] & Mr Creamer[4] are old acquaintances and I think could be influenced by Mr O'Connell.[5] I have never inquired from Mr McGuire how he stands but a letter to him, impersonal so far as I am concerned, but with the view that the movement should have at its head, as you say other than "faddists or cranks who seek to attach their visionary illogical isms as a "order" upon the legitimate trade union movement" would at least illicet a reply and perhaps an idea of what he will do. In view of the I.T.U.[6] having a Union Label the attitude of its officials and McCraith too is almost incomprehensible. The Iron Molders[7] could be written to in the same strain as McGuire. Write Mr. Fox.[8] Pardon length of this letter I thought it necessary to speak frankly and to assure you that anything you can consistently do with honor alike to yourself and our movement's work will reflect honor upon me and I will appreciate it.

Sincerely yours,   Saml Gompers.

Shall I [. . . ?] then I should like to know the [latest report from it?]

ALpS, reel 341, vol. 356, pp. 42-44, SG Letterbooks, DLC.

1. John Mahlon Barnes, secretary of CMIU 100 of Philadelphia (1897-1900), also served during the 1890s as corresponding secretary of the Philadelphia Central Committee of the SLP and as an organizer for the Philadelphia American Branch of the SLP.

2. Robert Ashe, a Somerville, Mass., machinist, served on the General Executive Board of the International Association of Machinists (IAM) between 1893 and 1897.

3. William L. Dawley, former general secretary-treasurer (1892-95) of the IAM, was working in Richmond as a grocer. He was not a delegate to the AFL's 1895 convention.

4. James J. Creamer, who represented the IAM at the AFL's 1895 convention,

was a Richmond, Va., gas inspector and former grand master machinist (1890-92) of the IAM.

5. James O'CONNELL was grand master machinist of the IAM (1893-1911) and third vice-president of the AFL (1895-1913).

6. The International TYPOGRAPHICAL Union.

7. The IRON Molders' Union of North America (IMUNA).

8. Martin FOX was president of the IMUNA from 1890 to 1903.

Excerpts from Accounts of the 1895 Convention of the AFL in New York City

[December 11, 1895]

M'BRIDE VINDICATED

The delegates to the annual Convention of the American Federation of Labor got down to business yesterday afternoon, hearing contests and deciding the claims of delegates to their seats. A stranger in the convention hall might have taken the gathering for a meeting of professional or business men. The men were well dressed and the language used in the speeches was temperate.

An attempt was made by the socialist element to unseat William C. Pomeroy,[1] delegate of the Chicago Trades and Labor Assembly, who has made himself obnoxious to them by his steady opposition to their influence in the labor movement in Chicago. The first protest against Pomeroy, made by the brewers,[2] was dismissed, and he was seated. Then W. Klapetsky,[3] who represents the Journeymen Barbers' National Union,[4] made the assertion that the Chicago Trade Council had affiliated with it a barbers' union[5] which was in opposition to the national union of the trade, and charged Pomeroy with falsehood in a statement made to him on this subject. Pomeroy gave the lie to Klapetsky. He was called to order by President McBride, who overruled the objection and declared Pomeroy seated.

LABOR STRUGGLES OF THE YEAR.

A lengthy report by the Executive Council concerning its work during the year was read at the morning session. . . .

. . .

M'BRIDE VINDICATED.

The most important part of the Council's report referred to the investigation of the charge made against John McBride, president of the Federation, to the effect that he had been bribed to effect a settlement of the American Railway Union's[6] strike.[7] Here is the Council's report of its investigation of the charges: —

"In the course of the year, as you all know, serious charges were preferred against our president in connection with the American Railway Union strike. The matter was thoroughly considered by your Council at its April meeting, and one of our members[8] was deputized to repair to Columbus, Ohio, and in conjunction with the central body[9] of that city make a complete investigation. Subsequently said member reported as follows, which was adopted by the Council: —

" 'New York, Dec. 9, 1895.

" 'As per instructions of the Executive Council, I visited Columbus, Ohio, and made investigation of the charges preferred by Mark Wild against John McBride, president of the American Federation of Labor. We had two all day sessions, May 8 and 9, 1895, of the committee of the Trades Assembly of Columbus, Ohio, to whom the charges had been referred. The committee had several sessions prior to my visit, and since then. But at no time did Mark Wild appear before the committee to substantiate his charges. Nor was there any evidence offered of a definite and conclusive character to show that John McBride had betrayed the interest of organized labor or been guilty of corrupt practices, as alleged by Mark Wild and others.

" 'P. J. McGuire.' "

Mrs. Eva McDonald Valesh,[10] of Detroit, was introduced after the reading of the report, and made a speech on the relation of women to trades unions. She said that she and her husband,[11] who is Deputy Labor Commissioner for the State of Michigan, were about to make a trip to Europe to study the conditions of the laboring people there. They will travel through Europe on bicycles, living among the workers, and Mrs. Valesh said that she would send regular contributions to the American Federationist, the official magazine.[12] A resolution to pay her for the articles was carried over her protest.

· · ·

CONVENTION WILL LAST TWO WEEKS.

It is likely that the Convention will last for about two weeks and will be the scene of a battle royal between the socialists and the old style trade unionists. The socialists will make a strong protest against the adoption of the parts of President McBride's address favoring legislative reform. Their chief opponents in the Convention are John

B. Lennon,[13] of the Journeymen Tailors' Union;[14] Henry Weismann, of the Bakers;[15] "Pat." McBride[16] and Penna,[17] of the Miners;[18] and Pomeroy, of Chicago. The socialists will, however, be an important factor in deciding the contest in the presidency, and the combinations thus formed may enable them to gain some slight advantages. At present the race lies between John McBride and Samuel Gompers, with Gompers slightly in the lead.

. . .

New York Herald, Dec. 11, 1895.

1. William Curtis POMEROY was the editor of the *American Caterer* (1896-98) and the *National Purveyor* (1897-99), journals of the Hotel and Restaurant Employees' National Alliance (HRENA; after 1898 the Hotel and Restaurant Employees' International Alliance and Bartenders' International League of America), and an AFL organizer (1896). He served as vice-president of the HRENA (1896-99).

2. The National Union of the United BREWERY Workmen of the United States.

3. William E. KLAPETZKY, of Syracuse, N.Y., was secretary-treasurer (1894-1904) of the Journeymen Barbers' International Union of America.

4. The Journeymen BARBERS' International Union of America.

5. The Barbers' Protective Association of Chicago.

6. The American RAILWAY Union.

7. See "John McBride's Presidency of the AFL," above, for a discussion of the charges brought against McBride by Mark Wild.

8. P. J. McGuire, first vice-president of the AFL, who was a representative of the United Brotherhood of Carpenters and Joiners of America at this convention.

9. The Columbus Trades and Labor Assembly was not affiliated with the AFL.

10. Eva McDonald VALESH was manager of the industrial department of the *Minneapolis Tribune* and a lecturer and treasurer for the Minnesota Farmers' Alliance. Around 1898 she moved to New York City where she worked for the *New York Journal* and served as an AFL organizer.

11. Frank Valesh was Minnesota deputy labor commissioner.

12. Eva McDonald Valesh's articles, entitled "Conditions of Labor in Europe," appeared in the *American Federationist* (3 [April 1896]: 23-26, [May 1896]: 41-43, [June 1896]: 64-66, [July 1896]: 83-85, [August 1896]: 111-13, and [October 1896]: 155-56).

13. John Brown LENNON was general secretary of the Journeymen Tailors' Union of America (until 1889 the Journeymen Tailors' National Union of the United States) and editor of the *Tailor* from 1887 to 1910. He was treasurer of the AFL from 1890 to 1917.

14. The Journeymen TAILORS' Union of America.

15. The Journeymen BAKERS' and Confectioners' International Union of America.

16. Patrick McBRYDE was secretary-treasurer of the United Mine Workers of America (UMWA) from 1891 to 1896.

17. Philip H. PENNA was vice-president (1891-95) and president (1895-97) of the UMWA.

18. The United MINE Workers of America.

[December 11, 1895][1]

THE LABOR CONVENTION.

. . .

Secretary Tracey[2] of the credential committee reported that they had considered the protest of A. W. McKinney[3] against James H. Sullivan[4] of the Painters and Decorators of America.[5] Upon the recommendation of the committee, the protest was dropped. James H. Sullivan protested W. E. Ward,[6] who claimed to represent a painters' union which is a dual organization.[7] The committee reported that Ward be denied a seat, and the convention concurred in the report. Several other committees reported progress, after which several new resolutions were offered and filed with the proper committee. Vice-President T. J. Elderkin[8] arose and said:

"I desire to call your attention to a great danger which confronts the federation, viz., the existence of a duality of organization within the ranks of the federation. This practice if continued will eventually place the federation in the centre of antagonistic elements. Take the case of the brewers as an instance; with 119 lodges represented in the Brewery Employees' National Union, they have a small minority of lodges attached to the Knights of Labor. These Knights of Labor assemblies have a national trade assembly[9] and meet in national convention and secretly legislate for the National Brewery Employees' Union. As a result a great national union attached to the federation is controlled absolutely by an inner circle of the Knights of Labor. That this is a menace to trades-unionism no sane person can deny. Your committee suggests as a remedy the following:

"Resolved. That the American Federation of Labor shall hereafter refuse to seat as delegates any representative whose organization has within its ranks any other organization comprising less than the total number."[10]

. . .

New York Evening Post, Dec. 11, 1895.

1. This excerpt is from a newspaper article reporting the proceedings of Dec. 11, 1895.
2. Thomas F. TRACY, a Boston cigarmaker, was a vice-president of the CMIU from 1896 to 1916. He represented the Massachusetts State Federation of Labor.
3. Joseph W. MCKINNEY, a Chicago painter, was prevented from taking office as general secretary-treasurer of the Brotherhood of Painters and Decorators of America (BPDA) after his election in 1894. After participating in forming the western faction of the BPDA, he served as its general secretary-treasurer from 1896 to 1897.
4. James Henry SULLIVAN, a Baltimore painter, served as general president of the BPDA from 1894 until 1898, leading the eastern faction of the divided trade. He was that faction's delegate.

5. The Brotherhood of PAINTERS and Decorators of America.

6. William E. WARD, Jr., was a member of BPDA 169 of Jersey City, N.J., and represented the western faction of the BPDA.

7. In 1894 the BPDA split into two factions. James H. Sullivan was associated with the one led by John T. Elliott, which remained headquartered in Baltimore. The other, led by Joseph W. McKinney, was headquartered in Lafayette, Ind. The 1894 AFL convention seated delegates from both groups, but the AFL Executive Council voted in February 1895 to recognize only the eastern faction. The split continued until 1900, when the two divisions amalgamated.

8. Thomas J. ELDERKIN was a leader in the Lake Seamen's Union in Chicago and general secretary of the International Seamen's Union of America (until 1895 the National Seamen's Union of America) from 1892 to 1899. He served as the fourth vice-president of the AFL in 1895 and represented the Seamen at this convention.

9. KOL National Trade Assembly 35.

10. The resolution was referred to the committee on organization, which reported that it was covered in substance by previous convention action.

[December 12, 1895]

MANY BOYCOTTS LAID.

With all preliminaries and disputes settled, the delegates to the National Convention of the American Federation of Labor devoted yesterday to practical business. There was little talking. Debates were cut short, and in many instances resolutions favorably reported by committees were declared adopted without a vote. In these short resolutions the power of the organization was expressed, for many of them related to boycotts against and vigorous fights to be waged on wealthy corporations in various cities of the country.

. . .

A DAY FOR BOYCOTTS.

Many other boycotts were ordered by the convention at the request of delegates, who explained the critical conditions of the local organizations. Most of these boycotts will not extend outside of their respective States.

There was much discussion over the efficiency of boycotts. Some delegates said that the weapon was losing its force. One speaker asked how he could be expected to remember the 233 firms now on the list. In many instances the boycotts amounted to nothing, it was declared, because no united effort was made to render them effective and the unions throughout the country soon forgot about them. The discussion on this subject lasted for an hour, its principal result being to stir up the delegates to further activity.

. . .

DARED TO RIDICULE GOMPERS.

Samuel Gompers proposed his perennial resolution denouncing capital punishment, and much to the convention's surprise a very energetic young man dared attack the big leader. Mr. [Pomeroy said the?] resolutions were sickly sentimental and hysterical, and he intimated that such was the condition of Mr. Gompers. The delegates held their breath expecting to see the ex-president oratorically slay him, but Mr. Gompers answered in a long dull argument to which Mr. Pomeroy simply replied, "Still sentimental and hysterical." Half a dozen voices voted for the resolution, and as nobody dared to say no, it was adopted.

Then the convention had to take up financial questions, and a resolution declaring in favor of free coinage at a ratio of 16 to 1 was adopted without discussion.

. . .

New York World, Dec. 12, 1895.

Thursday, Dec. 12, 1895.

FOURTH DAY—MORNING SESSION.

. . .

REPORT OF DELEGATES TO THE BRITISH TRADES UNION CONGRESS.

To the Members of the American Federation of Labor:
Fellow Workers:—

As your delegates to the Twenty-eighth Congress of the British Trades Unions, held at Cardiff, Wales, September 2d-7th, 1895, it becomes our pleasant duty to submit this our report:

. . .

POLICY OF THE CONGRESS.

At several of our conventions the attitude of the British trade unions has been frequently quoted as an inducement for us to follow in their lines of policy. In no instance has this been more ingeniously utilized than by those who sought to engraft the declaration in favor of collectivism on our organization. Following out this mode of citation we would call your attention to a resolution offered by the delegate[1] who was the author of the collectivist resolution adopted at the previous congress at Norwich.[2] The resolution he offered at Cardiff reads:
["]That agreeing with the remarks of the Parliamentary Committee

respecting the unemployed problem, we regret that during the past year they have taken no steps on the mandate given to them by the Congress of 1894, viz., to promote and support legislation in favor of the *nationalization of the land and means of production,* and which, in the opinion of this congress, was the only real solution of the ever-recurring problem of men, women and children starving in a land of plenty."

The vote on the resolution was: For, 186,000, against, 607,000. It was thus defeated by a majority of 421,000.

Thus the proposition of the collectivist principle failed of endorsement by an overwhelming adverse vote.

In view of the change of sentiment within a year upon such a vital issue we believed it our duty to make inquiry as to its cause. We soon learned that under the system of representation of organizations and voting power of delegates to the congresses, the gravest misrepresentation of the membership was possible and occurred.

In the first place each delegate to the congress had but one vote regardless of the membership represented, and since the larger organizations never could send their full quota of delegates by reason of the great expense involved, and as the smaller organizations were for some reason or another always fully represented, it can be easily appreciated how practically a minority view could prevail. This method of representation and voting power was changed at the Cardiff Congress, practically upon the equitable basis prevailing in the conventions of the American Federation of Labor: *i.e.,* each delegate now casts one vote for every member represented.

A further reason for the apparently changed sentiments is found in this fact. Many delegates at the Norwich Congress voted in favor of the collectivist resolution, believing, as they declared to us, that [it] would do no harm to the trade union movement, that it would satisfy the radical elements in the movement, and that all would thereafter act in harmony. It was found that after the close of that congress those who had secured the passage of the resolution, proclaimed that the adoption of the resolution carried with it the declaration that the trade unions were old and effete institutions, that their methods and tactics to secure better conditions for the workers were thereafter to be eschewed, and new lines, that of building a political party founded upon socialistic theories, was to be the principal work of the trade unions. When the trade unionists realized the full extent of the purpose of the resolution, they determined upon some course to demonstrate their true sentiments and belief.

It is but proper that we should also report to you that in conference with a number of delegates, they candidly admitted that the adoption of the collectivist resolution at Norwich was a mistake, but that "it would not do to acknowledge it to the world."

POLITICAL ACTION.

We would also call your attention to the adoption of the following at the Cardiff Congress: "That this congress endorses the principle of independent labor representation upon all local and government administrative bodies but would leave the power of selection in the hands of the constituencies, and where it is found advisable in the interest of the working classes. *This Congress is prepared to support candidates who are adopted by and receiving support from the political parties—either liberal, conservative, nationalist or unionist,* that in furtherance of this object, this congress instructs the parliamentary [committee] to use its influence in urging upon the government, the necessity of appointing workingmen upon the borough and county magisterial benches."

In reporting this matter fully to you, we do not wish to have it inferred that we took sides with either view. We have observed in our conventions and our movement, a worthy desire by all to learn the lessons taught by our British fellow trade unionists, all have pointed out their declarations and actions, and all have urged that so far as our own economic, politic and social conditions would admit that we follow them. In the interest of our movement, this matter should be fully understood.

In many industries of Great Britain, the workers are employed regularly a lesser number of hours than our workers in the same trades. From what we have learned, however, the so-called "overtime" is a greater general evil than exists among us; although great efforts are now being made to lessen it, and hopes are entertained that in the near future, except in great emergencies, to entirely abolish it.

In the matter of congress we found that its make up is much like our conventions. There are two features however which materially differ, one of which we can adopt with advantage, the other we think unpractical. In the congress very little if any new matter is brought up for discussion and action; other than such propositions which have been duly forwarded to the executive office at least six weeks before the meeting of the congress. These propositions are sent to all the organizations affiliated, which, if they desire, may forward amendments within four weeks of the congress. These propositions and amendments are sent to the delegates-elect two weeks before the meeting. We are aware that our Federation has adopted a similar measure, but we are of the opinion that until it is more generally accepted that new matter or measures which have not been regularly proposed and submitted before our conventions, we may be likely to have resolutions adopted for which there is insufficient time for consideration, as well as consultation with the rank and file of our membership.

The other feature to which we refer is the one which practically requires the congress to have as chairman a man recommended by the central body of the locality in which the congress is held. In our judgment the presiding officer of an important gathering such as the conventions of the trade unions of the United States or Great Britain should as with us be a responsible officer.

OUR RECEPTION.

At the time set apart for that purpose we were introduced to the congress with great warmth and cordiality of expression and demonstration. In addressing the men and women there assembled we felt as if we were standing upon ground consecrated by ages of suffering, self-sacrificing and devoted men. That we were facing and were surrounded by men and women who would stand or fall for the right; who would rescue the child from the factory, the mill or the mine and ennoble them through the influence of the schoolroom and the playground; whose every word and act sought the full enfranchisement and emancipation of the wealth producer, the attainment of the day when "man's inhumanity to man" shall be a question relegated to the barbaric practices of the past.

In our addresses we not only conveyed to our fellow unionists the fraternal greetings of their American brothers and sisters of labor, we reviewed the conditions prevailing among us, and the obstacles which stand in our way and which we hope and strive to overcome. We endeavored to represent the sentiments of our entire membership, reviewing the past, presenting the present and declaring our hopes and aspirations for the future.

It would be false modesty did we not mention that our remarks were received with enthusiastic fervor, hearty responses and fraternal good wishes. At the conclusion of our speeches, we were each presented with a medallion.

The week before the opening of the congress we went to Manchester, Liverpool and Dublin. At each place meetings of the Trades Councils[3] were previously arranged for, and we gleaned much which we regard as material information as to the prevailing conditions. Of course it is impossible, as it might be inappropriate to refer to many matters in this report, and for which we anticipate reporting in another way, but it is our manifest duty to say that the experience of our own workers is in line with that of our British trades unionists; that the unions based on low dues have been of but comparatively little benefit to the workers; that their membership has fluctuated, and many of them formerly the boast of the so-called "New Trades' Unionism," are but skeletons of their former existence.

CONSISTENT ACTION.

In our visit to Dublin we learned of an incident in the career of the Trades' Council of that city, which is not only noteworthy for the consistency of the trades unionists, but is also a tribute to the recognition of the principle that the labor movement in its essence is a class struggle in the interests of humanity. The incident to which we refer occurred a few years ago when the feeling and excitement ran high among Irishmen, each allying himself with the "Parnell" or "Anti-Parnell" wing of the Irish National movement.[4] Each wing insisted that the Trades' Council declare for its side of the bitter controversy. Despite the fact that every delegate was an ardent devotee to Ireland's cause, and an active disputant on the mooted question, the Trades' Council, as a council, decided that it would remain neutral. As a result, we found the trades unionists in Dublin as near a unit in spirit and action, as we have in any city on our travels.

FREE SPEECH.

Nor is it amiss to state that in every part of Great Britain we were most pleasantly surprised to observe the enjoyment and full exercise of the absolute right of free public assemblage and free speech. It is general in every city and town to hold public meetings particularly on Sunday afternoon, in the public parks or public squares. In the former any convenient article which will elevate the speaker above the heads of his hearers is utilized, while in the squares the pedestals of monuments are used as platforms. On several occasions we observed men on the four sides of the pedestal were addressing different assemblages upon as many widely differing topics. The police in attendance aided in maintaining order and supported the platform rather than the reverse which we have with regret too frequently observed in our own country in the past few years.

TRIP ON THE CONTINENT.

Taking advantage of the time which was at our disposal by reason of our inability to secure return passage earlier we visited Paris, France;

Hamburg, Germany; and Amsterdam, Holland; and were amply rewarded by much valuable information gathered, which we also hope
to lay before our workers at another time, but we refer to the visit
for the purpose of making known to you a few matters which should
be reported here.

In Paris the Bourse du Travail (the central body of organized labor),
the Typographical Union and the delegates who visited this country
during the World's fair of 1893, arranged meetings upon three successive evenings. From many of the addresses and conversations with
the workers we learned that an earnest effort is being made to thoroughly organize the workers in trade unions. The fraternal greetings
and cordial receptions accorded us were of the most gratifying character.

In Hamburg we had a "conference" with the executive officers of
the German trades union movement as well as a large number of
representative organized workers. While the trade union movement
in Germany is slowly forging ahead we find that it suffers much from
being deprived by the government of the full right of organization.
We also find that the trade union movement has been subordinated
by the political party[5] to which the workingmen of that country chiefly
belong. Hence through this repressive power of the government on
the one hand, and the political party domination on the other, the
difficulty for the growth and development of the trade unions in
Germany can be appreciated.

It is with pleasure we report that the Cardiff congress resolved to
send a delegation to our convention and we are heartily proud to
accord a hearty welcome to the two sturdy trade unionists[6] who are
with us today expressing the inarticulate yearning of the toilers for
a better and a nobler conception of human rights and human justice.

CONCLUSION.

In conclusion we beg to attest our sincere appreciation of the many
courtesies extended to us by all with whom we had the pleasure to
come in contact, and who as cheerfully aided us to make the work
connected with our trip so pleasant, and, we hope, successful; and to
return thanks to the American Federation of Labor for the mark of
respect and confidence in entrusting us with the mandate of America's
organized workers to our brothers and sisters of the "old world."

Earnestly expressing the hope that we have been in some measure
instrumental in attaining the goal, for which the whole past of the

human family has been but one continuous and preparatory struggle, the establishment of the Brotherhood of Man. We remain,

Fraternally yours,   Samuel Gompers,

P. J. McGuire.

. . .

AFL, *Proceedings,* 1895, pp. 44, 47-49.

1. J. Macdonald represented the Amalgamated Tailors, West London District, at the 1895 meeting of the TUC.
2. The TUC met at Norwich, Sept. 3-8, 1894.
3. The Manchester Trades Council (TC), Liverpool TC, and Dublin TC.
4. Charles Stewart Parnell (1846-91), although a Protestant and a wealthy landlord, was a forceful advocate of Irish home rule in Parliament. His personal and political fortunes declined dramatically in 1890 when he became involved in an adultery case resulting in divorce. The Catholic Church sharply condemned Parnell for his behavior, leading to a split within the Irish nationalist movement between those who supported the Church's position and those who remained loyal to Parnell for his commitment to home rule.
5. The Sozialdemokratische Partei Deutschlands (Social Democratic Party of Germany).
6. James MAWDSLEY and Edward COWEY were the delegates from the TUC. Mawdsley was general secretary of the Amalgamated Association of Operative Cotton Spinners (1878-1902); Cowey was president of the Yorkshire Miners' Association (1881-1903).

[December 14, 1895]

GOMPERS IS LEADING

The American Federation of Labor, at its Convention in Madison Square Garden yesterday, placed itself on record as emphatically opposed to the growing practice of carrying mails on street cars, in spite of the adverse report of its Committee on Resolutions, on the resolution to that effect introduced by O'Sullivan,[1] of Boston.

The resolution read that the Federation opposed the carrying of mails on street cars until such time as the street car lines were owned and operated by the government, and that Congress be asked to abrogate all existing contracts for such service. It was the last clause which caused the opposition in the committee, which is anti-socialist in its composition; but the adverse report aroused a storm of criticism. Furuseth,[2] of San Francisco, denounced the practice as dangerous to the liberties of the street car employes, as a violation of the thirteenth amendment to the constitution of the United States, in that it would deprive the employes of the right to quit their employment at any time, and reduce them, for a time at least, to a condition of involuntary servitude.

Mahon,[3] of Denver, representing the National Brotherhood of Street Car Employes,[4] referred to the tactics of the trolley companies in Brooklyn, who, during the recent strike,[5] placed a mail bag on their cars and thus compelled the motormen to remain at work or be imprisoned for interfering with the safe conduct of the United States mails. O'Sullivan, of Boston, declared that the street railway men of his city objected to the use of a postage stamp to compel them to accept reduced wages or longer hours of labor.

Socialists Rampant Again.

The floor of the Convention was a battle ground between the socialists and conservatives, and when the adjournment was taken last evening, Pomeroy, of Chicago, was holding the floor in a denunciation of the dangerous policy of his enemies.

The distinction between the collectivists and individualists, or between those who believe in governmental aid for labor and those who believe in reliance solely on the efforts of the organizations, was drawn at the morning session in a debate on a resolution asking Congress to establish governmental savings banks in connection with the post office system. The collectivists triumphed, but this is in no sense a triumph for the socialists, who are not at all in sympathy with the collectivists, of whom McBride, the president, is the leader. Weismann, of Brooklyn; Pomeroy, of Chicago, and Samuel Gompers led the individualists.[6]

. . .

The Eight Hour Day Report.

The special committee on the eight hour agitation reported that a general eight hour strike on May 1 will be inexpedient, but that all national and international unions be advised to prepare for such a movement, and that the Executive Council be instructed to correspond with the various unions and select one trade to begin the fight. The report was adopted and the Council was instructed to levy a tax, the amount to be determined later, and to concentrate the whole power of the Federation upon winning the fight for the trade selected.

There was some discussion between the socialists and conservatives on the report of the committee appointed to study the president's report. It was largely composed of socialists, and they made some changes in the report, notably in the the part dealing with the financial question. The committee substituted for a free coinage declaration the declaration that "all plans of finance are equally useless so long as the wage workers are compelled to sell their labor to those owning the means of production and transportation." The committee's report was adopted and the socialists won another barren victory in securing the tabling of a declaration against the violation of contracts with employers by sympathetic strikes.

The real fight came up, however, at the end of the Convention. An invitation was read to send delegates to the International Socialist Workers' and Trade Union Congress,[7] to be held in London in August. Weismann, of the bakers, opposed its acceptance. "The Congress is run," he said, "by the Delegates to the German Reichstag of the social democracy." Tobin,[8] of Massachusetts, a socialist delegate, objected to Weismann's remarks, but was overruled. Pinner,[9] of the miners, made a speech in favor of the delegates, indicating thereby that the McBride men are playing for the support of the socialists at the election for the presidency, which will be held to-day.

Linehan,[10] of Chicago, denounced Pinner for his support of the socialists and there was an angry interchange.

POMEROY ATTACKED AGAIN.

Then Barnes, of Philadelphia, a socialist, got the floor and made an attack on Pomeroy, of Chicago. Barnes is young and enthusiastic. Pomeroy, however, is undoubtedly the orator of the Convention. When Barnes had finished he made him ridiculous. He referred to the socialist as "a terpsichorean economist, an economic hula hula dancer."

"We trade unionists cannot compromise with you," he said. "You are out for defeat. We are out for plain, everyday, selfish, non-illusionist, non-confusionist work. We want no Utopia, but we are after the smallest amount of work for the greatest amount of money." Pomeroy was still on the floor when the hour for adjournment arrived and will finish his speech this morning.

. . .

New York Herald, Dec. 14, 1895.

1. John F. O'SULLIVAN, a reporter and labor editor for the *Boston Globe*, served as president of the Atlantic Coast Seamen's Union (1891-1902) and a vice-president of the International Typographical Union (1897-1902). He represented AFL Federal Labor Union 5915.

2. Andrew FURUSETH, a delegate of the National Seamen's Union, was secretary of the Sailors' Union of the Pacific (until 1891 the Coast Seamen's Union) for almost half a century (1887-89, 1891-1936). He lobbied for the AFL in Washington, D.C., from 1894 to 1902, and continued as legislative representative of the International Seamen's Union for the rest of his life.

3. William D. MAHON of Detroit was president of the Amalgamated Association

of Street Railway Employes of America (after 1903 the Amalgamated Association of Street and Electric Railway Employes of America) from 1893 to 1946, and represented that union at the convention.

4. The Amalgamated Association of STREET Railway Employes of America.

5. On Jan. 14, 1895, between 5,000 and 6,000 employees of several Brooklyn streetcar companies struck, under the auspices of KOL District Assembly 75, demanding improvements in working conditions and pay and the resolution of grievances precipitated by the conversion from horse-drawn to electric-powered streetcars. The car lines rejected offers of a compromise settlement and a proposal to submit differences to arbitration. When local police failed to protect strikebreakers and trolleys, the mayor requested intervention by the state militia. The troops arrived on Jan. 19, and by Feb. 16 the walkout had collapsed.

6. The convention proceedings record SG as absent from this session.

7. The International Socialist Workers' and Trades Union Congress met in London, July 27-Aug. 1, 1896.

8. John F. TOBIN served as general president of the Boot and Shoe Workers' Union from 1895 to 1919 and was one of its delegates at this convention.

9. Philip Penna.

10. James J. Linehan was a delegate of the United Brotherhood of Carpenters and Joiners.

[December 14, 1895]

SOCIALISM CROPS OUT.

It appeared evident yesterday at the Convention of the American Federation of Labor that the chief interest of the convention will centre in the election of officers which is to take place to-day. The Assembly Room of Madison Square Garden where the convention is being held, was comfortably filled with delegates and their friends and critics when the forenoon session opened yesterday.

. . .

Then the question of fixing a time for the election of officers came up. The friends of Samuel Gompers, who is a candidate for President, in opposition to President McBride, wanted it fixed for 3 P.M. to-day. Others wanted the election held yesterday afternoon, but they were overruled, and the battle will take place to-day. The Socialists who are opposed to Gompers, say that this is a skilful move on the part of his friends, as a number of Western delegates who are opposed to Gompers will leave for home this forenoon.[1]

. . .

New York Sun, Dec. 14, 1895.

1. Only one western delegate, Alfred McCallum, a cigarmaker representing the Duluth Federated Trades Assembly, failed to vote in the presidential election; he

would have cast a single ballot. The other delegates who did not vote included two from Brooklyn (with one and twenty-five votes, respectively) and one from Millville, N.J. (one vote).

[December 15, 1895]

GOMPERS PRESIDENT

Samuel Gompers, elected eight times previously to the presidency of the American Federation of Labor, and defeated last year in Denver by John McBride, was elected again yesterday, after a bitter struggle. In spite of the fact that the socialists threw their strength to McBride, contrary to the expectations of all who have been watching the Convention in Madison Square Garden, Gompers received a majority of 18 votes. His vote stood 1,041, against 1,023 for his opponent.

Canvassing had been going on actively throughout the morning session and at the recess, and it was thought that there would be several new men nominated. Prescott,[1] of Indianapolis; Khapetsky, of Detroit, and Pomeroy, of Chicago, were all spoken of, but at the last moment they withdrew, and only Gompers and McBride were nominated.

The election was a clean cut contest between the East and the West.[2] With the exception of the socialist vote, which comes principally from the East, Gompers received all the Eastern votes. The Western men voted solidly for McBride. The large organizations were almost equally divided. The shoeworkers,[3] who are socialists, cast 100 votes for McBride. Barnes, of Philadelphia, a cigarmaker, gave McBride 69 votes, but the other 207 votes of the cigarmakers went to Gompers. The printers cast their entire 291 votes for McBride, while the carpenters[4] split their vote, giving 150 to Gompers and 50 to McBride. Garland,[5] of the iron and steelworkers,[6] cast 40 votes for each of the candidates.

P. J. McGuire, of Philadelphia, was unanimously re-elected first vice president, and Augustin McCraith,[7] of Boston, and John B. Lennon, of New York, were re-elected secretary and treasurer without opposition. The other officers are James Duncan,[8] of Baltimore, second vice president, and James O'Connell,[9] of Chicago, and M. M. Garland, of Pittsburg, third and fourth vice presidents.

M'BRIDE DISAPPOINTED.

McBride was much disappointed by his defeat. He had confidently expected to be re-elected, and would have been had it not been for the absence of Gelson,[10] of the International Printing Pressmen's Union,[11] whose illness prevented his casting twenty-five votes promised to McBride. Barnes, of Philadelphia, however, violated his instructions by voting against Gompers. McBride, in his speech of congratulation for his successful opponent, said:—

"I came here to-day with a nice little speech all prepared for this occasion, but 'Sam' has made it."

The socialists were defeated all along the line yesterday. In a clean, clear cut fight at the morning session it was demonstrated that they were only a very noisy minority. On the test question, that of adopting a socialistic political platform, they polled 214 votes against 1,796 by the conservatives.

The struggle began at the opening of the session, when the debate on the proposition to send delegates to the International Socialist Congress in London was resumed. Pomeroy, of Chicago, resumed his speech interrupted by the adjournment on Friday, and fiercely denounced the socialists, and particularly Barnes, of Philadelphia, and Tobin, of Massachusetts, for their treachery to the Federation, in advocating the formation of a socialist trade alliance,[12] to take the place of the Federation, at the socialist meeting in Cooper Union on Friday night.[13] The proposition was tabled by an overwhelming vote.

FIGHT OVER THE PLATFORM.

The question of adopting the political platform then came up. It had been adopted at the Convention in Denver last year plank by plank, but a motion to adopt it as a whole had been defeated.[14] The president, in his address, had drawn attention to the doubt existing as to the position of the Federation, and asked that it be cleared up.

Pomeroy moved that "we declare the failure to adopt the twelve planks as a whole equivalent to a rejection, and we declare that the American Federation of Labor has no political platform."

The socialists opposed the resolution with their usual bitterness, and Barnes attacked the Federation. "I will not be surprised at anything you do," he said. "I have seen the Federation before accomplish the feat of swallowing itself without choking, and I suppose it can do so again."

Samuel Gompers said:—"It is true that in every movement the time comes for the parting of the ways, and it is time to let all the world know that the parting of the ways has come in this labor movement. We can no longer tolerate men in our ranks who are going out into the world and asking others to join a movement antagonistic to ours. Within twelve hours of the present moment delegates to this

Convention, at a public meeting, urged the adoption of a resolution whose purport was to disrupt the Federation."

John B. Lennon compared the socialist labor party to the A.P.A.,[15] and said that its only purpose was to cause dissension among the workingmen. Pomeroy's motion was adopted by a vote of 1,796 to 214, and then a motion to accept the platform as an abstract declaration of principles, with no political significance, was carried. The tenth plank, however, has been altered from a declaration for the public ownership of all the means of production and transportation to its present form.[16]

. . .

The election of Gompers to the presidency places the Federation squarely in opposition, not only to socialism, but to the principle of paternal legislation which McBride favored. Gompers is an advocate of the improvement of the condition of labor by the efforts of the laborers themselves, organized on the trade union plan, and believes in as little State interference as possible. To such an extent does he carry his advocacy of this principle that he is called a philosophical anarchist by his opponents.

New York Herald, Dec. 15, 1895.

1. William Blair PRESCOTT served as president of the International Typographical Union (ITU) from 1891 to 1898, and was one of its delegates.

2. An examination of the vote indicates no clear East-West division.

3. The BOOT and Shoe Workers' Union.

4. The United Brotherhood of CARPENTERS and Joiners of America.

5. Mahlon Morris GARLAND represented the National Amalgamated Association of Iron and Steel Workers of the United States (NAAISW). He served as president of the NAAISW from 1892 until 1898 and as fourth vice-president of the AFL from 1895 until 1898.

6. The National Amalgamated Association of IRON and Steel Workers of the United States.

7. August McCRAITH, the secretary of the AFL, was a representative of the ITU.

8. James DUNCAN served as second vice-president of the AFL (1894-1900), acting president of the AFL during President McBride's illness (1895), secretary of the Granite Cutters' National Union of the United States of America (GCNU; 1895-1905), and president of the Baltimore Federation of Labor (1897). He represented the GCNU.

9. James O'Connell was a delegate of the International Association of Machinists.

10. James GELSON of Brooklyn was secretary-treasurer of the International Printing Pressmen's Union of North America (after 1897 International Printing Pressmen's and Assistants' Union of North America) from 1892 to 1898.

11. The International Printing PRESSMEN'S Union of North America.

12. On Dec. 13, 1895, a meeting at Cooper Union under SLP auspices established the Socialist Trade and Labor Alliance (STLA). Several thousand people attended, including representatives of KOL District Assembly 49, the New York City Central Labor Federation (CLF), the Newark, N.J., CLF, the United Hebrew Trades, and the

Socialist Labor Federation of Brooklyn. The STLA embodied the "new trade union-ism" of Daniel DeLeon and his supporters in the SLP, a strategy to commit trade unions to the support of the party. It represented an abandonment of the SLP's efforts to capture the AFL and the KOL by "boring from within."

The STLA's efforts to defeat and replace the AFL centered on creating dual unions in competition with AFL affiliates, an approach that alienated many socialists and that, for the most part, proved ineffective. This, along with DeLeon's domineering style, helped deflate the movement by 1898. At its peak, the STLA did not exceed 30,000 members; its appeal was strongest among Jewish and German unionists in the New York City metropolitan area, particularly those in the clothing and shoe trades. In 1905, with about 1,450 members, the STLA joined the newly organized Industrial Workers of the World.

13. The meeting that organized the STLA was held on Dec. 13, 1895. See "An Article in the *People*," Dec. 22, 1895, below.

14. See "The Political Program," in *Unrest and Depression*, pp. 419-22.

15. The American Protective Association.

16. Plank 10 of the AFL's political program adopted at the 1894 Denver convention called for "the abolition of the monopoly system of land holding and the substituting therefor of a title of occupancy and use only" (AFL, *A Verbatim Report of the Discussion on the Political Programme, at the Denver Convention of the American Federation of Labor, December 14, 15, 1894* [New York, 1895], p. 62). The convention proceedings give the vote as 1,676 to 214.

[December 15, 1895]

GOMPERS'S MAJORITY 18.

Samuel Gompers, of the Cigarmakers' Union, was yesterday elected president of the American Federation of Labor. It was expected to be a very close fight between ex-President Gompers and his only opponent, the retiring President John McBride.

Although President McBride has frequently during the convention at the Madison Square Garden Assembly Rooms, disclaimed any connection with the revolutionary Socialists, it was known that the party who favored the introduction of a political platform into the Federation was ranged on his side.

As foreshadowed in yesterday's Journal, the poll was very close. Out of a total vote of 2,064 Gompers was elected by a majority of only 18. The predictions published in this paper yesterday proved accurate in almost every particular. The Typographical Union and the United Mine Workers went solid for McBride. Those two important trades control a combined vote of 472 and it needed the array of many unions in opposition to offset this powerful support. Gompers, however, secured the new delegates of the International Association of Machinists,[1] who were on the fence until the last moment, and, as was predicted, their allegiance was rewarded by the election of their leader, James O'Connell, to a seat in the executive council as third vice-president.

The unknown and carefully guarded intentions of the Brotherhood of Carpenters and Joiners, which it was prophesied was the key to the election and might sway the result, when crystalized into action actually did so, and was the means of electing ex-President Gompers. Vice-President Patrick J. McGuire got two[2] of his three men into line with himself, thus giving 150 votes to Gompers, but Delegate D. P. Rowland[3] bolted his leadership and recorded 50 for McBride.

Among his other most substantial supporters, Gompers numbered the Bakers', the Brewers', the Longshoremen's,[4] the Seamen's,[5] the Cotton Spinners',[6] the Tailors', the Tobacco Workers'[7] and the Barbers' unions.

McBride had the solid support of the Socialists, led by Delegates J. Mahohn Barnes and John F. Tobin, the Boot and Shoe Workers and the Horseshoers,[8] in addition to the Printers and Miners. The votes of the Iron Moulders, the Garment Workers and the Iron and Steel Workers were divided almost equally between the two candidates.

. . .

New York Journal, Dec. 15, 1895.

1. The delegates of the International Association of MACHINISTS were James O'Connell, Robert Ashe, and James J. Creamer.

2. A reference to James J. Linehan and William F. Plumb, delegates to the convention representing the United Brotherhood of Carpenters and Joiners of America (UBCJA).

3. D. P. Rowland was a member of UBCJA 667 of Cincinnati and a delegate of the Brotherhood.

4. The International LONGSHOREMEN'S Association.

5. The International SEAMEN'S Union of America.

6. The National Cotton Mule SPINNERS' Association of America.

7. The National TOBACCO Workers' Union of America.

8. The International Union of Journeymen HORSESHOERS of the United States and Canada.

[December 15, 1895]

GOMPERS JUST GETS IN

. . .

"We cannot fairly compare England and the United States on the same basis," said Mr. Gompers yesterday as he sat in an ante-room of the convention hall. "We make comparisons in advancement with the conditions of five years ago. The Englishman points to his grand-father's trade union. The men themselves are different; the conditions are different. In Great Britain organization is perfected and discipline to a remarkable degree results. Owing to class distinction it is difficult there for a man to rise in the world, therefore a leader stands out in greater prominence. In America all men have a chance to rise and a multitude of leaders aspire.

"Americans would never go into the market to buy brains.[1] True, it is a great idea to purchase the highest talent in the cause of an organization, but such a man as Lord Randolph Churchill[2] could never lead an American army of workingmen. Nor in my opinion would the Englishmen ever accept him, as Mr. Mawdsley suggests. In the ranks of American workingmen are leaders just as great, who only await the opportunity to develop themselves. An outsider would soon find himself like a general without an army. His methods would be his alone, not of the unions.

"The strength of a chain is equal to that of its weakest link. So it is with labor organizations in their fight for advancement. Their progress is equal only to the movement of the mass. Therefore what we need and what we shall strive for is the improvement of the body politic. As that is raised so we shall gain. The brilliancy of a single leader will not win the victory for labor. That must be done by the workingmen themselves.

"The Federation of Labor has four main objects in view now. First is the shortening of the hours of labor, which will bring with it many improvements.

"The second is the abolition of all child labor and the regulation of woman's labor.

"In a single third group can be enumerated improvements in san-itary conditions, inspection of shops, factories and mines and methods to render the labor of man as pleasant and healthful as possible. The last is the changing of laws that now favor capital and oppress labor like the iniquitous power of injunction.

"Many people do not understand the scope of the eight-hour move-ment. Its adoption will not only shorten the hours of the man em-ployed, but it will cause the employment of the idle and thus regulate the economic conditions of supply and demand for labor.

"In again becoming the executive head of this great organization, I have three methods in mind to accomplish the results which we all desire. The first and greatest is better, closer and more effective organization in trade union principles. That will mold the workers into a compact body, bring discipline and render them stronger.

["]Then I favor higher dues to be paid by each man in order to accumulate a great fund with which to carry on the fight. We are frequently hampered by lack of money, and leaders are unable to accomplish what might otherwise be secured. Money is a requisite for fighting capital with its own weapons and winning certain victories.

"My third plan is a broad one, having for its aim the carrying on of agitation everywhere, the education of the workingmen and the raising of them all to the plane which many have already reached. Then we shall have a thinking, intelligent body of men, deserving of every recognition."

. . .

New York World, Dec. 15, 1895.

1. In an interview in the *New York World,* Dec. 14, 1895, Mawdsley stated that trade unions in the United States lacked leadership and discipline, and should "meet capital upon its own ground" by hiring experienced individuals such as Randolph Churchill to manage their affairs: "Let them go into the market and buy brains and pay the market price for those brains."

2. Lord Randolph Henry Spencer Churchill (1849-95) was a Conservative party member in the House of Commons (1874-95) and served as chancellor of the Exchequer in 1886.

New York.   December 16. [1895]

ONE MORE DAY OF WORK

. . .

At the afternoon session the committee on organization reported favorably for the appropriation of a sum not exceeding $500 for the organization of the textile workers in the south, and one from the north to look after the work.[1] The resolution making the appropriation was adopted.

. . .

Detroit Free Press, Dec. 17, 1895.

1. The resolution read: "That a sum of money, not to exceed $500, be appropriated for the purpose of organizing the textile workers of the Southern States, and that the Executive Council select two organizers, one to be a resident of the South and one from some union of the textile industry" (AFL, *Proceedings,* 1895, p. 74).

[December 18, 1895]

SOCIALISTS VOTED DOWN.

The Convention of the American Federation of Labor resumed its session yesterday morning at the Madison Square Garden assembly-rooms. . . .

. . .

There was a long discussion on the question of organizing a political party devoted to the interests of labor. The result was defeat for the Socialists by an overwhelming majority and the adoption of the following resolution:

Resolved, That this convention declares that party politics, whether Democratic, Republican, Socialistic, Populistic or any other, should have no place in the Federation of Labor.

. . .

New York Tribune, Dec. 18, 1895.

An Article in the *People*

[December 22, 1895]

OUR MEETING.

On Monday evening, the 9th instant, despite the aid of a brass band, only about 600 people, fully 200 of whom were Socialists on the watch, cared to respond to the call of the "pure and simple" A.F. of L., to hold a meeting[1] in Cooper Union. The following Friday, without the brass bands, but moved by the vigorous breath of New Trade Unionism, that large hall was crowded; hundreds could not get in; and the audience was held till after 11 P.M. in enthusiastic rapture at the gospel of deliverance preached; and it launched, amid thunderous applause, the new national New Trades Union organization—the Socialist Trade and Labor Alliance—by the unanimous adoption of the following resolutions:

"*Whereas,* The issue between the capitalist class and the laboring class is essentially a political issue involving such modifications of our institutions as may be required for the abolition of all classes by transferring to the whole people as a corporate body the land and the machinery of production;

["]*Resolved,* That we, the Socialists of New York, in mass meeting assembled, urge upon all our fellow-workingmen throughout the United States the necessity of joining the Socialist Trade and Labor Alliance, now being organized for the purpose of placing the American labor movement on its only true and natural lines—the lines of international Socialism."

The chairman of the meeting was William L. Brower,[2] D.M.W. of D.A. 49; secretaries Ernest Bohm for C.L.F., and Emil Kirchner[3] for the S.L.P. The speakers were Comrades Sanial,[4] Tobin, delegate to the A.F. of L. from the shoe workers, Barnes, delegate from the cigar makers, DeLeon and Carless.[5]

The argument of the speakers was that the pure and simple union in America was an importation from England; that it started there at a time when even the capitalists had no clear conception of their own system, and much less clear was the conception thereof by the workers. To these capital appeared as a natural thing with rights that had to be respected; when the British delegate, Mr. Mawdsley, said Socialists and trade unionists (meaning the old-style union) wanted all that they produced, and consequently wanted the same thing, he erred, because the old-style union means by "all" that portion only of the wealth produced that remained after capital's "just share" was paid. Capital represented the accumulated stealings of capitalists; it was the product of labor, and not of the capitalists; consequently when the Socialists said labor should have "all" that is produced, they meant every speck of wealth in existence or brought forth. Another misconception of the capitalist system by the old-style union was the opinion of the other British delegate, Mr. Cowey, who held stoutly that the union should deal with the commodity labor the same as the capitalist deals with his commodities, and insist upon getting its price before taking its goods—labor—"from the shelve." The absurdity of this view was illustrated by quoting the remarks of the superintendent of the Pennsylvania Railroad who declared that the only solution of the labor problem was to starve out the worker seeing that "if you put a silver dollar on the shelf you had a silver dollar at the end of a year, but if you put a workingman on the shelf you have a skeleton at the end of a month." A third fundamental error in old-style unionism was its belief that a modus vivendi could be established between capital and labor, whereas the fact is that the very essence of capital is to crush out smaller holders and render independence wholly inaccessible to the proletariat. A fourth equally fundamental error of the British old-style union proceeded from conditions; it was the divorce of the political from the economic movement. This proceeded from the fact that the English worker was originally wholly disfranchised, and even now could not be said to be in the full and actual enjoyment of the suffrage. As a result of that, the British, or old-style union, used exclusively the weapons of the strike and boycott, because it had none other.

It was next shown that the tremendous influx of British old-style trade unionists forty years ago fastened on the American labor movement the errors of the old unions, including the blunder of excluding the unity of political action in a country where the ballot was common property. The British old-style unionist was a monomaniac on the subject, and introduced here, where the political weapon was accessible to the worker, the lame duck of the old country. It was a remarkable fact that the leading old-style trade unionists in America were all of English birth and importation, from the decoy duck Arthur,[6] who enriched himself at the expense of the lives of the locomotive engineers, down to the clown Gompers.

As a revolt against the concentrated folly of old-style British unionism in America, the Order of the Knights of Labor was launched. Uriah S. Stephens,[7] born here and keeping his eyes wide open, saw that labor alone produced all wealth; that the worker, stripped of capital, became more and more subject to the capitalist and less able to uphold his end of the plank; that there was no such thing as establishing permanent relations between the proletariat and the capitalist, but that the system had to be overthrown and substituted by the Co-operative Commonwealth; and, finally, that it was insanity for the worker to throw away his most potent weapon, the ballot. Stephens' native genius perceived that the British trade union was repellant and repulsive to, and a denial of the political rights our people enjoyed, besides being founded on economic fallacies. Accordingly, he founded the Order of the Knights of Labor upon the four cardinal principles: First, that all wealth was produced by labor, and should be labor's; second, that machinery destroyed the basis of "labor aristocracies" and compelled the solidarity of the proletariat; third, that the wage system had to be overthrown to make room for co-operation; fourth, that the independent political action of the worker should go hand in hand with his economic struggle. In forming his plan Stephens was aided greatly by the Communist or Socialist manifesto of Marx and Engels. He planted the Order squarely on the lines of international Socialism.

His work failed, however. The British old-style union had to such an extent poisoned the air in advance that it affected Stephens' organization, and when he finally was virtually deposed the British union took full possession of the labor movement in America. Since that time K. of L. or A.F. of L. was tweedledum and tweedledee. The result was disaster all around. The organizations of labor were smashed to pieces, or had shrunk mainly into bodies on which the labor fakir carried on his nefarious traffic with the capitalists. The machine had created such an overplus of labor that all strikes could be peacefully broken by the unemployed—as was now happening with the glass workers; or capital was so replete with fleecings that it did not care for the unemployed to come in and could wait until labor, starved out, "came down from the shelves" and went to work at the employers' terms—as happened with the great hatters' strike at Danbury;[8] or if capital grew impatient it would order the State to come down upon the strikers like a pile of bricks and bayonet them into submission— as happened in Chicago,[9] Homestead,[10] Buffalo,[11] Brooklyn, etc. The British or old-style trade union had become a crying crime against the workers; it now answered only the purpose of furnishing the labor fakirs who are union officers or hold jobs under the union, with charter fees and dues on which to live, while the worker was saddled with the additional burden of these miscreants.

Another revolt against the British trade union form was now on foot. D.A. 49 had repudiated the fakirs who controlled the offices of the K. of L., had issued a call[12] for all sister bodies of decent and progressive instincts to join it, and had joined the New York and Newark Central Labor Federations,[13] the Brooklyn Socialist Federation[14] and the United Hebrew Trades which already had shaken off the pure and simpledom of the A.F. of L., and together they had established a new national organization—the Socialist Trade and Labor Alliance.

The economic field of battle between Capital and Labor was one where Labor stood at a tremendous disadvantage; the political field of battle was one at which the disadvantage lay on the side of Capital. The new organization would unite the economic with the political struggle; shelter itself with the temporary shelter of the economic organization; fight when occasion required with the economic weapons of the strike and the boycott; but it would transfer its main force to the political field where it could meet Capital in larger numbers and with equality of weapons—the ballot. In the meantime, it would spread education, and not ignorance, as pure and simpledom did.

The new organization would demand of the union man that he resist starvation wages, starvation hours and starvation politics. It would throw to the wind the pure and simple trick of bluff; it would march slowly and firmly; it would gather the wage slaves in its fold as fast as they got tired of being deceived by fakirs; it would urge the toilers to leave the poor old stranded wreck of British or pure and simple trade unionism, and it would aim at complete emancipation, knowing that aught else is futile.

The Lieder Tafel sang several beautiful selections, and at the unusually late hour of 11.15 the monster mass meeting adjourned with three cheers and tigers for the S.L.P. and the Socialist Trade and Labor Alliance.

People (New York), Dec. 22, 1895.

1. On the evening of Dec. 9, 1895, a mass meeting of New York City trade unionists

convened at Cooper Union to hear addresses by AFL convention delegates. Speakers included SG, John Lennon, Henry Weismann, John McBride, James O'Connell, British fraternal delegates James Mawdsley and Edward Cowey, and Eva McDonald Valesh.

2. William L. Brower (b. 1860?), a shoemaker and subsequently bookkeeper and clerk in Brooklyn, became master workman of KOL District Assembly (DA) 49 in 1895 and later secretary-treasurer of District Alliance 49 of the Socialist Trade and Labor Alliance (STLA). He also headed the General Council of Shoe Workers, which became STLA District Alliance 7, and in 1898 became general secretary of the STLA.

3. Emil Kirchner was a member of the SLP's New York state committee in 1896.

4. Lucien Delabarre SANIAL was a prominent leader of the SLP.

5. Harry Carless, a Newark, N.J., silver plater and SLP member, became an organizer for the STLA.

6. Peter M. ARTHUR was grand chief engineer of the Brotherhood of Locomotive Engineers from 1874 until 1903.

7. Uriah Smith STEPHENS was a founder (1869) and first grand master workman (1878-79) of the KOL.

8. Probably a reference to the lockout of Danbury, Conn., hatmakers, trimmers, and finishers by the Danbury Hat Manufacturers' Association, which lasted from Nov. 25, 1893, to Jan. 31, 1894. The hatters, who were resisting a demand for concessions in the face of the general economic collapse of 1893, returned to work on the employers' terms.

9. See "The Pullman Strike," in *Unrest and Depression,* pp. 521-26.

10. See ibid., p. 189, n. 1.

11. See ibid., pp. 214-15, n. 3.

12. At a meeting of KOL DA 49 on Dec. 1, delegates associated with Daniel DeLeon won approval of a motion to withdraw recognition from the KOL General Assembly and KOL general officers and to unite with "progressive" KOL assemblies and central labor bodies to form a national labor alliance committed to socialism (*New Yorker Volkszeitung,* Dec. 2, 1895). The KOL expelled the leaders of this faction, who then met with like-minded socialists from the New York metropolitan area on Dec. 6, setting the stage for the founding meeting of the STLA on Dec. 13.

13. The Newark Central Labor Federation was established in 1894 and became District Alliance 4 of the STLA.

14. In 1895 the Brooklyn Socialist Federation became District Alliance 3 of the STLA.

To William McKinstry[1]

Jan. 2 / 1896.

Wm. H. McKinstry,
318 S. Burdock St., Kalamazoo, Mich.
My Dear Friend: —

I am in receipt of your favor of the 26th of December, which was forwarded from New York here, and hasten to reply, and to assure you that I regret exceedingly to learn that your affairs have not been bright for the past few years and to express the hope that Dame Fortune will deal more kindly with you in the near future.

Relative to your question let me say that I think it entirely proper for you to place it before me and I shall be equally frank with you in my answer.

It is true that I had no other ambition in the Cigar Makers International Union than to be of some service to it, and to occupy no office than that of 2nd Vice President, but when I learned that Mr. Neuroth declined the First Vice Presidency, that I had been nominated for that position, and further, that [. . .] element in the International Union had resorted to unfair means to nominate a candidate[2] for that office I concluded that it became my duty to allow my name to come before the members of our organization and give them the opportunity to vote intelligently either for a man who stands for the very opposite of what I do in the trade union movement, or to vote for me and thus retain the historical as well as intelligent method of practical and progressive trade unionism.

Since most of the enemies of the trade union movement from within as well as without, direct their shafts against me, I was perfectly willing that a new opportunity should be given them to show how thoroughly at variance they are with the organized workingmen of our country.

Of course I know that the office entails additional work, and I need not tell you that I have considerable work on hand now, but I am willing to do anything within my power for the purpose of having our organization a clean out trade union, and as I can weather the attacks of our enemies I am also willing to perform additional work. So far as any remuneration is concerned I have not thought of it at all.

You also know that the term of offices to be elected to the International Union will only commence January 1, 1897 and by that time, in the varying processes going on in the labor movement, your humble servant may well be a high private in the rear ranks.

For the reasons already mentioned as well as the fact that my declination now would not only take me entirely out of the Executive Board of the International Union, but also that the antagonists would regard it as a humiliating retreat, I cannot take action but that already indicated.

If you should decline to be a candidate, as you say you will, I shall esteem it one more of the many compliments you have paid me. However, I do not wish you to consider yourself bound by that statement in your letter.

Kindly convey my best wishes to Mrs. McKinstry[3] and [all?], and accept the same for yourself, from

Yours sincerely,   Saml Gompers.

TLpS, reel 9, vol. 14, pp. 88-89, SG Letterbooks, DLC.

1. William H. McKinstry was a member of CMIU 24 of Muskegon, Mich., and served as an AFL organizer.
2. Besides SG, three candidates appeared on the ballot for the position of CMIU first vice-president: McKinstry, Michael Raphael, and Elmer E. Greenawalt.
3. Probably Delia McKinstry.

A News Account of an Address in New York City

[January 4, 1896]

LABOR AGAINST WAR.

Before leaving for Indianapolis, the headquarters of the American Federation of Labor, Samuel Gompers made a farewell speech to the New York Central Labor Union on last Sunday, in which he denounced in scathing terms a policy looking to war between the United States and England. He said:

"Those who are stirring up this war scare[1] are covering themselves with a mask of patriotism behind which is hidden nothing but bluster and pomposity. Around, below and beneath this so-called patriotism is a scheme to enlarge the army and the navy.

"The true patriot is not looking for war. He wants peace. The workers of our country have no quarrel with the workers of other countries. They will not be swayed by political schemers. While they have the warmest hearts of all Americans, they can keep the coolest heads.

"I will be second to no man in devotion to my country, but I will not join with the mob of ignorant barroom shouters who, influenced by the rantings of political demagogues, are shouting for war. This war scare is nothing but pie for the political tricksters. Sensible workmen will never be influenced by these.

"In the ranks of the sensible, cool-headed workers and true American citizens you will find that this so-called war scare has had no effect. With them common sense rules. I know the feelings that the workers of England entertain for us. If it comes to a fight they will never join in willingly. They might be forced to it. But you won't find one among them who belongs to organizations among the volunteers.

"I have been very unwilling to express myself on this question. The question is so weighty that I have been forced to say something. Labor is never for war; it is always for peace. It is on the side of liberty, justice and humanity. These three are always for peace. The intelligent organized workingpeople bear no ill-will against any man. If they fight an individual, it is not because they dislike him personally, but they are simply warring upon the system he represents. I have never been in favor of war. If I could settle a strike by arbitration I would do it. I am convinced that the sentiment of the American people is not for war. It is for peace. The organized workingmen of the United States constitute the backbone of the great plain people.

"Who would be compelled to bear the burden of a war? The workingpeople. They would pay the taxes, and their blood would flow like water. The interests of the workingpeople of England and the United States are common. They are fighting the same enemy. They are battling to emancipate themselves from conditions common to both countries. The workingpeople know no country. They are citizens of the world, and their religion is to do what's right, what is just, what is grand and glorious and valorous and chivalrous. The battle for the cause of labor, from times of remotest antiquity, has been for peace and good-will among men."

Delegate Robert Winston,[2] of the Cab-Drivers' Union,[3] said: "The workers are shaking hands across the ocean. No matter what happens, it is labor that must pay the fiddler. Every decent workman in England to-day regards the American toiler as his brother. He cannot be influenced by a war scare. One nation of workers will no longer consent to fight another nation of workers. It is not the fight of brother toilers against brother toilers that is engaging the attention of the workingman to-day. It is the universal fight of labor against capital."

Delegate McDermott, of the Plasterers' Union,[4] said he had been a citizen of the United States for fifty years. Mr. McDermott is an Irish-American. He said: "I don't believe in this sentimentality about fratricidal war. I'm an American, and I'll fight—yes; I'll fight! We've been bulldozed by England long enough. Let us fight."

Delegate George K. Lloyd, of the Tin and sheet-Iron Workers' Union,[5] said: "I am in favor of war if the United States Senate and the House of Lords will meet in midocean and fight it out."

As Mr. Gompers was leaving the hall he stopped at the door and turning around, sa[id ex]pressively, with uplifted finger:

"If it really comes to a crisis, you will find that the men who counseled cool, calm action will be the first to fight when necessary."

At this the hall rang with hearty cheers, and dozens crowded eagerly about Mr. Gompers to grasp his hands and say a few words of encouragement. A rising vote of thanks was given Mr. Gompers for the sentiments he had expressed and his services as a leader of workingmen.

Paterson Labor Standard, Jan. 4, 1896.

1. In July 1895 the Cleveland administration attempted to arbitrate a longstanding boundary dispute between Venezuela and British Guiana, indicating that British pressure on Venezuela would constitute a form of European interference in the Western Hemisphere proscribed by the Monroe Doctrine. In November the British rejected the call for arbitration and refused to acknowledge the legal standing of the Monroe Doctrine. Amid growing popular hostility toward Britain, Congress reviewed the issue and in December reasserted the position of the United States. Britain then acceded to American mediation; a boundary commission began meeting on Jan. 4, 1896, and its work culminated in a treaty between Britain and Venezuela on Feb. 2.

2. Robert Winston was a New York City cab driver.

3. Probably the Liberty Dawn Association of Coach and Cab Drivers.

4. Possibly the Operative Plasterers' Society of the City and County of New York.

5. The United Tin and Sheet-Iron Workers' Protective and Benevolent Association.

An Interview in the *Indianapolis Sentinel*

[January 5, 1896]

NEED OF ORGANIZED LABOR.

Samuel Gompers, the newly elected president of the American federation of labor, assumed charge of his office on New Year's day. He at once engaged bachelor's quarters in this city, preferring, as he expressed it, not to "remove his wife and children from their parents, grandparents, uncles and aunts on an uncertain tenure of office." In personal appearance Mr. Gompers forms a striking contrast to his predecessor, John McBride. He is below the medium in height and of more than average weight. Among the organized labor advocates of the city he already has many acquaintances owing to his long identification with labor movements.

Yesterday Mr. Gompers was asked for an interview on questions that concern very nearly the interests of the labor masses of the country. He readily consented, as it is one of the characteristics of his nature to act courteously toward newspaper men. He was first asked what is likely to be done looking to the establishment of an eight-hour day. He said:

"The first thing that is necessary is a thorough organization of the wage workers and the trades unions and their federations so that they may agree in concert of action. First let them obtain eight hours by agreement with their employers and eight hours for all government employes either by statutory law or by order of the executive and departmental officers of the nation, state and municipalities. To accomplish this organization of the wage workers is essential. Although there is a fair degree of organization now I recognize that much more will have to be done in this direction before we achieve the full attainment of that desirable object — the eight-hour day. All thinking men agree that existing conditions are unfair, unequal and improper and require a change of remedy. It would seem even that those who run[?] could read that with the vast improvement of machinery and the application of new forces to the production of wealth as well as the division and sub-division of labor, that the most rational movement to meet these new conditions should be a reduction in the hours of labor of those employed, thus enabling work to be found for the workless.

["]In my judgment the reduction of the hours of labor is the first great living issue before the people and is demanded upon patriotic as well as upon economic and social grounds. I think that eight hours as a maximum is long enough for any laboring man to work in this area when steam and electricity drive machinery at its full force and speed."

As to Arbitration.

"There are propositions before congress looking to some permanent form of arbitration between labor and capital. Do you think that arbitration should be compulsory?"

"This question," said Mr. Gompers, "like many others is still in a tentative state both in the public mind and in the form in which it has found expression in the bills pending in congress. The people see that the great industrial troubles which occur disturb trade and commerce and frequently, as in the instances you refer to, they desire to accomplish a change which in effect would be more dangerous than the evil of which they complain. There is no thinking man whom I have yet met in the ranks of organized labor who does not favor arbitration, but it should be remembered that there is quite a distinction between voluntary arbitration and compulsory arbitration. In fact the terms in themselves 'compulsory' and 'arbitration' are the very antithesis of each other and arbitration which is compulsory will at no time be looked upon as fair or impartial by the party against whom a decision is rendered. Then, again, to compel arbitration and to compel the parties to it to abide by the decisions in so far as it relates to the labor problem presents this fact against which the intelligence revolts and freedom rebels, namely, to compel workmen to toil under conditions onerous or objectionable to them under fine or imprisonment. This is slavery. I would favor voluntary arbitration between workers and employers. I would favor compulsory investigation by an impartial board of disputes between corporations and their employes, the board being empowered to render an opinion as to which side of the controversy is the right and to allow the intelligence of an enlightened public opinion to do the rest."

"What is to be done looking to limiting the power of federal courts in injunction cases?"

"It seems that it will require an act of congress to accomplish that purpose. We have had a bill drawn up looking to the limitation of the powers of the courts to issue injunctions, more particularly in labor disputes.[1]

"The injunctions granted in the last few years by some of our federal courts have been universally recognized not as statutory, but as 'court-made' law. The theory of the law has always been that an injunction should never be issued where there is another remedy at law. The injunctions in the cases in question have entirely ignored and been entirely at variance with the long established principles.

"The bill which we have had prepared will be introduced in congress and we shall keep a sharp lookout as to the action of members of congress on this important and grave public question. We shall have a committee[2] at Washington during the session in constant attendance—in fact one of the committee is already there."

"How did the recent panic effect labor organizations?"

"In most instances it reduced their memberships, in some few to a great extent, while on the other hand there are three national unions which not only maintained their membership, but even during the greatest stress the membership increased.

"However, the organizations have come out of the panic remarkably well equipped. There are only isolated instances where a local organization has entirely gone to the wall and looking over the reports I see that there is generally a constant increase in growth and membership of unions. In all previous panics the labor unions were crushed out of existence and with every recurring era of business revival they have lost much valuable time in the work of reorganizing. This has been happily averted through the foresight of the active men in the movement who knew that these panics come periodically under our present haphazard method of industry and commerce and finance, and who assisted the passage of such measures in the trade unions so that they might be placed in a position to withstand the dire effects of these crimes. I look forward to a great revival of [the] trade union movement of our country within the next few years."

"What specific measures of legislation do you think labor demands?"

"We want improved conditions for labor generally on employers' liability for injury or death to employes resulting from their employment; better treatment to our seamen in our merchant marine; wages to be the first lien on all property; compulsory education for all children in our public schools; the abolition of the labor of all children under fourteen years of age; the limitation of the courts to issue injunctions; a law recognizing the labels issued to unions equal protection to that now given to trade marks; in short, the passage of such legislation, both national and state, as will meet the altered conditions of our industrial life.

"I am clearly of the opinion," concluded Mr. Gompers, "that all earnest well wishers of our people must be concerned in this grave and ever pressing industrial problem. It illy becomes men who flaunt their patriotism in the eyes of the public to antagonize every effort made by the organizations of labor to rationally effect a practical and evolutionary solution to this, the burning question of our time, which means either the reversion to barbarism or the perpetuation of our republic along intelligent, progressive and humane lines."

Indianapolis Sentinel, Jan. 5, 1896.

1. The measure may have been the basis of a bill (S. 2984, 54th Cong., 1st sess.) that Sen. David Hill of New York introduced on Apr. 30, 1896. It distinguished between direct contempt committed in the immediate presence of the court, and indirect contempt such as violations of injunctions, and provided for jury trials rather than summary judicial punishment in the case of indirect contempt of court. The bill was of importance to organized labor because violations of injunctions fell into the indirect contempt category. The measure did not become law.

2. The 1894 AFL convention had elected Andrew Furuseth and Adolph Strasser to serve as a legislative committee in Washington, D.C., to secure seamen's legislation. When the next convention did not reappoint them, the AFL Executive Council asked Furuseth to continue as the Federation's lobbyist to press the AFL's legislative goals in general; SG joined him later in the 1896 congressional session. The 1896 and 1897 conventions reelected Furuseth as the AFL's representative, but the 1898 convention referred the matter to the Executive Council, which thereafter appointed a legislative committee that varied in number from one to six members but usually consisted of two.

To G. W. Rogers[1]

Jan. 6 / 1896.

G. W. Rogers,
110 E. B St., Pueblo, Col.
Dear Sir & Brother: —

Your favor of Dec. 31 came duly to hand and contents noted.

In replying to your question I will say I have no desire to revoke any appointment of any general organizer made by ex-President McBride, providing only that the men who hold the commissions will devote such time as they can to the work, on trade union lines. It matters nothing to me what theory a man may hold, but when representing the American Federation of Labor, as the executive officer of the trade union movement, I only insist that he shall exert his usefulness and authority upon the lines laid down by our general movement.

Knowing you, personally, as well as I do I believe that you can accomplish a very great deal in the shape of organizing our fellow workers in Colorado and I can assure you that on the lines indicated I will second your every effort.

Under another cover I forward you a number of documents and blank forms which may aid you further in the work.

Reciprocating your kind wishes, thanking you for your congratulations and hoping to hear from you frequently as convenient, I am

Fraternally yours,　Saml Gompers.
President　A.F. of L.

TLpS, reel 9, vol. 14, p. 109, SG Letterbooks, DLC.

1. The recipient was probably Louis William ROGERS, an AFL organizer in Colorado. He was publisher and editor of the *Industrial Advocate* (Pueblo).

To William McKinstry

Jan. 24 / 1896.

W. H. McKinstry Esq.
Dear Friend: —

In reply to your other letter let me say that you can use your own judgement, but I firmly do believe that the lesser number of candidates there are running against me for First Vice-President the higher the compliment it would be to me, hence if you care to follow out your suggestion of declining do so.

Truly yours,   Saml Gompers

TLpS, reel 341, vol. 356, p. 54, SG Letterbooks, DLC.

To W. D. Mahon

Jan. 27 / 1896.

W. D. Mahone,
Pres. A.A. of S.R.E. of A.
Philadelphia, Pa.
Dear Sir & Brother:—

Owing to illness I have been unable to give the matter of your letter of the 16th inst. earlier attention.

You say that cigar makers union 100 of Philadelphia has passed resolutions censuring the national officers of your organization in the matter of the recent strike[1] in that city and that said union has resolved to forward a copy of the same to this office with the request for its publication in the *American Federationist.*

You also enter a protest against the publishing of the resolutions in the *American Federationist.*

Replying to these matters let me say that thus far I have not received the resolutions you refer to, but I beg to assure you now that should they reach me you may rest assured that I shall take advantage of the occasion to administer to the union in question such a lesson in the ethics as well as the principles and autonomy of the trade union movement that they will not be likely soon to forget.

I have tried to keep myself fairly informed as to the strike in Philadelphia and feel satisfied that the officers of your organization together with Brother McGuire acted in the best interests of labor, and certainly the men involved in the contest. You need have no misgivings in reference to me that I would allow any matter to enter our official magazine of the character in consideration.

Wishing you and your organization every possible success, and with kindest wishes I am

Yours Fraternally,   Saml Gompers
President   A.F. of L.

TLpS, reel 9, vol. 14, p. 129, SG Letterbooks, DLC.

1. On Dec. 17, 1895, Philadelphia members of the Amalgamated Association of

Street Railway Employes struck against the Union Traction Co., demanding wages of $2.00 for a ten-hour day, better working conditions, and an end to discrimination against union members. The workers returned to work on Dec. 24, after the company agreed to address their grievances and reinstate those who had been fired for union membership.

To George Perkins

Jan. 30 / 1896.

George W. Perkins,
Chicago, Ill.
Dear Brother: —

Your favor of the 18th Inst. was placed in my hands a few days ago. I have been critically ill and passed through a siege of suffering that few men could withstand and were it not for my pluck and robust constitution I should certainly have succumbed. If you would see me now you would scarcely believe I am the same man. I can scarcely walk a block and then at a gait that seems like crawling along. I have only been able since Monday to spend about an hour or so each day at the office but believe that I shall finally overcome everything and be strong and energetic again.

Let me say that I appreciate your kind work and I know that it springs from your very heart and conscience.

Yes, I want you to do all you possibly can to push the eight hour agitation. I fear, however, that the New York convention gave very little impulse to the movement. It was a [well?] worded document, sounding well, but really meaning little or nothing. The report was read and adopted during one of the sessions when I was on a committee visiting the American Tobacco Company,[1] and after reading it, I must say I am chagrined. To my mind it means only agitation this year preparatory for something in the future. Certainly it has designated nothing and directed nothing. I write this to you in candor, and still in confidence, as the innermost expression of my conviction in the matter.

Wherever you see an opportunity to say or write a word or push along the agitation for the greatest reform of our time, the movement to reduce the hours of labor, do it, Friend Bill, with all the energy you can.

Why not use some of our Eight Hour matter which is published in pamphlets? It would make good reading in the "Journal."

With kindest regards to you and hoping to hear from you soon and often, I am

Sincerely yours, Saml Gompers.

TLpS, reel 9, vol. 14, p. 150, SG Letterbooks, DLC.

1. SG was a member of the committee appointed by the 1895 AFL convention that met with the president of the American Tobacco Co. in New York City in an attempt to unionize the company. When the committee was unsuccessful, the convention voted to boycott the firm.

To John Sheehan[1]

Jan. 30 / 1896.

J. F. Sheehan,
General Organizer,
59 Front st., Holyoke, Mass.
Dear Sir & Brother:

You are, no doubt, aware that the Building Laborers International Protective Union[2] is about to hold its annual convention in your city Feb. 4, and it would be greatly to the advantage of the laborers themselves and the general labor movement if the International Union in question would become affiliated with the American Federation of Labor.[3] As our general organizer for the city of Holyoke I commission and request you to appear before the convention of the organization in question and, with their permission, to address the assembled delegates with the view of influencing them to become affiliated with the American Federation of Labor.

The recent convention of the A.F. of L. held in New York City instructed the executive officers of our organization to call a convention, if necessary, for the purpose of forming a national union of the unskilled laborers of our country. No doubt the affiliation of the building laborers International union may obviate the immediate necessity, or in fact, the necessity at all, for calling such a gathering and forming such a union.

We desire the affiliation of all trade unions, whether of skilled or unskilled workmen. We guarantee the autonomy of every trade union. We endeavor to so blend the consensus of opinion of the organized workers as to bring about the best results to the wage workers of our country. We have the greatest amount of liberty in the federation for each organization and yet an efficient cohesiveness to accomplish all practical results.

With this I mail to your address a few documents which will aid you further in the presentation of the subject to the assembled delegates and hope you will do the very best you can to accomplish the desired result.

I ask you to report the conclusions arrived at by the convention.

With kindest regards and hoping to hear from you soon and frequently, I am

Fraternally yours,   Samuel Gompers
President   A.F. of L.

TLpSr, reel 9, vol. 14, p. 149, SG Letterbooks, DLC.

1. John F. Sheehan.
2. The Building LABORERS' International Protective Union of America (BLIPU).
3. The 1895 AFL convention adopted a resolution of P. Costello of AFL Laboring Men's Protective Union 5287 of Newport, R.I., calling upon the Federation to form a national union of laborers' organizations affiliated with the AFL. John F. O'Sullivan attended the 1896 convention of the BLIPU at Holyoke, Mass., and encouraged the union to join the AFL. The BLIPU affiliated in 1898.

From W. D. Mahon

President,
Amalgamated Association of St. Railway Employes of America.
Detroit, Mich. Feb. 4th, 1896.

Dear Sir & Bro:—

Your communication of Jan. 27th[1] received and in reply will say I would of answered sooner but owing to my absence in the west it has been impossible. Your assurance in regard to the resolutions received, it was just what I expected as I know how you look on these things; but I felt it best to write you so there could be no misunderstanding. It was the same old crowd and the same tactics were used that there always is. They desired to see a failure of the strike. First, 5000 men out of employment would mean discontent and that would add to the ranks of the "ghost chasers." Second, a failure of trades unionism, through its strikes to win would have been proof of the arguments produced by such men as Barnes, Kershner[2] and the gang, but we did not allow it; hence the resolutions. I was pleased to learn through Mr. Lacey and Ford,[3] whom I met Sunday in Chicago, that your health was improving and that you were again able to be at your post. I hope that you may soon be restored to perfect health, for I feel that if ever the movement needed valuable workers it does now and it will be a serious blow to organized labor of America to lose such a valuable advocate and worker as yourself. I have just returned from Milwaukee where I have been convinced that the trades union movement needs just such firm trades unionists as yourself and Bro. McGuire. The Socialists at that place are ranting worse than in New York City and I fear in the near future there will be a volcano in the central body[4] of that city. Another matter that I desire to call your attention to— you are aware that Bro. McGuire lost some $1800 in bailing Kershner[5] of Philadelphia. I feel that he is unable to stand such a serious loss as he is a poor man like the rest of us and has had much sickness in his family during the past year. Don't you think something could be done in raising this money for him? President Perkins of your International brought it to my attention yesterday. As it is a delicate question with him on the account of the connections of which you are aware, don't you think you could suggest some way by which we could raise this amount? It would have to be done I think without Mr. McGuire's knowledge as you know his disposition as well as I do; but after we had raised it he could not refuse. Give it your consideration and whatever you advise I will assist you in doing. You will give my regards to Bro. McCraith, with hopes that you will be restored to health and vigor of your former years, I remain

Yours fraternally,   W. D. Mahon

TLS, Street Car Employes' Association Records, reel 142, frames 750-51, *AFL Records*.

1. Above.
2. Emil Kirchner.
3. Thomas Lacey and Sheridan Ford of Detroit worked as advertising agents for the *American Federationist*.
4. The Milwaukee Federated Trades Council.
5. John S. KIRCHNER was a member of CMIU 100 of Philadelphia.

A Circular

Indianapolis, Ind. [February 12, 1896]

THE AMERICAN FEDERATION OF LABOR

Has issued the following splendid symposium of what the organization stands for. It is circulated in form of a flyer and should find its way into every workshop of the country:—

The American Federation of Labor endeavors to unite all classes of wage-workers under one head, through their several organizations to the end:

1. That class, race, creed, political and trade prejudices may be abolished.

2. That support, moral and financial, may be given to each other.

It is composed of International, National, State, Central and Local Unions, representing the great bulk of organized labor in the United States and Canada.

It gives to any organization joining its ranks recognition in the labor field in all its phases.

It secures in cases of boycotts, strikes, lockouts, attentive hearing before all affiliated bodies, and it renders financial aid to the extent of its ability.

It is not a moneyed institution. It allows each organization to control its own funds, to establish and expend its own benefits without let or hindrance.

It aims to allow—in the light of experience—the utmost liberty to each organization in the conduct of its own affairs consistent with the generally understood principles of LABOR.

It establishes inter-communication, creates agitation, and is in direct and constant correspondence with a corps of representative organizers throughout the country.

It watches the interests of the workers in National Congress; it endorses and protests in the name of LABOR, and has secured vast relief from burdensome laws and government officials.

It is in communication with reformers and sympathizers in almost all classes, giving information and enlisting their co-operation.

It assembles once a year all classes of wage-earners, in convention, to exchange ideas and methods, to cultivate mutual interest, to secure united action, to speak for LABOR, to announce to the world the burdens, aims and hopes of the workers.

It asks—yea, demands—the co-operation of all wage-workers who believe in the principle of UNITY, and that there is something better in life than long hours, low wages, lack of employment, and all that these imply.

Its existence is based upon economic law to wit:

That no particular trade can long maintain wages above the common level.

That to maintain high wages all trades and callings must be organized.

That lack of organization among the unskilled vitally affects the organized skilled.

That general organization of skilled and unskilled can only be accomplished by united action.

Therefore, FEDERATION.

Again,

That no one particular locality can long maintain high wages above that of others.

That to maintain high wages all localities must be organized.

That this can best be done by the maintenance of national and international unions.

That any local union which refuses to so affiliate is inconsistent, non-union, and should be "let alone."

That each national or international union must be protected in its particular field against rivals and seceders. Therefore, FEDERA-TION.

That the history of the labor movement demonstrates the necessity of a union of individuals, and that logic implies a union of unions— FEDERATION.

Fraternally,　Sam'l Gompers, President.

Aug. McCraith, Secretary.

Bakers' Journal and Deutsch-Amerikanische Bäcker-Zeitung, Feb. 12, 1896.

To Lee Hart[1]

Feb. 17 / 1896.

Mr. Lee M. Hart,
Pres. National Alliance Theatrical Stage Employers.[2]
Dear Sir & Friend:

From many quarters I am in receipt of letters of complaint against the N.A.T.S.E. in its conduct towards local unions of musicians affiliated with the American Federation of Labor.

Of course, what your organization may do towards musical unions not affiliated with the A.F. of L. can be of little or no concern to us, but when the action proposed to be taken is not only of a drastic character but goes to the root of striking at the autonomy and existence of such a union it is our concern when they are affiliated.

In St. Louis I learn upon high authority that a local of your national union has gone so far as to organize people, claiming to be musicians and furnishing them at a much-lower rate than is set by the musicians' local union and setting forth in an advertisement that they urge union workmen not to employ members of our affiliated unions.[3]

It is unnecessary for me to say to you how sincerely I sympathize with your brotherhood, and how much I desire it to prosper, but I desire to call your attention to a few facts. One is, that a trade union never yet succeeded by trying to drag another down. That it is against the highest ethics of unionism to try to organize workers in any trade or profession for the purpose of having them work at lower wages and under poorer conditions than demanded by the union of the trade.

The latest information is that a convention[4] is to be called by your national alliance and that one of the principal objects of the convention will be to attempt crushing out the local unions of musicians affiliated with the A.F. of L. This (I need but call your attention to the fact) is one of the greatest wrongs that can be committed by one labor organization to another. Some of the largest organizations of the National League of Musicians[5] have instructed their delegates to become affiliated with the A.F. of L., and if patience and practical action is taken there is no doubt but what the Musicians National League, which meets in the course of a week or two,[6] will decide to become affiliated with the A.F. of L.

You can readily understand such action as is proposed by St. Louis and other places will affect [. . .] action on [the] part of the League. You will readily agree with me, [I believe] if any one attempted to organize carpenters or others as the Theatrical Stage Employes to coerce your union into certain line of action, you would resent it with all the power at your command. What you would regard as an injustice to yourselves you could not make to appear just to the musicians.

I do not say that you are blameful for every thing, or that the musicians are blameless. I only urge you to be careful in this matter. Do what you can to prevent an injury that cannot be remedied. For our old friendship's sake, for the sake of the cause we love so much, for the future which we hold so dear, I ask you to do everything within your power to prevent so calamitous a proceeding. Do what you can to appease the anger of the men. Make them see their duty as unionists, according to the rights that they would claim for themselves and I am confident good results will follow.

Trusting that you will give this matter your earliest and immediate consideration, with kindest regards, I am

Yours fraternally,   Saml Gompers
President   A.F. of L.

TLpS, reel 9, vol. 14, pp. 190-91, SG Letterbooks, DLC.

1. Lee M. HART served as president of the Illinois Brotherhood of Theatrical Stage Employes (1895-96) and subsequently as secretary-treasurer of the National Alliance of Theatrical Stage Employes of the United States (NATSE; 1898-1914).

2. The National Alliance of THEATRICAL Stage Employes of the United States.

3. Relations between St. Louis musicians and stage employees were particularly

strained in early 1896. During the winter the KOL had organized workers who were taking the place of striking members of NATSE 6 at five St. Louis theaters. Local musicians organized in AFL local 5579, many of whom were also members of KOL Local Assembly 5938, refused to join the strike in sympathy with the stage employees. The St. Louis Trades and Labor Union was able to announce in early March, however, that the stage employees' and musicians' locals had settled their differences.

4. The NATSE convention met in Detroit, July 13-18, 1896. It took no action regarding local unions of musicians.

5. The National League of MUSICIANS of the United States (NLM).

6. The NLM convention took place in Washington, D.C., Apr. 7-12, 1896. The League declined to affiliate with the AFL.

To the Executive Council of the AFL

Indianapolis, Ind. Feb. 18 / 1896

To The Executive Council, American Federation of Labor.
Dear Sir:

A few years ago a charter was issued to Federal Labor Union No. 5335[1] for the city of Cincinnati, Ohio. It was then in the hands of our best trade unionists, who performed excellent work. Subsequently a larger number became members and the older unionists had neither influence nor power to prevent indiscreet and anti–trade union action being taken. This so incensed them that they withdrew from the Federal Labor Union. The remaining members then saw an opportunity of diverting it into another channel and have accepted some persons as members who have always been known as antagonists to the trade union movement and who, being active in the old K. of L., did all they possibly could to disrupt and destroy the trade unions of Cincinnati.

I need but mention the names of some of the active members in the organization to show you into which hands it has fallen. Hugh Cavanaugh,[2] John Malloy, Wm. Leonard, H. Willis and others of the same kind. They are now endeavoring to split the movement in Cincinnati. I have received complaint from many sources, particularly from Mr. F. L. Rist,[3] who refers me to Martin Fox, P. F. Fitzpatrick,[4] D. P. Rowland, Harry Ogden, T. G. Donnelly,[5] Martin Walters,[6] and others of the loyal trade unionists of that city.

You are, no doubt, aware that these parties have been preying upon the reputation and influence that the labor movement gave them in former years and upon which they still desire to trade under cover of the honored name of the American Federation of Labor.

It is also charged against the Federal Labor Union that for the purpose of retaining the power they possess they refuse to accept any one as a member unless he is willing to work on the lines laid down by the parties named.

I am assured if the charter of Federal Labor Union No. 5335 is revoked these people will be rendered absolutely defenseless in their attacks upon our movement and that there will be unity and harmony prevailing, and further, that the convention[7] which will meet in Cincinnati at the end of the year will be greeted by a united body of harmonious organized workers.

In view of these facts I submit to you the proposition that the charter of Federal Labor Union No. 5335 be revoked. It is believed that the charter may be taken up by the original members and with better care a live and energetic body for organizing purposes will be put into existence. Kindly submit your vote[8] on this proposition to this office at your earliest convenience, and oblige.

Yours fraternally   Saml Gompers.
Prest.   A.F. of L.

TLpS, AFL Executive Council Vote Books, reel 8, frame 129, *AFL Records.*

1. The AFL chartered Federal Labor Union 5335 in 1891.
2. Hugh Cavanaugh was the manager of a Cincinnati shoe store; in the 1880s he served as secretary (1884-86) and district master workman (1886-88) of KOL District Assembly 48 and as a member of the KOL auxiliary board (1886).
3. Frank L. Rist, a Cincinnati printer and AFL organizer, was a leader of International Typographical Union 3 and the Cincinnati Central Labor Council (CLC), and was the founder and editor (1892-1918) of the CLC's organ, the *Chronicle.*
4. Patrick Francis FITZPATRICK was an officer of Iron Molders' Union of North America 4 of Cincinnati.
5. Probably Thomas J. Donnelly, a Cincinnati printer.
6. Probably Martin W. Walter, a Cincinnati printer.
7. The 1896 AFL convention was held in Cincinnati, Ohio, Dec. 14-21, 1896.
8. The Executive Council voted to revoke the charter.

From William Carter[1]

Editor and Manager.
Locomotive Firemen's Magazine.
Peoria, Illinois, Feb. 19, 1896.

Dear Sir:—

About six months ago, I wrote to Mr. McBride, requesting that he should contribute to the Firemen's Magazine, an argumentative article, wherein he would set forth the advisability of the Railway Labor Organizations, especially the Brotherhood of Locomotive Firemen,[2] in affiliating with the American Federation of Labor. He immediately replied saying that he would comply with my request, but seemingly he misunderstood my intention, in-as-much as he wrote a letter to Grand Master F. P. Sargent,[3] which the latter took as a personal communication. The result was that after waiting until shortly before your session in New York last December I wrote him again, and he advised me that such had been forwarded to Mr. Sargent. Things have changed, and I now make the same request of you.

When you were our guest at the Harrisburg Convention[4] in September 1894, although but a private in the ranks at that time, I am in position to say that there were many reasons why your invitation to the B. of L.F. to affiliate with the A.F. of L. was not given the consideration due a question of that much importance. I believe that at the Convention is not the best place to extend an invitation of this kind, that is when the question has not been discussed or considered by the membership in the local branches throughout the country. Delegates, as a rule, are somewhat cautious in taking new departures.

I am exceedingly anxious that at our next Convention,[5] consideration will be given, and action will be taken that will result in the Brotherhood of Locomotive Firemen becoming affiliated with the American Federation of Labor. Our Convention is held in September next in the city of Galveston Texas, and I believe that if you would contribute an article[6] over your own signature, for publication in the Magazine in an early number, inviting the Brotherhood of Locomotive Firemen to affiliate with the A.F. of L.; and in this article offer arguments against certain arguments that I know will be offered by our membership, thereby preventing a criticism of the plan. I find that there are three leading objections, if such they may be called, among our members, to becoming affiliated with the American Federation of Labor, and I believe that you are in position to answer each one of these effectually.

In the first place, our members will never consent to admitting the negro firemen of the South to membership in our Organization, but I do believe that they will consent to eliminating the word "white" from our Constitution, and depend upon each Lodge to regulate its own affairs as to who shall become members. The negro firemen have demoralized our Organization in the South on roads where both are employed. The negro willingly accepts the same class of work at greatly reduced wages. They never contend that they should receive union pay. If it were not for the opposition of the Brotherhood of Locomotive Firemen to the employment of negro firemen, I feel confident that wages would decrease over 50%. There are runs where two similar engines are pulling two similar trains, but one is fired by a white man, who receives 25% more pay for the same work than the other run fired by a negro. The negro is willing and content to fire an engine for $1.00 per day, as is the Chinaman to make cigars at less than half the scale of union wages. Now I believe that if we would remove the word "white" from our Constitution, the American Federation of Labor would accept our application, and not compel us to admit negroes as members.

If disposed to write, please touch on this point in your article.

Second: — We have always believed that a very close federation of the railway labor organizations is necessary. We believe that there should be a union of the railway labor organizations similar to the union of states. When I say "we," of course I refer to the firemen. You are aware, of course, that other railway organizations are opposed to any kind of federation. Some of our members believe that if we should affiliate with the American Federation of Labor, it would destroy or prevent a closer union or federation between railway unions. Of course, I know that this is not a fact. I see where the metal trades have federated in a closer union,[7] although a part and parcel of the A.F. of L. I would have you explain this in your article.

Third: — A great many of our members are of the opinion that should we affiliate with the American Federation of Labor, we would be called upon to strike or boycott, which would compel us to violate any contracts or agreements we may have with railway companies. For instance, I have seen the argument advanced that if the employes of a brick-yard or rolling-mill or other establishment, who were affiliated with the American Federation of Labor, should become involved in a strike at some town on a railway on which members of our Brotherhood were employed, that if a boycott was declared, on these goods, we would be called on to not haul them, and would be expected to refuse to haul these goods, and enter into the boycott, which of course would abrogate our contracts, and be virtually a strike. I have argued that no such thing would be expected by the A.F. of L., but that all that would be expected would be our moral and financial support, and that the latter would be purely voluntary. A reply from you to that effect would bear much more weight than anything I could say.

I hope that you will pardon me for going into detail and encroaching upon your time to such an extent; but I am a firm believer in pure Trade-unionism, and believe that all Trades Unions should affiliate with the American Federation of Labor. I believe that if you will carefully prepare the article in question, which I will give a prominent position in our Magazine, that it will result in the B. of L.F. becoming affiliated with the American Federation of Labor before the close of the present year. If we do this, it will encourage the Trainmen,[8] Trackmen[9] and others to do likewise, and if these Trades Unions of railway employes affiliate with the A.F. of L., at least Four Hundred Thousand workers will be added to the Federation in the near future. I believe that if the existing Railway Trades Unions affiliate with the A.F. of L., we can jointly organize all other classes in Trades Unions of their own.

If you do not think these plans judicious, or if you do not think it would be right for you to contribute the article in question, please do not hesitate to say so, but I assure you that if you will thus "break the ice," I shall do all in my power to assist you from an editorial standpoint.

Yours truly,   W. S. Carter.

TLS, Files of the Office of the President, General Correspondence, reel 59, frames 224-25, *AFL Records.*

1. William Samuel CARTER edited the *Locomotive Firemen's Magazine* from 1894 to 1904 (after 1901 the *Brotherhood of Locomotive Firemen's Magazine*).

2. The Brotherhood of LOCOMOTIVE Firemen (BLF).

3. Frank Pierce SARGENT was grand master of the BLF from 1885 to 1902.

4. The BLF convention at Harrisburg, Pa., met Sept. 10-20, 1894.

5. The BLF held its 1896 convention in Galveston, Tex., Sept. 14-24. The union did not affiliate with the AFL-CIO until 1956.

6. See "To the Members of the Brotherhood of Locomotive Firemen," July 1896, below. Other letters to the BLF urging affiliation, written by John Lennon and George Perkins, appeared in the January 1897 issue.

7. After two years of preliminary discussions among metal working unions initiated by the International Association of Machinists (IAM), the IAM, the Brotherhood of Boilermakers and Iron Ship Builders of America, and the International Brotherhood of Blacksmiths (later joined by the Pattern Makers' National League of North America) organized the Federated Metal Trades (FMT) on Oct. 20, 1894, at Indianapolis. The lack of salaried officers and waning interest among its constituent unions weakened the FMT, although it apparently continued at least through mid-1897.

8. The Brotherhood of RAILROAD Trainmen.

9. The Brotherhood of RAILWAY Trackmen of America.

To Herman Metz

Feb. 26 / 1896.

Mr. H. F. Metz,
Secy. Ft. Wayne Textile Union No. 6619,[1]
61 Elm st., Ft. Wayne, Ind.
Dear Sir & Brother:

Your favor of recent date came duly to hand and also the manuscript for your By Laws. You ask us to have them printed in German. I desire to ask you whether it is your intention to bear the expense entailed. Kindly advise me as to this and then I will make further inquiry.

I can recognize how necessary, under the circumstances, it is to have your By-Laws printed in the German language, although I earnestly hope that every effort will be made by our fellow-workmen, who speak the foreign languages, to speak the language of the country as soon as possible. I am sure that greater results will follow.

Your communication would have received earlier attention but for a very serious and dangerous illness through which I am just about passing and which has been nearly eight weeks duration.

Fraternally yours,   Saml Gompers.
President   A.F. of L.

TLpS, reel 9, vol. 14, p. 240, SG Letterbooks, DLC.

1. The AFL chartered Textile Union 6619 in January 1896.

An Editorial by Samuel Gompers in the *American Federationist*

[February 1896]

Fellow-unionists, greeting.

Presumably, it is but proper to say a word to my friends and fellow-unionists upon resuming the duties of the presidency of the American Federation of Labor, after an absence from that office for a year.

Many may mistake the real point involved in my election to that office and count it as squelching and annihilating a certain school of thought in the ranks of the American Federation of Labor. I would say that nothing can be farther from the purpose than that. I recognize as fully as any one what was intended to be accomplished by my election. But it is only fair to say that, as I have ever been in the trade union movement, and in all matters connected with my life, I believe in the fullest opportunity for thorough discussion and proper presentation of all schools of thought in the labor movement. My only insistence has been, and is to-day, that a man shall be true to his trade union in season and out of season, in spite of friend or foe, and that, apart from that, it is his province to believe in and advocate any reform which, in his judgment, is calculated to best advance the whole line of the trade union movement.

I have ever believed that the trade union platform was the broadest of any in existence. There is room enough for the most radical as well as the ultra conservative—in fact, I have always regarded the existence of both these elements as essential to the success of our movement. The radical, and perhaps impulsive, moving the conservative from a lethargic stand, while, on the other hand, the conservative acting as the safe anchor and check upon the illy-considered and hastily-conceived plans and panaceas for the immediate abolition of all wrong—the bringing about of the millennium of the world in a day. I recognize the energy and sturdy common sense of all the active forces in the trade union movement. None appreciates them more than I do, for the great good they have done and can do. The movement needs their services. It needs their intelligence. It needs their energy, and, in the compact whole, it will blend our cause into the great factor of an aggressive, moving body of the grand army of labor, determined to secure present amelioration in the conditions of the toilers, and finally to secure their entire emancipation. It requires earnestness, energy and persistency. We want the work of all.

The near future, promises, no doubt, a revival in the organization of the workingmen of our country. Every indication points that way. Let us subordinate our fads and isms; let us endeavor to meet this rising tide of organization by a united solid front; let us welcome it into our ranks and gather its full fruit, so that the toilers may be benefited and the movement placed another milestone on the road to labor's disenthralment. The times are ripe. It requires the concentration of effort of all. Let us be up and doing. Let us bear in mind the men, women and children who work in the mills, the mines, the factories and the stores. Let us remember the miserably paid and the overworked and the unemployed. Let us remember the great struggle yet before us and the great obstacles that have yet to be overcome. Let us unite in the interest of all. Let us be true to the struggles of the workers of the past. Let us be worthy sons of those who have struggled before. The cause of labor and the cause of humanity cries out to every man to organize and to every worker to become an organizer. Let it be the watchword all along the line throughout the country in this year of grace: That the downtrodden, that the cause of the weak and helpless, as well as the hope for the future, demand that this year every man shall do his duty.

In this solemn appeal and urgent call for unity, harmony and co-operation, in the work to bring about a thorough organization of the workers of our country, will be found in the front ranks,

Yours sincerely and fraternally,   Samuel Gompers,
President   American Federation of Labor.

American Federationist 2 (Feb. 1896): 224-25.

To J. F. Brown[1]

Mch. 2 / 1896.

Mr. J. F. Brown,
Secy. Tobacco Workers Union #6468,[2]
1403 St. Charles st., St. Louis, Mo.
Dear Sir & Brother:

Your favor of recent date came duly to hand and contents noted. In reply I would say I doubt the advisability of your union sending delegate to the convention mentioned.[3] The convention at New York, of the American Federation of Labor, resolved *not to send a delegate* and I presume that that action would have influence showing the course usually pursued by our affiliated organizations. However, it is a matter for your union to decide for itself. I merely mention it as a relative subject.

I am sure that any one who charges organized labor as being antagonistic to the colored race must be entirely ignorant of the history of our organization, or willfully and maliciously misrepresent it. At several of the conventions of the American Federation of Labor we had as many as half a dozen colored delegates from unions of colored men. In many of our organizations where the white and colored workers are organized together we have elected them to some of the most responsible offices. One of [our] great International unions[4] was kept out of the American Federation of Labor for five years until they struck the discriminating "color line" from their constitution. There are so many instances that it would fill pages if I attempted to relate them all. I merely record these as they occur to my mind to give the lie to the statement made by detractors of the good name of our movement.

I see that there is considerable force in what you say relative to having a colored m[an] go among our colored workers of the South, among the textile workers and endeavor to organize them, but the question is whether it would not be most advisable to have a textile worker or whether some worker in another branch of industry could accomplish as good results.

Let me hear from you relative to this in the course of a few days, after thinking it over, and I shall be glad to give it earnest consideration.

With best wishes for the success of our movement and hoping to hear from you at an early date, I am

Fraternally yours,   Saml Gompers.
President   A.F. of L.

TLpS, reel 9, vol. 14, p. 267, SG Letterbooks, DLC.

1. Probably James Brown, a black organizer in the South, first for the Tobacco Workers' International Union and, after the turn of the century, for the AFL.
2. The AFL chartered Tobacco Factory Laborers' Protective Union 6468 in 1894.
3. Probably the International Socialist Workers' and Trade Union Congress.
4. The International Association of Machinists.

To Carroll Wright[1]

Mch. 4 / 1896.

Hon. Carroll D. Wright,
Commissioner Department of Labor,
Washington, D.C.
My Dear Commissioner:

I have the honor to acknowledge the receipt of your favor of Feb. 25, the contents of which have been carefully noted.

I have given the subject matter quite some thought and cordially comply with your request for my opinion thereon.

You say that you have long contemplated the question of endeavoring to secure a complete list of the labor organizations of the country for publication in your reports. Let me say that I think that feature an exceedingly good one, but I also think that it should not be undertaken until the end of this year or the beginning of next. We will soon be in the throes of a presidential campaign and the political parties are not averse to resorting to rather unquestionable means for the purpose of obtaining some partisan advantage.

If such a list were published during a presidential campaign our unions would be flooded with all kinds of "appeals" from all parties and party hacks to the annoyance, disturbance and injury of our movement.

Then again the mote [motive?] for the request for such information at this time might, in all likelihood, be questioned from many quarters to whom you would be required to make application.

The census of such unions would be valuable and those unions which have stated benefits would only be too willing to comply with the request for information upon these points.

It is unnecessary to say to you that the trade union, the permanent movement of labor of the United States, is practically in its infancy and hence there are not so very many unions which have adopted a regular system of benefits, although nearly all of them have adopted some beneficial features, though of a local character.

I should be pleased to hear from you at any time and to discuss this question with you further.

More than likely I shall have an occasion, in the near future, to come to Washington and when I do I shall regard it as a pleasure, as well as a duty to call on you for the purpose of further discussing this and other subjects.

Serious illness has prevented me from giving your letter earlier consideration and reply.

Very truly yours,   Saml Gompers.

TLpS, reel 9, vol. 14, pp. 274-75, SG Letterbooks, DLC.

1. Carroll Davidson WRIGHT was commissioner of the U.S. Bureau of Labor (after 1888 the Department of Labor) from 1885 to 1905.

To the Officers and Members of the Cuban Revolutionary Party[1]

Mch. 5 / 1896.

To the Officers and Members of the Cuban Revolutionary Party,
c/o Jose R. Villa Lou,[2]
127 East 23rd st., New York City.

Permit me to take the earliest opportunity at my command to tender you, on behalf of the organized workers of our country, under the banner of the American Federation of Labor, my hearty and unfeigned congratulations upon the advanced step already taken by the United States government[3] for the recognition of the belligerent rights, and I trust, independence of the Cuban Libre.

I trust that the opportunity may soon be afforded me to tender you the congratulations upon Cuba's final recognition, not only as a belligerent, but as a Nation, free and independent, recognized by all as one of a family of nations, working on and on for man's disenthralment.

Very truly yours,   Saml Gompers.
President,   American Federation of Labor.

TLpS, reel 9, vol. 14, p. 290, SG Letterbooks, DLC.

1. In January 1892 expatriate José Martí organized the Cuban Revolutionary Party to lead the struggle against Spanish rule. It was based in New York City where Cuban cigarmakers invited SG to attend meetings of the revolutionary junta. He did so frequently, coming to know several of the movement's leading activists and to champion their cause within the labor movement. The CMIU and the AFL vigorously

backed the revolutionists. SG organized a mass meeting in 1895 in New York to support the junta, and the 1896 AFL convention passed a resolution urging Congress and the Cleveland administration to accord belligerent status to the rebels.

2. José Ramon Villalón was a Cuban revolutionary and a civil engineer educated at Lehigh University. In November 1898 he was a member of the Cuban Assembly Commission that met with Secretary of State John Hay in an unsuccessful attempt to raise funds. In 1899 Leonard Wood, commander of the Cuban occupation, appointed Villalón secretary of public works.

3. On Feb. 28, 1896, the U.S. Senate passed a resolution calling on the U.S. government to grant belligerent status to the Cuban revolutionaries.

To Adolph von Elm[1]

Mch. 9 / 1896.

Mr. A. von Elm,
17 and 19 Shaefer Strasse, Hamburg, Germany.
My Dear Friend:

No doubt you almost give up the idea of hearing from me in reply to your favor of recent date, and it is necessary to relate a circumstance scarcely of an encouraging nature which interfered.

You know that the headquarters of the American Federation of Labor were transferred to Indianapolis a year ago. I arrived here January 1 and went right to work with energy. But on the 7th I was stricken with a severe attack of acute gastritis which developed into a number of complications and I have gone through a siege of illness that, were it not for my will-power, as well as strong constitution, I could never have survived. In fact my most intimate friends gave up entire hope of my recovery. However, through my will-power and with the kindness of my physician,[2] who placed his carriage at my disposal—he called for me in the morning at my house and with the assistance of his coachman almost carried me from my room to the carriage, brought me to the office and there I worked for a few hours when many believed I would not leave the office alive, but this work seemed to divert my mind from my sufferings for a while and I believe really helped me along. I am just now convalescing although exceedingly weak, but doing the office work and shortly will be enabled to be in full trim to work as energetically as ever to carry on the work necessary to advance our movement.

I take the first real opportunity to answer your letter fairly and freely. It is needless to say how much I appreciate your congratulations upon my re-election to the presidency of the American Federation of Labor. I am sure that your words are the sincere expression of a consistent trade unionist who has the movement at heart, and who understands its philosophy and its missions.

Let me say to you that the statements made by the New York correspondent[3] as published in the Hamburg *Echo* attributing certain remarks to me, are wholly untrue and misrepresenting the statements I made upon the floor of the convention of the American Federation of Labor at New York, relative to the question of the agitation for "Das Coalition's Recht" in Germany.

When the correspondent says that I declared that the Social Democratic Party of Germany refused to consider or opposed the question of obtaining the right of coalition for the trade unionists of Germany he says that which is untrue. What I did say was that the right of coalition had not yet been obtained by the workingmen of Germany and that when the General Commission of the German trade union movement[4] proposed to submit the question for the German trade unions to undertake an active campaign to secure the right to coalition from the German Government the party leaders of the Social Democrats frowned down upon the effort and finally secured the abandonment of the proposition.

I used that circumstance as one of the arguments against the proposition of some of the delegates to commit the movement here to the same policy prevailing in the socialist party of Germany.

First it was known that I would be a candidate for re-election and that I would stand a chance to be elected, hence the New York party organs deemed it necessary in the Volks Zeitung to misrepresent every word I uttered at the convention so that a few party members might be kept in line to vote against me. When I was elected, in spite of all the chicanery and trickery, they set up a howl as if the whole world of labor had been destroyed. It is no wonder that DeRossi (who never appears in a public meeting, and whom I repeat is not known to the labor movement, either of the United States or in the city of New York in which he is supposed to live) took his information from the Volks Zeitung and sent on the slanderous statements attributed to me.

I think that I should mention a fact to you which may be of some interest. In all my connection with the labor movement, the various positions of responsibility that I have been placed in, I can honestly say that I have never asked any one to either nominate me for office or to vote for me, either directly or indirectly, and that I never subordinated my judgement and convictions, or failed to express them, regardless of what consequence they would be to me or what influence they would have upon votes cast for or against me. I challenge any one of my traducers to show a similar record. Perhaps

Professor (?) DeLeon, without a professorship, and Lawyer Hugo Vogt,[5] lawyer without a brief, the head and front of the new fangled "Socialist Trade and Labor Alliance of the United States and Canada" can truthfully make a similar statement.

As a matter of fact, by their own confession, they bargained with the K. of L. last year for the position of editor for the statistician, Lucien Sanial (who finds statistics for both the dominant political parties) to be editor of the K. of L. Journal.

I send you with this copies of the February and March issues of the *Federationist,* of which you know, as president, I am editor. I want you to read the editorials and see whether they are not tolerant. Read the [signed] editorial in the February issue. You will note there that I call for the toleration and unity.

I also forward a few documents that we have issued since my coming into the position of president again. I think you will find them interesting and somewhat apropos to the discussion.

The New York section of the Socialist party seems to be the enemies of the trade union movement and the trade unionists. It was they who gave the world their latest offspring "The Socialist Trade and Labor Alliance of the United States and Canada." It originated in a beer saloon at one end and the Volks Zeitung and People at the other.

It consists exactly of the same members, with the same head, tail and middle as was formerly known under the name of the "Central Labor Federation." The labor press of the country, of which there are about 180 publications, weekly, entirely ignored the new so-called "Alliance." The German Socialist press other than that of New York generally condemn it.

You have probably seen the Brauer-Zeitung and Baecker Zeitung. If not I shall ask the Secretaries to send you a marked copy.

The Philadelphia Taggablatt, St. Louis Tagablatt, Volks Anwalt, of Cleveland, the Cincinnati Tagablatt, the Buffalo Volks Anwalt, the St. Louis Labor, all of them condemn the new scheme in the strongest terms. I have been compelled to send the clippings to different places, and only through the kindness of a friend can I send you the few enclosed from which you can glean some little information in reference to their attitude on this subject.

Undoubtedly they are attacking the trade unions with greater vehemence and bitterness than ever before.

You may receive the Volks Zeitung but if you should not I send to you the enclosed article that they have in their weekly issue of March 7[6] making a ferocious attack upon the United Garment Workers of America.

If you notice the affidavit of which they publish a facsimile is printed in English and signed by a poor dupe[7] who was compelled to put his signature in Hebrew. He of course did not understand nor was he able to read the affidavit which he signed.

They do not say in the article that this fellow became a member of the union during the strike, that he had never paid a solitary cent into the organization, notwithstanding the fact that the officers made provisions that he would receive the $7.00 he mentions.

I want you to also be informed of the fact that the United Garment Workers is only in existence about four and half years and that by persistency and self-sacrifice the "task" system has been abolished in the trade, the "sweat shop" system brought down almost to the minimum, the hours of labor of the workers reduced to 10 per day and in many instances 9, and in some branches half holiday on Saturday, when the hours of labor formerly were from early morning until late at night.

That organization having accomplished so much in the trade, the so-called Socialists of New York now seek to destroy it. Take my word for it though they count without their host. They will be disappointed, for the organization will grow stronger, more powerful and influential for good as time goes on.

Yes, I too, am pleased to know that our friend Strasser has been selected as fraternal delegate to the German Trade Union Congress[8] which convenes in Berlin, May 4. I informed him of the receipt of your letter. I am confident that you are right. That the delegates to your convention will learn to respect him as a man with convictions and who has done much towards the organization of the trade unions of America.

He has done much towards the clearer comprehension by the wage-earners of their duties and rights.

I regret very much to learn in your last letter that our friend Legein[9] has not been in good health, but trust, however, that long before this he has entirely recovered. I want you to kindly remember me to him and friend Demuth, Mrs. Steinbach, our friend the store clerk, whose name I have forgotten, the many friends I made in Hamburg, and to express the hope that your Congress may be entirely successful in establishing the trade union movement upon a firmer more aggressive basis, insisting upon its absolute right of existence to carry on the work of organization and emancipation of labor, I am

Sincerely and fraternally yours,   Saml Gompers.
President   A.F. of L.

N.B.—Kindly let me hear from you as often as convenient.

P.S. Have [just in the . . .] and [. . .] which our Friend Legien [. . .] sent me. [Thank] him sincerely for me.

S. G.

You can make whatever use you please of this letter.

S. G.

T and ALpS, reel 9, vol. 14, pp. 330-33, SG Letterbooks, DLC.

1. Johann Adolph von ELM was a German cigarmakers' leader and a member of the Reichstag representing the Sozialdemokratische Partei Deutschlands (Social Democratic Party of Germany; SPD) from 1894 to 1907. In the *Hamburger Echo* of Jan. 3, 1896, Elm charged that Hermann Schlüter had printed false statements about SG in the *New Yorker Volkszeitung* and then refused to correct them. In his response (*Hamburger Echo,* Feb. 7), Schlüter said he had published remarks attributed to SG by other papers; when he received two letters from SG presenting his side of the case, he had printed them in their entirety except for the "shameless and ungentlemanly insinuations and abuse for which we had no reason to serve as a mouthpiece." Elm's rebuttal (*Hamburger Echo,* Feb. 12) accused Schlüter of distorting the truth "with the sole intention of carrying your mischief-making into the German labor movement."

2. Louis M. Rowe was an Indianapolis physician.

3. Karl Derossi, a German journalist, immigrated to the United States in 1883. In 1895 he worked for several German-American labor papers and was editor of two, the *Kürschnerzeitung* (*Furriers' Journal*) and the *Textilarbeiter* (*Textile Worker*). Derossi's piece, unsigned and datelined New York, Dec. 20, 1895, appeared in the *Hamburger Echo* of Dec. 31. In it Derossi claimed that at the AFL's recent convention, SG had attacked the SPD for hindering the organization of trade unions.

4. The Generalkommission der Gewerkschaften Deutschlands (General Commission of German Trade Unions; GGD) was formed in 1890 to serve as a national body to unify the German labor movement and convene trade union congresses.

5. Hugo Vogt, a notary public and later a lawyer, was a leader of the SLP in New York City and a founder of the Socialist Trade and Labor Alliance.

6. Apparently one of the articles published on Mar. 2 and 3, 1896, in the *New Yorker Volkszeitung* charging national officers of the United Garment Workers of America and local officers of the United Brotherhood of Tailors (UBT) with mismanagement, corruption, and collusion with manufacturers in a recent lockout.

7. The Mar. 3, 1896, issue of the *New Yorker Volkszeitung* reproduced a deposition of Jan. 31, in English, by Abraham Levin, a member of the UBT in New York City. Levin stated that he had received $7 in strike pay during a recent lockout, not the $12 that union officials claimed to have paid him. The *Volkszeitung* cited Levin's case as an example of the corruption that it alleged plagued the union. Levin signed the deposition in Hebrew.

8. The Congress of German Trade Unions met under the auspices of the GGD May 4-8, 1896.

9. Carl LEGIEN was secretary (1890-1920) of the GGD (subsequently the Allgemeiner Deutscher Gewerkschaftsbund [General German Federation of Trade Unions]) and editor (1891-1900) of its organ, the *Correspondenzblatt.* He served as a socialist deputy in the Reichstag (1893-98).

To Alexander Saqui

Mch. 11 / 1896.

Mr. A. Saqui,
Pres't. H. in H. B. S.[1]
47 Carmine St., New York City.
Dear Sir:

Your favor of the 10th Inst. to hand and contents noted. I am obliged to you for the information that the claim has been paid. I repeat that I cannot ask my physician, who is still attending me, to go before a Notary Public and make an affidavit as to the truth of his certificate. He has been more than kind to me and I cannot impose upon his good nature. After all his attendance, in which he made more than 150 visits, night and day, in consideration for his regard for me and my circumstances, he has reduced his bill to $100.00, which I can pay any time within the coming year.

Were it not that he placed his carriage at my disposal, it would have been impossible for me to have done any work in the past 5 weeks at all in my office.

After all this generosity on his part it would seem like an insult to ask him to go before a Notary Public and swear to the truthfulness of his certificate.

I am free to say to you that, knowing me as you do, I am desirous always of abiding by the laws of any society of which I am a member, yet I would prefer to refund the money than ask my doctor to do as requested.

Trusting you will appreciate the position which compels me to take this attitude, with kindest regards to you, officers and members of the society, I am

Very truly yours,   Saml Gompers.

TLpS, reel 341, vol. 356, p. 59, SG Letterbooks, DLC.

1. The Hand-in-Hand Benevolent Society.

To D. W. O'Fallon[1]

Mch. 13 / 1896.

Mr. D. W. O'Fallon,
General Organizer,
527 Woods st., Piqua, O.
Dear Sir & Brother:

Your favor of the 10th. inst. came duly to hand and contents noted. I laid your letter aside in order that I might think over the situation you describe in connection with the East India Matting factory, its removal from your city and the effect it has upon the Mattress Makers Union No. 6475.[2]

You say that the men having been on strike for a long time and that the matting factory in question was the only one in town, and that now it having removed from the city, you ask my opinion as to what the men should do, both in matter of their union and their own course in reference to employment.

In answer let me say that the question is one that does not often occur inasmuch as it is seldom that there is but one factory of a certain industry in a city. But since this was so in the instance referred to I should say that there are but few alternatives and which I shall freely mention in order that a possible intelligent decision may be arrived at.

The first is that men usually follow where their occupations are in vogue, and if the members of the mattress makers' union can, it seems to me they should endeavor to find work at their trade where mattress factories are in existence. Even to the extent of following the factory in question to Brooklyn, N.Y.

So far as I am concerned I will say that the union should be maintained, but, of course, in such a city or town where the industry is in vogue, the members of the union may go.

I would gladly make such changes in the charter as would be applicable to the case.

Let me say that our friends may answer that they cannot easily follow this advice and beyond doubt it is evidently true, but yet we must bear in mind this fact—that the workers usually migrate to such cities, states or countries where their trade or occupation has drifted. We find thousands of Welchmen [Welshmen] in the mining districts of our country who crossed the ocean in order to obtain employment.

Within the past few years the tin plate industry has been largely transferred from Wales to the United States. We see that the tin plate industry of the country universally increased as it has in the last few years, is followed by men who left their country to come here in order to obtain employment.

We see too that many industries are transferred from one section of the country to another and the workers simply follow and usually find employment where the trade has gone.

If this cannot be followed out by the members of Mattress Makers Union it is evident they will have to turn their attention, for the purpose of endeavoring to secure employment, to some other trade or occupation. Certainly since the trade has disappeared from Piqua it would be idle to attempt to maintain the union of men who worked in that trade previously.

If they remain in Piqua and follow some other trade or occupation as wage earners they should join the union of the trade or calling into which they have drifted, or otherwise become members of a Federal Labor Union. In the latter event the change in the charter could be made in accordance with the practice of the A.F. of L.

As per your request I mail to your address with this a number of circulars and other documents setting forth the purposes of the A.F. of L.

I thank you for your kind words of congratulation and commendation.

With kindest wishes, I am

Fraternally yours,   Saml Gompers.
President   A.F. of L.

TLpS, reel 9, vol. 14, pp. 365-66, SG Letterbooks, DLC.

1. Probably Daniel W. O'Fallon, a Piqua, Ohio, molder.
2. Actually Mattress Makers' Union 6574 of Piqua, Ohio, which was chartered by the AFL in September 1895.

From John Phillips[1]

Secretary,
United Hatters of North America.[2]
Brooklyn, N.Y. Mar. 14, 1896

Dear Sir

Yours of 11th inst.[3] to hand. There is one part of it which in my opinion should be answered at once and it is where you say that you have no recollection of any explanation that was ever given to you why the hatters did not affiliate with the A.F. of L. I regret very much that your memory is so poor on that point, but I will try to give you an explanation

I received an invitation to attend a convention of the A.F. of L. in Phila. in 1885,[4] *I think*. At the time I received it, the above-named organization (U.H. of N.A.) was just about becoming connected with the K. of L. I wrote to Secy.-Treas. Turner[5] of the K. of L. asking him if the convention about to be held in the vicinity of Broad and Market Sts., Phila. was antagonistic to the K. of L. and he said that it was. That settled the matter. Good faith, honesty, fair play and manliness preclude the possibility of being attached to two organizations at the same time that are working in direct antagonism to each other.

I gave you this explanation on one occasion at least and you seemed to be perfectly satisfied with it. I asked you to name one organization that belonged to the K. of L. and the A.F. of L. at the same time, and you failed to do so. Your failure redounds to the credit of honesty in labor organizations. We were compelled to join the K. of L. Local Assemblies of scab hatters were being formed. Union Labels other than ours were making their appearance. We checkmated the scabs, we have lived in peace. If we should become connected with the A.F. of L. we will settle up our affairs man fashion with the K. of L. giving ample notice of our intentions and fully prepared for results.[6]

Yours Resp.   John Phillips,
Sec'y.

ALS, Hat Makers' National Association Records, reel 140, frame 727, *AFL Records*.

1. John PHILLIPS was secretary of the United Hatters of North America (UHNA) from 1896 until his death in 1904.

2. The United HATTERS of North America.

3. Reel 9, vol. 14, pp. 349-50, SG Letterbooks, DLC.

4. The FOTLU's 1885 convention was held in Washington, D.C. The AFL held its 1892 convention in Philadelphia.

5. Frederick TURNER, a goldbeater and later a grocer, had been general secretary-treasurer of the KOL from 1883 to 1886 and general treasurer from 1886 to 1888.

6. The UHNA affiliated with the AFL in September 1896.

To Andrew Furuseth

Mch. 20 / 1896.

Mr. Andrew Furuseth,
Washington, D.C.
Dear Sir & Brother:

Your favor of the 18th Inst.[1] to hand and contents noted. Let me say that my physical condition does not warrant me in making an engagement earlier than the one stated in my last letter[2]—April 8, and then, of course, it will be necessary for me to obtain the privilege of the Executive Council.[3]

It should be superfluous for me to say that had I not been suffering as intensely as I have within the past few months, I should have regarded it as my absolute duty to be in Washington, and say a word on behalf of our Bills.

I read your criticism on the Arbitration Bill[4] both last year, and in your last letter, and I am satisfied that it is quite justified. You are right, particularly in this one thing: If the men representing the railroad organizations favor the provisions of the Bill, it is a matter entirely for them to decide so far as it applies to the employes of the railroads, and I am sure if I were you I would insist upon it, that under no circumstances, should you consent to its either being reported favorably or enacted into a law unless it exempts seamen and all other workers than the railroad employes from the operations of the law.

The Executive Council meets here Monday and I shall lay the matter before them.

Thanking you for your kind wishes and reciprocating them as well as hoping for every success, I am

Fraternally yours,   Saml Gompers
President   A.F. of L.

TLpSr, reel 9, vol. 14, p. 416, SG Letterbooks, DLC.

1. National Seamen's Union of America Records, reel 142, frame 511, *AFL Records.*

2. Mar. 9, 1896, reel 9, vol. 14, p. 326, SG Letterbooks, DLC.

3. In a trip lasting from Apr. 6 to 27, 1896, SG visited Washington, D.C., Baltimore, Philadelphia, New York City, Fall River, Mass., Boston, Hartford, Conn., Pittsburgh, and Chicago.

4. In February 1895 Constantine Erdman, a Democratic congressman from Pennsylvania, introduced a bill in the House of Representatives (H.R. 8556, 53d Cong., 3d sess.) calling for compulsory arbitration of labor disputes in firms involved in interstate transportation. SG and Furuseth opposed the measure, arguing against its compulsory provisions. A modified bill excluding seamen became law on June 1, 1898 (U.S. *Statutes at Large*, 30: 424-48). The Erdman Act of 1898 provided for the resolution of labor disputes on railroads in interstate commerce by voluntary mediation or arbitration by the chairman of the Interstate Commerce Commission and the commissioner of the U.S. Department of Labor. Unresolved disputes were to go to a three-person arbitration board for a binding decision. The act prohibited employers from threatening union workers or blacklisting discharged employees, and it outlawed contracts that prohibited employees from joining a union or that released employers from legal liability for injuries.

To Andrew Furuseth

Mch. 27 / 1896.

Mr. Andrew Furuseth,
Keystone Hotel, Penna. ave., Washington, D.C.
Dear Friend:

The Executive Council of the American Federation of Labor has been in session here the 23rd, 24th and 25th Inst., and it was indeed a most interesting session. I am confident that the work done and laid out will bear good fruit in the interest of our fellow-workers.

Enclosed you will find a draft of a bill for the amendment of the Eight Hour Law. I desire you to place it in the hands of both a member of the House and a Senator, in each instance having in mind the fact that the introducer will push it.[1]

I think it would be advisable to have a republican introduce it in the House and a democrat introduce it in the Senate. More than likely Senator Hill[2] would be pleased to father it. He has expressed himself for many years in favor of the movement to reduce the hours of labor and I heard from him on the 24th Inst., in which he reiterates his sentiments on that subject.

By all means I should like to see this bill introduced by a member of the Senate "on his own hook" and not "by request." It makes considerable difference when a bill reaches the committee. The influence of the "by request" is inimical to its progress and passage.

The Council decided that I should go to Washington and appear before the committee on labor, as per my previous statement to you, April 8th.

I wish you would arrange this with Mr. Phillips,[3] chairman of the committee on labor. I will write him also upon completion of this.

If nothing unforeseen should arise I shall be on hand. I hope to meet you there and anticipate the opportunity with pleasure.

With every wish for your success, I am

Fraternally yours,   Saml Gompers.

N.B. — Let me hear from you on receipt of this as to whether arrangement has or can be made.

TLpS, reel 9, vol. 14, p. 464, SG Letterbooks, DLC.

1. The AFL sought to amend the federal eight-hour law of 1892 (U.S. *Statutes at Large*, 27: 340), which limited the length of the workday for craftsmen and laborers in federal employment, to prevent subcontractors from avoiding its provisions by performing work off government property. The amendment went forward in April 1896 as part of S. 2705, introduced by David B. Hill, and H.R. 7939, introduced by Thomas W. Phillips (both 54th Cong., 1st. sess.); but these bills failed to become law.

2. David Bennett Hill, a Democrat, served as a U.S. senator from New York from 1892 until 1897.

3. Thomas Wharton Phillips (1835-1912) was a Republican congressman from Pennsylvania (1893-97).

To John O'Sullivan

Mch. 28 / 1896.

(Personal and private)

Friend Jack:

In your letter to Gus you say that Mary[1] will leave Boston for Chicago today and if it is at all possible for her she will stop over here to see me on her return from Springfield. Of course, I should be most pleased to see her but if her return is delayed beyond the 6th I will have left the city, providing my health permits; and I should very much dislike for her to go to the special trouble of coming here and then both of us be disappointed in not meeting. For that reason I write with this mail to our friend Mike Carroll of Chicago requesting him to inform Mary of this state of affairs and the fact that I am going to Boston and in all likelihood will meet her there.

I suppose this meets with your approval.

It will please you I am sure to learn that I am very much improved within this last week and think that I can now be counted on the list among the "dangerously well" as you were pleased to put it some time ago.

I know that it will be too early for you to meet me on the incoming of the train from Fall River but I expect you to call at the Quincy as soon as you can make it convenient. I also want your cordial co-operation to bring this machinists' dispute[2] to an end.

My trip to Washington is to appear before the committee on Labor on all our Bills; at the same time to appear before the National League of Musicians, which holds their convention there, on the 9th and urge affiliation. In Baltimore, a conference with Elliott[3] on the Painters' trouble. In Philadelphia the Central body[4] has decided to affiliate and somewhat of an investigation is necessary. In New York and Jersey for organizing purposes of an important nature and see "Mamma" and the folks. Boston, the machinists' dispute, etc., etc., Pittsburgh with brewers.[5] Chicago for general purposes, and back again to head quarters.

So you see I shall be pretty busy but anticipate our meeting with keen pleasure.

Sincerely yours,   Saml Gompers.

TLpS, reel 9, vol. 14, p. 487, SG Letterbooks, DLC.

1. Mary Kenney O'SULLIVAN was an organizer of women workers and a labor journalist.

2. The International MACHINISTS' Union of America (IMUA) disbanded in 1895 after the International Association of Machinists (IAM) agreed to drop the racial ban

from its constitution. In Boston, however, IMUA 28 continued to hold its seat in the Boston Central Labor Union (CLU). The CLU refused to accept representatives of IAM 264 until the local resolved the question of admitting members of IMUA 28. SG later reported that his visit to Boston, in mid-April, helped resolve the difficulty. By May 1896 IMUA 28 had disbanded, turning over its treasury to the Boston CLU.

3. John T. ELLIOTT served as general secretary-treasurer of the Brotherhood of Painters and Decorators (after 1899 Painters, Decorators, and Paperhangers) of America from 1887 to 1900.

4. The Philadelphia United Labor League (ULL).

5. In 1895 the National Union of the United Brewery Workmen of the United States (NUUBW) charged that several breweries in Allegheny Co., Pa., had been involved in forming KOL Local Assembly 92 in 1894 to serve as a de facto company union in opposition to NUUBW 22. NUUBW officers initially requested that the AFL boycott sixteen of the seventeen local breweries. The AFL Executive Council objected on grounds that such a boycott would be impractical, and that a report of the ULL of Western Pennsylvania—an unaffiliated regional central labor body—indicated that there were no nonunion breweries in Allegheny Co. SG's attempt to mediate the dispute in April 1896 failed, and the AFL convention in December endorsed a boycott of three local breweries.

An Editorial by Samuel Gompers in the
American Federationist

[March 1896]

A PROTEST AGAINST MILITANCY.

The United States Senate is now considering a bill[1] introduced by Senator Lodge,[2] of Massachusetts, appropriating $88,000,000 for coast defense, and incidentally many more millions for otherwise increasing and improving the army and navy. In other words, under the mask of the jingo spirit inaugurated a few months ago the schemes of the capitalist, the monopolist class of the country, is bearing fruition in the shape of an increased army.

We are free to say that we expected better things from Senator Lodge than a bill of that character. He must know, as all students of history know, that peace is as essential to successful industry as air is to lung-breathing animals; that the military spirit is dangerous to industry and commerce; that militancy is inconsistent with free institutions; that an increase of our army or navy does not imply greater ability to assert our rights in the affairs which concern our people; that an effort to make militancy one of the chief, if not the chief, considerations among our people is giving the lie to the assertion that we live under a government resting upon the consent of the governed.

Last December, when addressing the Central Labor Union in New York City,[3] we called attention to the fact that it was our earnest judgment that the "war message" was only a covert and first attempt of corporate wealth and its servants to increase the military power, to the detriment and injury of the masses of our country.

Recognizing this fact to be the condition of affairs, upon the day the bill came up for consideration in the United States Senate, we sent the following telegram to the Vice-President of the United States:

Indianapolis, Ind., Feb. 28, 1896.

Hon. Adlai E. Stevenson,
President United States Senate,
Washington, D.C.:

The workers of our country recognize in Senator Lodge's bill a covert attempt of corporate power to overawe the masses. It is inconsistent with and dangerous to free institutions. In the name of half million members, American Federation of Labor, I enter most emphatic protest against its passage. Please place before Senate.

Samuel Gompers,
President.

To which we received the following reply:

Vice President's Chamber,
Washington, Feb. 29, 1896.

Hon. Samuel Gompers,
Indianapolis, Ind.
Dear Sir—

Your telegram reached me last evening. It will be duly laid before the Senate when it convenes on Monday. There is no session of the Senate to-day. Your telegram will be referred to the committee having in charge the bill to which you refer.

A. E. Stevenson.

We believe it the duty of every worker in the United States and every union throughout the country to send in their emphatic protests to Congress against the passage of any bill by which militancy is sought to be encouraged or by which the spirit of peaceful industry and commerce is or may be checked or hemmed in [in] its development. We see so many of these conditions prevail in other countries; we see the workers—the masses—crushed under the burden of enormous taxation to support the armies and navies, which, in turn, are used to crush out the spirit of liberty, independence, justice and right. There is no danger from any foe now or prospective from which we cannot fully protect and defend ourselves. In time of real need we, as citizens, are all soldiers. It is the conscious fear of monopoly and capitalism of their wrong doing which makes such assinine or brutal exhibitions and propositions possible. The man who loves war is an enemy to the human race.

American Federationist 3 (Mar. 1896): 13.

1. An amendment proposed by Henry Cabot Lodge provided for the issuance of $100 million in bonds to cover some $87 million of expenditures in a coastal fortifications bill introduced by Watson Squire (S. 1159, 54th Cong., 1st sess., 1896). The amendment was tabled and evidently not added to the bill, which failed to pass.

2. Henry Cabot Lodge (1850-1924) was a Republican U.S. congressman (1886-93) and senator (1893-1924) from Massachusetts.

3. See "A News Account of an Address in New York City," Jan. 4, 1896, above.

To P. J. McGuire

April 1 / 1896.

Mr. P. J. McGuire,
First Vice-President A.F. of L.
Dear Friend:

Your favor of March 31st to hand and contents noted, and am more than pleased to learn of the success which has attended you on your trip. I am sure that your presence among our fellow-workers at the different points always has, and necessarily must have, the effect of stirring them up to renewed activity.

Many thanks for your suggestions in the Cornice Workers[1] and Box Makers[2] matters. I shall give them immediate attention. I think we can be of practical aid to the former at this time, in St. Louis. It is rather a rare opportunity which presents itself there and which I certainly shall take advantage of.

Relative to the United Garment Workers, let me say that I have just written[3] to our Friend Reichers.[4] I have caused a duplicate of that letter to be made and enclose it herein for your perusal. After noting its contents please return here for filing.

In addition to what I say in that letter let me add that Mr. Reichers has no cause to feel sore at the A.F. of L. nor at me, personally or officially. I organized the first Local of that trade in the Federation and if asked, he will admit that I practically conducted its affairs for a long time in order to bring life into the organization, and really founded the national union. Then when the great lock-out occurred in New York in the early part of 1893, I spent nearly two weeks for the purpose of bringing victory to the organization and it was secured. I appeared as counsel for the organization before the manufacturers' association and helped to secure the substantial victory[5] and it has redounded to their advantage ever since, and it was during that lock-out that the Federation made a loan to the organization of $1,500.00 which it subsequently donated to them.

Under these circumstances I think you will agree with me that there is no occasion for grumbling on their part against the A.F. of L.

I shall try to be at Baltimore about 5 P.M. April 9th and shall be pleased to meet you in the lobby of the Utah House at that hour. I shall write our friends Duncan and Elliott and ask them to meet you and I there at the time stated.

I have already notified the parties in interest that I shall arrive in Boston on the morning of the 18th, remaining there for the 19th to attend the meeting of the C.L.U.[6]

On the 20th the Association[7] meets in New York (the Association with some of whose members I am to confer relative the organization of the people in Jersey city. You will remember which I mean). It is necessary for me to be there on that date if I desire to be successful in my mission.

I wish you could make it so that I could meet you in Boston on either the 18th or 19th Inst. I know you could be of great assistance in helping me straighten out the dispute between the C.L.U. and the Machinists. I will stop at the Quincy while in Boston.

Will you please try and arrange your dates so as to be enabled to meet me there?

I am doing fairly well and am continually gaining. Many thanks for your good wishes.

With every hope for success, I am

                                   Sincerely yours,   Saml Gompers.

TLpS, reel 9, vol. 15, pp. 13-14, SG Letterbooks, DLC.

1. Tin, Sheet Iron, and Cornice Workers' International Association 36 of St. Louis appealed to the AFL to mediate its dispute with Mesker Brothers, a staunchly anti-union firm. When SG learned that the company was the subcontractor for cornice work on the auditorium in which the Republican national convention was to meet, he asked David Kreyling, president of the St. Louis Central Trades and Labor Union, to exert pressure on Mesker Brothers through the contractor for the project. The contractor subsequently withdrew the award from the firm. Mesker Brothers, however, continued to operate on a nonunion basis.

2. Probably AFL Tobacco Boxmakers' Protective Union 6042 of St. Louis.

3. SG explained the AFL's difficulty in responding to the United Garment Workers

of America's (UGWA) request for financial assistance (Apr. 1, 1896, reel 9, vol. 15, p. 11, SG Letterbooks, DLC).

4. Charles F. REICHERS served as general secretary (1891-95) and president (1895-96) of the UGWA.

5. See "Excerpts from a Report on the Mediation of the New York City Clothing Cutters' Strike," Apr. 12-20, 1893, *Unrest and Depression,* pp. 305-40.

6. The Boston Central Labor Union.

7. SG addressed members of the Trade Mark Association of Tobacco Manufacturers while in New York City.

To the Editor of the *Hamburger Echo*

April 6 / 1896.

To the Editor *Hamburg Echo,*
Dear Sir:

I am in frequent, but regret to say, not regular receipt of your valued journal, and have often seen therein references made to the labor movement in the United States, and particularly of the men whom your correspondent, Derossi, has stigmatized as dishonest, dishonorable and insincere.

Of course, it is entirely out of the question that I could attempt to cover all the ground of his malicious charges, false statements and unmanly insinuations, but having before me a few copies of your paper of recent dates I shall undertake, with your permission, to correct some of the statements he either ignorantly or viciously makes.

He seems to have selected Mr. A. Strasser, ex-President of the Cigar Makers International Union and your humble servant the special targets for his venomous arrows and while it is not within my province to come to the defense of another yet I will say a few words in reference to him before speaking of others or myself.

Then let me say that in 1877 when Mr. Strasser was elected president of the Cigar Makers International Union there were 1017 members in the United States and Canada without a dollar in the treasury. The cigar makers worked from early morning until late at night for any wage the employers were kind enough to give and in most instances married men were expected to take their wages out in trade or "truck"; the single men to board where the employer directed and for the balance of wages due the cigar maker, cigars were given to be sold by the workman for anything he could get. It can readily be seen what demoralization prevailed in the trade at that time. When he, Strasser, voluntarily retired four years ago, we had about 26,000 cigar makers organized, a fund of over a half million dollars in the treasury, expended nearly two and a half million dollars in ten years for strike and other benefits for the members, and an eight hour work-day for the cigar makers, a bond of unity throughout this country which is regarded by every workingman as the best trade union in America.

Let me add that after the first four years of his position his salary was $5.00 per week. In season and out of season he has been indefatigable in his effort to spread organization among the workingmen, has contributed both by his voice and pen, and his energy and ability so that the workers have felt his influence for good.

This is the man that Derossi tried to decry. This man who, after years of devotion and self-sacrifice in the cause of labor, is today practically without a dollar to his name.

One would think from reading Derossi's letters that the whole aim and object of the officers of the trade union movement of America was to obtain some political office, some snug place to buy and sell the workingmen and their votes as if they were so many cattle. I am sure that the first of these men whom he terms leaders in the labor movement of America who would attempt anything of the kind would soon be confronted with a storm of intelligent indignation of the American workingmen that Derossi can neither understand nor appreciate. I make this bold assertion without fear of contradiction from any quarter that the organized workingmen of the United States and their representatives are fully as honest, zealous, sincere and self-sacrificing as any on the face of the globe. That an occasional one will go wrong I will not dispute, but the conspicuousness with which a character is exposed proves what I say to be the rule.

So far as his statements in reference to me are concerned I shall speak of them after referring to another subject.

One would imagine from Derossi's letters that the "Cigar Makers Progressive Union," so-called, was divided from the Cigar Makers International Union by questions of principle. Let me show by almost one word how utterly ridiculous he makes himself. In 1881 the Cigar Makers International Union had a convention and recommended that the dues of members be increased from 15 cents to 20 cents per week. This was done, first, to pay larger benefits to the members, and secondly, to create a greater reserve fund. The proposition was adopted by a referendum vote of the members. The weak-kneed and disgruntled, as we find some in every organization, objected. Taking advantage of this dis-satisfaction of a minority a few men inaugurated a secession movement from the International Union and organized the Progressive Cigar Makers Union, retaining the dues at 15 cents per week while the International Union continued to pay the increased dues of 20 cents per week. Stripped of all verbiage this was the cause of the existence of the Progressive Union.

First, with a greater fund at our command, secondly our better organization throughout the country, and thirdly the co-operation of the organized workers of America, brought about, after five years, the amalgamation of the Progressives with the International Union.

Whatever struggles occurred between '81 and '86 were caused by the division existing and the alliance of the Progressives with the K. of L. whose trickery and scabbism is the by-word and reproach in the American labor movement. There may be differences of tactics in and among our different unions in the International Union, but not-withstanding this we are a unit in our organization and it illy becomes a man like Derossi to attempt to pass judgement on a struggle which occurred before he came to the United States and of which he could positively know nothing and upon which he manifests absolute ig-norance, if not worse.

I had almost forgotten to say that during the time the so-called Progressive Cigar Makers Union was divided from and opposed to the Cigar Makers International Union, we had increased wages throughout the United States in the cigar trade from 40 to 100 per cent, and we had more than 5000 union shops in the United States in which no cigar maker could work unless he was a member of the International Union.

Against me the most poisonous thrusts are attempted. When I was in Hamburg last summer I had an opportunity to freely speak to a number of its fore-most workmen representing the different shades of opinion and there went over fully my career in the labor movement of America. Of course, I shall not attempt anything of the kind here. It might take too much of your space and too much of my time and another thing I do not desire [is] to enter upon my biography. I will say that since my fourteenth year I have been a member of the union of my trade, have been active in the general labor movement, have held positions of trust and honor in my local union, in the state organization and the American Federation of Labor for years without receiving recompense in any way either for loss of time or work performed. I hold membership card No. 1 in the Cigar Makers In-ternational Union where the numbers run nigh on to 50,000. It is only within the past few years that a salary has attached to the office of president of the American Federation of Labor, when the orga-nization directed that I should give my entire time to its interests, its up-building and the organization of our fellow-workers throughout the country. Last year I held no office and worked consistently and thoroughly to the very best of my ability in the same direction.

But let us consider what Mr. Derossi has particularly to say against me. Coupling me with others he speaks of our selling votes to one or the other of the political parties and hankering after office. Let us see what truth there is in that. I remember once having cast a vote for one of the dominant political parties and that was my first vote in 1872. I challenge Derossi or any one else to show any one instance where I have written or uttered a word, directly or indirectly, which could be construed as favorable to either of the dominant parties. His charge is a pure fabrication born of the diseased mind of a vicious opponent.

He speaks of my nomination as senator and says I went to the "Conservative Central Labor Union of New York" asking for their endorsement. Let me give you the truth. I was nominated for senator by the Republican party. The largest faction of the Democratic party also nominated me. Election was practically assured. I did not wish the position and desired to administer to both parties the severest rebuke that I could. I talked the matter over with Mr. Henry Emrich,[1] General Secretary of the Furniture Workers National Union[2] and George Block[3] of the Bakers National Union and one or two others whose names I cannot now remember. We decided to go over to Mr. Schevitch,[4] editor of the New York Volks Zeitung and discuss the matter and to arrive at some result. We had to travel several miles, cross the river, and at nearly two o'clock in the morning roused Mr. Schevitch from his sleep. We discussed the question in all its phases and concluded that the best course would be not to appear before the "Conservative Central Labor Union" but the "Radical Central Labor Federation," all of us knowing full well that endorsement could not be had. It was our joint intention to show an example by my conduct to the workingmen of America that before they would dare accept any office at the hands of any party organized labor should be consulted. My letters to both parties declining the nomination are documents of which I am proud and which it would be well for those who pretend to be more radical to follow as an example.[5]

Derossi says I was a candidate of the Republican party. I shall be equally frank with you in this matter. I was a delegate from the local union of New York to the convention of the Cigar Makers International Union in 1893. In the early part of that year the industrial crisis had thrown a large number of workmen out of employment. We organized a local labor organization for the purpose of relieving our members. It gained some influence and since delegates were to be elected by people to the state convention to revise the constitution of the state of New York, some thought was given as to whether the workingmen of New York should not be represented directly in that constitutional convention. During that time, or to be exact, September, 1893, the convention of the Cigar Makers International Union took place at Milwaukee, Wisconsin, 1,100 miles from New York. While there, and engrossed in the work, I learned subsequently that the Democratic party wanted the conference to name two union men to be nominated for that convention and they would endorse them. This our conference declined. On my way from the convention I learned that the conference had nominated a number of workingmen as delegates to the state constitutional convention, among others being myself. I saw in the newspapers that the Republican party also nominated me. Having to stop over at Washington in the interest of some labor measures then pending before congress, I could not at once return to New York, but sent a telegram to the state officially declining the nomination and requesting them not to print my name on the official ballot. When I returned to New York City I learned for the first time that a declination by telegraph was not legal, that they could not take cognizance of it and that the time for declining had already elapsed and that my name would be printed on the ballot. Finding that I could not withdraw, we entered in earnest on the campaign, and during it I can challenge Derossi or any other man to say that I uttered a word other than adverse criticism and opposition to the Republican party as well as the Democratic.

He says that I ran behind the ticket. This is as untrue as his other statements. As a matter of fact the highest candidate on the Republican ticket received little more than 9,000 votes, while I received nearly 10,500. This too was in the district dominated by the worst corrupt practices of the Taminy organization which was then dominant in New York, the exposure of which I have no doubt you have read in the press.[6]

Time and again I have been approached by representatives of both parties who, saying that they desired to give labor an opportunity to be heard in the halls of Congress, offered to nominate me, each of which I have consistently declined.

In 1886 the legislature of the state of New York passed a law creating a State Board of Arbitration. The law provided for the Appointment of one Democrat, one Republican and one member of organized labor in good standing. The salary of the office was $3,000.00 per annum and traveling and incidental expenses beside. The Governor[7] of the state of New York telegraphed me that he desired to see me, and calling upon him he offered me the appointment as *the member in good standing in the labor organizations of the state.* I peremptorily declined the offer, as well as many other offers made by different parties and officers to me.

Let me say that I regret more than I can find words to express, the necessity which I [find] calls for me to make these statements. Nor do I make them because they [reflect] my [conduct but] because I [know] that the course I have pursued is the rule prevailing among the most active and foremost of trade unionists of our country.

As I said, I cannot attempt to cover all the ground of Mr. Derossi's abuse and untruths, but the above is sufficient to [hail] him as one of the greatest falsifiers of our time.

What I have said in this letter respecting Mr. Derossi is susceptible to proof if necessary.

I had almost forgotten that he questions my ability and [quotes] the New York Volkzeitung as proof of my lack of ability. He might as well quote Kaiser Wilhelm[8] as an authority on Karl Marx. [The truth is] I have been a working man all my life. Yes, a worker [when I was a little?] more than ten years of age. I have [. . .] to be a student and to learn, and whatever I do know, be it much or little, is [. . .] of the organized labor movement [to redound to] the workers' [advantage]. I have endeavored, and [now] praise myself, saying with some degree of success, to organize the workingmen of America. If I have done something towards that end I feel that [what little I have accomplished has been?] in the proper [. . . .] Who can say what Derossi has done[?]

Mr. Schleuter[9] in his letter says that he practically published what I said, but that I used abusive language. I ask who would have suffered the most had he published my letters as they were sent, if they were abusive? No, in my plain blunt style I have called a spade a spade. I have not minced matters and when a man deserved to be adversely criticised I have always had the courage of my convictions to apply the term most proper.

Mr. Schleuter not only suppressed the most important portions of my letter[10] but distorted what I said so that the reader could form no conception of what I had in mind when writing the letters. As a matter of fact with the paper at his command he [dares?] not publish my letter as it was written; and this is the reason why it was suppressed and distorted. By reading his letter closely you will see that he even objects to any one having the spirit of fair play sufficiently developed in him to defend a man when he knows that he has been unjustly dealt with.

There are a number of matters that crowd upon my mind, but I have a great amount of work to perform which precludes the possibility of my entering fully upon them. However, I have written this in [length?] so that the workingmen of Hamburg may know that the statements published reflecting upon the honor and integrity of the labor movement or the so-called leaders of the labor movement of America have no other basis than the imagination of malignant hostility.

Very respectfully yours, Saml Gompers.

TLpS, reel 9, vol. 15, pp. 69-73, SG Letterbooks, DLC.

1. Henry EMRICH, of New York City, was secretary of the International Furniture Workers' Union of America from 1882 to 1891 and treasurer of the AFL in 1888 and 1889.

2. The International FURNITURE Workers' Union of America.

3. George G. BLOCK, of New York City, was secretary of the Journeymen Bakers' National Union from 1886 to 1888, a founder of the New York City Central Labor Union, and a leader in the Henry George mayoralty campaign.

4. Sergius E. SHEVITCH served on the editorial board of the *New Yorker Volkszeitung* after 1878, edited the paper in 1890, and was an important figure in the SLP in New York City.

5. See "A Translation of a News Account of a Nominating Convention for the New York Seventh Senatorial District," Oct. 26, 1889, "To the Committee of Notification of the Republican Party of the New York Seventh Senatorial District," Oct. 28, 1889, and "An Excerpt from a News Account of a Meeting of the New York City Central Labor Federation," Nov. 2, 1889, in *The Early Years of the AFL*, pp. 244-47, 249-51.

6. See "To the Board of Aldermen of New York City and County," ca. Nov. 15, 1893, in *Unrest and Depression*, pp. 410-11.

7. David B. Hill.

8. Wilhelm II (1859-1941) was king of Prussia and German emperor from 1888 to 1918.

9. Hermann SCHLÜTER was editor-in-chief of the *New Yorker Volkszeitung* from 1891 to 1919.

10. In the letter, part of which Schlüter deleted as being "too coarse and rude," SG defended nonpartisan politics and denied that he had made disparaging remarks about the French workers' support of the Carmaux strike ("Billig und schlect" [Cheap and Bad], *New Yorker Volkszeitung*, Oct. 30, 1895).

To Adolph von Elm

Chicago, Ill. April 25, 1896.

Mr. A. von Elm,
Schäfer str., 19 part, Hamburg, St. Pauli, Germany.
Dear Friends:

In compliance with a resolution of the Executive Council of the American Federation of Labor, I have been on a lecturing and organizing tour through the eastern part of the country for the past few weeks, and on my homeward trip stopped over here. I desire that this letter should reach you before the closing of your congress, and hence forward it from this place.

There is a something which has arisen and which I desire to communicate to you, since it may be of some interest to you, should the question of the American Federation of Labor be brought up.

You, of course, have heard much of the new fangled organization started in New York, and called the Socialist Trade & Labor Alliance of the United States and Canada. When the New York faction of the socialist organization party organized it, they decided to hold a convention in the City of New York May 4, 1896, but the organization met with such little success that the convention would have proven an entire fiasco. This, of course, would have made them the laughing-stock of the labor movement of America, and has shown how little there is to their pretended movement and how weak is their following. This, of course, they wanted to obviate, and they postponed the convention until June 29th.[1] This in itself would be nothing. But it must be borne in mind, that the Socialist party will hold its congress[2] on July 4, 1896; just five (5) days after the convention of the so-called Socialist Trade and Labor Alliance. The active spirits in the party have divided up and gone through the country urging the Sections of the Party to send delegates to the Alliance's congress, and you will find, that the same parties who will act as delegates to the Alliance convention will be delegates to the party congress, so that, as a matter of fact, when the one ends, the other will begin, and that, in truth, they are nothing more than one and the same body—one and the same people. The informed will know the truth but to the uninformed, it will appear as if the convention has not been a flat failure that it otherwise certainly would have been. The party congresses were usually made up of about 15 to 30 men, one-half of whom were from the locality in which the congresses were held; they being selected as proxies—proxy-delegates, by the sections of the party situated some distance from where the congresses took place.

When the convention and congress are held, you will see the proceedings published in the Volkszeitung, and with the information herein imparted, you can see the true inwardness of the situation, as I know it to exist.

More than likely, when this reaches you, you will be exceedingly busy with the work of your congress; and I almost hesitated to send this letter to you at such a time, but, believing that the information can be of advantage to you, I assume that it will not be entirely unwelcome.

With every wish for success, and hoping to be remembered to our friends in the movement, I am

Sincerely, Saml Gompers.

N.B.: I shall be at headquarters, De Soto Block, Indianapolis, Ind., in a few days.

S. G

TLpS, Minutes of Meetings, Executive Council, AFL, reel 2, frames 1114-15, *AFL Records.*

1. The Socialist Trade and Labor Alliance convention met in New York City June 29-July 2, 1896.
2. The SLP convention met in New York City July 4-10, 1896.

An Interview in the *Chicago Tribune*

[April 25, 1896]

GOMPERS IS FOR PEACE.

"There will be no industrial upheaval in May in the United States," said Samuel Gompers last night.

"The workingman," he continued, "the true trades unionist, is conservative in thought and action. The workingmen of the American Federation of Labor recognize present conditions of returning prosperity. They will not assail those conditions. They will promote them if they can."

The President of the American Federation of Labor, representing nearly a million trades unionists, arrived in Chicago at 7:25 P.M. over the Pan-Handle from Pittsburg. He was met at the Union Depot by George William Perkins, International President of the Cigarmakers' Union; J. J. McGrath,[1] Treasurer of the Bricklayers' Union;[2] James O'Connell, third Vice-President of the federation and President of the International Association of Machinists; James J. Linehan, J. J. Lynch,[3] John J. Ryan, M. R. Grady,[4] and D. Douglas Wilson,[5] editor of the Machinists' Journal.

MR. GOMPERS CONSERVATIVE.

Mr. Gompers' direct official mission was the installation of the Bricklayers' Union, with its 4,000 members, as an affiliated body of the federation. This ceremony he performed at 10:30 o'clock last night. The Reception committee escorted Mr. Gompers at once to Bricklayers' Hall. On his way there he said:

"There will be no great strike. Reports I have said there might be are untrue and possibly malicious. There may be isolated demands on May 1 for an eight-hour day or a nine-hour day. But that the federation has planned, contemplates, or will undertake a general upheaval of labor forces in an attempt to secure the eight-hour day is not only false but preposterous. The men whose minds are the directing forces of the federation are ultra-conservative, I believe. It was upon the platform of conservatism they were elected to office last December. They recognize the slow emergence of the country from conditions of depression. They feel that disturbance of rising trade and industrial barometers would be criminal. They will not disturb them. They will not permit others to disturb them if they can help it.["]

EIGHT-HOUR DAY.

"The eight hour day is coming. I have said—and herein is where I have been misquoted, either by ignorance or malice—that in my judgment a hundred thousand wage workers early in May will receive from their employers the concession of a shorter day. This does not mean a strike of half a million men. It does not mean a strike, a general strike, at all. These concessions have been made voluntarily, after application, discussion, conference. I am not speaking loosely either, for the records of the federation, its recent correspondence, accurately indorse the figures I use.

"Socialism is dying out of trades unionism. Its advocates are leaving us to flock by themselves. The true trades unionist has no use for these blatant advocates of impossible frothings. Their teachings are vicious. The workingman is finding it out.

"The federation grows. It is greater than ever and gains strength each week. Part of my mission here will relate to the union of your two great central labor bodies, the assembly and the congress,[6] under one wing. It is well this amalgamation should take place. It is ill it has been so long delayed. Labor must not divide its energies and influence. From the information I have I am convinced there will be actual harmony and a spirit of fraternity within the reconstructed assembly."

Chicago Tribune, Apr. 25, 1896.

1. John J. McGrath, a leader in the Trade and Labor Assembly of Chicago (TLA) and earlier connected with Bricklayers' and Masons' International Union of America (BMIU) 21 of Chicago, was treasurer of the Chicago-based United Order of American Bricklayers and Stonemasons (UOABS).

2. The UOABS of Chicago, launched by secessionists from the BMIU during a

dispute over assessments in 1888, joined the AFL as directly affiliated local 6636 in February 1896 and became part of BMIU 21 in April 1897.

3. John J. Lynch was a Chicago cigarmaker and longtime business agent of CMIU 14 until becoming a partner in a cigar manufacturing firm in early May 1896.

4. Michael R. Grady, a Chicago bricklayer active in the UOABS, served as president (1895) and secretary (1896) of the Chicago TLA. He was also secretary and general manager of the National Accident Adjustment Co.

5. Duncan Douglas WILSON was the International Association of Machinists' grand foreman (title changed to vice-president in 1899) from 1895 to 1901 and the editor of its official organ, the *Monthly Journal of the International Association of Machinists* (after 1902 the *Machinists' Monthly Journal*) from 1891 to 1915.

6. In January 1895, several Chicago unions led by CMIU 14 seceded from the Chicago TLA and formed the Chicago Trade and Labor Congress (TLC). The TLC drew individuals strongly committed to independent political party activity, many of whom were socialists. SG and other AFL officers took part in negotiations in November 1896 that united the two bodies as the Chicago Federation of Labor. The new organization, chartered by the AFL on Nov. 16, 1896, admitted only AFL-affiliated unions.

To Eva McDonald Valesh

April 30th, [1896]

Mrs. Eva McDonald-Valesh,
7 Rue du Port Mahon, Paris, France.
Dear Friend:—

Your kind favor of the 15th inst. to hand and contents noted and it affords me much pleasure to learn that the trip of yours and Frank has been so safe, pleasant, and interesting. You certainly have not allowed much grass to grow under your feet, judging by the territory you have covered. The places you have visited and the incidents you recount, are indeed worth reading more than once and I am sure will go far to make an interesting volume of your work. It is more than kind of you to speak so encouragingly of my work in conducting the Federationist. I know that I am trying to do the best I can and it is some gratification to be commended by those I am confident have the power to discern and the courage to criticise. Beg to assure you that any suggestion that you or Frank can make, which may be of aid to me either in the movement or for the magazine, will be gratefully received and appreciated. It must indeed have been a delight for Frank to visit his birth place and meet the friends of his infancy. As for you, of course you were not in it since you do not speak "Cesky." You fling this at Frank and say also "Demaci Praci."[1] He certainly will think you have made decided progress as a polyglot.

Your third article reached here by the same mail as your letter. It is indeed excellent. Of course I expect you to keep us well supplied so that we may continue publishing until the full series is closed.[2] In order that you have the Federationist complete, I mail to your Paris address, a copy of each of the issues since I resumed its editorial management. You are right in your judgment that the editorials were dictated during my illness. I could not then hold pen or pencil in hand and even my dictation was with broken voice and seldom two syllables connected. I am sure you will be pleased to know that I have nearly recovered my old time health and except for weakness and an occasional twitch reminding me that I am not yet fully recovered, I am nearly my old self again. Yes, perhaps enjoying less physical annoyance than for the past few years. I do earnestly hope that Frank has found health, strength, and vigor by the trip and will come home to impress his friends that he is a typical British "beef eater." Of course it goes without saying that the same wish goes for you.

April 6th, I left here and went through to Washington, Baltimore, Philadelphia, New York, Fall River, Boston, Hartford, New York, Pittsburg, Chicago, and returned to this office on the 27th. Of course this makes it rather rushing just now, in getting out the May Federationist and to attend to the accumulated work, but I am sure that I shall get through. During my trip, friends say I did some good work, addressing public meetings and stirring up considerable thought and action among our people. We have made considerable progress with the past four months, with an increase in the income of the A.F. of L. of over 50%, as compared to the four months of last year, or in fact any four months of last year. We have issued a lot of printed matter and sent out broad cast throughout the country. I enclose a few of the matters in the copies of the Federationist. Look for them there.

When I write home today or tomorrow, I shall advise Mrs. Gompers that I have heard from you and that when you return, you and Frank will call upon her, or better still, why not write her, giving the name of the ship you will return on and the time of your scheduled arrival. I know that she will make it a point and try to be on the dock to meet you on the incoming of the steamer. When you come here, do you contemplate making your head-quarters in the East? At any rate, I hope you will be able to make it convenient to come to Indianapolis. You will greatly favor me if you will write in reply to this at your earliest convenience.

Our friends McCraith and Prescott, join me in wishing you and

Frank and Frank Jr.,[3] the very best of health and for myself, accept for both of you, the love of,

Yours sincerely, Saml Gompers

TLpS, reel 9, vol. 15, pp. 93-95, SG Letterbooks, DLC.

1. *Český* means the Czech language; *Demaci Praci* is probably a corruption of *Domácí Práce*, meaning "domestic work" or "home work."
2. See "M'Bride Vindicated," Dec. 11, 1895, n. 12, in "Excerpts from Accounts of the 1895 Convention of the AFL in New York City," above.
3. Eva and Frank Valesh's son, Frank M. Valesh, Jr.

To Samuel and Rose Mitchell

Indianapolis, Ind. May 3rd 1896.

Mr & Mrs Samuel Mitchell
New. York N.Y.
My Dear Children, Sam. & Rose:—
Upon this the Fifth Anniversary of your Marriage let me offer you the congratulations of a devoted father.

During the years of your wedded life I have felt a great solicitude for your happiness and prosperity; and assure you that I cannot find words to adequately express my gratification at the fact that I have seen the growth of your mutual love, confidence and devotion.

Let me express the hope that with each recurring year additional cause may come for the strengthening of the bonds of your affection for each other. And with health, prosperity to you and the blessing of a beautiful, loving child, like Darling Henrietta may your future be as bright and joyous as the sincere wish of

Yours Affectionately Saml Gompers.

ALS, George Meany Memorial Archives, Silver Spring, Md.

To the Editor of the *Chicagoer Arbeiter-Zeitung*

May 4th, [1896]

Editor Chicago Arbeiter Zeitung,
28 South Market St., Chicago, Ill.
Dear Sir:—
My attention is called to your article[1] published April 28th, and I beg to say in reply that your criticism is based upon a misquotation

from my remarks[2] to the Bricklayers on the evenings of April 25th or April 26th, since I addressed them upon both dates. I am not quite so ignorant of the industrial affairs of our time as to declare that the sum total of our movement is *simply* to obtain "remunerative" employment. Upon no occasion in my more than thirty years' connection with the labor unions of America, have I given utterance to such a statement and I am surprised that you should give credence to anything that would appear to place me in so false a position.

My contention has always been that the workers should concentrate their efforts to obtain more of the products of their labor and when securing that, to still strive for more; and if this should lead to the elimination of all profit on labor, that is the goal to attain [for] which we should strive.

Kindly publish[3] the foregoing explanation and oblige,

Yours very respectfully,   Saml Gompers.
Pres.   American Federation of Labor.

TLpS, reel 9, vol. 15, p. 135, SG Letterbooks, DLC.

1. "Samuel Gompers," *Chicagoer Arbeiter-Zeitung*, Apr. 28, 1896.
2. On Apr. 24, 1896, SG attended a meeting of the United Order of American Bricklayers and Stonemasons of Chicago to initiate the body into the AFL. The following evening the union held a banquet in SG's honor, during which he spoke about the growth and importance of the AFL.
3. The May 6, 1896, issue of the *Chicagoer Arbeiter-Zeitung* printed a summary of SG's letter; the paper claimed it was justified in assuming SG had made the statements since he had failed to challenge their publication in the local press.

To Robert Askew[1]

May 6th, [1896]

Mr. Robert Askew,
Pres. Northern Mineral Mine Workers Progressive Union,[2]
Ishpeming, Mich.
Dear Sir and Brother:—

Your favor of the 4th inst. just to hand and contents noted. After some deliberation I have concluded to reply at once, in order that I may at the earliest possible moment, give you what you ask, the result of my experience in just such cases as the members of your organization are confronted with now. You say that the Mining Companies are discharging union men and putting non-union men in their places. That you are now consulting with your National Executive Board and that the men at Ishpeming are "foaming with rage," and can hardly be restrained from striking.

I know that which I am going to say to you is probably not the most popular thing to say and to say much under such circumstances often makes enemies of men who were formerly friends and devoted adherents. You have organized what exists of the mineral mine workers' union. It has been accomplished at great risk, expense of time and money and the undivided devotion and sacrifice of its leading men. The mining Companies have had a taste of the power of your organization. Theretofore they have had undivided authority and sway in conducting their business. When recently your organization succeeded in preventing an encroachment upon the rights of the members, it evidently dawned upon the managers of the Companies that a new factor had come into life, with which they would have to count.

You can understand that this was not the most palatable thing for these managers and that they would, at the first opportunity which presents itself, take such action as will destroy that organization, that power, that factor, which proposes to discuss with them, or as they would put it, "dictate it to them the conditions, wages, hours, and other conditions of employment."

The Company evidently is going subtly to work about this, depending upon the weakness of men to follow their impulses, rather than what cool and deliberate judgment prompts and what will secure the best possible results for all. Bear in mind that the struggle of labor is not only justice that we must have on our side, but we must have the power to enforce justice. That power comes to labor only when properly organized and prepared to either command the respect of the employers or to excite their fear of a greater financial loss in refusing, than conceding justice to Labor.

After all, it is a matter of organization, of power, of preparation and discipline. "Foaming with rage" is neither the expression or manifestation of judgment, coolness, deliberation, determination, or power. In fact, it is the very opposite. The organization of workers in trade unions does not lessen the enthusiasm for justice for the rights of labor. It does not lessen the feeling of wrong committed upon them, but it is manifested and expressed in a different manner. It means arriving at a result deliberately, calmly, confident that though one here and there is attacked and falls by the way, ultimate victory is ours.

It is evidently the purpose of the Companies you name, to irritate the union men and provoke them into a contest at this time. This would indicate that they are better prepared for a contest at this time than at any time within the near past and if this is so, then it is the exact time when it is the best policy to pocket the rage and indignation and bide your time when the corresponding position may be changed.

I once said and repeat here to you now that "it is a science not yet fully understood when to strike and particularly when *not* to strike." I should judge from the conditions you describe, that the latter alternative confronts your organization, your members today.

As President of your organization, it devolves upon you to see to it that the members do not allow their rage to get the better of cool judgment. It may be an unpopular thing for you to try and stem the tide and hold the men steady in their first devotion to the union, but this is a time in the history of your organization which puts you to the test whether you are made up of that stuff, which a man holding your responsible position, should be made of.

Most of us can organize men and earn their plaudits and if this were all for which we are active in the movement, this might be temporarily secure, but when an executive officer is himself swayed and influenced by the men who are foaming with rage, the organization will soon go. He will go down with them and he will be held responsible for the failure of the organization, the impotency of rage.

If, on the other hand, a man in a position such as you are today, will insist that the men act with a due regard for their present and immediate future interests, you may incur a wave of unpopularity just now, but you will stamp your individuality, your honesty of purpose, your wise counsel, so thoroughly upon the members of your organization, so that the time will not be distant when they will recognize your worth and have more confidence in you than ever before.

You have honored me by saying that I have at my command, the experience of years in the labor movement. In my life of just more than forty-six years, I have devoted more than thirty-two to the labor movement. I have seen all kinds of struggles, all sorts of phases in connection with the labor movement. You have asked that I speak plainly, to advise you from the result of the experience I have gained. These must stand for the plain, blunt manner in which I have addressed you. You know your organization is not bound by what I have written, you can follow your own volition. I at least have the consciousness of having given you the best thoughts I am capable of on a very trying situation and one which I am sure calls forth the highest characteristics and the nobility of our character, the steadfastness of our purposes to obtain justice and fair dealing to our fellow workers.[3]

Fraternally yours,   Saml Gompers.
Pres.   American Federation of Labor.

TLpS, reel 9, vol. 15, pp. 167-68, SG Letterbooks, DLC.

1. Robert ASKEW was president of the Northern Mineral Mine Workers' Progressive Union (NMMWPU) from 1895 to 1897.

2. The Northern Mineral MINE Workers' Progressive Union.

3. There was apparently no strike by NMMWPU members until Dec. 21, 1896, when workers at the Aragon Mine in Norway, Mich., struck for higher wages. The strike ended unsuccessfully in March 1897.

To Edward Hoffman

May 6th, [1896]

Mr. E. J. Hoffman,
Pres. Cream City Mirror Plate Co.,
Rockford, Ill.
Dear Sir:—

Your favor of the 1st inst. to hand and contents noted, and I have been advised of the trouble existing between your Company and your employes, which I am glad to learn has been adjusted.

There is a matter however, of which you speak and which, though adjusted, seems to me to have been founded upon a mistaken policy. You say that having found that some men shirked their work at times, as a consequence you introduced the "piece work system" and that you took the "scale on a basis of 500 feet for a day's work for five men, which they would have to turn out to make wages." I presume that you will see that the introduction of this new method was nothing more or less than the "task system," and either the one or the other is not only distasteful, but highly prejudicial to the best interests of industry and commerce and particularly so to the men employed. I can readily understand in such circumstances that the men object to the introduction of this system, though understanding the fact as you say, they would make good wages, under that system. I feel confident from the tone of your letter, that there is really no purpose on the part of your firm, to do the men an injury, but that the policy was mistaken, I [am equally sure. . . .] has been promulgated to that effect or not, an employer retains the right to discharge a man who does not perform a fair day's work. You can readily see then how non-essential it is to declare either for the piece work or task work system.

Of course it is often difficult to have our men present a matter of their grievances to their employers in "an intelligent and gentlemanly manner," but these traits you will bear in mind, are only the result of careful training and favorable circumstances surrounding the life of the laborer. It is expecting a great deal that all the workers shall be "intelligent and gentlemanly." When too frequently the effort made by them for self and mutual improvement, is antagonized most bitterly by too many employers and corporations.

It is certainly commendatory of your Company that during the hard times, it has not reduced wages when you say it had the favorable opportunity to do so, but I submit to your candid consideration the fact that because you were fair then, is hardly good ground for departing from that course and attempting to introduce a system of labor calculated to call out all that is mean and selfish in the worker and to debase him in his own estimation and in the estimation of his fellow workers, as well as to deteriorate his position. I feel sure that calm deliberation and for a moment putting yourself in their places, you will scarcely think their conduct unjust.

Your criticism is right when you say that "it is a mistake to suppose that labor unions are organized for the purpose of making their employers come to terms whether their demands for same are justified or not." Certainly a mistake may be made occasionally, but the history of the labor movement of recent years does not presuppose any such condition of affairs to exist. Your experience in the Glass Workers' Union and [mine] in all other organizations [of] labor, bear this out.

Hoping that the arrangements arrived at, by which the trouble was settled, may be mutually advantageous and satisfactory, I am,

Very truly yours,   Saml Gompers.
Pres.   American Federation of Labor.

TLpS, reel 9, vol. 15, pp. 176-78, SG Letterbooks, DLC.

To John Swift[1]

May 6th, 1896.

John Swift,
624 Twentieth Ave., South, Minneapolis, Minn.
Brown[2] twenty-nine Nicollet Avenue your city engaging men to take places striking railroad men Milwaukee.[3] Try prevent this.

Samuel Gompers.

TWpSr, reel 9, vol. 15, p. 154, SG Letterbooks, DLC.

1. John Swift was the AFL general organizer for Minneapolis.
2. J. C. Brown.
3. On May 4, 1896, Division 15, the Milwaukee local of the Amalgamated Association of Street Railway Employes of America (AASREA), struck against the Mil-

waukee Street Railway Co. The firm had refused to negotiate the union's demands for recognition, a wage increase, and the right of employees to buy their uniforms where they wished. The strikers boycotted the line until June 19, and remained out at least through the end of the year. SG reported in July that he, together with Wisconsin Governor William H. Upham, tried unsuccessfully to arrange a settlement by which the company would rehire the strikers, some 1,000 motormen, conductors, and electrical workers. In mid-October the AFL issued an appeal for financial aid on their behalf.

To L. H. McAtteer

May 8th, [1896]

Mr. L. H. McAtteer,
Rock Hill, S.C.
Dear Sir and Brother:—

Your favor of recent date came duly to hand and owing to my absence from the city on important work, I was unable to give it earlier attention. I regret to learn the awful condition, as you describe it, transpiring in the South, although I knew it to exist to a large extent. My trip South last year, gave me information on this score which I scarcely believed credible until my eyes witnessed the same. You are certainly deserving of the greatest possible credit for the disinterested interest you take in this matter and I only hope you will be successful in organizing our fellow workers, particularly of the textile industry. I learned recently that a successful effort was made at organizing the textile workers at Columbus, Ga. Perhaps a letter from you to Mr. W. H. Winn,[1] 438 Second Ave., Columbus, Ga., or D. G. Reid,[2] East 14th St., Columbus, Ga., would give you further information upon this move. I am sure if once taken hold of, it will spread with great enthusiasm and be taken up by our fellow workers.

It is simply something awful, yes criminal, to think of the cruelty and barbarism of working young and innocent children in the mills twelve and fifteen hours a day and these children at the tender ages of six or seven years. When I spoke of this while in the South, the press rather severely criticised me for my audacity to interfere with their conditions. I cared little, however, what they said for I knew I was right and would go right on. I bid you, as I know you will, do likewise, whether you are praised or condemned for your ways and actions. It is worthy the best effort of man to devote some of his time, effort, and ability to rescue these innocent children from the grasp of greedy corporations, whose only hope is in the salvation of the almighty dollar.

With this, I mail to you under another cover, a number of documents to which I invite your attention and which I hope will be of some assistance to you in furthering the good work of organization. Kindly let me hear from you as frequently as convenient. With every wish for success, I am,

Fraternally yours, Saml Gompers.
President   American Federation of Labor.

TLpS, reel 9, vol. 15, p. 205, SG Letterbooks, DLC.

1. William H. Winn, a Columbus, Ga., printer, served as secretary and treasurer of International Typographical Union 220 in 1895. In 1896 he received a commission as an AFL general organizer to assist in a drive to unionize southern textile workers; he continued as general organizer into the next decade.
2. Probably David G. Reed, a Columbus, Ga., factory worker.

To the Superintendent of the Big Four Railroad[1]

May 21st, [1896]

Supt. Big Four Railroad,
Indianapolis, Indiana.
Dear Sir:—

Having been a passenger on the train of your road, leaving Peoria to this city yesterday, I have a grievous complaint to make against the lack of consideration on the part of the management of your Company for its passengers. The train left Peoria a little after seven and reached this city a few minutes before three in the afternoon. This necessitates a traveler to take a very early breakfast and yet there is no stop made by your train to enable passengers to secure a mid-day meal or lunch. I doubt if less consideration would be shown to cattle. It is not my desire to call public attention to this matter, but I believe you should be made acquainted with what nearly all passengers expressed as an outrage.

Very respectfully yours,   Saml Gompers.

TLpS, reel 9, vol. 15, p. 291, SG Letterbooks, DLC.

1. The general superintendent of the Big Four—the Cleveland, Cincinnati, Chicago, and St. Louis Railway—was J. Q. Van Winkle.

To Thomas Tracy

May 21st. [1896]

Mr. Tom Tracey,
332 East 8th St., New York City.
My Dear Friend Tom:—

I learned from a mutual friend of ours, that you are spending a few days in New York City and he also advises me that you are angry at my abrupt departure from Boston. First let me say that you are aware of the fact that I had made arrangements to go to Roxbury and that it was already later than I had expected to leave the meeting[1] of the C.L.U. Of course there is no use my mincing matters. I felt very much chagrined, very much hurt. You know I told you before the meeting, that I would necessarily feel that way if I were compelled to leave Boston without this matter being adjusted and it would have been adjusted if you had followed the course of your consistent record as a trade unionist, instead of which you took the side of a sentimental regard for persons, rather than follow trade union law, trade union necessity. Of course I admire the quality of sentiment in you as well as I like it in any other man, but I was led to expect something more than sentiment from you when an urgent case demanded it. That I was hurt is unquestionably true. You assisted as much as any man in electing me to my office as President of the American Federation of Labor and when on an important mission in line with my duty and in line with straight trade unionism, you rendered that mission a failure. However, this thing is done and over. It is settled in a manner, credible to all parties concerned and in trade union lines, and I am sure that you and our friend O'Sullivan have brought about this adjustment and I see no reason why the same warm, cordial friendship should not prevail among us as it has for years, yes, since our acquaintance. I know [you] too well to believe for a moment that you harbor any resentment. I am sure that pique is not in my makeup and I therefore offer you my hand and say shake, and let that incident drop. I am sure I owe much to you and Jack, for the cordial treatment I have always received when in "Beantown," and I want you and Jack to feel the same way when you see me any where we meet. Why not call at my house while you are in New York? I am sure Mrs. Gompers will appreciate the call. My address is 308 East 125th St. When you go to Boston, I wish you would show this letter to Jack and say that

I want him to consider this letter applicable to him also. I would appreciate it very much if you should write to,

Yours sincerely,   Saml Gompers.
Pres.   American Federation of Labor.

TLpS, reel 341, vol. 356, p. 67, SG Letterbooks, DLC. Handwritten notation: "Pr."

1. See "To John O'Sullivan," Mar. 28, 1896, n. 2, above.

To James Kelly[1]

May 26th, [1896]

Mr. J. F. Kelly,
Secy. Natl. Brotherhood of Electrical Workers,[2]
904 Olive St., St. Louis, Mo.
Dear Sir and Brother:—

I presume that you are aware that the trade unions of Washington, D.C. having become thoroughly dissatisfied with the conditions prevailing in that city and particularly the machinations of the K. of L., recently were organized into a Central Labor Union by direction of the Executive Council and that body is now working under a charter from the A.F. of L.[3]

The old and almost defunct central body[4] having seen that nearly all the unions have left them and joined the new and affiliated C.L.U., are anxious that those good unions represented therein, should remain with them and thus retain an excuse for continued existence.

On the other hand, it would be of the utmost importance if your local union[5] could be induced to become attached to the new C.L.U. and the purpose of my writing is that you may use your good offices with your local in Washington, to the end that they may act consistent with trade union law and principle and in the interest of labor generally by becoming attached to the new C.L.U. I should say too, that in the old body, there is represented a seceding and a suspended local[6] from the Brotherhood of Carpenters and Joiners.

Sincerely hoping that you will see your way clear to comply with the request herein contained, feeling assured that it is in direct line with the interests of our movement, and with every wish for your success, I am,

Fraternally yours,   Saml Gompers.
Pres.   American Federation of Labor.

TLpS, reel 9, vol. 15, p. 323, SG Letterbooks, DLC.

1. James T. KELLY served as grand secretary-treasurer (1891-95) and grand secretary (1895-97) of the National Brotherhood of Electrical Workers of America (NBEWA). He edited the *Electrical Worker* from 1893 until 1897.

2. The National Brotherhood of ELECTRICAL Workers of America.

3. The Washington, D.C., Central Labor Union was formed in March 1896 and received a charter from the AFL the following month.

4. The Washington, D.C., Federation of Labor.

5. NBEWA 26.

6. Formerly Brotherhood of Carpenters and Joiners of America 1.

To John Lennon

June 2nd, [1896]

Mr. John B. Lennon,
Gen'l. Sec'y. Journeymen Tailors Natl. Union,
Bloomington, Ill.
Dear Sir and Brother:—

Your favor of the 28th ult., relative to the San Francisco tailors union[1] and the central body[2] of that city, came duly to hand and I feel confident that you have every desire to help the movement, nor can there be any question that the attitude you take is absolutely correct. However, I want to say that the writing of a letter at this time to San Francisco, may result in graver injury than at this moment can be foreseen. You know the throes through which the movement in San Francisco has gone in the last few months.[3] They have had a kind of movement, such as prevails among the New York Socialist party men and it required all the efforts of our fellow unionists to prevent the movement from being entirely disrupted and wrecked. Of course you are aware that I contributed something towards saving the day, but I am apprehensive that writing a letter now, just before this so-called Socialist Trade and Labor Alliance is about to hold its convention, would simply bring "grist to their mill." Of course with you, it is not a question of a few weeks, it is a matter of principle and also a matter of winning the opportunities for a better organization on the Pacific coast. Better work can be done in this direction after the first of July than between now and that date.

I am sure you will not attribute my attitude to timidity, but rather to caution and from the stand point of what is likely to accomplish best results for your National Union and the general labor movement.

With every good wish, I am,

Fraternally yours,   Samuel Gompers.
Pres.   American Federation of Labor.

TLpS, reel 9, vol. 15, p. 355, SG Letterbooks, DLC.

1. Probably the Journeymen Tailors' Protective and Benevolent Union.

2. The San Francisco Trades and Labor Council organized in 1892 and changed its name in 1893 to the San Francisco Labor Council (LC).

3. SLP supporters launched the San Francisco Central Trades and Labor Alliance on Mar. 15, 1896, as a result of differences with the leaders of the San Francisco LC over political action.

From Andrew Furuseth

Washington D.C. June 5. [18]96.

Dear Sir & Bro

Just a few words to let you know how the matter stands. Your eight hour bill was refered to a Subcommittee of which McCleary[1] of Minesota, our Proffesser, wer ja gar nichts von die Arbeiter frage wessen cann,[2] was chairman and there will be no favorable report this session, which is now drawing to a close. It may be in its death trows [throes] when you get this letter. The reason for the non action seems to be that it is deemed so farreaching that it would in reality cause an eight hour day throughout the Country. At any rate our freinds will not report it to the house this session and I believe that Phillips is the real cause of preventing an unfavorable report but that is mere rumour. Now I shall leave here in a few days and unless something turns up shall see you at Indianapolis.

Fraternally yours   A. Furuseth

ALS, National Seamen's Union Records, reel 142, frame 521, *AFL Records.*

1. James Thompson McCleary (1853-1924) was a Republican congressman from Minnesota (1893-1907).

2. "Who can't know anything about the labor question."

To Jennie Finnie

June 12th, [1896]

Miss Jennie Finnie,
Secy. Victor Trades Assembly,
Victor, Col.
Dear Sister: —

I am in receipt of a letter from the executive office of the Retail Clerks National Protective Association,[1] calling attention to the fact that a committee of citizens called upon your Trades Assembly at its last meeting, with the request that your Assembly should sanction the movement for the opening of the stores and business houses in your city on Sunday. I am asked my opinion upon the matter and in order that I may express it in a manner calculated to be most clear, I write direct to you and through you to your Trades Assembly.

In the first place let me say, that upon economic, social, as well as upon moral grounds, the request of the committee of business men is entirely unjustifiable and wrong in principle. The beasts of burden have their day of rest and recuperation and certainly what nature and nature's laws intended for them, can not be less so to civilized men.

If there were a great famine for food or the other necessities of life, for the people of your city, to work almost incessantly would be justifiable; but in our day when the earth yields up its fruit in abundance, when the laborer is more than a hundred fold more productive than was his father, [when,] with [the aid of the latest improved machinery and tools of labor, with steam and electricity applied to] wealth's production, when the steamship and the railroad rush from one end to the other of our country and of the world, it does seem beyond reason that any one should make a request by which the toiling masses or any portion of them, be required to toil seven days of the week.

So sure as the stores and business houses are open seven days in the week, just so sure will the seven days work week become the general rule among our fellow workers, and just so sure will larger numbers of workmen become unemployed by reason of the extra labor required of those who are over-employed. This will mean not seven days pay for seven days work, but will mean seven days work for six days pay and less.

The whole history of the labor movement is replete with the evidence that when the hours of labor or the days of labor are increased, wages are reduced and on the other hand, a reduction in the hours of labor has always produced higher wages, better conditions, better surroundings, better homes, better citizens, better fathers, better husbands, better men.

The request made by the committee of citizens to your Trades Assembly, is an insult to your intelligence. It is an infringement upon your rights and ought to be rejected with the scorn and contempt it deserves. Stand by your organization, stand by your principles. Reduce the hours of your labor and the labor of your fellow workers. Relieve the burdens of your fellow workers, find work for the unemployed and the day of labor's disenthrallment from injustice and wrong will soon be at hand.

Fraternally yours, Saml Gompers.
Pres. American Federation of Labor.

TLpS, reel 9, vol. 15, pp. 408-9, SG Letterbooks, DLC.

1. The Retail CLERKS' National Protective Association of America.

To Samuel J.,[1] Sophia Dampf,[2] and Florence Gompers[3]

June 12th, [1896]

My Dear Children and Grandchild: —

I have your loving letter of the 8th inst., and hasten to answer it. I assure you that I regret to learn that both dear Sophia and darling baby are so ill and suffering. Of course the operation should be performed on Sophia's eye, but certainly every care ought to be exercised. I wonder when the family of Samuel J. Gompers & Co. will be out of the woods of illness and trouble. I hope however, that this will be the last and all will go better for the future. I think your move is one which will do you considerable good in becoming proficient on your instruments and I wish you every success in it.

You say that a member of Union 101 is publishing a paper[4] in the interests of the movement, but I have not yet seen a copy of it. Will you send me its name and place of publication? Upon receipt of this, you might also see the publisher and have him place our office on his list. I will gladly exchange with him. We are having the list of labor papers printed and I should like to enumerate his upon it.

In reference to the matter about which you inquire, I would say that an old gentleman by the name of John R. Vandervoort has documents which go to show that he is the real owner of the great estate of which Madam Jumel was possessed of when she died.[5] She left this to her son and he in turn assigned the property to his nephew, J. R. V. There has been a combination of possessors of this land which is worth millions and they, it is charged, have suborned judges, so that they are in possession of it and are keeping J. R. V. from the possession of his property. It is evident that they are considerably afraid of him, notwithstanding that he has little or no money. He spoke to me of this last year and I did not care to be bothered with it, since you know that I have no great desire for the possession of wealth. However, he has importuned me very much and while I have every belief that his statements are correct and that his papers are accurate, yet I do not underestimate the fact that the power which the possession of wealth gives, will overcome any question of right. It was for these reasons that I cared little about the matter at all. Of late, he has again addressed several letters to me and I thought it would not be amiss to have him make assignments of certain parts of the land to the members of our family and a number of our friends, they to form an association, have a good lawyer interested in the matter, give him possibly half interest in it, anything so long as he is reliable, have justice done this man and perhaps we be a part beneficiaries. I do not believe it would be wise for any or all of us to undertake any [great expense. If our family, or . . . a part of it . . .] it as fairly well explained as I know it.

I hope our darling baby is all right by this time and that her interesting chatter may soon again be sweet music to you.

With every wish for your success, happiness, and hoping to hear from you soon, I remain,

Your Dear Father and Grandfather. Saml Gompers.

TLpS, reel 341, vol. 356, pp. 69-70, SG Letterbooks, DLC. Handwritten notation: "Pr."

1. Samuel Julian GOMPERS, son of SG and Sophia Julian Gompers, was a member of International Typographical Union 101 of Washington, D.C.

2. Sophia Dampf GOMPERS was the wife of Samuel Julian Gompers.

3. Florence Gompers, born in 1892.

4. Probably the *Trade Unionist*, endorsed by the Washington, D.C., Central Labor Union and Building Trades Council.

5. Eliza B. Jumel, the widow of a wealthy New York City wine merchant, died in 1865 leaving a considerable estate. In 1873 George Washington Bowen, the illegitimate son of Mme. Jumel, unsuccessfully sued in an attempt to claim his mother's estate under an 1867 New York law. Upon Bowen's death the claim passed to his cousin, John Reuben Vandervoort. Vandervoort, a resident of Trenton, N.J., approached SG in 1894 for help in pursuing his claim to the Jumel estate, a tract of some thirty-two city lots. He proposed a joint effort to support his claim that would involve the transfer of some property to the AFL. SG informed him that because the AFL was not an incorporated body, it could hold no property. He suggested that Vandervoort "make

a man your heir whom you think would honestly dispose of the property in the interest of the organization" (SG to Vandervoort, Nov. 9, 1894, reel 8, vol. 11, p. 478, SG Letterbooks, DLC). SG, together with members of his family and a number of friends, subsequently formed an association to which Vandervoort deeded some property. By 1898, however, tiring of "the interminable legal meshes" into which the claim had fallen, SG offered to reconvey the deeds to Vandervoort, "desirous of washing my hands entirely of the affair" (SG to Vandervoort, Jan. 6, 1896, reel 9, vol. 14, p. 113, and July 22, 1898, reel 16, vol. 24, p. 298, ibid.).

To the Executive Council of the AFL

Indianapolis, Ind., June 13th, 1896.

To the Executive Council,
Colleagues: —

I herewith submit to you, a report of my actions during the trip[1] to Detroit, Cincinnati, Chicago and Cleveland.

I went to Detroit, per request of President Perkins of the Cigar Makers, with the view of endeavoring to effect settlement of the cigar makers' strike.[2] Had interviews with all manufacturers. Pres. Perkins and myself recommended to the strikers, a change of attack and to declare the strike off in all factories but one. The strikers voted by secret ballot 242 to 86 to continue on the same lines as heretofore. Their judgment may be at fault, but their energy and grit admirable.

At Cincinnati, the Central Labor Council had a demonstration and celebrated the tenth anniversary of the founding of the labor paper[3] of that city. The paper was started as a result of the eight hour movement of the German printers in 1886. There were fully 10.000 people at the celebration. I delivered an address to nearly 5000 in the open air at the Lagoon.

At Chicago, I had an interview with several active unionists and in the evening had a conference with the committee, representing the Trades & Labor Assembly and the Labor Congress. The matter of differences were entirely gone over and attempts to amalgamate [the] bodies on the terms of the agreement of the New York Convention,[4] were futile. I took notes of the evidence submitted. As a last resort, I secured the promise from both sides, that they would refer the question to their respective bodies, about resuming negotiations for amalgamation. I doubt if this will be successful however, since they are so widely apart. The feeling is not quite so bitter there against each other as it was some months ago, but the division does not seem as if it would be overcome of their own volition. Should they resume negotiations, the matter of proceeding under the alternative provision of the New York agreement will not be resorted to until failure to amalgamate is sure beyond peradventure.

At Cleveland, I attended the Convention of the Brotherhood of Boiler Makers & Iron Ship Builders and had the cordial co-operation and able assistance of Vice President O'Connell. We addressed the Convention and although up to this writing, not officially informed as to what action has been taken, I was assured beyond doubt of its affiliation.[5]

The machinists of Cleveland are on strike[6] and with Vice Pres. O'Connell, addressed them. We also held conferences with representative business men of Cleveland, with the object in view of adjusting the strike. Also addressed briefly the C.L.U. of that city.

The expenses of the trip to Detroit were borne by the cigar makers. Those to Cincinnati will, I believe, be borne by the C.L.C. the remainder falling upon the A.F. of L. In order to make the train connections and keep the engagements, the first of which came sudden, it was necessary to ride on the cars five nights out of the seven, but returned to the office and resumed duties there.

Fraternally submitted,   Saml Gompers.
Pres.   American Federation of Labor.

TLpS, AFL Executive Council Vote Books, reel 8, frame 152, *AFL Records.*

1. SG's trip to the Midwest lasted from June 4 until about June 10, 1896.

2. On June 4, 1895, CMIU 22 and 284 struck against eight Detroit firms that they charged used child and underpaid female labor to erode union wage rates. The walkout originally involved 384 men and women, 243 of whom were still on strike in September 1896.

3. The *Cincinnati Arbeiter-Zeitung.*

4. The AFL's 1895 convention endorsed an agreement by representatives from the Chicago Trade and Labor Assembly (TLA) and the Chicago Trade and Labor Congress (TLC) providing that the TLA should be the only central labor body in Chicago and should retain its AFL charter, but that it must adopt a new constitution and elect new officers. The new constitution was to make employers, persons not working at their trade, and political officeholders ineligible as delegates to the TLA. In the event that both the Chicago TLA and the Chicago TLC failed to ratify this agreement, the AFL Executive Council was to organize a new affiliated central body within three months and to revoke the current TLA charter. (See "An Interview in the *Chicago Tribune,*" Apr. 25, 1896, n. 6, above.) Efforts by SG to bring the two organizations together under the terms of this agreement broke down in September 1896, and SG convened a meeting of Chicago unions on Nov. 9 to organize a new central body. The AFL issued a charter for the Chicago Federation of Labor on Nov. 16; the new body adopted a constitution in December, and elected its first permanent officers in January 1897.

5. The Brotherhood of BOILER Makers and Iron Ship Builders of America held its convention in Cleveland, June 9-16, 1896. The delegates voted to affiliate with the AFL.

6. On May 24, 1896, the Brown Hoisting and Conveying Machine Co. of Cleveland locked out 800 employees, among them 208 machinists, over workers' demands for shorter hours, overtime pay, and union recognition. Together with the state board of arbitration, International Association of Machinists' President James O'Connell negotiated a settlement with the firm on July 27 that included extra pay for overtime, a Saturday half-holiday, formal grievance procedures, and the rehiring of locked-out union men. The men struck on July 31, however, claiming the firm had reneged on the agreement by not rehiring all union members. One of the strikers unsuccessfully sought injunctions against Cleveland's mayor for using the state militia to support the company and against the firm for arming its strikebreakers and violating the July 27 agreement. The strike apparently dissipated in the subsequent months.

To D. Douglas Wilson

June 16, [1896]

Private
Mr. Douglas Wilson,
330 Monroe Block, Chicago, Ill.
Dear Sir & Brother:—

Your favor of the 15th to hand and contents noted. In reply to your question I would say that I was badgered from morning until night with questions on politics and political parties, each of which I refused to express an opinion upon. While I expressed my admiration for the personality of Mr. Debbs, it seemed to me that it was a reflection upon the intelligence of the men of our movement to pay idolatrous worship to any man, and that certainly seemed to me to be the case with some of our unionists in Cleveland, and I so stated and it was published by the press of that city.[1] The reporter asked me who would be the candidate of the Peoples' Party and I said that I thought that Debs would be the logical candidate,[2] he asked further whether I thought he would make a good run and I answered that I thought he would make as good a run as any man on that ticket. This is about the sum and substance of the talk I had with the reporter, or rather upon the subject. I had made up my [mind to] remain as free as the air during this campaign and be most careful in my expressions yet I find myself quoted and questioned. Every man's word is exaggerated and distorted by the politician to the parties' ends. No man seems to be safe from them.[3]

Hoping this explanation will be satisfactory I remain,

Fraternally yours,   Saml Gompers.
Pres.   American Federation of Labor.

TLpS, reel 9, vol. 15, p. 435, SG Letterbooks, DLC.

1. SG apparently made the remark as part of his speech to the convention of the Brotherhood of Boiler Makers and Iron Ship Builders of America in Cleveland.

2. The 1896 People's party convention endorsed the presidential candidacy of Democrat William Jennings Bryan.

3. In a June 17, 1896, circular to AFL affiliates, SG disavowed newspaper reports that he had endorsed one of the contenders for the presidency. He warned unionists to regard the use of his name "coupled with either advice or urging the workers to vote for any particular candidate of *any* party for the office of president of the United States . . . as a falsehood, manufactured out of whole cloth" (*American Federationist* 3 [July 1896]: 105).

To Joseph Labadie[1]

Indianapolis, Ind., June 22, 1896.

Mr. Joseph A. Labadie,
Detroit, Mich.
Dear Friend Joe: —

I am in receipt of your favor of the 20th inst. the contents of which I note with great interest. Yes, it is true that the occurrences you mention are too frequent. In my case, however, I think that it is pardonable when the fact is taken into consideration that I usually make my arrangements following so closely upon each other, that I really have little or no time for social purposes in the places I go, except possibly at such unseasonable hours that I cannot ask any one to meet me. I seldom get through my work before very late at night, and then one cannot expect to put friends at such an inconvenience as to call at such times. However there is no question but that you are right, and if I can in the future so change my plans, I shall not so easily overlook the amenities of life by failing to meet old time comrades in the movement.

Should my local union honor me with a credential to the Cigar Makers convention,[2] I shall be at Detroit in September for about two weeks and then I shall try to make amends for seeming slights, and then of course I shall expect you and our friend Ogg[3] and a few of the old time coterie to give me some of your and their time.

I trust that the spirit will move you p.d.q. in order that you may be in the mood to write as per my request for the Federationist.

Hoping that you are enjoying good health, with kindest wishes and hoping to hear from you at your earliest convenience, I am,

Sincerely yours,   Saml Gompers.

Pres.   American Federation of Labor.

McCraith also sends good wishes and he is thinking up some notes.

TLS, Labadie Collection, MiU.

1. Joseph Antoine LABADIE, a labor journalist, was a founder and first president (1889-90) of the Michigan Federation of Labor. He was appointed clerk of the Detroit Water Works in 1893, a post he held until about 1920.

2. The CMIU convention met in Detroit, Sept. 28-Oct. 15, 1896; SG represented CMIU 144.

3. Robert Y. Ogg, a Detroit printer, had been a KOL officer and a member of the International Typographical Union. He became a clerk with the Detroit Board of Public Works in 1892, assistant collector of the Detroit Water Commission in 1896 and its assistant assessor in 1897, and secretary of the Board of Public Works in 1898. See also *The Early Years of the AFL*, p. 213, n. 4.

To Theodore Perry[1]

June 23, [1896]

Mr. Theo. Perry,
c/o Journal of Labor,
Nashville Tenn.

Dear Sir & Bro.:—

I beg to acknowledge receipt of your favor of the 18th inst. sent by yourself and a number of your colleagues. The contents of the letter have been given careful consideration and I am constrained to say that the attitude which has been assumed by both your Trades and Labor Council[2] and your Federal Labor union[3] is untenable, both from a standpoint of ethics, principle and interests of the trade union movement. The United States Marine band consists of enlisted soldiers; even though they are understood to be musicians, they are paid, clothed, and quartered by the people of the United States and receive a monthly salary, besides they are hired by private parties frequently to take the place of civilian musicians who are thus deprived of an opportunity of earning a livelihood, nor can the civilian enter into competition with the U.S. Marine Band for employment in consequence of the advantages which the latter have of which I have enumerated but few.

You say that the Musicians' Union both in your city and in other places have not always acted in the interests of [the] labor movement. I am not unmindful of the truth of this statement, but the simple fact that men will make mistakes against the interests of labor cannot in any way justify us in trying to make the mistake worse, or by our actions, do them an injury. In fact, as I understand it, the labor movement is in its nature an effort to overcome the shortsightedness of our less intelligent fellow workers and we cannot overcome or undo a wrong of theirs by committing a mistake or wrong ourselves. We have seen it in the case of labor troubles, where say, our street railroads, or our great railroads, where policemen have turned switches, have given instructions to ignorant men who have taken the places of our striking brothers, and yet they have not escaped our denunciation because the railroad organizations have thus far held aloof from the general labor movement. In both cases it is a question of employment, in both cases it is a question of principle, and I can very well see how pleased the Secretary of Navy[4] was when he secured the request from your Federal Labor Union for the U.S. Marine Band to officiate at the event of your Centennial celebration.[5] This document will, I am sure, be used not only for a particular instance, but in the future when there is any controversy the present incumbent or his successor will look upon it with satisfaction and justification for any occurrence that may be pursued relative to the Marine Band.

Relative to what you say was published in a Chicago paper of decided democratic tendencies and attributed to Mr. Hahn,[6] more than likely he may have expressed some indignation at the course pursued by your union, and that it may have been distorted into all conceivable shapes by the imagination and will of the reporter. I will say, that so far as he is concerned, he has in every convention of the National league urged an affiliation of that body with the A.F. of L. He is one of those who organized the national federation of musicians and applied to the A.F. of L. for a charter. I know him to be a thorough going union man and merely mention this, not in any defence of Mr. Hahn, but to convince you that he is not so ignorant of trade union principles as you convey in your letter.

In writing you as I have in my last as well as this, I know that what has been done cannot be undone, but I do hope that in the future that all of us may act upon the high ethical ground of trade union principles, though at times we may be deprived of a temporary pleasure and advantage. With every wish for success, believe me to be as ever,

Sincerely yours,   Saml Gompers.
Pres.   American Federation of Labor.

TLpS, reel 9, vol. 15, pp. 476-77, SG Letterbooks, DLC.

1. Theodore Perry was a Nashville printer and treasurer of International Typographical Union 20.

2. The Nashville Trades and Labor Council was organized in 1896 and was chartered by the AFL in September of that year.

3. Possibly AFL Federal Labor Union 6617, chartered in January 1896.

4. Hilary A. Herbert (1834-1919), a Democratic congressman from Alabama from 1877 to 1893, was secretary of the navy from 1893 to 1897.

5. The 1896 Tennessee statehood centennial.

6. Charles F. Hahn was secretary of AFL Chicago Musical Society 5484.

To Frank Weber[1]

June 24, [1896]

F. J. Weber,
966 10th St., Milwaukee, Wis.
Dear Sir & Bro.:—

Your favor of the 18th inst. to hand and contents noted with very great interest. Relative to what you say of the Building Trades Council,[2] I would say that so far no charter has been issued to such body although several applications have been made. It has been the policy not to grant such charters, but as to the wisdom of that action I am not sure. It is more than likely that some action will be taken at the next convention of the A.F. of L. I know the arguments that will be adduced against such a step. They are briefly, that that would bring triple or quadruple representation at the conventions. First through the local unions, then through the national or international, then through the central body, then through the Building Trades Council. Then again if the charter is issued to the Building Trades Council, the allied Printing Trade Council may make the same demand and the Metal Trades Council, etc. etc. I believe however, that the convention should definitely decide upon questions of this character and it will be made a subject of my report.[3] I note what you say relative to the formation of federal labor unions by the anti-unionists for the purpose of seeking representation at the conventions and either control or ruin the A.F. of L. I thank you for the timely warning and assure you that I am keeping a pretty good watch on current events. I wish you would keep me advised on this line of the development of the matter in your city.

The newspaper dispatches of Saturday reported the strike and boycott declared off and a letter of the same date from President Mahon says that the fight is yet being carried on with determination. Will you give me some information on this point. With very best wishes for success and hoping to hear from you soon, I am,

Sincerely yours,   Saml Gompers.

Pres.   American Federation of Labor.

TLpS, reel 9, vol. 15, p. 489-90, SG Letterbooks, DLC.

1. Frank Joseph WEBER, a Milwaukee sailor, was the chief officer of the Wisconsin State Federation of Labor from 1893 to 1917 and an AFL organizer.

2. The Milwaukee Building Trades Council was organized in 1895 and affiliated with the National Building Trades Council of America, an independent body established by union organizations in the building trades. In 1907 it joined the Milwaukee Federated Trades Council, an AFL affiliate.

3. SG made no mention of this matter in his report to the 1896 AFL convention.

A Circular

Indianapolis, June 27, 1896.

TRADE UNIONS AND PARTY POLITICS.

To Affiliated Unions—

Greeting:

We will soon be in the throes of a political campaign.[1] The passions of men will be sought to be aroused, their prejudices and supposed ignorance played upon and brought into action. The partisan zealot, the political mountebank, the statesman for revenue only, as well as the effervescent, bucolic political party, cure-all sophist and fakir, will be rampant. The dear workingman and his interests will be the theme of all alike, who really seek party advantage and success, though civilization fail, labor be crushed and relapse in barbarism be the result.

We are on the eve of events which will place our members, our unions and our entire movement to a most critical test, a test which may mean either a partial dissolution of our organizations, or their growth, extension and development. It is because of the great trust committed to my care that a timely word of advice and warning is given lest our members be taken unawares, fail to profit by the experience of labor organizations which have weathered the storms, and those others whose only evidence of former greatness or existence are their epitaphs, folly, blunders, calamities. "Learn to see in another's calamity the ills which you should avoid" is a maxim which Syrus declared more than nineteen hundred years ago, and it is as applicable to our times as it was when first penned.

Whatever labor secures now or secured in the past is due to the efforts of the workers themselves in their own organization—the trade unions on trade union lines, on trade union action. When in previous years the workers were either unorganized or poorly organized, the political trickster scarcely ever gave a second thought to the Dear Workingman and his interests. During the periods of fair or blossoming organization the political soothsayers attempted by cajolery and baiting to work their influence into the labor organizations; to commit them to either one party or another.

There are many organizations which may declare that their unions are safe from such influences, and, lulled into a fancied security, permit the virus of political partisanship to be injected into their very being; laying their unions liable to the most malignant diseases of division, antagonism and disruption. Bear in mind that the modern political party freebooter finds his prototype in the one who "For ways that are dark and for tricks that are vain the heathen (political) Chinee is peculiar."

The movement of labor now is growing stronger day by day. It is becoming more far-reaching than at any time within the history of our country. Each city, town and village now has its unions of labor. The time is coming, if we but meet the intruder at the doors of our meeting rooms, compel him to turn about and take his departure, when there will be few if any of our fellow toilers outside the beneficent influence of organized labor.

The industrial field is littered with more corpses of organizations destroyed by the damning influences of partisan political action than from all other causes combined. Nor must it be at all lost sight of that this does not only apply to local or national trade unions, but also to previous efforts of labor at national federation. The National Labor Union, in its time a great federation, after it committed itself to political partisan action, went to the limbo of movements which no longer moved. After that act it acted no more. No convention of that organization was ever after held.

In the light of that experience, the American Federation of Labor has always declared and maintained that the unions of labor are above, and should be beyond, the power and influence of political parties. It was with these great object lessons still dangling before our vision, like the famous writing on the wall, or like the sword of Damocles hanging over our heads by a single thread, which, severed by a failure to profit by past experience, may leave us headless, and the whole body of organized labor bleeding to death, a hapless victim to our folly, serfs or slaves to the cupidity of corporate monopolistic greed, that the American Federation of Labor at its last convention resolved that

"Party politics, whether they be democratic, republican, socialistic, populistic, prohibition, or any other, shall have no place in the conventions of the American Federation of Labor."

This action, while it directly decrees the course for the conventions of the American Federation of Labor, is also a declaration of policy and principle, and hence applies equally to all affiliated organizations.

The power of the trade unions is extending to all classes and influencing public sympathy and public judgment. Let us build up our organizations upon a solid basis as of adamant, that they may endure for all time; that they may be our protectors, our defenders, in our struggle for justice and right; that we may turn to them in the hour of our trials with the confidence of our manhood maintained, and in the hour of our triumphs to pay them the meed of praise and glory of victories won, men, women and children saved, our civilization and emancipation assured.

Let the watchword be: No political party domination over the trade unions; no political party influence over trade union action.

Long live the trade union! Long live the American Federation of Labor!

> Fraternally yours, Samuel Gompers,
> President American Federation of Labor.

American Federationist 3 (Aug. 1896): 129-30.

1. A reference to the presidential campaign of 1896 in which William McKinley, who ran on the Republican ticket, defeated William Jennings Bryan, the nominee of the Democratic and People's parties.

From Horace Eaton[1]

General Secretary.
Boot and Shoe Workers Union
Boston, Mass. June 29 1896

Dear Sir & Bro

Our late convention[2] has so entirely absorbed my time that I now have the first opportunity of answering your letter of June 13th.[3]

The "Fraternal" did not present himself at our convention a sin of omission which for many reasons I very much regret.

I quote from your letter the following—:

"The position the B. & S.W.U. is now in is exactly that of many other National trade unions of a few years ago, that too tried to work together on progressive lines with men who call themselves socialists but who use that term as a cloak for their iniquity and treacherous conduct to the best interests of Labor."

I take exception to the above statement in its unqualified application to socialists in the trade union movement.

As for myself I am a trade unionist first last and all the time but being a *free silverite* and approving the stand taken by the A.F. of L. convention on that question of political economy,[4] I trust I am liberal enough to grant the same rights to those who may differ with me and who may with equal sincerity advocate other legislation reforms.

I hold that if organized labor is to contend successfully with the forces of organized capital, it must bring to bear at the ballot box that same unity of action that is characteristic of its efforts in trade disputes, to the end that the law making powers may be used in our favor instead of in favor of our enemies.

Realizing that the organized labor movement in its present weak condition with only a small part of the workers organized, is not strong enough to wrest the law making powers from the hands of our oppressors, and feeling also that it is among the possibilities that the political movement for the emancipation of labor is not yet born, I am entirely opposed to any attempt to commit the movement to partisan politics, but do not believe we should refrain from expressing our approval of economic principles which are valuable as educational factors and which may be considered without engulfing ourselves in the quagmire of partisan politics.

This being my position I have charity for all who are sincere no matter what they may advocate provided they are loyal trade unionists.

If they are not loyal trade unionists no one is more ready than I to condemn their action no matter what school of economics they may represent.

We have in our organization many socialists radicals and conservatives. The brainiest and brightest among them are loyal to this union and to the A.F. of L. and entirely opposed to the S.T. & L.A. of the U.S. & C.[5]

One of the delegates[6] from Rochester N.Y. to our late convention goes to N.Y. city to the S.L.P. Convention to oppose the policy of the "union wreckers" and to bolt the party if that policy is endorsed. Such sincere and consistent trade union socialists as these, and there are many of them, should at this time recieve sympathetic support and encouragement and not wholesale condemnation.

It is always my purpose to consider these matters impartially and without prejudice.

With due respect to yourself personally and to your official position I fear that your past experience has biassed your judgement as evidenced in the quotation from your letter.

Since our organization started in the spring of '95 it has been a *trade union* movement. As soon as it was considered to be good policy it joined the A.F. of L. and has been and is now loyal to that body and desires that all organized labor shall be affiliated therewith.

In proof of the above I shall take pleasure in sending you a copy of the proceedings of our late convention as soon as printed.

Our membership like that of all other National organizations embraces members of all shades of opinion political or otherwise; they pay the bills and are entitled to all the protection and cooperative assistance they pay for, and for other organizations affiliated with us in the A.F. of L. or for any individual officer or member to be lukewarm in the support of our cause and our label because of the mere fact that we have socialists in or at the head of our organization is a rank injustice on our membership including those who are not socialists and who are in a great majority as well as a violation of all of the basic principles and laws of the A.F.L.

I have had reason to beleive that we have received very indifferent support in some sections because of the reason above stated.

I hope in the near future to be able to view the matter differently.

In Rochester N.Y. our locals withdrew from the chartered central body as I am informed because the central body did not enforce one of the provisions of its constitution and not with any desire to oppose the A.F. of L. as I think you will see when their side of the case is presented to you.

As a sample of the work done with intent to injure our organization and to victimize some of its members I inclose clipping from Rochester paper which is said to have emanated from a Mr. Wright[7] a member of the "Typo's" and also M.W. of the K. of L. District Assembly[8] in Rochester. It is an article that misrepresents in every line and is particularly unjust to Sieverman who is as stanch a trade unionist as he is a socialist and who assured me yesterday that our locals in R.— would go back to the central body soon. There will be no "Rupture."

In Lynn we have a contest with the last remnant of the K. of L. in our trade and in the central body[9] we have found a majority of the delegates from the carpenters,[10] printers,[11] Moulders[12] and machinists[13] voting with the K. of L. and against us on nearly every question that affected our interests.

With our own large representation the united support of the cigar makers[14] (whom we have ever found loyal) and the scattering delegates from the other trades that were true to the cause we were able to beat them until finally 3662 K. of L.[15] withdrew from the CLU and soon after the Carpenters Union #108 also withdrew and it is rumored that others are to follow in order to break up the C.L.U.

K. of L. leaders go into shoe stores and tell the dealers they will not buy shoes bearing our label and delegates from Typos, vote to back them up in their fight against us not withstanding the Typos got an advance of $2.00 per week for every man in the office in Lynn where our work is done and solely on account of our work as a written acknowledgment from their Sec[16] now in my possession will show.

We are good fighters have beaten them so far and will in the future. Our present plan is to have the C.L.U. take out a charter in the A.F. of L. and then put the Carpenters and others to the test and see where they stand.

This would mean a new A.F. of L. central body the transfer of a K. of L. assembly of coal handlers[17] to the A.F. of L. and possibly later might bring the local organization of street R. Employes into the A.F. of L. and we hope also would in time make Lynn a powerful "Federation" city.

In closing permit me to say that at all times we stand ready to advance the interests of the A.F. of L., not one of our locals is attached to DeLeon's side show and not one to our knowledge is working against the interest of any body affiliated with us in the A.F. of L.

It is on behalf of the membership of an organization that can show this clean record, that I feel warranted in addressing you in this way asking you to use your influence to remove any false impressions that may exist, to bring to the support of this union that undivided support of the A.F. of L. to which it is entitled, and to do justice to its members.

If you will consider those frank expressions that appear to criticize, to be prompted by my earnestness in the cause and not by any motives of a personal nature you will greatly oblige

Fraternally Yours   Horace M. Eaton.[18]

ALS, Boot and Shoe Workers' International Union Records, reel 139, frames 35-46, *AFL Records.*

1. Horace M. EATON was general secretary and treasurer of the Boot and Shoe Workers' Union (BSWU) from 1895 to 1902.

2. The BSWU met in convention at Boston, June 15-19, 1896.

3. SG to Eaton, June 13, 1896, reel 9, vol. 15, p. 420, SG Letterbooks, DLC.

4. The 1895 AFL convention passed a resolution reaffirming the Federation's endorsement of the free and unlimited coinage of silver at 16 to 1. It provided that copies of the resolution be sent to the president and to the chairmen of the House and Senate finance committees.

5. The Socialist Trade and Labor Alliance of the United States and Canada (STLA).

6. At the 1896 SLP convention Frank A. Sieverman, secretary of BSWU 46 (Lasters) of Rochester, N.Y., opposed the party's endorsement of the STLA; Daniel DeLeon

consequently condemned him as a traitor. By 1900 Sieverman had gone into business as a shoe merchant. In 1904 he was again associated with the BSWU as an organizer.

7. Charles H. Wright, a Rochester newspaper reporter, was a leader in International Typographical Union (ITU) 15 of Rochester. In 1896 he was master workman of KOL District Assembly (DA) 36.

8. KOL DA 36.

9. The Lynn (Mass.) Central Labor Union, formed at least as early as 1890, received an AFL charter in September 1896.

10. United Brotherhood of Carpenters and Joiners of America 108.

11. Probably ITU 120.

12. Iron and Brass Molders' 103, the Lynn local of the Iron Molders' Union of North America.

13. Probably International Association of Machinists' Lodge 334.

14. CMIU 65.

15. KOL Boot and Shoe Cutters' Local Assembly 3662.

16. George L. Bray was a Lynn stenographer.

17. Lynn coal handlers affiliated with the AFL as local 6852 in February 1897.

18. Responding to Eaton, SG wrote that he was not opposed to socialists per se, but to those such as Daniel DeLeon and the members of the STLA. He maintained that trade unionism could comfortably embrace both radicals and conservatives, and stressed the labor movement's need to shun attachment to any political party while exercising the vote in its self-interest.

From John O'Sullivan

President.
Central Labor Union
Boston, Mass., June 29th, 1896

Dear Sam: —

We are to have the question of the withdrawal of all organizations, not affiliated with their National unions,[1] up at our next meeting and I want some information as to the position taken by the Ex. Council on the matter.

It is being maintained by the Street car men's[2] officers, that they are a Federal union and hence they are not compelled to join the Amalgamated association of Street r'y employes. In their arguments against getting out of this union, they offer that if they were required to do so, their charter would be revoked by the AF of L and as that has not been done they make the claim that the opposition to their seating in this union comes from personal opposition to them.

They further claim that so long as they pay per cap tax to the AF of L they are in good standing and there are those who believe this to be a correct position. I am glad to say that we have only two organizations in the CLU that are not affiliated with their national unions—these are the street car men (FLU 2873) and the clothing cutters and trimmers union. I personally attended the last meeting of the car men and urged them to apply for membership in their national organization explaining to them our position if they did not do so. Tom Tracy was present and also urged them to do so. It develops now that the circular which Sec. O'Donnell[3] sent them bearing upon this matter and explaining that we would have to drop them, was never read to the members of the union and Mr. Patrick Duggan,[4] one of the officers of the union [says] that he never knew such a notice was sent to their organization and that he never misses a meeting of either his union or its executive council.

He naturally was indignant that he was kept in the dark about this whole matter, and says there are other officers in the same fix.

On this account there has sprung up a good deal of feeling against Sec. Ratigan,[5] and I am blamed for it because I called the attention of the members to this. Of course I am leading the fight for their withdrawal and it now looks like a personal quarrel, but I think you know me well enough to know that friend or foe it would be just the same, and who would lead the fight if I did not?

The secretary says the reason he did not bring the matter before [the] union was that there was not a quorum present at the meeting, but they passed motions there just the same and one of these motions was to invite J F O'Sullivan to address the meeting.

The union is [in a] horrible condition numerically and any one who dares to criticise the secretary is called an APA. This has disgusted the membership so that their meetings are poorly attended and instead of having 3000 on the books, I am told they have but about 150.

Some of the best men in the union are calling for a new organization but we don't like to form a new one while this one is recognised in the CLU and even then our organizing committee will go slow about doing this.

Ratigan was at the Denver convention, as you will remember and it was agreed there that his union would go into the National organization.

He feels sore against the national union for some reason or other, and is very unfair in his criticism of it, misrepresenting it at the meeting at which I spoke.

Now Does the Federation now recognise the union as a trade union, and if it does not, will you please say so over your signature, or will you explain explicitly just what relation the union bears to the AF of L?[6] I want this stated without any question of a doubt, for whether it is for or against our position, I mean to read it at the next meeting of the CLU before action is taken.

The six months will have been up before we meet again and the question will come up at our next meeting, for a protest against the further recognition of the union is to be made, by a temperance crank who objects to one of its members holding the office of the Vice pres. of the body while working, temporarily as a bar tender.

Do you regard the Silver question as a political party question, and if so where are we at having adopted a resolution on this matter at the conventions of the Federation?

I haven't worried you for some time, so thought you might think I was not on earth and that I would drop you a line upon this matter. Best wishes to Gus.

Sincerely Yours   John F. O'Sullivan
Pres

Mary is improving rapidly, you will be glad to know. Geo Schilling[7] called to day. He only remains here for a day.

Sincerely yours,   Jack

Mary sends love The Angel kid[8] is fine and grows more and more like Gus.

T and ALS, Street Car Employes' Association Records, reel 142, frames 752-54, *AFL Records.*

1. A resolution of the 1895 AFL convention required all AFL state federations and city central bodies to insist that affiliated unions join the respective national or international unions of their trades within six months of Jan. 1, 1896, or face suspension.

2. AFL Conductors' and Motormen's Union 3873 of Boston, chartered in 1889.

3. Edward O'Donnell was secretary of the Boston Central Labor Union and a member of International Typographical Union 13 of Boston.

4. Probably Patrick W. Duggan, a Roxbury, Mass., motorman.

5. James H. Ratigan was secretary of AFL 3873 of Boston.

6. AFL 3873 had long refused to affiliate with the Amalgamated Association of Street Railway Employes of America (AASREA), and on July 2, 1896, AASREA president W. D. Mahon asked SG to enforce the AFL convention's resolution banning independent unions from AFL city central bodies. SG wrote James Ratigan on July 3, urging his union to join the AASREA. He sent a copy of this letter to John O'Sullivan the same day, requesting him to encourage the local's officers to comply. On July 13, after the Boston union had again refused to affiliate, SG ordered it to surrender its charter.

7. George Adam SCHILLING, a Chicago cooper, served as commissioner of the Illinois Bureau of Labor Statistics from 1893 until 1897.

8. Probably Kenney O'Sullivan, John and Mary O'Sullivan's son, born in 1895.

Edward Boyce[1] to August McCraith

Office of Western Federation of Miners[2]
Butte, Montana, June 30. 1896.

August McCraith,
Indianapolis Indiana.
Dear Sir:

Yours of the 22. inst to hand and contents noted. In regard to our standing as an organization we are only in our infancy, we are only three years old on the 19th of May 96; there is fifty two unions in the Federation from the following states Colorado 20. Montana 14 [12?]. Idaho 10. Nevada 3. S. Dakota 3. Utah 3. Arizona 1.

Our last report showed 10.000. members in good standing but we confidently hope that by our next annual Convention,[3] to be held in Salt Lake City on the second monday in may to double that number.

This is the first time that they officers devoted all their time to the office to which they have been elected, or recieved any salary, other than what each convention paid the Secretary; the slump in Silver was a very sever blow to our organization, men were compelled to leave their homes in Silver producing districts, and engage in other business, thus our organization lost the best portion of its members, for a time: however most of them is again returning to the mining industry in new fields and doing splendid work for the organization where it was practically unknown.

Our prospect for the future is very encouraging, Every thing between the Nation body and locals is harmonious infact I never saw a body of men so interested in organized labor, every member trying to assit all he can.

I enclose you P.O. Order for charter, and will forward per capita tax upon receipt of same.

We have not been able to collect any statistic's up to this time owing to imperfict condition of the Organization.

Fraternally yours.   Edward Boyce.

ALS, AFL-CIO Charter Files, Inactive, International Union of Mine, Mill, and Smelter Workers' Records, George Meany Memorial Archives, Silver Spring, Md.

1. Edward BOYCE was president of the Western Federation of Miners (WFM) from 1896 to 1902.

2. The Western Federation of MINERS.

3. The 1896 WFM convention met in Denver, May 11-19.

To Eva McDonald Valesh

July 13, [1896]

Mrs. Eva McDonald Valesh,
Minneapolis, Minn.
My dear friend:—

Your favor of the 1st inst. came duly to hand but I have been out of the city for more than a week, among the mineral miners of Northern Michigan, down at Negaunee, Ishpeming, and Iron Mountain, and only on my return did I see your welcome letter, and now take first opportunity of replying. I, too, regard it as a mistake that our Friend Strasser did not attend the German Trade Union Congress, but you know that his connection with the labor movement has not brought him financial advantage, and he wrote me that it was impossible to go there and remain four months in Europe at his own expense in waiting to attend as a delegate to the convention of the British Trade Union Congress at Edinburgh.[1] I felt, too, that while we should like to have had him there, the Federation could not afford the expense of keeping him there that length of time. Even the progressive attitude towards trade unionism which the German Congress took would have been much more advanced had he been there. His individuality and character would have stamped itself upon the Congress, but there is no use fretting about matters which cannot be remedied.

Yes, I remember to whom you refer as the lady who always keeps our friend Von Elm in sight. Her name is Mrs. Steinbach. In my judgment, too, it is an ill-assorted companionship. She seems entirely enamoured of him and his talents, and I wonder sometimes, that a man of his disposition should at all find geniality or pleasure in her company. I knew him well when he was in this country, and when I met him in Hamburg, and found him the same staunch and true trade unionist, I was more than pleased to meet him. I presume that he mentioned to you that I addressed a number of German working men in the language of their country, and though by no means a German linguist, he flattered me by saying that I acquitted myself creditably and with honor to our cause. Of course, I am pleased to learn of his good opinion of me.

With this, I mail you a copy of the July Federationist. You will see both your article[2] in it, and also one from Miss Emily Greene Balch,[3] contributing an article on the German Trades Union Congress. While it is not exactly what I wanted, yet it is better than entirely ignoring the subject. I will say that the receipt for check was not enclosed, as you said. Unless you have sent one to Bro. McCraith, kindly make out another and forward it. (Just informed you sent receipt.) It is, indeed, a pleasure to me to learn that though like Macawber, you have been waiting for "something to turn up," you are somewhat more fortunate than he, that it has partially turned up, and I can only hope that the future may be bright for both you, Frank, and Frank, Jr. Frank making cigars must be quite a novelty to him and a sight fit for the Gods. Has he been elected delegate to Detroit?[4] I think it will please you to know that not withstanding the fact that I have been absent from New York these several months, Union #144 has honored me with an election as one of its delegates, and gave me thirty-nine votes more than any of the other candidates. It is indeed gratifying, and shows that the Union is not so forgetful of the men who have tried to perform their duty by them. It rather disproves the old maxim of "out of sight, out of mind." I feel really proud of this election; more so, than of many other incidents which have occurred in my connection with the movement.

I was sure you would be pleased with Mrs. Gompers' photo, and she took especial pride in having it forwarded to you.

In reference to the matter you spoke of, Mr. Swift, —[5] I will make further inquiries and do as the best interests of our movement warrant.

While I was in Northern Michigan among the iron miners, they requested me to come for their Labor Day demonstration but I convinced them of your ability to fill the bill. They thought that by my talk, I was a pretty good judge, and they authorized me to ask you to come to Norway, Michigan. It is but a two hour's ride from Lake Superior, and they will be willing to pay your expenses, and of course, give you a honorarium for your services. I trust that you will accept the invitation which they extend through me. They are most interesting people and full of energy, earnestness and enthusiasm. There is to be a joint demonstration of the iron ore workers and mineral miners at that place. I am sure you will make a hit with them, and at the same time, you will gain valuable information, which may be of service to you in your literary work. If you accept, and I wish you would, kindly communicate with Mr. Daniel Bjork,[6] Box 304, Norway, Mich., and also please advise me. Will write again to-morrow.

With kindest love and good wishes to you and Frank and the boy, I am,

Sincerely yours,   Saml Gompers.

TLpS, reel 9, vol. 15, pp. 566-67, SG Letterbooks, DLC.

1. The TUC met at Edinburgh, Sept. 7-12, 1896.

2. "Conditions of Labor in Europe," *American Federationist* 3 (July 1896): 83-85.

3. Emily Greene Balch, "German Trades Union Congress," *American Federationist* 3 (July 1896): 86-87. Balch was an economist, pacifist, and social reformer, and was a cofounder in 1902 of the Boston Women's Trade Union League.

4. Frank Valesh was not a delegate to the 1896 CMIU convention.

5. Probably John Swift, an AFL organizer in Minneapolis.

6. Daniel Bjork immigrated to the United States from Sweden in 1887. By the turn of the century he was a confectioner in Norway, Mich.

An Excerpt from an Article in the
Rocky Mountain News

[July 13, 1896]

GOMPERS AND GOLDBUGS

The meeting of the Denver Trades and Labor assembly was proceeding with more than usual quietness and celerity yesterday, even for a time when no election was on the programme, when a circular[1] was read from Samuel Gompers, president of the American Federation of Labor. John Bramwood,[2] who had just been relieved of his duties as president, was immediately on the floor, and with an intense irony moved that 5,000 copies of the letter be ordered printed and sent over the West to show what a master of language Mr. Gompers was. In two seconds the air was sizzling, as nearly every delegate wanted a whack at Gompers.

The letter was a most intricately worded one, abounding in rounded periods and allusions to the classics, and its substance was to entreat all labor bodies owing allegiance to the American Federation of Labor to avoid partisan politics.

After Bramwood had fired off some hot crackers, using words nearly as lengthy and sounding as those in the letter, Roady Kenehan[3] moved that the circular letter be returned to Mr. Gompers with the request that he send out copies of the free silver resolution[4] adopted at the last meetings of the federation.

Bramwood moved that the language and sentiment of Gompers' letter be condemned, and in doing so made another fiery address. He accused Mr. Gompers of being a McKinley goldbug and being in the employ of the money power to misrepresent the working men. The letter, he declared, was a rhetorical effort to blind the silver men of the West and keep them out of politics while he (Gompers) tried to disseminate goldbug opinions among the workers of the East.

Mr. Kenehan suggested that the assembly should not be too hasty, but Hamilton Armstrong, Andrew Chalmers,[5] Frank W. Lee[6] and other delegates severely condemned the federation president, all declaring they believed that he was in the employ of the gold power. Hamilton Armstrong told that, when he was in the East, he asked Gompers what 150,000 circulars setting forth the action of the Federation of Labor on the silver question would cost. "Mr. Gompers," said Armstrong, "said he would print them for $1,100, and I told him a few things about himself." Derisive laughter followed this statement, and Mr. Lee asked: "Did you pay him the $1,100?" "Certainly not." "Well, don't this circular show where he got the $1,100?"

IN TOUCH WITH PLATT.[7]

Continuing, Mr. Armstrong said that when in New York Mr. Gompers introduced him to numerous public men, "and the first of them," said Armstrong, "was the great Republican boss, T. C. Platt." Mr. Gompers' honesty was assailed and with the strong showing made by Mr. Armstrong, who was on the committee that reported him a defaulter to the federation.

C. W. Rhodes[8] and C. L. Merritt endeavored to still the troubled sea. Mr. Rhodes disagreed with Mr. Gompers and thought he was working for the money power rather than organized labor, but would not have the assembly lose its dignity. Mr. Merritt could see nothing in the letter but an ornate and wordy entreaty to unions to keep out of politics. This again brought out the storm, and a resolution was introduced asking Mr. Gompers to mind his own business. An amendment was offered requesting him to get out of politics before he was so free with his advice. Several speakers declared he was working for McKinley and the Republican party and endeavoring to neutralize the effect of the fight union labor was making for free silver.

Finally all amendments were voted down and following resolution passed:

Resolved, That the Denver Trades and Labor assembly condemn both the language of the letter of Samuel Gompers, president of the American Federation of Labor, and the sentiments expressed therein, and request him to publish to the world the free silver resolutions adopted by his body at its annual sessions.

. . .

Rocky Mountain News (Denver), July 13, 1896.

1. "A Circular," June 27, 1896, above.
2. John W. BRAMWOOD, a printer, was president of International Typographical Union (ITU) 49 of Denver from 1895 to 1896 and secretary-treasurer of the ITU from 1896 to 1908.

3. Roady KENEHAN, secretary-treasurer of the International Union of Journeymen Horseshoers of the United States and Canada (IUJH; before 1892 the Journeymen Horseshoers' National Union of the United States) from 1890 to 1910, represented IUJH 29 in the Denver Trades and Labor Assembly.

4. See "From Horace Eaton," June 29, 1896, above.

5. Andrew Chalmers was a Denver granite cutter.

6. Frank W. Lee was a Denver machinist and a member of the Executive Committee of the Colorado State Federation of Labor.

7. Thomas Collier Platt (1833-1910) was a New York state businessman and politician who served as a Republican in the U.S. House of Representatives (1873-77) and Senate (1881, 1897-1909).

8. Clarence W. Rhodes was a Denver printer and member of ITU 49.

To Samuel J. Gompers

July 14, [1896]

Mr. Samuel Gompers,
Washington, D.C.
My dear children:—

Your favor of the 6th inst. to hand and contents noted, and I am pleased to learn that some progress is being made in the health of the family, and trust that at this time, you are all enjoying the best of health, and that prosperity may attend your every action.

I do not think that you ought to allow yourself to be elected as president of the the C.L.U., with as little experience as you have in conducting the affairs of an organization. A friend would not have advised you to do a thing of this kind, and I am sure you know that Mr. Kennedy[1] does not wish you well. Nothing would give him greater pleasure than to try to show off on you. If you had had some experience in society affairs, I should say,—go right ahead, and even a little diffidence and retiring disposition would not hurt you then, but without the experience of even a membership on the floor of an organization, it is not the easiest thing to preside in dignity, and use prompt dispatch in business. Then, again, a lack of knowledge of Parliamentary rules, your enemies as well as mine, would take up in order to "put you in a hole." I am glad that you have seen through his wiles, and did not even nibble at his bait.

Our dear Florence must be all that your hearts can desire: vivacious, bright, laughing and happy. I would love to see her and you, too, and trust that I may have an opportunity soon. Will let you know later. I received a letter from home to-day, and all seemed to be getting along well, except that as I know, they are missing me more every day. Of course, that applies with greater force to me here, but I am doing the best I can and performing my duty as I see it. To-night, I leave for Streator, Ills., and shall be gone a few days. I feel that I am improving in strength and health, but would recuperate much faster, and do much better, were I able to get regular rest. Sleep and I are often strangers.

I am glad to learn that you are at last learning to play your banjo well. You do not say a word about how dear Sophia is progressing with her guitar.

I am in a very great hurry just now and cannot write more than to wish you the very best of everything.

Believe me as ever,

Your dear father,   Saml. Gompers

N.B. Write soon.

TLpSr, reel 9, vol. 15, p. 568, SG Letterbooks, DLC. Typed notation: "Dict. by S. G."

1. Probably John L. Kennedy (see *Unrest and Depression*, p. 120, n. 8), a Washington, D.C., journalist and member of International Typographical Union 101. In 1898 President William McKinley appointed him to the U.S. Industrial Commission.

To Charles Reichers

July 14, [1896]

Mr. Charles F. Reichers,
New York, N.Y.
Dear Friend:—

I write you on a personal matter and which I trust will not be a disagreeable mission for you to perform. You know that my boy[1] has been in his House now for more than a year and a half. There has been no promotion nor advancement scarcely in his position since then, although he feels that he has made decided improvements and enough to warrant a change in his condition in the establishment. He tells me that the cutting board is now vacant, and that if you were to see Mr. Rosenthal, no doubt he would give him the present chance. He is a young man now over twenty years of age and feels keenly that with the responsibility which rests on my shoulders, and also that with his advancing years, he should be enabled to not only look out for himself, but be more of a contributor to the family's support. You undoubtedly know that my illness has meant my getting into a debt of nearly $400, and then keeping up my establishment in New York makes my expenses pretty nearly what they were when I was at home, and my own maintenance here really reduces my salary fully $500 for the year, so that taking all in all, I am not occupying a beautiful bed of roses, financially considered. If you think you can do this for me, you know that I shall always esteem it a great favor, and appreciate it very highly.

Trusting that you may be able to see your way clear to do this for me, and with best wishes, I am,

Sincerely yours,   Saml. Gompers

TLpSr, reel 9, vol. 15, pp. 570-71, SG Letterbooks, DLC. Typed notation: "Dict. by S. G."

1. Abraham Julian GOMPERS, son of SG and Sophia Julian Gompers, was a cutter in the clothing industry.

To Abraham Gompers

July 14, [1896]

My dear son: —

Your favor just came to hand, and I am always more than pleased to hear from you. It has been such a long time since you have written. It is a pleasure to me to learn that the entire family are well, and that you are having as good a time as it is possible for you to have under the circumstances and my absence. Of course, I appreciate the fact that you feel my absence very much but you must bear in mind that I am here and alone; that this is by no means a pleasant life to lead; but I am engaged in a great work, and must perform what I regard as my duty to my fellow workers. I have written to our friend, Mr. Reichers,[1] and I am confident that if he can, he will do this service for you and me. I would suggest that you go to see him after receiving this letter, and say to him that I have asked you to call upon him, so that you could talk the matter over.

It is also a pleasure to me to learn that our Al[2] has at last found something to do, but you do not mention what it is. Let me know. I trust that it is something of advantage and which may prove permanent and successful. Mr. Vandavoort, in a letter to me, says that mother is not well. I hope that before this reaches you, she will have entirely recovered, and that she and Sadie are having a pleasant time in Brook[lyn].

That is the right course for you to pursue. Stand by the old Union, and do not allow the would-be union wreckers to take your interests or affections away from the true union of your trade. Perhaps, I may be enabled to come home in the early part of next month. At any rate, I shall try to, and then we may be enabled to spend a few days together.

Give my love to mother, Sadie, Sam, Rose and Al, and the entire family and friends, and accept the same for yourself. Write soon to your dear father,

Saml. Gompers

TLpSr, reel 341, vol. 356, pp. 75-76, SG Letterbooks, DLC. Typed notation: "Dict. by S. G."

1. See "To Charles Reichers," July 14, 1896, above.
2. Alexander Julian GOMPERS, son of SG and Sophia Julian Gompers, was a cigarmaker.

To H. Francis Perry[1]

July 16th, [1896]

Rev. H. Francis Perry,
Pastor Baptist Church,
Hyde Park, Mass.
Dear Sir:—

I am in receipt of your favor of the 8th inst.,[2] contents of which have been noted. The questions you propound require more than passing notice, and yet, to be answered accurately and fully, would demand more of my time than I have at my disposition just now. I would say, however, to your first question,—

"What reason would be given by your (my) associates who do not attend church, for their absence from church?"—

My associates would answer that the spirit now dominating our churches is no longer in touch with their hopes and aspirations; that the churches have no sympathy with the real causes of the misery or severe burdens which the workers have to bear; that the pastors and ministers have no conception of the workers' rights denied them and wrongs borne by them, or should they have the conception and knowledge, they have not the courage to publicly proclaim it from their pulpits; that the means and methods which my associates have by experience learned to be particularly successful in maintaining their rights and securing improved conditions, i.e., organization of the trade unions, have been generally frowned down upon with contempt, treated indifferently or openly antagonized by the ministers and the apparently staunch supporters of the church.

The church and the laborers have drifted apart, because the latter have always had their attention directed to the "sweet bye and bye," to the utter neglect of the conditions arising from the bitter now and now.

The reason my associates would further give for their non-attendance at church, would be that they have come to look upon the church and the ministry as the apologists and defenders of the wrongs committed against the interests of the people, simply because the perpetrators are the possessors of wealth, who manifest little fear that it will be more difficult for them to enter the kingdom of heaven than it is for a camel to pass through an eye of a needle; whose real God is the *almighty dollar* and who contribute a few of their idols to suborn the intellect and eloquence of the divines, and make even their otherwise generous hearts callous to the sufferings of the poor and struggling workers, so that they may use their exalted positions to discourage and discountenance all practical efforts of the toilers to lift themselves out of the slough of despondency and despair.

To your second question:—

"What remedies would you (I) propose to bring your (my) associates into closer touch with the church?"

I would say, a complete reversal of the present attitude as indicated in my answer to your first question, would be most likely productive of the results you desire.

It needs but casual observation to discern that the honorable exception to the ministry above enumerated, those men who preach from their pulpits and breathe with their every word, their sympathy with the great struggling masses of humanity, the wrongs and injustice from which labor suffers, their willingness to co-operate with and aid the workers to secure better conditions of labor; lesser hours of burdensome toil; more security in work; better remuneration while at work; removal of the onerous task of over employment from those who toil and to find an opportunity for employment for those who can find no work at all to do. These ministers of these churches you will find always interesting and not only interesting, but their churches filled with the workers who go to hear them. Who go to hear the ministers who preach the gospel in the spirit of Him and His Sermon on the Mount; who go to hear the ministers who have something to say and have the courage and manhood to say it, though it may offend the keen sensibilities of many pastors and many worshippers, so long as the best interests of the masses are subserved, their manhood and womanhood heightened and broadened; their hearts and minds touched to the core by deep and everlasting sympathy.

He who fails to sympathize with the movement of labor, he who complacently or indifferently contemplates the awful results of present economic and social conditions is not only the opponent of the best interests of the human family, but is *participas criminas* to all wrong inflicted upon the men and women of our time, the children of to-day, the manhood and womanhood of the future.

Very truly yours,   Saml Gompers.
President of the American Federation of Labor.

TLpS, reel 9, vol. 15, pp. 560-63, SG Letterbooks, DLC.

1. H. Francis Perry was subsequently minister of the Englewood Baptist Church of Chicago.

2. Perry sent a letter of inquiry to SG and other labor leaders and workingmen. It was reprinted, together with extracts of their replies, in his article "The Workingman's Alienation from the Church," *American Journal of Sociology* 4 (Mar. 1899): 621-29.

To Henry Rice[1]

July 20, [1896]

Mr. Henry Rice,
New York, N.Y.
Dear Sir: —

It is now nearly four months since I heard from you notwithstanding the fact that, at your request, I issued you credential in order to secure advertisements in the American Federationist. Although I have not written to you, I cannot say that the subject matter of your treatment of me has escaped my mind. Knowing well that you have been considerably engaged in work, and that when you work, you have a fair return from it, it seems to me that your oft repeated assertion to me that any to whom you owe money would always be paid, should have been some incentive to you to keep your word. I think the trouble has been that I have always treated you with too much consideration and have been last to lose confidence in you, and this treatment of you by me instead of earning the reward it should (your fair treatment of me), and your payment to me of the money you owe, has simply brought about your indifference, — yes, your positive ignoring of the claim I have upon you, the debt you owe. I cannot see how you can look an honest man in the face after the way you have utterly ignored your obligation. I once before told you that there was a limit to even my patience. I repeat it now, and assure you that I shall expect to hear from you in a substantial manner in a very short time.

Very respectfully yours, Saml Gompers.

TLpS, reel 341, vol. 356, p. 79, SG Letterbooks, DLC. Handwritten notation: "Pr. Bk."

1. Henry Rice, a New York City clerk and agent, was an advertising agent for the *American Federationist* and had use of SG's bank account. Rice used that privilege in late 1894 or early 1895 to finance the performance of a play, *The Weavers*, without SG's knowledge. In the process, he spent all of SG's savings—several hundred dollars—on the project, which subsequently failed. SG arranged with Rice to receive some of Rice's advertising commission income to repay the debt but thereafter found Rice's performance as a *Federationist* agent wanting in both energy and ethics.

To George McNeill

July 23, [1896]

Mr. George E McNeill,
Boston, Mass.
Dear friend: —

I do not know whether you receive the American Federationist regularly, and if you do, I presume that in your busy work-a-day life, you can give it but little attention. However, you may have seen since its publication, a number of articles[1] contributed by Fusitano Tokano, a Japanese, giving expression to excellent economic views, and a thorough believer in the trade union movement. In the current issue of the Federationist, I think I shall publish another article[2] just received from him upon the industrial development of Japan. He was in this country for several years and worked hard at manual labor in order to secure a collegiate education, particularly on economics. Columbia College laid the foundation, and I think that it is not boastful for me to say that I put the finishing touches to it, so that he now is a strong advocate of the trade union form of organization. So much am I and was I impressed with him, that before he left for Japan, nearly two years ago, I gave him a commission as organizer for his country. I am in constant correspondence with him, and within the last week, have received two letters from him at his Japanese home.

The burden of all this preamble is to the effect that he writes that in the development of the cotton industry, the same awful conditions are manifest as in the early history of the introduction of machinery in England and New England,—women and children working long hours of labor and at last, the conscience of the people becoming pricked, calls for some amelioration at the hands of the government. Mr. Tokona says that there are little girls of nine and ten years of age, who attend two mules for twelve or more hours a day. A Board of Health has made up an array of facts which is appalling; the Government has appointed a committee to recommend the necessary regulations or restrictions & our friend is anxious to have all the possible information he can obtain. He wants a copy of the laws of Massachusetts bearing upon the cotton operatives limiting the hours of labor and for sanitary conditions and inspection of the mills and their safety in case of fire. He also would like to have the history of the cotton spinners' struggle for the shorter work day in Massachusetts, and their present condition, and a copy of the Constitution and by-laws of the Cotton Mule Spinners' Association.

I earnestly hope that you will be enabled to furnish the desired information, and deem it of sufficient importance to comply not only in the interest of our Japanese workers, but the indirect influence it is bound to have upon the workers of our own country.

If you cannot furnish all the information, then as much of it as you can. Kindly communicate direct with Mr. F. Tokano, addressing him as follows,—

146 Higashi-Kata St., Komagome, Hongo, Tokio, Japan, and advise me in substance, what you have been able to do in the matter.

Hoping for an early reply, and with kindest regards, I am

Sincerely yours,   Saml Gompers.

Pres.   A.F. of L.

N.B. Have also just written to our friend Bob. Howard.[3]

Regards to Mrs McNiell.

T and ALpS, reel 9, vol. 15, pp. 663-64, SG Letterbooks, DLC.

1. "Labor Movement in Japan," *American Federationist* 1 (Oct. 1894): 163-66; "The Japanese Workers' Condition," ibid. 2 (Sept. 1895): 119-20; "Chinese Tailors' Strike in Shanghai," ibid. 3 (Mar. 1896): 5-6.

2. "Labor Problem in Japan," ibid. 3 (Sept. 1896): 133-35.

3. Robert HOWARD, a spinner, served as secretary of the Fall River (Mass.) Mule Spinners' Association from 1878 until 1897 and was an AFL organizer in the mid-1890s.

An Excerpt from an Article in the
Rocky Mountain News

[July 27, 1896]

. . .

GOMPERS HAS A KICK.

A communication[1] from President Samuel Gompers of the American Federation of Labor, in answer to the newspaper reports of the last meeting,[2] was objected to, but finally allowed to be read. He complained that great injustice had been done him by some of the members in their remarks, particularly the statements of J. W. Bramwood. Mr. Gompers called attention to the fact that the 16 to 1 circular[3] had been sent out under date of March 16, 1896. He also criticised Hamilton Armstrong, and denies that Gompers had ever introduced Armstrong to T. C. Platt. The further statement was made that Armstrong's charge with reference to a defalcation was untrue, and a strong plea for support was made. The letter was received and placed on file.

Mr. Bramwood defended his previous remarks, and said he had no doubt still that Gompers was in the employ of the money power. He declined to retract anything he had said about Mr. Gompers. The letter was ordered turned over to Mr. Bramwood and Mr. Armstrong for answer.

. . .

Rocky Mountain News (Denver), July 27, 1896.

1. SG to Harvey Schamel (secretary of the Denver Trades and Labor Assembly), July 21, 1896 (reel 9, vol. 15, pp. 649-53, SG Letterbooks, DLC).

2. Actually the meeting of July 12, 1896. (See "An Excerpt from an Article in the *Rocky Mountain News*," July 13, 1896, above.)

3. On Mar. 16, 1896, SG and AFL secretary August McCraith addressed a circular to all affiliates, calling their attention to the resolutions of three successive AFL conventions supporting the remonitization and free coinage of silver at 16 to 1. The circular requested the affiliates to send a copy of a resolution supporting this position to one of their U.S. senators and to Colorado Senator Henry M. Teller, a leading free silver advocate.

To Samuel Mitchell

July 29, [1896]

Mr. Sam Mitchell,
761 Third Ave., New York city.
My Dear Son:—
Your letter came duly to hand and contents noted, and I am more than pleased to learn that all the members of the family are well.

Enclosed, you will find duplicate of a letter[1] I have just sent to Mr. Vandervoort, and also the letter he sent you and the one he sent me. I presume the tone of the letter will not at all please him. If I ever had any desire to please him, that has ceased since he has assumed his patronizing air.

Our family and friends and their ancestors, have lived for many centuries without being land owners, and I presume the germ of our family will not become extinct if we surrender all further rights to the estate.

I presume that the letter I send you will meet the approval of all.

I am pleased to inform you that in consequence of business connected with our movement, I am undertaking a trip east, and shall arrive in New York on the evening of August 5th. Primarily, my work in New York city will be for the interests of the locked-out tailors.[2] I have written to Mr. Henry White, 28 Lafayette Place, that meetings may be arranged the 5th and 6th, during the evening, and the 7th, during the day.[3] Anything that I can do during that time will be gladly performed, for the tailors. On the evening of the 7th, I want to be at home, and then I should like to meet the members of the family and the friends.

I do not think it would be wise for you to have a regular or formal meeting of the Association[4] for that purpose. There will be a number of us present and we can have an informal talk without marring the pleasure of each other's company.

I have considerable work to do between now and my departure from here; hence, must be very brief. I shall have to visit — Brooklyn, N.Y.; Trenton, N.J.; go to Connecticut, a day or two; then to Syracuse, Buffalo, Sharon, Pa.; Columbus, O.; and to other places before returning here, so that you may see that although I may have the pleasure of being with you a few days, it will by no means be merely a trip for pleasure or rest, although the opportunity of meeting you all, will be compensating to the highest degree.

With love to you, Rose and the Darling Henrietta, I am your Dear Father

Saml Gompers.

T and ALpS, reel 341, vol. 356, p. 82, SG Letterbooks, DLC. Handwritten notation: "Pr. Bk."

1. SG to John R. Vandervoort, July 27, 1896, reel 341, vol. 356, p. 80, SG Letterbooks, DLC.

2. On July 22, 1896, between 10,000 and 12,000 New York City garment workers, including members of the Brotherhood of Tailors, a local affiliate of the United Garment Workers of America, struck manufacturers over the return of sweatshop conditions in the trade. The Clothing Contractors' Protective Association, repre-

senting subcontractors, initially joined with the Brotherhood to oppose cuts in the prices large firms paid subcontractors. This alliance soon broke down, however, and the strike evolved into a struggle between the subcontractors and the Brotherhood, with the union emerging victorious by the end of August.

3. July 28, 1896, reel 9, vol. 15, p. 707, SG Letterbooks, DLC.

4. See "To Samuel J., Sophia Dampf, and Florence Gompers," June 12, 1896, n. 5, above.

To John Lennon

July 30, [1896]

Mr. John B. Lennon,
Bloomington, Ills.
Dear Sir:—

Your favor of the 28th inst. to hand and contents noted. In reply, permit me to say that at present it is beyond my power to say whether a council meeting will be held previous to the convention. It will depend upon developments in the course of a month or so. One thing is sure, I cannot now positively assert whether there will be a meeting, and if there is one, when it will take place. I presume, however, that none will be held to interfere with the trip you contemplate making through Indiana shortly.

I will suggest the name of Mr. John Turner[1] for your Labor Day speaker. I have Mr. Turner's consent to assign him to any place for that day, and have written him to that effect to-day. He will communicate with you direct and you may rely upon his coming. He is the President of the London Shop Assistants' Union, which is the same as our retail clerks here. He is the gentleman who wrote the article, "A Peculiar Policy"[2] in the July Federationist. I feel confident that he will give satisfaction.

Many thanks for hints as to the political situation in Bloomington. I certainly agree with you as to the situation.

In the course of a few days, I shall leave here for a trip to Washington, Philadelphia, New York, Brooklyn, Patterson, Trenton, Syracuse, Buffalo, Sharon, Pa. and Columbus, O. I presume you saw that the tailors of New York, nearly 22,000, are on a strike. It is at their urgent request that I make a few addresses to the people and to help in the fight for a few days, that I undertake the trip, but I shall, at the same time, have the pleasure of being in the old home for a few days.

There is matter which I want to write to you about, for I think you should know it, and I prefer telling it to you myself than having it come to you in a garbled way.

I had some material, enough for a suit of clothes. You know that I am rooming with Mr. A. Lobenberg,[3] for five years, the organizer of the Retail Clerks National Association. He was one of the founders. Was a delegate to several of the A.F. of L. conventions, and a man who has lived here nearly forty years, on whose judgment in union matters, every one seems to rely. I asked him whether he could recommend me to some good tailor; a member of the Journeymen Tailors' Union of Indianapolis,[4] and one who could put the label of that organization on my suit. He made inquiries and reported to me in the evening that he knew of such a tailor, who would fill the bill entirely. The following morning, I took the material to the tailor; was introduced to him by Mr. Lobenberg, and he took my measure. I then asked him whether he was a union man; whether he could put the label on my clothes, to both of which questions, he answered affirmatively. The second day, in going there for a second measurement, before leaving, I remarked to Mr. Smith (that is the tailor's name) that he should positively not forget to put the label on the suit, and incidentally remarked that while other men might wear clothes without a label, I could not and would not. He assured me that it would be all right. The suit was brought to the office on the 3rd of July, within a few hours of my departure for Northern Michigan. The bill was presented to me; I paid it without a question, without having previously asked him what the cost would be. I expected to pay a union man's price for his work. Imagine my surprise after his departure. I put on the clothes, and upon examination, failed to find the label. Of course I thought it was a mistake or oversight in the haste to get the suit finished for me. I was very indignant, but went off on the trip with the new suit on. Had I had time to go to the house or send for another suit, I should not have worn the new one. Of course, I expected that on my return, the defect would be remedied. When word was sent over to the tailor, he said: — "Well, have Mr. Gompers send his suit over and I will fix that all right." Imagine my surprise when the suit was sent to me the second time with still no label in it, and then I learned the truth, — that he was a non-union tailor, and could not furnish the label. Mr. Christofferson,[5] Mr. Lobenberg and I, endeavored to take advantage of the situation for the purpose of persuading Mr. Smith to unionize his shop, but although we gave the matter several hours' attention, we were unsuccessful. In the presence of these gentlemen, Smith admitted what I said to him, but later, he said privately that he thought I meant the label with his name on it. You can readily understand how shallow this pretext is for I never would have said to him that I could not wear a suit without *his label* on it. I believe that there is some comment made on my conduct in this matter but the above is a true version of the whole matter, without coloring of any kind. I am conscious of having acted sincerely and consistently as a union man and one making a fight for union labelled work. There was no oversight or indifference on my part. It is a case of deception and imposition which could occur to any man, no matter how careful he might desire to be. It is now more than three weeks since this occurred, and I have not worn the suit since, although it is light and pleasant to wear, while I have nothing else but those garments which had to do service last winter.

Pardon my bothering you with a matter of this kind, but I thought it would be better to give you the story direct.

With best wishes to yourself and Mrs. Lennon, and hoping to hear from you soon, I am,

Sincerely yours, Saml Gompers.

TLpS, reel 10, vol. 16, pp. 5-7, SG Letterbooks, DLC.

1. John TURNER, of London, president of the United Shop Assistants' Union (after 1898 the National Union of Shop Assistants, Warehousemen, and Clerks), delivered a Labor Day address in Bloomington, Ill., during his tour of the United States in the summer and fall of 1896.
2. "A Peculiar Policy," *American Federationist* 3 (July 1896): 81-83.
3. Abraham B. Loebenberg, a retail clerk from Indianapolis, was a founder and leader of the Retail Clerks' National Protective Association of America.
4. Journeymen Tailors' Union of America (JTUA) 157.
5. Probably Elias S. Christopherson (variously Christophersen), a Rockford, Ill., tailor and JTUA organizer.

To Francis Thurber

July 31, [1896]

Mr. F. B Thurber,
148 Chambers St., New York City.
Dear Sir:—

I have your favor of the 23rd inst., and note with very great interest what you say relative to the money question. If you remember rightly, you will remember a statement that I made to you one evening last year, when I had the honor of dining at your house. It is to this effect, that the matters of the silver question and gold question are, in my judgment, both over-estimated in their importance, by the men who take the one or the other side. That the cause of our ills lies far deeper than the question of gold and silver.

Although in favor of bi-metallism, and I mean independently of any other nation, if necessary, I am of the same opinion as there expressed. Having said this much, I want you to believe me that I am seeking for the truth, and up to this time, I am certainly inclined to the opinion that the free coinage of silver would contribute to the improvement of the conditions of the real workers of the country. That it would not, as many would feign have us believe, cut the value of the dollar earned in two, but on the contrary, tend to make money cheaper, manhood dearer.

You say that you believe that with free coinage, "*another* panic is possible, which would throw great numbers out of employment which are now employed." Let me say that I concur with you in this view; that is, I do not believe that it would be a natural panic, but one created for a purpose and for its effect. In truth I am inclined to the belief that the moneyed interests of this country will precipitate a panic large or small, as the circumstances and conditions may demand in order that the present intelligent discussion of the question may be stopped and fright and panic held up to take its place.

You express no doubt that we would recover from the panic in time, and that "nothing can permanently stop the progress of this country." With this, I also agree, and taking into consideration the awful panics that have come upon our people, the terrible sufferings they have had to endure during these panics when gold was the single standard and silver demonetized as money, is it unfair to say that inasmuch as these panics come and go with periodical regularity that a new venture should be attempted, and that one which even as you express, we will "surely overcome," and which many believe, will have the effect of preventing so few of the people controlling its money, its medium of exchange, its means by which business is fairly and prosperously conducted.

I regret that I have not time to discuss this question at greater length. I have so much else to do that it is out of the question at this time.

I am confident that your attitude is what you believe to be the right one. I am sure that a very great majority of the organized workers of the country differ with you. In their belief, I am a sharer upon this subject.

With kindest wishes and regards for yourself, I am,

Yours very truly,   Saml Gompers

N.B. I will shortly be in N.Y. and if I can at all take the time from important engagements already made I shall be bold enough to call on you at your office.

S. G.

T and ALpS, reel 10, vol. 16, pp. 25-26, SG Letterbooks, DLC.

To the Members of the Brotherhood of Locomotive Firemen

[July 1896]

WHY AFFILIATE WITH THE FEDERATION?

To the Members of the Brotherhood of Locomotive Firemen:

When I ask why affiliate with the Federation? I have in mind the affiliation of the Brotherhood of Locomotive Firemen with the American Federation of Labor; and my answer to the question is in the affirmative, because it is right, because it is logical, because it is practical and must redound to the interests of the firemen, as well as all wage workers of the country.

Of course, in considering a step of such importance the members of the B. of L.F. would wish to see some good reasons adduced which will convince them that the course proposed is one calculated to advance and not injure their interests. I shall endeavor to give convincing proof for the belief I express. But before doing so, I prefer for the sake of convenience, as well as for a clearer conception of the subject, to answer some of the objections I know to exist among some members of the Brotherhood of Locomotive Firemen to affiliation.

The objections succinctly stated are:

First. — A close federation of railway labor organizations is essential, and that affiliation with the American Federation of Labor will defer the achievement of the first object.

Second. — Affiliation with the A.F. of L. would mean sympathetic strikes of firemen to enforce demands made by strikers of other trades, or to enforce boycotts, which may involve the abrogation of contracts of local lodges or the Brotherhood, as such may have with their employers.

Third. — The admission of the colored firemen of the South to membership in the B. of L.F. For the purpose of the clearest understanding I shall treat the objections in the order stated.

First—Is it at all likely that the affiliation of the B. of L.F. with the A.F. of L. would interfere with the federation of the railroad brotherhoods and orders? I am sure that to admit this would be to assert, because we have organized some members into our lodges or unions that, therefore, the effort to secure new members must be deferred or delayed. That because we can strengthen our workers in one particular trade or calling, that for that reason we cannot afford to strengthen it by taking the hand of fellowship offered by the organized workers of other trades and callings. That because we are strong in our own organization we shall weaken our position by allying ourselves with those who are equally organized, equally strongly intrenched.

Just as well might the individual workman contend that to organize with the other fellow workers of his trade, would weaken his position in any matter in which the interests of the workers and the employers may differ. The positions taken by the advocate of isolation of the labor organization when affiliation is necessary is just as fallacious and illogical as is the belief of isolation of the individual worker from his union, when organization is so essential to him in order to protect and further his and his fellow workers' interests.

In affiliation with the A.F. of L. the other organizations of labor would undoubtedly receive the support and strength that the prestige of the B. of L.F. can give, but the B. of L.F. would receive the assistance and support, the strength and prestige which the other affiliated organizations can and will surely give in return. Affiliation and non-affiliation presents the contrast between cohesion and repulsion, or between co-operation to aid each others' interests and indifference to each others' conditions. In a word the recognition of the true meaning of unionism versus non-unionism.

Second. — Does affiliation mean sympathetic strikes and sympathetic boycotts by which the lodge or the Brotherhood would violate contracts with their employers? I say no, emphatically no. The A.F. of L. has been in existence for nearly fifteen years, and in all that time it has never required any such action on the part of any affiliated organization. On the contrary, every expression, every declaration, every action has been in the direction by which organized workers have been urged to faithfully abide by agreements with employers. In well regulated trade organizations it is a matter of honor as well as of interests that contracts shall be observed. The sympathy of organized workers and affiliated organizations can be expressed and manifested by honorable and legal methods far better calculated to aid labor than by the enforced cessation of work involving violations of plighted faith and agreements.

Third. — Does the A.F. of L. compel its affiliated organizations to accept the colored workmen? I answer no! Decidedly no. No more than it compels organizations to accept Americans, Germans, Frenchmen, Englishmen, Irishmen, or even Hottentots.

What the A.F. of L. declares by its policy, [is] that [an] organization should not declare *against* accepting the colored man *because he is colored.* I am sure that if any man of the nationalities mentioned should ally himself with the employers as against the interest of the workers the B. of L.F. would reject his application for membership, regardless of how frantically he might wave the banner of his country. And yet, no one would think of declaring that "no American, no German, etc., shall become a member of this organization."

This is the attitude of the A.F. of L. on the color question. If a man or set of men array themselves for any cause against the interest of the workers their organizations have the right to say that their membership is barred. It should be at the wrong-doer against labor, it should not be a nationality or a race against whom the doors are barred.

The International Association of Machinists formerly had the "color line" provision in its constitution. It eliminated the objectionable declaration and became affiliated with the A.F. of L. Thus it will be seen that the I.A. of M. was relatively in exactly the same position on this question as the B. of L.F. is to-day. Yet, I venture to say, that any question, no matter how searching, directed to the officers of the I.A. of M. would bring forth the response that they are more than pleased with their affiliation, that their autonomy and independence is as fully recognized to-day as any time in the existence of their organization.

Thus then, the objections having been fairly met and answered I deem it necessary to say that inasmuch as the Brotherhood of Locomotive Firemen is about to hold its convention, the subject matter of its affiliation with the A.F. of L. should receive very earnest consideration of all the members in their meetings, so that the delegates to Galveston may be fully prepared to vote intelligently and I trust affirmatively upon this important subject.

Of course, it is well known that since 1881 the American Federation of Labor has endeavored to bring together the great national trades unions of America into intelligent, fraternal relations, to further and advance and protect the interest of the wage earners of America. With what success our efforts have been crowned is probably as well known to you as to myself, and needs but little, if any, mention in this article.

However, it will not be out of place for me to say that launching our Federation fifteen years ago, it was upon the troubled sea of industrial affairs, and following close upon a calamitous industrial crisis. There was much to discourage the efforts made, and many looked askance upon our project. They saw previous efforts made in this direction fail, and the path of federation strewn with corpses of the noblest thoughts and highest aspirations.

In building the basis of the American Federation of Labor, we laid the foundation stone which has proven to be almost magical in its advantages and permanency. In our declaration for the *autonomy* of the affiliated trades unions, we laid the corner stone upon which our organization rests, and from which, I am confident, it will never depart.

In the American Federation of Labor we endeavor to bring about a co-operative effort in order to advance the interest of the toiling masses, to bring to the aid of any organization engaged in dispute the practical sympathy and aid of their organized brothers and sisters of labor. It is an effort to accomplish the greatest good to all concerned without inflicting upon any the evil of governmental authority by any individual or any number of individuals.

In the face of antagonism of all kinds and from all sides, the A.F. of L. has steadily forged its way to the front, until to-day it stands out pre-eminently as the living, aggressive organized labor movement of our country, expressing the hopes and aspirations, the practical and ideal, to enforce the demands of the discontented workmen of America; to protest against unjust conditions of toil, so that all real reformers and thinkers now look to and place their confidence in its ability to accomplish the aims and purposes to which our general movement is devoted.

It aims to give intelligent expression to the yearnings of the weak, as well as the will of the strong. It creates a healthier public sentiment in the minds of the people. It helps to instill a broader view in the wage worker's mind as to his rights and duties, and with each step places the mile-stone behind us, inscribed with the progress made in the path of industrial and social reform. To aid in this work is the duty of every national and international trades union. To become affiliated with the American Federation of Labor is to manifest a duty which every trade union must readily recognize.

Let me assure you that in becoming a member of the American Federation of Labor, your organization surrenders no right it now enjoys, places itself in no position to lessen its power and influence.

We all maintain that it is the duty of the wage earner to join the union of his trade. We deem it wrong for a local union of that trade to remain outside of the national or international union of that trade, and I maintain that it is equally wrong for any brotherhood, national or international union to hold itself aloof from the family of trades unions in the American Federation of Labor.

It is true that single trades unions have been often beaten in pitched battles against superior forces of united capital, but such defeats are by no means disastrous; on the contrary, they are useful in calling the attention of the workers to the necessity of thorough organization, of the inevitable obligation of bringing the yet unorganized workers into the union, of uniting the hitherto disconnected local unions into national unions, and of effecting a yet higher unity by affiliation of all national and international unions in one grand federation, in which each and all trade organizations would be as distinct as the billows, yet one as the sea.

In the work of the organization of labor, the most energetic, wisest and devoted of us, when working individually, cannot hope to be successful, but by combining our efforts all may. And the combined action of all the unions when exerted in favor of any one union will certainly be more efficacious than the action of any union, no matter how powerful it may be, if exerted in favor of an unorganized or a partially organized mass.

The rapid and steady growth of the American Federation of Labor, arising from the affiliation of previously isolated, together with newly formed national unions; the establishment of local unions of various trades and callings where none before existed; the spontaneous formation of federal labor unions, composed of wage workers following various trades in places where there are too few persons employed at any particular one to allow the formation of local unions of those trades, thus furnishing valuable bodies of auxiliaries and recruits to existing unions upon change of abode, this steady growth is gratifying evidence of the appreciation of the toilers of this broad land of a form of general organization in harmony with their most cherished traditions, and in which each trade enjoys the most perfect liberty while securing the fullest advantages of united action.

Nor are the financial requirements of our affiliated organizations burdensome. The charter fee is but $5.00 for your Brotherhood and the per capita tax *one-fourth of a cent per month,* or in other words three cents per year. This does not mean $5.00 for each lodge, but for the Brotherhood entire, and the charter fee and the per capita tax being paid by the Brotherhood. Besides this, there is a provision made by which, with the consent of the affiliated organizations, an assessment of *two cents* per member may be levied, for *five* consecutive weeks. However, in the history of the A.F. of L. this has been levied but once. The financial contributions other than the per capita tax are generally of a voluntary character.

Perhaps there are other questions upon which the members of the B. of L.F. may desire further information, and to supply which it would not only be my pleasure but my duty, and for that purpose will gladly furnish printed matter and documents to any or all of your local divisions, that may request them.

Sincerely hoping that uninterrupted success may attend the future course of your grand organization, the Brotherhood of Locomotive Firemen; that this appeal for its fraternal affiliation with the great body of organized unionists may not go unheeded; that the Galveston convention will resolve to march shoulder to shoulder in affiliation with the greater body of workers under the banner of the American Federation of Labor.

I have the honor to subscribe myself,

Fraternally yours, Sam'l Gompers,
President American Federation of Labor.

Locomotive Firemen's Magazine 20 (July 1896): 64-67.

To George Perkins

Aug. 23, [1896]

Mr. George W. Perkins, Pres.,
Chicago, Ills.
Dear Sir: —

While in New York, I received your letter in reference to complaints you say were made through the recommendation of Mr. John Turner, because some say he claims to be or is charged with being an anarchist. Let me say that I know nothing as to that. He may or he may not be, for aught I know. I do know this that he is president of the London Shop Assistants' Association, which is another name for what we call the Retail Clerks Protective Union. The membership of the London Association is nigh upon three thousand. It is unnecessary for me to say how thoroughly conservative are the store clerks here, and they are no less nor no more so in London. It seems to me that if he has the confidence of his fellow-members, and that if they will elect him as their President, he ought to be a pretty good trade unionist. When he arrived in this country, the Boston C.L.U. recommended him. I received a letter from the organizer of Boston, in which it was said that he could do some good as a trade unionist. I gave him a letter of recommendation to the trade unionists of the country, not as an anarchist, but as a trade unionist. At a meeting he held in this city, I had the honor of presiding, and there was not one word which fell from his lips, from which one could detect anarchy. His lecture was on trade unionism, as true trade unionists understand it. Mr. Turner was not sent out by me or by any of the officers of the American Federation of Labor, nor at its expense. The only money he received from us was for an article he contributed for the American Federationist, which was published in the July issue, under the head of "A Peculiar Policy." I commend that article to your consideration, and I am inclined to think that you will not so widely disagree with him. On the contrary, I can find nothing in it to which I will not give my support. After all, it is the concern of no man what the belief of another is, whether he be Socialist, Anarchist, Prohibitionist, Republican, Democrat or Populist. What we, as trade unionists, set as a standard for a wage worker is,—are you a trade unionist? Are you true to your trade union? Do you regard your trade union as the first organization to which you owe allegiance? and these tests being answered in the affirmative, we will relegate all his other beliefs to himself and his conscience. I have no excuse to offer for recommending Mr. Turner to the fraternal consideration of the trade unionists of America. I believe him to be true to trade unions. With his other beliefs, if he has any, I have no concern. I think you will agree with me that this conclusion and stand is accurate.

Fraternally yours,   Saml Gompers.
President.   A.F of L

N.B. I learn that Monday's Chicago Record contains what purports to be an interview with me.[1] Will you try and get it for me and send it here in an envelope? Look out for Squibs in September Federationist,[2] which will be out in a few days.

S G

TLpS, reel 341, vol. 356, pp. 88-89, SG Letterbooks, DLC. Handwritten notation: *"official."*

1. "Gompers Speaks for Silver," *Chicago Record*, Aug. 24, 1896, reported SG's remarks in Indianapolis (*Indianapolis Sentinel*, Aug. 23) that as "a loyal union man" he would vote for free silver in the coming election and expected "a great many of the members" of the AFL would "feel obligated" to do likewise since the measure was one of the Federation's economic demands.

2. The September *Federationist* carried a brief account of Perkins's near-drowning in Lake Michigan on Aug. 16, 1896, and his rescue by James J. Linehan (*American Federationist* 3 [Sept. 1896]: 144).

From Erastus Peeke[1]

New York, Aug. 26th, 1896.

Dear Sir:—

Your valued favor of the 22nd inst.[2] to hand, and in reply to this beg to fully inform you of the matter which the writer desired to submit to your consideration.

Upon making due inquiry I ascertain that there is no Federation of Labor controlling the Liquor Trade, hence you are the party to be consulted.

The writer desires to bottle a whiskey, and put [it] on the market under your label with certain conditions. Providing sole control of the Brand, and label can be obtained with the sanction of your body, I will agree to handle a certain amount annually, and pay the American Federation of Labor a certain stated amount for each label used on each bottle. Further to agree to handle none but union bottles, cases, labels &c., and for this business of bottling, and casing, the goods to use none but Union help. Again, if this matter can be arranged through you, the business mentioned will in the aggregate do considerable, and will undoubtedly result in a large and continual income to your honorable body.

A personal interview would be much more desirable though if you can obtain an idea of what the writer requires by this letter, everything might be arranged by correspondence.

Should you agree that a personal interview would be of greater benefit, and you so inform me, I would be pleased to have the honor of calling upon you any time you should happen to be in the city, and so inform me.

Kindly address me personally in this matter.[3]

Awaiting the favor of your early reply, I beg to remain,

Yours very truly,   (Signed) E. C. B. Peeke.

TLpSr, AFL Executive Council Vote Books, reel 8, frame 167, *AFL Records.*

1. Erastus C. B. Peeke wrote on behalf of Cook and Bernheimer, a New York City distillery.

2. Reel 341, vol. 356, p. 87, SG Letterbooks, DLC.

3. SG agreed to furnish the labels after Peeke's employees organized and were chartered in January 1897 as AFL 6836, which meant that the whiskey itself—as well as its bottles, cases, etc.—would be union made.

To Daniel Harris

Aug. 27, [1896]

Mr. Daniel Harris,
New York, N.Y.
Dear Friend:—

Of course you understand that there will be quite a contest at the Detroit Convention against the trade union spirit and the trade union movement. The socialist party men have used the tactics of the "balance of power" to secure quite a representation at the Convention,— you know those tactics which they condemned in trade unionists when we proposed to secure labor legislation. Be that as it may, they have got quite a representation. I am informed that the delegates[1] from 141 are practically the same who attended the last convention of the international union, which by the vote for their officers, 141 stands for clear cut trade unionism. Yet, by mistake or misunderstanding, the delegates, to the last convention, of 141, voted in favor of the preamble committing the international union to socialist party doctrines. I think we ought to do what we possibly can to prevent so injurious a declaration from even standing the ghost of a chance of passing. For that reason, I would suggest the advisability of some of the members engaging the delegates in conversation and showing them in a clear way the injury which would result to our movement. You can look to every organization in the country which has committed itself to that policy and you will find it weak and impotent to do anything to defend, much less, advance the interests of its members or the crafts. Use your own discretion in the matter, but I should think it necessary that there should be more concert of action among the trade unionists than there has been heretofore. It is only by the persistency of the party socialists and the dependence of trade unionists upon the justice of their cause without agreeing upon policy or course of action, that has allowed these people to appear formidable in our ranks.

I hope that you are enjoying the best of health and that the same is true of our friends, to whom kindly remember me.

Hoping for success, and with kindest wishes that I may hear from you soon, I am,

Fraternally yours, Saml Gompers.

TLpS, reel 341, vol. 356, p. 90, SG Letterbooks, DLC. Handwritten notation: *"Private."*

1. The delegates to the 1896 CMIU convention from New York City CMIU 141 were I. Goldstein, Anton Krchov, Josef Wodika, and Karl Ransburg.

To William Stokes[1]

Aug. 27, [1896]

Mr. W. H. Stokes,
Muncie, Ind.
Dear Sir:—

Your favor of the 26th inst. came duly to hand, and contents noted. I should like to be in a position to answer your questions absolutely and accurately, but the Department of Labor Statistics and the Census Department[2] combined have thus far, been unable to ascertain even approximately the figures about which you inquire. Let me answer as nearly accurate as I can by saying that while I cannot give the percentage of skilled mechanics who are colored men, either in the North or the South, I do know that the percentage is very small. The reason there are not more colored skilled mechanics in the North than there are, is not because they are discriminated against but because of two reasons. One is, that to a very limited extent, do they at this time possess the required skill, and secondly, in too many cases, while our white fellow workers are engaged in disputes, making sacrifices, bearing the brunt of severe struggles to maintain the wages and conditions of labor, our fellow workers who are colored men, take the place of our victimized workers and help the monopolistic class to tear down comparatively fair conditions of labor and to fasten the shackles of servility upon the lives of the workers.

There are few instances that I know of where the colored workers are discriminated against by reason of their color. If workers will not organize to protect their own interests and the interests of their fellow workers, or if workers are so lost to their own self-respect and interests as to turn the weight of their influence on the side of the capitalists as against that of the workers, these men are the enemies of progress, regardless of whether they be white or black, Caucasian or Mongolian.

You are mistaken when you say that the colored men are in no union save the Barbers. The different unions of which a number of them are members are too numerous to mention in this letter. If you think I have not answered your questions fully write again but give a little more information as to yourself and the purpose of your questions.

Fraternally yours,   Saml Gompers.
President.

TLpS, reel 10, vol. 16, p. 129, SG Letterbooks, DLC.

1. William H. Stokes was a Muncie, Ind., barber.
2. The Census Office within the U.S. Department of the Interior.

To James O'Connell

Aug. 28, [1896]

Mr. James O'Connell, Vice-Pres.,
Chicago, Ills.
Dear Sir & Bro:—

I am in receipt of a letter from the officers of the Northern Mineral Mine Workers' Progressive Union, which is affiliated with the A.F. of L., requesting me to accompany Mr. Askew, President of the organization, in a visit to Mr. M. A. Hanna,[1] who, they say, is to be in Chicago in a short time. The object of the visit is to lay before Mr. Hanna, a number of grievances the men have who are employed in the mines owned by the Company, of which Mr. Hanna is President. I have written these officers,[2] that owing to a number of important engagements which will take me from headquarters, it is impossible for me to go to Chicago at this time. You are aware that this is no idle excuse. They have since asked that I write you with a view to your accompanying Pres. Askew in his mission. I do so, and if you can at all make it convenient, I should regard it as your duty to comply.[3]

Let me say that in my letter[4] to Mr. Mudge,[5] I called attention to the fact that while we hope that some good may be accomplished in the interest of the organization, and the men, as the result of such a call, we want it distinctly understood that no political or partisan capital is to be made out of the incident, and I am sure that it requires no reminder to you of that fact at my hands. I only state it here so that there need not be unnecessarily any compunction about the visit to a large employer of labor to secure advantage for union men, simply upon the grounds that that same employer occupies a conspicuous position in a political party.

Trusting that you may be enabled to comply with the request, I am,

Fraternally yours Saml Gompers.
President.

TLpS, reel 10, vol. 16, p. 143, SG Letterbooks, DLC.

1. Marcus A. Hanna (1837-1904) was an Ohio businessman and a Republican politician. Engaged in the coal and iron trade through his Cleveland firm, M. A. Hanna and Co., he also had interests in banking, newspaper publishing, and Cleveland street railways. In 1891 he became a political advisor to William McKinley, managing his successful Ohio gubernatorial campaign that year and McKinley's presidential campaign in 1896. Hanna served as a U.S. senator (1897-1904), was chairman (1901-3) of the Industrial Department of the National Civic Federation (NCF), and later president (1903-4) of the NCF.

2. SG to William Mudge, Aug. 18, 1896, reel 10, vol. 16, p. 142, SG Letterbooks, DLC.

3. Askew and O'Connell subsequently met with Hanna, apparently in early September 1896.

4. SG to William Mudge, Aug. 28, 1896, reel 10, vol. 16, p. 142, SG Letterbooks, DLC.

5. William MUDGE, a Negaunee, Mich., iron ore miner, was secretary of the Northern Mineral Mine Workers' Progressive Union (1895-97).

To Ernst Kurzenknabe[1]

Aug. 31, [1896]

Mr. E. Kurzenknabe,
St. Louis, Mo.
Dear Sir:—

I am in receipt of a letter from Dan Harris, Pres. of the N.Y. State Branch of the A.F. of L., in which he says:—

"There is only Ale and Porters' union[2] in Albany at the present time. The K. of L. Assembly[3] which had received a charter from the National Brewery Union[4] through the manipulations of Joseph Mansion,[5] has now really no existence at all. All breweries in Albany are now organized, which was not the case in the past. These Journeymen Brewers are, and always have been willing to affiliate with their national union, and if harmony prevails, I cannot see why they should be debarred except from prejudice on the part of some people. Cannot you intercede and have these people granted the charter to which they are entitled?[6] They number about 120 men and they include *all* the former members of the K. of L. Assembly. I hope you will interest yourself in this matter."

I cannot begin to tell you from how many sides this matter is being pushed and pressed by the trades unionists of the State of New York and also of Connecticut. It certainly ought to be settled, and I trust that it may be soon. In a letter received to-day from Mr. Philip Strong,[7] Gen. Secy. of the Coopers' International Union,[8] he enclosed a matter of charges brought by Local Union No. 7,[9] of the Coopers' International Union against L.A. 9426 and Unions 19 and 34[10] of the Brewery Workers, being a reflection on the jurisdiction of your national union. I enclose a copy of the same to you herein for your consideration. In Mr. Strong's letter, he says that the copy of the letter which I sent to him of Mr. Mansion, reflects the character of the man. That he has for years vented his miserable spite on the Coopers of Albany and vicinity. He says that he has letters in his possession of

1893 and 1894, written by Mansion, demanding that certain coopers be transferred into the Assembly of the K. of L., in which Mansion was master workman. That these members at the time belonged to Coopers L.A. 4333,[11] now Local Union No. 7. That Mansion's continued efforts to control them, brought them out of the K. of L. He says that No. 7 has been in existence for many years. That the X Rays is used by Mansion to abuse union men who do not wish to be subservient to him. He says too that Mansion's imagination serves him rather than facts in his attacks upon coopers, "Albany scabs." That Mansion has always tried to force L.U. No. 7 out of existence. Mr. Strong says that he has letters in his possession to substantiate the charges that L.A. 9426 Unions 19 and 34 take coopers into their membership.

You can readily see how this conflict of authority, this division of allegiance brings conflict and division of the organized workers of your own trade and I hope that soon the Gordion knot will be cut and this problem solved. Of course, I imagine that for a few weeks or months, you may have a fight on the other side, but with the decadence of the K. of L. and they are now almost totally extinguished as a labor organization, as well as the aggressive attitude of the trade unionists of Albany, Troy and of the rest of the country, will settle the trouble in pretty short order and to the advantage of your national union and the general labor movement.

Fraternally yours,   Saml Gompers.
Pres.   A.F. of L.

TLpS, reel 10, vol. 16, pp. 176-77, SG Letterbooks, DLC.

1. Ernst KURZENKNABE was national secretary of the National Union of the United Brewery Workmen of the United States (NUUBW) from 1888 to 1899.

2. The independent Ale and Porter Brewery Union 1.

3. Probably KOL Local Assembly (LA) 8546.

4. Probably NUUBW 19 (Ale and Porter Brewers), of Albany, N.Y.

5. Joseph R. Mansion, a Troy, N.Y., stovemounter and president of NUUBW 34, served as a secretary in the state factory inspector's office in Albany beginning about 1897. He was connected with KOL District Assembly (DA) 68 in the late 1880s and early 1890s, and with KOL DA 147 beginning in 1895.

6. Some time between September 1896 and September 1897, the remnants of NUUBW 19 merged with Ale and Porter Brewery Union 1 to become NUUBW 129.

7. Philip STRONG was general secretary of the Coopers' International Union of North America (CIUNA) from 1892 to about 1897.

8. The COOPERS' International Union of North America.

9. CIUNA 7 of Albany, N.Y.

10. NUUBW 34 (Ale and Porter Brewers) of Troy, N.Y.

11. KOL LA 4333 of Albany, N.Y.

To Louis Berliner

Sept. 3, [1896]

Mr. L. Berliner
728 Lexington Ave., Brooklyn, N.Y.
My dear friend Lew: —

Your favor of the 31st inst. to hand and contents noted. I am delighted to think that you had such a good time at the house and very much regret that I had not the opportunity of being with you. You know that when the chance offers, there is no one who appreciates fun and amusement more than I. After all with the hard work and serious side of life connected with our movement it is not amiss to take advantage of any opportunity which may arise to while away dull care and to rub off the rough edges of this struggling, seething world of labor. I read the clippings which you sent and also the Press, for which I thank you. There can be no question as to the ability with which that paper is edited but it is also true that at least now, it is on the wrong side of the fence, and so are you. I think you know me well enough to know that I am not partisan, but there are very many things which at this time should make every man who believes in improvement from progression rather than revolution as the result of misery and depravity; I say there is much that should make those who believe in the former, take a definite stand and fight for improvement to-day. However, I will not attempt to argue with you, for in your politics you are and always have been a "tindorfer." You remember you tried to defeat Einstein[1] by voting for Yahelka.[2] While I am dictating this, I am enjoying the pleasure of many reminiscences of the days when we were more often together, both in the shop and at our respective "mansions," particularly, the one you had where the landlord required you to pay $1.00 more because there was "a hole in the wall."

To be serious, let me say that I am glad to learn that your folks are all well, and trust that they may continue so. I want you to write that article for the Federationist. You need not [check?] yourself at all; just write freely, the same as if you were talking, and you will find that it will come quite readily to you. I regret that business is not better but hope that it will be soon.

With best wishes to yourself and all members of the family, believe me as ever,

Yours sincerely,   Saml Gompers

Write soon

T and ALpS, reel 341, vol. 356, p. 94, SG Letterbooks, DLC. Handwritten notation: "Pr Bk."

1. Edwin Einstein.
2. John Jahelka. See *Unrest and Depression*, p. 18, n. 5.

To James Linehan

Sept. 8, [1896]

Mr. James J. Linihan,
Dear friend Jim:—
Your letter of the 4th inst. to hand and contents noted. To each and every one of the counts in your indictment, I plead guilty but justification. In the first place, as the representative of the Windy City, you accorded me its freedom, hence, I come and go just as I feel like it without let or hindrance from a blooming Irishman, who, having failed to rule Ireland, settled in Chicago and proposes to rule America.

I have a positive grudge against you for saving the President of the Cigar Makers International Union. You probably had not time to think of the fact that I have been elected first vice-president of that organization, and if you had allowed him to have become poisoned by drinking too much water, I should have been his Constitutional successor. Can you blame me for my anger? I said it was bravery on your part. Now you can understand my grim humour. I am positively down on you and cannot for the life of me, think of a time when I shall forgive you for standing between me and my greatest ambition,— NIT.[1]

There have been so many proceedings of the Convention printed that we don't know what to do with them, and hence, it consequently follows that they're of so little value, that I did not wish to show such disregard to you by sending you a copy.

The same applies to the Federationists.

Oh, yes, Gus and I divided that fifty cents. You never need fear about that. You say, may his Satanic majesty whip me. If Perkins informs me right, you did not know what you were doing when you saved him except that you were between the devil and the deep sea; that you did not know where you would land. Let me relate to you a dream I had.

I dreamed that you were drowned, and at the gate of St. Peter announced yourself, when the wicket opened and you gave your name. It was closed again and your record looked up. The door opened and you were invited to step into the elevator. When you got in, you asked, "how far the elevator goes up." The reply came, "this elevator don't go up!"

When I awoke, I was sorry it was a dream.

In all candor, I want to say that I had but a few hours in Chicago, and expressed my desire to see you and really regretted that I did not have a chance, but I had to leave for headquarters that same evening. Those who saw me can tell you that I was so busy that I scarcely had time for meals during the day, and was on the go from the time of my reaching Chicago to the time of my departure.

I shall certainly send the printed matter as requested. Whenever I get a chance to come to Chicago, I do hope to have the pleasure of seeing you, which was denied me on this last trip.

Sincerely yours,   Saml Gompers.

TLpS, reel 10, vol. 16, pp. 247-48, SG Letterbooks, DLC.

1. An emphatic negative.

To Henry Rice

Sept. 9, [1896]

Mr. Henry Rice,
E. 114th St., New York City.
Dear Sir: —

I am in receipt of your favor of the 6th inst., contents of which are noted. I cannot say that it is at all reassuring, for as a matter of fact, you have kept me off on promises which have never been kept and deferred from one time to another [facing an?] obligation you undertook with me. I will not for the sake of this letter, doubt your statement that things are not as bright with you now as they should be, but I am positively aware that within this past year and a half, you have been employed and have had many an opportunity to make a payment if you were so inclined. It is simply that you thought more of an immediate pleasure or excitement than the payment of a debt not contracted upon a flimsy pretense but for actual cash money placed in your hands in a business way upon which you realized you were in a position to pay. You say that I speak in a way as if I doubted your honesty and that you intended to cheat me. I never like to use phrases that mean nothing nor to evade the plain meaning of my word. I say that you could have paid me considerably if you had been so inclined during the past year and a half. To say that I will see that the debt will be paid is simply to again indulge in promises which, though you intend to keep when you write the letters, pass out of your mind until you again possibly hear from me; in the interim again being careless of your obligations so long as your own present and immediate wishes are gratified. You know you have not treated me right and I too long made excuses to myself for your conduct. I say that even when things are only going fairly with you, you can, if you so determine, occasionally make payments. I trust you will do it; I expect you to do it, and show by your actions that you propose to keep your word.

With this, I mail to your address a number of Federationists which may be of service to you. I regret to learn that you are ill, and hope that you have recovered before this. Again I repeat, try to act squarely by one who has been your friend to the very last.

[Respectfully] yours,   Saml Gompers

TLpS, reel 341, vol. 356, p. 97, SG Letterbooks, DLC. Handwritten notation: "Pr Bk."

From Edward Lynch[1]

Meriden, Conn. Sep. 12th, 1896.

Dear Sir & Bro: —

I have just received a letter stating that a question of law or right has been left to you for a decision. The case is whether the International Polishers' organization[2] and the Stove Mounters[3] have a right to Boycott the product of the Detroit Stove works.[4]

The case is as follows. The Mounters in this firm were reduced in their wages. They would not stand the reduction and struck. The firm tried to fill their places and were succeeding. But when victory seemed to crown the company's efforts, they having the mounters' places almost filled, the Polishers struck, claiming that they could not do work for scabs. Their strike crippled the firm again. Since the polishers have struck they have been trying to fill the places of both polishers and mounters. The Iron Moulders have a Union[5] in Detroit, and members of that Union work in the Stove Shop. The Iron Moulders International Union will not allow their men to strike. They are doing work for scabs. The two International Unions whose men are on a strike have endorsed a boycott[6] on the product of this firm. The Iron Moulders International Union come to the assistance of the firm and declare that the Boycott is illegal. The claim been [being] that so long as Union men work in the firm a boycott cannot be placed. Now they have been pushing this matter in Cleveland. The agent there claims that if the Boycott is not removed he can not dispose of any stoves. The Iron Moulders International are fighting against it been [being] placed. They have therefore appealed to you for a final decision.

Now Brother Gompers this is a very important matter. At first thought it seems not very important, but by a close scrutiny of the matter it means either the destruction or the maintenance of the A.F. of L. There is no disputing the question but a firm can replace their old hands. The only thing they fear is a boycott. If you declared this one illegal in Detroit, because Iron Moulders are willing to assist at scabbing, all that any firm throughout this country got to do is organize a few of their men and the same obstacle will stand in the way. If that could be accomplished, you no doubt see what prestige the A.F. of L. would lose. We are organized to protect one another. That seems to me to be the fundamental principles of the Federation. If that is not so then Individual Unions are as good if not better that [than] by been [being] affiliated with the Federation. As International Unions not affiliated with the Federation we could order a strike when we felt aggrieved. Can it be possible that affiliation with the Federation denies us of this right?

The enemies of the Federation are all around. They could at a moment's notice organize a few socialists in any shop, and claim that they were Union Men. Your decision will then be thrust in the face of any committee that goes there, and firms that we have spent thousands of dollars in fighting will with the organizing of a few so-called scabs defeat our entire work.

The Iron Moulders think perhaps that they get a cinch on the Federation with their one hundred and fifty votes. That things will have to be decided in their favor or they will move. Remember it is the small organizations that are keeping them so numerically strong. If we decide to let them fight their own battles and when scabs fill their places, be content, and not strike, the Iron Moulders will soon be a thing of the past.

They have always maintained their contempt for those that were fighting for justice. Whenever the opportunity presented itself they have resorted to the same tactics they have in Detroit. The time is just now and here when we will show them that the intelligence of the American Federation of Labor do not all use rammers.

I know their past history. They always want others to assist them but they will assist nobody. We can retaliate, and if we are forced to do so the day is not far distant when one of the proudest organizations and best in this country will be rent assunder.

I have only striven to place this matter before you so as you will be prepared to give your decision. I know all that possibly can be done will be used to influence you to act in opposition to us. But I believe furthermore that your love and patriotism for the Federation of Labor will be above party prejudices and that those who are struggling for their rights will not by you be trampled on.

Allow me to remain,

Fraternally Yours,   Edward M. Lynch,
Int. Pres.   M.P.B.P. & B.U. of N.S.[A.]

TLS, Metal Trades' Records, reel 141, frames 249-52, *AFL Records.*

1. Edward J. LYNCH was president of the Metal Polishers', Buffers', Platers', and Brass Workers' Union of North America.

2. The METAL Polishers', Buffers', Platers', and Brass Workers' Union of North America (MPBPBW).

3. The STOVE Mounters' International Union (SMIU).

4. On May 26, 1896, the Detroit Stove Works locked out forty-eight members of Stove Mounters' Union 1 of the SMIU over a conflict involving the use of apprentices. On July 15 twenty-six members of Polishers' Union 1 of the MPBPBW walked out in sympathy. The mounters and polishers settled with the company on Sept. 15, agreeing to its work rules on condition that it dismiss nonunion workers hired during the dispute. Except for a few cases involving assistant foremen, the company complied.

5. Iron Molders' Union of North America 31.

6. The AFL Executive Council voted in August 1896 to endorse the boycott on the Detroit Stove Works.

From Henry Van Holland

Eastmans Company,
New York, Sept. 15/[18]96.

Dear Sir:—

We are just in receipt of your communication of the 8th inst.[1] and note complaint lodged with you from butchers[2] who were formerly in our employ, claiming that a most unjust, unreasonable and unnecessary reduction in wages was offered the cattle butchers, and, that in consequence of which they have been out on strike,[3] in the defense of the already scant wages paid them, since July 22nd. We beg to say that this is not so, that the skilled labor which we have on the plant are men who have been in our employ for a long while, and, as per copy of Pay-rolls which we enclose you, you will note that they are making more money and are better paid than they were previous to July 22nd. We had just completed alterations in our building, cutting down our killing beds from 33 to 15, and, as we are not doing the volume of business we were six months ago, found it necessary to reduce the number of laborers about 50%. You will note that the reduction in killing beds is a little more than 50%. Of course those who were shut out, or, those whom we were unable to employ, took it upon themselves to annoy us by saying that they were out on strike. The Central Labor Union harbored them without asking for any explanation. We are glad, however, that when it reached your office you gave us an opportunity to lay the facts before you.[4] We beg to call your attention to the fact that the Committee of Arbitration Commissioners for the State of New York waited upon us in regard to the rumored strike, but withdrew, deciding that there was nothing to arbitrate. In the Pay-rolls, copy of which we enclose you, you will find that the skilled laborers were paid $25.00 per week previous to July 22nd, since then we have been paying them 45 cents per hour, which you will also note averages $31.50 per man, so that, rather than decreasing their wages we have increased them, financially bettering the condition of the men.

Thanking you for your communication, we are,

Yours very truly,   Eastmans Company of New York,
Henry Van Holland
General Manager.[5]

TLS, Amalgamated Meat Cutters and Butcher Workmen of North America Records, reel 141, frames 208-9, *AFL Records.*

1. Reel 10, vol. 16, p. 238, SG Letterbooks, DLC.

2. The AFL chartered Cattle Butchers' Protective Union 6647 of New York City in February 1896.

3. On July 22, 1896, about 20 cattle butchers employed by the Eastmans Co., a dressed beef firm in New York City, struck against a reduction of wages. They were soon joined by 140 other butchers who claimed that wages had been severely reduced for the two previous years. Despite efforts to mediate the difficulty through the New York Board of Mediation and Arbitration, the strike continued for several months and ended unsuccessfully after the company hired nonunion butchers.

4. In notifying Herman Robinson of his letter of inquiry to the Eastmans Co., SG wrote, "Of course, it is necessary to at least go through the form of giving them an opportunity of being heard, but apart from this, I have had quite an experience that

in a number of instances, we have been enabled to secure an adjustment of the difficulty without going further; and resorting to a request of labor and the sympathetic public to give the products of such Company a wide berth" (Sept. 8, 1896, reel 10, vol. 16, p. 240, SG Letterbooks, DLC).

5. On receipt of this letter, SG expressed concern that "if this statement of the Company's is true, then misrepresentations have been made to the local labor men of New York and also to this office. . . . This is an important matter and we cannot afford to be wrong." He subsequently learned from one of the commissioners of the New York Board of Mediation and Arbitration, however, that the firm had refused the Board's proposal of a conference between the company and its employees. SG concluded that "in a matter so important as this, when a Company will deliberately say that which is untrue, its word in other respects is unreliable, particularly in connection with the labor movement." He placed the company on the AFL's "We Don't Patronize" list and wrote the London Trades Council to ask its support against patrons of the firm in England (SG to Daniel Harris, Sept. 26, 1896, p. 340, ibid.; to Charles Lachenmeyer, Oct. 17, 1896, p. 351, ibid.).

To Jere Dennis[1]

Sept. 23, [1896]

Mr. Jerry Dennis,
Sturdivant, Ala.
Dear Sir and Brother:—

I am in receipt of your favor of the 19th inst. the contents of which are carefully noted. Permit me to congratulate you and we may say to congratulate the workers of your state upon your election to the legislature of Alabama.

It will afford me pleasure to give you all the information within my power relative to the questions which you ask upon the labor laws and labor legislation. Of course I cannot attempt to positively say as to the absolute accuracy of information given. But in any case where there may be a doubt you will find it so stated.

First, I believe the best Employers Liability Law exists in Massachusetts.[2] I think that New York,[3] Ohio[4] and Illinois[5] follow in the order named.

Second, Anti-convict labor. The constitutional convention of 1894 in the state of New York adopted an amendment[6] to the constitution of that state which forever prohibits the labor of convicts being let by contract or coming in competition with free labor.

Third, Lien Law, a law for the collection of wages due to workers in New York State.[7] And is perhaps the best of any of the laws now extant in any other state.

Fourth, The simplest and best election law prevails, I think, in either

Massachusetts[8] or New York.[9] That is, by the best and simplest, I understand you to mean under the Australian system of voting.

Fifth, Anti-Commissary Law. I do not know what is meant by this term. Is it the Companies' store or Truck store system to which you refer? Let me know, so I may answer intelligently.

I would call your attention to a book recently published by Chas. Scribners Sons of New York and written by F. J. Stimson,[10] entitled "Hand-book to the Labor Laws of the United States." In my judgement it is one of the best things published on the subject and will unquestionably be of great service to you in your future work.

There is one matter which you did not mention in your letter and which I think should receive the earliest possible attention of every lover of the human family. Last year when lecturing and organizing through the South, you remember I went in many places of Alabama. I soon learned that the legislature of your state in '94 repealed the state law prohibiting the employment of children for more than 10 hours a day. I was not only horrified by this outrageous piece of legislation, but I was dumbfounded at the absolute ignorance of the working men of the state upon the fact that this crime that had been committed by that legislature in sacrificing young and innocent children to the greed and rapacity of the profit mongers. Alabama has the unenviable distinction of being the only state in the world where a law for the protection of children has been repealed. And the man that shall lead in the fight to redeem the good name of your state, in this regard, and come to the rescue of those who can be in [the?] position to save themselves will make his mark and be performing his duty to the children of to-day; the men and women of the future.

I note what you say relative to Mr. Oates.[11] On this matter I prefer to say nothing at this time.

With every wish for success and hoping to hear from you frequently I am

Fraternally yours,   Saml Gompers.

President   A.F. of L.

TLpS, reel 10, vol. 16, pp. 300-301, SG Letterbooks, DLC.

1. Jere Dennis (b. 1861), a Birmingham, Ala., printer who published and edited the *Labor Advocate* (Birmingham) from 1888 to about 1896, ran as a Populist for the Alabama House of Representatives in 1896. A committee of the house awarded his Democratic opponent the seat, a decision disputed on the grounds of vote fraud. Born in Alabama, Dennis served International Typographical Union 104 of Birmingham as an executive board member (1888) and vice-president (1893). He was president of the Birmingham Trades Council in 1893 and an AFL organizer in the early 1890s. By 1900 he had become a lawyer.

2. Acts of 1894, chap. 499.

3. New York apparently did not pass an employer liability law until after the turn of the century.

4. Sec. 301 of the Ohio revised statutes of 1888 applied to employer liability in coal mines. The Ohio Acts of 1890, p. 149, related to railroad employers' liability.

5. Chap. 13 of the Illinois revised statutes of 1891, and sec. 4 of the Illinois Acts of 1895, p. 250, applied to employer liability in coal mines.

6. Art. 3, sec. 29 of the New York constitution forbade the farming out, contracting, or sale of prison labor to any person or corporation after Jan. 1, 1897.

7. The New York mechanics' lien law (Laws of 1885, chap. 342) was strengthened by amendment several times; the most recent amendment extended it to cover more work sites (Laws of 1895, chap. 673).

8. Acts of 1889, chap. 413 (amending Acts of 1888, chap. 436) provided for the public printing of and distribution of ballots and privacy in voting.

9. Laws of 1891, chap. 296, which amended Laws of 1890, chap. 262, "An act to promote the independence of voters at public elections, enforce the secrecy of the ballot, and provide for the printing and distribution of ballots at public expense."

10. Frederic Jesup Stimson, *Handbook to the Labor Law of the United States* (New York, 1896).

11. Probably William C. Oates (1835-1910), the Democratic governor of Alabama from 1895 to 1897. Oates had previously served as a member of the state House of Representatives (1870-72) and as a U.S. congressman (1880-94).

To Mr. Beckly

Sep. 24th. 1896

(*Confidential*)

My Dear Mr. Beckly.

[. . .] I am in receipt of your favor of the 15th. It reached here, however, during my absence from the city. I appreciate what you say and repeat that it would afford me pleasure to meet Mr. Bryan[1] for the purpose of talking over matters of interest, but engaged as he is and busy as I am I can not see how it can be conveniently arranged.

To-day I received a letter from Mr. Bryan in which he mentions the good work, he learns, I am doing for the silver cause. He also expresses the hope that we may meet before the campaign closes but that his time is so completely occupied that he must trust to meet me en route. I would write him direct but I do not know his route nor his dates, and since I see that he is and will be a few days longer in the East, I depend upon you to convey my appreciation of his sentiments and kind words and to assure him that they are earnestly reciprocated.

He should certainly come to Indiana for a few days and most certainly to Indianapolis. I shall be in Detroit from Sep. 28 until Oct.

10. Then I return here and except for a day now and then (which I can easily postpone) I will be here all the balance of the year.

Should you see Mr. Bryan, I have no objection to your showing this letter to him, to all others, however, I shall be obliged to you if you will regard it as strictly confidential.

Should you wish to address me while I am in Detroit, write to Griswold Hotel. Always mark your envelopes as well as letters "Confidential.["]

Very truly yours, Saml Gompers.

TLpS, reel 341, vol. 356, p. 102, SG Letterbooks, DLC.

1. William Jennings Bryan (1860-1925), Democratic congressman from Nebraska (1890-94), U.S. secretary of state (1913-15), and unsuccessful presidential candidate in 1896, 1900, and 1908. In 1896 Bryan was nominated by both the Democratic party and the People's party.

To Louis Berliner

Sept. 25, [1896]

Mr. L. Berliner,
2406 Myrtle Ave., Brooklyn, N.Y.
My dear friend Lew:—

I am in receipt of your favor of the 23rd inst., and assure you that I was delighted by its perusal. After I read it, I gave it to our friend McCraith, who also enjoyed it, and pronounced it O.K. There is no doubt in my mind but what to a very large extent, you are right, but I imagine that our industrial affairs depend less upon the legislation of Congress and the States than you seem to think. I am under the impression that you place too much stress upon the effect of political legislation on industry. As a matter of fact, you know as well as I can say that the development of the trade unions clarifies public opinion to such an extent that it finds this consensus of expression and judgment into public law. It is seldom, if ever, that political legislation precedes the demand evolved from the industrial conditions brought about by the trade union movement. I believe with you that absolute free trade can only come when industrial conditions in the world are more highly developed, and when the organizations of labor have kept pace with them. Yet, I imagine you attach too much importance to the policy of protection, for as a matter of fact, in free trade England, the organizations of labor are further advanced and more highly developed than in protective tariff America. Mark you, I do not use this as an argument against the protective tariff policy; I merely mention it as a fact, which I believe you will not dispute. If your letter dealt less with political policies, and more with trade unionism, I would have taken the liberty of publishing it in the Federationist, but of course, to do so under the circumstances, would simply open up channels for the discussion of protection vs. free trade, in the columns of our paper, and you know that opens up a vista of discussion to which there is scarcely an end. I call your attention to the discussions in Congress for months upon months at a time, which last for years, and yet, there are few converts from one to the other side. Truly did Payne[1] say that "Time makes more converts than reason," and as industry develops and organizations of labor grow, will the conditions change so much as to compel men to break away from old notions and prejudices. While I am an advocate of the silver cause, I have said, and say to you now, that I believe that both sides attach too great importance to the question. The fact of the matter is, that act as we will, there are few men, who, in voting for either Mr. Bryan or Mr. McKinley, can really say that either represents the voters' full judgment. There are thousands who are silver advocates and protectionists like you. There are silver advocates and free traders. There are advocates of the income tax and other propositions in the platforms of the one or the other party. Yet, when voting for one party, the voter must swallow the whole platform, and favor certain policies repugnant to his conscience. In the coming issue of the Federationist, I have a little editorial utterance[2] on that subject. I think the time is ripe for a greater agitation of the principle initiative and referendum, that is, direct legislation. Thus the people could have the opportunity of voting upon every proposition separately, and to have a fairer consensus of their judgment, and have such legislation as would secure the greatest good to the greatest number.

I repeat that I was delighted to read your letter. You know that my remark of "Tindorfer," was said playfully, for I am sure there are few who have given the labor cause closer study than you, and I am sure it should go without saying that I have the greatest respect for your notions, even if we sometimes disagree. I see that you have not lost your old force of character and expression, and I now, more than ever, request you to write an article on trade unionism.

Remember me kindly to the folks and friends, and let me hear from you soon. With best wishes, I am,

Sincerely yours,   Saml Gompers.

TLpS, reel 10, vol. 16, pp. 323-24, SG Letterbooks, DLC.

1. Thomas Paine (1737-1809) was an English-born propagandist and pamphleteer

of the American Revolution. He was the author of, among others, *Common Sense*, the *Crisis* papers, and *The Rights of Man*.

2. "Political Intimidation," *American Federationist* 3 (Oct. 1896): 162-63. SG noted incidents of large employers coercing workers to vote for candidates and argued that only when workers maintained their economic independence through trade unions could they be genuinely independent politically.

Excerpts from News Accounts of the 1896 Convention of the CMIU in Detroit

[October 3, 1896]

SOCIALISTS WHIPPED

"I am a socialist, but I am opposed to mixing politics with trades unionism."

This remark, made at the opening session of yesterday's convention of the International Cigarmakers' union, by Chas. Specht,[1] of St. Louis, Mo., was so different from all that had gone before in the discussion of the previous day that it created a decided sensation. Mr. Specht said he favored political action by organized workingmen, and believed they could maintain a party outside of their unions which would command great beneficial influence.

Addresses were also made by A. Jablinowsky,[2] of New York, socialist; Alfred McCallam,[3] of Duluth, trades unionist; M. Benditt,[4] Philadelphia, socialist; Delegate Heimerdinger, New York, anti-socialist; L. Greenman,[5] Boston, socialist; and the discussion was closed by President G. W. Perkins in a very pleasing and eloquent summary, which was a resume of the achievements of the organization during the past three years.

Before the vote was taken on the first socialistic preamble,[6] which had been submitted by H. H. Acton,[7] Mr. Acton insisted that he had a right to make a closing argument. The chair held otherwise. J. Mahlon Barnes, the recognized leader of the socialists, appealed from the ruling, and Vice-President Gompers was called to the chair. The convention sustained the chair, and the vote on the first of the eleven socialistic resolutions was taken by roll call and resulted 73½ for, to 273½ against. The other votes were taken by acclamation and all the eleven preambles were bowled down, one after the other by the same relative vote. This was also the fate of a non-socialistic preamble, which declared that the organization was formed on trades union lines solely. It was plain that the convention meant to stick to its present attitude—organization pure and simple. When the last socialistic sentiment had been knocked out, Delegate Acton asked that the clerk be instructed to record him as having favored them all. Chairman Gompers ruled the request out of order, and an interchange of great bitterness took place.

Delegate J. Mahlon Barnes, socialist, rose to a question of information, and the chair ruled him out of order without hearing his question. Then Mr. Barnes asked:

"When is a question for information not in order?"

"A question for information is not in order when it is not in order," replied Mr. Gompers.

This passage in the proceedings was immediately reduced to writing by Barnes, and its discussion took up most of the afternoon session. Barnes denounced Gompers' conduct in the chair as "high handed tyranny," and moved that his question and Gompers' reply be placed in the records. Gompers tried to get a modification of his language by introducing an amendment, but it was so manifestly different from what had taken place that the amendment was voted down.

"If the president of the American Federation of Labor is ashamed of the exhibition he made," said Fred Schaefer,[8] of New York, "let him come before the convention and apologize like a man, and we may let him off."

Mr. Gompers was plainly angry at the failure of his efforts at modification and the tantalizing remarks of the socialists. With a flushed face he arose and for ten minutes hurled defiance at his baiters, assuring them that trades unionism would live and occupy an honored and enviable place in the hearts of the working people long after socialism was dead and universally abhorred. He denounced socialism as the implacable foe of trades unionism. Mr. Barnes replied in a sarcastic vein, and the convention then voted, refusing to place the question and answer in the journal.

So intense had been the spirit aroused that during the remainder of the afternoon, when the proceedings were on minor changes in the constitution, the feeling of the two factions cropped out. . . .

. . .

Detroit Free Press, Oct. 3, 1896.

1. Charles A. Specht, the secretary of CMIU 44 of St. Louis, represented his local at the convention.

2. Ludwig Jablinowski was a member of New York City Cigar Makers' Progressive International Union (CMPIU) 90.

3. Alfred McCallum, active in the Duluth Federated Trades Assembly, represented CMIU 212 of West Superior, Wis., and CMIU 294 of Duluth, Minn.

4. Morris Benditt, secretary of CMIU 165 of Philadelphia, represented his local at the convention.

5. Leon Greenman represented CMIU 97 of Boston.

6. Of the ten proposed preambles, nine were generally socialistic and called for the abolition of the wage system, worker ownership of the means of production and distribution, and the employment of political as well as economic power to achieve workers' goals. The remaining one called for the CMIU to be organized strictly along trade union lines.

7. Harry H. Acton represented CMIU 192 of Manchester, N.H.

8. Fred Schaefer represented CMPIU 90 of New York City.

[October 6, 1896]

IN THE FIELD OF LABOR.

Although the socialistic element in the cigarmakers' convention has been turned down by an overwhelming majority at every attempt to foist its principles and ideas upon the Cigarmakers' International Union, the radicals still continue to make trouble and delay the regular business. Another effort on their part to introduce politics into the union was effectually squelched last evening by the adoption of the following resolution, introduced by Delegate Samuel Gompers:

"Resolved. That the Cigarmakers' International Union declares anew its unreserved and unqualified fealty to and faith in the trade union form of organization and the trade union movement; that we hold the trade union movement as paramount to any other in the struggle for labor's amelioration and the laborer's emancipation; therefore, the introduction of party politics, of whatsoever kind into the Cigarmakers' International Union is contrary to the best interests of our craft, our organization and our cause, and should therefore be discountenanced."

The discussion of this resolution was so animated that neither President Perkins nor any of the delegates seemed to notice that the time for adjournment was long past until the vote had been taken. Delegate Blum,[1] of San Francisco, socialist, moved as an amendment that all after the word "emancipation" be stricken out. About thirty or forty voted for it, but a thundering "No" from the big majority easily showed the fate of the amendment. The resolution was then enthusiastically adopted, only a handful of socialists voting against it, Delegate Blum insisting that he be recorded as voting "no." A storm of applause greeted the announcement that the resolution had been adopted.

A previous turn down of the socialists occurred toward the close of the morning session. After a number of amendments to the constitution had been acted upon, most of them being rejected, one was introduced in reference to the publication of reports. There was a move to get the official journal out of the hands of the president and the executive board and turn it over to the press committee. Delegate Schaefer, of New York, who led the supporters of the amendment, charged that the journal was in the interest of a few and for the purpose of slandering the socialists. Delegate Acton asked the privilege of the floor for Daniel DeLeon, of New York, member of the general executive board of the socialist trade and labor alliance. This motion brought forth howls and hisses, and was indignantly rejected. Delegate Jablinowski, of New York, then challenged Vice-President Gompers, who was in the chair, to meet DeLeon in debate at Social Turner hall in the evening. Mr. Gompers declined to accept. He said DeLeon was totally unworthy of regard, that he had been in the city under cover for a week and had directed all the attacks of the socialists. "If my record as a trades unionist," said Mr. Gompers, "will not stand without entering into a debate with such a fellow, then it must fall." (Loud applause.)

J. Mahlon Barns, of Philadelphia, the leader of the socialists in the convention, jumped upon the stage and tried to speak, but his voice was drowned in the confusion, amid the yells, catcalls and hisses, and he had to desist.

. . .

Detroit Free Press, Oct. 6, 1896.

1. Nicholas Blum represented CMIU 228 of San Francisco.

Excerpts from the Minutes of a Meeting of the Executive Council of the AFL

[October 21, 1896]

WEDNESDAY MORNING.

Called to order at 10. All members present.

. . .

The secretary then suggested that we dispose of the matter of organizers mixing in politics, and read letter from Brittania Workers[1] of Meriden who had withdrawn owing to action of Organizer Crowley[2] Duncan—Must we drop declarations as soon as we enter politics.

If a political party adopted the 8-hour day must we drop the question. Must we debar members from speaking for the question. Garland stated that an officer expressing himself individually did not draw his organization into politics. The liberty of the individual must be considered; he would not go on the stump because of his official position, yet he had the right to express his individual opinion

The secretary took the stand that no officer or organizer had a right to express himself publicly or privately on political questions. If he did not like this, he had the privilege of resigning. But he could not speak as an individual; he would always be quoted as the representative of his organization. His individuality was merged into his office.

O'Connell had heard much dissatisfaction in certain quarters. An organizer or other officer should relinquish his position when entering politics. He would at next convention submit a resolution relative to officials so withdrawing.

The secy moved that the commissions of all organizers actively engaged in politics be revoked.

O'Connell thought it was kind of late to take action now

. . .

MGuire seconded motion of secretary relative to organizers.

Gompers opposed it at this time. It would place us in peculiar position. Would be accused of accepting Mark Hannas money.

The secy stated such accusation could not be made inasmuch as it would apply to some of those working on the Hanna end.

Lennon opposed the motion

Duncan favored it

Garland opposed it. Individual had a right to express himself.

O'Connell in favor

McGuire in favor

McGuire moved to amend to insert "actively engaged—using the name of the American Federation of Labor."

The secretary opposed the amendment He would not admit that any organizer or officer could enter politics to any extent, active or otherwise, without dragging his position or organization after him.

Vote on amendment by roll call:

    Yes—M'Guire, Duncan, OConnell

    No—MCraith, Garland, Lennon Gompers

Vote on original motion—

    Yes—O'Connell, Duncan MCraith

    No—MGuire, Garland, Lennon, Gompers.

The secretary stated if he had known this would be the result he would have voted for the amendment

MGuire moved to reconsider

No second

MGuire moved to expunge from the records in order to bring up again.

Vote — Yes — MGuire, Duncan, O'Connell.

No — Gompers, Lennon, Garland, MCraith

WEDNESDAY AFTERNOON.

. . .

Duncan moved

That the commissions of organizers using the name of the AF of L or their official position for political purposes, be revoked

Seconded by O'Connell & MCraith

. . .

Garland moved as a substitute that the commissions of Pomeroy, Carney[3] and Crouley [Crowley] be revoked.

Vote on the substitute

Yes — Gompers, Lennon, MGuire, Garland

No — McCraith, Duncan, O'Connell

. . .

Resolved, that while the A.F. of L. can ~~and should~~ declare in favor of and work for certain legislative matters, in accordance with ~~the~~ our general anti-political principle, it should not by any means or in any manner, by insinuation or otherwise, indirectly ~~endorse~~ advocate ~~such matters~~ or declare for such legislative matters at the request of any political party, its agents, through the newspapers during a political campaign or otherwise.

Resolved, that this applies to all persons holding official position in the A.F of L. either as general officer or organizers.

MGuire — moved be referred to convention

adopted[4]

A and P and TD, Minutes of Meetings, Executive Council, AFL, reel 2, frames 1126-31, *AFL Records.*

1. Britannia Workers' Union 5809 of Meriden, Conn., received an AFL charter in 1892.

2. Timothy M. CROWLEY, who had worked as a grocer, orchestra leader, and piano agent in Meriden, Conn., was president of the Connecticut State Branch of the AFL and an AFL organizer.

3. William A. CARNEY was an organizer for the AFL and the National Amalgamated Association of Iron and Steel Workers (NAAISW). He had served as vice-president of NAAISW District 1 (1890-95) and second vice-president of the AFL (1891-93).

4. The 1896 AFL convention adopted delegate Frank L. Rist's resolution that no Federation officer be allowed to use his official position in the interest of any political party.

To Saverio Merlino[1]

Indianapolis, October 30, 1896.

Sig. Arv. Saverio Merlino,
Segretario Camera Del Lavaro,[2]
Naples, Italy:
My Dear Sir—

Your favor of recent date came duly to hand, and contents noted. I was in attendance at the convention of our organization, which lasted some weeks, and was exceedingly busy with other work, hence, could not reply earlier.

Of course, I remember you well—the incident of our meeting in the office of the Amalgamated Iron and Steel Workers, in 1892, where we discussed the immigration question generally, and particularly that of the Italian workmen.

I am inclined to believe with you that much better results would follow if there would be some understanding between the organizations of labor of the United States and Italy, than are now accomplished by existing laws, but the fact is, that up to the present time little communication has been had between our respective workmen, while, at the same time, much injury has been done. I am also informed that there are few workmen in your country who are organized into trade unions. I refer to trade unions such as exist in the United States and Great Britain. As a consequence, there is little concert of action among the workers of Italy on economic lines; hence, when workmen in the United States are engaged in any dispute relative to wages, hours of labor, or other conditions of employment, one of the first threats which American workmen have to face from their employers, whether private or corporate, is that Italian workmen will be brought to this country to take their places. Yes, even before conflicts arise, and in anticipation of them, large influxes of Italian workmen are brought here and held as a menace over the heads of our workers to prevent either an improvement in their condition or to force them lower down in the economic scale.

I presume your observations in this country have convinced you, as mine have me, that the American people are as generous as any people on earth. They are swayed, too, by the sentiment that the United States should be an open and free asylum to the oppressed of the whole world, and that a free entry into our land should be accorded to all. But, counter to this feeling and this sentiment, is presented the fact that we have a hard and bitter struggle to maintain or to make any progress in our standard of life, and that what with the inventions and introduction of machinery, and the application of new forces to industry, on the one hand, and the wholesale immigration of low-paid workers from other countries, on the other hand, we have a conflict that increases in intensity and bitterness with each recurring day.

However much our workers are therefore imbued with the feeling and sentiment I refer to, they are confronted with a very serious situation which compels them to resort to some means by which immediate relief from an impending danger forces them. It is because of this that they have demanded from congress the enactment of laws either restricting immigration or for the prevention of workmen and laborers coming into this country under written or implied contracts, and a more stringent enforcement of these laws.

At a convention of the American Federation of Labor, held a few years ago, a resolution was adopted declaring that a further restriction of the immigration laws was not necessary,[3] but if I read the temper of our people aright, I am inclined to the belief that they will soon make another declaration, and of a different character.

You will bear in mind that, although the United States is a country quite young in years, it is now quite matured in industry and commerce. To-day we have myriads of men and women unemployed. There is not an industry which is not overcrowded, and there are numberless workers vainly pleading for an opportunity for employment; hence, the immigration of large numbers of working people into the United States can only have a hurtful influence.

Nor is the view taken by our fellow-workers upon the immigration problem an entirely selfish one. The old and effete monarchical institutions of several European countries are perpetuated by the outlet of thousands upon thousands of workmen who seek our shores. These governments—these institutions—are thus relieved of the acute industrial and economic situation, when, as a matter of fact, if these people would remain at home, concessions, improvements and reforms would be a matter of absolute necessity, and would soon be forced or conceded.

I trust that you will not misunderstand me and believe for a moment that I am an advocate of great restriction of immigration, or that I look to such restriction as a means by which labor can be emancipated from our present economic wrongs. I merely submit these thoughts to you which I know are understood and felt by American workmen.

It would be pleasurable information if you could advise me of the full extent of organization of Italian workmen in trade unions, and what other organization, if any, exists, having for its purpose the betterment of the condition of the Italian workmen.

Let me say, too, that I should be exceedingly pleased to be one of the instruments by which a better understanding may be reached between our respective countries, not only upon the question of immigration, but upon those lines in which we all have an identity of interest, and in the hope for the establishment of a common polity.

With kindest wishes to you, and in the expectation of hearing from you at an early date, I have the honor to remain,

Yours fraternally, Samuel Gompers,
President American Federation of Labor[4]

American Federationist 3 (Dec. 1896): 219-20.

1. Francesco Saverio Merlino, a Neopolitan lawyer, was an influential socialist writer.

2. A *Camera del Lavoro* (Chamber of Labor) was a locally based central labor body that coordinated activity among its constituent unions, promoted organization, provided educational and employment services, and settled labor disputes. The first one was organized in Milan in 1891, and others appeared throughout Italy during the decade.

3. The 1894 AFL convention adopted a resolution declaring that further restriction of immigration was unnecessary except for the exclusion of contract laborers, non-political criminals, and people who were likely to become public charges.

4. When this document was published in the *American Federationist*, Commissioner General of Immigration Herman Stump wrote SG that it might give the impression that Gompers thought federal enforcement of the contract labor laws to be lax and ineffectual. "As you have officially and personally been kind enough to state on several occasions that you believe our Bureau to be honestly endeavoring to enforce the immigration laws in the interest of the working classes," Stump continued, "I feel that it is but proper to call the matter to your attention in order that the erroneous impression thus disseminated may be rectified." Further, Stump asked SG to report "any new cases of evasion or violation . . . of the Contract Labor Laws . . . in order that suitable steps may be promptly taken to prosecute them to the fullest extent of the law" (Stump to SG, Dec. 11, 1896, Records of the Central Office, Letters Sent, vol. 32, p. 274, RG 85, Records of the Immigration and Naturalization Service, DNA).

To William Montgomery[1]

Nov. 3 [1896]

Mr. Wm. H. Montgomery,
1633 Champa St., Denver, Colo.
Dear Sir & Friend:—

Your telegram of the 2nd inst. came duly to hand and contents noted. In reply permit me to say that I do not know whether Mr. Dewar's[2] telegram of Saturday evening, was unfair toward you or not. I will quote it. It is as follows:—

"Was Montgomery officially authorized to investigate strike,[3] and advise settlement on any terms?"[4] to which the following answer was forwarded,—

"Montgomery not authorized by us to interfere with your difficulty, nor any other person."

You can readily see that this was the only course left for us, immaterial whether your intentions were good or otherwise, or whatever you propose to do. The trade unions have absolute authority and jurisdiction to decide for themselves in the matters of their trade disputes. As a printer, you would refuse to allow a miner to interfere between you and any newspaper proprietor with whom you were engaged in a contest. Of course, if the printers' union sought the services of a miner, the case would be different. If the union objected to the miners interfering in any way, the common law as well as the written law of trade unionism would compel the miner to keep his hands off, and if we were asked the same question in this instance, we should be required to answer as we did in the case of the miners.

As president of the American Federation of Labor, I have no authority to take any action in this direction unless my services are first requested by the men in interest. It is then only that the authority of the Federation can be exerted. Mark you, I do not wish you to infer for a moment, that I said that you claimed authority to settle the question with the miners. I was merely asked the question quoted above. My answer was to the question. There was no assertion that you claimed authority either in the telegram to this office or in the reply. At best, the question was hypothetical.

As to whether the miners are wise or not in refusing an offer which you say is fair, this also is a matter for them to decide, and until they ask the good offices of the Federation, I am compelled, even if it were not my desire, to stand by the men who are engaged in this conflict. They are bearing the burdens; they are making the sacrifices. If they win, it will be their gain; if they lose, it will be their loss. They are making what everybody admits is a heroic struggle against great odds, and I earnestly hope, as I am sure you do, that victory may be theirs.

With kindest regards, and hoping to hear from you soon, I am,

Very truly yours,   Saml Gompers.

TLpS, reel 10, vol. 16, p. 457, SG Letterbooks, DLC.

1. William H. Montgomery was a Denver printer and an AFL general organizer.

2. Ewen J. Dewar was a miner from Leadville, Colo.

3. The Leadville strike. See "The Western Federation of Miners and the AFL," below.

4. SG had received complaints about Montgomery from the president of the Leadville miners' union and secretary of the Leadville Trades and Labor Assembly. The charges included accusations that Montgomery had met with the mine managers before consulting with union officers, had demoralized the strikers through his remarks to them, and finally had demanded that their leaders call off the strike within ten days because it was not authorized by the AFL (SG to William Montgomery, Nov. 12, 1896, reel 10, vol. 17, pp. 36-37, SG Letterbooks, DLC).

To Benjamin Tillett[1]

Nov. 4 [1896]

Mr. Ben Tillett,
5 Melita Villas, Old Charlton, London, S.E., Eng.
Dear friend Ben: —

Both your letters came duly to hand and you are right that I owe you a letter. I owed you one previous to the receipt of your last, but I was in attendance at the Convention of the Cigar Makers International Union, which lasted three weeks. Upon my return, the Executive Council of the A.F. of L. held a session here which lasted nearly a week. This brought me nearly up to the time of the receipt of your last letter. I was pleased to receive both of them, — yes, even the one announcing that you "have been very seriously ill," that portion particularly, which says that you *have been* ill. I do hope, however, that you have taken care of yourself, have rested, and that now you are enjoying the very best of health and strength. The movement needs you and your services, and it needs you "mighty bad." Illness always comes at an inopportune time, but possibly never more so with you than at the time it did. Perhaps it is better that you go slow and preserve yourself; in other words, follow the advice you are giving to the boys affiliated with your new employment, — "Ca Canney."[2] It may, in the long run, give you better opportunity to do better work and more years of it. I know, of course, that it is one of the easiest things in the world to give others advice. I know that I have been advised in the same line for the past few years, and particularly this year, and yet every time I feel some little returning strength, I work on and on with an intensity that would kill many others, and does leave me much weaker. I suppose it is the same with yourself, — Of a high nervous temperament, excitement at a high pitch, and the nervous strain at a great tension. Do the best you can for the movement and perhaps a little application of "Ca Canney" will be good for it, as well as for yourself and those you love and who love you.

Thus far, I have not seen Mr. McHugh,[3] nor have I heard from him more than that the day following his arrival, I read an account in the newspapers of his coming here. Nor have I heard anything of his being in conference with the officers of the Seamen's or Longshoremen's organizations. He has not written here. More than likely, his work is of such a nature that privacy or secrecy may be necessary, and that he does not care to write here. However, be that as it may, I regret that I have not thus far been of very great assistance to the organization or the movement.

At the Council meeting of the A.F. of L., I broached the subject of your International movement, and a resolution was adopted authorizing us to co-operate with the Seamen's organization in attaining the desired ends of both national organizations. I do not know how far-reaching this will be, but I would be pleased could I be of some tangible service. I shall make mention of the points you give. Many thanks for the notes which you have given. I shall use them in the Federationist.

No, I am taking no part in the financial discussion. The Federation has adopted resolutions on the subject at three successive conventions. If asked in regard to the matter, I simply place my index finger upon them and say not a word. With you, I believe that there are other and more important subjects which affect our wage earners more directly, more intensely, to which they should give their undivided attention. These middle class issues simply divert attention from their true interests.

You will know the result of the election long before this reaches you. Indications point that it has gone one way, and that is for McKinley. Since both of them are blessed with the same Christian name, I cannot be charged with being partisan if I shout to you "Hurrah for William!"

Since March I have not seen either of our delegates who went to the Edinburgh Congress. Mr. Sullivan[4] went to Paris, and I learn that he will remain there for several months yet. The weather in Scotland was so inclement that Mr. Strasser returned within a few days after the close of the Congress, but with the exception of his going to Baltimore and returning to New York, he has not travelled anywhere, and as I say, I have not seen him, hence, have had no opportunity of learning of their treatment at the Congress, that is, I have not learned from any one but yourself. Yes, I should say that the second or third day of the Congress, Mr. Sullivan wrote here stating that he and his colleague were being well chaperoned. Of course, it is a great gratification to me to learn that they made such a good impression upon the Congress. There is no question but that they are both very able men. We published Mr. Sullivan's address to the Congress in the November issue of the Federationist,[5] a few copies of which I will mail to your address under another cover.

I, too, am disappointed that you are not coming over and that I shall not have the pleasure of seeing you. Yes, no doubt I should treat you as if you "deserved starving." I want to get a chance at you sometime, and in the latest language of our streets, "I won't do a ting to you."

Of course you know that the headquarters of the Federation are about 900 miles from New York City. I have only been in the latter place twice since last Christmas, although my family and my home is located there. It is quite something to be deprived of even occasional pleasures with wife, children and home.

I learn that Mr. McHugh attended a luncheon in New York City last Friday evening, after a big political meeting[6] by our labor friends. This is the second time I have heard of him, and this, too, was through the Press. I send the clipping to you herein.

I read the splendid article you wrote on "Government and other Things" and enjoyed it very much. The similes can be well adapted to our own Federal Congress.

Thus far, I have not been informed when Messrs. Woods and Mallinson,[7] your delegates, will leave for these shores. I have written to our central labor union of New York, and a committee will undoubtedly be appointed to receive them. I do not think they will have much time to weigh heavy on their hands while here. Cincinnati itself is not a very beautiful city, but its suburbs and surroundings are delightful. Of course, the time of year in which our Conventions are held gives a visitor a very poor impression of our country. It is then practically at its worst. Many years ago, we held our Conventions earlier in the year, but the temptation to use the movement for partisan political purposes became such a fad among many that it demanded changing the date of the Convention until after elections were held, whether local, state or national.

We had a most interesting Convention of the Cigar Makers' International Union, and the most practical action was taken by it that I have seen for some time. I have asked our President to send you a copy of the proceedings, which may be of interest to you. I commend to your attention especially, the report of President Perkins. It is an excellent document.

I do not know whether I am indebted to you or our friend, Tom Mann,[8] for sending me a number of clippings on the experiences of yourself in Belgium and he in Hamburg. It was outrageous. These old monarchial governments seem to appreciate the tendency of trade unions and the trade union movement. That is plainly evident. If anything should arise in connection with the matter, let me hear of it. I would also be pleased to have you write to me upon any new phase developed in your international movement.

I am more than pleased to hear that your family are enjoying the best of health. Give my best wishes to Mrs. Tillett[9] and the children.[10]

Hoping for your renewed health and strength and success, believe me as always,

Yours sincerely,   Saml Gompers.

Love, luck and a good grasp of your hand. Shake! "Old bard."

T and ALpS, reel 10, vol. 16, pp. 469-71, SG Letterbooks, DLC.

1. Benjamin TILLETT was a founder and general secretary (1889-1922) of the Dock, Wharf, Riverside, and General Labourers' Union of Great Britain and Ireland.

2. *Ca' canny*, a Scots term meaning "slow down" or "go easy," had by the early 1890s acquired the specific meaning of a work slowdown (as an alternative to a strike) among organized British seamen and longshoremen.

3. In 1896 the International Federation of Ship, Dock, and River Workers sent Edward McHUGH, a Scottish printer and dockworkers' organizer, to the United States to organize longshoremen on the east coast. McHugh founded the American Long-shoremen's Union with the assistance of Henry George in October 1896 and served as its president from 1896 until 1898, when it disbanded.

4. James William SULLIVAN, a New York City printer and editor, was active in International Typographical Union 6.

5. "An Address," *American Federationist* 3 (Nov. 1896): 183-85.

6. On Oct. 30, 1896, a meeting was held under the auspices of organized labor at Cooper Union in New York City in support of William Jennings Bryan's presidential candidacy. Among the speakers were John Swinton, Henry George, George McNeill, Charles Adams, Henry Lloyd, Thomas B. McGuire, Joseph R. Buchanan, John J. Junio, Thaddeus B. Wakeman, and Jacob E. Bausch.

7. John Mallinson, an Edinburgh cordwainer, was secretary of the Edinburgh Trades Council and served as chairman of the Parliamentary Committee of the TUC in 1896.

8. Thomas MANN, a British machinist, was secretary of the Independent Labour party from 1894 to 1896.

9. Jane Tompkins Tillett.

10. Jeanette and Mabel Mary Tillett.

To Robert Howard

Nov. 11 [1896]

Mr. Robert Howard, Secy.,
Fall River, Mass.
Dear Sir & Brother:—

Your favor of the 6th inst. to hand and contents noted. In connection with the organizing trip for the Textile Workers of the South, I would say that Mr. Fred J. Estes,[1] of Columbus, Ga., has been appointed as your colleague. Mr. Estes is a member of Typographical Union No. 220, and I am informed is a fluent talker, has had some experience and is also a Congregational minister, and is now employed on the "Evening Call." I will write him upon the completion of this and will advise him that you will write him at once.[2]

You may be aware of the fact that through the assistance of our organizers and some of our unions in Columbus, Ga., a number of Textile Workers' Unions were organized and through the efforts of this office, these locals were attached to the Textile Workers' Unions.[3] I saw by a paper a few days ago that Mr. Littlewood,[4] Secretary of the Textile Workers National Union, calls attention to the fact that he has influenced the Textile Workers of Georgia to form an organization which he says has declared for the "principles of the socialist trade & Labor Alliance,["] an organization, by the way, which the Convention which elected Mr. Littlewood secretary, repudiated by refusing to affiliate with it. The result of Mr. Littlewood's action has already alienated the co-operation of the trade unions, and those who give their active sympathy towards the new movement of the Textile Workers of the South. I will advise our fellow unionists and friends to do all they possibly can to stand by the Textile Workers' Unions, notwithstanding any impracticable step which they may take, but I believe it is the first duty of yourself and Mr. Estes to do all you possibly can to see that the Textile Workers of Columbus, and all through Georgia, as well as through the other sections of the South, are organized into trade unions so that the workers may have the first benefit resulting from their organized effort. For this reason, I believe you should make your initial move at Columbus, Ga.

You can write to Mr. Estes, C/o "Evening Call," Columbus, Ga. You can write him as to route of travelling, and such other matters as will occur to you.

Please keep me advised when you start and also write a report of the progress made by you and your colleague on this trip. I have thus far not heard from the new C.L.U.

Fraternally yours, Saml Gompers.
President A.F. of L.

Enclosed please find Commission as Chief Special Organizer.

TLpS, reel 10, vol. 17, p. 7, SG Letterbooks, DLC.

1. Fred J. Estes, a Columbus, Ga., printer, served as an AFL organizer assisting Robert Howard in his campaign to unionize textile workers in Georgia, Tennessee, and the Carolinas in late 1896.
2. SG to Fred J. Estes, Nov. 11, 1896, reel 10, vol. 17, p. 8, SG Letterbooks, DLC.
3. The National Union of TEXTILE Workers of America (NUTWA).
4. Herbert LITTLEWOOD was general secretary and organizer of the NUTWA in 1896; by early 1897 he had been succeeded by James Reid. In a letter to William H. Winn of Feb. 25, 1897, SG referred to the discontent caused by Littlewood's visit to the South and to the "peculiar rumors afloat in reference to his doings and by whom he is employed" (reel 11, vol. 18, p. 190, SG Letterbooks, DLC).

Samuel Gompers about 1898 (George Meany Memorial Archives).

Samuel Gompers (second from right), Benjamin Tillett (second from left), and two of Tillett's associates, near London, 1895 (George Meany Memorial Archives).

Rose Gompers Mitchell, daughter of Sophia Julian and Samuel Gompers (George Meany Memorial Archives).

Henrietta Mitchell, daughter of Rose Gompers and Samuel Mitchell, about 1893 (George Meany Memorial Archives).

Florence Gompers, daughter of Sophia Dampf and Samuel Julian Gompers, 1915 (George Meany Memorial Archives).

James Duncan, 1896

Frank Morrison, 1897

John B. Lennon, 1896

James O'Connell, 1899

August McCraith,
about 1896

John McBride presiding at the 1895 AFL convention (*New York Journal*).

P. J. McGuire (left) and an unidentified associate, possibly Gabriel Edmonston (United Brotherhood of Carpenters and Joiners of America).

Samuel Gompers shortly after his arrival in West Virginia during the miners' strike in 1897; the photograph was taken by a coal company detective (George Meany Memorial Archives).

Eugene Debs addressing striking miners in the vicinity of Pittsburgh, 1897 (*Pittsburg Post*).

Robert Askew, 1900

Samuel Ross, about 1897

M. D. Ratchford, 1897

Frank Weber

W. D. Mahon

George Perkins, 1897 (George Meany Memorial Archives).

Eva McDonald Valesh, 1895 (*New York Journal*).

Henry Weismann, 1896 (*Eight-Hour Herald* [Chicago]).

A Noble Movement and a Valiant Leader.

A RECITATION.

INSCRIBED TO MR. SAMUEL GOMPERS, PRESIDENT A. F. OF L.

A wondrous vision met my gaze one lovely springtime day ;
A mighty host in phalanx true, that stretched for miles away,
And oft above the music's harmonious, joyous noise
I heard the words "Hope," "Freedom," from a million gladdened throats.

Back to the age of chivalry my ardent spirit fled,
And then my eager fancies conjured up the myriad dead
Who offered up their valiant lives o ı many a bloody field,
Till civilization conquered and ignorance did yield

But hold ! in all that column no glittering steel I see,
But good and honest citize s, who step full light and free ;
All horny-handed sons of toil, ɪhə pride of every land,
And on their banners "Labor's Rights" in bold outline did stand.

Never marched a nobler host through ancient Gaul or Rome,
No gayer banners caught the gleam of Heaven's sunlight dome ;
No prouder hearts did ever beat in any age or land,
No truer lover of this kind than he who held command.

"At last, ' I cried ; "O God ! at last, our days of bliss are nigh ;
No longer with our burning sweat our life blood they shall buy;
No more we'll face the "Master, ' "!Boss," with heart in dire suspense,
And learn that a human heart was valued less than cents.

And in my joy I sprang ahead and joined their glorious ranks:
And joined my humble voice with theirs in pouring forth glad thanks.
Hurrah ! hurrah ! we're free at last ; hurrah for labor's rights !
Away with wroug, less hours for toil, and more for home delights,"

And far away, and far away the winds our voices bore,
And still our ranks did grow apace, recruited from each store,
And people blessed the noble mind of him who wrought the plan
By which Labor Federation brought joy to toiling man.

We've won the right to name our price, to name our length of day :
We've cleared the path of Industry of weeds that o'er it lay ;
Where erst was squalor and distress, and ignorance most rude,
The hand of plenty and the school doth scatter each rich food.

The American Federation of Labor is the cause
Of additions to our statutes of "Reformed Labor Laws"
And down the distant ages our Gompers' name shall go
As bright as the happy smiles he caused around our hearths to glow.

T. C. WALSH

Thomas C. Walsh's poem "A Noble Movement and a Valiant Leader," published in the *Paterson Labor Standard,* 1896 (George Meany Memorial Archives).

The Western Federation of Miners and the AFL

When the Western Federation of Miners (WFM) voted to join the AFL in May 1896 and officially affiliated in July, its decision marked a significant development in the effort to build a national labor organization. While the AFL and its affiliates had chartered a number of local, federal, and central labor unions in the West up to this time, their organizing efforts had been hampered by considerations of cost and distance. As a consequence, Samuel Gompers welcomed the WFM's affiliation both as an extension of trade unionism and as an opportunity to dispel the notion that the AFL had little interest in western workers. But despite initial expectations, relations between the AFL and the WFM quickly deteriorated. After the WFM was defeated in the Leadville, Colorado, strike of 1896-97 and, in part, blamed the AFL for this failure,[1] long-standing regional tensions and philosophical differences came to a head. By 1898 the WFM had broken its ties to the AFL and had launched the Western Labor Union as an alternative, regional labor federation.[2]

Founded in Butte, Montana, in May 1893 as an industrial union pledged to "unite the various miners' unions of the west into one central body," the WFM offered membership to all workers in and around the mines including drillers, shot-firers, engineers, carpenters, and those employed by concentrating mills and smelters.[3] Focusing on traditional trade union concerns at its founding convention, the WFM's constitution called for payment of fair wages in lawful money rather than scrip, enactment of mine safety laws, accordance of preference in employment to union members, exclusion of Pinkerton detectives, prohibition of child and contract convict labor, and use of "all honorable means to maintain friendly relations between ourselves and our employers, and . . . arbitration and conciliation to . . . make strikes unnecessary."[4]

Despite its hopeful beginnings, the union soon languished. The collapse of the nation's economy, the repeal of the Sherman Silver Purchase Act, and a sharp drop in the price of silver seriously weakened both the hard-rock mining industry and the WFM. Moreover, the union lacked effective leadership—the presidents elected at its 1894 and 1895 conventions both resigned while in office, as did the secretary-treasurers elected in 1893 and 1894; the union had to re-place the secretary-treasurer elected in 1896 when he could not be located.[5] The revival of the industry and then the election of Edward Boyce in early May 1896, however, seemed to promise the rejuve-nation of the union. A militant veteran of the 1892 Coeur d'Alene strike, a dedicated supporter of the People's party, and a tireless organizer, Boyce was the WFM's first full-time president. Yet hardly more than a month after assuming office, he found himself embroiled in a strike that significantly affected both the WFM's development and its relationship to the national labor movement.

"Were it not for the Leadville strike," Boyce reported to the WFM's May 1897 convention, "I could have organized twice as many unions as I have during the past year." The conflict began on May 25, 1896, when Boyce led a committee of miners to request a fifty-cent wage increase from mine managers who paid less than the union's rate of $3 per day. When the managers turned down this proposal, the com-mittee submitted a written request on June 19. That evening, miners in Leadville voted to call out their coworkers who were receiving less than the minimum rate — 968 men employed in thirteen mines. In response, mine managers throughout the district not only shut down their mines and resolved to protect each others' property, but also secretly agreed not to "recognize or treat in any manner or at any time with any labor organization" without the consent of a majority of the managers. With the lockout in force by June 22, some 2,250 men had been idled.[6]

The strike remained relatively peaceful until the end of June. Ten-sions rose, however, when strikers began threatening and assaulting nonunion workers and when members of the strike committee pur-chased and distributed rifles and revolvers to strikers and to the sympathetic sheriff of Lake County, M. H. Newman, ostensibly to protect life and property against destruction that might be charged to the union. A strong supporter of the miners' cause, Newman opposed the managers' request to the governor for military assistance and allowed striking miners to prevent "suspicious-looking men" — strikebreakers — from entering Leadville. His chief assistant went so far as to deputize strikers to preserve the peace.[7]

Violence erupted shortly after midnight on September 21, when a dynamite explosion and fire destroyed the buildings and surface ma-chinery at the Coronado mine and led to a riot that left three miners and a fireman dead. The Coronado was the first mine to have resumed production in Leadville (work had begun there on August 17), and its workforce, all of whom were residents of Leadville, had been armed by the managers. Another riot broke out shortly thereafter at the nearby Emmet mine—which strikers assaulted with bombs and "an improvised cannon"—but this time well-armed company "defenders" drove off their attackers with buckshot and rifle bullets, leaving another miner dead. Although the WFM contended that the operators had staged the explosion to obtain the military protection they had so far been denied, Sheriff Newman had little choice but to accede to the call for armed assistance. Within twenty-four hours, 653 militiamen were reportedly encamped in Leadville. While the strike would continue into the spring, the events of September 21 and their consequence—the involvement of the state on the side of the mine managers—spelled the defeat of the miners' cause.[8]

Boyce and P. H. Clifford, the WFM's delegates to the AFL's Cincinnati convention, reported on the strike at a meeting of the AFL's Executive Council in Cincinnati on December 15. They maintained that few strikers had gone back to work and that the managers had been able to bring in no more than 160 strikebreakers; they admitted, however, that the strike had cost the union some $67,000. Boyce and Clifford did not wish to alert the press—or the mine managers—to their financial difficulties, but they did hope that the AFL would publicly support the strike; the two agreed that a circular to the AFL's affiliates, acquainting them with the situation and asking them to contribute, would prove helpful. In response, the Executive Council submitted a resolution to the AFL convention, approved by Boyce and Clifford, that called on member unions to extend "moral and financial support" to the strikers; the resolution was adopted. According to Gompers, Boyce did not expect the circular to generate significant contributions—indeed, it apparently brought in barely enough to cover its cost—but the WFM subsequently made a formal request for financial aid, which Boyce maintained he sent to Gompers in February 1897. It received no response, however; Gompers insisted that he never received the letter but that, if he had, he would certainly have referred it to the Executive Council.[9]

Apparently of greater significance to Boyce than this lack of financial support was his experience as a WFM delegate at the AFL's 1896 convention. Chagrined by the fact that his fellow delegates were still debating the silver question and that some went so far as to urge the AFL to reverse its position on this issue, Boyce delivered a stern lecture affirming the AFL's free silver stance.[10] Similarly, when his resolution recommending that union members refrain from joining the state national guard or militia failed to win the support of the Committee on Resolutions on the grounds that it interfered with individual liberty, Boyce was outraged. Again taking the floor, he argued that the militia's primary purpose was to break strikes, and he and Clifford recounted the miners' experiences at Leadville. Although the two eventually persuaded the convention to adopt the resolution, Boyce was critical of what he considered the delegates' inability to face economic and political realities, what he termed "the low intellectual plane" of the convention's deliberations, and the AFL's conservative response to the needs of its western constituency.[11] His long experience in the hard-rock mining industry had convinced him that trade unionism could not fight effectively against corporate capital. He informed Gompers that the time had come "to do something different than to meet in annual convention and fool away time in adopting resolutions, indorsing labels and boycotts," and made it clear that he favored the formation of a "Western organization" since western workers were "one hundred years ahead of their brothers in the East" and had little in common with them.[12]

At the same time that Boyce's relations with Gompers and the AFL were approaching the breaking point, Boyce was establishing contact with Eugene Debs. He asked Debs for help in effecting a settlement at Leadville and, gratified by Debs's prompt decision to come there and to remain in the West for several weeks, Boyce praised him warmly in his presidential address at the WFM's 1897 convention: "Although Brother Debs was an entire stranger to me, I appealed to him to come to Leadville. . . . He did not hesitate nor offer any excuse for his inability to come to our assistance. On the contrary, he left his duties at home and repaired to Leadville immediately."[13]

The program Boyce outlined in his 1897 presidential address underscored the evolution of his thinking. Arguing that corporate concentration had rendered the American workingman "a dependent suppliant, on bended knees," he recommended that local unions purchase available mining property that could be developed as cooperatives. He further advised the miners to organize more aggressively, break their ties with established political parties, distribute "reform literature," prohibit members of the national guard from joining the WFM, and boycott "all companies and individuals or organizations" that employed or admitted militiamen to membership. In his most controversial statement, he urged local unions "to provide every member with the latest improved rifle which can be obtained from the factory at a nominal price," announcing that he looked forward to the day when "we can hear the inspiring music of the martial tread of 25,000 armed men in the ranks of labor."[14]

Boyce subsequently participated in the September 1897 Chicago conference called to bring an end to "government by injunction," using the meeting to build support for the formation of a western federation of labor. In December, the WFM's executive board voted to poll the membership on the question of organizing such a body; acting on the affirmative responses that were received, Boyce, early in 1898, called for a meeting to be held in Salt Lake City in May "for the purpose of bringing all labor organizations of the West into closer touch with one another upon all matters pertaining to the interest of labor."[15] Members of the WFM dominated the conference, which ran concurrently with the WFM's annual convention, but the delegates also included representatives of various other trades. On May 11, 1898, the conference launched the Western Labor Union, an organization that endorsed industrial unionism, political action, and "the unification of all labor unions and assemblies east of the Pacific ocean and west of the Mississippi river."[16]

Notes

1. *Miners' Magazine* 2 (Nov. 1901): 9.

2. As Melvyn Dubofsky makes clear, the Western Labor Union may have "never amounted to much," but it did count several federal labor unions and locals of international unions as affiliates (Melvyn Dubofsky, *We Shall Be All: A History of the Industrial Workers of the World* [Chicago, 1969], p. 71).

3. Ibid., p. 34.

4. Richard E. Lingenfelter, *The Hardrock Miners: A History of the Mining Labor Movement in the American West, 1863-1893* (Berkeley, 1974), pp. 221-22; John Ervin Brinley, Jr., "The Western Federation of Miners," Ph.D. diss., University of Utah, 1972, p. 37.

5. Vernon H. Jensen, *Heritage of Conflict: Labor Relations in the Nonferrous Metals Industry up to 1930* (Ithaca, N.Y., 1950), pp. 56-57.

6. *Rocky Mountain News* (Denver), May 11, 1897; Carroll D. Wright, *A Report on Labor Disturbances in the State of Colorado, from 1880 to 1904 . . .*, U.S. Congress, Senate, Docs., no. 122, 58th Cong., 3d sess. (Washington, D.C., 1905), pp. 87-88. For a full discussion of the strike, which the Leadville miners' union declared ended "on the basis of *status quo antebellum*" on Mar. 9, 1897, see Melvyn Dubofsky, "The Leadville Strike of 1896-1897: An Appraisal," *Mid-America* 48 (1966): 99-118. The quotation is on p. 117.

7. Wright, *Report*, pp. 89-98.

8. Ibid., pp. 92-94; Dubofsky, "The Leadville Strike," p. 108; Jensen, *Heritage of Conflict*, p. 59. For President Boyce's account of these events see *Rocky Mountain News* (Denver), May 11, 1897.

9. "Excerpts from the Minutes of a Meeting of the Executive Council of the AFL," Dec. 15-21, 1896, below; SG to William Blackman, Mar. 21, 1898, reel 15, vol. 23, p. 84, SG Letterbooks, DLC; Jensen, *Heritage of Conflict*, pp. 59-60; "From Edward Boyce," Mar. 16, 1897, and "To Edward Boyce," Mar. 26, 1897, below. It is doubtful whether the AFL could have provided any effective support at this late date: the mines had "resumed full operations" the previous autumn, Sheriff Newman was removed from office in December, the state withdrew most of its troops from Leadville in January, and, by February, most strikers had either gone back to work on the mine owners' terms or left town (Dubofsky, "The Leadville Strike," pp. 110, 112, 116; Wright, *Report*, pp. 96, 101).

10. AFL, *Proceedings*, 1896, p. 59.

11. Ibid., pp. 75-76. Boyce's observation on the AFL convention is to be found in John H. M. Laslett, *Labor and the Left: A Study of Socialist and Radical Influences in the American Labor Movement, 1881-1924* (New York, 1970), p. 251.

12. "From Edward Boyce," Apr. 7 and Mar. 16, 1897, below. Boyce may also have been annoyed by the fact that William Montgomery, an AFL organizer, had reportedly demanded that the Leadville miners call off their strike because it had not been approved by the AFL ("To William Montgomery," Nov. 3, 1896, below; "Excerpts from the Minutes of a Meeting of the Executive Council of the AFL," Dec. 15-21, 1896, below).

13. *Rocky Mountain News* (Denver), May 11, 1897.

14. Ibid. Although Boyce's recommendation to buy rifles drew harsh public criticism, his supporters defended the anger that inspired his words. As W. S. Willis, president of the Salt Lake City typographical union, explained to the press, Boyce had "spent six months in jail for some mythical offense at the time of the Coeur d'Alene strike. When he went to Leadville last winter he was arrested the moment he left the train on a charge of inciting a riot, although he had not been in the city for six weeks. . . . The real revolutionists are those who have overridden all law in their effort to coerce workingmen. They have sown the wind, now let them seek their cyclone cellars" (*Salt Lake City Tribune*, May 13, 1897).

According to SG, the WFM's 1897 convention voted to remain affiliated with the AFL, and newspaper accounts indicate that it elected a delegate to the AFL's 1897 meeting in Nashville. SG wrote that Boyce subsequently decided to disaffiliate; Boyce returned the union's charter to the AFL in 1898.

15. "To the Executive Council of the AFL," Mar. 1, 1898, below; *Miners' Magazine* 1 (Jan. 1900): 24-25.

16. *Salt Lake City Tribune*, May 12, 1898.

To the Executive Council of the AFL

Indianapolis, Ind., Nov. 28, 1896.

To the Executive Council, A.F. of L.,
Colleagues: —

Since last June, the miners, engineers, stationary firemen, pump-men, and mine mechanics, of Leadville, Colo. have been on strike. Very many sacrifices have been borne by the men in order that they may be successful. Every effort has been made by the mine owners to destroy confidence among the men, but thus far, the men have stood nobly together, even when incendiarism and murder were committed and falsely laid at their door. The miners belonging to the Western Federation of Miners are receiving benefits from that organization. Our members of engineers, firemen, pumpmen and mine mechanics have had little or nothing to sustain them in this long struggle. In order that they may be encouraged, Secy. McCraith and I have deemed it wise to submit a proposition that may show our desire to be of some practical aid to them. Therefore, the following is submitted for your consideration: —

Resolved, That the sum of $200 be and hereby is appropriated in aid of engineers, firemen, pumpmen and mine mechanics' union 6745,[1] A.F. of L.

Please return your votes[2] upon the above proposition at your earliest convenience, and oblige,

Yours fraternally, Saml Gompers.
President A.F. of L.

TLpS, AFL Executive Council Vote Books, reel 8, frame 180, *AFL Records.*

1. The AFL chartered Cloud City Stationary Engineers, Firemen, Pumpmen, and Mine Mechanics' Union 6745 of Leadville, Colo., in June 1896.
2. The Executive Council approved the resolution.

From Philip Thomas[1]

St. James Hotel Scranton Pa. Nov. 29th 1896

Dear Sir and Brother,

I hope that you will excuse me for being a little tardy in answering your last letter,[2] I was delayed collecting the information relative to the Circle Cheque System,[3] therefor you will please excuse me. I received the commission as organizer all right with the documents pertaining to that office it reads for the City of Scranton, am I confined to this City or have I a roaming commission as it were to go wherever I like I dont want to intrude upon the other fellows territory but I have been thinking of paying Wilkesbarrie a visit in the interest of our organization. I will go anyhow and take the chances.

We need somthing to put new life into the Trades Unions of Scranton this last Election seems to have demoralized them we cant even get them to attend the meetings and when they do attend they only stay long enough to pay their dues then they ar off again, At A Special meeting of the Carpenters[4] last Friday night called for the purpose of voting upon the ammendment to our Constitution made at our General Convention[5] at Cleveland Ohio, out of a membership on our books numbering nearly 350 the total members present were 39 and myself and two other members had all we could do to keep them together until the voteing was all over, as soon as it was they left the room in a body leaving 6 of us to finish the buisness although there was some vital questions to come up for their consideration, concerning the wages paid in Scranton which during the last year has virtualy been reduced twenty five cents a day the bosses have done this gradualy the men them selves being willing to take whatever was offered them they kick on the job and street corners but never attend the meetings to devize meens to justify themselves They even go so far as to put the blame of such a state of affaires upon the shoulders of the half dozen of us who are raising heaven and earth to keep the Union together. This may seem a sorry tale to you but it is nevertheless a true one They even voted down the advance in our dues from 60cts to 75cts and I noticed that it was those only who attended our meetings regularly that voted for it and those who voted against were members who are never in attendence some of them in [fact] were total strangers to me, and I have no[t mi]ssed a meeting in two [yea]rs. I would also say here that while I have been three years delegate to the C.L.U.[6] yet I have missed but one night and then I was attending our Convention at Cleveland.

The fact of the matter is this, it is no use minceing matters when we see that the life of our Organization is at Stake, the members here are at loggerheads and will not pull together and the reason for all this is the A.P.A. now I myself have been brought up a Protestant and I hope to die one. and nothing in this world would change my ideas engrafted into my mind in my younger days and strengthened by myself by observation and study in my mature years yet rather than join a body such as they who are banded together for the sole purpose of disfranchising and keeping out of Public office free born American Citizens just because they happen to profess a certain re-

ligious creed when I do send me to Siberia for I am sure that the life
of the Russian prisoners would be bliss to the life that we should lead
here Now there are all Creeds and Nationalities in our Union we
have as many A.O.H.[7] as A.P.A. and they all know each other so no
matter how important the measure that should be brought up in our
meetings the one faction will oppose the other thereby stoping all
progress, unless somthing is done and done quickly, (and God knows
what we cane do to put a stop to this state of affairs, for I am sure
it will take a wiser head than mine to handle the job.) Trades Unions
will be a thing of the past, in this City whatever for elsewhere.

There has been surgested in the C.L.U. that we do somthing at
once to create new interest in Federation and Trades Unionism it is
proposed that we hold a weeks Jubillee here, that is, that we rent one
of our large halls for one week, then each Union Represented in the
C.L.U. shall have come here the best speaker in its order. That is
that we write head quarters to send on the best man available for
that week, Then we would have say, Carpenters night, Typos night
Plumbers night, and Painters night and so on for the week, we think
that this scheam would be conducive of much good. I would like to
have your oppinion and any suggestions that your vast experience
would seem best upon this matter. I would like you to give Special
attention to this

I am very glad to hear that you are about to take some action[8]
relating to the Circle Cheque System, at the Cincinattie Convention
I fully expected to be there to give whatever assistance I could, but
I am afraid that all my hopes in that direction has gone to the dogs,
while I have been duly elected a deligate yet there is no money in
the C.L.U. Treasury to pay my expences, we are in the hole some
60 dollars from our Labor day picnic for while the Parade was the
best ever seen in Scranton yet the Picnic was a total failure so as I
cant at the present time afford to pay my own expences which I
certainly would do if I could. I am afraid I will not be there. Therefore
in my absence I will now try and give you all the information in my
possesion so that you may yourself have something tangable to work
upon.

I[n] the early part of August last a Glib tongued little fellow about
28 or 30 years old giving his name as Eugene Peltier, presented himself
for a hearing to our C.L.U. we would not admitt him without some
sort of Credentials he therefore brought somewere in the neighbor-
hood of 30 endorsment from Different Central Labor Unions and
Trades Unions throughout the country they all seemed right as they
were duly signed and sealed by the several Unions so we heard what
he had to say. he told us that the Trades Union Circle Check Asso-

ciation was endorsed by nearly all the international Unions and by the A.F. of L. (see enclosed letter head) therefore we thought that they would hardly dare print such assertions on their letter heads if such was not the case and then the comunications from other Central bodies being taken into consideration we took it for granted that the Fellow was all right. so he unfolded his scheam which I must say if carried out honestly and fairly would be a good one, it was this. we were to have all the Merchants handleing Union Goods give to each purchaser a check bearing the ammount is [of his?] purchase the purchaser would then turn it in to the Union to which he belonged, then the Union would in turn send them in to the C.L.U. for Collection thereupon the C.L.U. would then present them back to the Merchant and Collect 3 Per Cent upon their face value (the Mercant signing a Contract to this affect) the C.L.U. would then retain 1 Per cent of the sum for its trouble the other 2 Per Cent would then be turned over to the Union to which the purchaser belonged we all thought this a pretty good thing but would not take any action upon it until after it had been refered to our several Unions for their consideration so it whent at that for that night, this was on a Monday night The Carpenters met on the following Friday he presented himself there and they refused to have anything to do with it but were willing that the C.L.U should go ahead upon their own responsability in the meentime the agent Petier Called upon the R.S. of the C.L.U. who is a clerk in one of our leading clothing stores (Miles J.K. Levey)[9] and told him that every thing was all right, that the Merchants were jumping at the scheme but that he was handy capped in approaching them on account of not having the endorsment of the Scranton C.L.U. anyhow how he worked upon poor Levey so the [that] he wrote him out a endorsment stamped with the seal of the C.L.U and signed his own name as R.S. and forged my name as president it was about two weeks after that Sec Levey told me of this action taken by him and told me he had signed My name to the endorsment saying that he hoped that I would not kick about it as he knew that I would sign it any way, it was just at this time that I began to be a little suspicious of the System so I told him that I did not think [I w]ould but knowing that Levey was was a pretty good fellow I promised to say nothing about it providing he never done such a thing again, so Bro Gompers this is a secret between myself and him and you are the first to know anything about it and I hope it will be kept sacred by you unless you should deem it nesasary for the good of our Order to make it Public then do so by all means,

I enclose 15 contracts entered into by the agent Peltier and the Leading Merchants of our City you will find he did not go for the small fry. with the exception of one or two he Collected 5 dollars from each and here is where he puts himself amenable to the law he promised that for this 5 dollars the Merchants should have certain advertising in Books and papers furnished by his Co and that all the nesasery papers would be furnished by them none of this has been carried out therefore the Merchants are looking to the C.L.U for some redress and we have wrote repeatedly to 8 John St. New York but can get no reply therefore we have come to the Conclusion that it is a skin game and I can assure you it has put us in a very bad light with the Merchants I hope that you wil[l] take care of the Contr[acts] an[d] return [them] when you are through with them as they belong to the C.L.U so far I think that I have given you a rough sketch of their doings I could keep on writing all night but as it is now 12 oclock I will wind up for the present and if there is anything else that I can do please remember that I am always at your command. and I am very sorry that I will not be able to meet you at the Convention.

I have 25 Machine Woodworkers ready to organise and I am making some progress with the brewers. we intend to try our hand with the factory girls at once we have enlisted the Young Womans Christian Association in their favor the Local Editor of the Elmira Telegram is doing all he can in the cause also. By the way I have not seen anything of Federationist up to date and I would sugest that you put the name of Scranton Branch Elmira Telegram upon your list of exchanges the Local Editor P. Barrett[10] is a down right good fellow and always willing to put in a good word for us, so I will close with best wishes from yours

Fraternally   Philip J. Thomas

ALS, Files of the Office of the President, General Correspondence, reel 59, frames 268-77, *AFL Records.*

1. Philip J. Thomas was a member of United Brotherhood of Carpenters and Joiners of America (UBCJA) 563 of Scranton, Pa., and president of the Scranton Central Labor Union (CLU).

2. SG to Philip Thomas, Nov. 16, 1896, reel 10, vol. 17, p. 49, SG Letterbooks, DLC.

3. The consumers' circle check system was meant to encourage trade unionists to buy union-made goods from local merchants. A consumers' "circle," or association, authorized participating shops to give customers an official check as proof of purchase, and the merchants in turn eventually paid the circle a rebate based on the redeemed checks. The system did not necessarily include all businesses handling union-made goods, and proved subject to fraud.

4. UBCJA 563.

5. The 1896 UBCJA convention was held in Cleveland, Sept. 21-29.

6. The Scranton CLU was organized about 1894 and received an AFL charter in 1895.

7. The Ancient Order of Hibernians, a secret Catholic Irish-American fraternal organization.

8. The 1896 AFL convention adopted a recommendation in SG's presidential report opposing the circle check scheme.

9. Myles J. K. Levy.

10. Patrick A. Barrett.

To Ernst Kurzenknabe

Dec. 5 [1896]

Mr. E. Kurzenknabe,

Secy.,

St. Louis, Mo.

Dear Sir: —

Although I have acknowledged several letters since the receipt of your favor of the 21st., yet I have been unable to give its contents the consideration they deserve, this owing to the work preparatory to the Convention. Although even now having considerable work to perform, I take time in order to reply, if not fully, then at least in a measure, to your suggestions and advice.

Before starting out, let me say that I appreciate most sincerely your expressions of friendship and good will, hence, whatever remarks you make in your letter, I am sure are prompted by the very best intentions to further the interests of our great movement and good will towards me personally.

You say, "The American workman must go into politics, but into the independent labor politics, they must start a class movement to secure their right to live as men and not as slaves."

Let me answer by saying that the American workmen do go into politics and the organized workmen into independent labor politics. It is not necessary for them to *start* a class movement. The trade union movement is the only working class movement in the country or in the world. The movement often called a class movement is often nothing more than a party movement, and in the same degree as this party movement increases, in the same ratio does it lose its working class character.

You believe that I should advise workmen to "sever their connection with *both* old political parties." I prefer to go further and to recommend to the workers of this country to sever their connection with *all* political parties, and I am sure that as workers are weaned from the political parties and are more staunch and true to the interests of their class movement, the trade union movement, the more distinct will the line of interest become and the advances of labor accelerated, gathering strength as they go, and growing until final emancipation is achieved eliminating class interests in the interest and disenthrallment of all from their false economic, social and political conditions.

You ask me to be "a leader of the American Federation of Labor and not only an officer." Where would you have me lead them? Where they have demonstrated their unwillingness to go? You say that thousands of honest workingmen will co-operate with me and give me their hearty support if I take the step you suggest. While this may be true, the other fact cannot be ignored, that if I were to take this step though thousands were to co-operate with me and give me their support, there are millions who would antagonize me, and after all, it is not the question of the support given me but what will best serve the interests of the movement, to protect and improve the condition of the workers of the movement, so that a better foundation may be laid to-day for the structure that is constantly being built.

There are some who have said that the reason I do not, as they are pleased to term, go further, is that I am so anxious to retain the position I occupy. I think that our relations are such that I should speak freely and frankly with you on this matter. I do not wish to go over my life's history except to say that as a factory operative for twenty-six years, I have never been outside of the labor movement. While working at my trade and since, I have ever tried to do my duty to my fellow workers, and to be fair, open, upright and courageous. I would be feigning were I to say other than that I regard the position I occupy as one of the greatest honor and the gravest responsibility, and though perhaps, if reasonable requests are complied with, I should like to perform the duties of that office as long as it shall please our workers in the movement, I could not and would not accept such a position of trust if it conflicted with my conscience and my convictions.

These thoughts lead me to the conviction that the best interests of the movement and all labor and all progress in our movement, lie in encouraging and keeping up the trade union movement, and such a movement growing constantly must inevitably secure betterment for all. It is the underlying thought of my action that prompts me to keep as near to the workers as possible, marching with them at the head of their column, willing to face the dangers and bear the brunt of battle. I prefer this for the movement's sake, not for the position. You may regard this as a mistake. If so, that is where we differ.

If the workingmen have always dinned into their ears that it is useless to struggle for better conditions to-day and this comes from the men who are supposed to give the labor cause their best thought, is it any wonder that a feeling of impotency sets in? The weak want encouragement and they then will soon demonstrate their ability to contend for their rights, and when people are fully imbued with a determination to accomplish their ends, the whole history of the world bears testimony to the fact that they have finally won. This is so, too, of labor.

Sometime when we are together, if ever we get the chance, I should be most pleased to discuss this question further. I have too little time to discuss this matter further now. More anon.

With kindest expressions of friendship and good-will, I am,

Fraternally yours,
Pres. A.F. of L.

TLp, reel 10, vol. 17, pp. 191-92, SG Letterbooks, DLC.

Excerpts from the Minutes of a Meeting of the Executive Council of the AFL

Dennison Hotel, Cincinnati, O. Dec 15, 1896

Present — Gompers, Lennon, O'Connell, Garland, McGuire, Duncan, Secretary McCraith being absent, Mr. Duncan took his place.

. . .

The president stated the Leadville miners desired to present some facts relative to their strike and also to secure financial aid.

Delegate Boyce of the miners said that there were 3000 men involved; only 10 had gone back on them: 20 union sympathizers had caused damage to property. 35 men were charged with same and the miners had been at a cost of $67,000, and now desired help from the council. The United States had been scoured for men and only 160 had been found to go into the mines, and then only by presence of militia. Their were 3000 on strike and 7000 were involved.

Del Clifford,[1] also of the miners, said they did not want public press to report they were looking for money. They did want it known that the A.F of L was back of the Western Fed of Miners, as it would help them materially. He also stated their principally industry was gold mining, next lead, silver nearly run out. The mining company could not afford to shut down the silver mine on account of political reasons. The new governor[2] takes office Jan 12; he was expected to withdraw militia when the scabs would depart.

Both delegates thought a circular sent to organizations would do good, and would not be objectionable, as it would not be matter of press report.

Delegation withdrew.

President Gompers moved

Resolved, That this convention of the American Federation of Labor hereby expresses its most emphatic and earnest endorsement of the attitude of the Western Federation of Miners in the rightful struggle of its members located at Leadville, Col., against the attempted encroachment upon their rights. That we hereby, and to the utmost of our ability tender them the support of the American Federation of Labor and call upon the [natio]nal and local unions herein affiliated, as well as on our central bodies, to extend to [them our moral] and financial support to the end that victory may reward our fellow-[workers of Leadville, Colorado, in their patriotic and determined stand for right.]

It was decided that the proposition be submitted to the delegates of the miners and if satisfactory the same be presented to convention.[3]

. . .

Dec 21. 96

All present, except McGuire who came in shortly after opening.

Del Kenehan of the Horseshoers was admitted. . . .

. . .

Del Kenehan also spoke on the resolution[4] before convention asking for a representative of labor in presidents cabinet. This was for the purpose of giving to the Western Senators an argument to defeat the Western Mine Owners, who would make a similar request to have a representative of theirs [. . .] would doubtless act in the interest of the mine owners, and order out militia when necessary.

Moved by Lennon that request be granted to ask for representative in presidents cabinet. Carried.

The president asked Kenehan for information on Montgomery's action[5] in the Leadville strike

Kenehan said Montgomery had gone to Leadville stating he was sent by the A.F. of L. to settle the strike. He aroused the ire of the miners and was told to get home which he did as quick as he could. In answer to further inquiry he said Montgomery was not a safe man to have connections with.

. . .

A and PD, Minutes of Meetings, Executive Council, AFL, reel 2, frames 1137-40, *AFL Records.*

1. Patrick H. CLIFFORD, an Aspen, Colo., miner, was a Western Federation of Miners' delegate at the 1896 AFL convention.

2. Alva Adams.

3. The AFL convention adopted this resolution on Dec. 18, 1896.

4. The 1896 AFL convention directed the Executive Council to draft a bill to establish a U.S. department of labor. However, because Rep. David K. Watson of Ohio introduced such a bill on Jan. 28, 1897 (H.R. 10179, 54th Cong., 2d sess.), the Council turned the matter over to SG, who decided that no further Federation action was required. H.R. 10179 failed to pass.

5. See "To William Montgomery," Nov. 3, 1896, n. 4, above.

Excerpts from News Accounts of the 1896 Convention of the AFL in Cincinnati

[December 16, 1896][1]

GET OUT OF LINE

. . .

POLITICAL DISCUSSIONS.

. . .

The long expected report of the Committee on Credentials was next called for, which recommended that the committee be relieved from further action in the Pomeroy matter[2] and the case decided by the convention. Delegate Warner,[3] Secretary of the committee, read the charges preferred against Pomeroy. He said that the committee had waited upon Pomeroy, who stated that so far as the charges of the Illinois State Federation was concerned, he was entirely innocent, for the reason that he was attached for several hundred dollars and could not pay the amount due the federation until certain pending litigation was settled. Pomaroy admitted that he had signed certain documents during the recent campaign, but had only done so after deciding to surrender his commission as General Organizer to the American Federation of Labor. Secretary Warner concluded his report with the recommendation that the matter should be settled by the convention, that being the proper tribunal in a matter of such importance.

A HOT DEBATE.

Delegate Morrison[4] then introduced a motion to the effect that the report of the Committee on Credentials be received and the credentials of Pomeroy rejected. It was lost, and then the fun began. Politics threw everything else into the shade, and during the balance of the afternoon session there reigned the utmost excitement. Every delegate who spoke did not mince matters. Insinuations, threats and almost insults were hurled back and forth, and many eloquent speeches were delivered. The battle started when Delegate Warner urged that no action on the matter should be taken until both sides were heard. Delegate Christopherson[5] concurred in this, and made a motion that the charges against Pomeroy be read. Carried. Delegate Warner then read the charges, as detailed above, and concluded by saying that at the recent meeting of the Executive Council at Indianapolis Pomeroy's commission as organizer was revoked. Delegate Morrison asked whether it was a fact that the commission was revoked, or that Pomeroy resigned of his own will. Secretary McCraith replied that the commission had been revoked. Then Delegate Weissmann[6] claimed the attention of the convention, and for the next fifteen minutes the delegates and visitors were treated to a brilliant oration.

He spoke against excluding Pomeroy, and said: "Are we ready to constitute ourselves a court of equity? We would be going outside our jurisdiction if we excluded this man. He has stolen nothing, committed no crime, but he has simply exercised his right as an American to choose his own political beliefs. This organization is so far above politics that it should not consider such a question for a moment. If we do we shall be adopting the tactics we have repudiated time and again. There are no proofs against Pomeroy, and I hope that the delegates will not allow personal feeling to enter into their minds when called upon to vote on this matter. This is one of the schemes carefully laid to bring the discussion of politics into the convention, and if I can prevent it I shall do so, and behind me is a strong organization that will stand by me."

THE CHICAGO TROUBLE.

He concluded by urging the delegates not to reject the credentials of Pomeroy.

Delegate Morrison followed with an eloquent appeal in behalf of the motion to reject the credentials. He asked why, if Pomeroy had committed no offense against the federation and the trades union movement, his commission should have been revoked by the Executive Council of the federation. He gave a resume of the Chicago trouble, which resulted in the breaking up of the Chicago Labor Congress and the subsequent establishment of the Chicago Federation of Labor, which he attributed to the actions of Pomeroy. Concluding, he asked, in the name of organized labor, that the delegates consider well this matter.

Delegate O'Donnell[7] said that he was willing to waive all the charges excepting the last, that of signing his name to political documents and using his official title as Organizer of the Federation. That offense, he thought, could not be overlooked. Delegate J. B. Lennon[8] spoke in favor of the motion to reject Pomeroy's credentials. He said that the question before the convention was a moral one, and that a man who brings discredit upon the labor movement should not be allowed a seat. At this point Delegate Weissmann asked for a construction of a clause in the constitution, but was ruled out of order. He then called for information, and asked if Section 8, Article 3, of the constitution did not provide that the question of politics should be debarred from the sessions of the federation. He then asked if the present debate was in order. Chairman McGuire[9] decided that it was, and the debate continued and grew warmer.

Delegates Ashe[10] and James O'Connell[11] spoke against the seating of Pomeroy, the latter saying that Pomeroy's actions had already cost the International Association of Machinists several lodges. O. E. Woodbury,[12] delegate from the Illinois State Federation of Labor, then said his say. He denied that he had any personal spite against "Billy" Pomeroy, and that he wished this to be understood. He then asked why Pomeroy's commission was revoked, and Chairman McGuire replied that it had been annulled with other organizers who took an active part in the recent campaign. Delegate Kidd[13] created quite a sensation when he said that Pomeroy was not to be trusted. He said that Pomeroy had told him, in answer to a question, that he was only in the labor movement for what there was in it. He said that Pomeroy had organized a woodworkers' union[14] in Chicago when there was one[15] already in existence, and asked if such action as this was not enough to condemn him as antagonistic to the labor movement.

AMENDMENT OFFERED.

Delegate Duncan[16] at this point offered an amendment to the motion already before the convention that the report of the Committee on Credentials be received, that the credentials of Pomeroy be accepted, and that the charges against Pomeroy be referred to the National Alliance of Hotel and Restaurant Employes[17] for action. In support of his motion he said that all the arguments made so far were made against Pomeroy, and not the organization he represents. He said that the Waiters' Alliance should be accorded representation. If Pomeroy has committed any offense, said Delegate Duncan, he has already been punished by the Illinois State Federation, and his offense, if any, against the Federation of Labor has been punished by the revoking of his commission. The question to be decided, he said, was whether the credentials of the Waiters' National Alliance should be questioned.

Delegate H. Lloyd[18] spoke in favor of the original motion. He said that some of the speakers had very ingeniously dragged the convention into a political discussion, and blamed Delegate Weissmann for so doing. At this Delegate Weissmann claimed the attention of the Chair. He said: "The eagle has screamed. My friend Lloyd has made a charge against me which he knows to be false. Mr. Lloyd himself took an active part as a Democrat in the recent campaign, and he is not in a position to throw stones." Here Chairman McGuire ruled the speaker out of order. Continuing, Delegate Weissmann said that Delegate Lloyd had charged him with being dishonest, which charge he repudiated. "Again I urge you all not to open the floodgates of political discussion in this convention. For three years we have succeeded in keeping such matters out of our sessions. I agree with Delegate Duncan that Pomeroy should be seated, and that the charge brought against him be referred to his own organization. Because there is a personal feeling against Pomeroy among many of the delegates is no reason why the Waiters' Alliance should be debarred representation here."

A PERSONAL FIGHT.

Delegate O'Sullivan,[19] Chairman of the Committee on Credentials, then made an earnest appeal in behalf of the alliance and the seating of Pomeroy. He said that the cause for so much antagonism against Pomeroy was due to the fact that he had supported the sound-money cause. He added that there would not have been a word of opposition had Pomeroy committed the same offense in the interests of the silver cause. By debarring Pomeroy from a seat in this convention, said the speaker, you will be denying the right of free speech. Do not let this convention take any such action. The National Waiters' Alliance should be recognized, and Pomeroy is equipped with the proper credentials. Delegate Askew[20] denied that he was a socialist, and that as one [who was not], he was opposed to the seating of Pomeroy. Delegate O'Neill,[21] the oldest delegate at the convention, spoke in favor of the original motion, and Delegate Phillips[22] thought that Pomeroy was guilty of a capital crime, and should be electrocuted.

At this point Delegate Yarnell[23] moved for the consideration of the previous question, which effectually put an end to further discussion. The motion was seconded and carried with a rush. The roll call was called for and a vote taken on the amendment offered by Delegate

Duncan, which resulted in its defeat. The question before the house then reverted to the original motion to reject the credentials of Pomeroy, which was carried,[24] Delegate Penna[25] declining to vote. . . . Chairman McGuire declared the motion carried, and Pomeroy will be debarred from his seat as a delegate. Delegate Prescott[26] asked to have his vote reversed, which was refused. . . .

Cincinnati Commercial Tribune, Dec. 16, 1896.

1. From a newspaper account of the proceedings of Dec. 15, 1896.

2. The convention was considering several charges against William C. Pomeroy who represented the Hotel and Restaurant Employees' National Alliance. These included his failure to honor a publishing contract with the Illinois State Federation of Labor (FL) and the signing of a political statement in his official capacity as an AFL organizer.

3. George H. Warner was a delegate of the International Association of Machinists (IAM); he served as directing business representative of IAM District 15 of New York.

4. Frank MORRISON, a delegate of the International Typographical Union (ITU) and a member of ITU 16 of Chicago, was elected secretary of the AFL at the 1896 convention. He served in that post from 1897 to 1935 and as AFL secretary-treasurer from 1936 until his retirement in 1939.

5. Elias S. Christopherson was a Journeymen Tailors' Union of America (JTUA) delegate.

6. Henry Weismann represented the Journeymen Bakers' and Confectioners' International Union.

7. Edward O'Donnell represented the Boston Central Labor Union.

8. John B. Lennon, AFL treasurer, was a JTUA delegate.

9. P. J. McGuire, first vice-president of the AFL, represented the United Brotherhood of Carpenters and Joiners of America (UBCJA).

10. Robert Ashe was an IAM delegate.

11. James O'Connell, AFL third vice-president, was an IAM delegate.

12. O. E. Woodbury, a Chicago carpenter, represented the Illinois State FL.

13. Thomas Inglis KIDD of Chicago was general secretary (1895-1905) of the Amalgamated Wood Workers' International Union of America.

14. Possibly the Machine Wood Workers' National Union.

15. Amalgamated WOOD Workers' International Union of America.

16. James Duncan was second vice-president of the AFL and a delegate of the Granite Cutters' National Union of the United States of America.

17. The HOTEL and Restaurant Employees' National Alliance.

18. Henry Lloyd represented the UBCJA.

19. John F. O'Sullivan represented the Massachusetts State FL.

20. Robert Askew was the delegate of the Northern Mineral Mine Workers' Progressive Union.

21. George McNeill represented AFL Federal Labor Union 5915.

22. John Phillips was a delegate from the United Hatters of North America.

23. Samuel Yarnell, a member of UBCJA 584 of Victor, Colo., represented the UBCJA.

24. SG voted with the majority.

25. Philip Penna represented the United Mine Workers of America.

26. William Prescott was a delegate from the ITU.

[December 17, 1896][1]

THIRD DAY'S WORK

. . .

. . . at this point the matter[2] was laid over by the introduction of Mr. Edward E. Clark,[3] General Secretary of the Brotherhood of Railway Conductors,[4] who represented the five great railroad brotherhoods.

A Distinguished Visitor.

The federation for some time had been desirous of having these brotherhoods affiliated, and the delegates gave Mr. Clark a rousing reception. The distinguished visitor was escorted to the platform and introduced to the convention by President Gompers. Mr. Clark read a paper on the subject of "Arbitration," written with especial reference to National legislation looking toward the settlement of differences between the railroad companies and employes by arbitration. Mr. Clark said he extended the greetings from the Brotherhoods of Locomotive Firemen, Conductors, Engineers,[5] Trainmen and Telegraphers,[6] which elicited great applause. Replying to a number of questions on arbitration, Mr. Clark said that the bill pending in Congress was considered a good thing, for it would bring matters properly before the public. Mr. Clark spoke of the State Boards of Arbitration as being ineffectual,[7] and all that he knew, he said, were political machines. Delegate McBride[8] protested against the speaker being subjected to such a volley of questions, and they at once ceased. The address of Mr. Clark will be printed. His suggestions were referred to a special committee. . . .

. . .

Resolutions Adopted.

The report of the Committee on Resolutions was next in order, and Secretary Morrison, of the committee, reported the following:

. . .

11. By Delegate O'Neill, calling for prompt action in recognizing the belligerent rights of Cuba.

Cuban Discussion.

The last resolutions occupied the attention of the convention during the balance of the session. Delegate Black[9] spoke against their adoption, arguing that the federation would be going outside its jurisdiction by adopting them. This raised a storm of indignant feeling, and one after another the delegates spoke in behalf of the patriots. Delegate White[10] said that the resolutions should be adopted on economic principles, and Delegate Weissmann made a stirring address in favor of their adoption. President Gompers also spoke in favor of the resolution and eloquently referred to the sufferings being endured by the brave Cubans now struggling for independence. He said that it was proper that the convention should take immediate action upon this matter. "I am always on the side of the oppressed and the weak. It is one of the great principles of trades-unionism. If I am in America I am a union man; in England, I am a trades unionist; in Germany, I would be a Socialist, and in Russia, I would be a Nihilist. The Cubans are fighting for their rights, and I hope that these resolutions will be adopted without a dissenting voice."

Delegate O'Neill followed with an earnest appeal for the adoption of the resolutions, and Delegate Warner said that it was the duty of the federation to assist the patriots. Delegate Donnelly[11] protested against their adoption. He said that it ill-befitted a trades union to take such action as might lead to a war. He thought that it would be better to discuss the better organization of the working people of this country and devote all the energies in that direction. Delegate Sam Yarnell hoped that the federation was not built upon such narrow principles that it can not extend the hand of sympathy to struggling fellow-men. He said that if our forefathers were living today they would be found in Cuba. "We want to show Spain that when she sheds innocent blood and allows its soldiers to outrage defenseless women and slaughter babies that the working people of the United States will not allow such things. It is time this butchery was stopped. The resolutions should censure the President for not taking a decided stand upon this matter."

Delegate Furuseth,[12] of the Seamen's Union, spoke against the adoption of the resolutions. He said it would bring on war with Spain, which would result in this country being burdened with an immense army and navy. At this point the previous question was called, which ended further discussion. Delegate Black asked for privilege to explain his position, which was granted. He said that it was his privilege to differ with others without being abused by some of the delegates. A vote was then taken, which resulted in sixty delegates voting in favor of the resolutions and nine against.

. . .

Cincinnati Commercial Tribune, Dec. 17, 1896.

1. Covering proceedings of Dec. 16, 1896.

2. The issue under discussion was a dispute between New York City brewers and coopers.

3. Edgar Erastus CLARK was grand chief conductor of the Order of Railway Conductors of America.

4. The Order of RAILWAY Conductors of America.

5. The Brotherhood of LOCOMOTIVE Engineers.

6. The Order of RAILROAD Telegraphers of North America.

7. The railroad brotherhoods favored the Erdman bill because it made arbitration settlements binding on corporations and contained unprecedented bans on blacklisting, ironclad contracts (stipulating an employee's agreement not to join a union as a condition of employment), and harassment of union members.

8. John McBride was a delegate from the United Mine Workers of America.

9. David Black, a delegate of the Iron Molders' Union of North America (IMUNA), had been a member of IMUNA 28 of Toronto; after moving to Cincinnati he was editor of the *Iron Molders' Journal* from 1895 until his resignation in 1903.

10. Either Henry White of New York City, representing the United Garment Workers of America, or John White of St. Louis, a delegate of the National Tobacco Workers' Union.

11. Thomas J. Donnelly, a Cincinnati printer, represented AFL Federal Labor Union 6697.

12. Andrew Furuseth represented the International Seamen's Union of America.

Cincinnati, Ohio, Dec. 17. [1896]

SILVER AND UNIONISM

Delegate Mahone,[1] of the Street Railway Union, sprang a surprise at the morning session of the Federation of Labor, by rising to a privileged question, and stating that very grave rumors were being circulated against the general officers, and moving that a committee of five be appointed to investigate these charges. Many delegates insisted on specifying the charges or putting them in writing, but these objections did not prevail.

The subject was debated for a time, and finally postponed to the late afternoon session. On reassembling at 4:30 o'clock, the Federation went into executive session to consider the charges.

The executive session continued from 5 P.M. till 8 P.M., and resulted in the vindication of President Gompers and the retirement of Secretary McCraith, whose term expires next month. While the rumors of charges surprised President Gompers and all others except a select few of the delegates, there seems to have been much agitation during last night in consultation rooms over the sensation that was to be sprung to-day. Ex-Secretary A. G. Wines[2] and Secretary August McCraith were separated by friends while quarreling in a room at the Dennison House in the early morning hours, and revolvers are said to have been drawn.

POLITICS CAUSED THE TROUBLE.

The trouble was between President Gompers and Secretary McCraith, and dated back to the last campaign. In the absence of President Gompers it is said that Secretary McCraith edited the Federationist. McCraith is considered a Socialist, and was afterward a silver man, but in the absence of President Gompers he kept out articles on the silver question that had been previously appearing in the organ of the Federation. At a subsequent meeting of the executive council this matter, with other differences between the President and Secretary, were considered, and Secretary McCraith was compelled to apologize to President Gompers.[3]

It is charged that after this action of the executive council Secretary McCraith conspired against President Gompers, and tried to make a case against the President on the correspondence of the latter with certain prominent political leaders in the silver movement. Secretary McCraith held that in replying to the letters of silver leaders President Gompers went beyond the power of the President of the Federation. While Secretary McCraith is called an anarchist by many delegates, he is recognized by all as a consistent trade unionist and as being averse even to any sort of affiliation with political parties. It is claimed that President Gompers does not affiliate with any party, but that his correspondence with the advocates of free silver was in accordance with resolutions adopted at the last three national conventions of the Federation. It was out of this correspondence that the rumors sprang about President Gompers being closely associated with National Chairman Jones[4] and others.

DELEGATE MAHONE'S CHARGES.

In the executive session Delegate Mahone, who sprung the question on the rumors of charges earlier in the day, read a paper setting forth the rumors that President Gompers had acted with politicians, and even negotiated with them during the recent campaign. Mr. Mahone said he would not present it as a charge, and that there was a rumor of only one offense, and that was that President Gompers had participated in politics.

Secretary McCraith, who originated the rumors on which the charge was based, then made a statement about keeping politics out of the Federation, and read all the letters that President Gompers had written and received from political leaders during the campaign. These parties wanted President Gompers to meet Chairman Jones in Chicago. This proposition was declined. Then it was proposed to have President Gompers meet other silver advocates in Chicago. President Gompers replied that he was too busy to leave his office, but would talk the matter over if the parties would come to Indianapolis. It was admitted that at least one representative of the silver cause did come to Indianapolis to see President Gompers. None of the letters had been filed away with the private papers of President Gompers, but all were filed with the official correspondence of the President, and labeled "Politics." Secretary McCraith and any others could get the letters and read them, and the Secretary did produce all of them in evidence.

Secretary McCraith said he felt President Gompers had done wrong, and called the attention of the executive council to the matter. Mr. McCraith also stated that President Gompers had been at Chicago at least once during the campaign. On investigation the executive council reported that they knew where President Gompers was while in Chicago; that he did not meet Chairman Jones or any other politician there, but that he went there to confer with a President of an international union.

PRESIDENT GOMPERS' STATEMENT.

President Gompers was requested to make a statement, but he said only a few words, and announced that all his correspondence and his actions in the official capacity of President of the Federation were as open to the delegates and the world as the correspondence which Secretary McCraith had seen fit to bring to the convention.

After considerable discussion, which reflected more on those who had circulated the rumors of serious charges than on President Gompers, Delegate Penna, of the Miners' Union, offered the following:

"Having heard the charges of alleged wrong-doing by President Gompers during the recent political campaign,

"Resolved, That we indorse the President's position, dismiss the charges, and exonerate him from all blame."

During the informal hearing of the case there was an exciting discussion of the silver question, but there were only three dissenting votes, and the three voting in the negative announced that they did so on account of their opposition to the free coinage of silver, which they would not indorse in any form, although they desired to indorse President Gompers.

RESOLUTION OF CONFIDENCE ADOPTED.

The following, offered by George W. McNeill, was then unanimously adopted:

"Resolved, That the delegates to the Sixteenth Annual Convention of the American Confederation of Labor do hereby declare in unqualified language their confidence in President Samuel Gompers as a man worthy of the cause he has espoused and for which he has sacrificed his time, health, and ability."

A similar resolution of confidence was unanimously adopted in indorsing the five members of the executive council. During the debate it was brought out that only two of the five members of the executive council knew anything about these rumors, circulated by Secretary McCraith and others against President Gompers, until Delegate Mahone called attention to them in the convention hall to-day.

After the action of the convention in executive session, Secretary McCraith announced that he would retire, and the friends of Delegate Morrison, of the Chicago Typographical Union, are now confident of Morrison's election to-morrow afternoon without opposition. It is the general opinion that all of the old officers will now be re-elected except Secretary McCraith.[5]

Since the silver question was such a feature of the executive session, when the charges against Gompers were being considered, it is now announced that a resolution will be offered to-morrow to strike out the indorsement of the three previous national conventions of free coinage at the ratio of 16 to 1, and a long and animated discussion is expected.

Washington Post, Dec. 18, 1896.

1. W. D. Mahon was the delegate of the Amalgamated Association of Street Railway Employes.

2. Apparently Abner G. WINES, secretary-treasurer of the International Typographical Union from 1893 to 1896, though Wines was not actually a delegate to the AFL convention.

3. The *Cincinnati Commercial Tribune* of Dec. 18, 1896, reported that McCraith had been accused of accepting a bribe to withhold publications from the *Federationist* while editing the journal in SG's absence, and had apologized to SG after the matter came to the attention of the Executive Council. Speaking before the convention, delegate George Warner labelled the story "a malicious falsehood," and the meeting voted to support McCraith if he sued the newspaper (AFL, *Proceedings*, 1896, p. 59). The *Tribune* published a retraction on Dec. 22.

4. James K. Jones (1839-1908), a Democratic congressman (1881-85) and senator (1885-1903) from Arkansas, was chairman of the Democratic National Committee in 1896 and 1900.

5. The convention reelected SG, P. J. McGuire, James Duncan, James O'Connell, M. M. Garland, and John B. Lennon, respectively, as president, first through fourth vice-presidents, and treasurer; it elected Frank Morrison secretary.

SG subsequently wrote this evaluation of August McCraith: "Mr. McCraith, so far as financial honesty is concerned, can not be questioned. He was also a competent official. He did seek to impose his own theories upon the mo[ve]ment, regardless of the attitude of the organization. It was this which first caused any friction between him and me. He seemed to suspect every one of wrongdoing who did not agree entirely with him in his theories of philosophical anarchy. This, with an additional failing of overweening conceit which prompted him to imagine that he 'knew it all[']; that there was 'no depth' to any one whose studies and convictions of the social problem did not coincide absolutely with his, was his gravest fault. These faults made it exceedingly difficult for any one to get along with him, and which brought about his retirement" (SG to James Bell, Jan. 31, 1901, reel 28, vol. 40, p. 569, SG Letterbooks, DLC).

[December 18, 1896]

. . .

ADVOCATES HIGHER DUES.

The most important question decided upon by the convention yesterday, outside of the charges brought against Gompers, was a resolution introduced by Delegate P. J. McGuire, of the Carpenters' International Union, advocating higher dues. It recommended that affiliated locals not having a National head should, within the next six months, so change their constitutions as to place the minimum membership fee at fifty cents per month. There was considerable opposition to the resolution from delegates representing the local unions, and three amendments were submitted, but afterward voted down. Delegate McGuire made a stirring address in behalf of the motion, and when it was put to a vote it was adopted.

. . .

Cincinnati Commercial Tribune, Dec. 18, 1896.

[December 19, 1896][1]

. . .

Resolutions were next introduced and adopted extending the aid of the federation and its affiliated unions to the Colorado miners. The next resolution read proved to be the long-expected one relating to the silver question. It was drawn up by Delegate Weissmann, of New York, and called for the repeal of the resolution adopted by the federation three years ago, which recommended the free and unlimited coinage of silver at the ratio of 16 to 1. The resolution was given to the Committee on Resolutions two days ago, and in its report yesterday it recommended that when the federation adopted the resolution three years ago it was then an economic question, but that now it had assumed a political aspect, and the committee therefore recommended discussion. At this point President Gompers vacated the chair, which was taken by Delegate Tobin.[2]

Delegate Weissmann was the first speaker, and made an earnest and eloquent plea in behalf of the resolution. He said: "This question should be properly settled here today. By allowing the resolution adopted three years ago to stand you will be declaring in favor of a political party, which would be an action that would call forth considerable dissatisfaction on the part of the trades unions. The federation in its constitution declares that it will not mix up in politics, but it will be doing so if it allows the resolution adopted three years ago to stand. It will also be the means of diverting the interests of labor from the basic principles of trades unionism. I was instructed by my organization to bring this matter before the convention, for we bakers believe that the one principle upon which the federation should center all its energies is the eight-hour question, and not go outside its jurisdiction in declaring in favor of something which can never do the wageworkers any good. We believe it essential for the best interests of labor that every effort should be made to shorten the work day, and not take issue with any political party. If the federation adopted a resolution favoring the free coinage of silver three years ago, it was done because at that time the question was an economic one. Today it is entirely different, for it has now become a political question, and the federation is opposed to taking sides with either of the parties. At the Denver convention I opposed the resolution."

At this point the speaker was interrupted by Delegates Kenehan[3] and Mahon, the latter immediately launching forth into an hysterical plea for free silver. Delegate Kenehan then asked to make an explanation, but Chairman Tobin told him the explanation had been made. Delegate Kenehan protested and said that the Chair was not a mind reader, and charged Chairman Tobin to tell of what he (Kenehan) was thinking. Delegate Ashe spoke against the resolution, and hoped it would be voted down. He was followed by Delegate Yarnell, of Cripple Creek, who said that the bakers worked such long hours that it was no wonder they did not understand the silver question. Delegate DeLong[4] then made a motion that the whole matter be laid on the table. A roll call was demanded, which resulted in the defeat of the motion by a vote 1,367 to 931.

A substitute was next introduced by Delegate Yarnell declaring in favor of indorsing the previous actions of the federation in the free silver resolution. This led to another long discussion, until Delegate Lennon offered an amendment to the substitute to the effect that the convention reaffirm the stand taken at the Denver Convention, but emphatically deny that in the adoption of this measure the federation indorses any political party. Delegate Yarnell, after some dispute, accepted the amendment, but Delegate Garland[5] wanted to offer another amendment declaring in favor of a high protective tariff. He was ruled out of order. Delegate Weissmann spoke against the Lennon amendment, and said that by adopting it the federation would be pledging itself to a political party. He urged the delegates not to vote for such a principle. A vote was taken and the roll call again demanded, which resulted in the adoption of the amendment by a vote of 1,915 to 326. . . .[6]

. . .

Cincinnati Commercial Tribune, Dec. 19, 1896.

1. Covering proceedings of Dec. 18, 1896.

2. John F. Tobin represented the Boot and Shoe Workers' Union.

3. Roady Kenehan was the delegate of the International Union of Journeymen Horseshoers of the United States and Canada.

4. Charles J. DeLong was the delegate of AFL Engineers' Progressive Association 6614 of Chicago.

5. Mahlon M. Garland was the delegate of the National Amalgamated Association of Iron and Steel Workers.

6. The convention proceedings give the vote as 1,915 to 362 (AFL, *Proceedings,* 1896, p. 60).

Cincinnati, Ohio, Dec. 19. [1896]

LABOR CONVENTION

. . .

The matter of moving the national headquarters was then brought before the convention by the Law Committee. A motion was made that the word Indianapolis be stricken out, and the delegates given a chance to vote their choice. Delegate Weissmann of the New York Bakers' Union spoke for five minutes, the time limit, against the motion. President Gompers vacated the chair and gave the convention his views on the subject, which were strongly in favor of removal from Indianapolis.

His chief arguments were that the city lacked adequate facilities for the dissemination of federation and labor news through the public press, the great news associations having their own correspondents, who could not put anything on the wires without first receiving orders from headquarters in some larger city, and that it was equally lacking in printing facilities. He did not speak in favor of any other city. There were several other speeches on the subject, most of them favoring the motion, and on the roll being called the motion to strike out was carried by a vote of 1,594 to 730, and Indianapolis was ordered stricken from the constitution.

Delegate Silver,[1] of Washington City, moved that the word Washington be substituted, and Delegate Kennehan, of Denver, moved that Chicago be substituted.

Delegate Weissmann entered a protest against Washington, holding that there was great danger that the Executive Council and permanent officers of the federation would become contaminated by the degrading and corrupt practices and influences that would there surround them, degenerate into professional Congressional lobbyists and lose the influence which they can now exert with members of the nation's legislature as honest men, asking only that which is right in behalf of the nation's wage-earners.

"I hope Washington will not be chosen," said he, "but I know it will. There is a combination in this convention that has already accomplished the passage of several measures of doubtful propriety, and it will accomplish this one." There was a general murmur of disapproval of this remark, and the chair promptly called the delegate to order.

First Vice President P. J. McGuire advocated the selection of Washington for the good of the Federation and all wage earners. In Washington City the Executive Council would be always in touch with national legislation and it would be impossible for the introduction of and action upon bills affecting wage earners affiliated with the A.F. of L. without the knowledge of the officers, as has frequently occurred in the past.

He hoped to see the time when the organization will buy ground and erect a temple in the national capital for the permanent home of the American Federation of labor.

The vote resulted in the selection of Washington by 1,705 against 487 for Chicago. . . .

Unidentified New York City newspaper, Dec. 20, 1896, Scrapbook 1, reel 24, *AFL Records.*

1. William S. Silver, a stonecutter, represented the Washington, D.C., Central Labor Union.

[December 22, 1896][1]

ITS LABOR ENDED

. . .

The first matter discussed was the Erdman arbitration bill. The special committee to which the bill had been referred for analysis recommended that it be not indorsed by the convention. Some discussion followed, and on motion the matter was referred to the Executive Committee for final disposal. . . .

. . .

DISCUSSING IMMIGRATION.

The report of the Committee on Immigration, read by Delegate P. J. McGuire, attracted great interest. It recommended that the Executive Council hire a competent attorney to draw up a bill for presentation to Congress for the restriction of immigration. It also recommended for passage House Bill 7864,[2] bearing on this subject; that the United States Inspectors be urged to see that the laws bearing on immigration be strictly enforced; that punishment should be inflicted upon those who violate the alien contract labor law; that all immigrants be required to state that they intend becoming naturalized citizens within one year after they land, and that copies of this report be printed and sent to all Congressmen and Representatives. Delegate Fursueth objected to the recommendations referring to the compulsory naturalization of immigrants and the authority of the Consuls at foreign ports. He said that no immigrant should be compelled to state whether he will or will not become a citizen of the United States. Delegate Lloyd said that organized labor should not advocate the Lodge bill. "We must not join issue with the capitalist in keeping out foreign labor," said Mr. Lloyd. "Why should we keep out honest labor? The foreign labor is the bulwark of our organizations, and I hope the whole matter will be voted down."

Delegate O'Sullivan said that the question of restricting immigration has been agitated since the seventeenth century. He produced an old document signed by workingmen in 1677, petitioning the General Court of Boston to restrict immigration. He said that it comes with poor grace from this convention should it indorse the report of the committee. He asked by what right foreigners, who have established their homes in this country, shall say who shall and who shall not come here. Delegate McGuire spoke in favor of the committee's report. He defended the Lodge bill, which gives an educational test to immigrants, which, should they fail to pass, provides for their reshipment back to their native countries. He ably defended the report of the committee, and said it was due the labor movement to keep out the foreigners who flock to this country and take the places of American citizens.

A long and interesting discussion followed, in which nearly all the delegates took part. Both sides of the question were given a thorough hearing, although an effort was made several times to table the report. Delegate Ashe succeeded in offering an amendment which recommended that the whole matter be referred to the Executive Committee with instructions to make a thorough investigation[3] and then submit the report to the various unions affiliated within the next six months. After a long and tedious debate, it was adopted by a vote of 32 to 20. . . .[4]

. . .

Cincinnati Commercial Tribune, Dec. 22, 1896.

1. The article describes the proceedings of Dec. 21, 1896.
2. The major provision of H.R. 7864 (54th Cong., 1st sess., 1896), known as the Lodge-Corliss Bill, was to restrict the immigration of illiterates. It also barred male aliens from repeated travel to the United States to work unless they declared their formal intent to become citizens. President Grover Cleveland vetoed the measure on Mar. 2, 1897.
3. On June 10, 1897, the AFL Executive Council issued a circular soliciting the views of affiliates on a series of proposals for regulating immigration: greater restriction, banning of paupers and criminals, greater governmental enforcement powers, imprisonment of violators of the alien contract labor law, steamship company liability for the character of their passengers, stricter civil and educational requirements for naturalization, and admission only of immigrants declaring their intent to become citizens. The circular called on affiliates to instruct their delegates to the next AFL convention on the immigration question. See "Under Its Old Regime," Dec. 19, 1897, n. 3, in "Excerpts from Accounts of the 1897 Convention of the AFL in Nashville," below.
4. The proceedings give the vote as 30 to 22 (AFL, *Proceedings,* 1896, p. 82).

From August Donath[1]

Real Estate Broker,
Washington, D.C., December 24, 1896.

Dear Mr. Gompers:

I am glad that your headquarters will be located here, for you will find that there is much in being "on the ground" when legislation is being enacted. But what prompts me to write this letter is the deplorable state of the labor element here. Not that the workingmen, at different occupations, are not organized. On the contrary, they are organized too much. I believe there are three different Unions and Assemblies of carpenters,[2] two of plasterers,[3] &c., and one pulls against the other.

I have long left the active discussion of Labor topics to other men, but as I believed in Union principles when employed at my trade, (printing), I still have the desire to have those principles upheld. But as at present constituted, the workingmen of this town stand in their own light, and he who will once teach them the wisdom of turning all their energies in one direction, will do a good work indeed. Just now the local Knights of Labor are on the point of revolt from the national body, on account of arbitrary action against them[4] at the recent General Assembly, and it might be the best time that will ever present itself, to make advances to them. The District Master Workman, Mr. H. G. Simmons,[5] is an earnest, sincere man. I believe he wants to do what is best for the wage-workers. The president of the local Federation of Labor is Mr. McHugh,[6] and he is also, I believe, the National Secretary of the Stone-cutters. He is well spoken of. The president of the Central Labor Union is a member of the Bricklayers' Union,[7] of unusual intelligence, and the last man, I am assured, to stand in the way of that union of forces that must be secured before the interests of Labor can be advanced in this city. His name is Mr. Spohn. If you can begin your work in this town by bringing these different and rival organizations to a realization of the suicidal course they are pursuing, you will make glad the hearts of all who, like myself, are not now actively working for a living, but to whom the cause is still dear and holy.

With kind regard, August Donath.

TLS, Files of the Office of the President, General Correspondence, reel 59, frames 281-82, *AFL Records.*

1. During the mid-1890s August Donath (1845-1913) operated a real estate, loan, and insurance business in Washington, D.C. An emigrant from Westphalia in 1857, he settled in Roxbury, Mass., where he learned printing. After Civil War service he moved to Washington, D.C., in 1863, where he worked for the government printing office (GPO) and for Washington daily papers, as a clerk and examiner for the Bureau of Pensions, and ultimately as Superintendent of Documents in the GPO. He was active in the Columbia Typographical Union (International Typographical Union [ITU] 101) and in 1883 helped found the *Craftsman,* which served as the ITU's organ. He edited the paper through early 1884 and returned to serve as its associate editor in the late 1880s. His publishing work also included editing the *Chester* (Pa.) *Times* and the *West Chester* (Pa.) *News.* He was elected president of the ITU board of Childs-Drexel trustees and served in that office for six years, until the Home for Union Printers was opened in Colorado Springs, Colo.

2. United Brotherhood of Carpenters and Joiners of America 190, Amalgamated Society of Carpenters and Joiners Branch 683, and probably KOL Local Assembly (LA) 1748.

3. Operative Plasterers' International Association of the United States and Canada 96 and KOL LA 1644.

4. The 1896 KOL General Assembly, which met in Rochester, N.Y., Nov. 10-21, preferred charges against three members of KOL District Assembly (DA) 66 for complicity in libeling national KOL officers in the *Washington Times.* The three were C. G. Conn, editor-in-chief of the paper, William H. G. Simmons, vice-president of the paper's parent company and master workman of DA 66, and James K. Potter, secretary of the company. The General Assembly subsequently decided to expel Conn and to demand a retraction from Simmons and Potter.

5. William H. G. Simmons was a Washington, D.C., tinner and master workman of KOL DA 66 in 1896. He was a member of KOL LA 2031.

6. James F. McHugh was secretary (1891) and secretary-treasurer (1892-1912) of the Journeymen Stonecutters' Association of North America.

7. Milford Spohn, a former president of Bricklayers' and Masons' International Union of America 1 of Washington, D.C., was the first president of the Washington, D.C., Central Labor Union (1896-98) and president of the Washington, D.C., Building Trades Council (1899).

From Michael Donnelly[1]

Sheep Butchers Protective Union No. 6146.
405 E. 19th St. Kansas City, Mo. Decr. 29 1896

Dear Sir & Bro.

The action of the Armour Pckg Co. in forcing us to Strike[2] is in keeping with their past record. They were no doubt aware that a National organization of Butchers[3] is under way, and that this Union is the Prime mover in the enterprise. This is the first time in my nine years connection with Packing House Butchering, that a national organization has been contemplated and it is a sad blow to our future welfare to see our national Union about to be nipped in the bud. As the Writer sees things now our only salvation lies in getting our Fellow Craftsmen in Chicago organized. I mean Beef Sheep and Pork Butchers. The financial condition of the Three Locals[4] here is at such a low ebb, that it would be impossible for them to send an organizer to the Windy City at present. Pork Butchers #6453 and Beef Butchers #6496 have been assisting in the Armour Boycott, which is a continual drain on their Treasuries and our union being so small has not been able to accumulate a large Treasury Our Delegate's[5] expenses to the Cincinati Convention almost left our Treasury depleted.

In Chicago the Butchers have got the same opposition to contend with, that we had when we first organized that is the fear of being discharged which was the penalty for becoming a member of a Trades Union When organizing care must be taken to do the work with as little publication as possible, in fact I would be in favor of carrying on the work almost secretly. In organizing the Butchers here we just got a few of our most reliable men together, talked the matter over, applied for a Charter and got down to business. We were affiliated with the Central Body[6] Three months before our Employers or the Public generally were aware of the fact, during which time we kept recruiting our forces right along, so that when The Packers became cognizant of the existence of a union, They were amazed to find every Sheep Butcher in Two out of the Three Establishments which slaughter Sheep members of our Union. The same tactics were pursued by the Cattle and Pork Butchers, with what degree of success you are already aware the Pork Butchers now being the largest Trade Union in the city. So my belief is if a start could be made in Chicgo our success nationally would be virtually established In the event of getting the Chicago Butchers organized, it would be a comparitively easy matter to organize Omaha, St. Louis, and other large Packing Centers.

If you can spare the time to give this matter your earnest consideration and be able to give us some encouragement and advice you will have conferred a great favor on

Yrs Fraternally, M. Donnelly,

Secty #6146

ALS, Amalgamated Meat Cutters and Butcher Workmen of North America Records, reel 141, frames 213-15, *AFL Records.*

1. Michael J. DONNELLY, secretary of AFL Sheep Butchers' Protective Union 6146 of Kansas City, Mo., was a founder in 1897 of the Amalgamated Meat Cutters and Butcher Workmen of North America.

2. On Dec. 26, 1896, members of AFL 6146 walked out over a reduction in piece rates. They regarded the wage cut as an effort by Armour to rid itself of unions in the wake of unresolved struggles with firemen and other workers that had begun in May. The Federation endorsed the strike the following month. On Apr. 9, 1898, the AFL Executive Council approved a settlement negotiated by the company and an AFL committee by which Armour agreed to recognize and negotiate exclusively with unions of its employees and to experiment with a shorter workday.

3. A reference to the forthcoming organization of the Amalgamated Meat Cutters and BUTCHER Workmen of North America.

4. AFL Beef Butchers' Union 6496 and AFL Pork Butchers' Union 6423 (both chartered in 1895), of Kansas City, Kans., and AFL 6146 (chartered in 1893).

5. George Byer, of Kansas City, Mo., represented AFL 6146.

6. The Kansas City (Mo.) Industrial Council, chartered by the AFL in 1895.

To Gabriel Edmonston[1]

308 E. 125th St. New York Jan. 9th 1896. [1897]

Dear Friend Gab: —

Yours of the 7th to hand last night and am very much interested in the information you impart relative to office rooms.

By this mail I write our friend Duncan asking him to meet you in Washington, Monday or Tuesday. Whatever you and he decide upon I know will be satisfactory to me because it will be advantageous to the A.F. of L. and the facility to do its work.

When there *is elevator service* in the building the fact that a suite of rooms is one floor higher makes no difference to us, the saving of $10.00 per month in the rent is quite an item however.

Enclosed find two letters on the subject of office. I think it too far from *The Avenue.* Don't you?

Should you and Duncan decide favorably on a place, hire it and let me know by mail or wire the address.

Pardon the trouble I am putting you to but I know that your devotion to the cause and willingness to aid me in this difficult matter, will prompt you to do this cheerfully.

I saw Pete and spent some pleasant and interesting hours with him. Of course we spoke of you and old times; and the fact that once sincerely enlisted in the cause it was almost impossible to get right out.

I found my folks in good health and we were much happy in the re-union. Well we will take up housekeeping in the District by the end of the month.

Thanking you for many kindnesses and best wishes to you and yours I am

Yours Sincerely   Saml Gompers.

Pardon paper.[2]

ALS, Papers of Gabriel Edmonston, reel 1, *AFL Records.*

1. Gabriel EDMONSTON, a Washington, D.C., builder, was a founder and the first president of the Brotherhood of Carpenters and Joiners of America (1881-82) and from 1886 to 1888 served as treasurer of the AFL.

2. The letter was written on a sheet of plain paper rather than AFL stationery.

Julius Reinhart[1] to Frank Morrison

Secretary
Musicians Mutual Protective Union[2]
Butte City, Montana, January 23rd 1897

Dear Sir and Bro:—

Yours of recent date advising this Local of the National League of Musicians of the United States to affiliate with the so-called American Federation of Musicians[3] (certainly not a federation of *American* musicians) at hand and the Board of Directors of this Local has instructed me to reply to the insulting communication as best I know how.

As representative of this organization, I desire to impress upon you, in the first place that this Union owes its existence and its charter to the National League of Musicians of the United States, a Trades Union from which *all* charters of Musicians' organizations should emanate; this fact being verified by the frantic effort of the A.F. of L for three consecutive years to almost beg upon its bended knees for affiliation of our National body.

The League is the sire of all Bona Fide and True Musicians' Unions and any so-called Musicians' Union owing first allegiance to some other organization or claiming another organization as its fountain head is born out of legitimate wedlock has an illegitimate Sire and must per se be deemed a bastard organization.

A more impudent proposition than that made by the A.F. of L., which hitherto has been held in the highest esteem by this Local, can by us hardly be conceived and a continuation upon those lines will soon place the A.F. of L upon the low plane now occupied by the formerly powerful organization known as the Knights of Labor. How an organization of the standing of the A.F. of L and commanding the respect not only of the laboring masses of the United States, but to a certain extent, also that of the capitalists and corporations, for the fair and manly stand usually taken upon all propositions affecting the two classes could so stultify itself as to recognize a few disgruntled office seekers of a National Craft, who have outlived their usefulness, and endeavor to start a Fountain head in opposition to one organized and recognized for many years fails to be understood by this writer and it sorely grieves me to see the old A.F. of L following in the footsteps of the late lamented K. of L. who, at the moment that they infringed upon the rights of trades unions fell and lost the power that they wielded in the land and the respect of the craftsmen was lost to them forever. It is not too late for the A.F. of L to retrace this step backward and to assume among the craftsmen of the United States the standing which should be its due.

Now for our individual case:—We protest that the stand taken by the A.F. of L. in asking us to withdraw from the National League of the United States and unite with the A.F. of M. is one of the most unreasonable and untenable propositions ever made by such a body as yours has always been supposed to be, to an organization like ours. You issued to us many years ago a charter which purported to give us the protection of the A.F. of L; you never hesitated to receive our per capita tax (it probably came in handy about the house) and then you pick up an assortment of ex office holders and office seekers of our Fountain head and throw in a few expelled scabs and unprincipled scoundrels and then in Shylockian manner kindly ask us to pay a new charter fee to the baby A.F. of M (Lord save the name) and particularly get a new line of supplies. How great must be this new organization greater even than its so-called parent when the older child is entirely forgotten and asked to follow the steps of a foster father in place of its own legitimate and true parent. What a travesty upon Unionism is this.

For years have we been affiliated and now you ask us to quit and join hands with the new born child. What fearful labour pains must have been borne in bringing this new child into the world, for it is said that the greater the mother suffers in bringing a new child into the world the greater is her love for the same. There is somewhere published if my memory is not at fault, a book entitled "Parturition made easy"; it were advisable for the A.F. of L to get a copy if it expects to continue in this business, for there is little doubt but that the pains will increase and a new National body will be organized to occupy the place formerly occupied by not only itself but also the almost defunct Knights of Labor.

We are not affiliating at the present time with any and every organization that comes along; we are strong enough to stand upon our own bottom; we were organized fighting the strongest labor Union in this town; it numbers between three and four thousand, we number about a hundred and beat it; we are locally strong because this is a town of legitimate unions and unionism and while we regret the action taken by your body in this matter, we are compelled to bid you an affectionate adieu. Ta-ta.

Yours etc.   J Reinhart
Secretary   Local No 39 of the Nat League of
Musicians of the U.S.

TLS, American Federation of Musicians' Records, reel 141, frames 680-81, *AFL Records.*

1. Julius Reinhart was a Butte, Mont., musician and mercantile agency manager.
2. AFL Musicians' Mutual Protective Union 5533 of Butte, Mont., was chartered in 1891. It was local 39 of the National League of Musicians of the United States.
3. AFL 5533 did not affiliate with the American Federation of MUSICIANS.

To N. J. Svindseth[1]

Jany. 26th. [1897]

Mr. N. J. Svindseth.
H. of R. Salem, Oregon.
Dear Sir & Brother:—

Your favor of recent date to hand and contents noted. As per your request I shall endeavour to secure copies of the best laws on State arbitration and have them sent to you direct. I fully agree with you that thus-far the State boards of arbitration have been of very little practical value for organized labor.

The fact of the matter is that in the struggle of labor there are few if any who can be impartial. We are most of us bound to take sides with one or the other in a controversy of this character. Then again who is to decide what is fair? Legislatures are not apt to give a board power to call for books and papers, to compel employers or companies to disclose their private and business matters. It is regarded as an invasion of their rights. Without this a thorough investigation can not be made. Then again there is one commissioner appointed from the organizations of labor and more usually because of his political affiliations. Then again the representative of the employing class and one who is supposed to be disinterested. Pray, who will you find of that character who is not swayed by his interests of class feeling? Then again let me add an employer of labor may be able to prove that he cannot afford to pay the wages demanded or that to successfully carry on the business a reduction is necessary, and yet as a matter of fact be paying lower wages than others following the same business.

Arbitration usually means compromise and although it would be fair to a particular employee it would not be fair so far as the trade in general is concerned. Your general suggestion of insufficiency and inefficiency of this character brings this thought to me.

When labor is well organized and well equipped we will have conciliation sought by the employers. Until then labor is practically in the woods and groping in the dark. I hope you may be successful in securing the passage of laws really in the interest of labor and that your legislative career may be entirely successful and satisfactory to yourself, your constituents and our cause.

Let me hear from you frequently and oblige

Yours Fraternally, Saml Gompers.
President A.F. of L.

TLpS, reel 10, vol. 17, p. 356, SG Letterbooks, DLC.

1. N. J. Svindseth was secretary of AFL Columbia River Fishermen's Protective Union 6321 of Astoria, Ore., and a Populist member of the Oregon House of Representatives in 1897.

To Frank Sargent

January 28, [1897]

Mr. Frank P. Sargent,
Grand Chief of Brotherhood of Locomotive Firemen,
Peoria, Ill.
Dear Sir & friend:

Your favor of recent date to hand and contents noted. It was owing to a very great amount of confusion which reigned in our office caused by the removal of Headquarters which interfered with my earlier acknowledgment of your kind favor of recent date, nor could I then give any information upon the subject about which you wrote. You have seen a copy of the proceedings of the Cincinnati Convention. In order that you may have one beyond peradventure, I mail a copy to you under another cover. Your attention is respectfully called to pages 47, 79 and 86. This will indicate what action was taken by the Convention on the Railway Arbitration bill. The Executive Council directed me to secure the opinion of competent attorneys upon the subject, and to see whether the defects pointed out by the committee (on page 86), could be eliminated from the bill. Our friend Mr. Hine[1] of the B. of L.F. was invited to appear before Attorneys Ralston[2] & Siddons[3] and to invite any one he chose to argue in favor of the bill. I have received the opinion of the Attorneys and enclose a copy thereof to you herein.[4] You will observe that the opinion characterizes the bill as thoroughly inimical to the interests not only of railroad employees, but also to that of all labor and labor organizations.

Inasmuch as this bill is so dangerous to the interests of all labor, our Executive Council has decided that the bill should be defeated by all means, since it is absolutely impossible to amend it if any of the important features which it now contains are retained in it. I deemed it my duty to advise you of this course, and hope that you will see in it naught but the desire to do that which will best promote the best interests of our fellow-workers and our great movement, which is intended to protect and advance their interests. I feel confident that after a careful perusal of the opinion rendered, you will agree that the action of the Federation has saved us from going too far in a very dangerous direction.

While in Galveston I had the opportunity of conversing with (his name has escaped me) the Counsel[5] for the B. of L.F., and he stated to me at the time that he thought it contained nothing of practical value to the B. of L.F., or any other organization, and that it might prove detrimental in some instances. So you will observe that your [own] counsel, without having the opposition [stated to him is in practical agreement with?] the opinion rendered by Messrs. Ralston and Siddons.

In connection with this matter I would call to your attention the decision rendered this week by the Supreme Court of the United States in the case of Robert Robertson versus the United States.[6] Justice Harlan[7] in delivering the minority opinion called attention to the fact that "involuntary servitude," which was abolished by the 13th amendment to the Constitution, has been re-established by the decision. The Court held that when workmen entered into an agreement to labor for a particular period, that the labor can be specifically enforced; in other words, workmen engaged in interstate commerce, or in coastwise or foreign trade, if they enter into an agreement to work for a specified time, should they for any reason, individually or collectively, refuse to work, they can be arrested and either enforced to work or suffer imprisonment. You can easily see what the result of such a decision means if fully carried out.

Of course, I have no doubt that the enforcement of the full effect of this decision will be held back. It is not intended to cover the ordinary force, but if for some reason or other, the workmen on railroads suffering from poor conditions of labor should determine to quit work after an agreement to labor for a time has been entered into, either individually or collectively, and the movement should become of large proportions, you will find the civil and military forces of our country utilized and backed up by this decision, which to-day is the law of our country. Why, injunction proceedings are not to be compared to it in enormity and effectiveness.

Kindly let me hear from you relative to th[is] at your earliest convenience.

I wish you would say to Brother Carter that I will write to him in the course of a few days. I shall have an interview with Mr. Kidd of the Wood-Workers, who will be enabled to give me more information of which he writes.

With kindest regards to yourself and your Colleagues, I am

Yours fraternally,   Saml Gompers.

President   A.F. of L.

N.B. I enclose copy of opinion (first proof) of Ralston & Siddons

S. G.

T and ALpS, reel 10, vol. 17, pp. 397-98, SG Letterbooks, DLC.

1. William F. Hynes of Brotherhood of Locomotive Firemen (BLF) Denver lodge 77 served on the BLF's grand executive board (1888-90) and board of grand trustees (1890-96).

2. Jackson H. Ralston (1857-1945), a printer and a member of International Typographical Union (ITU) 101 of Washington, D.C., and ITU 59 of Quincy, Ill., during the 1870s and 1880s, was a partner in the Washington law firm of Ralston and Siddons. The AFL retained him as counsel on several occasions, most notably when SG and others were under indictment during the protracted Buck's Stove and Range case (1908-14).

3. Frederick L. Siddons, a partner in the Washington, D.C., law firm of Ralston and Siddons, became an associate justice of the District of Columbia Supreme Court, serving from 1915 to 1931.

4. Ralston and Siddons to SG, Jan. 23, 1897, Files of the Office of the President, General Correspondence, reel 59, frames 290-99, *AFL Records.*

5. Thomas W. Harper of Terre Haute, Ind., served as general counsel for the BLF.

6. In May 1895, Robert Robertson, John Bradley, P. H. Olsen, and Morris Hanson, four seamen who had signed on to the crew of the barkentine *Arago* in San Francisco for a voyage to the Pacific Northwest, Valparaiso, and other foreign ports, left their ship in Oregon. The *Arago*'s captain arrested the men and brought them back to San Francisco in chains. The four had thought themselves immune from arrest under the Maguire Act of 1895, which prohibited imprisonment for desertion in the coastal shipping trade. The International Seamen's Union of America subsequently took up their cause as a test case, arguing that their arrest had violated the involuntary servitude provision of the Thirteenth Amendment. On Jan. 25, 1897, in *Robertson* v. *Baldwin* (165 U.S. 275), the U.S. Supreme Court rejected that defense and held the seamen liable to arrest for violating their contract.

7. John Marshall Harlan (1833-1911) was associate justice of the U.S. Supreme Court (1877-1911).

To J. P. McDonnell[1]

Feby. 17th. [1897]

J. P. McDonnell.

c/o Patterson Labor Standard.

Paterson, New Jersey.

Dear Friend Mc: —

Your favor of recent date came duly to hand after traversing from Indianapolis to New York, thence to Washington. I note what you say relative to the awful strain you are undergoing and fully realize it. I know the sacrifices you have borne in order to keep the Standard afloat. I should be only too pleased if it was in my power to aid you. I believe you understand that fully.

In the matter of asking Col. Wright for any favor I am in very great doubt that he would comply. As a matter of fact I have on two occasions made a request of him of a simple character but without avail. Recently something has occurred which I imagine will not bring me in much favor with him. It is in relation to the Erdman so-called arbitration bill. You have undoubtedly seen what I have had to say in the Federationist of Feby.[2] on that. He takes a decidedly opposite view and not only that but he is actively engaged in securing its enactment and more than likely you may hear something sharp in relation thereto.

I want to thank you very much for your kindness for printing the poem dedicated to me.[3] I did not see it in the Labor Standard and it was only on the last day of the convention that I unearthed a number of copies which you so kindly sent to me. I do not know what purpose Mr. McCraith had in view but he certainly did not go out of his way to see that they were placed in the hands of the delegates. Perhaps his action towards me in the convention and elsewhere will explain these matters. As a matter of fact I have not a copy now and if you have one or two copies you could spare send them here in an envelope and I shall appreciate it very much.

I was in hopes that with the issuance of a charter to the musicians as a National Union that part of my troubles on that score would be ended instead of which it seems to have rebounded and come with more terrible force and effect. In all my connection with the labor movement I have never seen or heard less harmony than emanates from the organized musicians.

I trust that you may soon get out of at least some of the troubles that you are now surrounded with and that better health and success may attend you and yours. Let me hear from you frequently and believe me as ever,

Yours sincerely,   Saml Gompers.

P.S. The above was dictated two days ago but with a large mass of matter and only written to day. Your letter received this [P.M.]. Will give it immediate attention.

Yours.   Sam.

T and ALpS, reel 11, vol. 18, p. 101, SG Letterbooks, DLC.

1. Joseph Patrick McDONNELL was editor of the *Labor Standard* from 1876 until

his death in 1906. He helped organize the New Jersey Federation of Trades and Labor Unions in 1883 and served as its chairman until 1897.

2. "Danger Ahead," *American Federationist* 3 (Feb. 1897): 257-59. SG explained that the AFL opposed the Erdman bill because it interfered with the unqualified right of workers to quit their employment.

3. The poem, written by Thomas C. Walsh and entitled "A Noble Movement and a Valiant Leader," was published in the *Paterson Labor Standard*, Dec. 12, 1896.

To Henry White

Feby. 20th. [1897]

Mr. Henry White.
22 La Fayette Place. New York City.
Dear Friend: —

I am in receipt of your favor of recent date but owing to my absence from the office on a trip West[1] in the interest of our movement, and the work accumulated in the office, I have been unable to reply earlier. However let me say that I shall appreciate very much the receipt of your article[2] on the question of immigration. I have something already for this issue[3] upon the subject giving proposed measures for Congressional action. As per your suggestion I will issue the commissions to the gentlemen you name.

I received the note which you enclosed for Mr. Nolan. My boy[4] is here with me. I did not care to leave him in New York without employment. I preferred that he should then eat at my table and sleep in my home. If there is any position open for him in that house or in the house you name he will go on to New York by the first train after receiving a letter or telegram as the case may be. You may communicate with me on matters of this character to my house #327 H Street N.E. I went to the store here but learned that Mr. Saks[5] was making a trip to Virginia and Indiana and in all likelihood will not return here until about a week from now. Perhaps he would go to New York soon thereafter. When you see him please keep this matter in mind and let me know.

Appreciating your kind words and hoping that you may be entirely successful I am,

Very Truly Yours,   Saml Gompers.

I may see you before this letter reaches you. No. It cannot be before Tuesday.

S. G.

T and ALpS, reel 11, vol. 18, p. 167, SG Letterbooks, DLC.

1. SG's trip, from Jan. 29 to Feb. 11, 1897, included stops in Racine, Kenosha, and Janesville, Wis., Rockford and Chicago, Ill., and Indianapolis and Red Key, Ind.

2. "Immigration Restriction as a Necessity," *American Federationist* 4 (June 1897): 67-69.

3. "The Immigration Laws. Proposed Administrative Amendments," ibid. (Mar. 1897): 16-17. See also "The Immigration Laws. Proposed Administrative Amendments, No. II," ibid. (Apr. 1897): 37-38.

4. Abraham Julian Gompers.

5. Probably either Isadore Saks or Andrew Saks, partners in the Washington, D.C., clothing firm Saks and Co.

To Edward Boyce

March 9th, [1897]

Mr. Edward Boyce,
President, Western Federation of Miners,
Butte, Mont.
Dear Sir and Brother:

It is quite some time since I have heard from you in any way connected with our movement and particularly as to the struggle in which the members of your organization have been so long engaged and so heroically standing for their rights. A few weeks ago the Engineers' Union stated that in a short time from then that a request would be made by the officers of your organization for the Executive Council of the American Federation of Labor to levy an assessment upon the membership in aid of the men of Leadville who are on strike. I am free to say that I have expected that application to reach me any day.

Of course, I am aware that your organization is about to hold its convention at Salt Lake City,[1] and I shall be pleased to learn that ways and means may be devised by which not only the men who are standing so nobly for their rights may be successful, but also that the Western Federation of Miners may be absolutely and permanently so, that the bond of union existing between the organized workers of our country may be strengthened in the interest of all.

Within the last ten days I am in receipt of a number of letters from different sources, stating that a sentiment has been studiously worked up with a view of having the Western Federation of Miners withdraw from the A.F. of L., upon the plea that financial support was not forthcoming, and that a new organization should be formed for the West, as distinct from all other organizations of the workers of the other sections of the country. I cannot vouchsafe for the absolute accuracy of these statements made to me, but coming as they do from so many different sources and places I cannot but believe that either the rumors are founded upon fact, or there is an organized effort to malign the officers of your organization.

I do not wish to assume that the rumors are correct, but would say that even if it is harbored in the mind of any one, it is most unjust, improper, and destructive to the best interests, not only of the Miners, but of all labor of our country.

All know that our affiliated organizations pay but one-quarter of a cent for each member per month into the funds of the American Federation of Labor. No one can conceive of the idea that a great fund can be created from such a small contribution, and it is equally known to all that we have no mysterious power by which touching a rock, great riches can be had and given to our fellow workers. Even the fact that our fellow unionists may be engaged in a most just and righteous struggle, does not give us the means by which to create large funds to help them, unless the members in our organizations in the first instance are willing to pay their share and bear the burden by which such a fund can be created. Hence, upon this score I am sure there is no fault which can be laid to the door of the American Federation of Labor but which will reflect upon each and every one of us. Some of us may have the satisfaction of performing our duty in advocating the creation of such funds, but until we can convince our fellow-workers of its necessity we will all have to bear the blame, and the inconvenience of its absence.

As to the fact of attempting to divide the workers upon sectional lines, it seems to me, if the thought should be harbored by any one, a gross misconception of our duties to ourselves and our fellow-workers. On every hand we see concentration of wealth in corporations, combinations and trusts; the wealth possessors do not allow themselves to be divided on sectional lines when their interests are at stake; they do not divide their forces; they concentrate, they federate, anything that will make their power and influence more potent is resorted to. How should labor act under such circumstances? Should we not profit by these examples set us? Should we not take advantage of every opportunity which presents itself to us? Should we not recognize that our interests are one and the same? Should we not try to unite, federate and if possible concentrate our efforts upon a given line of policy and activity? We all maintain that it is morally wrong for a worker engaged at his trade or calling to remain outside of the union of his trade. It follows that it is morally wrong for a local union of a trade to hold aloof from the national union of that trade, and we maintain that it is equally wrong for any national union of a trade to remain outside of the great family of trade unions of the country.

I am as conscious of the defects in the American Federation of Labor as any one [who] can point them out to me. With some others we have endeavored to remedy these defects; we have tried by all honorable means to organize the workers in their respective unions, to make these organizations in their national unions and in our Federation as effective as possible. That we have not accomplished more is not due to the men who recognize its shortcomings. It is because the great mass of labor have thus far failed to realize their full duty to themselves and to each other. Our unions and our Federation is and can be only that which we make it. If it does not fill the expectations of some of us, it becomes our duty to struggle on and on, in order to make it a most thorough, compact and perfective organization to fight the battles of labor to-day, and to secure the rights of the toilers for all time. These changes and improvements are not brought about in a day, nor are they accomplished by divisions in our ranks. Unity is the essential element to success, not only in the West, or in any other one particular portion, but in the entire domain of our broad country.

The times require the exercise of the best judgment which we are capable of; conditions are such which should call forth the very best that is within us to stand more firmly together than ever before. There is nothing in this world which so gladdens the gaze of the enemy in battle as to divide the forces with which it is to contend. If you learn of any one believing that division in the ranks of organized labor can or is likely to be of benefit to our cause, I trust your good judgment will lead you to dispel the illusion.

I sincerely hope that your convention may be entirely successful, and that harmony will prevail and that success will come to the Miners and toilers in general, and that unity and solidarity will be the outcome of your convention, and that it will infuse courage and hope among the toilers of our land to struggle on for the day of emancipation.

Fraternally yours,   Saml Gompers.
President   American Federation of Labor.

TLpS, reel 11, vol. 19, pp. 34-37, SG Letterbooks, DLC.

1. The Western Federation of Miners' convention met in Salt Lake City, Utah, May 10-18, 1897.

To Daniel Kirwan[1]

March 9th. [1897]

Mr. D. M. Kirwan.
#1227—19th. Street. Denver, Colorado.
Dear Sir & Brother:—

Your favor of the 3rd came duly to hand and contents noted. Let me say in connection with both this letter and your previous one that you made it exceedingly difficult for me to publish. You know that there is a rule in every printing office that matter intended for publication should be written only on one side of the paper. This is essential in order that when the manuscript is cut up it will not be lost. I really do not know how I shall get over this. The thought has occurred to me that perhaps you might find time to write it over on one side of the paper and at the same time condense it.

Let me say too that I should be opposed to any scheme by which a fund should be created providing the same were left in the hands of the general office or in the hands of the organizers. I believe a fund when created for the purpose of defence and progress in the labor movement should be held by the organizations for transmission to any point where it may be used to effect, but I am not in favor of placing a large sum of money in the hands of one or a few officers. I do not want to question the honesty of any man—I prefer that no one should question mine—but I believe that men should be protected against themselves, against their poverty, against severe temptations. Then again you must also bear in mind that the matter of having men pay large sums of money into the union is not so easily accomplished; it takes time to develop; this goes not by jumps but by slow stages. Having had an experience of activity in the labor movement for nearly one third of a century I speak from my own personal knowledge and observation.

Let me assure you that I appreciate your kind words and your earnestness and I believe ability to wield a good influence in the cause of labor. I trust that you may give the movement the benefit of your active participation.

With kindest regards and hoping to hear from you soon I am
                              Fraternally yours,   Saml Gompers.
                                        President   A.F. of L.

TLpS, reel 11, vol. 19, p. 43, SG Letterbooks, DLC.

1. Daniel M. Kirwan was a Denver streetcar conductor.

An Excerpt from a News Account of an Address in New York City

[March 12, 1897]

RATIFY THE TREATY.

A mass-meeting[1] called to ratify the pending peace treaty[2] between this country and Great Britain, held at Cooper Union last evening, brought together one of the largest and most representative audiences that has ever been seen in that historic old hall.

. . .

WAR'S BURDENS ON LABOR.

The Speech of Samuel Gompers, President of the American Federation of Labor, particularly appealed to the large number of wage-earners present. He based his argument on the fact that the burdens of war rested on them necessarily. He said in part:

"I imagine that in the establishment of the Republic of these United States our forefathers not only had in view the establishment of an independent nation, but at the same time to give to the world a new meaning of the rights of man. (Applause.)

"And in the Declaration of Independence, being the new magna charta of the human race, it declared that all men were born free and equal, and in that declaration it did not confine itself to the people of these colonies, but it was a declaration as broad as the universe. (Applause.)

"After this declaration the seed was sown for wider comprehension of human rights and the furtherance of human sympathies. It meant, too, that the day of militarism should be put an end to (applause); that the day of government by force ought to stop; that the government of reason, the government of intelligence and the government of human interests should be paramount over the prowess of any man or set of men.["] (Applause.)

MILITARISM IS BARBARIC.

"At best the profession of militarism is the profession of slaughter. At best it is barbaric. At best it is destructive, and there are few questions in the history of the world that have been settled right by the arbitrament of force. (Applause.) And certainly even among those questions which may have been settled right few have been settled satisfactorily or humanely.

"In Continental Europe we see to-day, and have seen for more than one-third of a century, the people burdened by standing armies never before equalled in numbers and equipment; where people are by force of circumstances compelled to flee from the rigors of their own government into ours in order to escape military service and to make the struggles of the toilers of our country more desperate and more acute. (Applause.)

"These countries, with their continued increase in their standing armies and their naval resources, seem to impel and give encouragement to many in our country who too often care to ape the manners of those on the other side and who want to play with military and naval forces. (Applause.)

"We have seen, as we see now, numbers of men advocating a great increase in the army of our country. Ah, my friends, that in itself is a declaration that government by and for and of the people is not the success that we would have it. (Applause.)

"My friends, let me say this, that before this proposition for the great armament of our people, before the creation of our standing armies and increasing the military forces of our country, we should look well and should endeavor to find a way by which we can still maintain the simplicity of the form of our government, while at the same time defining and maintaining the honor, the integrity and interests of our country. (Applause.)

"Here right in our own city we see this militant spirit being cultivated and developed. We see children of the people of our city in large numbers having the doors of our schoolrooms closed to them without the opportunity of an education to be given them. (Applause.) We see at the same time the drill masters employed in the night schools that the boys who attend school by day may be drilled in military tactics at night. (Applause.)

"Let me say, my friends, that with this jingo spirit the people of our country have no interests and no sympathy. (Applause.)

"We are proud of the country which we claim as our own; we are proud of its history, proud of its heroes and proud of its traditions, and we hope as we struggle for its glorious future.

"But we maintain that patriotism does not mean the hatred of our neighbor. (Applause.) Nor do we believe that it is a wise policy, as some would advocate, that a foreign war might be a good cure for our domestic evils.

"The burdens of war have always fallen upon the masses of labor. (Applause.)

"I want to discuss this question not only from the standpoint of a citizen and a man, but I also want to express my judgment from a standpoint of the men who labor. (Applause.) And when I say labor I mean those who labor in the factories, in the stores, in the mills and in the mines. I mean the men who are known as the great body of wage-earners of our country. Upon them has always fallen the burden of war, to furnish the sinews of war while war lasts, to bear the burdens of increased taxation when war has ended and to be shot to death upon the battle-field while war is in progress. (Applause.)

"Labor has had to make these sacrifices for the stupidity, for the inhumanity and for the viciousness of monarch and false statesmen. (Applause.) While our honored Chairman[3] was addressing the meeting, I heard some gentlemen in the audience say 'Yes, but England is starving her people in India.' I want to say to you, my friends, that so long as the people of India will not manifest to England, or to the world, that they have rights that are bound to be respected, the people of India will be starved the same as the people of all countries will be. (Cheers.)

"Let me say, my friends, that as between two countries such as the United States and Great Britain, each a master in his own domain with the wonderful resources of each country, I believe that there can be no danger to the interests of our people in submitting to arbitration within the limits as prescribed in the treaty now pending before the United States Senate. (Applause.)

"I want to say a word if there are any wage-earners here, and I believe there are a large number. I want to say a word particularly to them. You bear in mind, fellow-workers, that during the eras of war that government is accorded greater powers than during eras of peace, and the apparent power exercised to maintain order is used oppressively and to suppress and to repress and often prevent the right of public meeting and public speech and free speech.

"In the exercise of great powers often requisite under military control, the right of free meeting, the right of free speech, and free press is endangered. And when the smoke of battle is gone these rights, taken from the masses of the people under often necessary conditions, are seldom freely given back to the people.

"The attitude of labor has always been in favor of arbitration. It has sought arbitration in the disputes it has had with employers, and if arbitration has not been more successful it cannot certainly be laid at the door of labor. (Applause.) We want to settle these questions of controversy that arise and can be settled by an appeal to reason and an appeal to our judgment, an appeal to our sense of honor, an appeal to our interests. They can and they should be settled around the table where discussion and judgment and truth and justice shall decide.

"I have said that the organizations of labor have always stood for the unification of the human race, the recognition that after all we are brothers of one human family. We want to over come the petty jealousies, the strife and discord, that has made countless myriads of widows and orphans and thousands and thousands of men sent to untimely graves. We want to accomplish peace on earth and good will toward all men."

. . .

New York World, Mar. 12, 1897.

1. The call for the meeting was signed by prominent religious, civic, and business leaders. In addition to SG, the speakers included New York City Mayor William Strong, Columbia University President Seth Low, former Secretary of the Treasury Charles F. Fairchild, Bishop Henry C. Potter, Judge Henry E. Howland, and former Congressman John DeWitt Warner.

2. On Jan. 11, 1897, Secretary of State Richard Olney and British ambassador Sir Julian Pauncefote signed a treaty providing for the settlement of unresolved diplomatic disputes through courts of arbitration. The Senate rejected the treaty on May 5, 1897.

3. William L. Strong (1827-1900), a Republican, was mayor of New York City from 1894 to 1897.

From Edward Boyce

Butte, Montana, March 16, 1897.

Dear Sir and Brother:

Your welcome letter of the 9th inst.[1] is received and contents carefully noted. In answer, I will say that *I know nothing about the western federation of miners withdrawing from the A.F. of L.;*[2] whoever wrote you on that point knows more about the future of the organization than I do. In the first place, we could not withdraw until the Convention so decided.

With reference to us making application to the A.F. of L. for financial assistance to carry on the Leadville strike, I wrote you to that effect on the 16th of February, but received no reply. I presume you did not get my letter or I would have received an answer. However, I will say that is of little consequence, *there is an easier way of winning the battles of labor;*[2] much easier than sitting down in idleness until the capitalists starve us to death in idleness and hunger.

With reference to the organization of union of forces among the laboring men of the West it is something that I have always favored, and am very enthusiastic on that point at all times, for the interest of labor. Do not think me egotistical when I say that I think the laboring men of the West are one hundred years ahead of their brothers in the East. You will remember that I told you in Cincinnati that I had not been East in fifteen years, and I never was so much surprised in my life as I was at that convention, when I sat and listened to the delegates from the East talking about conservative action when four million idle men and women are tramps upon the highway, made so by a vicious system of government that will continue to grind them further into the dust unless thay have the manhood to get out and fight with the sword or use the ballot with intelligence.

You know that *I am not a trades unionist;*[2] I am fully convinced that their day of usefulness is past; and furthermore, since last election there is little sympathy existing between the laboring men of the West and their Eastern brothers.

I leave for the Black Hills in a few moments, so you will please excuse the brevity of this letter. I will be in Butte about the first of April, and will be delighted to hear from you, when I will have an opportunity of writing you more fully.

Fraternally yours,   Ed. Boyce.

PLSr, *An Address. To the Western Federation of Miners, in Convention Assembled, Salt Lake City, Utah* (Washington, D.C., 1897), pp. 2-3.

1. Above.
2. Italics probably added by SG for emphasis when publishing the letter.

To George Bettenhausen[1]

March 18th. [1897]

Mr. George A. Bettenhause.
#29 Spring Street; Lynn, Mass.
Dear Sir & Brother: —

Your favor of the 16th to hand and contents noted. I am obliged to you for the information you gave and also for the clipping of the paper. Replying to your question let me say that generally among those who know the man best say that Daniel DeLeon is simply an alias and that his right name is Daniel Loeb. The one is a translation of the other, meaning "the lion." Several years ago he was a single taxer and generally denounced the socialists as "beer guzzling socialists." He then became a member of the "Nationalist" club to follow out the theory of Edw. Bellamy[2] in his work "Looking Backward" and he was charged by many with malfeasance of the club's funds. The club subsequently disbanded. Then for the sake of getting the position as editor of the socialist party paper "The People" he became an avowed socialist. He joined the K. of L. with the understood purpose of becoming General Secretary or Grand Master Workman. He sought to control what there was left of that order and when that failed helped to destroy it. He has encouraged secession from established unions and brought about divisions in a number of local unions in trades in which wages have since been reduced and other obnoxious conditions forced upon labor. He sought to control the A.F. of L. and when he failed in that by reason of the determination of the trade unionists who have given their lives to the work he has sought to destroy that organization and to malign the characters of the men who have been its staunchest advocates and friends. He is now simply in a wild rage because of his inability to do as he desires.

You can imagine the wonderful progress which is made in Germany which is the main country in which the socialist party movement exists and which this DeLeon wants us to follow. The hours of labor range from 12 to 18 and in many instances more among the workers of Germany. Wages are of the very lowest of the countries of continental Europe, certainly much lower than England, Ireland, Scotland, France and Belgium and several others and at the bottom when compared with the wages, hours and other conditions of employment in the United States. In Germany the Socialist party has been in existence for over thirty years and they have not a law upon the Statute books which they can show as the result of their work and even they themselves admit that conditions have become much worse. The Imperial Executive of Germany issued a decree[3] about a year ago limiting the hours among bakers. The limit is practically that the hours of labor shall not exceed 14 hours with the exception when the boss baker may think sufficient to warrant more and that can be applied to seven days a week. You can imagine what the conditions must be when an Imperial decree calls for anything like this.

I understand of course that we have a great struggle in our country. Our trade unionists are making the fight for better conditions and if we can not make the progress for which we hope, yet if we were to follow on the lines of DeLeon we would go back at a rate so fast as to bring us to actual slavery and barbarism.

Let me say that when I was first notified to address the meeting at Lynn[4] no intimation at all was given me that DeLeon was to be there. It was only upon my request to find out who else was to speak at the meeting that I learned that DeLeon was to be there and that was after I had made arrangements to be elsewhere on the evening of the 13th. There was unquestionably a purpose in Mr. Carter's[5] letter in suppressing from me the knowledge that DeLeon was to be at that meeting. There was no indication to me from him that I was to be expected to enter into a debate or joint discussion with anybody. He was guilty of an effort to inveigle me into a controversy with one who was prepared while I was to remain unprepared. I am not surprised though. It is only in keeping with the tactics of these men who are following the tuition of a dreamer or a villain or both. That DeLeon was quite mild in his talk and made few if any personal references is due to the fact of my letter more than to anything else.

Let me call your attention to another fact that in my travels through the country to discuss and lecture upon the labor question and the labor movement frequently the members of local committees have invited the Mayor or the Governor or some other public man who may perhaps be in sympathy with our movement. Over this I have no control but this DeLeon and his satellites condemned this in the severest terms and say that it is an evidence that the capitalistic class is in sympathy with me and our movement; yet, as a matter of fact we see that the Mayor[6] of your city presided over the meeting at which he extolled his theory and belittled the trade union movement. I do not know whether your Mayor is in sympathy with the movement or not, nor is this intended as a criticism or a reflection upon him, but it is merely cited to show the inconsistency of these people. They are a sorry lot blowing hot and cold in one breath so long as it will suit their purpose.

Fraternally yours,   Saml Gompers.
President   American Federation of Labor.

TLpS, reel 11, vol. 19, pp. 169-70, SG Letterbooks, DLC.

1. George A. Bettenhausen of Lynn, Mass., was active in CMIU 65 and an AFL organizer.

2. Edward Bellamy (1850-98) was a Massachusetts lawyer, journalist, and reformer whose widely read utopian novel, *Looking Backward, 2000-1887* (Boston, 1888), created a popular following for his idea of a voluntary and gradual introduction of planned state socialism to replace industrial capitalism. Under the name "nationalism," Bellamy's vision became the basis of the Nationalist clubs through which individuals, primarily from the middle and upper classes, discussed and disseminated his ideas. Two Boston papers promoted "nationalism," the *Nationalist* (1889-91) and the *New Nation* (1891-94), the latter under Bellamy's editorship.

3. Sec. 120 of the German trade regulations (Gewerbeordnung) decreed Mar. 4, 1896, and effective July 1, 1896, limited the workday of regular employees in bakeries and confectioners' shops to no more than twelve hours a shift (or thirteen including a one-hour break), mandated eight hours' rest between shifts, and no more than seven shifts a week. The law also provided exceptions for overtime and the special circumstances of apprentices.

4. The Lynn Central Labor Union invited both SG and Daniel DeLeon to speak at Lasters' Hall on Mar. 13, 1897.

5. Frederick S. Carter, a Lynn, Mass., laster, was secretary of Boot and Shoe Workers' Union 32 and a member of the SLP.

6. Walter L. Ramsdell, a former printer, was the Democratic-Populist mayor of Lynn, Mass., 1897-98.

To Edward Boyce

March 26th, [1897]

Mr. Edward Boyce,
President, Western Federation of Miners,
Butte, Montana.
Dear Sir and Brother:

I am in receipt of your favor of the 16th,[1] contents of which I have carefully noted. I beg to assure you that I read its contents with more than ordinary interest and I am pleased to learn from you that you know nothing about the Western Federation of Miners withdrawing from the American Federation of Labor.

I am frank enough to say to you that there have been people who have done you the injustice of advising me that you had declared your purpose of insisting upon the forthcoming convention of your organization to secede from the American Federation of Labor. If you will re-read my last letter[2] you will note that I refer to this. I could scarcely believe that you as President of the Western Federation of Miners, an organization that has so recently become affiliated with the A.F. of L., would at a convention so soon after its affiliation advocate separation, withdrawal and division in the ranks of labor.

If there is anything that experience demonstrates more than another it is the necessity for the combined forces of labor in this country to unite more thoroughly than ever before, to bear with each other's faults, to endeavor to enlighten each other to the best of our ability, and to help those who still fail to see the necessity of organizing, to enter with earnestness and zeal within the ranks, to try and teach those who have not yet recognized this necessity; to teach those who have but a very faint conception of the main purpose and underlying principles of the labor movement; to teach them the first primer in the union of labor.

I am sure you will agree with me that little can be expected upon a higher plane of action from men who, through ignorance and short sighted greed, fail to register themselves on the side of their fellow workmen in the "cause" of labor. It certainly requires a peculiar conception, for anyone to imagine that the working people of our country have a higher aim, when they fail to perform their first duty to themselves and their fellow workers, by organizing upon a common plan of unionism in defense of their immediate interests. It is as sure as day follows night and night follows day that men who will not defend their immediate interests cannot be relied upon to strive manfully for a future, a better state of society.

I beg to assure you that I did not receive the letter you say you sent on the 16th of February requesting financial assistance. Had I received it the matter would certainly have been referred to the Executive Council who would perhaps have approved ordering an assessment being made, or an appeal made to all labor in favor of the striking workers of Leadville.

It grieves me, however, to learn that you believe that there is an "easier" way of winning the battles of labor than as you describe them "sitting down in idleness until capitalists starve us to death in idleness and hunger." This is not the language of the man I imagined as the hero of the Leadville strike; this is not the language of the man I know you are; it is not the language of men who have fought great battles and have stamped the progress of their struggles on the pages of human history and human progress.

The most victorious armies in the world have at times had their set-backs. The heroes in our revolutionary war were heart sick, foot sore and hungry. It was then to arouse their drooping spirits that a man of the time arose and declared "now is the time that tries men's souls." In the face of apparent defeat, in spite of all appearances of a hopeless struggle the men of the revolution took on new courage and with words of cheer as substitutes for good food and good clothing and proper equipment, fought on and on until victory was achieved and a new Nation born. The whole history of the world is replete with evidence of this character, this disposition, this manhood, this heroism. Without it the world would be barren; or barbarism and slavery would be the order of the day and all hope of future emancipation blotted from the memory and hope of men.

Hunger? Idleness? Yes, even in the struggles of labor they must be sometimes borne in order that right and justice shall prevail; or at least such a protest made against wrong and injustice that shall thrill the world with a new sense of responsibility and determination to struggle more manfully than ever that right shall prevail.

Speaking of an "easier" way of winning the battles of labor; were it not so serious it would be ridiculous to think that the battles of labor can be won "easier." Those who imagine that the road to labor's emancipation is "easier" will have their labor for their pains and are deluding themselves into a false position and helping divert their fellow workers from the real struggle which the toilers are of necessity required to make into a channel which secures them nothing but despondency, despair and real hunger, permanently established as their condition of life, and servility and docility to take the place of a struggling earnest manhood to establish a greater degree of happiness and a fair standard of life which will enable them to struggle on more manfully still, more persistently until the day of labor's emancipation shall be achieved.

I do not wish to discuss the proposition that "the men of the East are one hundred years behind their Western brothers." I do not think so and I think you will admit that the pressure of industrialism and commercialism and the evils resulting from our present false economic conditions are much severer and bear much more heavily upon the workers of the East and the North than in the West.

The men who have not seen the industrial centers for a long time can scarcely form a conception of the great burdens the toilers of these sections have to bear and the manly struggles, too, that they make in order to permit themselves to stand erect and face the contest, bear the brunt of battle, endure sacrifices, and yet never give up the hope of achieving their independence and battling for labor's emancipation. The discussion of whether men of the West and other portions of our country are either in advance or behind each other is not calculated to advance or solidify the interests of labor and for the [that] reason I think we may well afford that to remain without further comment.

Do you think for a moment that the delegates to the Cincinnati convention, or the men in the East, North or South sympathize less with what you say, the "four millions of men and women idle who are tramps upon the highway" than do the men of the West? Don't you believe that they would take any action which in their judgment would seem wise and best to change such condition of affairs, if the slightest prospect of success presented itself? They realize, however, as all should realize, that words are not actions, that there is a difference between declarations and deeds; that resolutions are not revolutions and that alleviation and emancipation never yet was secured and never can be secured by an "easy" process and that all the declarations in the world made by a few men to go forth with the ballot will not relieve, much less remove the evil of which we complain.

Nor do I wish you for a moment to be deceived into the belief that the men of the other sections of the country, the delegates to the Cincinnati Convention, are less impressed than you with the necessity of effective political action and the proper use of the ballot by labor in labor's own interests. Let me assure you that the trade unionists whom you met at Cincinnati are not at all backward or too conservative, they simply desire as a result of their experience and knowledge to couple practical action with their enthusiasm; and immaterial in which way or upon which field the labor course is contested they have been, are and will be shoulder to shoulder with the advance guard of the grand army of labor.

As for your suggestion that the resort must be to the sword I prefer not to discuss. I only want to call your attention to the fact, however, that force may have changed forms of government but never attained real liberty.

Liberty! the conception of which is a matter of growth, a matter of education, and is a matter of progress, proceeds in the same ratio that the people conceive their rights and will manfully, heroically and with self-sacrifice stand for it and which no power in the form of government can withstand. It is the purpose of the trade union movement to instill this greater manhood, this greater self-reliance, this intelligence, this independence in the hearts and minds of the workers which when once conceived cannot be driven out by sophistry, poltroonery or by force.

You say that I know you are "not a trade unionist." No, I did not know this and I assure you that when I read your statement in the letter I was more than surprised. I have heard quite a number of strange statements in my life, but it was reserved for you to make the strangest of all, that of being President of a great trade union to declare that you are not a trade unionist. I really cannot see how you can reconcile your action to your declarations. I know that if I were not a trade unionist I should not only declare it but I should act it. I would not be president of a trade union; I would not even be a member of a trade union. I would, if I were not a trade unionist, if I were an opponent of trade unionism, I would get out of the trade union and out of the trade union movement and I would fight it. I would not occupy so questionable a position as being the President and member of a trade union and declare myself an opponent of it.

You say that "there is little sympathy existing between the laboring men of the West and their Eastern brothers." I doubt it. I believe that there is more real sympathy between them than many would have us believe. I think such declarations a great wrong in the face of existing conditions when all the forces antagonistic to labor are united and uniting still more in their effort to hold the workers in check, to suppress their efforts and oppress them in their struggles for emancipation.

The forces of wealth understand the necessity for common concert of action. They do not divide upon theories; nor do they divide upon geographical lines, from some men coming from one portion of our country and others from another, and I regret to see a man of your intelligence and of your position and of your influence declaring that there is little sympathy between the working people of the West and other portions of our common country; we cannot overcome the slightest antagonism to our efforts; we cannot achieve the slightest advance or progress in our interests; we cannot achieve the smallest right which belongs to us by scattering our forces.

I earnestly hope that the Convention of the Western Federation of Miners will stand true to the colors of their union and though they have been defeated in their Leadville strike, they will declare with other men who have fought in the great battles of life that though defeated they are not conquered and that they will organize more strongly and firmly, more earnestly and aggressively than ever before; and while organizing the men in their own trade or calling and allying themselves with their fellow organized workers from all parts of the country without regard to trade, calling, nationality, religion or whatever section of the country they may come from. Let us stand united in defeat as well as in victory. It is only by such sterling qualities called forth in defeat which shows our true manhood, our ability to take up the battles of labor and never say "die."

And yet Brother Boyce I say it to you in all candor and all friendliness and I ask you to consider this matter well; I ask you in the name of the great interests committed to your care, the great influence you wield with your fellow workers of the Western Federation of Miners that you use that great power to unite and solidify the forces of labor of our country and fight, and fight hard, against any attempt that will seek to force an entering wedge to divide the workers in our movement.

With assurances of my high regard I am,

Fraternally yours, Saml Gompers.
President A.F. of L.

N.B. I am writing this to you not for publication, but what I regard as my highest duty toward you and your organization and towards the workers both East and West, North and South.

S. G.

TLpS, reel 11, vol. 19, pp. 313-19, SG Letterbooks, DLC.

1. Above.
2. "To Edward Boyce," Mar. 9, 1897, above.

From Edward Boyce

Butte, Montana, April 7, 1897.

Dear Sir and Brother:

Yours of the 28th ult.[1] is received and contents noted with much care and interest. After mature deliberation I am fully convinced that no two men in the labor movement differ so widely in opinion as the President of the A.F. of L. and the writer. If you will show me what good results can accrue from trades unions without action we might understand each other? The trades-union movement has been in operation in our country for a number of years, and through all these years the laboring masses are becoming more dependent. In view of these conditions, do you not think it is time to do something different than to meet in annual convention and fool away time in adopting resolutions, indorsing labels and boycotts?

If force never attained real liberty, then your letter is conflicting in its parts. However, that is something unworthy of space at this time.

Well, if I have made the strangest statement you ever heard in your life, in declaring that I am not a trades unionist I hardly see how you could escape strange things so long. I believe I will partially follow your advice and get out of the trades-union movement — but I digress when it comes to fighting it. I may also inform you that I am not the president of a trade union, or a member of one.

I presume we are all striving for the same purpose. That purpose is to elevate the laborer, not to array one against the other, or imitate the present deplorable struggle between the A.F. of L. and K. of L.

I can assure you that, no matter what action the Western Miners take with reference to the A.F. of L., it will not be hasty, nor calculated to injure the labor movement; but now, as ever, I am strongly in favor of a Western organization.

Fraternally yours,   Edward Boyce.

PLSr, *An Address. To the Western Federation of Miners, in Convention Assembled, Salt Lake City, Utah* (Washington, D.C., 1897), pp. 5-6.

1. Actually Mar. 26, 1897, above.

To Joseph Cosgrove[1]

April 10th. [1897]

Mr. J. T. Coxgrove,
Organizer.
#318 W. 4th. St.; Muscatine, Iowa.
Dear Sir & Brother:—

Your favor of the 7th inst. bearing post mark 9 P.M. Apr. 8th to hand and noted. I am therefore somewhat in doubt that this will reach you in time for Monday although I write immediately upon its receipt. Under the circumstances you mention I should say that the young lady button workers can organize separately as a union and have a charter issued to them as such.[2] While this is so it is reluctantly issued because it is not the best or wisest step. These men and women all work together and their interests are identical and each one discussing them should discuss them jointly in order to arrive at the best possible conclusions. However as I say if they insist upon organizing a separate union it is better to have them organized in that way than not organized at all.

With every wish for success I am,

Fraternally yours,   Saml Gompers.
President   AF. of L.

TLpS, reel 11, vol. 19, p. 523, SG Letterbooks, DLC.

1. Joseph T. Cosgrove was a Muscatine, Iowa, tailor, AFL organizer, and secretary of AFL Federal Labor Union 6309.

2. The AFL had chartered Button Workers' Protective Union 6861 in March 1897. Extant records do not indicate the chartering of a women's button workers' union in Iowa in 1897.

From William Griscom[1]

Secretary
The Tribune of Labor and Trades Unionist[2]
Chattanooga, Tenn. [ca. April 13] 1897

Dear Sir and Brother:

In reply to your favors of April 2 and Mch 23d I desire to say that the Trades-Unionists, the Tribune of Labor and myself as organizer have pursued the cause outlined by you. We have at all times advised the men to stand by their Union, and warned them against the folly of casting away the only anchor they had.[3] I am glad to say that during the past month the influence has been such as to bring in twelve reinstatements and was informed to-day of two other applications.

I desire to state further that the Trades-Unionists of Chattanooga, most fully appreciate the cause of the molders dissatisfaction. Even more fully than does Bro Fox if I can judge the tenor of his letter to you by your favor to me. While to a man the Union men of Chattanooga opposed any insubordination on the part of the iron-molders—they to a man endorsed the strike. We knew at the time, the strike was not sanctioned by the international, but after two weeks of negotiation, and making of every proposition that honorably could be made—by a committee appointed by the Central Labor Union[4]—we advised the men to come out. We believed then and still believe that the strike was justified by every principle for which labor is contending. If there is any short-sightedness it occurs to me, it is at the other end of the line.

To state the case in brief. There was a class of cheap work which was being done by white workmen by the peice. The proprietors came to the conclusion they could get the work done cheaper by employing negro moulders by the day and called the chairman of the shop committee to consult with him. They were then informed that molders had determined that the negro should not gain further foothold in the shops of Chattanooga, and they could be compelled in self defence to refuse to work with them. The offer was made to the proprietors that rather than have the negro further encroach on the trade the molders would take turns in doing this work at the same scale they would pay the negro. But this was not listened to. It was negro or bust. Then the matter was referred to the Central Labor Union, and a committee appointed—who waited on the cahill people[5] the propositions made them were so fair and liberal that they were finally forced to the admission that they preferred the negro to the white man from the fact that he "was more docile and more easily controlled.["] That is as long as he could make a $1.00 a day he would stick by the job. If those men were not fighting against a degraded condition, then Labor has never made such a fight.

I am frank to say that we have little patience with the sentiment of trying to uplift the negro. We know our international officers do not realize the gravity of the menace the black-man in the South is to Labor organization. They have no conception of the prejudice and distrust that exist between the two races. They do not seem to realize that the employer is not using the negro from any philanthropic or christian motives for the elevation of the race, but only as a club to bring the condition of the white mechanic to the level of the negro. So far as making friends of the negro, if that means to Unionize him, there is just About the same chance of doing this as there would be of christianizing him. The negro knows that at anything near the same price, the white man would have the preference. In fact he is constantly threatened with being displaced by the whites. They are reduced to poor beasts of burden, for no purpose but to satisfy the greed of unprincipled employers. They make only enough, to live ni [in] the poorest hovels, on the cheapest food—and to wear cast-off clothing. In Gods name when do you think it will end.

In the ten foundries in this city in only one has the white man an equal chance with the negro. They have driven the Boilermakers away, reduced the carpenters to starvation wages. Are driving out the railway firemen and trackmen, the stone masons Union has become only a skeleton; the operators of wood working machinery are debarred from organization because the negro stands ready to take his place whenever he asks for better conditions. The Harness makers and leather workers are under the same conditions, and they are gradually walking into other trades.

He is without a sense of honor, distrustful by nature, and previous education, has no conception of the higher duties of citizenship and is debarred by prejudice from exercising them if had. He believes the white man is responsible for his condition, that he is entitled to consideration politically and industrially because he is black—and the only thing that can be said in his favor is that he has sense enough to be clannish and to erect no foolish or senseless social conditions within his own race. The condition described for Chattanooga is the condition in every southern city that I have been in. It is not a fight against the negro as a man, it is simply a question of shall the southern mechanic come to the level of the negro; shall he leave the country or shall he bring about a condition that will to a limited extent bring the negro to him. Surely this last is more desirable, but can never be done by allowing the negro, unorganized to gain the ascendency.

If our international leaders have a solution, I would be glad to render all aid in my power. But it will take more heroic action than sentiment built upon a far away view. You will pardon the length of this, but I want you [to] see our side—and want your help.

> Fraternally and Sincerely   Will S. Griscom

ALS, Files of the Office of the President, General Correspondence, reel 59, frames 304-10, *AFL Records*.

1. William S. Griscom, a Chattanooga printer, who became an AFL organizer in the fall of 1896, was apparently secretary of the Chattanooga Central Labor Union (CLU).

2. The *Tribune of Labor and Trades Unionist* was the organ of the Chattanooga CLU.

3. Griscom was referring to the aftermath of a spring 1896 strike in Chattanooga in which Iron Molders' Union of North America (IMUNA) 53, without the sanction of the national union, unsuccessfully opposed the employment of black molders. In his letter to Griscom of Mar. 23, 1897 (reel 11, vol. 19, p. 235, SG Letterbooks, DLC), SG advised him that for the members of IMUNA 53 to consider secession from the national union would place them "entirely in the wrong." SG's letter of Apr. 2 relayed the views of IMUNA president Martin Fox, whose opinion he had solicited. According to Gompers, Fox maintained that the strike had been both unconstitutional and impractical, and that "rather than make enemies" of the black molders the IMUNA advised attempting "to make friends of them." In SG's opinion, the Chattanooga molders were blaming their national officers for the loss of the strike rather than admitting "their own short sightedness." "If these moulders are trade unionists," SG concluded, "the best way they can demonstrate that is to make their peace with the organization, join it and help build it up" (ibid., p. 372).

4. The Chattanooga CLU organized at least as early as 1896 and affiliated with the AFL in July 1897.

5. Probably the Cahill Iron Works, a Chattanooga firm.

To William Griscom

April 16th. [1897]

Mr. W. S. Griscom,
Organizer.
#829 Chestnut St.; Chattanooga, Tenn.
Dear Sir & Brother: —

I have your favor[1] which you omitted to date and have read it carefully and with very great interest. Let me say that I appreciate every word you say and to assure you that there is no false sentiment, in fact no sentiment at all, about the matter connected with the negro laborers whether they be moulders or other workers. I know too that the officers of our National and International organizations are not governed by sentiment in the premises. They realize the danger which lurks in every step taken to drive the negro further into a position where he will be more docile, and regard the white workman as his mortal enemy. You observe that the employers under the pretense of philanthropy give the negroes employment. They may say to the white workers that their real purpose in hiring the negro is because they are more docile and will work for less wages, but they will studiously inoculate the black workman with the vilest of prejudices against the white workman and demonstrate by incidents that their friendship is founded upon truth. The negro will then look upon the white workman as his mortal enemy and their white employers as their steadfast friends.

You must bear in mind that this industrial struggle is one of judgement, one of tact, and when there are two forces in antagonism to each other it is the policy of each to win friends from the other side. It is this policy which the officers of the National and International organizations are following and whether they be upon the grounds or far from the scene of action this judgement is founded upon practical action and that which is calculated to bring the best results.

Even if the officers of the International had approved the strike of the locals in your city, it might have been prolonged but it could have had no other ending and that is borne out by the fact that they were right.

I do not for a moment entertain the belief that by our simple declaration that we shall make friends of the negro laborers. Their previous condition, their former absolute dependence upon their masters (and now their employers) have deprived them of learning that it is necessary for them to rely upon themselves and upon each other, but I am confident that if organized workingmen will take a more liberal view of the situation, or rather a more practical view, that the negro workman will to a very much greater extent make common cause with us in our struggles. I am sure no one can entertain the belief that the negro is going to die out. He is a living fact and a factor and regardless of all the prejudices that may be entertained he must be counted with and the way to count with him is the question that must be considered. I beg of you to believe me that in this matter I strip myself absolutely from all sentimental considerations and base it upon what I am confident will best serve the interests of labor to help, though it may be slow and gradual, in the solution of this great problem.

It is very gratifying to me to learn that there have been a number of reinstatements of the old members into the union and I sincerely wish that the time is not far distant when everyone shall be counted upon the roll of membership. Hoping to hear from you soon and often I am,

Fraternally yours,   Saml Gompers.
President   A.F. of L.

TLpS, reel 11, vol. 19, pp. 602-3, SG Letterbooks, DLC.

1. "From William Griscom," ca. Apr. 13, 1897, above.

An Article in the *Baltimore Morning Herald*

[April 17, 1897]

LABOR LEADERS ARRIVE.

Samuel Gompers, president of the American Federation of Labor, and James O'Connell, grand master of the International Association of Machinists, arrived in this city yesterday from Washington.

On their arrival the well-known labor leaders were met by President James Duncan, of the Federation of Labor; Ed. Hirsch,[1] delegate of the International Typographical Union, and others prominently identified with the trades unions of this city.

Messrs. Gompers and O'Connell came here on the invitation of President Duncan to attend a conference for which he had previously arranged with Joseph Friedenwald, president of the Crown Cork and Seal Company, an institution which has a difficulty of long standing with the International Association of Machinists. The local machinists' union,[2] which is identified with the national body and with the Federation of Labor, has been endeavoring to make Mr. Friedenwald's establishment a union shop, and though there is no question of wages involved in the discussion, the relations between the Federation of Labor and the Crown Cork and Seal Company have been strained for a considerable time. It was hoped that the conference which was arranged for yesterday would lead to the settlement of the trouble, but according to a statement made to a Herald reporter last night by President Gompers it is now further from settlement than ever. The works are located at 309 Girard avenue.

"While we were conferring with Mr. Friedenwald today," said Mr. Gompers, "we asked that Mr. O'Connell, who is the grand master of the International Association of Machinists, be permitted to go through the factory and talk to the employes, in order to get their side of the story. Mr. O'Connell was willing to go through during the dinner hour, and interview the men at a time when the objection could not be made that he was interfering with their work or wasting their time. Mr. Friedenwald refused point blank to give Mr. O'Connell this privilege, saying that he would not be coerced and that he did not want anyone to meddle in what he regarded as his private business and the business of the company. This caused us to abandon further efforts to come to any understanding with Mr. Friedenwald. We will now do our utmost to demonstrate to this concern the responsibility it is incurring in fighting organized labor."

In reply to a request from a Herald reporter to explain the nature of the trouble Mr. Gompers said: "Some time ago several of the machinists employed by the Crown Cork and Seal Company joined the local Machinists' Union, which is affiliated with the Federation of Labor. Three were discharged within a few days of joining the Union, and they were plainly given to understand that their dismissal was due to their identification with organized labor. Immediately after this several other machinists who worked at the Cork and Seal Company's place asked for withdrawal cards from the Union, and as their reason they gave the explanation that they had to withdraw or lose their jobs. Later on 15 non-union employes of the same concern, who had been proposed in the Union and who had paid their initiation fees, failed to show up for initiation, and didn't even ask their money back from the Union.

"The Federation of Labor took the matter in hand after the foregoing facts had been reported to it by the Machinists' Union. President Duncan and a committee waited on Mr. Friedenwald and inquired if it was a fact that he had denied his employes the right to join the local union. Mr. Friedenwald failed to give any satisfactory answer, and then the Federation threatened a boycott.

"On the 29th of March last Mr. Friedenwald got up a circular which he caused all the employes to sign, which stated that the Crown Cork and Seal Works was in no way inimical to union labor, and that the company would not discharge any employe for belonging to a labor union. Mr. Friedenwald had this circular reproduced and the signatures photographed, and sent copies to his customers and to various organizations throughout the country. This was, I suppose, an effort on his part to convey the impression to the trade that his shop was a union shop, and in this way he hoped to offset the threatened boycott. There are several union men in Mr. Friedenwald's employ, but they are afraid to let the fact be known, fearing they would be discharged like some of their fellow employes were some time ago. The status of the affair is now that we will have to show the strength and influence of organized labor."

Messrs. Gompers and O'Connell returned to Washington last night.

Baltimore Morning Herald, Apr. 17, 1897.

1. Edward Hirsch was a Baltimore printer, member of International Typographical Union 12, and president of the Baltimore Federation of Labor (1897, 1899-1900).

2. International Association of Machinists 186.

Excerpts from the Minutes of a Meeting of the Executive Council of the AFL

Headquarters, Washington, D.C. April 19th, 1897.

MONDAY.

MORNING SESSION.

. . .

Meeting called to order at 11:30 with Gompers, Duncan, O'Connell, Garland, Lennon and Morrison present.

President Gompers gave a review of what the Advisory Board[1] had done at the two meetings it had held, and reported that they advised that a memorial be presented to Congress by a large body of representative union men, who should meet at the Capitol before the Congress convened Wednesday Morning, April 20th, 1897.

Adopted.

Moved by Mr. Lennon that the Executive Council call upon the President of the United States at three o'clock this afternoon for the purpose of having a conference with him relative to labor matters, measures and conditions, but more particularly in relation to the eight hour work day.

Ex-Congressman Phillips called at Headquarters and was admitted to the Executive Council, when a general discussion took place as to who would be the logical candidate for chairman of the labor committee. Mr. Phillips expressed his opinion as to who would be the most favorable to labor.

Moved by Mr. Lennon that objection be raised to the appointment of Mr. T. V. Powderly as Superintendent of Immigration in New York.

On motion it was decided that the Executive Council in their conference with the President, should request that he refer to labor legislation and labor interests in his message to Congress, and particularly to the Eight Hour Law, American Seamen's Bill,[2] Contempt Bill,[3] and Anti-Trust Bill.[4]

. . .

AFTERNOON SESSION.

. . .

Reconvened at 4:30; all the members present.

Moved by Mr. O'Connell that the Secretary make a minute note of the Council's conference with President McKinley and spread them on our record. (By request of President Gompers I have adopted the following as the minutes of the interview):

The President discussed with the Executive Council fully and freely the existing conditions of labor and the various matters and measures which could redound to labor's interest. President McKinley suggested that the requests for legislation be submitted in writing in order that it may appear in tangible and practical form for his consideration and action.

During the interview the request was made for the exercise of executive clemency to the only surviving member of the unfortunate crew, Ephraim W. Clark, who is now in Thomaston Prison, Maine, undergoing a life sentence for mutiny on board the Jefferson Borden nearly twenty years ago. The provocation and awful suffering and brutality endured by the mutineers were urged upon the attention of the President, who immediately directed that the papers on file be submitted to him for consideration, and he gave further indications that the matter would receive his early and we earnestly hope favorable action.

It had been mooted through the press that the President would appoint Mr. T. V. Powderly to the position of Superintendent of Immigration and that the appointment was intended as a compliment to and a recognition of labor. When this statement went uncontradicted for several weeks and the appointment seemed about to be made, the Executive Council of the American Federation of Labor felt it to be its duty to call the President's attention to the unwisdom of such an appointment. It was urged that the immigration laws and particularly the contract and many other features of these laws were the result of the efforts of the workers, and that one in sympathy with labor or at least having the confidence or even the respect of labor, should receive the appointment to such a position.

The President certainly seemed to entertain the belief that Mr. Powderly possessed these qualifications; he was assured, however, that the appointment would be regarded as an insult rather than a compliment or recognition. The Executive Council would recommend no one for the position but protested against the appointment contemplated.

The conference lasted nearly an hour, and was entirely devoted to the discussion of matters of primal importance to labor. The President expressing his interest and desire to do what laid in his power to further the interest of the wage earners and the public generally. At the conclusion of the interview it was felt by all that a duty to the toilers had been performed and would result to their advantage. At least it is certainly devoutly wished that the results may prove so and pave the way for legislative and executive action.

. . .

President Gompers reported a movement on foot for the Western Miners to secede from the American Federation of Labor and organize a "Western Federation." The letters of President Boyce of the Western Federation of Miners, were read by President Gompers, also President Gompers' reply.

Mr. Debs' letter[5] in the New York Journal was read by Treasurer Lennon. On the call for the standing of the Western Federation of Miners, by Mr. McGuire, the records show that on June 20th, 1896, their strike, began, and they were admitted into the American Federation of Labor on July 7, 1896,

Moved by Mr. Lennon that the letters of President Gompers and President Boyce of the Miners, with an argument against a "Western Federation" being formed, be printed[6] and forwarded to the delegates to the Convention of the Western Federation of Miners at Salt Lake City, Utah. Carried.

On motion the Council adjourned until 7:30 P.M.

EVENING SESSION.

Meeting called to order at eight o'clock; with all the members of the Council present.

. . .

In case of the resolution[7] passed at the Cincinnati Convention asking help to organize the women employed in electrical manufacturing establishments and which was referred to the Executive Council, moved by Mr. Garland that it be referred to the President with instructions to give such aid as the finances of the Federation would justify. Carried.

. . .

T and PD, Minutes of Meetings, Executive Council, AFL, reel 2, frames 1144-46, *AFL Records.*

1. The 1896 AFL convention created an advisory board, consisting of representatives of national and international affiliates living in Washington, D.C., to meet monthly with federation officers and plan the eight-hour campaign. The board's recommendations were subject to Executive Council approval.

2. In 1896 New York Congressman Sereno E. Payne introduced H.R. 6399 (54th Cong., 1st sess.), which, as modified in committee, included a ban on imprisonment for desertion, limits to the practice of allotting seamen's wages to family members, creditors, or other individuals, improvements in shipboard fare, and penalties for masters whose cruelty caused crewmen to desert. It failed to pass. In December 1896 Maine Senator William P. Frye introduced an amended version in the Senate containing a provision for up to one month's imprisonment for desertion. It, too, was unsuccessful.

3. The House Judiciary Committee reported a substitute (H.R. 2471, 54th Cong., 2d sess.) on Jan. 8, 1897, for Sen. David Hill's contempt bill (S. 2984, 54th Cong.,

1st sess.; see "An Interview in the *Indianapolis Sentinel*," Jan. 5, 1896, n. 1, above), but the measure apparently failed to pass.

4. Probably S. 1546 (55th Cong., 1st sess.), a bill to amend the Sherman Antitrust Act; it was introduced on Apr. 1, 1897, by William V. Allen of Nebraska.

5. Eugene Debs's letter of Apr. 16, 1897, appearing in the *New York Journal* of Apr. 17, predicted the launching of a grand industrial cooperative movement covering all fields of labor—with the workers "virtually being their own employers and receiving the whole product of their labor"—at the forthcoming American Railway Union convention to be held in Chicago in June. "The old methods have been outgrown," he wrote, and "nothing more can be accomplished on present lines." (See "To John O'Sullivan," June 25, 1897, n. 3, below.)

6. *An Address. To the Western Federation of Miners, in Convention Assembled, Salt Lake City, Utah* (Washington, D.C., 1897). These letters (to Boyce, Mar. 9, from Boyce, Mar. 16, to Boyce, Mar. 26, and from Boyce, Apr. 7, all 1897) are reprinted above.

7. The resolution was introduced at the AFL convention on Dec. 17, 1896, by James Kelly of the National Brotherhood of Electrical Workers.

From Martin Fox

Office of the Iron Molders' Union of North America
Cincinnati, April 20 1897.

Dear Sir & Bro.

Yours[1] with the inclosed letter[2] from our friend, brother Griscom came duly to hand. I have no desire to criticise his position on the race question, only to say, that when men of his intelligence so plainly express their prejudice against the negroe, no matter what qualifications the black man may have as a workman and mechanic, what can be expected of those who have not had the same oppertunities in life as our friend. If men of his standing were to use their efforts on the lines we have always indicated, I am satisfied they could educate the workingmen of the South that they must recognize the mechanical abilities of the black man, let their social conditions take care of themselves. I am glad that this question was so prominently brought to our notice, it gives us an oppertunity to place our position squarely before them in a way so that there will be no misunderstanding in the future.

The effect has been beneficial to our members in Chattanooga, and I am in hopes they will in the future come to their Union for relief and not shift the responsibility on the black man for all the ills from which they suffer. A little stiffening of the back-bone would do them no harm.

Comment is unnecessary on the Article of our friends in Sheboygan.[3] Their statement reminds me of the boy story, "Its not me but the other fellow''. The position of our members is still safe, and I do not care to push the boycott, unless we find it necessary as a last resort. With kindest regards I am as ever

Fraternally Yours in U   Martin Fox.

Prest

ALS, Files of the Office of the President, General Correspondence, reel 59, frames 313-14, *AFL Records.*

1. SG to Fox, Apr. 16, 1897, reel 11, vol. 19, p. 604, SG Letterbooks, DLC.
2. "From William Griscom," ca. Apr. 13, 1897, above.
3. In mid-March 1897 Iron Molders' Union of North America (IMUNA) 286 of Sheboygan, Wis., requested IMUNA approval to strike Kohler, Haysen, and Stehn Manufacturing Co. to resist proposed reductions in wages paid for molding on bathtubs, sinks, reservoirs, and cuspidors. The IMUNA sanctioned the strike, which lasted at least through the end of the decade.

The Executive Council of the AFL to the President, Cabinet, and Congress

Washington, D.C. April 21st, 1897.

To the President, Cabinet and Congress of the United States of America.

Gentlemen:—

Multitudes of our working people—American citizens—at this hour are suffering humiliating poverty and countless privations and look to you for speedy relief. Last Fall they were promised helpful legislation and they expect it from you without unnecessary delay. In no party spirit we appeal to you to heed their wants and to promptly meet this unparalleled situation in the true spirit of American patriotism.

With industry half paralyzed, trade stagnant, values depressed and shrunken, with enterprise stifled and the productive powers of labor palsied, with our commerce listless on the seas and our immense resources blighted, we bid you haste the return of better times, to inspire confidence and bring cheer and comfort to the homes of the millions of citizens who now seek work and wages in vain.

In the name of the producers in shop and factory, in mill and mine, in the fields and on our lakes and seas, in behalf of the toilers out of work and of those underpaid, we urge on you the necessity of legislative relief. The destitution among the honest, proud and industrious people of our land, though half hidden, is ever increasing and becoming more and more appalling. The hopes they had are fast turning to gloomy despair. Invention, machinery, the subdivision of labor, and the countless labor dispensing appliances to cheapen production even in the best of times, disturb permanency of employment, tend to reduce wages and intensify competition in nearly every field of labor. Added to this the unrestricted flow of immigration from abroad, the organization of trusts, the centralization and concentration of capital in the manifold industries—all make the existence of the workingmen more hard and precarious. These changing conditions, unknown in our forefathers' times, must be met not by promises broken to the hopes, but by substantial and remedial legislation at the hands of Congress.

We therefore most respectfully memorialize the President, Cabinet and Congress of the United States for the enactment of these measures:

1. Amendment to the Federal Eight Hour Law, so to secure its practical enforcement on all public work by or for the United States Government, whether done by contract, sub-contract or day's work.

We are sternly opposed to the evasions and violations of the present eight hour law by the heads of Departments and officials in the Federal service.

2. A remodelling of our immigration laws so as to secure an enlarged protection to American citizens and their families.

3. Reform in the National Banking System and in the issuance of the currency of the United States so to secure the people from the possibilities and disasters of financial crises.

4. Liberal appropriation for government public works and for the improvement of rivers and harbors.

By the prompt adoption of these relief measures at the hands of Congress, we firmly believe some degree of prosperity may be restored and the conditions of the people bettered. We assure you the millions are now in no disposition to be trifled with. They are fast becoming desperate, and deep are their mutterings of discontent. They desire to realize some of the prosperity so freely promised on the stump six months ago.

Over three millions of willing workers are idle; shall they appeal to you in vain? Shall the interests of trusts, syndicates, monopolies, corporations and moneyed men remain of more importance than the welfare of the toilers? We trust not. We still believe the people's Representatives are not dead to the public welfare. We ask that they rise to the patriotism of this great occasion and hasten to bring relief to the masses of their fellow citizens.

Very respectfully yours,   Saml Gompers.

P. J McGuire

James Duncan

Jas O'Connell

M M Garland

John B. Lennon

Frank Morrison

Executive Council American Federation of Labor.

TLS, RG 46, Records of the U.S. Senate, Committee on Education and Labor, DNA.

An Excerpt from an Article in the
Washington Evening Times

[April 21, 1897]

CONGRESS URGED TO ACT.

The American Federation of Labor through its highest representatives, called on Speaker Reed today to urge that remedial legislation be had at the earliest practical day, without, however, indicating any time definitely. The executive council of the Federation is now in session in this city.

Speaker Reed met these representatives in his room, heard argument on behalf of certain propositions presented, and made a reply. The case was presented by President Gompers, First Vice President Maguire, of Philadelphia, and Mr. Duncan, of the executive council. In addition to the oral presentation of their requests the Federation submitted to the Speaker a memorial referring, among other things, specifically to the enforcement of the eight-hour law. This memorial is given below.[1]

President Gompers first addressed the speaker, saying that the delegation consisted of the officers above mentioned, the executive council and the advisory board. He explained the functions of these bodies, and what relation they bore to the workingmen of the country.

He premised that neither he nor the delegation came in the spirit of taking part in any controversy as between the Republicans and Democrats in respect to the contention that the House should at once proceed to business. What was asked by the labor people was not that remedial legislation should be had tomorrow or next week, but that there should be legislation in aid of the laboring men of the country.

Mr. Gompers said that it was unnecessary to repeat to the Speaker the condition now existing, of which he was so well aware. He might, however, suggest that his aid and that of Congress could well be invited in reference to the eight-hour law, to Government appropriations and to some modification of the immigration laws. He had not come prepared to make a speech, as the matters were largely covered in the memorial.

Mr. Maguire addressed himself to two subjects—the currency and the enforcement of the eight-hour law. He described the condition of the workmen in Philadelphia, which, he believed, was a fair statement of their condition in cities elsewhere and throughout the country. He did not refer specifically to any particular currency, but impressed the point that it was the duty of Congress to pass such measures as would prevent the panics and other money movements that affected workingmen and the country so disastrously from time to time.

Mr. Duncan spoke largely on the eight-hour law. He said that it was unfortunate that there was a belief, and that it had grounds of verification, that the Government itself was not disposed to be as friendly as it should be to this eight-hour law agitation. In fact, it had, on appeals to it, rather opposed than favored it. Mr. Duncan recited the condition, especially, of the granite cutters, with whom, he said, Mr. Reed ought to be familiar, on account of the importance of that branch of industry in Maine. He made a very strong appeal for assistance on all the subjects set forth in the memorial.

President Gompers asked if any other member of the delegation desired to speak, and none replying, he made an additional statement. He said that apart from the specific things asked for, he would call the attention of the Speaker to an important consideration. There was, he said, a growing sentiment throughout the country that the Federation, and, in fact, all labor bodies were of no avail to secure legislation from Congress.

This Mr. Gompers did not believe, nor did he assume that because the last Congress did nothing for labor that such was the future intention of the body. The existing facts, however, gave some ground for the unfortunate belief that existed among some laboring classes who were rapidly coming to the conclusion that there was only one remedy, and that was might, brute force, instead of waiting on the processes of the law.

He expressed the hope that something would be done to encourage the workingmen of the country, and in general to ameliorate their condition.

The Speaker said that he was pleased with the spirit in which he had been approached by the president as one not intending to disarrange any of the plans of the House.

He said pithily that matters of legislation were now being driven tandem and not abreast, and he was glad to note from the remarks of Mr. Gompers that the Federation recognized that fact. Mr. Reed said that in return for the appeal to him he might make an appeal to the Federation to aid in the plan of the House, and that they might wait until the tariff bill[2] had been passed or rejected.

He would not expect the laboring men to add anything to the inertia of the large body which now had the affairs of the country in hand. Mr. Reed promised to bear in mind the representations of the committee to him, just as he would those of any important body of citizenship. This closed the interview, both sides being apparently pleased with what had taken place.

All of the speakers for the Federation indorsed Mr. Garner,[3] of New Jersey, for chairman of the Committee of Labor when that committee should have been appointed by Mr. Reed.

. . .

Washington Evening Times, Apr. 21, 1897.

1. See "The Executive Council of the AFL to the President, Cabinet, and Congress," Apr. 21, 1897, above.

2. On Mar. 18, 1897, Rep. Nelson Dingley of Maine introduced H.R. 379 (55th Cong., 1st. sess.) to raise import tariffs. Known as the Dingley Tariff, it became law on July 24, 1897 (U.S. *Statutes at Large,* 30: 151-213).

3. John J. Gardner (1845-1921) was a New Jersey businessman and Republican congressman (1893-1913).

From Charles Bechtold[1]

National Union of the United Brewery
Workmen of the United States.
St. Louis, Mo. May 4, 1897

Dear Sir & Bro.:—

In order to show you how little the different officers of the locals of the International Coopers Union care for the interest of our organization, I send you enclosed a copy of a letter from the Chicago coopers' Union to Anheuser-Busch.[2] You find in this letter where the gentleman threatens to write to you, if we would not permit their members to take away part of our work in the washhouse and pitch-yard department in said brewery. Cooper work is done in a cooper shop and not in a brewery. Driving hoops[3] is no particular cooper work and has always been done by brewers. The coopers in Boston[4] are raising the same racket against our local unions there. It is time that such an unnecessary racket is stopped entirely. No doubt if it is allowed to go on it will make the brewery bosses feel as if there was a bad feeling amongst the different Organizations, and the result will be that neither the coopers nor we can make much headway.

Therefore, I kindly ask you to write to those people, the coopers, and stop them from causing unnecessary troubles for our local unions and thereby benefit their own interests more than by raising the devil all the time.

Fraternally Yours,   Chas. F. Bechtold
Nat'l Sec'y.

TLS, National Union of the United Brewery Workmen Records, reel 139, frames 271-72, *AFL Records.*

1. Charles F. BECHTOLD was a secretary of the National Union of the United Brewery Workmen of the United States from 1892 until 1901.
2. Robert McPherson to Anheuser-Busch Brewing Co., Apr. 27, 1897 (National Union of the United Brewery Workmen Records, reel 139, frames 275-76, *AFL Records*). McPherson was secretary of Coopers' International Union of North America (CIUNA) 94 of Chicago.
3. Driving hoops involved tightening loose barrel hoops.
4. CIUNA 89.

To Alonzo Caldwell[1]

May 10th. [1897]

Hon. A. B. Caldwell.
Syracuse, N.Y.
My Dear Sir & Brother: —

It is with profound gratification that I read the contents of your interesting favor of the 8th inst. advising me of the compliment paid by Court United States #1050 I.O.F.[2] in electing me an honorary member thereof. I beg to assure you and Court United States that I appreciate the very high honor paid me and shall to the very best of my ability endeavor to prove worthy of the confidence and respect manifested. In the early days of the movement of Independent For-restery in the United States it required some courage, some conviction, to hold the banner of our movement aloft. The grand results accomplished, the great membership gained and the prestige achieved is a high testimonial to your foresight, your unswerving devotion and high attainments. It is a pleasure for me to recall the fact that I was of some aid to you and our Brothers in launching this great organization.

For nearly 25 years I have devoted my entire time to another movement, the movement of the masses of labor, to secure that justice from which they have been for centuries deprived. That movement is destined to accomplish what the I.O.F. holds as a sincere sentiment— Liberty, Benevolence and Concord for and among mankind.

The seventy years of your life have been fruitful of results far beyond the hopes, struggles, achievements of most people. There are few who can look back upon life so worthily spent in the interest of humanity and who have accomplished so much towards the betterment of those who associated themselves with the Order.

Permit me to reciprocate the very warm words of friendship and confidence and well wishes which you express and to add the hope that health, happiness and prosperity may attend you in the evening tide of your well spent life.

Sincerely & fraternally yours,   Saml Gompers.
President   A.F. of L.

N.B.:— Is there a Court of the I.O.F. in the District of Columbia?

TLpS, reel 11, vol. 19, p. 832, SG Letterbooks, DLC.

1. Alonzo B. Caldwell was a New York–born journalist and lawyer. In 1874 SG, Caldwell, and others founded the Independent Order of Foresters (IOF)—a fraternal organization—in Newark, N.J. Caldwell moved to Syracuse, N.Y., about 1891 and practiced law there until his death in 1901.

2. The IOF Court United States 1050 was one of five chapters in Syracuse.

To the Executive Council of the AFL

Washington, D.C. May 10th. 1897.

To The Executive Council,
American Federation of Labor.
Colleagues:—

May 4th I visited Rochester, N.Y. and had a conference with representative labor men of that city in reference to the subject matter discussed at the last meeting of the Executive Council particularly the growth of trade unionism and the difficulty of the National Brewery Workmen's Union and the K. of L.

I had a conference with the Bartholomay, Rochester and Genesee Brewing Companies. It is evident that they have contracts with the K. of L. These contracts expire Jany. 1st. 1898. The Companies did not dispute that they did not wish to have two organizations of the brewers, but they expressed no hostility toward the A.F. of L. It appears that if they could have their employes organized in the National Union they would have no objection but they are evidently indisposed to incur the hostility of the K. of L. I did not urge them to break the agreement which they have with the K. of L. but insisted that before a new agreement was entered into we should be considered and consulted: that is our National Union should. They are positively opposed to the breaking of the agreement with the K. of L. The managers of the Companies, and I saw them all, seemed very much pleased with my visit and suggestions.

On my departure from Rochester to Syracuse I met Mr. T. B. McGuire,[1] of the G.E.B. of the K. of L. on the car. I got into a conversation with him and the entire matter was gone over as well as a suggestion from him for unity between the A.F. of L. and the K. of L. We agreed that whatever we said to each other should be considered as no matter for publication other than among the officers of our respective organizations. He incidentally remarked that the agreement with the Brewing Companies of Rochester called for the payment of $10.00 for the lowest wage in the Breweries. While I was at the Brewery office the pay rolls were shown me and it appeared that the lowest wage paid was $12.00, a discrepancy of $2.00 and I was convinced that the Statement of the officers of the National Union of United Brewery Workers of a secret understanding between the Brewing Cos. and the K. of L. by which lower wages should be paid than the prevailing scale of the National Union was founded upon fact. When Mr. McGuire made this statement to me not knowing that I had seen the pay rolls I asked him whether I could use this publicly if necessary. He said that I might. I ask the members of the Executive Council to consider this confidential for the present. I shall communicate with you later as to the suggestion made by Mr. McGuire for unity.

While at Rochester I had a conference with the proprietors of the Rochester Herald, a paper on which the printers' union members have been on strike[2] for the past ten weeks. It is more than likely that the negotiations will result in a complete success for the union. The officers who were the committee on conference requested my co-operation and say that it was a most fortunate incident for them that I came to the city and that their success if achieved will be due to the influence of our movement and my presence there at the time.

There was an excellent meeting at Buffalo[3] and also at Syracuse, on the night previous and after my visit to Rochester.

Mr. McGuire, with me, deplored the division and antagonism which exists in the labor movement as exemplified by the A.F. of L. and the K. of L. His attention was called to the fact that the treaty[4] which we once proposed might perhaps still hold good. He stated that the mixed assemblies were a positive failure and that the movement could only be successful based upon the question of wages and hours. He suggested that the Executive officers of both our organizations should unite in a common movement not to take organizations from each other, that there might perhaps be joint action between the Executive Council and the Executive Board of both organizations and mentioned other details in connection with it. He stated that if we are not united, if we keep apart as we now are, it would simply be a continuation of the present conflict. You will remember that the main points of the treaty were that the K. of L. would desist from organizing trade locals, should concede the trade jurisdiction to the National unions of the trade and issue no label to rival the label of any trade union. We continued to discuss these matters until the train arrived at Syracuse the understanding being that they would be discussed by the officers of our respective organizations.

I deem it my duty to advise you of this and to hope for your opinions in the matter which I ask you to freely and fully express.[5]

Yours fraternally,   Saml Gompers.

President   A.F. of L.

TLpS, AFL Executive Council Vote Books, reel 8, frame 194, *AFL Records.*

1. Thomas B. McGuire, a New York marble polisher and truck driver, was a member of the KOL General Executive Board from 1886 to 1888 and 1892 to 1897.

2. Members of International Typographical Union 15 struck when the *Rochester Herald* locked out its employees on Mar. 7, 1897, for refusing to accept a wage cut. The *Herald*'s ownership changed hands on Sept. 1, 1897, and on Sept. 25 the union, through the good offices of State Superintendent of Public Works G. W. Aldridge, negotiated a settlement. The strikers returned to work on Oct. 4.

3. On May 3, 1897, SG addressed a meeting of the Wesley Club, a Buffalo, N.Y., organization composed of young men affiliated with the Methodist Episcopal Church.

4. See "A Committee of the Philadelphia Trade Union Conference to the Cleveland General Assembly of the KOL," May 18, 1886, in *The Making of Union Leader,* pp. 395-96.

5. The AFL Executive Council voted to cooperate with the KOL Executive Board to end the organizations' raiding of each other's affiliates.

To Martin Fox

May 13th. [1897]

Mr. Martin Fox,
President, Iron Moulders Union of N.A.
P.O. Box #388; Cincinnati, Ohio.
Dear Sir & Brother: —

I am in receipt of a letter from our organizer at Chattanooga[1] in which he makes some reference to the negro question again but I firmly believe he has somewhat changed in his views for I have argued it very strongly with him.[2] In his letter he says that there are very good prospects to organize a Federal Labor Union[3] and that in all likelihood in a short while it may number hundreds of members. Yes, he asks me whether your National Union would be willing to allow the negro moulders to become members of the Federal Labor Union and to "await the process of evolution before attempting that they be made members of the Iron Moulders Union or form a separate local." He adds that he does not know that he can accomplish this but that he may have the movement on foot and would like to proceed on sure lines. In my reply to him I have stated that I would write to obtain your decision and whatever that would be will be binding upon me and must govern his course. Kindly reply to this at your earliest convenience and oblige,

Fraternally yours,   Saml Gompers.
President   A.F. of L

TLpS, reel 11, vol. 19, p. 881, SG Letterbooks, DLC.

1. See "From William Griscom," ca. Apr. 13, 1897, above.
2. See "To William Griscom," Apr. 16, 1897, above.
3. The AFL chartered Federal Labor Union 6898 of Chattanooga on May 17, 1897.

To William Winn

May 17th, 1897.

Mr. Will. H. Winn,
Columbus, Ga.,
Dear Sir: —

I am in receipt of your favor of the 13th Inst., and note its contents with a great deal of interest and pleasure. In connection with the label on the textile products, I would say that the consideration of it was, as I told you, deferred until some other time. It was necessary to take this action for obvious reasons. Mr. Reed,[1] the former general secretary, in his circular letter,[2] calling for the convention,[3] declared that he was going to recommend that the textile workers national union should withdraw from the A.F. of L., and affiliate with the socialists' alliance, which you understand is another name for the socialist party. If the Convention had followed that course, I would have stood instructed, as per the Cincinnati A.F. of L., to immediately take steps to organize a national trade union of textile workers on true union lines. In other words, that the interests of the textile workers were no longer to be trifled with by theorists and blatherskites, if we could help it. The Philadelphia Convention, however, turned its back upon these would-be union wreckers and planted its foot down, flat, for trade unionism. I would say that the action has been sent to the referendum of the matters [members?], but I am assured that there is little doubt of the outcome.[4] This, of course, changes the situation completely. Now, the National Union will have absolute jurisdiction in the issuance of a union label. I shall correspond with Secretary Mills[5] upon the subject and advise you as soon as I hear from him. I hope that the matter will take tangible shape soon, so that it may soon be put in operation. I learn that Mr. Green[6] rendered quite good service at Philadelphia in standing for true trade unionism. Of course, being an old friend of yours, there would be no doubt as to the stand he would take. I appreciate, too, very much your words of commendation, in re my eight hour work-day article[7] and, also, the memorial.[8] We do not profess to have the "open sesame" to heaven, but we have the determination to try and do as near right as we know how, and we are putting forth every effort to accomplish the right.

Hoping to have a revival of industry soon, and with it a great impetus for organization, and with kindest regards and best wishes, I remain,

Yours Fraternally,   Saml Gompers.

President   A.F. of L.

TLpS, reel 11, vol. 19, pp. 962-63, SG Letterbooks, DLC.

1. James P. REID was an Olneyville, R.I., weaver.
2. Reid sent SG a copy of the circular in mid-March 1897.
3. The National Union of Textile Workers of America (NUTWA) held its eighth annual convention at Philadelphia, May 3-5, 1897.
4. The NUTWA did not disaffiliate; its 1897 convention rejected the proposal of the union's socialist officers to withdraw from the AFL and turned them out of office.
5. Henry S. MILLS was general secretary of the NUTWA from mid-1897 until at least 1898.
6. Prince W. GREENE was elected vice-president of the NUTWA at its 1897 con-

vention. Later in the year he became president of the organization and served in that office until 1900.

7. SG's articles entitled "The Eight-Hour Work Day: Its Inauguration, Enforcement and Influences Discussed," appeared serially in the *American Federationist* in 1897 (4 [Mar.]: 1-2, [Apr.]: 23-25, [May]: 47-49, [June]: 69-71, and [July]: 87-88). They were also published in the Michigan Bureau of Labor and Industrial Statistics, *Fourteenth Annual Report* (Lansing, 1897), pp. 200-216.

8. See "The Executive Council of the AFL to the President, Cabinet, and Congress," Apr. 21, 1897, above.

To Levi Schrader[1]

May 24th. [1897]

Mr. Levi P. Schrader,
Organizer.
#411 Ferry St.; Ludington, Mich.
Dear Sir & Brother:—

Your favor of the 17th to hand and noted. I note the complaint which you make on behalf of Laborers Protective Union #6869[2] in the matter of the Government contract work but it is scarcely sufficient in detail to base a complaint upon although I shall do what I can and go before the Department at Washington.

Let me say that there is no provision in the laws of the U.S. which interferes with the employment of workmen from one city or any other part of the country. For that reason the complaint which you make, that the contractors employ help from other cities, can not be made a matter of complaint before the Department. I readily see the injustice and inadvisability of such a scheme, and if the work were performed by the Government under the day-work system then I could urge it as a matter of justice and practicability. This might also be urged as well as you can in your locality upon the contractors and perhaps with the same effect.

The U.S. law passed Aug. 1st. 1892 provides that eight hours shall constitute a day's work for all government work. I want to call your attention, however, to a recent decision of the courts[3] in which it was held that the work done by contract is not government work until after it has been completed and turned over to and accepted by the Government. You can readily see how far reaching such a decision is. Yet we must endeavour to overcome it by the best means at our command.

There is no standard of wages provided by either law or the rules of the Department for work done under contract. I believe it to be the duty of your Union to insist by all means within its power that the contractors shall not be permitted to work members of your union, and labor generally, for long hours of labor and low wages. Anything I can do to help you in this will be cheerfully performed. I ask you to do what you can to force the unwilling contractors to deal more fairly with labor. That is the primary purpose of your union. Please give me further detailed information in regard to these matters and oblige,

Yours fraternally,   Saml Gompers.

President   A.F. of L.

TLpS, reel 12, vol. 20, p. 57, SG Letterbooks, DLC.

1. Levi P. Schrader was a Ludington, Mich., carpenter.
2. AFL Laborers' Protective Union 6869 of Ludington, Mich., was chartered by the AFL in March 1897.
3. Possibly *United States* v. *Ollinger* (55 Federal Reporter 959-61), decided May 10, 1893, in the U.S. District Court, Southern District, Alabama. The court ruled that the defendant, William Ollinger, had not violated the federal eight-hour law even though his employees had worked nine-hour days while filling a federal contract for two barges. It maintained that Ollinger was not amenable to the law because he was neither an officer nor an agent of the U.S. government, nor a contractor or subcontractor on public works, since the barges remained his own property until they were completed and sold to the government.

To the Executive Council of the AFL

Washington, D.C. June 16th. 1897.

To The Executive Council:

Colleagues: —

Owing to the decision of the Supreme Court, U.S. in the case of the Trans-Missouri Traffic Association which declared such pooling in violation of the Sherman Anti-Trust law,[1] Senator Foraker,[2] Ohio, introduced into the Senate some time ago a bill[3] practically legalizing such pooling.

It is currently rumored here, and it has been published, that the Senate Committee on Interstate Commerce proposes to report the bill favorably. You are also aware that under the Sherman Anti-Trust law the decisions were rendered affecting organizations of labor.

The thought has occurred to me that before this bill is reported to the Senate an effort should be made by the representatives of the A.F. of L. to secure an amendment to the law by which lawful labor organizations should be exempt from the provisions of the law. It seems to be an opportune time when if the trusts and corporations can secure modification of a law which impedes their growth or development the organizations of labor should not be the only ones who should remain the parties liable under the old law, but be among the ones who will find relief by the amendment.

At the last meeting of the Executive Council it was agreed that in the event of matters arising of this character the subject should be attended to by Mess. McGuire, Duncan, Morrison and the undersigned by reason of the close proximity that each of these members resides to the National Capital.

If the members of the Executive Council approve that affirmative action be taken on these lines the members thereof, enumerated above will be asked to act in the premises.[4]

Kindly return your vote upon the above matter at your early convenience and oblige,

Yours fraternally,   Saml Gompers.
President   A.F. of L.

TLpS, AFL Executive Council Vote Books, reel 8, frame 201, *AFL Records.*

1. The court decided Mar. 22, 1897, in *United States* v. *Trans-Missouri Freight Association* (166 U.S. 290), that the Trans-Missouri Freight Association—a rate-fixing consortium formed by eighteen railroads in 1889—was not a "pool" as prohibited by the Interstate Commerce Act. It ruled, however, that the association did represent an agreement in restraint of trade in violation of the Sherman Antitrust Act.

2. Joseph B. Foraker (1846-1917), an Ohio lawyer and judge, Republican governor of Ohio (1885-89), and U.S. senator (1897-1909).

3. On Mar. 30, 1897, Foraker introduced S. 1479 (55th Cong., 1st sess.) to amend the Interstate Commerce Act. The bill was referred to committee and failed to pass.

4. The AFL Executive Council approved SG's proposal.

To G. A. Hoehn

June 19th. [1897]

Mr. G. A. Hoehn.
#3430 Tenn. Av.; St. Louis, Mo.
Dear Sir & Brother:—

Your favor of the 15th containing manuscript for your article on Karl Marx came duly to hand. I have not been able to read it all yet but what I have interested me very much and I shall begin its publication[1] at the earliest possible moment. You have seen the continued articles[2] as they are running through the American Federationist and as soon as these are completed, which will be shortly, I shall commence the publication of yours. I beg to thank you very much for your kindness in giving us the opportunity of their publication first. I was glad that you enumerated what Mr. Sorge[3] wrote in the Die Neue-Zeit.[4] I had the privilege of reading the original about the time of its publication my attention having been called to it by Theo. Cuno[5] of N.Y. I regret to learn that you have been ill but hope that you are now enjoying the privilege of good health. With kindest regards and best wishes I am,

Yours fraternally,   Saml Gompers.
President   A.F. of L.

N.B. How would you like the change of the title to
"Karl Marx.
His Meritorious Work in Behalf of the Modern Labor Movement.
Marxism vs. Pseudo-Marxism." — It seems to strike me as the [. . . .]

T and ALpS, reel 12, vol. 20, p. 291, SG Letterbooks, DLC.

1. "True Socialism. Marxism and Pseudo-Marxism" appeared serially in the *American Federationist* in 1898 (5 [Aug.]: 107-9, [Sept.]: 130-32, [Oct.]: 153-54, and [Nov.]: 175-77). Hoehn outlined Marxist theory and argued that ameliorative labor legislation and trade unionism—rather than the SLP activism of a "pseudo-Marxist clique of shyster lawyers of New York"—were authentic expressions of working-class interest and power as defined by Marx and his associates (ibid. [Sept.]: 131).

2. SG's series on the eight-hour workday (see "To William Winn," May 17, 1897, n. 7, above).

3. Friedrich Adolph SORGE, a leading American socialist and former general secretary of the International Workingmen's Association (1872-74), worked in Hoboken, N.J., as a music teacher.

4. Hoehn had translated passages from a series of articles by Sorge on the American labor movement. Sorge had written them on the suggestion of Friedrich Engels; they were published in *Die Neue Zeit,* the journal of the Sozialdemokratische Partei Deutschlands (Social Democratic Party of Germany), between 1891 and 1895. In one Sorge called for an end to the divisions within the New York City labor movement. "If, from reasons of honesty, a harmonious working *together* has become impossible," he argued, "then a *modus vivendi* must be found to enable a working *side by side* in a peaceable way" (*American Federationist* 5 [Sept. 1898]: 132). In another, Sorge claimed that the AFL, with "all its faults and defects," was deserving of respect because it was "a *bona fide*, a true labor organization—an organization of wage workers, pure and simple, without clauses and back doors in its statutes through which middle class and wealthy capitalists, would-be reformers and politicians, might creep in" (ibid. [Nov.]: 176).

5. Theodore F. Cuno was a German-American socialist and journalist. A native of Prussia, he was expelled from Germany, went to Milan and organized the local section of the First International, and in 1872 immigrated to the United States. He joined the Spread-the-Light Club—KOL Local Assembly 1562 of Brooklyn—and in 1881 was elected grand statistician of the national order. Cuno was on the staff of the *New Yorker Volkszeitung.*

A Circular

Washington, D.C., June 21, 1897

To Whom It May Concern:

Having had occasion, in connection with my duties, to be in St. Louis, Mo., June 4th and 5th, the undersigned called with a committee upon H. S. Block,[1] of H. S. Block & Co., with the view of an amicable adjustment of the differences[2] existing between the cigar makers' unions and the firm in question. Mr. Block refused to consider the question of his firm paying the "union scale." His language was gross and vile; his manner harsh and overbearing. He spurned organized labor, its power and influences, and sneeringly defied labor "to do its worst." It remains with the workers and the sympathizers with our movement to demonstrate to H. S. Block & Co. that labor has rights which even this firm is bound to respect.

Samuel Gompers,
President   American Federation of Labor.

Cigar Makers' Official Journal, July 1897.

1. Henry S. Bloch was a St. Louis cigar manufacturer who had moved his firm from Cleveland after a labor dispute in 1896.
2. On Sept. 28, 1896, CMIU 44 and 281 struck H. S. Bloch and Co. over a wage cut. A lengthy struggle ensued during which the firm hired new workers and obtained a KOL charter for them, while the AFL boycotted the company. A settlement on Aug. 19, 1897, restored the union scale and provided for the rehiring of CMIU members and the firing of their replacements.

To John O'Sullivan

June 25th. [1897]

Mr. John F. O'Sullivan.
c/o Boston Globe; Boston, Mass.
Dear Friend:—

Your favor of the 22nd to hand and many thanks for the things of interest you communicate in regard to the convention[1] of the Boot & Shoe Workers Union. It is a most interesting spectacle. Just to think of it that in all the conventions of National unions which have been held within the past two years there has been a steady growth toward trade unionism, true, pure and simple and a weaning from the alluring spectacle of the chimerical, speculative theories. The Boot & Shoe workers Union being the outcome of the different branches of the trade declared almost emphatically against practical trade unionism and our friend Tobin was carried along to the chief executive position upon that issue. Today as a result of experience and responsibilities I believe he stands nearer the trade union movement than ever before. As a matter of fact the so-called socialists (which is now used as another name for anti-trade unionist) now regard Tobin as not of their kind and he is not allowed to train with them. I have every faith that the near future will witness a very great impetus to our movement on true trade union lines.

I suppose you noticed that the Textile Workers convention at Philadelphia elected trade unionists as officers and refused to be longer continued in the entranced state. The Carpenters at Cleveland, the Cigar Makers at Detroit, the Iron Moulders and hosts of others, all have taken a firm stand upon this matter.

I am sure that the outlook a few years ago was anything but promising in this direction. It required heroic and determined action at the Denver convention of the A.F. of L. and though it involved the defeat of trade unionists it was the triumph of trade unionism for there was a reaction awakening all along the line which culminated at New York and since then there has been a constant realization of the trade union issue and a clearer comprehension of the trade union movement.

You perhaps may remember that at the mid-day banquet we had at the Quincy House[2] a month after Denver when we predicted that such would be the case and that my defeat at Denver would be productive of good to our movement. It drew the lines and compelled men to show their colors. I feel great gratification at the result of the work of our sincere men who always hewed strictly to the line.

By the way I protest against your constant reminder that I am not getting young or prettier. If I am not very much mistaken "there are others" and I imagine that O'Sullivan the sailor is one among them.

I hope you and Mary and the friends of our movement are well and doing well and entertain the hope that we shall make still greater progress until there shall be no question as to the full field of labors' struggles being conceded to the trade unions.

There was a balloon ascension in Chicago[3] a few days ago labelled "co-operative commonwealth." There were brass bands and fireworks galore. Have you seen or heard anything of it in your region since?

Let me hear from you often.

Sincerely yours,　Saml Gompers.

President　A.F. of L

TLpS, reel 12, vol. 20, pp. 352-53, SG Letterbooks, DLC.

1. The Boot and Shoe Workers' Union convention met at Boston, June 21-26, 1897.

2. See "An Article in the *Boston Herald*," Jan. 9, 1895, above.

3. The American Railway Union held its final convention June 15-17, 1897, in Chicago. It voted to dissolve and establish a new movement, the Social Democracy of America (SDA). The founding convention of the SDA then met under the leadership of Eugene Debs, June 17-21, and announced plans for establishing a socialist communitarian colony—the National Co-operative Commonwealth—in Washington state.

To Sofus Jensen[1]

June 30th. [1897]

Mr. Sofus Jensen,
Secretary, Columbia River Fishermens
  Protective Union #6321.[2]
P.O. Box #472; Astoria, Oregon.
Dear Sir & Brother:—

I am in receipt of a letter from Bro. P. J. McGuire, Secretary of the United Brotherhood of Carpenters & Joiners of America, in which it is stated that when your Union started the Co-operative Packing Co. it was the understanding that you would build your cannery and have your work done exclusively by white labor, instead of which, it is charged, your Union entered into a contract with a Chinese boss to furnish the labor and that now they are all Chinamen who are working there. It is also stated that you have a sign board posted on the building on which there is the notice that "no white labor need apply." Of course I do not know whether these charges are true, but certainly if they are true they are most reprehensible. I am unwilling to believe that men could be banded together in unionism to protect themselves and each other who would be guilty of the conduct charged in the letters referred to. I ask you to kindly advise me in reference to this at your earliest possible convenience and oblige,[3]

Yours fraternally,   Saml Gompers.
President   A.F. [of L.]

TLpS, reel 12, vol. 20, p. 392, SG Letterbooks, DLC.

1. Sofus Jensen was secretary of AFL Columbia River Fishermen's Protective Union 6321 and an AFL organizer.

2. The union received its AFL charter in 1894.

3. Jensen subsequently wrote SG to deny that the union had erected such a sign and to explain that it had taken steps to replace "Chinese and coolie labor" with "American workmen" (SG to P. J. McGuire, Aug. 7, 1897, reel 12, vol. 20, p. 910, SG Letterbooks, DLC).

To James Porter[1]

July 1st. [1897]

Mr. J. E. Porter,
Secretary, Colored Laboringmens Alliance.
#927 Perdido St.; New Orleans, La.
Dear Sir:—
Your favor 26th to hand and noted and I beg to assure you that [I] appreciate very highly the very kind words of commendation of your Alliance as expressed by them in regard to the recent interview had with Hon. Wm. McKinley, President of the United States. Let me say that the President and I were discussing the amendments to the anti pooling bill[2] and we became very much interested, the President exhibiting thorough acquaintance with the matter under discussion and he expressed himself then as you no doubt have seen published; that is that he is favorably inclined toward the organizations of labor and that they were a natural result of present economic conditions.

We shall do our very best in order to secure the elimination from any law now in existence any feature which applies, or is construed to apply, inimically to the organizations of labor.

I trust that the workers of the South both white and colored will lose no time to organize as swiftly upon trade union lines for in them after all is the only hope labor has to protect and advance its interests.

How is it that the Colored Laboringmens Alliance is not in affiliation with the labor movement under the A.F. of L.?

It is quite some few years since I heard from you and should be pleased if you can write again taking an interest in the movement.

I presume you have seen that our friend Flemming[3] has started a new paper *The Southern Economist,* and also that our friend Leonard[4] is still in the ranks. Should you see them kindly remember me to them.

With kind regards and best wishes I am,

Yours fraternally, Saml Gompers.
President A.F. of L.

TLpS, reel 12, vol. 20, pp. 403-4, SG Letterbooks, DLC.

1. James E. PORTER was an AFL organizer and a member of International Longshoremen's Association 231.

2. Probably either Sen. Joseph Foraker's S. 1479 (see "To the Executive Council of the AFL," June 16, 1897, n. 3, above), or H.R. 2808 (55th Cong., 1st sess.) introduced by Richard C. Shannon of New York on Apr. 14, 1897, to amend the Sherman Antitrust Act. Both bills sought to loosen restrictions on railroad pools.

3. Robert P. Fleming was a New Orleans printer and editor of the *Southern Economist and Trade Unionist.*

4. James Leonard.

An Article in the *Pittsburg Post*

Washington, July 3. [1897]

STRIKE FOR LIVING WAGES.

Following is the statement of President Samuel Gompers, of the American Federation of Labor:

"The mine workers are striving for living wages.[1] No industry has a right to exist which cannot pay living wages. Such an industry would be a blot on civilization and a menace to our institutions. It is absurd to argue that between the coal mine and the $4 to $5 a ton the consumers have to pay for coal there is not profit enough to pay the miners living wages. There must be a readjustment. Coal is a necessity of our modern industrial civilization. It must pay its producers enough to live on.

"I shall do everything which lies in my power to aid in bringing this momentous struggle to a successful end. The mine situation was never so wretched as now. But the Federation was never so strong as at the present time. Less than 1 per cent of the members of labor organizations have received charitable bequests outside of the organizations themselves. This despite one of the most marked periods of industrial depression in the history of the country. If necessary, I may go into the coal field, but at all times I shall be in constant communication with the leaders of the strike. The following telegrams will explain themselves:

" 'Columbus, O., July 2, 1897.

" 'Samuel Gompers, President A.F. of L.,

" 'Washington, D.C.:

" 'The miners of the United States will suspend work to-morrow in a demand for living wages. Hope this will meet your approval.

" 'M. D. Ratchford.'[2]

" 'Washington, D.C., July 2, 1897.

" 'M. D. Ratchford,

" '53 Clinton Building, Columbus, O.:

" 'If miners suspend work in demand of living wages, I not only sincerely hope that they may be successful, but that no compromise will be accepted that does not involve the establishment of that principle. At any stage where I can be of assistance to the miners in this contest I am yours to command.

" 'Samuel Gompers.' "

Pittsburg Post, July 4, 1897.

1. After several years of declining wages and dwindling membership in the bituminous coalfields of the East and Midwest, the United Mine Workers of America (UMWA) issued a call for a strike to begin July 4, 1897. More than 100,000 miners quit work at the outset, and their numbers eventually grew to 150,000; the strike was particularly effective in Illinois, Indiana, Ohio, and western Pennsylvania (the Central Competitive Field). When the UMWA sought the labor movement's support in West Virginia—strategically important and largely nonunionized—SG and other prominent trade unionists met at Pittsburgh on July 9 to coordinate their efforts. They subsequently sent organizers to the state and mounted protests against harassment by local officials and state courts. Eugene Debs and James Sovereign also campaigned on behalf of the miners. A compromise settlement ratified Sept. 11 ended the strike for most miners (see "To Frank Weber," Sept. 10, 1897, n. 1, below), but some 20,000 men were still idle in early November. A conference between representatives of the UMWA and operators in the Central Field in January 1898 forged an agreement raising wages and providing for arbitration of differences and ongoing union-management consultation (see "To John George," Apr. 29, 1898, n. 3, below). By March most operators in the Central Field—with the exception of the DeArmitt mines of western Pennsylvania—had subscribed to its terms. Operators in West Virginia continued to resist unionization and the interstate agreement, prompting the UMWA to place a boycott on all West Virginia coal in June (see "To P. J. McGuire," July 8, 1898, n. 2, below).

2. Michael D. RATCHFORD was president of the UMWA (1897-98).

An Excerpt from an Article in the
Philadelphia Public Ledger

Pittsburg, July 9. [1897]

HELP FOR THE COAL MINERS

. . .

The greatest gathering of labor leaders that ever assembled in this country during a strike was held in this city to-night to devise means to assist the coal miners in their contest for increased wages.

The conference was called suddenly, but the officials responding represent nearly every branch of organized labor in the United States.

Those present were Samuel Gompers, President of the American Federation of Labor; M. D. Ratchford, National President of the United Mine Workers of America; M. M. Garland, President of the Amalgamated Association of Iron and Steel workers; Stephen Madden,[1] Secretary of the Amalgamated Association; J. M. Huges,[2] First Vice President of the Federation of Metal Trades;[3] M. J. Counahan,[4] National Secretary of the Journeyman Plumbers' Association;[5] M. P. Carrick,[6] President of the Brotherhood of Painters and Decorators; L. R. Thomas,[7] President of the National Pattern Makers League;[8] W. B. Mahon, President of the Amalgamated Association of Street Railway Employees; Patrick Dolan,[9] District President of the United Mine Workers of America, and W. M. Warner,[10] District Secretary of the United Mine workers.

The session was secret, and it was almost midnight before it was over. The Press Committee, Messrs. Gompers, Ratchford and Counahan, then gave out the following statement, in which was incorporated, they said, all that was done at the conference:

A MANIFESTO ISSUED.

"After an informal discussion, reports were made by Messrs. Ratchford, Dolan and Warner in regard to the situation of the movement, and it was demonstrated that the suspension was practically general in the competitive bituminous coal district extending also to Kentucky and Tennessee, excepting a few points in West Virginia.

"It was realized that the situation in West Virginia required attention, in order that the suspension should become absolutely general and success assured. With that object in view, action was recommended by President Gompers, of the American Federation of Labor, and it was determined to overcome this feature of the contest.

"It was also determined that every effort be made on the part of those present to secure the co-operation and practical aid of organized labor for the struggling miners. All the circumstances warranted the firm conviction that the miners will ultimately achieve victory, and to this end the aid of labor and the sympathetic public be invoked.

"Conscious of the great interest which the public has in a contest so widespread as that of the miners, it gives us great satisfaction to know that the miners have not been and are not now opposed to arbitration.

"We therefore urge and advise that a conference be held by the representatives of the miners and the operators, with a view of arriving at a settlement of the present suspension."

Notwithstanding the positive announcement by the committee that the statement furnished the press covered all the proceedings of the conference, it is known that an organized effort to secure a general suspension of mining in West Virginia was decided upon.

After a thorough canvass of the situation, it was unanimously agreed that the West Virginia miners hold the key to the situation, and, without their united support, the success of the general movement would be greatly jeopardized.

In furtherance of this determination the officials present pledged themselves to send into this field a full quota of the best organizers in their several associations.

After adjournment, in response to the question whether a 2 per cent. assessment on all organized labor would be made as contemplated, President Dolan, of the Pittsburg district, said he thought such action would eventually be taken.

He would not admit, however, that the matter of assessment had been considered at to-night's conference, or that the question of a general sympathetic strike had been discussed.

Philadelphia Public Ledger, July 10, 1897.

1. Stephen MADDEN was secretary-treasurer of the National Amalgamated Association of Iron and Steel Workers from 1897 to 1898.

2. Probably James F. HUGHES, a Pittsburgh tinner who served as secretary of the Tin, Sheet Iron, and Cornice Workers' International Association (TSICA) from 1895 to 1897 and as secretary-treasurer of the Amalgamated Sheet Metal Workers' International Association, as the TSICA was renamed, from 1897 to about 1900.

3. The Federated Metal Trades.

4. Michael J. COUNAHAN was general secretary (1892-93) and secretary-treasurer (1893-97) of the United Association of Journeymen Plumbers, Gas Fitters, Steam Fitters, and Steam Fitters' Helpers of the United States and Canada and editor of its official organ, the *United Association Journal,* from 1892 to 1897.

5. The United Association of Journeymen PLUMBERS, Gas Fitters, Steam Fitters, and Steam Fitters' Helpers of the United States and Canada.

6. Michael Patrick CARRICK, a founder of the Brotherhood of Painters and Decorators in 1887, served as general president of the western faction of the divided organization in 1896 and 1897.

7. Llewelyn R. THOMAS, a Pittsburgh patternmaker, was president of the Pattern Makers' National League of North America (from 1898 the Pattern Makers' League of North America) from 1894 to 1902.

8. The PATTERN Makers' National League of North America.

9. Patrick Dolan of Pittsburgh was president of United Mine Workers of America (UMWA) District 5 from about 1896 to 1905.

10. William Warner of Pittsburgh was a member of UMWA 524 in District 5 and secretary-treasurer of the district from 1897 to 1899.

To M. D. Ratchford

July 12th. [1897]

Mr. M. D. Ratchford,
President, United Mine Workers of America.
#81 Clinton Bldg.; Columbus, Ohio.
Dear Sir & Brother:—

As per our understanding I have today commissioned Mr. W. D. Mahon to go into the coal fields of West Virginia. I have wired to several of our other active, earnest and able trade unionists and there will be several others who will report to your office in the course of a few days to be assigned by you to the fields in which they shall work in order to help induce the miners of W. Va. to join their fellow workers of the competitive bituminous district and suspend work to the end that success may be achieved to secure a living wage for the miners. Mr. Robert Askew will leave Mich. tonight and report to you in the course of a few days. Mr. F. J. Weber of Wis. will also report to you. Mr. James Wood of New York will in all likelihood report and others whose names I can not now give because I have not yet heard from them. The expenditures for the work of these men will be borne by the A.F. of L.

Today I learn that the New York Central Labor Union appropriated $100.00 to aid you in your movement and that several of the unions there are going to do the best they can.

Pittsburg advises me that they will send you two organizers for W. Va. and other men for local help through Penna.

I am advised too from other sources that considerable effort will be made to help you along the lines to carry out the policy determined upon at Pittsburg last Friday night.

It is needless for me to assure you again how anxious I am that success shall attend your efforts. The men are certainly deserving of victory. They are making a splendid fight against combined wealth perhaps unparalleled in the history of the world. They are striving to attain some fairer recognition as a result of their labor. Anything that I can do to further their interest will be, cordially, sincerely and gladly. With every wish for a triumphant ending of this great struggle I am,

Sincerely & fraternally yours,   Saml Gompers.
President   A.F. of L.

TLpS, reel 12, vol. 20, pp. 515-16, SG Letterbooks, DLC. Typed notation: "Dictated S. G."

To M. D. Ratchford

July 13th. [1897]

Mr. M. D. Ratchford,
President, United Mine Workers of America.
#81 Clinton Bldg.; Columbus, Ohio.
Dear Sir & Brother: —

Enclosed please find check for $50.00 which has been donated by Hon. Ernst H. Crosby[1] of New York in aid of the miners' cause.

Mr. Crosby suggests that a clear statement of the case ought to be made and adds that with such an authoritative statement of facts a good mass meeting could be gotten up in New York and considerable good done to aid the miners in this struggle. I am in full accord with that opinion.

Let me say in connection with this that such a statement ought to be gotten out at the earliest possible moment and given the widest publicity. I was under the impression that you proposed getting out such a letter signed by your Executive Board. There are a number of noble spirited people whom such a statement of facts and appeal would reach and who would readily respond.

What do you think of the idea of asking the newspapers to open up a subscription in aid of the miners? I am inclined to believe that it would produce good results. If you think that the official sanction of the A.F. of L. Executive Council would add force to it I would gladly submit the matter to my colleagues for their approval.

Then again if the strike is not ended by the time the *American Federationist* goes to press what do you think of the idea of having it also published[2] and calling for subscriptions?[3]

Do you think it would be wise to issue a circular to the organizations asking them to contribute funds to carry on your contest?

Kindly give these matters your careful consideration and response at as early a date as possible and oblige,

Your sincere well-wisher,   Saml Gompers.
President   A.F. of L.

N.B.: — I have acknowledged Mr. Crosby's donation but would be pleased if you will send him a receipt for the same addressing him at Rhinebeck, N.Y.

S. G.

TLpS, reel 12, vol. 20, pp. 553-54, SG Letterbooks, DLC.

1. Ernest H. Crosby, a New York City lawyer, was president of the Social Reform Club.

2. An account of the strike's origins, "A Statement of the Cause of the Miners' Strike," was published in the August 1897 *American Federationist* (4: 122-23) and was signed by Ratchford and United Mine Workers of America Secretary William C. Pearce.

3. The call to aid the strikers appeared under "Appeal for the Miners" (ibid., p. 119).

To M. D. Ratchford

July 20th, [1897]

Mr. M. D. Ratchford,
President, United Mine Workers of America,
#81 Clinton Building, Columbus, O.
Dear Sir and Brother: —

Your several favors of the 15th and 17th insts. came duly to hand and contents noted. I am exceedingly pleased to learn the bright prospects for victory in the strike. I am sure that there is no one, who is more anxious for the success of your movement, or who will go to greater lengths to attain that end, than I. I am receiving reports by wire and mail daily from our friends Askew and Weber. I presume they also are in communication with you. Our friend Mahone has wired but not written, but I see accounts of his good work in the newspapers.

Weber held a meeting in McDowell Sunday and a warrant was sworn out for his arrest for violating the Sabbath law. He was doing good work and had a dangerous set to contend against. He learned of the warrant being issued and eluded the officers and went over into Cattleberg, Ky., just over the border. Inasmuch as they are looking for him for the purpose of putting him behind prison bars, ostensibly for violating a law, but in truth to deprive the cause of his splendid ability and energy, I do not know that he can be of much further service in this present contest in West Virginia. If he goes there they will arrest him, and to keep out of the State, he might as well be far removed from the scene of action. Of course, if he had not crossed the border to evade arrest and should have been jailed, it might have reacted against the operators and in favor of the miners, by creating a sentiment based upon outrageous injustice.

The last letters which Mr. Askew and Mr. Weber sent here I enclose herein so that you might note their contents. Both contain very important information, particularly where Mr. Weber calls attention to a spy who is acting as one of the officers of your local in the district he names. After noting the contents of both these letters, you will please return them to this office.

Yesterday I learned that the Brotherhood of Carpenters and Joiners voted the sum of $500.00 to aid you in your movement. Having been apprised of this fact I have written to the officers of our affiliated national and international unions, asking them whether it is possible to make an appropriation of $500.00. more or less immediately to help your contest.[1] I enclose copy of the letter herein for your information.

I have written Mr. Thurber[2] in connection with the matter of which you wrote, also Mr. Connor, and hope for good results at their hands.

If you think that a contribution from the funds of the A.F. of L. would be of any benefit to you, I wish you would make the application and it will receive prompt attention.

You remember in transmitting Mr. Crosby's check, I called attention to the suggestion he makes in regard to the issuance of some statement from you. I wish that it could be prepared for I am confident that it will arouse a great deal of additional interest in your cause. I would be pleased to publish it in the Federationist, and editorially comment on it and urge its wide dissemination and consideration.

With every wish for success, I am,

Sincerely and fraternally yours,   Saml Gompers.
President   A.F. of L.

TLpS, reel 12, vol. 20, pp. 653-54, SG Letterbooks, DLC.

1. July 19, 1897, reel 12, vol. 20, p. 648, SG Letterbooks, DLC.
2. SG wrote to Francis Thurber on July 20, 1897 (reel 12, vol. 20, p. 655, SG Letterbooks, DLC) asking that he urge New York financier Washington E. Connor to influence the mine operators to accede to the miners' demands.

To M. D. Ratchford

July 21st, [1897]

Mr. M. D. Ratchford,
President, United Mine Workers of America,
Columbus, O.
Dear Sir and Brother:—

A colored man by the name of M. J. Bailor,[1] Editor of the Pittsburg, (Pa.) Gazette, had a talk with me a few days ago relative to the effort to unite the workers, both white and black. He seemed very much interested in proper recognition being given to the colored worker.

He admitted that it would be necessary to have the colored workers act fairly towards their white fellow workmen, in order to receive the recognition they deserve. The conversation turned upon the coal strike and I asked him whether he would be willing to assist in appealing to the miners of West Virginia, particularly the colored men, to suspend mining until the successful termination of the present contest. He said that he would be willing. He came here to-day and repeated his willingness. He is an entire stranger to me, and I do not know whether it would be right or safe to have him do this work, but he is a candidate for Consul to Hayti[2] and has the endorsement of a number of representative Pennsylvanians. If you think that we ought to avail ourselves of his services, let me know and I will advise him. In either event, either write or wire.

　　　　　　　　　　　　　　　Yours fraternally,　　Saml Gompers.
　　　　　　　　　　　　　　　President　A.F. of L.

TLpS, reel 12, vol. 20, p. 670, SG Letterbooks, DLC.

1. Probably W. J. Bailor, who lived in Steelton, Pa., and published the *Harrisburg Sentinel-Gazette* from 1894 to 1897.
2. Bailor subsequently withdrew his application for the consulate.

To William Pearce[1]

　　　　　　　　　　　　　　　　　　　　　　July 22nd. [1897]

Mr. W. C. Pearce,
Secretary, United Mine Workers of America,
81 Clinton Bldg.; Columbus, Ohio.
Dear Sir & Brother: —

Your telegram of the 22nd in which you say that our friend Weber is doing good work in West Virginia, that the boys want him there and requesting that his time be extended came duly to hand. In connection with this let me say that I have extended Mr. Weber's time, but I should not have interfered with him at all were it not for the fact that he had left the State in order to avoid arrest upon the warrant issued against him for addressing a meeting last Sunday owing to which I presumed he could no longer continue in the work assigned him.

I understand from the press that President Ratchford has gone to West Virginia and will help in the fight. Does it not seem as if the denunciation of the operators at this time by our friends Debs & Sovereign[2] is likely to arouse greater bitterness on the part of the operators and make a settlement less likely? The strike is in the hands of the officers of the United Mine Workers of America and I do not wish to interfere at all in its direction or management, but I think it is a something which should commend itself to your consideration. I foresaw several things and plainly stated them in my telegram to President Ratchford of July 15th.[3] in which I said "A man who declared strikes ineffective and that he will never again participate in one should not be [permitted to interfere with] your strike now, particularly where prospects are so bright."

I do hope that you will win out in this contest. I am exceedingly anxious that you shall win and it is the fear that any one may do anything that may make the contest doubtful which makes me so anxious.

With assurances of high regard and best wishes I am,

Fraternally yours, Saml Gompers.

President A.F. of L.

N.B.: — What do you say about the matter I suggested in my previous letter[4] to President Ratchford in regard to Chris Evans.[5] I have asked James Wood of the Cigar Makers to report to headquarters as soon as possible.

S. G.

TLpS, reel 12, vol. 20, pp. 678-79, SG Letterbooks, DLC.

1. William C. PEARCE, an Ohio miner, was secretary-treasurer of the United Mine Workers of America (UMWA) from 1896 to 1900.

2. James R. SOVEREIGN served as general master workman of the KOL from 1893 to 1897.

3. SG to M. D. Ratchford, July 15, 1897, reel 12, vol. 20, p. 598, SG Letterbooks, DLC.

4. SG to M. D. Ratchford, July 21, 1897 (ibid., p. 666). SG offered to send Chris Evans to West Virginia to assist with the strike under Ratchford's direction.

5. Christopher EVANS, an Ohio miners' leader and secretary of the AFL from 1889 to 1894, was an organizer for the AFL and the UMWA.

To Executive Officers[1] of National Trade Unions

Washington July 24 [18]97

President Ratchford of the Miners just wired[2] that peaceable assemblage and free speech have been forbidden and suppressed in West Virginia. In compliance with his request I invite you to a conference[3] to be held at Wheeling, West Virginia at noon, Tuesday, July twenty-seventh. Similar invitation is extended to Executive Officers of all National Trade Unions. No duty now is more important than attendance at this conference. The very presence of all to whom this is addressed will arouse the miners to their full duty and decide the contest in their favor. If your presence impossible, send representative.

Samuel Gompers,
President,   American Federation of Labor.

TWpSr, reel 12, vol. 20, p. 708, SG Letterbooks, DLC.

1. This telegram was sent to executive officers of national or international AFL affiliates and the five railroad brotherhoods.
2. M. D. Ratchford to SG, July 23, 1897 (*American Federationist* 4 [Aug. 1897]: 119-20).
3. See "Excerpts from an Article in the *Pittsburg Post*," July 27, 1897, below.

An Editorial in the *Cleveland Citizen*

[July 24, 1897]

HELP FOR THE MINERS.

Wednesday evening the Central Labor Union voted fifty dollars to the miners. No national official made a request for funds, but had an appeal for aid been sent here, no doubt a handsome sum could be raised each week.

Why have not the Federation officials issued a general appeal for funds and thus aided in stiffening the backbone of the striking miners? Information comes from the Pittsburg district that women and children are starving to death, and there is want and destitution on every hand. The skinned and robbed miners are being driven to desperation while the operators smile as they rake in increased profits for their surplus coal, and now, just as the market is being cleared of the surplus product and victory seems to be in sight, breaks in the ranks of the men are reported as occurring on account of hunger. A stampede, an ignominious rout is not improbable. It might yet be prevented by quick action.

Where is Gompers, anyhow? Is he writing letters of sympathy again? Is he waiting for the December meeting[1] of the A.F. of L. to give him instructions—to push him along? We heard of him in Pittsburg several weeks ago, accompanied by his usual wise-look, and it was mysteriously given out that the Federation president would "do something." Up to date he has done nothing but draw his salary.

There are hundreds of unions and thousands of individuals that have been waiting for a call for contributions from some responsible official head, and it would have been freely responded to with sums from two cents to a hundred dollars or more a week.

Oh, what a shame, what a burning shame it will be if this great struggle for a living wage, this noble fight for suffering women and starving children, fails! We are informed that the public has but slight understanding of the awful conditions of poverty and slavery that exist in the mining regions. "God knows what Dan and I will do," wrote a miner of Cecil, Pa., even before the strike. "I think we will join the tramping bums and beg our living, for we have tried hard to make it honestly and failed, so we can't be much worse at anything, or rather nothing."

Another miner in the same district, working in W. P. Rend's mine, wrote to a Southern craftsman and friend:

["]An electric plant has just been put in here and it is making quite a revolution in the mining business. The company here gets its coal cut and loaded for 38 cents a ton, and the difference between that and the digging price is 22 cents a ton, quite an item in favor of the machines.

["]My thoughts are very dark indeed when I think of the sorrowful conditions here, and I become quite despondent and feel myself getting old under the plutocrat's rod of iron, and if something don't turn up soon I don't know what might become of me. . . . ["]²

These are Americans, ye patriots! Is their cry of distress to go unheeded? Where are the politicians that they do not help now? Has the middle class nothing but maudlin sympathy? And are these struggling wage-slaves to be deserted by their own class? If the members of the A.F. of L. Executive Board refuse to act, let them resign before they lose the respect of all honest men!

Cleveland Citizen, July 24, 1897.

1. The 1897 AFL convention met at Nashville, Dec. 13-21.
2. Ellipses in original.

Excerpts from an Article in the *Pittsburg Post*

Wheeling, July 27. [1897]

LEADERS IN CONFERENCE.

The convention called by President Samuel Gompers, of the American Federation of Labor, to discuss the strike situation in West Virginia and Pittsburg districts, assembled here to-day. It had been confidently asserted the convention would settle the strike. In fact, it settled nothing. It contained a greater number of representative labor leaders than ever gathered before to discuss industrial questions, yet they did little more than talk. The 26 delegates,[1] covering almost every conceivable labor industry, acted on behalf of over 200,000 workmen of the United States. Presidents Gompers and Ratchford, as well as other prominent officials, agreed that it was the most important gathering of the clans in the history of trade organizations. They declared likewise that it was a crisis in the history of organized labor. The delegates commenced assembling last evening, and every train this morning brought them in groups of four and five. A reception committee met all visitors. Owing to a number of important officials being delayed, the original convention hour of 9 o'clock was extended so that it was nearly noon before the convention was called to order.

The delegates exhibited a studied reluctance to talking before official action had been taken. Men came from as far south as Nashville, from the ore fields of Michigan, and from nearly every city of importance in the territory between. Some of them had traveled night and day to get here in time, and they all came with pledges of unwavering support from their organizations. As one of them expressed it, "We were eager to be here, not because we wanted to have any particular voice in the matter, but to help roll up the vote of confidence and support for the miners."

Sovereign an Early Arrival.

Grand Master Workman James R. Sovereign, of the Knights of Labor, was among the early arrivals, with Secretary Frank Morrison, of the American Federation of Labor. "We are in this fight to the last," said Mr. Sovereign, emphatically. "We will show these operators that if they whip one of us they must whip all of us. This is the decisive fight and we are going to win, no matter what the cost." Mr. Sovereign said there was no friction between the two great labor organizations at present. "All factional fights are buried in this one great event," he continued. "We are here to help the miners, and party lines cut no figure."

President Gompers, of the American Federation of Labor, regarded the convention as one of the most serious that had ever been called together. He said the Fairmont and DeArmit mines were the focal points of the entire situation, and that on them depended the outcome of the strike. "As far as calling the men out is concerned," said he, "we have a right to demand that they shall quit work, and they have an equal right to do so. The fact that the railroads in West Virginia are in governmental control[2] will not, to my mind, make any difference in conducting the fight."

. . .

The afternoon session consisted of a general discussion of the situation. Mr. Debs took an active part in the debate, together with Mahon and Sovereign. The entire ground was gone over and the delegates from a distance given a thorough understanding of the entire situation, mine by mine. Mr. Askew spoke on behalf of the mineral miners of the Masaba, Gogebic and Marquette ranges. He said they would cheerfully concur in the decision of the convention and do anything in their power to help the strike. With this discussion but little headway was made, and it was finally proposed that a committee be appointed to present ways and means to aid the strike. This was unanimously agreed to, and accordingly the purpose of the convention was placed in the hands of five delegates.

This committee consisted of John B. Lennon, Jesse Johnson,[3] P. H. Morrissey,[4] J. R. Sullivan[5] and George W. Perkins. This committee went into executive session at 5 o'clock and remained in session until 9:30, during which time the plan of putting organizers into the West Virginia field was discussed. President Ratchford will have personal supervision of this work, and it was stated by President Gompers that within a week about 100 men will be in that district.

SOLICITING FINANCIAL AID.

The officers of the American Federation of Labor were ordered to transmit to all trade and labor organizations in the country letters asking what they can do in the way of helping the strike along financially. President Gompers was empowered to appoint the speakers for mass meetings to be held on August 5. He will assign speakers for the various meetings upon application.

The real issue of the convention, as originally stated, that of deciding on a sympathetic strike and the calling out of railroad employes, was not acted upon. Both Mr. Gompers and Mr. Debs said that it was not even talked of seriously, both of them attributing much of the additional strike rumors to unfounded newspaper reports. It was stated by a member of the convention, however, that a hasty canvass revealed the fact that very few people favored a universal tie-up and the matter was therefore quietly dropped. The question of aid was then swung around to a financial basis, and the appeal formulated by the committee was the result.

. . . The convention adjourned at midnight, after receiving the report of the committee, which was adopted unanimously. The report was in the shape of a manifesto, and reads as follows:

An Appeal for Help.

"A wail of anguish, mingled with desperation, arises from the bowels of the earth and the miners cry for relief, for some degree of justice touches the reponsive chord in the hearts and consciences of the whole people, drudging at wages, when employed, which are insufficient and portend misery, starvation and slavery. The miners are confronted with a condition by which their scant earnings are denied them, except through the company pluck-[me] stores, which out-shylock the worst features of the nefarious system, and as a stigma on the escutcheon of our country and a blot on our civilization.

"We, the representatives of the trades unions and of all organized labor of the United States, in conference assembled, to consider the pending struggle of the miners for wages sufficient to enable them to live, and to enjoy at least to some degree the necessities of life, are determined to forever put a stop to a state of starvation in which they are now engulfed.

"The deplorable condition of the miners is well known to all of our people. They live in hovels, unable to buy sufficient bread to ward off starvation, in many cases not sufficiently clothed to cover their nakedness, and their children unfit to attend school because of lack of food and clothing, thus making them a danger to the future stability of our republic. We feel sure that all men and women who love their own families, or who have one spark of human sympathy for their fellows, cannot fail to give all the aid in their power to enable the miners to win their present battle.["]

Resent the Injunctions.

"The representatives of the miners have been restrained by injunction[6] when exercising their fundamental right of public assembly and free speech, to present to the world their grievances. We, as American citizens, resent this interference with the rights guaranteed to us under the constitution. In the ordinary affairs of life all enjoy privileges and rights which constitutions neither confer nor deny, but the guarantee of the right of free public assembly and free speech was intended to give opportunity to the people, or to any portion of them, to present the grievances from which they suffer and which they aim to redress.

"We denounce the issuance of injunctions by the judges of West Virginia, Pennsylvania and other states as wholly unjustified, unwarranted and unprecedented, more especially in the absence of any exhibition or manifestation of force on the part of the outraged miners. We call on the government of West Virginia, and upon the governors of all other states, and on all public officials, for full and ample protection in the exercise of our rights of free speech and public assemblage. We have no desire to trespass upon the rights of anyone, and we demand protection in the exercise of those rights handed down to us by the founders of the republic. We recommend that indignation mass meetings be held throughout the entire country, to give expression to the condemnation of the unwarranted injunction interfering with the free rights of free assemblage and free speech, and we also extend sympathy and support to the mine workers to the utmost extent.["]

A CALL FOR ORGANIZERS.

"We hereby call upon each national and international organization of labor to send representatives to act for and by the direction of the United mine workers, as organizers in West Virginia, Pennsylvania and such other states as may be necessary. Fully imbued with the heroic struggle which the miners are making for pure womanhood and innocent childhood, for decency for manhood and for civilization, and with the consciousness of the justice of their cause and of the responsibility of their actions, we call upon the workingmen of our country to lend all possible assistance to our suffering, struggling fellow-workers of the mines, and to unite in defense of our homes, our rights, our citizenship, and our country."

. . .

Pittsburg Post, July 28, 1897.

1. Attending the Wheeling conference for the AFL were SG and Frank Morrison, and, for their organizations, John Lennon (Tailors); M. M. Garland (Iron and Steel Workers); Theodore Perry (Typographical Union); Frank Sargent (Locomotive Firemen); Patrick Morrissey and Val Fitzpatrick (Railroad Trainmen); Charles Wilkins (Railroad Conductors); James Sovereign (KOL); James H. Sullivan, Michael Carrick, Joseph McKinney, and John Rae (Painters and Decorators); J. Kunzler (Flint Glass Workers); George Perkins (CMIU); M. D. Ratchford, William Pearce, Patrick Dolan, and T. L. Lewis (United Mine Workers); Eugene Debs; Michael Counahan (Plumbers); W. D. Mahon (Street Railway Employes); L. R. Thomas (Pattern Makers); W. H. Riley (Stogie Makers); Robert Askew (Northern Mineral Mine Workers); Jesse Johnson (Printing Pressmen); J. F. Mulholland (Bicycle Workers); and H. R. Jackson (Tobacco Workers).

2. On July 6, 1897, receivers for the Wheeling and Lake Erie Railway obtained an order from the U.S. Circuit Court, Southern District of Ohio, providing federal marshals to guard the company's right-of-way and mining properties against the actions

of strikers. On the following day, the road began moving coal from West Virginia to Ohio under the marshals' protection.

3. Jesse JOHNSON of Nashville was president of the International Printing Pressmen's and Assistants' Union of North America.

4. Patrick Henry MORRISSEY served as vice-grand master (1889-95) and as grand master (1895-1909) of the Brotherhood of Railroad Brakemen (after 1890 the Brotherhood of Railroad Trainmen).

5. James H. Sullivan.

6. On July 26, 1897, Special Judge John W. Mason of the Marion Co., W.Va., Circuit Court issued a temporary injunction barring Eugene Debs and others from speaking and organizing among the miners of local collieries. Four days later, at the request of mine operators, Mason made the injunction permanent. When Gov. George Atkinson's support of the strikers' right to peaceful activity weakened the ruling's effect, mine owners obtained even broader injunctions in mid-August—covering western Pennsylvania as well as West Virginia—from Judge John J. Jackson of the U.S. District Court of West Virginia and others. United Mine Workers of America officers and supporters, including SG, set out to test their legality by campaigning in the coalfields; their challenge apparently proved successful.

An Editorial by Samuel Gompers in the *American Federationist*

[July 1897]

HASTE IS NOT SPEED.

Recently a gathering took place in Chicago, heralded to the world as a movement for colonizing workers in a given State of the Union, for the purpose of capturing the political power of the State to introduce the co-operative commonwealth.[1] Public attention has been directed to the scheme and it has been scrutinized with a view of learning its real merit, or rather its real purpose.

To us the move appears neither new or novel; it is nothing more nor less than a very vain attempt to find a way out of a sad state of industrial affairs by which large numbers of our fellowmen have been thrown into a state of idleness.

Elsewhere we have said of this movement that no scheme is so alluring or justified as one which promises or really seeks to find employment for the myriads of men and women walking the streets of our cities and country roads vainly looking for an opportunity to earn their bread by the sweat of their brow; no cause so thoroughly appeals to the sympathies of thinkers and workers; none is more highly commendable. Hence, so far as the desire of any one to find work for the host of workless workers is concerned, that is highly commendable. But desires and sympathies are entirely different to actual achievements and successes.

In the history of our industrial development there have been many periods of panic and crisis. Each one of them has brought with it a scheme similar, or very nearly similar, to the one just launched. Universal and voluntary co-operation is perhaps the ideal life to which all reformers and sympathizers bend their effort. Colonization with that object in view has been undertaken time and again, and invariably with the same result—defeat, hopes deferred, aspirations destroyed and courage frozen.

Sympathetic men are continually devoting their attention to find a way out of the awful economic and social conditions which modern industry brings in its wake and there are too often men swayed simply by their sympathies and desires of finding a "shorter route" out of the industrial miasmatic atmosphere into the haven and elysium of social happiness. In this vain attempt actual conditions and facts are lost sight of. They hope to create a new state of society within the present and fail to perceive that the old must of necessity be at war with the new; and the old being so vastly extensive and so deeply entrenched that the smaller must of necessity be forced to the wall.

Modern industry and commerce admits of no side show or small competitor. The struggle for the attainment of labor's rights, for justice to the toilers, must be waged *within* modern society and upon the field of modern industry and commerce.

That struggle is the struggle of the trade unions and though apparently slow, is yet the fastest, truest and most successfully conducted by the trade unions. It takes up the gage of battle, wages the contest unceasingly; it is not diverted either to the right or the left, but consistently, persistently, and aggressively carries on the contest for the complete emancipation of labor from every thraldom of injustice; and along the road secures less hours of toil for the employed workers, and finding work for the unemployed; thus enlarging the economic, social, moral and political opportunities not only for themselves but for all mankind.

There is no field either economic, politic, social or moral upon which the trade unions do not exercise their power and influence. Success is not greater simply because of the comparative indifference, backwardness or ignorance of many. In the same ratio that the workers organize in the purely and truly trade union movement do they place the milestones of achievements and progress behind them.

The trade union movement is the natural and rational movement of labor. It deals not with the speculative nor the chimerical. It hews to the line, moves on and on as the collective intelligence and deter-

mination admits, and though spurned by some, ridiculed and antagonized by others, carries on the struggle for the attainment of labor's
rights and the laborer's ultimate emancipation.

All honor to men who seek a "way out," but after the illusions have
been dispelled and the effervescence of passing enthusiasts have sub-
sided, the trade unions will still be found battling and struggling as
opportunities afford to attain the right.

American Federationist 4 (July 1897): 95.

1. A reference to the formation of the Social Democracy of America (see "To
John O'Sullivan," June 25, 1897, n. 3, above).

To George Atkinson[1]

August 9th. [1897]

Hon. G. W. Atkinson,
Governor.
Charleston, West Virginia.
Dear Sir: —

I have the honor to acknowledge receipt of your favor of the 3rd[2]
in regard to the matter of the right of public assemblage and free
speech in the State of West Virginia, and I beg to assure you that
your declarations of rights enjoyed by the people under the Constitution of the United States and of the State of West Virginia are all
that can be expected, all that we require.

There is no desire on the part of the miners, their representatives
or their friends, to violate the laws of our country, or of the State of
West Virginia. I believe with you that you have a right to claim for
yourself, as we claim for ourselves, the privilege to "discuss politics,
religion, science, labor organization, or any other subject" we may
choose to discuss, in public halls, or on public highways. The bill of
rights of our constitution allows these privileges and no court can
impair them. It is indeed gratifying to learn from your letter that so
long as the workingmen of the State of West Virginia conduct their
cause in a peaceful manner that it will be your pleasure as well as
your duty to protect them. This is all that we ask.

You say that you have requested the Attorney General[3] of West
Virginia to "appear in the matter and assist in having an early adjudication by the Supreme Court of the State of this injunction proceeding."[4] May I ask whether the Attorney General will be advised

to urge its dissolution as involving an infringement upon the constitutional liberties of the citizen? Having taken the unquestionably constitutional and natural ground it seems to me, and I beg leave to suggest it to your consideration that the Attorney General might well be advised to pursue this line of action.

Permit me to assure you that I appreciate most highly the position you take in this matter and the emphatic language in which it is declared.

I have the honor to remain, dear sir,

Yours very respectfully,   Saml Gompers.
President   American Federation of Labor.

TLpS, reel 12, vol. 20, pp. 928-29, SG Letterbooks, DLC. Typed notation: "Dictated S. G."

1. George W. Atkinson (1845-1925), a lawyer and editor, was a Republican congressman (1890-91) and governor (1897-1901) of West Virginia.

2. The July 27, 1897, Wheeling conference delegated SG, James R. Sovereign, and M. D. Ratchford to meet Governor Atkinson to protest Judge Mason's injunction and the harrassment of strike organizers. When they met with the governor on July 28, he expressed support for the miners' struggle and civil rights and promised to make a public statement after studying the injunction. His subsequent letter of Aug. 3 (*American Federationist* 4 [Sept. 1897]: 154-55) maintained that, while as governor he could not intervene in a judicial proceeding, he had instructed the attorney general to expedite a state supreme court hearing on the injunction's constitutionality. He assured the labor leaders that he would protect the miners' rights to peaceable assembly and free speech.

3. Edgar P. Rucker was Republican attorney general of West Virginia from 1897 to 1901.

4. Apparently this adjudication proved unnecessary in view of the lack of prosecutions under the state injunction and the subsequent issuance of a broader federal injunction in mid-August.

To Patrick Dolan

Aug. 10th, 1897.

Patrick Dolan,
Pres.,
Pittsburgh, Pa.
My Dear Sir & Bro.: —
I received a telegram from the Secretary of our Fisherman's Protective Union of Astoria, Ore., advising me that they were desirous of sending one-hundred cases of Salmon in aid to the striking miners, and inquired where they would do the most good. Having been informed

that a large number of miners in your district are camping out, I have wired the organization to send its contribution to you at your headquarters at Diamond St.

The Fisherman's Protective Union by reason of a great strike[1] in which its members were involved, erected and operates a cannery, which uses the Union label of A.F. of L., furnishes the finest can Salmon now on the market. The gift from this Union, is I am sure prompted by the best interest of organized labor, and is a contribution from earnest men to earnest men, and I trust will contribute help and success to the splendid struggle now being made.

Fraternally yours, Saml Gompers.

TLpS, reel 12, vol. 20, p. 952, SG Letterbooks, DLC.

1. On Apr. 10, 1896, about 450 members of AFL Columbia River Fishermen's Protective Union 6321 struck Astoria canneries for a wage increase. After a ten-week strike, marked by the deployment of the state militia on June 15 to protect the canneries' operations, the firms accepted the union's terms and the strikers voted to return to work on June 20.

To the Executive Council of the AFL

Washington, D.C. August 21st, 1897.

To The Executive Council, American Federation of Labor.
Colleagues: —

Events in the Miners' strike have followed each other so swiftly, that I have been unable to communicate with you as I should have liked. There are some actions which I have taken upon which I should have your approval or otherwise.

On July 24th, I received a telegram from Mr. M. D. Ratchford, President of the United Mine Workers of America, a copy of which you will find on Pages 119 and 120 of the August issue of the American Federationist. You will observe that the telegram calls upon me "in behalf of the struggling miners to convene all the chief executive officers of all national labor organizations at Wheeling, West Virginia, on Tuesday, July 27th, for the purpose of meeting this crisis and achieving victory for the cause of labor." In the other portions of the telegram you will observe that it was necessary to take some action to meet the crisis by reason of the issuance of injunctions of the courts, abridging the rights of public assemblage and free speech.

When this telegram reached me, there was no time to consult the members of the Executive Council as to what course to pursue, if any, and for reasons which I shall explain, I deemed it necessary in the interest of the Miners, as well as our movement, to comply with the request, and on the 24th inst. sent a telegram[1] to the executive officer of each national trade union affiliated with the A.F. of L. and the railroad organizations. Each of the members of the Executive Council received such a telegram.

As stated above there were two reasons which prompted [me] to send this notice to attend the Wheeling Conference. One was, to [do] what we possibly could to further the interests of the Miners, and to defend the right of free speech and public assemblage; the second was, that this conference would have taken place had I sent the invitation or otherwise, and without my invitation it would have been confined to Mess. Ratchford, Pearce and Dolan of the Miners, Mr. Eugene V. De[bs,] Mr. J. R. Sovereign and perhaps one or two others. The others [who] attended the conference assured me that they would not have been present if it had not been for my invitation. Of course, I could not have refused to attend, and we might have had some very impractical action taken by the few who would have attended, un-restrained by those who did attend at my solicitation, and whose influence was manifestly felt along [the] lines of common sense and practical action. The articles in the August issue of the American Federationist under the headings, "The Story of the Wheeling Con-ference,"[2] and "The Appeal for the Miners,"[3] give substantially the action taken, and which, events have apparently justified.

You are requested to vote upon the endorsement or otherwise of the action of the President in calling the conference.[4]

In company with Messrs. Ratchford and Sovereign, we called upon the Governor of West Virginia, and had a lengthy interview regarding the right of public assemblage and free speech, and received from him a letter later which so far as he had power, justifies our position in regard to the exercise of these rights. You have, perhaps, seen copies of this letter in the public press.

The operators evidently realizing that Governor Atkinson's letter would about neutralize Judge Mason's (of the State Courts) order, then resorted to the Federal Courts and obtained injunctions from Judge Jackson (of the West Virginia district) and others in Pennsyl-vania. Having been called upon by President Ratchford, I went into the districts in which we were enjoined from public assemblage and free speech and held a number of meetings in West Virginia and Western Pa.;[5] although injunctions were served upon me, my meetings were otherwise uninterfered with, nor was I molested in any way by the Courts or the officers of the Courts.

You have approved the action of sending a number of organizers into the field to help the Miners in their contest. At first it was supposed that about two weeks would have been sufficient; events have demonstrated, however, that their services have been of incalculable benefit to the Miners' cause and that it would be most difficult and disastrous should they now be recalled. The men in the field are Chris Evans, W. D. Mahon, Robert Askew and F. J. Weber. Mr. Mahon is having his hotel and other expenses paid, but receiving no salary, that being paid by his own organization. The others are receiving salary of $3.00 per day and hotel and other expenses. The costs thus far for the four men are $1,000. The matter now submitted to you in connection with this is shall these organizers be continued in the field for a while longer.[6]

Kindly return your votes upon the above two matters at your early convenience and oblige,

Yours fraternally, Saml Gompers.
President A.F. of L.

Friend Garland. Can you return this copy to our office after noting and voting. We want it for filing purposes. Our 6th copy was too blurred for that purpose.

Sam.

T and ALpS, AFL Executive Council Vote Books, reel 8, frames 209-10, *AFL Records.*

1. See "To Executive Officers of National Trade Unions," July 24, 1897, above.
2. *American Federationist* 4 (Aug. 1897): 119-22.
3. Ibid., p. 119.
4. The Executive Council endorsed SG's action in calling the Wheeling conference.
5. SG's trip, lasting roughly from Aug. 9 to Aug. 19, 1897, included stops in Columbus, Ohio; McKeesport, Pa.; and the New River and Kanawha River districts of West Virginia.
6. The Executive Council voted to extend the tenure of the organizers.

An Editorial by Samuel Gompers in the
American Federationist

[August 1897]

ANENT CLASS CONSCIOUSNESS.

In another column we publish a letter[1] asking a very serious, yet fair question, and one which requires an equally fair and candid answer. Our correspondent quotes a sentence that we used in our last issue of the *American Federationist* as follows: "The trade unions are organizing the wage earners in the class conscious struggle against all profit mongers under whatever shape they may appear or form they may assume, to battle for the abolition of all human wrongs and the attainment of all human rights." This sentence, our correspondent says, has caused some discussion and the claim has been put forth that the trade union movement is not a "class conscious" movement. He does us the honor of expressing his confidence that we would not have used the term had there not been good grounds upon which to base it. Let the following be the answer to our friend:

Since the organization of the first trade union within modern society—that is, since the abolition of all forms of feudalism, and with its overthrow the free play and opportunities for the full development of the capitalistic system—these organizations have always possessed the exclusive characteristics of not only a class organization of the wage earners, but have exercised and demonstrated their unqualified class consciousness.

The term "class conscious" indicates that those who belong to that class are conscious of that fact, and are conscious, too, that their interests as a class are separate and distinct from any other class; and that while organizing in a class organization they may and do benefit all others, yet they organize in a class organization for the betterment of the conditions of that class.

Class conscious! As a matter of fact, there is no other organization of labor in the entire world that is a class organization or is so class conscious as are the trade unions.

In a political party, or any organization other than the trade unions, which sails under the name of labor, all sorts of persons are eligible to membership, regardless of their walks of life, regardless of the fact that their interests may be diametrically opposed to those of labor. So long as any one signs a declaration it is deemed sufficient for him to assume the functions and invade the domain of the real *bona fide* class conscious labor movement.

The trade unions, as their name implies, organize the wage earners of a particular trade or calling and the consciousness is not only declared but practiced that none who have interests hostile to the wage earners can find membership in the trade unions. No, not even Professor Garside,[2] who vowed his sympathy with labor but was a Pinkerton detective, or a professor sailing under an alias and who seeks to wreck the labor movement in the interest of the money power of the country.

While the trade unions court the sympathy, kindness or assistance, yet reject the attempt of anyone whose interests may be in the remotest antagonistic with that of the wage earners to dominate them; in fact, it excludes them from membership and the councils of trade unions.

In 1891, at the Detroit convention[3] of the American Federation of Labor, this class consciousness of the trade union movement was emphasized by the exclusion of one who came with credentials from an organization which was not based upon the same class interest and did not possess the same class consciousness.[4]

The British trade unions at their Congress in 1895, at Cardiff, Wales, eliminated from their councils some of those who had, through a loosely constructed rule, crept in and attempted to fasten themselves upon and rob the trade unions of this class conscious standing. All through the civilized world, wherever the trade unions are founded and growing, there the same plain, manifest class consciousness is exhibited and maintained. Where, pray, is there greater consistency, greater growth and more distinctly drawn the lines of class conscious action than those manifested by the trade unions? Nowhere in the world.

As a matter of fact the wage earning class of the world occupies the lowest rung in the ladder of economic life. With its emancipation comes the abolition of classes based upon possession of wealth and power; with its disenthralment comes the abolition of all profit or interest in any form. It realizes that those who would be free themselves must strike the blow; that the freedom of labor must be accomplished by the workers themselves. Therefore, they organize in the trade unions — the class conscious organization of labor — for the gradual and natural elimination of all classes and the emancipation of man.

American Federationist 4 (Aug. 1897): 115-16.

1. The letter, from George Roberts of Columbus, Ohio, was dated July 14, 1897 (*American Federationist* 4 [Aug. 1897]: 123).

2. Thomas Hamilton Garside served as an SLP lecturer and general organizer in 1888 and 1889, after which he became connected with the anarchist Johann Most. In 1890 he played a major role in the New York City cloakmakers' strike, raising money and serving as an intermediary between the strikers and the manufacturers. When he independently attempted to conclude a settlement that did not address the demands of the strikers, however, he was widely accused of being a paid agent of the employers. Garside subsequently worked as a reporter for the *Philadelphia Times* and as a detective.

3. The AFL's Detroit convention met Dec. 8-13, 1890.

4. The convention declined to seat Lucien Sanial as a delegate of the New York City Central Labor Federation because that body contained a non–trade union affiliate—the SLP—and no longer held an AFL charter. (See "Gompers and the Struggle between the Central Labor Union and the Central Labor Federation in New York City," *The Early Years of the AFL*, p. 192).

To P. J. McGuire

September 1st, [1897]

Mr. P. J. McGuire,
Philadelphia, Pa.
Dear friend Pete: —

Your favor of the 31st ult. to hand and noted. I was most pleased to note its contents; I agree with every word you say in it and in the light of the news paper despatches from St. Louis our decision independently reached that the calling of the Conference[1] was a sad mistake was more than justified. The idea of calling upon all the divisions and sub-divisions of organized labor, reform, educational and scientific bodies, they resolving to assess working men one day's wages. For years we have discussed the proposition of building up treasuries in times of peace to prepare for conflicts, and have also discussed the question of assessments to be levied in a well-regulated manner and the best we have been able to secure from our fellow workers is what we have in the laws of the American Federation of Labor. Now our friends, the Miners, who in their palmiest days never had a treasury and a few years ago resolved to abolish their defense fund and declared this to the world, Mr. Debs with his social democracy, who and which has declared the trade union tactics as failures, and who at every opportunity takes advantage of it to declare that he is not now affiliated with any organization of [labor], Mr. Sovereign of the Knights of Labor opposing strikes generally and having scarcely any membership and less responsibility, the Single Taxers, "Patriots of America,"[2] etc., this is indeed a great gathering to declare an assessment upon the wage earners of America.

You remember when I sent out the letters to the different national organizations, asking them to vote $500.00 more or less in aid of the Miners, the I.T.U. officers advised me that they were not in a position to do so owing to the conflicts in which many of their local unions were engaged. In response to the request to send an organizer in behalf of the I.T.U. in the coal fields, practically the same answer was given. Later I am informed that they had great trouble to enforce the assessment passed by the Colorado Springs Convention[3] for the extension to the Home.[4] It is an interesting question how the I.T.U. is going to enforce the assessment of one day's pay, and if the assessment is not enforced why is it an assessment; why call this mass meeting of all the reformers and reform scientific bodies of the country simply to *appeal* to or *request* the workers to make a donation of one day's pay, certainly little cause to call such a gathering for such a purpose.

You remember that Mr. Prescott wired me asking me whether I intended going to the St. Louis gathering, and said that he was in doubt as to what he should do, and that I wired him that I would not go. You have no doubt seen it published that he presided over the St. Louis Convention. Are not his actions strange after sending me the telegram he did?

I hardly think that Mr. O'Connell of the I.A. of M attended the Convention. I am confident that Mr. Henry Lloyd was not there notwithstanding the publication of his name in the papers to that effect for I this morning received a letter from him bearing the postmark and date of Boston, August 31st.

Many thanks for the clippings you enclosed. They are very interesting. I see that Mr. Sovereign is reported as saying "That the time has come for organized labor to re-organize." These people instead of organizing are continually trying to reorganize. It is the false basis of their organization which enables them to lay their entire hopes upon a given point and when that fails, their hopes fail and they want to reorganize or build something anew.

I can readily understand Mr. Ratchford's action; he is trying to make the best fight he can for the Miners and the calling of the St. Louis Convention was for the purpose of giving the Miners something to look forward to and the hope of strengthening their position and relief. The fact that the St. Louis Convention resolved to hold another "if necessary" September 27th[5] is in exact line with this policy. The principal wrong he did in this matter was to call that convention without advising those so as to make it representative in character, and also to use the name of a responsible officer of the American Federation of Labor without his authority or consent and declare that he had endorsed the call.[6]

To the lasting credit of the trade unionists can be recorded the fact that they could not be caught by the methods employed and that they did not go to St. Louis to attend the Convention. I never in my life felt more satisfied with any action, than I do in this particular case. Our absence from the St. Louis Convention was one of the best attestations of our loyalty and devotion to the trade union movement.

I am glad to know that you will be free next month and part of October. I shall think the matter over and if at all possible shall call the Executive Council together for a meeting in the real interests of the Miners or in the general interest of our movement.

I am glad to learn that you are feeling well and have your work in good shape. We started in on general work, but were unable to do much yesterday. We are catching up, though, and things are running in better shape.

With sincere regards, I am,

Yours fraternally,   Saml Gompers.

TLpS, reel 13, vol. 21, pp. 61-63, SG Letterbooks, DLC.

1. On Aug. 20, 1897, the Executive Board of the United Mine Workers of America issued a call for a conference of labor and reform leaders to be held in St. Louis. The conference met Aug. 30-31 with several trade unionists, including AFL Third Vice-President James O'Connell, in attendance. The delegates adopted resolutions condemning the use of injunctions in the coal strike and calling on workers to set aside the wages they earned on Sept. 3 as a donation to the miners. They also called for a second conference to be held in Chicago on Sept. 27 if the miners' strike had not been settled by Sept. 20.

2. William H. "Coin" Harvey and prohibitionist Howard Taylor established the Patriots of America in Illinois in 1895. The organization advocated the free coinage of silver and supported the presidential candidacy of William Jennings Bryan in 1896.

3. The International Typographical Union (ITU) convention met Oct. 12-19, 1896, at Colorado Springs, Colo.

4. The Childs-Drexel Home for Union Printers in Colorado Springs, Colo., opened in 1892 and accepted aged or invalid printers with at least ten years' membership in the ITU.

5. The conference was held in Chicago, Sept. 27-29, 1897. With the miners' strike already settled, it was sparsely attended.

6. SG's name had been appended to the call for the St. Louis conference (see "An Excerpt from an Article in the *Pittsburg Post*," Sept. 6, 1897, n. 2, below).

An Excerpt from an Article in the *Pittsburg Post*

[September 6, 1897]

GOMPERS WAS DENOUNCED BY UNIONISTS.

Samuel Gompers, president of the American Federation of Labor, will be given an unacceptable Labor day present this morning. The United Labor League of Western Pennsylvania[1] has, figuratively speaking, thrown him down on the floor and tramped all over his prostrate form. It was at one of the hottest and most exciting meetings ever held by the league last night. It was on account of expressions[2] made by Gompers in reference to the recent convention of labor leaders in St. Louis. He is credited with making unkind remarks about the gathering and casting reflections on those who were foremost in the meeting.

Gompers had a few defenders, and at one time there were remarks concerning somebody being thrown out of the window. One delegate made an eloquent plea, on the ground that a move to censure a labor leader at this time would militate against the best interests of organized labor in general, and the miners in particular. But he had no standing, and the delegates were emphatic in their denunciation.

A proposition to take some action on the platform adopted by the St. Louis convention brought out the discussion and subsequent action. The resolutions were read and reaffirmed. Remarks were called for when M. P. Carrick, secretary of the league and president of the Brotherhood of Painters and Decorators of America, made a long speech. He spoke of the action of Gompers in assailing some of the delegates to the St. Louis convention in the public prints, and maintained that it was time to call a halt. During the course of his speech he referred to Gompers as a "plug-hatted, greasy tool of capital." Among other things he said:

CALLED HIM A DEMAGOGUE.

"Samuel Gompers, president of the American Federation of Labor, has through interviews and non-attendance at the conference of labor leaders at St. Louis, proved himself a demagogue and no true friend of labor. This man should be exposed throughout the length and breadth of this land in order that every friend of the cause of labor, whether organized or not, may know him. Gompers has said that Debs and Sovereign are trying to disrupt trades unions. It is he that is doing his utmost to accomplish this. Debs has traveled about the country doing the work of a hero and a sincere man in the cause of the miners, at his own expense, and I believe he is the most honest man in the labor movement to-day. Sovereign made a most honorable statement at the Wheeling conference when he said that, while a member of and the general master workman of the Knights of Labor, he would lay aside the question of membership and assist in the cause of the miners, because it was a fight of humanity, of the working classes in general, and not the fight of any particular organization. Gompers never uttered such a statement, and his actions have been quite the reverse.

"I want to say that it was not the trades unions that came to the assistance of the miners; not Gompers nor the Federation of Labor, but the great mass of the unorganized labor and citizens who have no interest in organizations. Business men, politicians, sewing girls, sweat-shop workers and people from all crafts came to the relief of the miners, and their cause would have been utterly lost had it depended on trades unions and such men as Gompers. I think an investigation will bear out the statement that the trades unions did not give more than 20 per cent of the contributions for the miners' cause.

"It is time to call a halt on some of these labor fakirs who sit in their offices, look wise, and thank God they are not like the poor workingmen of this country. It is time that such people be taught a lesson, and this is the occasion to do it. Let us as trades unionists put ourselves on record. Down with all traitors who go into a fight as high-toned and all-wise advisers; then, just in the crisis of the battle, desert us and try to give us a chill before a grateful public. I say this is a shame and a disgrace to the honored cause of labor.

"If the workingmen desire redemption from wrongs, they will have to look to the great reform element of the country for reform legislation, and not to labor leaders who wear plug hats, sit in their offices in Washington and draw fat salaries from the ranks of the workingmen.["]

A DISGRACE TO TRADES UNIONS.

"Gompers is a disgrace to labor, I repeat, and I believe it is high time to call down the would-be aristocrats of labor and kick them bodily out of the movement. I make these assertions for the good of our common cause. Let us know where we are at and fire every traitor from our organizations as fast as they manifest themselves."[3]

During the delivery of his speech Carrick was pale with anger, and his denunications seemed to be a surprise. When he had finished he was greeted with round after round of applause. Calvin Wyatt[4] affirmed Carrick's remarks. He said Gompers was the president of his organization, but he was in favor of slapping any leader in the mouth that saw fit to make public censure in the middle of a fight. Peter Gallagher[5] said he was strongly in favor of taking some decisive action. He asserted that Gompers tried to get the miners into the middle of the stream, when he attempted to put a stone on their necks and drown them. Thomas Dicus,[6] of the Typographical union, offered the following resolution:

"Whereas, Samuel Gompers, president of the American Federation of Labor, in a recent interview in the public prints, attempted to belittle the convention held in St. Louis that was called to devise ways and means to aid the striking miners; therefore, be it

"Resolved. That the United Labor League of Western Pennsylvania disapprove of the utterances of Mr. Gompers for the reason that they are inimical to the best interests of organized labor, and we are liberal enough to believe that the great battle for the emancipation of labor cannot be won by trades unions alone."

SUGGESTED THE WINDOWS AS EXITS.

Thomas O. Schell[7] pronounced himself strongly against the resolution. He had just entered and made an appeal to the delegates not to take hasty action, as it would be to the detriment of organized labor. Schell jocularly intimated that some one should be thrown out of the window, when Dicus said he would be present when the throwing process was going on. One delegate wanted the resolution laid on the table, but his motion had no second. A vote was called for and the resolution was adopted, only nine delegates voting against it.

It was decided to send a delegate to the Chicago convention to be held September 27, and every delegate present was instructed to urge his local to do the same. A number of speeches were made favoring a good representation at the Chicago convention, whether the coal miners' strike was settled or not. There was a strong sentiment in favor of making a determined battle against government by injunction. Thomas Grundy[8] made a speech in favor of keeping up the agitation, and charged that labor organizations were sold out to political leaders. He said it was time to act, and the ballot should be resorted to. A. M. Bonsall also made a speech in the same strain.

. . .

Pittsburg Post, Sept. 6, 1897.

1. The United Labor League of Western Pennsylvania, a central body for Pittsburgh and Allegheny, was organized in 1895.

2. In an interview given on Sept. 3, 1897, SG indicated that his name had been appended to the call for the St. Louis conference without his knowledge or consent, and explained why he had not attended the meeting: "The call was issued to 'organized labor, its various divisions and subdivisions, and to all reform, social, educational and scientific bodies, who condemn government by injunction.' Under this call any body of men who are opposed to government by injunction would be entitled to a seat in the convention. In other words, persons entirely remote from and having no connection with labor movements could have been in attendance, and, by overwhelming numbers, directed the course, mapped out the policy and dominated the trade-union movement. As president of the American Federation of Labor, a responsible officer in the trade-union movement, I would not dare hazard the interests of our fellow-workers at the hands of persons who might be entirely irresponsible" (*St. Louis Globe-Democrat*, Sept. 4, 1897).

3. Gompers subsequently commented to George Perkins: "I presume you saw the attack of this man Carrick, of Pittsburgh. You know that he is an expelled member of the Brotherhood of Painters & Decorators—expelled, I am told, for dishonesty. He then joined the faction of the Painters, which has been refused recognition by the A.F. of L. He participated in the conference which sought to aim a blow at the trade union movement and the A.F. of L. and you can readily understand the animus of his attacks. You can judge the caliber of the man too when he posed as a trade unionist and denies that the assistance given the miners comes from the trade unions, when, as a matter of fact, you know and I know that with very little exception the sum total of the contributions in aid of the miners were the result of the offerings

and sacrifices of the true trade unionists of the country" (Sept. 10, 1897, reel 13, vol. 21, p. 145, SG Letterbooks, DLC).

4. Calvin Wyatt was a Pittsburgh printer.

5. Peter W. Gallagher was financial secretary of Brotherhood of Painters and Decorators of America 6 of Pittsburgh.

6. Thomas J. Dicus was a Pittsburgh printer.

7. Thomas J. O'Shell was a Pittsburgh clerk.

8. Thomas Grundy was a Pittsburgh real estate agent long active in such reform causes as the Greenback movement, the American Land League, temperance, and the KOL.

To Frank Weber

Sept. 10th. [1897]

Mr. Frank J. Weber,
Organizer.
Hotel Peyton; Charleston, W.Va.
Dear Sir & Brother:—

Your favor of the 9th to hand and noted. I note the surroundings and the situation which you describe. You say that you hope no mistake will be made at Columbus meeting[1] and add, that if the 65¢ compromise is accepted for Ohio and Penna. there will be trouble in W.Va. and that you may pay for it with your lives, that "brother Turner[2] has been threatened with a rope." Taking all these things into consideration I wired you just now that a check had been sent you last night and that immediately upon its receipt you should proceed to Charleston and remain there subject to my further orders. I have done this as it seems to me to be the wisest course to pursue and I hope that you have carried it out and will do so.

The convention at Columbus is necessarily largely composed of either unorganized or newly organized miners. They necessarily lack the experience so requisite in an emergency such as is now presented. It is possible that no mistake may be made; and, yet, if there is none it will be rather the unforseen. At any rate I do not think that I should leave you in a position which may involve such serious dangers and results when they can be obviated by the change of your location for a few days. Of course if the Columbus convention ratifies the proposition our organizers will repair to their respective homes. Otherwise they will remain subject to further orders from this office.

Fraternally yours, Saml Gompers.

TLpS, reel 13, vol. 21, p. 135, SG Letterbooks, DLC.

1. Delegates representing the striking bituminous coal miners met Sept. 8-11, 1897, in Columbus, Ohio, to vote on the settlement negotiated by the United Mine Workers of America (UMWA) and the mine owners. The convention ratified the terms, which included a temporary differential scale pegged to the rate of 65¢ a ton in the Pittsburgh district, with the final scale to be determined by arbitration. It also voted an assessment to support miners who remained on strike in western Pennsylvania, West Virginia, and Illinois.

2. Possibly W. H. Turner of the UMWA.

To P. J. McGuire

Sept. 11th. [1897]

Mr. P. J. McGuire.
#124 North Ninth Street. Philadelphia, Penna.
Dear Sir & Brother: —

Your favor of the 9th to hand and noted; also, enclosure. Many thanks for clippings. They were, indeed, interesting and tend to show what is really in the air by this proposed Chicago convention. The fact that the S.L.P. people propose to take it up and be represented by delegates is an evidence that many of the elements of disrupters will find common grounds of action, or at least propose to.

The murderous attack[1] upon the poor fellows at Hazleton, Penna. is going to have an awful effect and I am certainly under the impression will go far to influence the Columbus convention to reject the compromise proposal. While there is some horror expressed by the newspapers in regard to the shooting, yet in between the lines you can discern that that is in part an answer to the threats which have recently been launched against the government. If, perhaps, some of those who indulge in these harangues were to take the front rank and risk their lives there would be some show of justification for their utterances. As it is, advertisement is evidently what they are craving for and the other poor unfortunates are getting the bullets. This attack on the Hazleton miners is rank murder. I am glad to learn that you will be with us at the Council meeting promptly on Sept. 20th.

Sincerely yours,   Saml Gompers.
President   A.F. of L.

N.B. Received umbrella O.K. Thanks.

T and ALpS, reel 13, vol. 21, p. 160, SG Letterbooks, DLC.

1. On Sept. 10, 1897, Luzerne Co., Pa., Sheriff James Martin and his deputies opened fire on an unarmed and peaceful procession of three thousand miners marching toward Lattimer, Pa., where a strike was in progress over low wages and high prices at the company store. The gunfire killed nineteen and seriously wounded forty

of the miners. In a trial at Wilkes-Barre lasting from Feb. 1 to Mar. 9, 1898, Martin and the deputies were acquitted of murder and manslaughter charges.

To P. J. McGuire

Sept. 14th, [1897]

Mr. P. J. McGuire,
Philadelphia, Pa.,
Dear Sir & Brother:—

Your favor of the 13th Inst., with enclosures, came duly to hand. I am very much gratified that you have been in a position to have Governor Altgeld's Labor Day speech[1] published, and will have a large number of copies for gratuitous distribution. It is a splendid presentment of the living question of the day and it must have been a rare treat for fellow unionists of Philadelphia to have had the privilege of listening to him. I see that his address is quite extensively quoted through the press and editorially commented upon, and, as a rule, favorably so.

Enclosed, find the jointly written letter of Messrs. O'Connell and Perkins returned. Many thanks. I have made a copy of it.

Our friend Lennon wired me that he had received telegram from Denver, stating that his father[2] was dying there and that he, Lennon, was going to Denver and was not sure that he could return here in time for our Executive Council meeting. I have hopes that the old gentleman will recover and in time to allow our friend Lennon to be in attendance. I think there are circumstances connected with our movement, at this time, which makes it essential for every member of the council to be present to help steady the ship of labor.

While dictating this, I received your letter, containing the clipping from the Philadelphia "Tagablatt," giving the discussion on Debs and Socialism.[3] Yes, it is very significant of the policy of the S.L.P. Werner says that Debs will soon be in conflict with the trade unions. Of course, he (W) abuses us, but that counts as nothing. Perhaps his statements are correct, however, as to the possible conflict, but, if it comes, it will be because he will attempt to intrench upon the trade unions' territory and dominate the movement. In a letter received yesterday from Atlanta, Ga., I am informed that there are some who are going among our unions and trying to have them give up their charters and join Deb's Social Democracy. Our informant says that they have made no progress thus far, except with a few expelled, weak-kneed and suspended members. Yes, I am free to say that if this should continue and take a more aggressive form there may be a conflict and, perhaps, sooner than some might wish it. In my opinion, we have been tolerant too long of men who have gone about the country declaring the size of their hearts, and repeatedly offering up their necks for the hangmen's noose as their stock in trade for practical work in the labor movement.[4] I want to avoid conflict, or any appearance of a conflict, as much as possible, but, whether I succeed in it or fall under it, I am willing that our movement shall be clear cut and let us know who are with the trade unions and who are against them. The trade union movement has had to withstand edicts of government backed up by force, as well as the ignorance of a large number of masses. It has had to overcome the opposition of the vicious and the false friend, the Pinkerton agent, as well as the Agent Provocateur. It has been preached against and denounced. It has been proven (?) folly. It has been demonstrated (?) by the political economists to be a pure waste of time and effort, and yet the workers will organize and the trade unions remain [at?] the struggle better and more thoroughly than ever, and the real fights that labor will make to obtain just and fair dealing to the workers and to encourage a new order of things at the proper time, a new order of things based upon justice to humanity, if it is ever brought about, will be the result of the trade unions. Though I might be believed to be narrow, or fanatical, I have all my life and I now, more than ever, pin my faith and hope for labor's disenthrallment in the true trade union movement.

Pardon my taking up your time with writing you this, which is like bringing coal to your castle, but reading the clipping of the discussion which you sent me, and having in mind the recent events, opened up a number of instances to my mental vision and it required some effort to condense my thoughts into the above.

I am exceedingly pleased that you will be with us Monday. It is necessary.

Our friends Chris Evans and Robert Askew wired me Saturday night that the 65¢ rate had been accepted by the miners' convention of Columbus and from that I telegraphed congratulations to Mr. Ratchford. It is really the first advance gained by the miners in many years, amounting to, perhaps, twenty to twenty-five per cent increase in their wages and if it had not been for the aid and practical work of the trade unions of the A.F. of L. they would, probably, not have been able to hold out two weeks, and then it would have been positive failure. Well, we can stand the abuse so long as we help to attain tangible results for the workers.

I regret I could not be with you last week and enjoy the pleasure of the company of yourself, Chance[5] and Gallagher,[6] and the ozone of Atlantic City. With kindest regards and best wishes, I am,

Sincerely yours,   Saml Gompers.

President   A.F. of L.

TLpS, reel 13, vol. 21, pp. 194-96, SG Letterbooks, DLC.

1. John Peter Altgeld, former governor of Illinois, spoke on Sept. 6, 1897, in Philadelphia's Washington Park to a crowd of about two thousand, under the auspices of the United Labor League. He condemned corporate political influence and claimed that the use of court injunctions was threatening republican institutions.

2. Maj. John A. Lennon, a Denver merchant-tailor for forty years, died on Sept. 14, 1897.

3. On Sept. 12, 1897, the German Branch of the Philadelphia SLP met to discuss Debs and his recently founded Social Democracy of America (SDA). Some speakers dismissed the movement as not based on socialist principles and the class struggle, but Louis Werner, editor of the *Philadelphia Tageblatt*, was among those who saw promise in the SDA, arguing that "sooner or later he [Debs] must come into conflict with the venal and cowardly leaders of the American trade unions, and if his movement served no other purpose, it would be good for that reason alone" (*Philadelphia Tageblatt*, Sept. 13, 1897).

4. SG was probably reacting to reports of the St. Louis conference that met on behalf of the striking coal miners (see "To P. J. McGuire," Sept. 1, 1897, n. 1, above). On Aug. 31 the conference adopted a resolution "that no Nation in which the people are totally disarmed can long remain a free nation, and therefore we urge upon all liberty-loving citizens to remember and obey article 2 of the constitution of the United States, which reads as follows: 'The right of the people to keep and bear arms shall not be infringed.' " In a speech to the conference later that day, Eugene Debs told the delegates, "I shrink from that bloodshed . . . but if this is necessary to preserve liberty and our rights—in that event I will shed the last drop of blood that courses through my veins" (*Pittsburg Post*, Sept. 1, 1897).

5. George CHANCE, a Philadelphia printer, was president of the Pennsylvania Federation of Labor and an AFL organizer.

6. Possibly Daniel J. Gallagher, owner of a Philadelphia printing shop.

Thomas Kidd to Frank Morrison

General Secretary
Amalgamated Wood-Workers International
Union of America
Chicago, Sept. 16, 1897.

Friend Frank:—

Your letter of the 13th inst. is before me and the contents of the same swallowed eagerly and with considerable pleasure. Your talk was radical all right and no talk is any good unless it is radical. There are degrees of radicalism. Yours is somewhat moderate, mine is away up in G.

Relative to the murder of the miners on a public highway in the State of Pennsylvania, I can only repeat what I said to Roberts[1] of the Dispatch, when he interviewed me upon the matter, that if one of the victims were a brother of mine, there would be a dead sheriff[2] to-day. I swear it by the Eternal powers that if any relative of mine had been a victim of this murderous assault, that I should have kept on Martin's tracks, until the scoundrel did not have a spark of life. I have no sympathy whatever with the remarks of Mr. Carrick in his attack on Sam Gompers. That is what the Plutocracy wants. Desires to see us quarreling among ourselves, and then it rubs its hands in glee, knowing well that so long as our leaders are divided, just so long will it be in a position to oppress labor with impunity. I should [have] liked to have seen Gompers come out with a more radical statement in relation to the shooting of the miners, than that which he gave to the Press, but then he is naturally conservative and I do not suppose he can help his conservatism any more than I can help my radicalism. I have always given Gompers credit for being honest and have never hesitated to put on the gloves with those who hinted otherwise, but I should like him much better if he would deal less in generalities and talk pointedly and explicitly when times warrant the use of strong language.[3]

You say that you are afraid that I have not been to church often enough to be good authority for the statements I made at Grand Rapids. One of the points I made was this: "At a church conference in Maine last month, the sum of $70,000.00 was raised for foreign missions. Raised to clothe people who do not need clothes. Raised to convert heathens who do not want to be converted and raised to civilize barbarians who are bound together by closer ties than the so-called civilized Christians. $70,000.00 raised to send to the heathens, at a time when hundreds of thousands of American coal miners, who were not heathens, were almost dying of starvation." That was one of the points I made and I will leave it to your good sense, and sound judgment whether it is necessary for a man to go to church to be able to see that the action of this conference was barbarous, cruel, inhuman and unchristian. I have nothing, Frank, against Christianity but I am opposed like the devil to churchianity. There is an awful difference between the two.

Replying to the question you ask if I do not believe it possible for the A.F. of L. to make a stand and absolutely refuse to have anything in a Central Body that is not affiliated with the A.F. of L. either direct or through their national organization, I will reply in the affirmative. The present system encourages unions to keep away from their national organization. They can fight their national organization through the Central Body and can snap their fingers at the American Federation of Labor. Look at the Chicago Federation for instance, at its last meeting, unseating the Chicago Musical Society,[4] a local union of the American Federation of Musicians, which is a part of the A.F. of L. It unseated a branch[5] of the Waiters' Alliance for the same reason, viz. that these two organizations had rivals,[6] not affiliated with the A.F. of L., that were fighting them. I will be frank enough to say that I have little use for either the Waiters or the Musicians, but as long as the American Federation of Labor recognizes them, the Central Bodies affiliated with the American Federation of Labor ought to be compelled to recognize them too. Unfortunately the woodworkers have a very poor delegation in the Chicago Federation of Labor. A delegation that is afraid to get up and make a fight for what it knows to be right. Sooner or later the American Federation of Labor will have to take the stand that you suggest.

When I returned from Grand Rapids I heard everybody say that there was a tie for first place between the carpenters and the Woodworkers. It did me good to have our union classed with the carpenters and painters, because, as you know, these are two of the strongest organizations in Chicago. I am glad that it pleased you to see in cold print that we had 1500 on parade.[7] Your pleasure implies that you take the same interest in our organization that you did when it was difficult for us to get a corporal's guard to a meeting. We are still growing and our capita tax will show that we are increasing considerably. We expect a falling off in Nov., Dec., Jan. and Feb., when the mills close down, but we will be better off than we ever were before in winter.

With best wishes, I am,

Fraternally yours,   Thos. I. Kidd.

P.S. Yes Hattie is still with me.

TLS, Amalgamated Wood Workers' Records, reel 143, frames 802-5, *AFL Records.*

1. William C. Roberts was a member of International Typographical Union 16 and labor editor of the *Chicago Dispatch.*

2. James Martin, a former mine foreman, was Republican sheriff of Luzerne Co., Pa., from 1896 to 1899. He led the group that opened fire on the miners at Lattimer, Pa.

3. In a subsequent letter to Morrison, Kidd wrote: "When I used the term generalities I used it in its fullest sense. Our friend Gompers simply makes a statement in which reference to 'our enlightened age' and 'flag of freedom' occurs. Strong language is not all that we want. Talk against injunctions is not all that we want. Accusing those elected to administer justice, as being servile is not all that we want. Such statements are generalities, pure and simple. What we want is a way to change the system so that miners will not be shot down when they make a demand for a

greater share of what they produce than the miserable item which they to-day receive" (Sept. 27, 1897, Amalgamated Wood Workers' Records, reel 143, frame 806, *AFL Records*).

4. American Federation of Musicians (AFM) 10.

5. Hotel and Restaurant Employees' National Alliance (HRENA) 40.

6. AFM 10—the Chicago Musical Society (CMS)—was competing with the American Musicians' Union (AMU), which contained former members of KOL Local Assembly 952. The Chicago Federation of Labor unseated the CMS at its Sept. 5, 1897, meeting and indicated it would bar the musicians until they reconciled their differences and merged. In 1898 the CMS withdrew from the AFM, but a portion of the membership launched the Chicago Federation of Musicians (CFM) in December 1898, which received a charter as AFM 10. In 1899 Kidd helped arrange a merger of the AMU, CMS, and CFM under the AFM 10 charter. The rival of HRENA 40 was the Chicago Waiters' League.

7. Members of seven locals of the Amalgamated Wood Workers' International Union of America—by some estimates as many as 3,700—marched in the Chicago Labor Day parade on Sept. 6, 1897.

To Andrew Furuseth

Sept. 18th. [1897]

Mr. Andrew Furuseth.
S.W. Cor. East & Mission Streets. San Francisco, California.
Dear Sir & Friend:—

Enclosed you will find clipping which I think you will be very much interested in. I do not know but what you may have seen it, but for fear that it might have escaped your notice I enclose it for your information.

I beg to assure you that I appreciate your suggestion and commendation in your recent letter more than I can find words to express. You know these howlers who are simply chasing rainbows and setting off fireworks, particularly great big pin wheels with their own countenances as the chief attraction, are not the brave men that they would have the world believe they are. If I have any knowledge of the men who are never cowards in any conflict they are those who do not prate about their willingness to shoot and be shot, or to be hanged. For a time, at least, the trancers are holding the boards, but I am quite confident that good judgement will prevail and with the dawn of calmness the effervescence of bombasto furioso will again become obscure. You know me well enough that I have always tried to perform my duty. I trust that you will not for a moment doubt that either now or at any other time I ever will shirk it. With best wishes to you and our friends on the Coast I am,

Fraternally yours, Saml Gompers.

TLpS, reel 13, vol. 21, p. 258, SG Letterbooks, DLC.

Samuel Gompers and Frank Morrison to P. J. McGuire

Washington, D.C., Sept. 18, 1897.

P. J. McGuire,
Mass Meeting,[1] Hazleton, Pa.
We join in expression of keenest sympathy for the murdered and butchered miners, their disconsolate widows and helpless orphans. The indignation of our entire people at the brutal monster Martin is boundless. The miscreant must meet his punishment but more than [that] all organized labor will create a more enlighted public opinion which will protect the lives and rights of our people and secure true freedom for all.

Samuel Gompers
Frank Morrison.

TWpSr, reel 13, vol. 21, p. 273, SG Letterbooks, DLC.

1. On Sept. 18, 1897, P. J. McGuire, George Chance, John Fahey, and others addressed a meeting of between two and three thousand miners on Donegal Hill in Hazleton, Pa.

A Circular Issued by the Executive Council of the AFL

[September 22, 1897]

A call has gone forth to the trade unions and public for a labor convention in Chicago next Monday. The ostensible objects are to take measures in aid of the miners on strike and to offset the sweeping powers of the courts in granting injunctions in defiance of popular rights during labor disputes.

These objects are very commendable, and worthy the active practical support of every trade unionist and of every lover of his fellow-man. But conditions have somewhat changed since that convention was agreed upon. This week fully 75,000 miners have gone to work on terms fixed jointly by the miners and operators, and which give a decided increase in wages and grant practical recognition to the United Mine Workers of America as an organized body. On the 21st instant the strike was generally ended, except in West Virginia, a few points in Western Pennsylvania, and a portion of Illinois. It is the greatest victory gained by trades unions in years. It was won against the combined power of wealth, judicial usurpations, and inhuman tyranny.

From the beginning of the contest, twelve weeks ago, the American Federation of Labor and the trades unions of the whole land have been in the forefront with money and men to back the miners. Thousands of dollars went out generously from the trade unions, and zealous union men gave their services freely to this noble cause. A liberal public, too, gave no inconsiderable share of help in various ways. All through this struggle the miners in their manly dignity displayed no brutish violence; their forbearance and discipline are at once the wonder and admiration of our age.

The American Federation of Labor, believing only in practical methods, has to-day decided to continue its support with organizers and money until a complete victory for the miners is won. To this end it calls on its unions and on the public to not halt in their full and unmeasured aid to this worthy movement. Many families still need support, and money will be required for some time to come, until the miners are more fully at work and able to help themselves. Let the trade unions be liberal in their donations until this struggle is crowned with complete success.

We can see no need for the labor convention in Chicago next Monday. We advise our unions not to be represented there. The money it would cost to send delegates had better go to help the suffering miners and their families. It is not by conventions, with irresponsible talk, inflammatory declamation, and revolutionary buncombe, that the cause of labor can be advanced. Violent appeals to the passions of the multitude can serve no good purpose. It is only by systematic organization of the working people in trade unions, with united hearts and united funds, and a fraternity of purpose which knows no bounds of creed, color, nationality, or politics, that will uplift the masses.

Trades unions are not the promoters of social disorder or the upholders of riot or revolution. Our course is along the lines of peace and historical orderly development. We are law-abiding citizens, and if the law or its administration at times is against us, we are confident that an enlightened public opinion will ultimately correct the wrong. Hence we here make appeal to all fair-minded molders of public thought, to our public men, to the clergy and the press, to make a decided stand henceforth with us against the unfair and unconstitutional use of judicial injunctions which are wholly subversive of popular liberty.

We further urge the citizens of our entire country to rise unitedly at the polls in every State and elect men to make and administer our laws who will root out and make forever impossible these new forms of judicial tyranny and political pliancy which now prevail in the service of corporate wealth.

Adopted by the Executive Council of the American Federation of Labor, at Washington, D.C., September 22, 1897, and indorsed by M. D. Rathford, President of the United Mine Workers of America.

PD, Minutes of Meetings, Executive Council, AFL, reel 2, frames 1155-56, *AFL Records.*

To the Executive Council of the AFL

Washington, D.C. Sept. 29th 1897.

To the Executive Council, American Federation of Labor.
Colleagues: —

In the published reports of the Chicago convention, which we advised our trades unionists not to be represented in, I see that some have advised the formation of a Western Federation of Labor. This recalls to my mind the fact that the evidence which Vice President McGuire submitted in support of a scheme and conspiracy upon the part of a few men to crush the trade union movement and destroy the American Federation of Labor, is [ante]dated by several months. If you will remember that the Western Federation of Miners were on strike during the Cincinnati convention last Dec.; that Debs went to Montana and sought to lead that strike, and did lead it into a disastrous failure; you will remember that I called your attention to the fact that I had received a confidential letter about that time stating that Mr. Edward Boyce would recommend to the convention of the Western Federation of Miners that the members arm themselves and particularly that the organization should withdraw from the American Federation of Labor and form a Western Federation of Labor. Mark the similarity of language. You remember the spirited correspondence had with Mr. Boyce, as published by your authority in a pamphlet, which in the light of current events, I ask you to re-read, and enclose copy of it herein for that purpose.

The address[1] which the Executive Council issued at its last session was undoubtedly one of the greatest acts which it can place to its credit in defense of the trade union movement and in the interest of all labor. You will note that it took the bottom out of the Chicago call and gathering, which has fizzled out, and the few responsible trade unionists who were at St. Louis were even consp[icuous] by their absence at Chicago. It is practically [now] the elements [of] failure which have gathered together and their impotent rage, as manifested in their tirades against the trade unionists and trades unions is the best evidence that they hold no commission either by voice or sympathy of [the wage earning] masses of our country.

The incidents noted herein are of such importance that I deem it my duty to communicate them to you and to congratulate you and [when] the opportune time comes perhaps be in a position to congratulate [the] wage workers of America from escaping the dangerous pitfall which was prepared for them.

Fraternally yours,   Saml Gompers.
President   A.F. of L.

P.S.:—The Chicago papers disclose the fact that Mr. Edw. Boyce is in attendance at the Convention there; and, also, that Mr. Debs is laboriously trying to prove that the miners' strike was lost and that all strikes are failures.

TLpS, AFL Executive Council Vote Books, reel 8, frames 214, 216, *AFL Records.*

1. See "A Circular Issued by the Executive Council of the AFL," Sept. 22, 1897, above.

To P. J. McGuire

Oct. 13th. [1897]

Mr. P. J. McGuire.
#124 N. 9th. St.; Philadelphia.
Dear Friend:—

I have your letter of the 12th; also, the report of Organizer Frank Weber, as well as our friend McGregor's[1] letter, for all of which I beg to thank you. I find them exceedingly interesting. During my trip East[2] I saw Weber and had a talk in connection with the matters which he investigated. Of course he was then able to give me more information, probably, than he would have opportunity to write. There is no question but what there is collusion between the prosecuting attorney[3] at Hazleton and Sheriff Martin's friends. Of course it would be most difficult to attempt to prove this legally, but I am morally certain this is true, and the letter of Mr. Loughran, the attorney for the prosecuting committee, is certainly indicative of that fact.

I have some doubts as to what we can do at this time in financially assisting the prosecution of Sheriff Martin although I am satisfied it ought to be done.[4] We have expended so much of our funds and have such a small balance that a call from that source is out of the question, and I doubt the wisdom of making a general appeal for such purpose. It might be regarded as vindictive rather than prompted by a spirit of justice. Money ought to be raised for the purpose from established funds and obtained in an unobtrusive manner rather than a public appeal. I am in some doubt as to how Mr. Loughran's letter should be answered owing to the matters already mentioned.

I see no reason why I could not go with you to Hazleton to address a meeting on Saturday and Sunday Oct. 30th & 31st.[5] Of course if arrangements are made I will leave here in time on Saturday in order to reach Hazleton in the evening. I certainly should like to know at as early a date as possible what arrangements you make in this matter. You may rely upon my keeping the engagement.

Dr. Rice,[6] of The Forum, advised me that he has been out of the city for some little time and for that reason has been unable to give the matter of which we corresponded earlier attention. You will, perhaps, hear from him in the course of a few days. I gave him the name of our friend McGregor and I am advised that he has already written him.

I see by the Philadelphia Tagablatt that they are following up the same tactics as Robert A. Pinkerton[7] did in his testimony before the Congressional Committee[8] which investigated the Homestead strike; that is, trying by all means within its power to prove that all strikes are accompanied by violence, force and murder. Of course the address[9] of the Executive Council is too important a document to allow these disruptionists to let go by without attacking; it is too good a trade union document, and doctrine, to allow [to] stand unchallenged, and I certainly agree with our friend McGregor's judgement that the document was not only timely but will stand for all time as a text of true trade unionism.

You say you had a talk with Debs while he was in Philadelphia. I suppose it was interesting: it certainly should have been very warm. There is no denying that Debs can say most pleasing things to one, and, yet, a short time before and after ascribe to that same person the most malevolent of designs, and even with all that he is not a bad fellow I firmly believe, but brainy, bright—but the apostle of failure. It is a pity he never, in his days of development, had the opportunity of coming in [close] contact with not only trade unionists, but sincere, sympathetic theoretical as well as practical trade unionists. Hence he has had his mind prejudiced against trade unions and trade unionists believing them to be bare and barren of sentiment.

Enclosed find returned McGregor's letter.

I regret very much that the suggestion was not made earlier to print the address issued by the Executive Council. It seems a little late now, but the importance of the document is such that it can be utilized at any time. As McGregor suggests it was not only [a] timely document, but one which will stand as a text for the future conduct of trade unionists. Being just in the course of preparation of the call for the Nashville convention I think it would be well to have the address go out with it. It would seem peculiar to send the address special so late after its issuance.

Please let me hear from you at your early convenience in regard to the arrangements for Hazleton.

With best wishes I am,

Sincerely yours, Saml Gompers.

N.B. Enclosed find credential in Stetson matter.[10] If you think well of it, I will go with you on the 30th.

It was absolutely necessary to hurry back here.

S. G.

T and ALpS, reel 13, vol. 21, pp. 471-73, SG Letterbooks, DLC.

1. Hugh McGREGOR had served as SG's secretary during the late 1880s, directing the AFL office during the president's absence. He helped organize seamen on the Atlantic coast and between 1890 and 1892 served as secretary of the International Amalgamated Sailors' and Firemen's Union.

2. SG's trip east (Oct. 4-10, 1897) included stops in Philadelphia, New York City, Hartford and New Haven, Conn., and Boston.

3. P. Frank Laughran, of Hazleton, Pa., was one of three private lawyers retained to assist the prosecution in the Lattimer case.

4. At its Sept. 23, 1897, meeting, the AFL Executive Council adopted a resolution condemning the Lattimer massacre and pledging to raise funds for the legal prosecution of Martin and his deputies.

5. SG, together with P. J. McGuire and George Chance, spoke in Hazleton, Pa., on Oct. 30, 1897, and in Freeland, Pa., the next day.

6. Joseph M. Rice, a physician and author, was editor of the *Forum* from 1897 to 1907.

7. Robert A. Pinkerton was a copartner in Pinkerton's National Detective Agency.

8. For Robert Pinkerton's testimony on July 22, 1892, before the House Judiciary

Committee, see *Employment of Pinkerton Detectives*, U.S. Congress, House, Reports, no. 2447, 52d Cong., 2d sess. (Washington, D.C., 1893), pp. 189-213, 217-18; and for his testimony on Nov. 26, 1892, before the Senate Select Committee, see *Report . . . in Relation to the Employment for Private Purposes of Armed Bodies of Men, or Detectives, in Connection with Differences between Workmen and Employers*, U.S. Congress, Senate, Reports, no. 1280, 52d Cong., 2d sess. (Washington, D.C., 1893), pp. 235-65, 269-70.

9. See "A Circular Issued by the Executive Council of the AFL," Sept. 22, 1897, above.

10. In September 1897, at the request of the United Hatters of North America, the AFL Executive Council appointed P. J. McGuire to accompany a local Philadelphia committee to meet with a representative of the John B. Stetson Co. about working conditions and union recognition.

To Andrew Furuseth

Washington, D.C. Oct. 26th 1897.

Mr. Andrew Furuseth
My Dear Friend:—

Your favor of the 20th to hand and contents noted. I beg to assure you that I appreciate the confidence you repose in me by writing me as fully and frankly as you do. I can say, too, that I have heard the same rumors which have come to you and I am not surprised either. You remember that we have passed through an era during the last year practically the same as took place in 1893.[1] Then the A.R.U. strike took place and because then I refused to "order" a general sympathetic strike all the elements of opposition were worked up and together with the trade unions' antagonists and all sorts of isms contributed to my defeat in Dec. of that year. Together with that fact was the additional one that the convention was held at a great distance from the industrial centers interfering with the opportunity of organizations being represented there. The past year has seen the great miners' strike, which, though largely victorious, yet, has given the same opportunity to the same elements and the convention again this year is far removed from industrial centers. Now in addition to this, however, I see recently that there is an effort been made by some persons who claim to represent the labor press to have a convention[2] at Nashville at the same time as the A.F. of L. convention takes place. I know that this call has really emanated from a source not entirely friendly to your humble servant; but, apart from this fact, it seems to me that there is an element of danger in it. If this call is fairly responded to it will mean that men will come there who have the means to say very ugly things of any one who will oppose any proposition which they may favor and there are not so very many men who can stand up for what they believe in the face of what this may mean to them — that is, opposition, antagonism &c — and the danger is that we may experience what the Populists did some years ago when the representatives of the Populist press determined upon having a convention take place at the same time as the Populist conventions and when they could not fully control them made the scape-goats of those who antagonized the schemes of the representatives of the papers and brought about schisms which were too wide to heal. I do not know whether these men have the same purpose as the populist editors had. In fact I do not know that the populist editors themselves had it in the beginning, but I have no doubt that the results may prove just as dangerous. I mention this merely as an additional incident showing the elements at work on the line indicated by you.

Let me repeat what I said in New York two years ago; that is, if the clear cut true trade unionists who attend the convention agree upon any good trade unionist who will stand for trade unionism before all else I am perfectly satisfied to retire in his favor and I say this with the full consciousness of all that it implies. I am by no means tired of the office, [or] of the work. On the contrary I am as much, if not more intensely, interested in the trade union cause than ever before and I have nothing that I can now see for myself in the future; but, be that as it may, I am willing to take my chances and voluntarily give way to some thorough trade unionist. But, so far as withdrawing and perhaps allow some one to be elected who, either through lack of experience, knowledge or steadfastness of character will deviate in his course and if not divert the movement himself allow it to be diverted by those secret as well as open enemies, that I will not do. Combinations, perhaps, may be effected to secure my defeat, but at any rate under such circumstances the results mentioned will not be achieved with my connivance, for to withdraw in face of such circumstances would be conniving at the mischief.

I want you to understand me fully. I do not believe for a moment that I am the only man in the labor movement fit and qualified to be President of the American Federation of Labor, or the only one who is honest and true to the cause. On the contrary, as you observe, I say that if our men can agree upon a man I should deem it my duty and would cordially retire in his favor. For instance, the danger which confronted the trade union movement within this past year is not appreciated nor understood: the St. Louis gathering; the Chicago gathering, all were the results of deep laid plots by a few men to disrupt the trade union movement. Had there been a man at this office who was either weak or not fairly well grounded in his unionism a pretty hard blow would have been dealt it which would have staggered it to a very great extent and it would have taken years to recover from. However, I need not dilate upon this matter at all. You understand it fully as well as I and all you need know is the circumstances attending the case and you will be fully aware as to the facts of which I speak.

It is needless for me to say that I appreciate exceedingly your words of commendation and confidence and know too that you can not be swerved from your purpose to aid your fellow seamen in their great struggle still before them.

I sincerely hope that I may have the pleasure of meeting you, at the convention for I believe better opportunities are opened up now than we have had for some years past. With assurances of highest regard as well as appreciation of your profferred assistance I am,

Yours fraternally and sincerely, Saml Gompers.

President A.F. of L.

N.B.:— I have sent you copy of the Oct. issue of the American Federationist in which you will note my article "Instead of an Editorial"[3] which though long I believe you will find interesting.

TLpS, reel 13, vol. 21, pp. 612-14, SG Letterbooks, DLC.

1. The Pullman strike occurred in 1894.

2. In October 1897 George Wilmot Harris, editor of the *Chicago Federationist* and a member of International Typographical Union 16, issued a call to the labor press to meet in conjunction with the AFL's Nashville convention in December to establish a labor press association. Representatives of forty trade union journals and general newspapers met in Nashville, Dec. 15-16, 1897, and organized the Associated Labor Press of America to furnish broad and reliable coverage of the labor movement.

3. In "Instead of an Editorial. On Filth, Folly and Faithlessness" (*American Federationist* 4 [Oct. 1897]: 191-95), SG defended his decision not to attend the St. Louis conference (see "To P. J. McGuire," Sept. 1, 1897, n. 1, above).

To Edward O'Donnell

Oct. 27th. [1897]

Mr. Ed. O'Donnell.

#45 Eliot St.; Boston, Mass.

Dear Friend:—

Your letter, poem[1] and clipping to hand and all read with the utmost interest. If it were not so late I would get the poem in the Nov. issue of the American Federationist. I will make an effort to find a place for it; but, if not, it will certainly go in the Dec. number. It is excellent. I should be pleased, too, to have your article, as you say you will write, on the subject of the displacement of the printer by machinery. Of course you are aware that notwithstanding the introduction of machinery the I.T.U. has steadily gained in membership and that the average wages of the printers are higher and their hours of labor shorter. Of course this is for the employed printers. The old time printer who has been crowded out by machinery and his younger competitor is suffering the ills so many of our fellow workers in other trades do who also have been displaced by machinery. It is an awful thing to think that because it is possible to produce the wealth of the world easier that for that reason with so large a number it is more difficult to earn a livelihood; and, yet, such are the facts in our present civilization. I can see no hope for the future, no real way out, other than that which the trade union promises—the reduction in the hours of labor. With all that that implies the workers will soon find a short route to the abolition of all injustice and bring about at least an equality of opportunity.

I was rather surprised to learn from your "labor echoes" that McCraith was "making war[2] upon Henry George."[3]

Yes, I see that Debs is booked for a number of talks[4] in the East and I am not surprised at the resentment by our trade unionists for his utterances decrying the trade unionists and trade union action. A few weeks ago he urged that where there was no social democratic ticket in the field that he would advise people to vote for Populists, or others who stood nearest to labor generally, ignoring the S.L.P. He was taken to task for this at a Philadelphia meeting and last Saturday I saw a signed article[5] by him in which he has made his peace with the S.L.P.—that is, so far as urging people to vote for their party. As a matter of fact he has advocated so very many different things and so near after and in opposition to each other that it is difficult to keep track of which is said first or last.

With kindest regards and best wishes I am,

Fraternally yours, Saml Gompers
President A.F. of L.

TLpS, reel 13, vol. 21, pp. 624-25, SG Letterbooks, DLC.

1. "Do Not Blame Me If I Sigh," *American Federationist* 4 (Nov. 1897): 207.

2. Possibly a reference to an article signed "A.M.," published under the title "Hard Words for George" (*American Craftsman*, Oct. 16, 1897), that attacked Henry George.

3. Henry George, a Philadelphia-born journalist, labor reformer, and antimonopolist, ran for mayor of New York City in 1897, dying four days before the election.

4. Eugene Debs's speaking tour in Oct. 1897 included New York City and Lynn, Boston, and Cambridge, Mass.

5. Debs's piece, dated Oct. 16, 1897, encouraged members of the Social Democracy of America to support the SLP candidates in the fall elections in New York, Pennsylvania, and other states (*Social Democracy*, Oct. 21, 1897).

To Mrs. Henry George[1]

Washington, D.C. October 29th [1897]

Mrs. Henry George,
Union Square Hotel, New York City.
Am shocked beyond description at news of death of your husband Henry George. The people have lost a great champion and humanity a devoted friend. Accept sincere condolence in your great bereavement.

Samuel Gompers.

TWpSr, reel 13, vol. 21, p. 650, SG Letterbooks, DLC.

1. Annie Fox George.

To Samuel Jones[1]

Nov. 4th. [1897]

Mr. Samuel M. Jones.
Toledo, Ohio.
Dear Sir:—
Upon my return to the office I find your favor of the 29th awaiting me, contents of which I have read with unusual interest. Let me assure you that I appreciate the sincerity of your words and the intelligent sympathetic action in regard to the effort to make the shorter workday more universal.

The advantages of the movement to reduce the hours of labor are so manifold, and while to one who has made the matter a study they are superficial, are yet too deep for those who have had neither the opportunity or ability to give it their attention and study. I read a good portion of your book on the eight hour day system and like it very much and think that coming, as it does, from a large employer of labor it will have additional interest and perhaps be more convincing than any production from the hands of either a workman, scientist or one who will advocate the proposition from an altruian standpoint. I do not know whether you have seen any of the matter which we publish on the subject of the eight hour workday and for that reason take pleasure in sending copies of our pamphlets to you under separate cover.

Your letter has very much interested me and I should like to publish it in the American Federationist, our official journal; yet, I feel that I ought not to do so without your consent.[2]

Permit me to express to you my sincere [thanks for the copy?] of your song "Divide The Day." I admire it very much and am distributing it among some of our friends in the movement. I hope it will have every success. I feel confident that it will materially aid us in our efforts for the success of the system to which it is dedicated.

With assurances of high regard and appreciation of your sympathetic co-operation in our movement I am,

Sincerely yours,
President   A.F. of L.

TLp, reel 13, vol. 21, pp. 708-9, SG Letterbooks, DLC.

1. Samuel Milton "Golden Rule" Jones, a Welsh-born manufacturer and reformer, was Republican (later independent) mayor of Toledo, Ohio (1897-1904).
2. The letter was published in January 1898 (4:264).

From Henry Fischer[1]

11/8/'97.

Dear Sir and Bro—:

With regard to yours of the 5th to Mr. Evans,[2] will say, I am glad of the stand you are taking in connection with the Circular sent you; that is, you will investigate the matter of the Brown Tobacco Co.,[3] and that it must have the indorsement of the Executive Council, before publishing it in the Federationist.

Now, Sam do not beat around the bush; why did you put Mayo's and Finzer's Ads.,[4] in the Federationist? Did they get the indorsement of the Executive Council?

I think you know as well as I do, that Mayo is one of the most oppressive Labor crushers in this country; and I have several times requested you not to advertise for firms who are antagonistic to our Organization. Now, I hope you will take the same stand with regard to these firms, that you have taken in the case of Brown.

When you were here last, you told me that Mr. McCraith made the Contract with the Mayo firm, and that as soon as it expired (which was to be in October, you told me),[5] you would not renew it; so how is it, that you are still carrying it?

Now I should like for you to notify me with regard to this, so that the case can be placed in a right light before the Convention.

Hoping to hear from you soon, I am

Fraternally yours, Henry Fischer.
Nat'l Pres.

TLpS, Tobacco Workers' International Union Archives, Special Collections, MdU.

1. Henry FISCHER was president of the National Tobacco Workers' Union of America (NTWUA; after 1898 Tobacco Workers' International Union [TWIU]) from 1895 to 1908.

2. E. Lewis EVANS was secretary-treasurer of the NTWUA and the TWIU from 1895 to 1925, and president of the TWIU from 1926 to 1940. For SG's letter, see reel 13, vol. 21, pp. 713-14, SG Letterbooks, DLC.

3. The Brown Tobacco Co. of St. Louis—apparently under pressure from larger anti-union firms—refused to meet its union employees' wage demands and then removed the union label from its products. After SG's unsuccessful attempt to arrange a settlement between Brown and the NTWUA in late 1897 and early 1898, the AFL Executive Council placed the firm on the AFL's unfair list in June 1898.

4. P. H. Mayo and Bro., Richmond, Va., and John Finzer and Bros., Louisville, Ky.

5. In his response to Fischer, SG denied making this statement (Nov. 10, 1897, ibid., pp. 828-29).

From Theodore Roosevelt

Navy Department,
Office Assistant Secretary,
Washington. November 15, 1897.

My dear Sir:

It will always be a pleasure to me to hear from you, and if at any time you call here in person I should like to go over the whole matter with you.

I went in to see the Secretary[1] today about the Marine Band, laying before him a communication from the Colonel Commandant[2] of the Marine Corps. Unless we doubled the rate of compensation now paid to the musicians of the Marine Band, we could not get them of the quality we now have them, provided they were prohibited from playing outside; and if we doubled their salaries we should have to double the salaries of all the other musicians in the naval service, which would cause a great expense. It is the Secretary's purpose not hereafter to send the Marine Band to big cities where it will be brought into competition with musical unions, unless for exceptional reasons it is deemed necessary. (I may explain that very frequently everybody, from the Governor and Senators down, will send a petition to have the band sent somewhere.) But the Secretary does not see any reason why the band should not be sent, for instance, to some of the Southern States, where no such first-class organization exists, and it would not be practicable to prevent their playing in Washington, to the same extent, and under the same limitations and regulations, which have hitherto been applicable to them. Forty-one of the members of the band belong to the Musical Union[3] of this city.

If you will come here I shall be delighted to show you all the correspondence we have had on the subject.

Very truly yours,   Theodore Roosevelt

TLS, American Federation of Musicians' Records, reel 141, frames 725-26, *AFL Records.*

1. John D. Long (1838-1915), a lawyer, was the Republican governor of Massachusetts (1880-82), U.S. congressman (1883-89), and secretary of the navy (1897-1902).

2. Maj. Gen. Charles Heywood was commandant of the U.S. Marine Corps (1891-1903).

3. The Columbia Musicians' Protective Association of Washington, D.C., was local 41 of the American Federation of Musicians.

To Charles Scribner's Sons

Nov. 18th, [1897]

Messrs. Chas. Scribner Sons,
157 5th Ave., New York, N.Y.,
Gentlemen:—

I am in receipt of your favor of the 13th Inst., and, also, a copy of Mr. Wyckoff's latest chapter on the "Workers,"[1] which I have read with very great interest. I am sure that Mr. Wyckoff has had most splendid experience and has portrayed them in excellent colors. It has already aroused a very great deal of interest, which is certainly likely to increase. Let me say, however, in regard to this matter, that while the experiment in itself is a most wholesome one, and one the narration of which is calculated to do considerable good, yet the fact, the knowledge that Mr. Wyckoff had, that, if the worst came to the worst, he could retire from the struggle and enjoy the advantages which his position in life could give him, would, of necessity, deprive him from feeling so intensely many of the things which the ordinary wage-earner would feel and experience, who is forever bound up with his condition as a wage earner.

I have not been in a position to carefully keep all the parts of Mr.

Wyckoff's article and would appreciate the possession of a copy of the book when issued.

Thanking you for your courtesy, I am,

Very truly yours,   Saml Gompers.

President   A.F. of L.

TLpS, reel 13, vol. 21, pp. 975-76, SG Letterbooks, DLC.

1. Walter A. Wyckoff, a Princeton University economist, had worked his way from Connecticut to California between 1891 and 1893 as a common laborer to gain firsthand knowledge of working-class life. He recorded his experiences in a series of articles, "The Workers. An Experiment in Reality," that appeared in *Scribner's Magazine* in 1897 and 1898. The articles also appeared in book form (*The Workers. An Experiment in Reality. The East* [New York, 1897], and *The Workers. An Experiment in Reality. The West* [New York, 1898]).

To Henry White

Nov. 20th, [1897]

Mr. Henry White,
#20 LaFayette Place, New York, N.Y.,
Dear Friend:—

Your favor of the 18th Inst., with clipping from New York "Times,"[1] came duly to hand, and I am obliged to you for the opportunity it gives me of seeing this matter. There is much to say on this question on both sides, and I am sure that we have no desire to do an injury to a bona fide organization of labor, whether they be musicians or others, but it must be borne in mind that the mutual musical protective union is a union only in name. I am confident if you knew the inner workings of that organization as I have had them rubbed up against me, you would have found the justification of the course pursued by the union and the other musical unions throughout the country.

You, perhaps, know that the mutual[2] which I shall, for the sake of convenience, call the "Bremer" faction,[3] made no attempt to protect the real working musicians. That is, the musicians who worked as musicians for a living. It seemed simply to exist by the sufferance of their employers. And, as a matter of fact, only until shame-faced by the Manhattans did they at all provide a place for the musicians to have shelter within a hall so that they could come together and wait, as they are required to wait, for engagements. It was a common sight, until recently, to see musicians shivering in the cold in the streets of New York, in front of the hall and then being plugged and clubbed by the policemen and continually compelled to "move on" or be arrested. The poorer the men were the more subject were they to this outrage, for they could not go into the saloons and be in shelter, warm themselves, for they hadn't any money to "spend over the bar." The employers were largely the members of the so-called union and dictated the policy as well as everything of the organization through Bremer. It was the revolt against this injustice which prompted the large movement to organize the musicians into the Manhattan.

Throughout the country musicians, and the very best of them, too, are often required to work at other trades or callings. Hence, they are usually union men in their other trades, and it was galling to them that in those trades they were union men while, as musicians, they were the reverse and stood in an antagonistic spirit to the labor movement. At a number of the Conventions, a large majority of the delegates would vote in affiliation with the A.F. of L., but Bremer would always secure enough proxy votes, which he carried in his pocket and cast against any such proposition, and, in fact, violated the constitution of the organization in at one time declaring the proposition lost when it was not lost. The general labor movement had a convention, after every honorable effort in this direction to give one further opportunity for a recognition of its standard and connection with labor, and, failing in that, that a new national organization be formed, the old line organization ratified the offer, under the circumstances as mentioned, and the new national union was formed under the name and title of the American Federation of Musicians, and I am confident that I speak but the truth when I say that it has just as high a class of musicians connected with it, and it now has a membership of more than four to one throughout the country, as compared to the old time organization. Perhaps it would not be amiss to say that Mr. Ruhe of Pittsburg, who is Mr. Bremer's right hand man and adviser, is an employee of the Carnegie Frick Company, and you can readily understand his opposition to an attempt for organized labor.

I do not know whether the present move on the part of the Manhattan is wise, but that is a matter which, likely, consideration will have much to determine. At any rate, it is deserving of the support of our fellow unionists.

I very much enjoyed reading your letter and clipping, and, particularly, the blessing which our friend Bushe[4] extends. They are appreciated, and will go far to save the soul of

Yours Sincerely,   Saml Gompers.

President   A.F. of L.

TLpS, reel 14, vol. 22, pp. 18-20, SG Letterbooks, DLC.

1. The *New York Times* of Nov. 17, 1897, reported on the unsuccessful efforts of the Manhattan Musical Union and other local musicians' unions affiliated with the AFL, working through the New York City Central Labor Union, to convince theaters to discharge musicians affiliated with the rival Musical Mutual Protective Union (MMPU). It described the latter as the largest and strongest local musicians' union in the country and reported that it claimed the best musicians as members and controlled all the city's orchestras. According to the *Times* article, MMPU president Alexander Bremer contended that the locals affiliated with the AFL contained poorly trained musicians and those expelled from the MMPU for such reasons as nonpayment of dues.

2. The MMPU.

3. Alexander H. W. BREMER, a New York City musician and clerk, was president of Musical Mutual Protective Union—National League of Musicians of the United States (NLM) 1—of New York City from 1893 to 1898 and president of the NLM from 1895 to about 1898. Other leaders of the faction opposing NLM affiliation with the AFL in the 1890s included C. H. William RUHE, a Pittsburgh bookkeeper and musician who was president of the NLM from 1892 to 1894, and Jacob Beck, NLM secretary from 1892 to 1895. Beck, who was a member of the Philadelphia Musical Association (NLM 2), also worked as a cigar dealer.

4. J. F. Bushe (variously Busche) had published the *Workmen's Advocate* from about 1887 to 1889 and was connected with a New York City printing firm.

To Eugene Reaves[1]

Nov. 22nd. [1897]

Mr. Eugene Reeves,
President, Trades and Labor Council,[2] A.F. of L.
#145 N. 3rd. St.; Hamilton, Ohio.
Dear Sir & Brother:—

Your favor of the 19th to hand and noted. In it you state that President Schwab,[3] of the Cincinnati Brewing Company, has consented to unconditional arbitration and I find his signature and endorsement to your letter. Yesterday I received a telegram from Mr. Schwab stating that he had read your letter and that "it is O.K." Under these circumstances it appears that all parties to the controversy have agreed that the writer shall be the arbitrator of differences existing between the Cincinnati Brewing Company and the Local Brewers Union #83,[4] both of Hamilton; that the arbitration is to be unconditional and that all have agreed to abide by the award. In accordance therewith I beg to advise you that I shall be in Hamilton on Saturday Nov. 27th. I may have to go to different points and therefore designate one o'clock P.M. of that day for both parties in controversy to meet. I shall notify Mr. Schwab and also the Union #83.

I should be pleased if you will appoint some good unionist who has not been committed fully to either one or the other sides of this question to act as my secretary and who has a quick conception and can write fairly rapid and take some notes of the proceedings. I do not wish a stenographer myself and will not allow either side to have one. The hearing and investigation will not be public only those in interest being present with their witnesses. The President of the Trades & Labor Council and the brother whom you may appoint as clerk, or secretary, being the exception to the rule. I think that if I have a large room at the hotel it will be sufficient; or, if there be no such large room then the parlor would, if there be sufficient privacy, do for the purpose. I do not wish to conduct a star chamber proceeding, but I do not think it would be wise nor conducive to the best results to throw it open to the public. On my arrival I will go to the hotel in Hamilton at once and ask you upon receipt of this to wire me the name of the hotel to which I should go. You need not wait to see the hotel proprietor. I repeat the request to wire at once, which I should receive Wednesday not later than noon, giving me the name of the hotel.

By this same mail I am writing to Mr. Schwab and the Secretary[5] of the Union giving them the requisite notice and information.

Hoping that I may be instrumental in adjusting this affair fairly and permanently I am,

Fraternally yours,   Saml Gompers.
President   A.F. of L.

N.B.: — After wiring me the name of the hotel which you have selected you will please notify both the Union #83 and President Schwab of that fact, where the hearing will take place.

S. G.

TLpS, reel 14, vol. 22, pp. 50-51, SG Letterbooks, DLC.

1. Eugene Reaves, a Hamilton, Ohio, molder, was secretary of Iron Molders' Union of North America 283 of Hamilton (1896-98).

2. The Hamilton Trades and Labor Council received an AFL charter in 1896.

3. Peter Schwab.

4. The dispute between National Union of the United Brewery Workmen of the United States 83 and the company had begun about eighteen months before. For the details of the case see "An Article in the *Hamilton Republican*," Nov. 29, 1897, below.

5. Henry Meyer. SG wrote Meyer and Schwab of his decision to come to Hamilton on Nov. 27 "to hear the evidence and determine the controversy." He added that "while the fullest latitude will be afforded for the introduction of testimony bearing upon the case I beg to advise you that I shall endeavour to have the rules of evidence governed by common sense, as it is likely to contribute to a fair adjustment of the differences, rather than a direct enforcement of the rules of evidence governing the courts of law" (Nov. 22, 1897, reel 14, vol. 22, pp. 52-53 and 54-55, SG Letterbooks, DLC; the quotation is from the letter to Meyer, p. 52).

An Article in the *Hamilton Republican*

[November 29, 1897]

MISSION A SUCCESS

Samuel Gompers, president of the American Federation of Labor, and arbitrator in the differences existing between the Cincinnati Brewing Co. and some of their employes, has handed in his decision. It is a compromise with both parties and satisfactory to all concerned. Mr. Gompers left yesterday afternoon for Washington, D.C.

His decision is as follows:

Hamilton, O., Nov. 28, 1897.

In the matter of the dispute between the Cincinnati Brewing Co., and the Local Brewery Workman's Union No. 83 of Hamilton, O., the undersigned was chosen as arbitrator, the parties to the dispute agreeing in advance to submit the entire controversy to unconditional arbitration and to abide by the award of the arbitration.

Agreeable to this an investigation was held at the St. Charles Hotel, at Hamilton, O., commencing at 1 o'clock in the afternoon of Saturday Nov. 27, and lasting until 10:45 in the evening or a session of nearly ten consecutive hours. The Cincinnati Brewing Co., was represented by its President, Peter Schwab and Brewery Workers Union 83, by its president, Mr. Conrad.[1] In all, there were twenty-nine witnesses heard—10 for the union and nineteen for the company. It is impossible in the brief time at the command of the arbitration to recount the entire history of the dispute or to receive in full the testimony elicited. It may be necessary however, to refer to a few essential matters which have had weight in arriving at the conclusions reached.

It is evident that the Cincinnati Brewing Co. had a mental reservation as to some of the provisions of the contract it entered into with [the] Brewery Workers' union on May 1, 1896. Its endeavor to prove that the contract was delivered in an unusual manner and with a verbal condition is a clear demonstration of that fact. The evidence which the company adduced on this point was successfully controverted by witnesses for the union and confounded by the witness the company called to corroborate its statement in this regard. But apart from this, the fact is that the contract was signed in the absence of sufficient testimony to impair the validity of any of its provisions, or in its entirety, it must stand and be interpreted in letter and spirit.

Hence it is clear that Henry Mayer was discharged from the company's employ, contrary to the provisions of the contract. Since the discharge of Meyer is the point on which this controversy turned it is well that some further mention be made of the matter.

It was clearly proven that more work could be performed by Meyer and the men in whose team he worked, but it was not clearly proven whether it was the fault of Meyer or the other members of the team. Union men are, by the nature of their obligation, to give, and certainly to a union employer, a fair day's work for a fair day's wages, and it should be the duty of the union to co-operate with the employer to accomplish that end. The company could and should have availed itself of the provision to complain to the union of any violation of its rights and its interests, as provided by the contract. The fact that it made no such complaint must logically be accepted that there was no real ground for complaint. It is submitted, however, not so much as a criticism of the past as a suggestion for the future. In-so-far as the Union's course in the dispute is concerned, that is immediately preceding the rupture of its relations with the company, it was not of that calm and deliberative character which is likely to succeed in winning the respect of the public nor the confidence of its members. Haste is not speed, nor is the enthusiasm of the passion of the moment, whether caused by real or imaginary grievances, calculated to mete out to others or attain for ourselves, justice.

The union erred, in the arbitrator's judgment, in placing the firm's product on the unfair list before every effort at a peaceful adjustment had been made. It is true that efforts had been made in that direction, but there were still, the Hamilton Trades council [and] the National union of the American federation of labor to endeavor to effect the purpose before final action should necessarily be taken. The members of the union who were employed by the company failed utterly to perform their duty to themselves, their employer or to the union. If they believed that the company was being unjustly dealt with by the union, they should have remained at the meetings of their Union and by their votes manifested their opposition. The fact that one of their members, who was previously suspended by the union for non-payment of dues, 5 or 14 (as it was variously claimed) others who were fined, were requested to leave the meeting room, was no justification for the remainder who were not affected in their rights in leaving the meeting room and thus surrendering whatever rights they had to these opposed to them and opposed to the company's rights and interests. It is evident that they regarded themselves not so much as members of the union as the company's representatives in the union. Even in this latter capacity they proved themselves unequal to its performance.

From the testimony itself and the manner in which it was given it is plainly evident that the policy of the Cincinnati Brewing company was not inimical to organized labor, nor to the Brewery Workman's union. On the contrary, it was quite favorable. Yet it is undeniable that the management was influenced to take unnecessary unfriendly action or to look suspiciously upon the work of the union. It was not elicited who was responsible for this but both the company and the union are commended to jointly endeavor to discover the real enemy to both and remove the evil genius. He is not a member of organized labor. For these and other reasons, too numerous to mention, the following decision is rendered:

First—That Henry Meyer be re-instated into his old employ in the company.

That all the employes of the company who were members of the union at the time the present controversy arose, shall be re-instated into the union regardless whether they were suspended for nonpayment of dues or fines, or whether they were expelled, upon the following conditions: That all fines imposed upon the members be reduced and a fine of $1 is imposed on all for violation of their obligation to the union and their failure to perform their duty as employes and workmen.

Second—That all be required to pay their dues to the union which have accumulated between their suspension or expulsion.

Third—That the company shall re-instate in their old positions, all its old employes it discharged by reason of their connection with this dispute.

Fourth—The union shall take the company off its unfair list and declare its product fair and entitled to the patronage of organized labor and its supporters and sympathizers.

Fifth—That the company discharge those whom it may have employed to take the place of the men whom it discharged because of their connection with this controversy or who left the company's employ by reason of the union.

Sixth—That the contract between the company and the union be renewed to terminate May 1, 1898 then to be renewed or amended as best suit the mutual interests of both.

Seventh—That the decision of the arbitrator be enforced by both parties within one week from the date thereof.

In view of the complications which have arisen and are likely to arise and with the object of avoiding them in the future and from the part that the system is wrong, the arbitrator recommends that employes who are not employed at the various branches of the brewing business, be required to join the bona fide unions of their trades rather than as now, when plumbers, engineers etc. are members of the Brewery Workman's union.

The task of the arbitrator has not been an easy one. He approached it with misgivings as to his ability to find a way out of which each could accept with honor and advantage. But prompted by a keen sense of duty and fairness to both he has arrived at the above conclusions and decision. With the sincere hope that all will cordially and promptly carry out, both in letter and spirit, the awards rendered, the undersigned begs to remain

Sincerely, Samuel Gompers,

arbitrator.

Mr. Peter Schwab was seen by a *Republican* reporter this morning and asked the question

"What do you think of Mr. Gompers' decision?" He replied, ["]I am satisfied with the decision and more than pleased with it. It sustains the company in the important points that were at stake.

["]Mr. Gompers says in his report that instead of being an enemy of labor, I have at all times been its friend; that the Brewers' union acted hastily declaring the product of our company unfair and we are now placed on the fair list. In regard to the failure on our part to follow certain rules in the contract we entered into with the Brewers' union were unintentional. Such as, reporting to the union any shirking of work, negligence of our employes to give us a fair day's wages. Mr. Gompers' decision is a fair and just one and a vindication for the company. At the same time the tenets of the union have been maintained and from now on we will all work in harmony." Mr. Schwab added, ["]I will say that Mr. Gompers is one of the most fair minded gentlemen I have ever met; he dealt squarely with us and is an honor to the association he represents."[2]

Hamilton (Ohio) *Republican*, Nov. 29, 1897.

1. Jacob Conrad was a Hamilton, Ohio, maltster.

2. Despite the apparent success of SG's arbitration efforts, relations between the local and the company deteriorated over details of the agreement and accusations of bad faith. When the arbitration award expired on May 1, 1898, the firm refused to renew its contract with the union; instead it concluded an agreement with the KOL. When the company rejected SG's request to arbitrate the matter, the AFL Executive Council placed the brewery on the boycott list.

Excerpts from Accounts of the 1897 Convention of the AFL in Nashville

[December 15, 1897]

LABOR MEN ARE GIVEN A BARBECUE[1]

. . .

AFTERNOON SESSION.

. . .

The Committee on Resolutions reported on a resolution offered by T. J. Elderkin,[2] opposing the annexation of the Hawaiian Islands by the United States.[3] The committee offered a substitute as follows:

"Whereas, there is at present pending in the United States Senate a treaty providing for the annexation of the Hawaiian Islands; and,

"Whereas, that annexation would be tantamount to the admission of a slave State, the representatives of which would necessarily work and vote for the enslavement of labor in general; therefore, be it

"Resolved, by the American Federation of Labor that we disapprove of annexation, and,

"Resolved, that we urge the United States Senate to reject the treaty of annexation and to take such other steps as may be necessary to maintain amicable relations with Hawaii."

AGAINST HAWAII'S ANNEXATION.

Andrew Furuseth[4] made a warm speech opposing the annexation, and George E. McNeill[5] suggested that the substitute be amended so as to provide for the incoming Executive Council laying the matter before Congress, and if necessary before the President, showing the opposition of the Federation to the annexation.

The substitute as amended was adopted.

. . .

Nashville American, Dec. 15, 1897.

1. This article, covering the convention proceedings of Dec. 14, 1897, begins with a description of the barbecue held on the evening of Dec. 14 for the delegates to the AFL convention.

2. Thomas Elderkin was a delegate of the International Seamen's Union of America (ISUA).

3. President William McKinley sent the Hawaiian annexation treaty to the Senate in June 1897; it was virtually identical to a treaty proposed but not ratified in 1893 after the overthrow of the Hawaiian monarchy. The Senate did not act on the measure before the outbreak of the Spanish-American War — the annexationists lacked the necessary two-thirds majority — but Congress subsequently approved annexation by joint resolution, which required only a simple majority in each house.

4. Andrew Furuseth was a delegate of the ISUA.
5. George McNeill represented AFL Federal Labor Union 5915 of Boston.

[December 16, 1897][1]

FOURTH DAY—AFTERNOON SESSION.

. . .

Delegate Lloyd[2] offered the following resolution, and asked immediate consideration, which was granted:

Resolved, That the American Federation of Labor reaffirms its declaration that it welcomes to its ranks all labor, without regard to creed, color, sex, race, or nationality, and that its best efforts have been, and will continue to be, to encourage the organization of those most needing its protection, whether they be in the North or the South, the East or the West, white or black, and that we denounce as untrue, and without foundation in fact, the reported statement of Mr. Booker T. Washington,[3] of the Tuskeegee University, to the effect that the trade unions were placing obstacles in the way of the material advancement of the negro, and that we appeal to the records of the conventions of the American Federation of Labor, and especially to the records of the Chicago convention,[4] as the most complete answer to any and all such false assertions.

It was moved that the resolution be concurred in.

Delegate Jones[5] said that the white people of the South would not submit to the employment of the negro in the mills, and said that the union of which he was a member did not admit negroes.[6]

Delegate Gompers said a union affiliated with the American Federation of Labor had no right to debar the negro from membership. The trend of the movement is against cheap workmen. It was a matter of record only yesterday, when it was brought out that the intelligent white workmen had to expend money to educate the textile workers. If we do not give the colored man the opportunity to organize, the capitalist will set him up as a barrier against our progress. Every time we help these men it helps to raise the laborer to a higher plane. It is our purpose to aid and compel organization of the workers. It is not a question as to the color of a man's skin, but the power that lies in organization.

Delegate Lloyd said that he knew no North, no South, no black, no white in the labor movement, and that he came from the home of Wendell Phillips and William Lloyd Garrison,[7] and did not ask our Southern friends to take the negro to their breast, but he did ask them to give to the negro the same bargaining power with capital that we accord to the white workers. The capitalist would be glad to use the black against the white. The only aristocracy that we recognize in the trade union movement is brains and brawn.

Delegate Fahey[8] said he believed that the negro of the South could be educated up to the principles of true trades unionism.[9]

Delegate O'Connell[10] said that the statement of Booker T. Washington, that the trades unions were keeping the blackman in the South down was as absurd as to say that the white man of the North was against the white man of the South. You will find that the negro man of the South is taken to the North to take the places of the white man on strikes. This question at this late day seems to me to be ridiculous. Shall we allow any professor to say that we stand in the way of the elevation of God's common family?

Delegate McGuire[11] stated that the intention of the resolution was simply to set us right before the world and the negro in particular. He said the trades unionists do not keep the white American boy or the black American boy from learning a trade, and claimed that the bulk of the industrial laborers in the South consisted of negroes, and that in trade contests they were just as good as our white brothers.[12]

Delegate Ratchford[13] said that this question affects the unskilled laborer, more than any other. The moment you draw the color line in the American Federation of Labor, you debar the organization which he represents. Is the organized labor of the South in any way responsible for it? He believed it was, to some extent. If you want to legislate against the colored man, legislate him out of the hotels, and let him take the place of the girls in the mills, and put the girls in the hotels.

Delegate Mahon[14] said that the remarks of Delegate Jones were not the sentiment of the trades unions of the South.[15]

Delegate Klapetzky spoke in favor of the resolution.

Delegate Glenn[16] raised the point of order that the time for the special order had arrived to go into executive session.

Delegate Jones demanded the floor.[17]

Delegate Kenehan[18] secured recognition from the Chair,[19] and said that he hoped that every delegate who wished to speak would be heard, and that every Southern brother would have an opportunity to express himself.

Previous question demanded.

The Chair stated that he did not believe that it was necessary, and put the motion and declared it carried, while several members were on the floor demanding recognition.

. . .

AFL, *Proceedings*, 1897, pp. 78-79.

1. Related newspaper coverage of this debate is to be found in the notes.

2. Henry Lloyd represented the United Brotherhood of Carpenters and Joiners of America (UBCJA).

3. Booker Taliaferro Washington (1856-1915), born a Virginia slave, attended Hampton Institute and subsequently taught there from 1879 to 1881. He was appointed superintendent of the newly founded Tuskegee Normal and Industrial Institute in Tuskegee, Ala., in 1881. Washington advocated industrial and agricultural training, thrift, and self-help to promote southern blacks' economic advancement and, at least publicly, disclaimed any interest in social and political equality with whites. With his stress on racial accommodation and individualism, he attracted the support of prominent northern and southern philanthropists and politicians. Throughout 1896 and 1897 he delivered speeches on the subject of industrial labor that charged white trade unionists with barring black workers from skilled positions in shop or factory and with refusing to work or organize with blacks.

4. The 1893 AFL convention in Chicago unanimously adopted P. J. McGuire's resolution reaffirming the labor movement's commitment to organizing workers "irrespective of creed, color, sex, nationality or politics" (AFL, *Proceedings*, 1893, p. 56).

5. Luther C. Jones, a Phoenix City, Ala., clerk, represented AFL Federal Labor Union (FLU) 6877 of Columbus, Ga.

6. According to the *Nashville American*, Jones argued that "the white laborer in the South could not compete with the negro laborer" but admitted that organization of the black workers "would no doubt improve the condition of things materially" (Dec. 17, 1897).

7. William Lloyd Garrison of Boston was a leading abolitionist and editor of the *Liberator*.

8. Charles P. Fahey, a harnessmaker and secretary of the Nashville Trades and Labor Council, represented FLU 6617.

9. The *Nashville American* reported Fahey's remarks as follows: "C. P. Fahey arose and announced himself as a Southern man, well acquainted with the negro's condition, and he did not believe the latter the equal of the white man socially or industrially. He said no one coming from what section he might, would go farther to aid the negro than the Southern man, who was familiar with his condition. Answering the strong expressions of President Gompers, favoring the negro in the labor movement, the speaker was very warm. He stated that the President of the Federation had not revoked the commission of a national organizer who had patronized a non-union white barbershop in preference to a colored shop which was union. The holder of the commission, he said, had been allowed to resign and no publicity had been given the matter except through the local press. As the party in question had been expelled from the Trades and Labor Council for acknowledging that no organization could make him patronize a negro in preference to a white man, the speaker said he did not think President Gompers practiced what he preached. One delegate inquired who the party referred to was, and the answer was Jesse Johnson, President of the Pressmen" (Dec. 17, 1897).

10. James O'Connell, the AFL's third vice-president, represented the International Association of Machinists (IAM).

11. P. J. McGuire was the AFL's first vice-president and represented the UBCJA.

12. The *Nashville American* reported that, in addition to criticizing delegate Jones, McGuire attacked Washington for "attempting to put the negro before the public as the victims of gross injustice and himself as the Moses of the race" (Dec. 17, 1897).

13. M. D. Ratchford represented the United Mine Workers of America.

14. W. D. Mahon represented the Amalgamated Association of Street Railway Employes of America.

15. Mahon reportedly contended that Jones "was not a representative of Southern trades unionism, but had only lately entered the movement" (*Nashville American*, Dec. 17, 1897).

16. S. B. Glenn, organizer for the IAM and a member of IAM 92 of Kansas City, Mo., represented the IAM.

17. The *Nashville American* reported Jones's remarks as follows: "Mr. Jones asked that the privilege be allowed him to say something in his own defense. He declared that he did not oppose the negro, but he did say that the negro laborer was lower than the white. He mentioned a case in Atlanta where a concern had employed negroes and the white employes had struck, but the sentiment of the public had fallen with the strikers. He admitted that he had only recently entered the movement, but he declared that he had a right to speak. He concluded by asking if there was any effort made in the East to organize the Chinese who came in conflict with union labor" (Dec. 17, 1897).

18. Roady Kenehan represented the International Union of Journeymen Horseshoers of the United States and Canada.

19. The *Nashville American* reported that Samuel Yarnell, a representative of the UBCJA, was chairing the convention at this point (Dec. 17, 1897).

[December 18, 1897][1]

MANY REPORTS

. . .

MORNING SESSION.

. . .

Whereas, The working people of the United States and the American Federation of Labor are on record as in favor of the formal recognition by the United States Congress of the fact that a state of war exists in the island of Cuba; and,

Whereas, The President of the United States and all the members of Congress were elected on party platforms pledging them such recognition; and,

Whereas, The policy of delay on the part of the present Administration has reached the point where discretion ceases to be a virtue and become national cowardice and disgrace; therefore be it

Resolved, That it is the sense of this convention that the United States Congress should waste no more time in useless debate and diplomatic chicanery, but should take such immediate action as may tend to put an end to the indiscriminate murder of the common people of Cuba by Spanish soldiery.

The committee[2] reported that the action had been taken at Cincinnati[3] and the resolution was useless. An amendment was offered indorsing the action taken at the last meeting. Andrew Furuseth made a speech opposing a war with Spain, which he thought would result if the Government took up for Cuba.

Edward Moore[4] said that the slaves of America should be freed before liberating those of Cuba was attempted. He spoke of excesses here, and the wrongs which, he said, were unrighted in this country. If it were assured, he continued, that the working people of Cuba would be made free, he would be willing to [have] a war with Spain.

Cuba Libre Humbug.

Delegate Miller[5] said that the sufferings of the American working people were greater than those in Cuba, and if a war came up with Spain, the burden would fall upon the laboring class. He was glad that the occasion offered itself for the debate, so that the delegates could express their ideas of what he thought was humbuggery.

Thomas Crosby[6] thought that the Cubans deserved liberty and did not think that a war would follow by recognizing their struggles for liberty. If a war did follow, he said, the Americans should remember their own struggle for liberty.

P. F. Doyle[7] arose and quietly said that the American labor movement was a movement of peace, and there was no peace where there was not liberty. He spoke for Cuban independence from the yoke of Spain.

Thomas I. Kidd[8] declared that he was very sorry to note a jingo sentiment which was growing in the country. He was not sure that a change for the Cubans to the rule of the American speculator would be preferable to the Spanish yoke.

Ernest Krepp[9] declared that if any one show him where the advantage to the Cuban wage-earners would be he would change his opinions, but as it was he was opposed to taking a step that looked as if it would involve the United States in a war that would no doubt be taken up by some other European power.

American Freedom First.

Robert Askew[10] said that his position was if he went to war to go to fight his own battles. First of all he was anxious to see the American wage-worker free.

Others spoke upon the subject and John F. Tobin[11] offered the following substitute:

"Resolved, that it be the sense of the convention that Cuba have industrial freedom from which will follow political freedom."

A motion was made to lay the substitute upon the table and the question was asked if such a procedure would carry the entire matter with it. The answer involved an appeal from the decision of the chair, which was withdrawn and an appeal taken by another delegate.[12] Finally it was decided that tabling the substitute would table the entire matter. The roll call upon tabling the substitute followed. Before the result was announced noon came and adjournment was taken.

AFTERNOON SESSION.

. . .

The vote upon the morning motion was announced as 854 for and 1,394 against laying the Cuban matter on the table.

The question of the substitute offered by Mr. Tobin was then called for. This was brought before the convention and the vote taken, and the substitute lost.

A motion which had been made by G. H. Warner,[13] and which reiterated the position taken at Cincinnati, was put to a vote and carried.

. . .

Nashville American, Dec. 18, 1897.

1. Covering the proceedings of Dec. 17, 1897.

2. That is, the Committee on Resolutions, reporting on resolution 117 on the subject of Cuba.

3. See "Third Day's Work," Dec. 17, 1896, in "Excerpts from News Accounts of the 1896 Convention of the AFL in Cincinnati," above.

4. Edward S. Moore, a Philadelphia hatter, represented the United Hatters of North America.

5. Owen MILLER, president of the American Federation of Musicians (1896-1900), represented that organization.

6. Thomas Crosby, a New Britain, Conn., printer, represented the Connecticut state branch of the AFL.

7. Peter F. DOYLE, a Chicago stationary engineer, represented the National Union of Steam Engineers. He was secretary-treasurer of the Chicago Federation of Labor and the Illinois State Federation of Labor.

8. Thomas Kidd represented the Amalgamated Wood Workers' International Union.

9. Ernst Kreft, a member of International Typographical Union 2 of Philadelphia, represented the Philadelphia United Labor League; he was president of the League between 1895 and 1897.

10. Robert Askew represented the Northern Mineral Mine Workers' Progressive Union.

11. John Tobin was a delegate of the Boot and Shoe Workers' Union.

12. Thomas J. Murphy, a Boston blacksmith, member of Journeymen Horseshoers' International Union of the United States and Canada 5, and president of the Boston Central Labor Union (CLU); he was the CLU's delegate.

13. George H. Warner represented the International Association of Machinists.

[December 19, 1897][1]

UNDER ITS OLD REGIME

. . .

MORNING SESSION.

. . .

Upon a resolution referred to the committee[2] instructing the President of the Federation not to insert in the Federationist any advertising matter coming from a non-union firm or corporation, the report was unfavorable for the stated reason that the adoption of such a measure would almost prohibit the receipt of advertisements for the journal. A motion to non-concur was lost and the committee report accepted.

EMIGRATION QUESTION.

The hour of 9:30 o'clock selected for making a special order of the immigration question having arrived, the recommendations of the committee were read. The report recommended that the Federation indorse a reasonable measure of restriction on the lines of an educational test as contained in the Lodge bill that failed of enactment in Congress last year. This step was advised in view of the result of votes taken by those organizations that complied with the instructions of the Cincinnati convention.[3] A resolution calling for the absolute suspension of immigration for a period of five years was unfavorably considered by the committee, as was a resolution opposing restriction.

A motion was made that the report be adopted. This brought on much discussion, in which a telling speech in favor of immigration was made by Henry Lloyd, though he announced that he was bound as delegate from the carpenters to vote otherwise.

C. H. Myers[4] spoke against immigration. He said he agreed with the words he had heard from Delegate Ratchford that what was breaking the backs of the miners of the country was the influx of those low-priced foreigners who lived by maintaining a standard of civilization below that of the American workman.

M. D. Ratchford said he hoped the better judgment of the convention would vote for the restriction of immigration along educational lines.

August Priesterberback[5] said it was the capitalist who feared immigration, that is the educated class of immigration. He said if such a step had been taken fifteen years ago many of those in the convention might have been in the old country at the time he was speaking.

BLIND IN THE FACE OF LABOR.

Samuel Yarnell pronounced the talk of the restriction of immigration a blind in the face of labor, put there by the politicians of both parties. He was opposed to any further action toward the restriction of immigration.

Edward Moore said that he was always willing to take those foreigners who come over to this country with a trades union card, but those who tended to lower the standard of living he was opposed to receiving. He declared himself a practical trade unionist in the matter.

Roady Kenehan declared that restriction was hypocrisy. If the resolution was carried he thought it would be well to stop sending fraternal delegates to England if the men of that country were to be kept out just because they were not educated up to American citizenship.

M. M. Garland[6] said that many of the members of the convention dared not go back home unless they voted for some kind of restriction. He announced that the sentimentalism which had been uttered in the convention might move the new delegates but the votes of the large organizations would carry the report.

A vote was taken upon the full recommendation of the committee regarding the emigration question. The roll was called and the result announced later.

. . .

AFTERNOON SESSION.

. . .

The announcement of the vote on the immigration question was made as 1,842 for and 352 against.[7]

The election was then taken up. . . .[8]

. . .

Nashville American, Dec. 19, 1897.

1. Covering the proceedings of Dec. 18, 1897.

2. The Committee on the President's Report.

3. The committee reported that affiliates responding to the AFL's poll on the subject favored immigration restriction and the convention adopted the committee's

proposals for restrictive legislation. See "Its Labor Ended," Dec. 22, 1896, in "Excerpts from News Accounts of the 1896 Convention of the AFL in Cincinnati," above.

4. Charles H. Myers, a member of the Granite Cutters' National Union, past president (1894) and secretary (1895) of the Baltimore Federation of Labor (FL), and chief of the Bureau of Labor Statistics in Maryland (1896-97), represented the Baltimore FL.

5. August Priestersbach (variously Priesterbach), a St. Louis driver and secretary of the Beer Drivers' and Stablemen's Union—local 43 of the National Union of the United Brewery Workmen of the United States (NUUBW)—represented the NUUBW.

6. Mahlon M. Garland was AFL fourth vice-president and represented the National Amalgamated Association of Iron, Steel, and Tin Workers.

7. The proceedings record the vote as 1,858 to 352.

8. The officers elected by the convention to serve during the following year were SG, president; P. J. McGuire, James Duncan, James O'Connell, and M. M. Garland, first through fourth vice-presidents; John B. Lennon, treasurer; and Frank Morrison, secretary.

[December 21, 1897][1]

. . .

MORNING SESSION.

. . .

. . . The committee[2] made a report in reference to a letter received from the W.C.T.U.[3] asking that the Federation pronounce against intemperance as a foe to the labor movement. The report stated that though the committee thought that temperance would be a material aid to the advancement of the movement it was not deemed an essential. The committee extended thanks to the temperance organization for its good wishes which the letter had expressed.

DIDN'T USE THE LABEL.

T. D. Fitzgerald[4] asked if it was true that the W.C.T.U. did not use the label of the Allied Printing Trades upon its printing. It seemed to be the impression that such was the case and after some discussion Delegate Crosby moved that the report of the committee be amended so as to convey the information to the W.C.T.U. that the employment on its part of union men would tend to secure the co-operation of organized labor in the cause of temperance. The amendment was adopted.

. . .

Afternoon Session.

. . .

The report of the Committee on Resolutions was then continued. The first resolution reported on was the one indorsing independent political action. The resolution offered by P. J. McGuire was as follows:

"Resolved, that the American Federation of Labor most firmly and unequivocally favors the independent use of the ballot by the trades unionists and workingmen, united regardless of party, that we may elect men from our own ranks to make new laws and administer them along the lines laid down in the legislative demands of the American Federation of Labor, and at the same time secure an impartial judiciary that will not govern us by arbitrary injunctions of the courts, nor act as the pliant tools of corporate wealth.

"Resolved, that as our efforts are centered against all forms of industrial slavery and economic wrong, we must also direct our utmost energies to remove all forms of political servitude and party slavery, to the end that the working people may act as a unit at the polls at every election."

The committee reported upon the resolution favorably and a motion to table it was lost.

Amendment Was Lost.

Ernest Kreft then offered an amendment to it designating the lines along which legislation would be favorable. The amendment advocated in substance collective ownership and declared against the present wage system.

The amendment was lost.

Mr. McGuire said in behalf of his resolution that to be independent in politics one must not be partisan. He was for clean cut labor without any isms that would take in every man who was willing to stand for a fair day's work and a fair day's pay.

James Brennock,[5] the oldest delegate in the convention, arose and declared with some feeling that he had always longed to see the day when the labor men would awake to their opportunities and use the ballot. He expressed the belief that if legislation was passed favorable to the whole people, that the labor men could take care of themselves.

Mr. McGuire said he did not believe in the establishment of a new party, that the labormen should assist legislation favoring the laboring class and finally it would come together just as the Republican party had on the question of the abolition of slavery.

"We've got to be cautious, moderate and reasonable," he declared.

A CRISIS APPROACHING.

Samuel Yarnell said he knew of no resolution in which he took more interest. He thought that the country was approaching a crisis as parlous as any that had risen during the century and it would effect not only the present generation, but generations yet unborn. "We must choose," he said, "between a monarchy ruled by unscrupulous men, or a republic governed by the people."

The resolution was then put to a vote and adopted.

. . .

Nashville American, Dec. 21, 1897.

1. Covering the proceedings of Dec. 20, 1897.
2. The Committee on Resolutions.
3. The Woman's Christian Temperance Union.
4. Thomas D. Fitzgerald, an Albany, N.Y., printer and Democratic alderman-elect, was a member of International Typographical Union 4 and president of the Allied Printing Trades Council of New York. He represented the New York State Branch of the AFL.
5. James Brennock, a Chicago carpenter, was treasurer of United Brotherhood of Carpenters and Joiners 1; he represented the Chicago Federation of Labor.

An Article in the *Nashville American*

St. Louis, Dec. 21 [1897]

AGAINST THE FEDERATION.

The National Building Trades Council[1] was permanently organized to-day. The delegates deeply resent the alleged unseemly action[2] of the American Federation of Labor in condemning the object of their meeting,[3] and with the apparent idea of meeting the Federation on a common footing, have decided to hold the next annual meeting[4] in Kansas City, in December, 1898, one week before the meeting of the American Federation of Labor,[5] in the same city. Officers were elected as follows: President, Edward Carroll,[6] Chicago; Vice Presidents, Theo. S. Jones,[7] Kansas City; J. P. Healy,[8] Washington; A. J. Franz[9] and J. F. Harvey,[10] Milwaukee; M. P. Garrick, Pittsburg; C. S. Leveling,[11] East St. Louis; Secretary and Treasurer, W. H. Steinbiss,[12] St. Louis.

Nashville American, Dec. 22, 1897.

1. The National Building Trades Council of America (NBTCA; after 1904 the International Building Trades Council of America) was formed to help the frag-

mented, locally based building trades councils achieve uniform wage scales and working conditions. It consisted of local councils, national and international unions—notably of painters, plasterers, electrical workers, and steam fitters—and independent local unions. SG attacked the NBTCA as a dual organization, and most national building trades unions shunned it because its structure favored local bodies. By 1903 dissatisfaction among major NBTCA affiliates and a growing desire by national and international building trades unions for a new body reflecting their interests led to the founding, in October, of the Structural Building Trades Alliance (SBTA). The Council was considerably weakened by defections to the SBTA, but apparently continued its formal existence until 1912.

2. On Dec. 18, 1897, the AFL convention approved a resolution by Henry Lloyd against the formation of a national building trades council.

3. The founding convention of the NBTCA was held in St. Louis, Dec. 20-22, 1897.

4. The 1898 convention of the NBTCA met in Kansas City, Mo., Dec. 12-16.

5. The 1898 AFL convention met in Kansas City, Mo., Dec. 12-20.

6. Edward CARROLL, a Chicago plasterer, was secretary-treasurer of the Operative Plasterers' International Association of the United States and Canada (1894-98) and president of the Chicago Building Trades Council (BTC; 1896-1900). He served as president of the NBTCA from 1897 to 1898.

7. Theodore S. JONES, a Kansas City, Mo., carpenter and municipal street inspector, was the NBTCA's vice-president (1897-98), president (1898-99), and vice-president again beginning in 1899.

8. John P. Healy was a member of Washington, D.C., Bricklayers' and Masons' International Union 1. He worked as a technical employee and as a building inspector for the District of Columbia between 1902 and 1921.

9. Henry J. Fanz was a Toledo, Ohio, tinsmith in the 1890s and early 1900s and was a member of Amalgamated Sheet Metal Workers' International Association 6.

10. James F. Harvey worked in Milwaukee as a brakeman and then an ironworker until at least 1909.

11. Probably C. J. Leveling, who served as president of the East St. Louis BTC in 1898 and 1899.

12. Herman W. STEINBISS was a St. Louis painter and member of Brotherhood of Painters and Decorators 46.

From Lyman Gage[1]

Treasury Department
Office of the Secretary
Washington, Dec. 22, 1897.

Dear Sir:

I have read with care the resolutions adopted the 20th instant at Nashville by the convention of the Federation of Labor, which recite as follows:

"Resolved, That we declare ourselves most positively opposed to the Gage financial bill[2] recently introduced in Congress by the Secretary of the Treasury. It is a measure that, if adopted as a law, will only the more firmly rivet the gold standard on the people of this country and perpetuate its disastrous effects in every form."

"Resolved, That we pronounce the Gage bill an undisguised effort to retire our greenback currency and all Government paper money, with a view to the substitution of National Bank notes in their stead, and thus fasten the National Bank system for years upon the American people."

Now if it be true that the Gold Standard—by which things have been measured as to price for the last sixty years in this country is inimical to the interests of the laboring classes of the United States—then I think it is inimical to all classes. In other words I do not believe that the exploitation of one class by another, either through false weights, partial laws, or a bad monetary system, can be made to work for the permanent benefit of the exploiting class itself, or for the general weal, even were it defensible on any ground of right or justice, which it is not. Granted, therefore, that the permanence of the gold standard (for which I argue) operates in this evil direction, then your resolutions of condemnation are well founded, and I am justly charged, either with an ignorance which constitutes me a foolish adviser, or with a perversity of motive which makes me an evil adviser.

I have a right to disavow the charge of perversity or evil purpose, since there is nothing in my whole life as related to my fellow men, either in word or deed, from which the possession by me of such characteristics can be inferred, much less demonstrated.

But ignorance often works unconsciously as deep injury as evil intent might do and to this sin of ignorance (if it be a sin) I must confess myself to be a possible victim. This confession, however, ought not to classify me as separate from my fellow men generally, whether they be considered as individual units or as congregated in groups. Ignorance is a relative, not an absolute term, since few are totally ignorant, and none is absolutely wise. Nor does the number constituting the group change this fact, since the wisdom of a group, however large, can not be greater than that of the wisest man in it.

This remains true whether the subject matter involving knowledge and judgment be astronomy, physics, or finance. The condemnation then involved in the resolutions referred to is measured by the just or imperfect apprehension of questions relating to monetary science held by the wisest men who supported them.

Laying these general considerations aside, let me say to you, and through you to the great body you so honorably represent, that if instead of denunciatory resolutions, which are not argument, you or any one on your behalf will show that the views I entertain and advocate are other than salutary to the great economic body of which we are all independent members, I will abandon them without hesitation. My present conviction, the honest fruit of sincere study and reflection, is that a breakdown in our present money standard would be a most disastrous blow to all our commercial and industrial interests, and that upon the wage workers, as a class, would be entailed the most serious effects of the disaster. Believing this I must so bear witness.

Respectfully yours,   Lyman J. Gage

TLpSr, William McKinley Papers, DLC.

1. Lyman Judson Gage, a Chicago banker, served as secretary of the U.S. Treasury from 1897 until 1902.

2. Gage drafted a comprehensive financial bill introduced in the House of Representatives as H.R. 5181 (55th Cong., 2d sess.) by Joseph H. Walker of Massachusetts on Dec. 16, 1897. It was designed to guarantee that holders of paper money issued by the government could redeem it for gold and silver coin and bullion. The bill was referred to committee and failed to pass.

To William McKinley

December 28th. [1897]

Hon. William McKinley,
President of the United States,
Washington, D.C.
Dear Sir:

Pursuant to instructions of the Convention of the American Federation of Labor held at Nashville, Tennessee, December 13-21, 1897, the undersigned were directed to transmit the enclosed petition and protest to you. In accordance therewith we have the honor to transmit the same herein, and trust that it may receive your favorable consideration.

We have the honor to remain,

Yours very respectfully,   Saml Gompers.
President   A.F. of L.
Attest: Frank Morrison
Secretary.

To the President of the United States:

At a convention of the American Federation of Labor, held at Nashville, Tennessee, this the 16th day of December, 1897, consisting of delegates from more than 500,000 organized workmen from all parts of this Union, it was unanimously

Resolved, That the rumored contemplated appointment of Edward M. Paxson[1] to be a member of the Interstate Commerce Commission has caused the most serious apprehensions among members of the American Federation of Labor, and may well arouse a protest from every friend of organized labor throughout the country.

Resolved, That the appointment of this man to the position named would be most unfortunate and unfit:

1. In view of his record while Associate Justice and Chief Justice of the Supreme Court of Pennsylvania, during a period of nearly twenty years, where a line of his opinions show a persistent leaning and bias in favor of corporate power and greed.

2. In view of that infamous charge to the grand jury in reference to the labor troubles at Homestead, Pa.[2]

3. In view of his conduct while one of the receivers of the Philadelphia and Reading Railroad, where he countenanced, upheld, and defended a tyrannical rule of that Company, forbidding any of its employes to continue to be or become a member of any body of organized labor, and commanding the members of the several labor unions along the line of said road to hand in the charters of their unions to the general manager of the Company.

4. And for other reasons which show his unfitness for a position which calls for the occupant to stand between the employer and the employee.

And the undersigned officers of the American Federation of Labor are requested to transmit the same to you.

Saml Gompers.
President   American Federation of Labor.
Attest: Frank Morrison
Secretary.

TLpS, reel 14, vol. 22, pp. 217-19, SG Letterbooks, DLC.

1. Edward M. Paxson, a retired jurist, was a Pennsylvania Supreme Court justice (1874-89) and chief justice (1889-93). He served as a receiver of the Philadelphia and Reading Railroad from 1893 to 1896. Paxson was not appointed to the Interstate Commerce Commission.

2. See *Unrest and Depression*, p. 233, n. 2.

To Lyman Gage

December 29th. [1897]

Hon. Lyman J. Gage,
Secretary of the Treasury,
Washington, D.C.
Dear Sir:

I have the honor to acknowledge receipt of your courteous and interesting favor of the 22nd inst.[1] in which you quote the resolutions adopted by the Nashville Convention of the American Federation of Labor in regard to the financial bill which you prepared, and which at your suggestion was introduced in Congress.

You take exception both to the position which our organization has taken upon your bill, as well as the language employed. Even if you are justified in the one, you certainly misapprehend the other.

The resolutions declare ourselves "most positively opposed to the Gage financial bill," and "we pronounce the Gage bill an undisguised effort to retire our greenback currency and all government paper money, with a view to the substitution of national bank notes in their stead." I submit that you will seek in vain for a single denunciatory word either in regard to your motives, your plan, or your bill. We realize that denunciation is not argument, but to declare our position and the statement of a fact in regard to a most important and far-reaching measure, affecting and changing the financial system of our country, can by no means be construed as denunciation.

Those resolutions declare against your plan for more thoroughly committing our country to the gold standard, a plan for destroying our greenback currency and substituting bank notes, a plan in fact for weakening the control of the national government over that most important of all measures, the measure of values, and strengthening the banks, a plan, aiming at what you call "currency reform," and which we call "bank monopoly."

That you should take offense at these resolutions I regret, for the right to express disapproval of the acts of their servants is one of the rights held sacred by the American people and one you will freely accord. To deny that right is to deny the people a voice in their own government. We do not question your right to give expression to your views neither should you question our right to dissent from them.

We do not charge you with "ignorance, relative or absolute," or allege any "evil purpose," or a "perversity of motive" on your part, as implied in your letter, nor upon rereading the resolutions will you find them either condemnatory or denunciatory, as you say they are. The resolutions are declaratory of the views of the American Federation of Labor, and are entirely impersonal, for of all men in public life, we have the greatest respect for your probity and integrity.

It is true that the resolutions referred to contain no argument in support of our declarations. But I would remind you that it is not customary to look to resolutions for argument anymore than it is customary to look in our statute books for arguments in support of the laws contained therein. Resolutions are meant to announce the opinions of the body adopting them.

The wage-earners of America represented in the American Federation of Labor, believe that the position you have taken in regard to the retirement of our greenback currency is antagonistic to their interests, and they are opposed to your plan for more thoroughly committing this country of ours to the gold standard.

The first of the resolutions of which you complain declares that your currency bill "is a measure that, if adopted as a law, will only the more firmly rivet the gold standard on the people of the country and perpetuate its disastrous effects in every form." It is only the latter part of this resolution to which you can take exception. You deny that the perpetuation of the gold standard at which you aim would have any disastrous effects, you declare that if it can be shown to you that the maintenance of the gold standard has been inimical to the interests of our people you will abandon your plan for perpetuating this system, you ask what evils have resulted from our adherence to the gold standard. I answer that the evils are those that have grown and ever must grow from a dishonest measure of values, a measure of values that interferes with the just distribution of wealth, that deprives some men of a part of their earnings that is rightly theirs, and confers it upon others who have earned it not. Any measure of values that thus forces an unjust distribution of the products of labor, that deprives producers of the fruits of their toil, cuts down wages and profits, thereby destroys the incentive to enterprise, leads to industrial stagnation, enforced idleness, distress, and public suffering.

The products of labor are divided into three general shares. One share goes as interest and rents to the money lender and landlord, to capitalists who do not productively use their own capital, who seek to avoid the risks of production. A second share goes as profits to employers, a third share goes as wages to wage earners. The interest charges and rents, in short the shares of the money lender and landlord, are to a great degree fixed, fixed in terms of dollars, and profits and wages, the shares of employer and wage earner, are subject to great fluctuations. This being so it is clear that anything that reduces the total money value of the products of labor must increase the share of the money lender and creditor though nominally fixed and decrease the share to be divided among employers and wage earners. It is equally clear that to increase the value of money must decrease the value of the products of labor and therefore enrich the creditor at the expense of the debtor, unjustly enrich the money lender at the expense of employer and wage-earner.

Now if our adherence to the gold standard has caused money to grow dearer you must admit that the gold standard has done injury to our people, brought distress to wage earners, and employers, and discouraged enterprise. Our adherence to the gold standard has caused money to grow in value, and, of course, forced the things measured in money to fall in price. This you may deny. But during the twenty years 1872-1891 prices, gold prices, fell in general 27½%. This is shown by the exhaustive tables to be found in Senate Report #1394, Second Session, 52nd Congress, — tables showing the movement in prices in the United States. Prices have in general further fallen since 1891. Now you may urge that this fall in prices and increased purchasing power of gold was due not to an increasing value of gold, but to general improvement, and a general cheapening of production. But admitting it was: did this make the rise in the purchasing power of gold right and just? Clearly with such rise the creditor classes with fixed incomes, classes that seek to shift the uncertainties of business upon other shoulders, have had their incomes increased, and suppose this increase has come from a cheapening of production and not a rise in gold, what have these creditors done to earn it? Nothing, absolutely nothing. It is the enterprise of the employer, the ingenuity of the wage earner that has brought about the cheapening of production, and they and they alone are entitled to the benefits of those efforts. However, it is not alone to a cheapening of the labor cost of production, but also to an actual appreciation of gold that the fall in prices since 1872 has been in great part due. And this appreciation has grown out of the demonetization of silver which has increased the demands for gold. This is a question that every producer can answer: has the fall in prices curtailed my earnings? If the fall in prices has been due only to general improved methods of production, a lessening in the true cost of production, he has suffered no loss from such fall. Moreover, the fall in prices since 1893, a fall in prices common to all gold-using countries, a fall in prices of 20%, has not grown out of improvement in machinery exclusively; that the labor cost of production has not been increased by one-fifth in these past four years and that therefore the cause of this fall in prices must lie, in what: if not in dearer money, and was due primarily to an appreciation in gold.

To one or two circumstances, however, I want to direct your attention, for if you ponder over them with due weight you will not claim that movements in prices are solely due to inventions of labor saving machinery, economics in production, cheapening of the means of transportation and that changes in the value of money have nothing to do with the movements of prices. Changes in the value of money have largely influenced the movements of prices during the last half century and were great factors in the price movements during one long period. During the quarter of a century following the gold discoveries in California there was much progress in the line of invention, much introduction of labor saving machinery, much cheapening in the labor cost of production. This on your theory should have caused steadily falling prices. But what happened? The outpouring of gold from the Californian and Australian gold fields cheapened gold, cheapened gold to a greater degree than commodities were cheapened and the result was that prices were in general 30% higher at the end of this period than at the beginning. Then what happened? We, along with many other nations, closed our mints to silver. We increased the demand for gold with the result that gold went up in value and prices of commodities down. You must abandon the advocacy of gold mono-metallism, unless you can show that the demonetization of silver and the doubling of the demand for gold resultant therefrom, has not caused gold to grow dearer and prices lower to the great injury of all producers of wealth. You should at least show that the perpetuation of the gold standard will not result in making money dearer and human flesh cheaper.

And now just one word as to the second of the resolutions to which you take exception adopted at the recent Convention of the American Federation of Labor. This resolution declares, and you admit it, that the purpose of your currency bill is to cause the retirement of our national greenback currency and all government paper money and the substitution of bank notes. This you hold to be desirable. Why? Would it not give the banks the power to regulate our foreign exchanges, the power to check gold exports by contraction and by screwing down accommodation to merchants so as to force them to throw their products on the market at prices at which our foreign creditors would rather take such products than our gold? Would it not thus relieve the Treasury of the burden of providing for gold redemptions, and make the banks supreme? This we hold to be undesirable. It would make the banks guardian over our volume of money and so of our measure of values; it would enable the banks working in the interest of the speculators to cause movements in prices with great certainty, enable them to depress prices by contracting the currency and raise prices by expanding the same. It would thus enable the few directing the banks to take advantage of the many, enable the few to enter into a gamble with the producers of wealth with the surplus products of labor as the stake and enter that game with loaded dice. In a word it would make the banks the masters, the many the slaves, and would enrich the few and impoverish the multitude.

In the statement you recently made before the House Committee on Banking and Currency in support of your bill you say, and repeat this truism, "That the less the Government owes, the less it will have to pay." Yet your plan involves the proposition of the retirement of our national paper currency and greenbacks, upon which we pay no interest at all, and the issuance of bonds in its stead in the sum of $200,000,000, which we shall owe, and upon which we shall be required to pay interest. The inconsistency of your statement and your plan seems glaring.

We oppose your currency bill because as has been well said, it is "a bill to provide for the abdication of the sovereign powers of the government to the banks, for strengthening the hands of the speculative cliques, enriching the few and impoverishing the many."

Very respectfully yours, Saml Gompers.
President American Federation of Labor.

TLpS, reel 14, vol. 22, pp. 226-33, SG Letterbooks, DLC.

1. Above.

To Henry Mills

Jany. 6th. [189]8

Mr. H. S. Mills,
Secretary, National Union of Textile
  Workers of America, A.F. of L.
#161 Division street; New Bedford, Mass.
Dear Sir & Brother: —

I am in receipt of a letter from our organizer, J. E. Courtney,[1] of Atlanta, Ga., in which he speaks of the awful struggle[2] in which the members of the Textile Workers Union #122, of that city, are engaged. He says that people are suffering from cold and hunger and that in spite of this fact having taken a secret ballot after the votes were counted there were only 12 out of 270 in favor of giving up the fight. He says that these people require assistance at the earliest possible moment in order that they may be enabled to maintain the fight and I desire to impress its importance upon you and the members of your Executive Board and in fact upon all in the textile industry. I understand that there is an effort being made by the corporations in your industry to reduce wages among the Eastern workmen and the excuse given for this offer of reduction is because of the cheap labor of the textile workers of the South. There are one of two alternatives which the Eastern textile workers now have; either to support the textile workers of the South who are now engaged in the struggle to either maintain or increase wages, or on the other hand for themselves be compelled to enter into the struggle to prevent reductions in their own wages. Self interest of the plainest character should prompt every textile worker in the New England States to contribute financ[ially to] the best of their ability in order to maintain these people[. . . .] If the people in the South [win this battle] your road will be a much smoother one to travel and it may prevent struggle and sacrifice the ending of which we can not now foresee. I believe it the duty of yourself and colleagues to take this matter up at once and vigorously inaugurate a campaign that shall solicit and secure sufficient financial assistance for the Atlanta textile workers as shall break the domineering and absolute rule of the Southern corporations in the textile industries and encourage the workers in order that they may win this first conflict and make future inroads upon their interests impossible. I would suggest, too, that you call upon Bro. Samuel Ross,[3] P.O. Box #367, New Bedford, Mass., of the Spinners National Union, consult with him in regard to the matter and I am sure that both his experience as well as his position will prompt him to co-operate with you to attain the desired result. Should you see him, and I wish you will at an early date, you may show him this letter as expressing my view of the situation.

The Union there, I understand, complains that out of the small amount which the A.F. of L. convention was enabled to donate in their aid they had to pay $35.00 for the expenses of President Green which they believe should have been borne by the National Union. They claim certainly that it should not have been taken from them when a few dollars will go so far to protect their interests. I know nothing of the matter of my own knowledge except that which is communicated to me for the purpose of advising you.

I again urge that every action will be taken by you and your colleagues to grapple manfully and heroically with the situation which is presented. It is an opportunity which may be fraught with great results to the advantage or interest or injury of your entire industry.

Hoping to hear from you at an early date I am,

Fraternally yours, Saml Gompers.

President A.F. of L.

TLpS, reel 14, vol. 22, pp. 290-91, SG Letterbooks, DLC.

1. James E. Courtney was an Atlanta tinner.

2. The Atlanta textile workers' strikes in late 1897 reflected the racial divisions among the city's workers. On Aug. 4 two hundred women and girls walked out of the Fulton Bag and Cotton Mill Co. in protest against the company's hiring twenty black women; four hundred men joined them in sympathy. The following day the company agreed to discharge the black workers and the strikers returned to work. A second strike began on Dec. 6, however, when the company fired several employees after a dispute over a pay cut. By Dec. 9 it involved some one thousand employees under the leadership of National Union of Textile Workers 122 of Atlanta and the Atlanta Federation of Trades. A mass meeting in support of the strikers on Dec. 15 claimed "the issue at stake means either the reduction of white labor to a level of social equality with negro labor, or the supplanting entirely of white labor by negro labor" and pledged aid "to the end that white supremacy may prevail" (*Atlanta Constitution*, Dec. 16, 1897). The strike ended in defeat for the workers in January 1898.

3. Samuel Ross served intermittently as secretary of the National Cotton Mule Spinners' Association of America (and of the organization as it was subsequently renamed) between 1891 and 1911. He was also a Republican member of the Massachusetts legislature (1892-99 and 1902-14).

To Samuel Ross

Jan. 19, [189]8

Mr. Samuel Ross,

Secretary Nat'l Cotton Mule Spinners Ass'n of America,

New Bedford, Mass.

Dear Sir and Brother:

Your favor of the 16th inst. to hand, and contents noted. I am obliged to you for the report you make in regard to your visit to the Textile Workers who are now on strike at Atlanta, Ga. It is a very interesting report, and indicates more thoroughly than ever the fact that without a fairly well organized Union, the workers are likely to be too easily moulded by impulses and persisted influences by those who have too little experience to guide them to practical action. More especially is this so, when the workers are engaged in the controversy with their employers, no matter how justified the causes are in which the people are engaged. I do not know how the strike has terminated for they have not kept me informed, within this past week or so. I understand that there was quite some little complaint in regard to Brother Green charging the Atlanta local for the expenses incurred in his trip, the money coming out of the appropriation by the Nashville Convention. Of course I do not know as to what basis there is to the complaint, and I have endeavored to show to our Atlanta friends that the action by Brother Green was not in any other light but in their own interest.

Of course I have noted the great strike[1] in which the members of your Union, as well as workers in other parts of [the] Textile Industry, are engaged. It is a splendid manifestation of independence, and I trust may prove entirely successful in turning the tables, that is, instead of accepting a reduction of wages, the fining system shall be abolished. I see by this morning's papers that our friend, Mrs. Eva McDonald Valesh is in New Bedford, the special representative of the New York Journal. Reading it in the papers is the first intimation that I have of the fact. I knew that she was on the Journal, for as a matter of fact, I was instrumental in aiding her to get that position, but the reason I write this is that you may trust her implicitly, and I feel sure that if you should suggest a matter to her which ought not to be published, she will not violate that injunction or request. Of course you are aware that she is a most excellent public speaker, as well as a good writer, and her heart is right in accord with pure Trade Unionism. I shall write her[2] by this mail, but do not know where she is stopping. For that reason, if you should see her, please ask her to make inquiries at the Post-office for the letter, if it has not already reached her. I am exceedingly pleased to learn that the Carders[3] and Loom Fixers[4] are acting in accord with you, and I trust that the trick the Companies are trying to apply, that is to divide workers in the different branches of the Industry, will not be successful, and that common cause will be made. If success is achieved in this controversy, it will mean a more thorough organization of the Weavers and workers of other branches of the Textile trade. It will give the movement such an impetus that will be of great advantage all over. You ask me whether I cannot make arrangements to come to New Bedford to address the public meeting. Let me say in answer that I shall deem it not only my duty, but a pleasure to do all that I possibly can to help to victory, and if you and your colleagues conducting this contest, think I can be of some service in aiding you by my presence in the future meeting, I want you to feel assured that I will come at the shortest possible notice. I only ask, however, that you may advise me sufficiently in advance, (if you have the time) so that it may entail the least possible disarrangement of our regular work.

Inclosed you will find a commission as organizer for the Textile Industries of the United States. This, I believe, will cover the jurisdiction you desire, and will be ample for all purposes. I herein inclose Manual of Common Procedure, which you will use in the work. Under separate cover I mail to your address, a number of blank applications for charters, and a number of other documents which will help you in the work.

I inclose you herewith check for $36.60 for your expenses incurred in your trip to Atlanta.

Please sign inclosed receipt, and accompany it by a bill, same as enumerated in your letter. Forward bill to this office at your earliest convenience.

Again sincerely expressing my hope for success in your movement, I am,

Fraternally yours,   Saml Gompers.

President   A.F. of L.

TLpS, reel 14, vol. 22, pp. 403-5, SG Letterbooks, DLC.

1. In response to wage cuts in textile mills throughout New England in early January 1898, some fifteen thousand members of the National Cotton Mule Spinners' Association of America and independent unions struck on Jan. 17, 1898, in New Bedford, Mass., and several other cities in the region. Although restoration of wage cuts was the principal issue, New Bedford weavers also demanded an end to the fines system and a uniform piece-rate scale. The strike weakened in late April when New Bedford weavers and loom fixers voted to return to work, and on May 20 New Bedford spinners conceded defeat.

2. SG to Eva McDonald Valesh, Jan. 19, 1898, reel 14, vol. 22, p. 413, SG Letterbooks, DLC.

3. Probably the Carders' Union of New Bedford, Mass., organized in 1893.

4. Probably the Loom Fixers' Association of New Bedford, Mass.

To the Executive Council of the AFL

Washington, D.C., January 24, 1898.

To the Executive Council:—
Colleagues:

You are undoubtedly aware of the great textile workers' strike now in progress in New England. Secretary Mills writes me saying that applications are constantly coming in for an organizer. He asks my services for two weeks in that capacity, but, owing to the great amount of work devolving upon me, that is, now, out of the question. I have expressed my willingness, however, to go to a few points agreed upon by him and Secretary Ross of the Spinners. This action is submitted to you for your approval, or otherwise.

I have suggested further that I would submit to you a proposition, and I do so now, that three local men, one in each of the places I may visit, be engaged for a week, for the purpose of devoting their entire time to organizing the textile workers, the men to be recommended by the officers of the textile workers' national union.

I, also, propose that Vice-President McGuire be requested to devote a few days in the interest of the textile workers.

Please return your vote upon the above propositions at your earliest convenience, and oblige.[1]

Yours Fraternally,   Saml Gompers.
President   A.F. of L.

TLpS, AFL Executive Council Vote Books, reel 8, frame 247, *AFL Records.*

1. The AFL Executive Council approved all three propositions.

To John Lester[1]

Jan. 25th, 189[8].

Dr. J. A. Lester,
Nashville, Tenn.,
My Dear Sir:—

Through the courtesy of our Vice-president, Mr. P. J. McGuire, I have your favor of the 4th Inst., contents of which are carefully noted. I beg to assure you that I, too, regret very much that we did not meet in Nashville during my sojourn there. Mr. McGuire and myself made quite an assiduous effort to find where your meeting took place, and, though raining and muddy, we walked the streets for fully two hours in search of the place of meeting, making inquiries in at least a dozen different stores for the place of meeting. There were dances and lodge meetings taking place, but we could not discover where you and your friends were holding forth. Inasmuch as this cannot be remedied now, so far as personal attendance is concerned, we can endeavor to do the next best thing, that is, in communicating with each other in the hope of accomplishing the desired purpose, that is, in aiding in the organization of our negro fellow workers of your city. Desirous of accomplishing the best results, I mail to your address, under separate cover, a number of documents, blank applications, &c., to which the attention of yourself and our friends are cordially invited.

I beg to thank you for your efforts in the direction to organize our friends and sincerely hope that every success will attend your efforts.

Kindly let me hear from you at your early convenience, and oblige.

Yours Very Truly,   Saml Gompers.
President   A.F. of L.

N.B. The name and address of our organizer in Nashville is, M. J. Noonan,[2] Care Journal of Labor, Nashville, Tennessee.

S. G.

TLpS, reel 14, vol. 22, pp. 473-74, SG Letterbooks, DLC.

1. John A. Lester was a black Nashville physician.
2. Martin J. Noonan, a Nashville tailor, was president of the Nashville Trades and Labor Council (1897-98) and a member of Journeymen Tailors' Union of America 85.

To P. J. McGuire

Feb. 2nd, 1898.

Mr. P. J. McGuire,
124 North Ninth St., Philadelphia, Pa.,
Dear Sir & Brother: —

Your favor of the 31st Ult. to hand and, by the same mail, I received one, by special delivery, from Mr. Mills. After consulting with Mr. Ross, they have come to the conclusion that it is necessary to cover as many places as possible and, hence, they are making arrangements for meetings for you in Biddeford and Lewiston, Me., and in Manchester, N.H., the dates of which they do not give me. I have written them asking them to advise with you direct in regard to the dates. The meetings which they have arranged for me, take place in Lowell, Lawrence and New Bedford, on the 7th, 8th and 9th Insts.

There is quite a conflict between the textile workers' organizations themselves. Mr. Cahill[1] seems to have either acted upon his own accord, or by authority of the local textile workers of Lawrence, to launch a "national union." In view of this conflict and the injury it may have, both upon the immediate struggle and the organization in the future, I have called a conference[2] of Mills, Ross and Cahill, and a few of our other friends, in Boston, for Sunday, and I trust that I may be successful in bringing them, if not to unity, at least closer together and to make a common cause in the present struggle.

Yesterday I learned that my married daughter[3] in New York was very dangerously ill, and I had to send Mrs. Gompers on there to her bedside. I know you will be pleased to learn that I have information that she is somewhat improved. Of course, this will make it necessary for me to stop in New York for a few hours, a time that I hoped to be enabled to spend in Philadelphia with you, in order to talk matters over. I shall try, however, to stop over for one train and, if I can, will advise you by wire. There are so many matters upon which I should like to have a talk with you, some of which cannot be well discussed outside of this office, for the papers are already here, and for this reason, as well as others already mentioned, I would like you to come here and appear before the Committee on Labor to-morrow, Thursday morning.

With kindest regards and best wishes, I am,

Sincerely yours, Saml Gompers.
President A.F. of L.

TLpS, reel 14, vol. 22, pp. 619-20, SG Letterbooks, DLC.

1. Thomas P. CAHILL, a Lawrence, Mass., weavers' union leader who served as general secretary of the National Union of Textile Workers of America (NUTWA) in 1895 and 1896, apparently founded a short-lived national organization known as the United Textile Workers of America (UTWA) after the expulsion of the NUTWA's Lawrence local in 1896. Cahill was serving as the UTWA's general secretary in 1898.

2. On Feb. 6, 1898, SG met in Boston with leaders of the striking textile workers and representatives of organized labor in Massachusetts to coordinate support for the strike. Among those attending the conference were Michael Duggan and Samuel Ross of the National Cotton Mule Spinners' Association, Henry Mills of the NUTWA, Thomas Cahill of the UTWA, J. D. Pierce of the Massachusetts Federation of Labor, John Tobin of the Boot and Shoe Workers' Union, Henry Lloyd of the United Brotherhood of Carpenters and Joiners, Thomas Tracy of the CMIU, Thomas Murphy of the Boston Central Labor Union, George McNeill, and AFL organizers Louis Weeks, John O'Sullivan, and George Bennett. The meeting appointed a committee to foster unity among the textile unions.

3. Rose Gompers Mitchell.

A News Account of an Address in Lowell, Mass.

[February 9, 1898]

CROWDS HEARD GOMPERS

Samuel Gompers, president of the American Federation of Labor, was the honored guest of the local labor unions last evening, when he addressed three largely attended meetings.[1]

The attendance at the three meetings aggregated upwards of 1000, and outside of a little interruption at the meeting in Burkes' Hall, all of the meetings were harmonious as they were all enthusiastic.

Thomas F. Connolly[2] was conspicuous by his absence at all of the meetings.

At Burkes' Hall.

Burkes' Hall was packed to overflowing when President Gompers, accompanied by District Organizer Louis W. Weeks,[3] Michael Duggan[4] of the Spinners' Union, Secretary James Smith of the Trades and Labor Council[5] and Mr. Morrow[6] of the Loomfixers' Union, filed into the hall.

Mr. Weeks opened the meeting by expressing regret that the city of Lowell has not a larger hall, after which he introduced Michael Duggan, president of the National Spinners' Union, as the presiding officer. Mr. Gompers, he said, holds the highest honor in the gift of the working people of America. He closed by introducing Mr. Gompers, who was given a rousing reception. He said:

Mr. Chairman, ladies and gentlemen and friends: I feel the responsibility of attempting to discuss a great problem in a time of great excitement. It is almost impossible to consider calmly the questions that enter into our every-day life; the life of our families. The time for such discussion is when passion is absent and just conclusions can be arrived at. Having attempted to do this in season and out, I trust I will be enabled to discuss calmly and fairly the conditions that the textile workers are called to face today. Today you find yourself face to face with the question of accepting a reduction in wages of 10 per cent. The Lowell operatives have accepted this reduction, but there is not one man or woman in Lowell who does not feel the pang and sting of this injustice, although they do not manifest it.

I come here tonight to discuss with you what should be done to protect your interests, not only today, but in the days to come. (Applause.) Let us see what reasons the manufacturers give for this reduction. They say that the industry has grown in the South to such an extent that they cannot compete with them. Nothing is farther from the truth than that. (Cries of "hear, hear," and applause.) I do not deny that they work longer hours and at lower wages in the South, but there never was an industry successfully conducted upon a basis of long hours and low wages. Where hours are shortest and wages highest, there you find the most successful industries and the most progressive people.

Go where you please, look where you please, at any industry you please, and you will find this absolutely true. If long hours and low wages tended to successful industry, then China ought to stand at the head. (Tremendous applause.)

Only a few days ago Mr. Samuel Ross had an interview with a mill treasurer, and the latter was compelled to admit that southern competition was not the reason for the cut. If any reason does exist for this cut, it is the presence of so much raw material. Then let them join with us and restrict the output. (Applause.)

But these men had another object in view. There was a conspiracy among the mill owners of New England to cut the wages. (Applause.) Supposing the mill owners are successful in this contest; what is going to be the result? Will the southern mill owners not take the same step? Is it not known that the operatives of the South have not the resisting qualities as the operatives of the North? They will prove easy victims to the cupidity of the mill-owners and the same differentiation between the wages of the North and South will still exist. (Great applause.)

The policy which the mill owners are pursuing is that of nibbling at the vitals of the operatives of the North and South. They are trying to Chinee-ize the American people, but I doubt their ability to do so. (Applause.)

The business men of Biddeford are organized to assist the operatives of Biddeford, because of this Chinee-izing process, and they realize that in such an event their business will have to go. (Applause.) I am told that the business men of Lowell are suffering for lack of trade, and it is for no other reason than that the mill owners have cut the wages of the operatives in order to squeeze another one per cent on dividends.

But they have reckoned without their host; the operatives are aroused as never before, and have rallied around the banner of organization and that banner will carry them to victory. (Applause.) Superintendent Kerr[7] of the Grinnell Mills, affected by the cut down, says that the labor leaders are responsible for the cut down. Yes, we went to the treasurers on our bended knees and begged them to cut wages. (Laughter.) That is what we exist for. (Laughter.) This meeting was held in Grace Church, New Bedford, and I presume it was opened with prayer and closed with the benediction. (Laughter.) Undoubtedly he believes in preying upon labor six days in the week and praying for labor one minute. (Laughter and applause.)

The same blackguardly accusations that are argued against the men who discuss the labor question were hurled at the head of Wendell

Phillips, Abraham Lincoln and all those who were opposed to slavery. (Applause.) Time came and went and who is there so contemptible, so entirely lost, that he would not do honor to the memory of Wendell Phillips, who was dragged through the streets and pelted with chickens unhatched. (Applause.)

The labor agitator is like a firebell, calling attention to the wrongs that exist and the dangers that confront us. Woe to the operative when agitation ceases! Mr. Kerr says the employers are without organization. Why, somewhere I heard the name Arkwright Club[8] mentioned. (Laughter and applause.)

Some few years ago I met a lawyer at the state house who represented an organization of manufacturers and was fighting the 58-hour law. This process cannot succeed. In contravention to the policy inaugurated by the mill owners, President Andrews,[9] your own fellow citizen, said that it is only by united action that "men can secure any increase in their wages; under such conditions charity would not be necessary." We want no charity; we want work at living wages. (Applause.) I say Amen to all that Professor Andrews has said. This earth cannot remain upon its axis if it stands still. There is absolutely no stagnant position for us to occupy; we either progress or recede. If the working people do not take a stand, they will be compelled to work longer hours and at lower wages.

Lowell Mail, Feb. 9, 1898.

1. On Feb. 8, 1898, SG spoke in three meetings in Lowell, Mass.; they were held at the Burke Temperance Institute, the Spinners' Hall, and the Building Laborers' Hall.

2. Thomas F. CONNOLLY (variously Connelly), a Lowell, Mass., mule spinner, was financial secretary of the Lowell weavers' union (1899-1902).

3. Louis W. Weeks of Lowell, Mass., was president of CMIU 255 and an AFL organizer.

4. Michael DUGGAN was president of the National Cotton Mule Spinners' Association of America.

5. The Lowell Central Labor Union, organized in 1889, was chartered by the AFL as the Lowell Trades and Labor Council on Feb. 16, 1898.

6. Dennis J. Morrow was a member of the Lowell Loom Fixers' Association.

7. Nathaniel B. Kerr was superintendent of the Grinnell Manufacturing Corp. of New Bedford, Mass.

8. The Arkwright Club, founded in 1880 and based in Boston, was a New England cotton textile manufacturers' trade association.

9. Probably the Rev. Elisha B. Andrews, president of Brown University (1889-98).

An Excerpt from a News Account of an Address in New Bedford, Mass.

New Bedford, Feb. 9 [1898]

IN AN UPROAR.

The Gompers meeting tonight proved the most exciting incident thus far since the strike began.

Since the inception of the resistance against the 10 percent reduction of wages the local members of the socialist labor party have been busy in spreading their doctrines. They were present at the meeting tonight in full force, and before Pres. Samuel Gompers of the American federation of labor had done speaking they were responsible for one of the biggest uproars ever seen in city hall.

This afternoon James T. Hancock,[1] the organizer of the New Bedford section of the socialist labor party, issued a challenge to Mr. Gompers to a joint debate on the theories advanced by the American Federation of Labor as opposed to the doctrines of the socialist labor party, and toward the end of his remarks Mr. Gompers saw fit to take the matter up.

He had been talking of the discord among the strikers, of which he said he had read since coming into New England, and which he said he had been told was not true, and he denounced such stories as calculated to injure the success of the strike.

"I know you will win," he said, "if you will only be true to each other. You cannot but win if you stand true, but if you find men who, under the pretense of advocating labor, will throw into the fight an issue which breeds discord, they should be branded by the name of traitor to the cause of labor. I care not who he is, or whether he is a member of a union or not.

"In this connection," continued Mr. Gompers, "I will say that a challenge has been issued to me.

"First let me say that I don't know how I should find time to take part in such a debate. My engagements are so made to speak in the cause of labor a word helpful to the men and women who are engaged in the struggle, that I couldn't find time, even if I had the inclination, to accept the challenge.

"Have I tried to do aught but what will be helpful? Have I said one word to contribute to their defeat?

"This challenge is made in the heat of a contest, when the men and women who are battling for their rights should, if ever, stand

together, and to challenge a comrade in arms at such a time is trai-
torous.

"The duty of the men engaged in labor's battle is to join shoulder
to shoulder and face the common enemy, and not to challenge a man
whose desires are all for your victory and who is working with you.

"I want to tell you—you who make the challenge—that it is good
for you that you are living among people who tolerate such conditions.
If you lived in the country where your ideas are best promulgated,
and if you would dare to do what you have done in the midst of a
contest you would not be permitted to show your faces among decent
working men.

"How dare a man, or any number of men, presumably in the
conflict, attack the principles and policy and tactics involved in such
an organization when it is engaged in conflict? Such things are per-
missible in times of peace, but any man or men who will divide the
forces of labor which will result in taking the bread out of the mouths
of the helpless women and children are the paid hirelings of the mill
owners.

"I do not say that there are not some misguided men among them—
some men who would not do such a thing of their own accord if not
urged by stronger minds—"

Before he had a chance to finish the sentence, Mr. Hancock, who
is a member of the spinners' executive committee, jumped to his feet
from his position in the rear of the hall.

"I challenge you right here," he shouted. "Give me five minutes
and let me come on the platform, and I'll answer you right now."

UPROAR IN HALL.

In a moment the hall was in an uproar. Several socialists in other
parts of the audience joined in the clamor, and the speech of one was
not distinguishable from the other.

At last somebody started the cry, "Throw him out."

"Don't do that," said Gompers, securing the attention of the meeting. "Don't do it. Don't sink to his level."

Thereupon the noise was divided between applause for the retort
and the demand of the socialists for a chance to be heard.

"I know this red button brigade," shouted Gompers, excitedly, when
he could make himself heard. "You will find a pinkerton agent, the
paid hireling of the mill corporations here Friday night to divide you
against yourselves."

The crowd took this to mean DeLeon, the socialist labor agitator
who is booked to speak in city hall Friday evening,[2] and there was
another outburst of applause, mingled with hisses.

Gompers saw that if he would not let the meeting break away from
him he must keep talking, and he made an effort to still the interference of the socialists by pouring out a steady stream of words.
During his effort he grew red in the face, and the veins in his forehead
swelled as though they would burst.

"Men who will not fight together are traitors to each other," he
continued. "I am willing that everybody should have a hearing, as
any man should, but in the face of a battle no division can be tolerated."

"Fight this battle at the polls, then you'll pull both ways," interrupted a socialist.

"That's just it," returned Gompers. "You'll pull both ways and get
nothing."

CHEERED BY CROWD.

"The movement of labor is composed of conflicting ideas, perhaps,"
Gompers continued, as the crowd quieted down temporarily, "but
you must bear in mind the fact that there are those who are way
down on the lowest rungs of the social and economical ladder, and
if you hope to attain success you must take the workers as they are
and not as you hope to find them.

"I am told that the collections are not coming in better for the
textile workers in New Bedford because of this very division. I have
been told that the money which comes into this city is not used to
relieve the strikers, but rather for the propagation of some particular
ism rather than for the help of those engaged in the strike.

"That is not so," he announced with fierceness, and he would have
gone on had not somebody reminded him that the time for the leaving
of his train was approaching.

"I am told," said Mr. Gompers, "that it is time for me to leave for
my train. I must go to Pittsburg, where I am to address a labor meeting
tomorrow night. But I tell you, I am coming back."

"Come back Friday night!" shouted an enthusiast.

"I am coming back," repeated Gompers, "but I can't come then;
some other time. Let me warn you, though, that the man who will
come into your city for the purpose of preaching the doctrine of
asking you not to believe in the strike in which you are engaged is
the man who is in the pay of the corporations. I don't know now
when I can come back, but I hope you will win. I ask you to be true
to yourselves. Depend upon yourselves and you will win the fight
which will make you free."

Then Gompers left the hall, and as he did so the crowd rose to
their feet and cheered and swung their hats in parting.

Immediately after his departure a rising vote of thanks to Mr. Gompers for his attendance at the meeting and his interest in the strike was taken. When the nays were called for the crowd looked around to see if Hancock would rise, but he did not make any show of himself.

. . .

Boston Globe, Feb. 10, 1898.

1. James T. Hancock was a New Bedford, Mass., spinner.
2. Daniel DeLeon's speech at the New Bedford, Mass., city hall on Feb. 11, 1898, advocated control by workers of the means of production, attacked trade unions in general and SG and Samuel Ross in particular, and urged striking textile workers to join the Socialist Trade and Labor Alliance.

An Article by Samuel Gompers in the *New York World*

[February 20, 1898]

SAMUEL GOMPERS ON THE LATTIMER SLAUGHTER.

The trial now going at Wilkesbarre of Sheriff Martin and his deputies for the murder of the nineteen men and the maiming of more than forty others at Lattimer on the 10th of September last is indeed harrowing in its details. Having undertaken a personal investigation in the trial, the affairs connected with it and the causes and incidents which have led up to the wholesale butchery, I shall endeavor to narrate what may prove an interesting story, and which I hope will be of some benefit in the lesson it teaches. Of course, with the thousand and one important incidents chronicled daily in the newspapers, it is exceedingly difficult to give more than a resume of each day's proceedings of the trial, and many of these are lost sight of by reason of the failure of the average man to keep a clear train of thought leading to a final conclusion and fair judgment. Having this in mind, The World asked me to go to Wilkesbarre for two days to watch the conduct of the trial. The first article appeared in Thursday's edition of The World;[1] the latter is dealt with now.

WHO IS TO BLAME FOR THE "CHEAP LABOR"?

To have a clearer understanding of the trial at issue it is necessary to say that upon entering the court where the trial is in progress one is immediately impressed with the fact that the issue involved is as much a question of the relations of employer and employed as the question of the trial of Sheriff Martin and his deputies for murder, and, as has been invariably the case, the representatives of corporate power assume a hauteur and domineering attitude toward all. The counsel for the defense, former Attorney-General Palmer[2] and Mr. Lenahan,[3] as well as Sheriff Martin and the deputies, assume an air of offended pride and indignation at being called upon to defend themselves against a charge of killing a score of mere laborers, and, think of it! foreign laborers at that!

We must bear in mind the fact that some years ago the miners throughout this district of Pennsylvania were Americans, Englishmen and Welshmen, who by their environments and higher conception of their rights received a comparatively fair wage. The miners of those days compared favorably in every way with the workers of other trades. It was owing to the overweening greed of the mine-owners that they combined and resorted to the means of "importing" the cheapest labor of Europe into this country by and under alluring contract, which, though on its face appearing an improvement of the condition in which they were placed in their own country, bound them to the companies as firmly as ever slave to master.

Intelligent Labor Forced Out.

Gradually the American, English and Welsh miners were supplanted by Poles or Italians, and there are few if any of the former in the anthracite regions now. Wages to miners were reduced to the lowest possible limit of human existence: the introduction of the companies' stores followed rapidly.

A number of companies were organized and men employed at mining at a vein of coal which could not be profitable in itself, but the company's store, in which the miners were compelled to purchase all their necessaries of life at prices from 20 to 200 per cent. higher than they could be purchased at other places, furnished the profit upon which these companies prospered.

It has been clearly proven that thousands of miners never received as much as ten cents cash in wages for a year at a time. Any miner who failed to patronize the company's store to the full extent of his wages was first warned, and if the "offense" was repeated, summarily discharged. Thus the miners were bondmen and bound to the earth and to their employers as rigidly as though they were the lawful slaves of their masters.

During the struggles of the miners of a decade ago against being supplanted by these cheap laborers the companies armed the "foreigners" to defeat the men who foresaw the dangers which were likely to follow, and which have come. No wonder, then, that the corporations formed a very low estimate of the value of the lives of their then allies. But the sordid greed for more dividends did not stop there, for they continually cut wages and increased the prices in their stores, thus reducing the income and increasing the expenditures of the miners. It was burning the candle at both ends.

No one but who has gone through the mining regions and has seen the poverty, misery and squalor of the miners can have a conception of the awful conditions prevailing.

Is it surprising, then, that these men turned at last and declared that they might as well starve in the free open air as to work and have the lives of themselves, their wives and their little ones crushed out of them by a system as damnable as was ever invented by human cunning?

How the Miner Was Cheated.

It was in the latter part of August that the discontent of these men made itself manifest, when they demanded that the price of powder, for which they paid $2.90 and which could be purchased elsewhere for $1.25, should be reduced and that some consideration should be given them in the matter of a small increase in the pittance for which they worked.

The mining companies regarded this simple request as a presumption not at all to be considered; they looked upon it as a rebellion of their slaves; they treated it as if those engaged in it were questioning the "divine right" of their masters. The thought that these laborers were men, and under the laws of our country were entitled to all the rights of manhood, never occurred to them.

Finally when the miners made an effort to exercise the natural and the lawful right to march upon the public highway, they were met by an armed band, who shot them down in their tracks, and as they ran away from the murderous bullets were massacred in cold blood, or, as one witness of the crime described it, "as if they were rabbits."

Perhaps not in all history, certainly not in modern history, has there been such a criminal slaughter of men who were fleeing for their lives.

We are justly indignant at the cruelty practiced upon Cuban non-combatants by the Spaniards. Yet here we have right at our doors men who are not only non-combatants, but who retreated in disorder, their very lives depending upon their running, and yet murderously shot in the back by a band of as irresponsible and blood-thirsty mercenaries as was ever brought together.

Local Police Overawed by Sheriff's Deputies.

It is not generally known that the men were advised by the Chief of Police, Evans Jones,[4] that they might take another route to Lattimer and that then they would be perfectly within their lawful rights and that if any one interfered with them he would arrest them. The men followed the advice given them and were fully assured that they not only were exercising their right, but had police protection.

In their march they had not a weapon of any kind with them; they carried the banner of our country before them and had implicit faith and confidence that so long as they were unarmed and acting as they were, its folds would protect them. Strange as it may appear, the bearer of the Stars and Stripes was the first target for the missiles of the deputies; the poor fellow was literally riddled with bullets, and these deputies further manifested their patriotism by tearing the flag of our country into shreds, throwing and tramping it upon the ground.

Some of the expressions of the deputies are interesting when considered in connection with the shooting which followed. While they were riding in a trolley car to intercept the men at Lattimer, one, raising his gun, said: "I should like to get a bead on some of them; I'd pull down six of them without moving." Another playfully remarked: "I'd like to shoot these fellows at one cent a piece, and I'd make money at that." The poor fellows after the shooting, in high fever from wounds, begged for a drink of water to assuage their thirst. They were kicked and cursed, and struck with the butt ends of guns.

Nor is it generally known that Sheriff Martin had no choice in the selection of those who constituted his posse commitatus. His posse of deputies was made up by the mine-owners. They were armed by the companies, handed over to the Sheriff with commands to him. They were neither organized, nor did they act in any other capacity than a private armed band, an armed band unknown to and in conflict with the law and the institutions of our country.

How the Trial Strikes Mr. Gompers.

To the one who studies the present trial and knows of the manner in which it has been brought before the courts, the results will not be surprising nor convincing. It is well known that D. A. Fell,[5] who was District-Attorney at the time of the shooting, was dependent upon the corporations and held himself always at their command.

The preliminary hearings were evidently conducted by him with the purpose of throwing every obstacle in the way of a trial calculated to convict. The indictment which he framed failed to include a count charging a conspiracy to k--- [kill], thus requiring the prosecution now to prove the shooting and killing by a certain deputy of a certain victim, an essential without which a conviction cannot be secured. When there were so many engaged in the shooting and so many were killed and wounded and the excitement of the time, the difficulty in clearly proving this fact is manifest.

JUDGE WOODWARD[6] AND THE COAL COMPANIES.

The Presiding Judge, Stanley Woodward, is married into a family of landholders of the district, who receive royalties upon every ton of coal mined. When a cessation of mining occurs from any cause Judge Woodward is to that extent a loser of part of his income. He is a member of the Westmoreland Club, of which the mine-owners are largely members and of which also a number of the so-called deputies are members.

His social surroundings, his financial interests, are all with the mine-owners. Is it difficult to discern toward which side his sympathies lean? At the opening of the trial he assisted practically in excluding any one from the jury box unless he was a "native" American. Jurors were accepted who expressed a prejudice against "foreigners" and who had strong opinions as to the innocence of the indicted men, which, as they said, would require strong evidence to remove.

He admitted the accused to bail, notwithstanding they were under indictment for murder in the first degree, and during the forty-eight hours when they were unable to renew bail they were paroled without bail, and simply upon their own recognizance, a proceeding unparalleled in the history of modern jurisprudence. He excluded testimony showing malignity, vindictiveness and the brutality of the accused, and allowed the defense to so frame their questions as to convey the idea to the jury that there was "a fight" at Lattimer, notwithstanding the fact that every particle of evidence showed that there was not the slightest resistance on the part of the miners.

He permitted the attorneys for the defense, or rather it may as well be stated as hinted, the attorneys for the companies, for they in truth are on trial, to browbeat the witnesses for the Commonwealth, though they are physical wrecks as the result of their wounds.

The counsel for the companies and deputies sneer at the death of the murdered men, laugh at the wounded witnesses, domineer the Court and browbeat the counsel for the Commonwealth.

The Innocent Indicted to Help the Guilty Escape.

Former District-Attorney Fell had some men indicted whom it was known were absolutely innocent of any participation in the murders, men who with more conscience than the balance refused to hunt and shoot men in cold blood and threw away their weapons. Yet some of these innocently indicted are placed in the front row among the accused, and their countenances stand out in strong contrast to the hard visages of the guilty ones; yet they are used as the foreground to this picture for its influence upon the minds of the jury.

Attention has already been called to the fact that most of the accused are usually reading novels or newspapers, that they look bored at the proceedings, seem to regard it as a huge joke, not for a moment having the faintest suspicion that there is anything serious likely to result to them. If the facts were not so tragical the proceedings would be farcical.

One can form an idea of the trial best by the following incident. The District-Attorney,[7] after making a vain attempt to protect a witness from the brutal attacks of the attorneys for the defense, and when Judge Woodward refused to protect a witness who was physically weak and mentally disturbed owing to his wounds and gruffly said that he would not interfere, declared that he would enter no more objections, that it was useless for him to enter any more objections against such proceedings; that he would make none thereafter, closing with "I am thoroughly disgusted."

A Talk with Counsel for Defense.

I had an interview with Mr. Lenahan, one of the counsel for the defense, inquiring as to the rights and principles involved in the trial and any other matter bearing upon the case, though it may not be brought out during the trial. He informed me that since I had made the request for the interview on the previous day he had consulted with his associates and "they had nothing to say."

In interviews with counsel[8] for the Commonwealth they were open and candid, expressing their full belief in not only the guilt of the accused, but that the killing was a cold-blooded conspiracy to murder. Neither the Court nor the defense seemed to rise to the importance of the case nor the dignity of the occasion. I was invited to be introduced to Judge Woodward, but I had some self-respect which I did not care to sacrifice by meeting a man whom I not only believed to be, but whom every one present knows is acting manifestly unfair.

The entire and combined influences of the companies, the Sheriff and deputies, who are but their hirelings, the Judge and counsel for the accused, who are their associates and beneficiaries, all seem to be prompted by the one motive which lies at the bottom of the murders as well as the trial — that is, that this shooting is intended to be "a lesson" to the working people that they have no rights which the corporations are bound to respect, and that if needs be human life, when that life is possessed by a worker — that worker being perhaps a "foreign" worker — is of no account and may be taken at the caprice or sport of their mercenaries.

No one among those who sympathize with the murdered or wounded men hanker after the lives of Martin and his fellow-conspirators and fellow-murderers. We have not yet become so brutalized as to want the blood of any man upon our hands, but it is a mistake to believe that human life can be toyed with and taken without finding its retribution. The men who went to Lattimer on that fatal day went unarmed, without so much as a stick to support them, and many of them were weary and footsore upon that hot summer's day.

They had previously decided, and carried out their purpose, to be unarmed and unprotected except by the justness of their cause and the American flag, in which they had absolute faith.

SHERIFF'S DEPUTIES WILL GO SCOT FREE

It is sad to contemplate when workingmen of either American or foreign birth have their faith and confidence in the emblem of our country destroyed, and perhaps sadder still is the possibility of losing faith in the justice of our courts.

It may do for awhile for the companies and the deputies to escape the just punishment which is their due for their crime, but outraged humanity and their own conscience will haunt them to their last day, and though for a moment victory be on the side of the corporations, it is written as plainly and as clearly as the day, that in the end these butcheries shall cease, justice prevail and men enthroned in the full possession of their rights, regardless whether they be wage-earners or mine-owners.

The workers of our country are organizing better and more thoroughly each day; we shall not only create a healthier public sentiment as to man's rights and man's duties, but we shall largely constitute that public opinion. And, when that day comes, the crime of Lattimer will be a red-letter day in the annals of our history to which all will look back upon with horror as the monumental crime of the nineteenth century.

Samuel Gompers.

New York World, Feb. 20, 1898.

1. SG's first article, "Sheriff's Deputies to Go Free Gompers Writes the World," was published Feb. 16, 1898.

2. Henry W. Palmer was a Wilkes-Barre, Pa., lawyer.

3. John T. Lenahan, of Wilkes-Barre, Pa.

4. Edward Jones was chief of police at West Hazleton, Pa., at the time of the Lattimer incident.

5. Daniel A. Fell, Jr., was Republican attorney general of Luzerne Co., Pa., from 1895 to 1897.

6. Stanley D. Woodward was president judge of Luzerne Co., Pa.

7. Luzerne Co. District Attorney Thomas R. Martin.

8. Other prosecuting attorneys in the case included John McGahren and John M. Garman of Wilkes-Barre, Pa., and James A. Scarlett of Danville, Pa.

To John Thomas[1]

Feb. 23, [1898]

Mr. John Lloyd Thomason,
180 Bleecker St., N.Y., N.Y.
My dear Sir:

Your favor of the 21st. inst. to hand, inclosing two tickets for the meeting of the Nineteenth Century Club[2] on March 10th.[3] I shall appreciate your call at the Ashland House at the time stated in your communication.

I observe that the invitation requests that gentlemen shall appear in "Evening Dress." In as much as I have never worn evening dress, nor do I expect to depart from this custom, I will ask that I be excused.

Anticipating with pleasure our meeting, I am,

Very sincerely, Saml Gompers.

TLpS, reel 14, vol. 22, p. 751, SG Letterbooks, DLC.

1. John L. Thomas was secretary of the Nineteenth Century Club (NCC).

2. The NCC was founded in New York City in 1883.

3. At the Mar. 10, 1898, meeting of the NCC in New York City, SG debated Edward Atkinson, a Boston industrialist, economist, writer, and public speaker, on the question "A Minimum Living Wage—Should It Be Recognized as a Principle and Rule of Life?" SG defended the position that a living wage for workers should have first claim on the profits arising from production and distribution. He defined it as "a minimum wage—a wage which, when expended in the most economical manner, shall be sufficient to maintain an average-sized family in a manner consistent with whatever the contemporary local civilization recognizes as indispensable to physical and mental health, or as required by the rational self-respect of human beings." He warned that while a living wage sustained the social and economic vitality of the community, substandard wages bred "mental and physical dwarfs," discouraged demand and consumption, and led to "strikes, riots, and destruction of life and property." Moreover, it was not only a matter of self-interest but also of justice for society to

insure the payment of a living wage: "As the countless ages pass away, each generation creates its share of wealth for those who come after them, and the entire stable wealth of the world, its great inventions, its enduring superstructures, of art and utility, are to a great degree the result of the patient toil of the mighty tribes that slumber in its bosom. The wealth of these past ages is certainly the inheritance of all; it provides, in many instances, easy access to natural opportunities; it is simply held 'in trust' by the present generation, and will be passed, with added wealth, to the succeeding generation. The 'State' certainly fails in its duty if it does not see, *de jure*, that each shall have an equality of opportunity to enjoy this wealth . . . which in itself provides an opportunity to every one to earn a living. It must provide, if necessary, protective measures to this end, both upon the score of humanity and sanitary grounds, and for reasons of economic existence." He argued, however, that the state should not fix the wage by statute—except in the case of public employees—because of the danger that "the minimum would become the maximum" (*American Federationist* 5 [April 1898]: 25-27, 30).

To Henry Mills

Feb. 25, [1898]

Mr. H. S. Mills,
Box 520, New Bedford, Mass.
Dear Sir and Brother:

I am obliged to you for the information relative to the matter submitted to the Executive Council of your National Union, and I trust it will prevail.

I am in receipt of a letter from T. P. Cahill, under date of February 20th, 1898, in which he says:

"I beg to inform you that I received the report of the Boston committee a few days after your visit to Lowell Mass. I am personally satisfied that the committee has acted with tact, and taken a step towards a reunion of all the textile workers in one organization. I have consulted some of our leading members and find that they are in thorough sympathy with the object to be obtained, and have already agreed to let the dead past remain buried, and the only questions to be solved are questions relating to the future welfare of organized textile workers which they desire assurances from the officials of the N.U. towards co-operating towards adopting a system of high p.c. tax with death and strike benefits paid from the general Treasury. Our members are always entitled to such benefits from the G.T. and you can realize the embarrassing position we would be in to abandon our present form for the old system which has been so disappointing to the textile workers in the past. Personally I have some doubts about those textile unions that have been started in on the old cheap plan, favoring the high tax plan or submitting, if carried in face of their opposition. No other individual exercised the influence in the N.U. that I did, yet I never could get them to realize the tremendous importance of such changes. I am willing to yield personal opinions, to secure unity. I understand that the G.E.C. of the N.U. is to repeal the action of their G.E.C. of 1896, in revoking the charter of Union #2[1] of this city, and my proclaimed expulsion. I do not care so much about that as I do about a proper system of organization for the future. I sent your letter to Lowell, to prove your anxiety to have Mr. Connelly[2] at that conference, as I understand that it was asserted that he was ignored and not desired by you. Any suggestion that you may offer will always receive careful consideration. Of course we have amongst us those that desire us to continue in our present course, and to refuse any overtures from the N.U., but I feel satisfied that 'common sense will prevail.'

> ["]Fraternally yours,   T. P. Cahill
> ["]Gen. Sec. U.T.W. of A."[3]

By this you will see that the conference as well as conclusion reached will accomplish its purpose in this instance, and further, of necessity, it will have its influence with the people in Lowell who are still so persistently holding back. They will soon find the error of following the mistaken advice of both Messrs. Connelly and Kinsella,[4] and perhaps in the near future an opportunity may be presented by which the good results can be achieved to the interest of your National Union.

I shall write to Mr. Cahill, and encourage him to keep on in the line to bring whatever of his organization there is into the National union. Of course it is unnecessary for me to say that I fully agree with the remarks which he makes, in so far as they apply to higher dues and benefits in the union. As a matter of fact they will have to be adopted if permanency and success are to be obtained. It may wean the textile workers from the insurance factions, but it will give them an opportunity of insuring themselves in the unions more cheaply and more securely, and give them also an opportunity of paying a salary to an officer who has the ability and willingness to do the work to protect and advance their interests. I am confident that under your administration great success can be achieved, and that a splendid opportunity will soon be opened up to you in the movement, and thus bring greater advantage to all.

This is the third letter[5] you will receive perhaps within one day, and I do not expect a full and complete answer to them all, for I know how your hands are tied. I ask you to advise me however, in reference to the meeting of March 4th,[6] which I hope will take place, and which of course will be during the day if at all, and also to let me know what conclusion has been reached by your Executive Board in regard to the proposition and recognition of our Committee to unite. When we meet in New Bedford, we can discuss the other matters.

Sincerely yours, Saml Gompers.
President A.F. of L.

TLpS, reel 14, vol. 22, pp. 780-82, SG Letterbooks, DLC.

1. Probably National Union of Textile Workers of America 2 of Lawrence, Mass.
2. Thomas Connolly.
3. A copy of this letter is in the United Textile Workers of America Records, reel 143, frame 355, *AFL Records.* Regarding the abbreviations, "N.U." stands for National Union (of Textile Workers of America), "p.c." for per capita, "G.T." for General Treasury, and "G.E.C." for General Executive Council.
4. William L. Kinsella, a Lowell, Mass., insurance agent and former textile operative, was president of the Lowell weavers' union in 1898.
5. SG's letters to Mills, dated Feb. 22 and 24, 1898 (reel 14, vol. 22, pp. 742 and 759, SG Letterbooks, DLC), dealt with various aspects of the AFL's support of the textile workers' strike.
6. On Mar. 4, 1898, SG met in New Bedford, Mass., with Thomas Connolly and Matthew Hart, secretary of the New Bedford weavers' union, in an attempt to promote unity among the striking organizations. He also addressed a strike meeting at the New Bedford city hall.

To John Tonsing[1]

Feb. 26, [1898]

Mr. John F. Tousing,
Secretary Cleveland Central Labor Union,
#40 Burton St., Cleveland, O.
Dear Sir and Brother:

I have the honor to acknowledge receipt of your favor of the 10th inst. conveying a series of resolutions adopted by the C.L.U. at its meeting of January 12th regarding an editorial which appeared in answer to a communication from the manager of the Cleveland Citizen.[2] As a reason for not replying earlier I desire to say that there has been more important work demanding my attention in the effort to organize our fellow workers, to be somewhat helpful to our struggling textile workers of New England, and to attend to the large correspondence connected with this office.

You say in your resolution that it is "basely false" when I charge the Cleveland Citizen with throwing obstacles in the way of the Brotherhood of Carpenters and Joiners in their effort to establish the eight-hour work day for its members in Cleveland.[3] Yet as a matter of fact what I charged is true and beyond a possibility of a doubt by those who have taken sufficient interest in our movement to keep informed upon events as they transpire. If you still doubt this I commend your attention to the columns of the Cleveland Citizen, and the public press of your City during the Carpenters' efforts to secure the eight-hour work day. If you have any doubts that my criticism of the Cleveland Citizen's editor's[4] action are accurate, I commend you for verification or otherwise to the Carpenters' unions[5] of your city, and to the general secretary of the Brotherhood, Mr. P. J. McGuire.

It is a fact beyond contravention that the attitude and anti–trade union policy of the Cleveland Citizen and because that paper sails under the flag of being your official Journal, has divided the labor movement of your city so much so that the Building Trades Unions of Cleveland have positively refused to have any connection with your Central Labor Union, and that between 25 and 35 other unions in your City are unrepresented in your C.L.U. at its weekly meetings.

In view of these indisputable facts your charge of "base falsehood" and prevarication will scarcely have much weight with thinking earnest men, who are giving their undivided devotion to the cause of wage labor.

If I apprehend conditions aright, the Cleveland Citizen, like all other official papers published by Central bodies, is intended to be the spokesman, advocate and defender of the struggles which labor makes to secure justice for the workers not only in the distant future, but today. In the case of the Cleveland Citizen, instead of it being what it was intended, it has become a menace to the true interests of the workers, and means to divide men of labor against each other, to tear down the general labor movement, to malign the men engaged in it, and to asperse their motives. In fact it has come to my knowledge that men engaged in the movement in your City have refrained from expressing their true sentiments in regard to the labor movement by reason of the whiphand which the editorial management of the Cleveland Citizen holds over the heads of men who dare differ with the policy of their paper. In a word in this instance, your C.L.U. has created its own Frankenstein, which if permitted to continue will either crush or cripple its own creator.

With a full knowledge of the above facts, and conscious of the accuracy of the laws, principles and policy of the American labor movement as understood and carried on by the American Federation of Labor, I think you will agree with me that it is impossible for me to comply with your request to retract the statements made by me regarding the Cleveland Citizen, except to restate them with greater emphasis.

I note that in each of the statements, resolutions, criticisms or denunciations of your C.L.U., they have been published in the Cleveland Citizen and given to the Press, and that any reply made from this office has invariably been suppressed. I should be pleasantly disappointed should this communication be an exception to the rule.[6]

In spite of all that has been said in bitterness or anger against me, I bid you accept the assurance that I shall ever do the very best which lies in my power to aid all our fellow workers, those of your city included, to organize, to battle for their rights, and to attain that glorious end for which our noble cause stands.

Fraternally yours,   Saml Gompers.
President   A.F. of L.

TLpS, reel 14, vol. 22, pp. 808-11, SG Letterbooks, DLC.

1. John F. Tonsing was a Cleveland painter and corresponding secretary of the Cleveland Central Labor Union (CLU).

2. The November 1897 issue of the *American Federationist* (4: 217) charged that the *Cleveland Citizen* was hostile to the AFL because the Federation had once turned down a Cleveland CLU proposal to make the *Citizen* the AFL's official organ. In an editorial in the January 1898 *Federationist* ("He Hides Behind You," 4: 262-63), SG published a communication from *Citizen* manager Robert Bandlow refuting this charge. Bandlow maintained that it was his paper's "privilege to point out the shortcomings of officials of any organizations at any time." In response, SG accused the *Citizen* of misrepresenting the trade union movement in Cleveland, discouraging unions from membership in the CLU, opposing the Cleveland carpenters' campaign to achieve the eight-hour day, and publishing "filth, vituperation and malicious representation in regard to officials of the A.F. of L." At its Jan. 12, 1898, meeting, the CLU adopted resolutions defending the *Citizen*'s record as a proponent of the shorter workday and demanding that SG publish a retraction in the columns of the *Federationist*.

3. On May 1, 1896, Cleveland locals of the United Brotherhood of Carpenters and Joiners of America (UBCJA) began a campaign of selective strikes for an eight-hour day; it had succeeded by August of that year.

4. Max S. HAYES was editor of the *Cleveland Citizen* from 1894 to 1939.

5. UBCJA 11, 39 (Bohemian), 398 (German), and 449 (German).

6. SG's letter appeared under the headline "Gompers, the Prevaricator" (*Cleveland Citizen*, Mar. 12, 1898).

To the Executive Council of the AFL

Washington, D.C., Mar. 1st, 1898.

To the Executive Council,
Colleagues:

I am just in receipt of a letter from one of the executive officers of an affiliated central body of the West (the writer asks that confidence be maintained, hence I do not use his name), informing me that Mr. Edw. Boyce has called a meeting[1] to be held at Salt Lake City May 10th, 1898, "for the purpose of bringing all labor organizations of the West into closer touch with one another upon all matters pertaining to the interest of labor. As the labor people of the West have never met together to discuss matters of interest to them or advance their interest, the executive board favors such action." My correspondent is a true union member and loyal to the A.F. of L., and is opposed to all division in the ranks of our movement. He has been invited, and, notwithstanding many overtures which have been made to him, he has still refused them. He urges that something may be done in the matter, in order to avoid the injurious results which would certainly follow a division of the movement.

You will observe that the invitation is adroitly drawn, since it does not even by indirection say anything regarding the secession or withdrawal from the general movement of the country. Kindly advise me in reference to this, apart from the matter as authorized by the last executive council meeting, that is, upon the appointment of an organizer.[2]

I beg to advise you and to congratulate you upon the decision rendered by the United States Supreme Court, sustaining the eight-hour law[3] of the State of Utah. Our eight-hour agitation is bearing good fruit. Vice President Duncan, Andrew Furuseth, Jno. C. Durnell,[4] George Chance and the undersigned, appeared before the Senate Committee on education and labor to-day, in behalf of our eight hour bill.[5] An interesting discussion ensued and an adjournment was taken until Monday morning, March 7th, 1898.

Fraternally, Saml Gompers.
President A.F. of L.

TLpS, AFL Executive Council Vote Books, reel 8, frame 253, *AFL Records.* Typed notation: "Dictated S. G."

1. Under the leadership of Western Federation of Miners' (WFM) President Edward Boyce, the delegates to the convention in Salt Lake City, held May 10-12, 1898— more than two-thirds of whom were WFM representatives—organized the Western Labor Union (WLU). In contrast to the AFL, the WLU favored organization by

industry over organization by craft and emphasized independent labor party politics. While the WLU attracted some support from a small cross-section of trades, it failed to expand significantly beyond its WFM base. Its convention in June 1902 adopted a proposal by Eugene Debs to change its name to the American Labor Union (ALU) and to challenge directly the AFL's leadership of the labor movement. The ALU attracted little support outside the West, where it remained heavily dependent on the WFM. It ceased to exist after participating in the establishment of the Industrial Workers of the World in 1905.

2. The 1897 AFL convention directed the Executive Council to carry out the mandate of the 1896 convention to appoint an organizer for the intermountain and Pacific regions. At its Feb. 22, 1898, meeting, the AFL Executive Council authorized SG to appoint two organizers to canvass the intermountain West in the spring. In April SG issued commissions to Walter MacArthur and E. M. Bannister.

3. Art. 16, sec. 6 of the Utah constitution mandated an eight-hour day on all public works and authorized the legislature to pass health and safety laws regulating factories, smelters, and mines. Under this provision the state enacted an eight-hour law on Mar. 30, 1896 (Laws of 1896, chap. 72). When the law's constitutionality was challenged, the AFL Executive Council appropriated $750 to defray legal expenses involved in its defense. On Feb. 28, 1898, the U.S. Supreme Court upheld the law's constitutionality (*Holden* v. *Hardy*, 169 U.S. 366).

4. John C. Dernell was a member of CMIU 14 of Chicago.

5. On Jan. 27, 1898, New Jersey Congressman John J. Gardner introduced H.R. 7389 (55th Cong., 2d sess.), mandating an eight-hour day for employees of either the federal government or contractors or subcontractors on public works. The measure passed the House but failed to pass the Senate.

To Frank Morrison

March 15th, [1898]

Mr. Frank Morrison,
Secretary, American Federation of Labor.
Dear Sir and Brother:

You are authorized and requested to appear before the Convention[1] of the Brotherhood of Painters and Decorators of America now in session at Buffalo, N.Y. The cause of the representation of the Executive Council by one of its members at this Convention is known to you and will be found completely stated in the printed proceedings of the Convention of the American Federation of Labor held at Nashville, Tennessee, December 16th, 1897. Your attention is called to Pages 116-117.[2]

To refresh your memory it would be perhaps advisable to go back somewhat and recall a few incidents leading to the facts, by which the American Federation of Labor has been called upon to take action in regard to the dispute between the Painters' organizations.

The Brotherhood of Painters and Decorators of America was organized as a national union and became affiliated with the American Federation of Labor. At a Convention[3] of the Brotherhood held at Buffalo some years ago, a dispute arose as to the proper succession to office. Mr. Elliott of Baltimore claimed to be the General Secretary, and Mr. McKinney of Lafayette claimed to be the Secretary. As a consequence, two rival organizations were brought into existence. Both Mr. Elliott and Mr. McKinney offered to pay per capita tax to the A.F. of L. This was during 1895, under the administration of Mr. John McBride as President. After investigation, the Executive Council of that year accepted the per capita tax of the Brotherhood of Painters and Decorators represented by Mr. Elliott as Secretary. This, of course, involved the recognition of that organization as the bona fide national organization of painters, in full affiliation with the A.F. of L.

The faction of the Brotherhood of Painters and Decorators, represented by Mr. McKinney, appealed from this decision of the Executive Council to the Convention of the A.F. of L. held at New York, December, 1895. The matter was referred to the Grievance Committee which submitted a report, published in the printed proceedings of the New York Convention (See Page 84).[4] You will also note the statements made by the parties in interest. Each party charges the other with bad faith, and the failure to live up to the agreement reached at the Convention, which, at the time, was regarded as a final settlement. You will understand that one of the conditions understood to be agreed to by both parties was that the officers of both factions should retire, and that neither of them did so.

The division continued and feeling ran high on both sides. A number of local unions, attached to the Brotherhood of which Mr. Elliott is Secretary, took action in regard to holding a convention to be held at Cleveland. It is disputed as to whether this call was properly demanded. Notwithstanding this, a number of local unions did go to Cleveland and held, what they termed, a convention of the Brotherhood of Painters and Decorators of America. A faction of the Brotherhood therefore represented by Mr. McKinney as Secretary, was holding a Convention at Cleveland at the same time.[5] Articles of agreement were reached and an amalgamation of both these factions accomplished, and there elected Mr. Barrett,[6] Secretary with Headquarters at Lafayette. The Brotherhood of Painters and Decorators of America with Headquarters at Baltimore claimed to remain practically intact and is affiliated with the American Federation of Labor. The faction of the Brotherhood represented by Mr. Barrett sent a representative to Nashville during the time that the A.F. of L. Convention was in session. This gentleman appeared before our Committee, but made no request to be heard during the Convention. In consequence of the report of the Committee already referred to above, and the statements made by Mr. Sullivan, delegate of the Brotherhood of Painters and Decorators to the Nashville Convention, who is at the same time, President of the Brotherhood, a representative of the A.F. of L. was invited to appear at the Convention now being held. You are empowered to act as that representative.

At the meeting of the Executive Council held here February 21-22-23, 1898 propositions[7] were adopted looking toward an adjustment of the differences between the still divided painters' organizations. These propositions you will find in the March issue of the American Federationist (Page 19). A copy of these propositions was furnished to both Mr. John T. Elliott and to Mr. John Barrett, Secretaries of the respective bodies referred to. Mr. Elliott did not reply to these propositions, evidently proposing to lay them before the Convention now being held, for action. Mr. John Barrett replied by direction of his Executive Board, saying that the intervening time between the receipt of the propositions and the action for which they called was insufficient, hence the matter is practically in the same position as when the Executive Council submitted the propositions.

Of course you know that this division among the Painters' organizations is causing most wide-spread dissatisfaction and dissension in the ranks of organized labor. Almost in every City organized labor is taking sides with one or the other, and in many the movement is rent asunder. How far wider the dissension and division may go will be measured with the severity and intensity with which each contends for his own side. I am quite sure that unless this breach is healed very soon, this added to the schemes of the natural enemy of labor, will not only retard the progress of our movement, but injure the cause of progress in the interest of the men and women of our time, which may take decades to overcome and heal, much valuable time will be lost, many heart-sores and injustices borne, all or many of which should and can be avoided. If unity can be accomplished many of the wrongs from which labor suffers can be righted, and many rights which are yet denied us can be achieved. The Eight-Hour work day will be more readily accomplished, and the road to labor's emancipation cleared of unnecessary obstacles.

I am firmly convinced that any man, or any body of men who or which will be recognized by organized labor as being manifestly in the wrong, who stands in the way of unity will be held to a strict accountability and will have no place in the regard and respect of the earnest men engaged in our cause.

It seems to me that the Brotherhood now in session should pursue a course which would ratify the propositions for unity submitted by the Executive Council, leaving the date and city blank, to be filled in by the Executive Council of the A.F. of L., after corresponding and communicating with the officers of both organizations. At least that ought to be done, or if some other more tangible proposition or suggestion can be evolved by the Convention now in session, certainly then no objection can be made, but from my observation I am firmly of the opinion that the proposition of the Executive Council are the means most likely to produce the best results.

You will, of course, use your best judgement while at the Convention and impress upon the officers and delegates in attendance their manly action as union men, as men engaged in the great cause, the fundamental principles of which are unity of hands, hearts and minds.

Sincerely hoping that you may be entirely successful, I am,

Fraternally yours,   Saml Gompers.
President   A.F. of L.

TLpS, reel 14, vol. 22, pp. 984-88, SG Letterbooks, DLC.

1. The eastern (Baltimore) faction of the Brotherhood of Painters and Decorators of America (BPDA) held its convention in Buffalo, N.Y., Mar. 14-18, 1898.

2. AFL, *Proceedings*, 1897, pp. 104-5.

3. The BPDA's earlier Buffalo, N.Y., convention met Aug. 6-11, 1894.

4. AFL, *Proceedings*, 1895, p. 68.

5. The eastern and western (Lafayette, Ind.) factions of the BPDA both held conventions in Cleveland in December 1897—separately Dec. 6-9 and then together Dec. 9-11. The rapprochement proved temporary, however, and the BPDA schism did not end until SG arranged a "peace conference" at AFL headquarters on June 18-21, 1900.

6. John H. BARRETT was secretary-treasurer of the western faction of the BPDA (1897-99).

7. The AFL Executive Council called on each of the rival BPDA factions to elect five representatives to confer on terms of reunification in Buffalo, N.Y., on Mar. 16, 1898. It advised that reunification be accompanied by the retirement of current officers and their replacement through an election.

To William Rausch[1]

March 16th, [1898]

Mr. W. E. Rausch,
Secy. Treas. Internation[al] Union of Bicycle Workers,[2]
201 National Union Building, Toledo, Ohio,
Dear Sir & Brother:—

Your favor of the 13th Inst. just to hand. I, also, received a letter from the National Cash Register Company, of which the following is a copy:

"March 10, 1898.

Mr. Samuel Gompers,
423-425 G. St., N.W., Washington, D.C.,
Dear Sir: —

Your letter of March 8,[3] inquiring in regard to a dispute between our Screw Making Department and ourselves, which culminated in a strike[4] of 47 men about three weeks ago, has been duly received and noted.

Attached you will find a statement marked "A." This statement was not gotten up for general distribution, but is addressed, as you will see, and was distributed only to our employes.

About six months ago I wrote to you asking you to pay us a visit at your leisure. We are trying to accomplish for labor about all the things for which you are seeking. Our object in sending that letter to you was to have you come here in order that we might have a conference with you, and to have you offer suggestions as to what we might do to further better the condition of our employes, but, probably, owing to your being very busy you were unable to attend. We think it is really a duty which you owe to organized labor for you to come here and see for yourself the conditions existing in this factory, which are such as cannot be found in any other institution either in this country or abroad. This condition of affairs is appreciated generally by our 1300 employes, the 47 screw-makers being the only ones involved in this dispute, and we think they would not have been involved had it not been for outside influence. This influence was exerted partly by men working in other shops under entirely different conditions, partly by manufacturers who did not like to see our ideas extended, but more especially, we believe, by certain politicians who were hostile to progressive schools, especially those which pertain to manual training, cooking, sewing and others, all of which tend to a large extent toward the betterment of labor. We believe that three-fourths of the men employed in our Screw-making Department regret their action, and that they would not have gone out had it not been for this outside influence, of which we believe they were not cognizant.

On February 12th, 1898, Mr. Rausch, secretary-treasurer of the International Union of Bicycle Workers, and two other gentlemen called at the factory and we had the terms of a settlement talked over and agreed upon, as we thought, as you will see in the printed statement above referred to, but outside influences were determined that our men should strike. On Monday, February 21, the opening day of our Twelfth Annual Convention,[5] just at the time when representatives of our Company, both in this country and from Europe, numbering in all about 300, were gathered for this Convention, this strike took place. The determination to go out on that day when it would mortify us and injure us more than on any other day of the year was very marked.

On Saturday, February 19, when our time should have been devoted to the preparations for the coming convention, we had a meeting with the shop committee of the Screw Making Department and we devoted about 2½ hours in an interview with them endeavoring to avoid the strike. We read to them the stenographer's report of the verbal agreement which we made with Mr. Rausch, and we believe that had he come back, as we requested, there would have been no further dispute in the matter.

On Monday, February 21, Mr. J. F. Mulholland,[6] president of the International Union of Bicycle Workers, came to the factory for the purpose of conference. On account of our convention, however, it was found impossible to arrange for this until Tuesday, March 1. Mr. Mulholland would not listen to reason, but made additional claims and demanded our signature to a contract within half an hour, and it seemed to us that he was determined to prolong the strike, as he demanded things of us which we could not possibly yield, because we could not secure the information to aid us in our decision within the time allowed. We insisted that he live up to the contract made with Mr. Rausch and he refused to do so.

The strongest endorsement we have in the attitude we have taken is that of our employes as evidenced by the voluntary testimonials which they have sent to us. Of each of these testimonials we send you, under this cover, a copy, and in order that you may know that these copies are absolutely true and correct, I have had them certified to.

We stated in our printed circular that we would be very glad to have all of our screw-makers come back to work, without discrimination, provided, they returned by Friday, March 4, and we waited for them to return until today. We are now running short on material and in order to keep the balance of our employes at work we were obliged to fill the vacancies with volunteers from the rest of our force. There are yet some twelve or fifteen vacancies in the department, and we instructed our foreman in filling these vacancies to give the preference to any of our old employes who might apply for the positions, providing they could accept them and remain in good standing with their union, as we have done all in our power to prevent discord in the ranks of the union men, because we have no desire to weaken or destroy the union, which is, no doubt, of necessity to the men in many places where they have to work and where, if it were not for the union, advantages would be taken of them.

The general feeling in the community here is all in favor of us and against the screw-makers. We cannot afford to do anything that would seem like unfairness towards labor, because it is our object to do all that we can to uphold it. If you could only see the good-will prevailing in our institution towards the officers and that prevailing between the officers and others, especially in relation to our clubs and special affairs, you would heartily endorse all that we do. This strike was precipitated just at this time, we believe, by people who are especially interested in doing us harm.

We also send to you a copy of Commissioner Ruehrwein's[7] report containing a brief account of the methods of organization and advantages offered to its employes by our Company. Mr. Ruehrwein paid our factory a visit and gave it a very thorough inspection.

I had several appointments to deliver what we call our "Factory Lecture," the same which I delivered in Paris, Berlin and London last year, but I have had to cancel all of these engagements, excepting one which I fill tonight in Cincinnati, in a hall where I understand you are to speak later on. I regret very much that I am obliged to cancel these engagements, because I had hoped by these lectures to induce a number of manufacturers in this country to adopt our methods of treating labor,[8] but they now meet me with the argument that these efforts on our part are not appreciated as is evidenced by the strike which we have just had. This strike has thrown cold water on a great many men who were about to adopt such of our methods as they could to advantage. We are still hopeful that in time all this will be overcome, and that we will be able to deliver this lecture all over the country. We were just on the point of sending out a lecturer, at a salary of $4,000.00. per year, to deliver this lecture not only in the principal cities of this country but in Europe as well. His main theme would have been that justice, shorter hours and the treatment of employes as men and women pay; that progressive schools, manual training schools all pay; that higher wages, shorter hours and proper education is at the foundation of the future of labor.

I remain,

> Yours very respectfully, Jno. H. Patterson,[9]
> Prest. The National Cash Register Co.

P.S. Kindly return to us the testimonials when you are through with them."

There are a number of enclosures, which are too voluminous to copy and I cannot forward them. One is a printed statement, issued by the Company in regard to a letter written by the Screw Makers

Union No. 23,[10] of Dayton, to Mr. Dohner,[11] Foreman of the Screw Department, under date of February 9th, and what purports to be a part of a verbatim conversation between yourself, Mr. Ellis and Mr. Theobald.[12] Another is various petitions signed by the individual workers in each of the departments. In view of this entire matter, it seems to me that it would be necessary to consult my colleagues of the Executive Council, to proceed under the law and practice of the A.F. of L. You will understand that I have no power to place the Company upon our unfair list without the consent of the Executive Council and then only when every effort has been made to have a thorough investigation and honorable adjustment has failed. I should like to bring this matter to a point whereby an adjustment could be reached at once. I am consulting my colleagues of the Executive Council by this mail,[13] and would like to ask you your judgment upon this suggestion, and I am to go west in the course of two weeks.[14] What do you think of my meeting either yourself or President Mulholland or both of you at Dayton and then have a conference with representatives of the Company with a view of bringing about an adjustment.[15] Mark you, I do not say that I should attend it. Any other member of the Executive Council would, perhaps, do just as well. I simply refer to myself in the matter, since I am to pass very near that territory.

I have merely acknowledged receipt[16] of the letter of the National Cash Register Co., promising [an] answer "after further investigation." Please let me hear from you as to these matters at your earliest convenience, and oblige.

Fraternally,   Saml Gompers.

Pres't.   A.F. of L.

TLpS, reel 15, vol. 23, pp. 30-33, SG Letterbooks, DLC. Typed notation: "Dict. S. G."

1. William E. RAUSCH was secretary-treasurer of the International Union of Bicycle Workers (IUBW).

2. The International Union of BICYCLE Workers.

3. SG to the National Cash Register Co. (NCR), Mar. 8, 1898, reel 14, vol. 22, p. 916, SG Letterbooks, DLC.

4. On Feb. 9, 1898, forty-seven members of the IUBW in NCR's screwmaking department in Dayton, Ohio, presented demands to management for union recognition, restriction of the number of apprentices, removal from the department of shopmates objected to by the union, and payment for work previously performed without pay. Negotiations began Feb. 12 but were inconclusive; the workers struck on Feb. 21. On Apr. 2 SG met in Dayton with representatives of the company and the IUBW, arranging a settlement in which the firm accepted unionization of its screwmaking department and conceded the other points at issue. The agreement provided that the strikers would return to work on Apr. 25.

5. Three hundred NCR salesmen attended the firm's twelfth annual convention in Dayton, Ohio, Feb. 21-26, 1898.

6. John F. MULHOLLAND, a Toledo, Ohio, machine operator, was president of the IUBW (subsequently the International Union of Bicycle Workers and Allied Mechanics and the International Association of Allied Metal Mechanics) from 1896 to 1904.

7. William Ruehrwein was commissioner of the Ohio Bureau of Labor Statistics (1896-98).

8. NCR had inaugurated a pioneering corporate welfare program for its employees that included improving workplace conditions, health care, and educational opportunities.

9. John Henry Patterson.

10. Apparently IUBW 23.

11. John H. Dohner.

12. Henry Theobald, Jr., secretary of NCR.

13. SG to the AFL Executive Council, Mar. 16, 1898, reel 15, vol. 23, p. 23, SG Letterbooks, DLC.

14. Between Apr. 2 and 21, 1898, SG visited Buffalo and Rochester, N.Y.; Dayton and Toledo, Ohio; Indianapolis and Evansville, Ind.; Ishpeming, Mich.; Rock Island, Moline, and Chicago, Ill.; St. Louis and Kansas City, Mo.; and Kansas City, Kans.

15. SG wrote NCR on Mar. 22, 1898, offering to come to Dayton, Ohio, to mediate the dispute (reel 15, vol. 23, p. 77, SG Letterbooks, DLC).

16. SG to NCR, Mar. 15, 1898, reel 15, vol. 23, p. 12, SG Letterbooks, DLC.

To Louis Berliner

March 31, [1898]

Mr. Louis Berliner,
728 Lexington Ave., Brooklyn, N.Y.
My Dear Friend:

Your favor of the 26th inst. to hand, and contents noted, and I assure you that upon reading it, I was shocked beyond expression. When I told the folks of it last evening, they were astounded. I cannot find language to express my regret and horror at what you say. The idea of having been in a good paying business, with the prospect of safety when in your declining years, to be financially ruined is something that is enough to appall any one, and I assure you it does so to me, particularly after the years of acquaintance and friendship which has existed between us. I am in doubt as to who you mean when you speak of your "son-in-law" being the cause of it. Do you mean Bernard Bomeisel.[1] I want to reserve anything I have to say in this matter until I hear from you upon that point. I trust, too, that matters are not as bad as they appeared at first. Let me say too, that I should be pleased to have you write me. You know you can do so in all confidence.

Sophie and the family join me in wishing you and the family health and better success.

With kindest regards, I am,

Sincerely yours,   Saml Gompers.

TLpS, reel 15, vol. 23, p. 316, SG Letterbooks, DLC.

1. Bernard Bomeisl was a Brooklyn dealer in painters' supplies.

To Walter MacArthur[1]

March 31, [1898]

Mr. Walter Macarthur,
Editor Coast Seamens Journal,
San Francisco, Calif., Sta. D.
Dear Sir and Brother:

The last Convention of the American Federation of Labor directed that one or more organizers be appointed for the inter-mountain country. These would have been appointed some time ago, but the fact of the matter is as you know the revenue of the A.F. of L. is very small, and the funds of the A.F. of L. in consequence is in keeping with it. It is necessary however, in the interest of our movement that every effort be made to carry out the instructions to the best of our ability.

The Executive Council has made it my duty to make the appointments, of course subject to their approval. Having this in mind, I am pleased, recognizing your ability, earnestness and sterling unionism, to tender you the position, and hope that you will be enabled to accept it, even if only for a brief period. I know, and am verified in that knowledge by our friend Furuseth, who is here, that your duties to the Seamens Union are such that you cannot be spared from your office for long periods, yet I hope you will be enabled to accept it even for one particular purpose, that is, to attend the conference which has been called by Mr. Edward Boyce, to take place at Salt Lake City, Utah in May. The expenses of your trip, together with salary, will be borne by the A.F. of L. It would perhaps be advisable if you went as a regular delegate to that Convention. You will be doing the movement a very large service by accepting this mission.

Inclosed you will find excerpts of a letter[2] which I have written to a friend in Olympia, Washington.[3] It may contain interesting information to aid you.

Inclosed you find commission as organizer for the inter-mountain country for one month.

With best wishes, I am,

Fraternally yours, Saml. Gompers.
President A.F. of L.

TLpS, reel 15, vol. 23, pp. 317-18, SG Letterbooks, DLC.

1. Walter MACARTHUR edited the *Coast Seamen's Journal* (1895-1900, 1901-13).
2. In his letter to William Blackman of Mar. 29, 1898 (reel 15, vol. 23, p. 304, SG Letterbooks, DLC), SG responded to Boyce's criticisms of the AFL's lobbying methods and its system of voting and representation.
3. William BLACKMAN, president of the Washington State Labor Congress and an AFL organizer, was a factory, mill, and railroad inspector of the Washington State Bureau of Labor in Olympia.

Excerpts from an Article in the
Chicago Federationist

Kansas City, Mo., April 7 [9]. [1898]

GOMPERS IN THE WEST.

. . .

At the conclusion of his address[1] Friday night Mr. Gompers picked up a piece of paper and said: "I received this note a moment before rising to address you. It says that some gentleman in the audience would like to ask me some questions. With your permission, I am now ready to answer them, if it is in my power."

Mr. Cunningham,[2] who was on the city ticket of the Socialist Labor Party, arose and said: "Mr. Gompers, you say we are living under a false economic system. What shall we put in place of it?"

"A true one; one that will be evolved out of the intellectual progress of our people."

"Do you prohibit the discussion of politics in labor unions?"

"No, sir!" Mr. Gompers pushed his head out beyond the footlights and glared. "I'll tell you what we won't allow, sir. We won't allow the labor unions to become the tail of any political kite, sir."

"Does it stand labor in hand to study political science?"

"Most certainly it does. There is no science which the working people should not study. The trade unions urge all members to study."

"Then how about the letter you wrote a year ago, forbidding the discussion of political science in labor unions?"

"The gentleman is talking about that of which he knows nothing. If you have any such letter of mine produce it and I will answer you."

Cunningham did not have the letter, but promised to be at the meeting the following night at Kansas City, Kan., with a copy of it, and then he continued:

"How about the sheriff who shot down the strikers at Lattimer? Was he not elected by the workingmen whom he shot?"

Mr. Gompers didn't know. He thought not.

In reply to another question of Mr. Cunningham's, Mr. Gompers said he could not state positively that there were any constituencies in the country in which the laboring people were not in the majority, the point urged by the Socialists being that the laboring people were responsible for their condition because they did not take the political power themselves.

. . .

The president of the A.F. of L. was interviewed, written up and talked to, and of, by Kansas Cityans. . . .

. . .

Regarding President McKinley's stand in the Cuban-Maine[3] affair, President Gompers thinks the president has acted very wisely. "It is to be hoped by everybody that war will be averted," said Mr. Gompers, "and that a peaceable and dignified settlement of the present deplorable affair can be consummated. If Cuba can be freed without war, so much the better. If not, we must be fully prepared for war, and any undue haste in the form of a sudden declaration of war without preparation would be a fatal blunder, which would cause this country no end of embarrassment. If the president should comply with the popular demand for war I think he would make a mistake.

"Now do not misunderstand me," said Mr. Gompers. "If we can avert war, and at the same time preserve our national dignity and honor, well and good. But if such can not be done, then I say war, and an unrelenting one.

"It is a melancholy theory to consider that every hope except one of averting war—and that hope the very slenderest—has been taken from us.

"I can see little chance of this government's maintaining peace with Spain. But I can console myself with the thought that if we are to be plunged into war with Spain we shall at least have done all in our power to prevent it. The only hope of maintaining peace is, of course, that Europe will protect the present Spanish dynasty so that when it makes the surrender of Cuba to the United States the other factors in Spain will not overthrow it.

"I can partly understand why Spain shrinks with such horror from yielding Cuba. The island is one of the oldest of her possessions and it seems the ruin of the monarchy to lose it."

When asked regarding the effect of war upon the laboring people, Mr. Gompers replied:

"It would make corpses of the men, widows of the women and orphans of the children, for it is the laboring man who must defend his country's flag and it is the laboring man—the common man, you say—who must die for its honor. Can you wonder that I shrink from the degradation of blood and murder and misery? And yet I would have war rather than retreat from the wise, firm and honorable position which this country has taken in regard to Cuba.

"You ask me whether or not war would be wholly a misfortune; whether it would not in some way relieve and rest us from the constant pondering and brooding over perplexing social questions. The answer is that we are exchanging conditions and questions of peace for those of blood. The thoughts which labor is now thinking—the harmonizing thoughts of home and family and comfort—are to be changed to the animal and brutish thoughts of slaughter. War makes men brutal. War is brutal, always and forever.

"And war cannot extinguish for all time the problem of employer and employed; war cannot make us forget forever the problem of machinery, of child labor, of closer human relations and of sanitary conditions. War can only displace them for a time with bloodier thoughts, which give way in turn and leave us learning over again the primer of social conditions."

Mr. Gompers left for the east via Moline, Ill., and will spend some time at Washington headquarters. During his absence Frank Morrison always holds the reins of the Federation machinery, and it is even said that the business is done by our Frank while Gompers is in Washington. However that may be Gompers has an able assistant, to say the least, and the "old man" knows it.

Morrison has made large numbers of friends in his position as an officer of the A.F. of L. and there is no doubt but that he will be Gompers' successor, provided, of course, the "old man" decides to retire from office.

Charles W. Fear.[4]

Chicago Federationist, Apr. 13, 1898.

1. SG spoke on Apr. 8, 1898, at the Gilliss Opera House in Kansas City, Mo.
2. Cornelius Cunningham, a Kansas City, Mo., tinner, was the SLP candidate for police judge in the April 1898 city elections.
3. Since 1895 Cuba had been wracked by an insurrection aimed at ending Spanish colonial rule. Alarmed at the island's chronic instability and the threat to American

lives and property there, the McKinley administration dispatched the battleship *Maine* to Havana harbor after a Jan. 12, 1898, riot in the city. On Feb. 15, the *Maine* exploded and sank, killing over 250 crewmen. Probably the result of an accident on board the ship rather than a Spanish plot, the episode nevertheless inflamed American public opinion, exacerbating longstanding tensions with Spain over the Cuban revolt and reinforcing the determination of many American political and business leaders to settle the Cuban question. On Mar. 9 President McKinley obtained an appropriation to begin military mobilization, and between Mar. 20 and 28 he demanded a number of concessions from the Spanish government aimed at ending hostilities and achieving eventual Cuban independence. When Spain rejected the demand for independence through American mediation, McKinley evacuated American citizens from the island and on Apr. 11 asked Congress for authority to go to war to pacify and liberate Cuba. Congress complied on Apr. 19, and, after a final ultimatum to Spain, a blockade of Cuba was declared and Admiral George Dewey was ordered to capture or destroy the Spanish squadron in the Philippines. Spain declared war on Apr. 24.

The Spanish-American War proved an easy victory for United States forces in the Caribbean and the Pacific. The belligerents signed an armistice on Aug. 12 and a peace treaty on Dec. 10; the latter was ratified by the U.S. Senate on Feb. 6, 1899. Under its terms the United States acquired the former Spanish colonies of the Philippines (for $20 million), Guam, Puerto Rico, and some smaller islands. Spain also agreed to relinquish Cuba and assume its $400 million debt obligation.

4. Charles W. Fear was a Kansas City, Mo., printer.

Excerpts from an Article in the *Kansas City Times*

[April 10, 1898]

GOMPERS IS MUCH EXCITED

Cornelius Cunningham, who charged President Samuel Gompers of the American Federation of Labor with being the author of a letter disapproving of the study of political economy by laboringmen, and who promised to produce a copy of the letter at a meeting of laboringmen in the chamber of commerce at Kansas City, Kan., last night, failed to put in an appearance or to send an excuse for his absence, and a majority of those who heard Mr. Gompers last night and his emphatic denunciation of the charge were persuaded that he never gave utterance to such a sentiment. . . .

Mr. Gompers made an eloquent talk last night to the large audience that was present, and at the conclusion of his lecture called upon Mr. Cunningham to bring forth the letter.

"Is the man in the house?" asked Mr. Gompers, leaning over the table and looking down upon the assemblage.

For a time there was no response, and the audience began to shift about uneasily.

"If he is here, I call upon him to produce the letter," said Mr. Gompers.

"Guess he didn't come," someone remarked.

"He was afraid to," said someone else.

"Wait a minute," said Mr. Gompers. "I beg of the audience not to make any comment. Is the gentleman in the house?"

Mr. Cunningham was not present. The great labor leader mopped the perspiration from his forehead and waited.

"I have written more than 10,000 letters in my life," Mr. Gompers finally began, "but I never wrote such a one as this man accuses me of. I would be a fool to advocate such a thing. Why, the idea of my opposing the study of political economy by laboringmen! Political economy is the science of life, and why shouldn't laboringmen study it? I would consider myself a fit subject for the insane asylum had I been guilty of such a thought. I never wrote anything that could be exaggerated into such a statement as this man accuses me of having made over my own signature. A man who would rise up in a public meeting and make such a false charge can place no value upon his conscience." Mr. Gompers spoke rapidly and with much earnestness, and finished the sentence with a gesture that showed that he was thoroughly aroused. And before the words were cold upon his lips half a dozen men were upon their feet asking his attention.

COULD NOT FIND THE LETTER.

"The gentleman who made the charge is absent, and in his defense I wish to state that he was unable to find the letter, though he is positive that it was published," said a friend of Cunningham's.

"It was not published," quickly retorted Mr. Gompers.

"I would like to state," said another of the audience, "that the letter was published in the Midland Mechanic some time in June or July last."

"I say that it was not published in the Midland Mechanic or any other paper," said Mr. Gompers, excitedly.

"But it was," said still another, "and if the files of the paper had not been lost we could confront you with it."

"Pray, sir, is there not a copy of the Midland Mechanic in all this city of that date? That man promised me that he would be here tonight with that letter, and he has failed to keep his word. Suppose I had failed to be here tonight, you would have called me a coward."

"You should blame the Midland Mechanic and not Mr. Cunningham, for he only read it in the paper," interposed someone as Mr. Gompers began to apply the lash to his absent adversary.

"I would stake my life that he didn't do any such thing. I would like to have that man here." The speaker grew visibly excited and paced up and down the rostrum, wringing his hands. "Isn't he here somewhere. O, I wish you could get him. Here, won't somebody take down what I say, so that the papers can get it straight?"

Someone consented to write as he dictated, and the speaker began his statement.

"Write it down that this man claims that Mr. Lewis,[1] formerly editor of the Midland Mechanic, some time during June or July of last year, charged through the columns of his paper that Samuel Gompers discouraged workingmen studying political—"

"He didn't say that," yelled Charles Richardson,[2] a brother Socialist of the absent man.

"Well, my God, what did he say?"

Mr. Gompers was very angry, and his usually red face grew pale under the excitement. Suddenly he seemed to recover himself, and raising his hands beseechingly, he dismissed the subject.

"We will not talk any more of it. These little controversies and battles of words are good things," said Mr. Gompers, with a smile. "They cause us to think and bring us wisdom. We should not be angry, but should all work in unison for the great cause of labor. By discussing our work we become better acquainted with it, and can better fit ourselves for the duties that we have to perform. Let us all lend our energies and influences for the strengthening of our forces. Trades unions have withstood the edicts of kings and potentates, have suffered their representatives to [be] guillotined and hanged, but they still exist, and will continue to exist. Every labor organization is a link in the chain of toilers that are striving for better conditions and better opportunities for the great masses. There is nothing that can secure the protection for the toiler that the labor union does not do. I beseech you to organize and pray you to be loyal to each other. Don't say that you can't pay the little dues that are required, for if you don't pay it to the union you are paying it tenfold into the coffers of the money power. Organized labor has had her victories and her defeats, but she will triumph in the end."

. . .

Kansas City Times, Apr. 10, 1898.

1. J. Harry Lewis, advertising manager of the *Kansas City World*, had edited the *Midland Mechanic* until about 1896.

2. Charles L. Richardson was a Kansas City, Mo., traveling salesman and an SLP member.

An Excerpt from a News Account of a Meeting of the Chicago Federation of Labor

April 17. [1898]

CHICAGO FEDERATION

. . .

GOMPERS MAKES A SPEECH.

President Dunn[1] at this juncture of the proceedings caught a glimpse of the president of the American Federation of Labor in the rear of the hall and invited him on the stage. As Mr. Gompers made his way up the hall he was given a regular ovation, a delegate from the cigarmakers calling for three cheers for the "president of the greatest labor organization in the world," which was given in a hearty manner.

Mr. Gompers later, on motion, was invited to say something, and in the course of his remarks went into the history of Chicago's central labor body, saying it was the most aggressive the city ever had and was to be congratulated on the vast amount of work it had accomplished. "Within a few days," said Mr. Gompers, "we may be brought face to face in deadly conflict with another nation. I have said elsewhere, and I repeat it here, that war should be avoided at all times when it can be avoided honorably. The highest legislative body in the land has taken action that proves it is inevitable. I am for Cuba free and independent. In New York I have ever helped the Cuban Junta. My advice has been sought, and as a representative of the laboring men and women of the country I have assured the Cubans of our support. My devotion to the cause of Cuban liberty extends back for many years. In the long struggle that preceded the present war for years I devoted a part of my wages for the support of the Cuban cause.

"I do not believe in war for war's sake. But if war is necessary to free Cuba, I say go to war. (Applause.) We want Cuba free! (Applause.) The massacre of innocent men, women, and children must be stopped. Starvation of thousands must be tolerated no longer. We want due reparation for the killing of our men and the destruction of our battleship. (Applause.) Cuba is too far away from Spain to belong to Spain. It is a part of this hemisphere, and will be enrolled among the list of American republics.

"Again, a revival of healthy industrial conditions is at hand. The impetus of increased work is felt on all sides. War means an interruption of this. The laboring man of today, the man in the ranks of organized labor, was never thinking as much as he is at the present time, and he is not crying for war. Is it necessary that, because a pro-Weylerite,[2] for political reasons, destroyed our Maine, we should seek reparation by shedding the blood of other men? Are there not other honorable modes of reparation to be obtained? When it is determined there are not such modes then consideration of war will be another question."

Of labor organizations Mr. Gompers went on to say: "They were never stronger. I think capitalists and the workingmen are closer together than ever, and we have reached that point where there is no human power that can destroy the labor organizations of this country. The fact that these organizations have gone through the period of industrial depression without becoming disorganized has increased the confidence and respect in them on the part of the employer. Further, there is more work for labor to-day than there has been for some time past. Labor is more in demand, and, while here and there some differences exist, they are not serious, and the general situation is most excellent. Of course the preparations for war have increased the work in certain branches of labor enormously, but to offset this is the fact that, while war is imminent or when it becomes a certainty, there will be much capital withheld from investment because of capital's timidity. This will affect industrial conditions to a certain extent. The Cuban question will trouble everything until it is settled, and that is one of the powerful reasons why labor wishes for the freedom of Cuba. A more powerful reason is that the granting of political freedom to a people but precedes the securing for them of economic freedom. After political freedom is secured for Cuba the great questions will arise of economic freedom, and in all this American labor is vitally interested and opposed to the existence of any rotten Spanish autocracy in Cuba."

. . .

Chicago Federationist, Apr. 20, 1898.

1. William T. Dunn, a member of International Union of Journeymen Horseshoers 4 of Chicago, was president of the Chicago Federation of Labor.

2. General Valeriano Weyler y Nicolau was commander of Spanish forces in Cuba (1896-97). The American press gave him the soubriquet "Butcher" for the brutal conduct of his anti-insurgent campaign.

To the Executive Council of the AFL

Washington, D.C. April 29th, 1898.

To The Executive Council, American Federation of Labor.

Colleagues:

We have had quite some correspondence with the Secretary[1] of the Trades and Labor Congress of the Dominion of Canada[2] in regard to the subject matter of financial assistance necessary for their securing legislation in the interests of labor of the Dominion. You will remember that the subject matter was discussed at our Convention and at our Executive Council meeting and the undersigned authorized to act in the matter but I prefer to consult your wishes and have your approval on any tangible proposition. Secretary George W. Dower states that if the sum of $100.00 was set aside each year by the A.F. of L. to aid their legislative committee, the arrangement would be satisfactory and appease any dissatisfaction which may exist among the labor organizations of Canada, and inasmuch as the local unions of Canada are attached to the National and International Unions of America having their Headquarters in the United States and affiliated with the A.F. of L., it would seem that some apportionment is due them for the work indicated. I therefore, submit to you the following proposition:

Resolved, That a sum not exceeding one hundred dollars (100.00) be set aside each year by the A.F. of L. for the purpose of aiding the legislative Committee of the Trades and Labor Congress of the Dominion of Canada, the same to be drawn upon by order of the legislative committee subject [to] the approval of the Secretary and President of the A.F. of L. Please return your votes upon this proposition and oblige,[3]

Yours fraternally,   Saml Gompers.
President   A.F. of L.

TLpS, AFL Executive Council Vote Books, reel 8, frame 273, *AFL Records.*

1. George W. DOWER was a Toronto printer and member of International Typographical Union 91. He was secretary-treasurer of the Dominion Trades and Labor Congress (DTLC) and the Trades and Labor Congress of Canada (TLCC; as it was renamed in 1892) from 1888 to 1900, except for the 1890-91 term.

2. Toronto unionists formed the Canadian Labor Congress in 1883; it was reorganized in 1886 as the Trades and Labor Congress of the Dominion of Canada. It was later renamed the DTLC (1888) and then the TLCC (1892).

3. The AFL Executive Council approved the proposal.

To John George[1]

April 29, [1898]

John E. George, Esq.,
#10 Oxford St., Cambridge, Mass.
Dear Sir:—

Your favor of the 26th inst. to hand, and contents noted. It is very gratifying to learn that you are engaged in writing an article[2] on the joint convention[3] of miners and mine operators in Chicago last January. I presume that you have the data and full information upon the subject. Should you require any additional, I feel confident that our friend, Mr. M. D. Ratchford, President of the United Mine Workers of America, Stephenson Bldg., Indianapolis, Ind., would be pleased to aid you.

It is quite a mistaken notion to believe that this case "is about the only example of what is in England called 'collective bargaining' on a large scale" that we have in this country.

The Amalgamated Association of Iron and Steel Workers have a wage committee meet about two weeks before the annual convention of the association. The committee reports to the convention. The convention appoints a committee to meet the iron and steel manufacturers jointly or otherwise, generally jointly. There "collective bargaining" takes place for the ensuing year.

The Iron Molders Union of North America has had a system of "collective bargaining" annually for a number of years. A few weeks ago I met President Martin Fox (of Cincinnati, O.,) at Chicago, Ill. where a renewal of agreement was just consummated.

The American Flint Glass Workers Union,[4] William J. Smith,[5] Pittsburg, Pa., have had—I am not sure whether they now have—a system of "collective bargaining."

The rule in the United States is that the "collective bargaining" takes place between organized labor and employers more largely in localities. Quite a number of national unions undertake local "collective bargaining" from national headquarters.

Then again, there are a number of national organizations which stipulate a minimum wage rate for all localities.

I hasten to reply to your questions as per your request, and, if possible, to avoid your making any statement in your paper which could easily be upset.

When your article is published, will you kindly let me have a copy of it, and oblige,

Yours very truly, Saml Gompers.

President A.F. of L.

TLpS, reel 15, vol. 23, pp. 451-52, SG Letterbooks, DLC. Typed notation: "Dic. S. G."

1. John E. George, a former Braidwood, Ill., miner, was a graduate student at Harvard University.

2. "The Settlement in the Coal-Mining Industry," *Quarterly Journal of Economics* 12 (July 1898): 447-60.

3. Efforts by coal miners and mine operators to forge an industry-wide agreement resulted in a joint conference in 1886, initiated by the National Federation of Miners and Mine Laborers. The conference established a joint scale of prices with regional differentials that were designed to create similar rates of wages and profits throughout the industry. With diminishing success, subsequent annual conferences through the early 1890s attempted to maintain the agreement; it collapsed completely in the wake of the 1893 depression. The desire of the United Mine Workers of America (UMWA) to restore it was an impetus behind the 1897 coal strike and the subsequent convention of UMWA delegates and mine operators that met in Chicago, Jan. 17-26, 1898. The convention agreed on a differential price scale for much of the interstate bituminous region and provided for an eight-hour workday and boards of conciliation to adjust grievances. The delegates agreed to meet again in 1899.

4. The American FLINT Glass Workers' Union of North America (AFGWU).

5. William J. SMITH of Pittsburgh served as president of the AFGWU from 1885 to 1900 and, in addition, as the union's treasurer from 1887 to 1900.

An Editorial by Samuel Gompers in the *American Federationist*

[April 1898]

SOCIALISM vs. SOCIALISTS OF NEW YORK.

"BY THEIR ACTS SHALL YE KNOW THEM."

Recently we called attention to the fact that the Socialist party, under the leadership of an individual known as Daniel DeLeon, of New York, makes it a point to enter into negotiations with employers of labor during periods in which their employes are engaged in a trade dispute or strike, no matter whether it be for improved conditions or against a reduction in wages, and through him throws its assumed influence against the workers' efforts. This was manifestly so during the textile workers' strike of New Bedford, Mass., where this person used the same arguments that every greedy capitalist and their apologists, advocates, and allies make when speaking of trade unions, and the active men in the trade unions.

Three weeks ago the members of the Cigar Makers International Union of New York working for Seidenberg & Co. went on strike[1] against a reduction. The DeLeonite Socialist party of New York entered into an agreement with the firm with a view of supplying socialist (?) workers to take the strikers' places. The International Union controlled the situation, and with the assistance of the A.F. of L. office scored the victory, wages being restored, and a complete union establishment being effected. That the firm did not succeed in enforcing the reduction is no fault of the so-called socialists of New York.

Of course these incidents are but a small part of the destructive work and tactics which the parties referred to undertake to accomplish, happily for the workers, without success. They gloat over every attempted invasion of the workers' rights by employers, denounce trade union action to resist, and preparation to resist, capitalist encroachments; they have disrupted several unions and then called them "advanced" bodies. In so doing they rendered the workers in those trades helpless victims to the rapacity of the employers; and yet, all this is done under the pretense of advancing the cause of socialism. How much at variance they are, however, with the socialist writers and thinkers a few facts will show.

The last international socialist congress was held in London in 1896. There resolutions were adopted declaring that the organization of local and national trade unions should be encouraged and are essential to the emancipation of labor. We quote from the official printed proceedings:

["]The trade union struggle of the workers is indispensable to resist [the] economic tyranny of capital, and thereby better the actual condition of the toilers. Without trade unions no living wage, and no shortening of hours of labor can be expected.

["]The Congress considers strikes and boycotts are necessary weapons to attain the objects of trade unions. What is most essential is the thorough organization of the working classes; as the successful management of a strike depends on the strength of its organizations.["]

The Congress declared it to be the duty of all to make the trade unions as effective as possible, to organize national trade unions in their respective countries—

"Thus avoiding waste of power by small individual or local organizations. *Especially difference of political views ought not to be considered a reason for separate action in the economic struggle.*"

In a book written by one of the two authoriticians on Socialism, Frederic Engels ("The Condition of the Working Classes in England"), the following passages in regard to trade unions and strikes occur. He says:

["]Every manufacturer knows that the consequence of a reduction not justified by conditions to which his competitors also are subjected would be a strike, which would most certainly injure him, because his capital would be idle as long as the strike lasted and his machinery would be rusting, whereas it is very doubtful whether he could in such a case enforce his reduction. Then he has the certainty that if he should succeed his competitors would follow him, reducing the price of the goods so produced, and thus depriving him of the benefits of his policy. Then, too, the unions often bring about a more rapid increase of wages after a crisis than would otherwise follow. For the manufacturer's interest is to delay raising wages until forced by competition; but now the workingmen demand an increased wage as soon as the market improves, and they can carry their point by reason of the smaller supply of workers at his command, under such circumstances.["]

Further on in the same work Engels, discussing the causes which prompt workers to sometimes strike in spite of the fact that the prospect for success is bad, says:

["]It will be asked: 'Why, then, do the workers strike in such cases, when the uselessness of such measures is so evident?' Simply because they *must* protest against every reduction, even if dictated by necessity; because they feel bound to proclaim that they, as human beings, shall not be made to bow to social circumstances, but social conditions ought to yield to them as human beings; because silence on their part would be a recognition of these social conditions—an admission of the right of the bourgeoise* to exploit the workers in good times and let them starve in bad ones. Against this the workingmen must rebel, so long as they have not lost all human feeling; and that they protest in this way, and in no other, comes of their being practical English people, who express themselves in *action,* and do not, like German theorists, go to sleep as soon as their protest is properly registered and placed *ad acta* there, to sleep as quietly as the protesters themselves.["]

What is true of the workers of England is equally true of the workers of our own country, who, being eminently practical, express themselves in action and make that action known and felt in the every day struggle to not only maintain the vantage ground gained, but ever battling and preparing to battle along rational common sense lines to secure better material, social, political, and moral conditions for the

* Wealth possessing or capitalist class.

workers, and the attainment of that justice for which the human family from time immemorial have yearned and struggled.

The so-called socialists of New York are all at variance and in conflict with the best writers, thinkers, and actors in the socialist movement in every other part of the world. And this state of affairs has been the sum total of a professional late recruit's activity or deviltry in the socialist movement of New York. He has aroused the honest indignation of every sincere wage-earner engaged in the effort to emancipate labor; he has made the name socialist synonymous with cheap, unfair workers, and strike breakers; and has alienated the good will of thousands of earnest, honest, faithful, and intelligent workers.

If there is not a dishonest combination between the DeLeonites and employers of labor when in dispute with their workers, it is a very peculiar agreement of thought between avarice and a strange cult, known only to a professorial *pseudo* socialist, who lives under an assumed name and who, assuming to advocate a principle, is guilty of the gravest offenses against the honor and interests of the working class.

American Federationist 5 (Apr. 1898): 37-38.

1. On Mar. 14, 1898, cigarmakers and packers of CMIU 144 and nonunion employees struck the New York City firm of Seidenberg and Co. over a wage cut. According to a report by a CMIU 144 member, the Socialist Trade and Labor Alliance's Pioneer Local Alliance 141 supplied workers for the firm during the strike. Nevertheless, CMIU 144 achieved a settlement on Mar. 22 that restored the wage cut, required union membership for all cigarmakers doing board rolling, and excluded members of the Pioneer Alliance from the shop.

To the Executive Council of the AFL

[May 7, 1898]

[To the Executive Council,] American Federation of Labor.
Colleagues:

As you are already aware, the textile workers of New Bedford have been on strike since January 17th, 1898, against a reduction of 10% in their wages. The only union in the textile trade affiliated with the A.F. of L. was that of the local[1] of the Cotton Mule Spinners' National Union. The workers in the other branches of the textile trade were partly organized, but not attached to the Textile Workers' National Union. Notwithstanding this fact, the Cotton Mule Spinners' National Union, and the Textile Workers' National Union's officers requested that we aid the people on strike by securing them voluntary contributions. This has been done, and a large sum of money was secured in the interest of the strikers. Through this peculiar combination of circumstances, together with the one that the secretary[2] who was authorized to receive the moneys was an opponent of trade unions (a member of the S.L.P.) who declared that the trade unions were not contributing the money which the strikers were receiving, the contributions fell off considerably. A little more than a week ago, the strike was officially declared off by the organizations other than the local of the C.M.S. and the Carders. The money received from voluntary contribution has been given entirely to the workers in the branches other than the Cotton Mule Spinners, the latter having been supported out of the funds of the National union. The National Cotton Mule Spinners' Union for the past three weeks has supported the Carders, in order that they might also be continued on strike. The result of this has been that the expenditures of the Cotton Mule Spinners' reaches about $800 over and above their income, notwithstanding that they levied an assessment of $2.50 per week on their employed members at New Bedford, and about $1.00 a week on other members outside of New Bedford.

The Cotton Spinners' National Union recently held its Convention,[3] and Mr. Samuel Ross, as secretary, was directed to make application to the A.F. of L. for the enforcement of Article 10 of the A.F. of L. Constitution, that is, "for the Executive Council to levy an assessment of 2¢ per member per week upon their National, International and Local bodies affiliated with the Federation."

A conference[4] was held with Mr. Samuel Ross and Mr. Donnelly,[5] of the Cotton Spinners' Union, and Mr. P. J. McGuire, Vice-President A.F. of L. and myself in regard to this application. The matter was fully discussed, and the gentlemen of the Cotton Spinners' Union believe that they can win the strike, if they are assisted for a few months. The matter of issuing a circular requesting voluntary contributions for the Cotton Spinners and Carders, instead of levying an assessment, was discussed, and they fully agreed that whatever seemed most advisable to the Executive Council would be agreeable to them. You will therefore please vote upon the following propositions:

1. That the Executive Council levy an assessment of 2¢ per member per week for five continuous weeks, as per sections [1] and 2, Article 10, Constitution of the A.F. of L.

2. That a circular be issued by the officers of the A.F. of L. to affiliated unions for financial support to the Cotton Mule Spinners' National Union.

The above are intended as alternative propositions, and although the Executive Council are entitled to vote for or against both, if the desire is to financially assist the Mule Spinners, one of the propositions should be approved, and the other disapproved.

Please return your votes to this office at your earliest convenience, and oblige,[6]

Fraternally yours,   Saml Gompers.

President   A.F. of L.

TLpS, AFL Executive Council Vote Books, reel 8, frames 278-79, *AFL Records.* Typed notation: "Dis. [Dic.] S. G."

1. The New Bedford (Mass.) Spinners' Union.

2. William Cunnane, a New Bedford, Mass., weaver, was secretary of the Joint Strike Committee.

3. The National Cotton Mule Spinners' Association of America held its semi-annual convention in Boston, Apr. 5-7, 1898, where it changed its name to the National Spinners' Association of America (NSAA).

4. The conference apparently took place in New York City on May 4, 1898.

5. Probably Thomas O'DONNELL, an officer of the NSAA, who served as secretary or treasurer of the spinners' national union from the early 1890s into the second decade of the twentieth century. He was the union's treasurer in 1897.

6. The AFL Executive Council voted against levying an assessment but in favor of issuing a circular.

To Samuel Goldwater[1]

May 10th, [1898]

Mr. Samuel Goldwater,
Detroit Michigan.
My dear friend:

Through the kindness of a friend, I learn that you have been very ill, and that you are still suffering. Of the nature of your illness, I have not been informed, but am told that you have been confined to the house for some time. I do not write this as a letter to console you, because that is unnecessary for a man of your sterling qualities, earnest character and devoted principles and high mind. I write you as a friend and say to you that there are more friends of yours than you have any knowledge of, who hope that your great strong will will help you to overcome your illness. I have in mind many cases, among them my own, in which I firmly believe that grit and determination has had much to do with bringing about recovery and health, and I want you for the sake of your family and your friends, yes, for yourself, to just grit your teeth and make up your mind that you are going to overcome the illness from which you are now suffering, and make it possible for all those who love you to greet you again in your old time health and vigor. The very many years of friendship and personal good will which has existed between us prompts me to express the sincere hope that I may for many years more count you as an old time friend and worker in our great cause. If you can find it convenient to drop me a line, even by a friend, I shall appreciate it very much.[2]

Sincerely yours,   Saml Gompers.

Tom Tracey is here and says Amen!.

T and ALpS, reel 15, vol. 23, p. 529, SG Letterbooks, DLC.

1. Samuel GOLDWATER had served as a vice-president of the CMIU in 1895. He died on May 26, 1898.

2. On May 11, 1898, SG wrote Henry Barter that "it causes me great regret to think that our old friend Sam Goldwater is near his end. I wrote him a letter yesterday, and I do hope it may reach him in time, reach him and encourage him. You can readily understand that it is rather a delicate undertaking to write a man under such circumstances; when you see him please remember me to him with my sincere wishes for his recovery and health" (reel 15, vol. 23, p. 565, SG Letterbooks, DLC).

To Frank Gill[1]

May 11th, [1898]

Mr. Frank H. Gill,
125 E. Pico Street, Los Angeles, California.
Dear Sir and friend:

Through the courtesy of Brother Hawkins[2] Secretary of the County Council of Labor,[3] I have your address and am glad to have the opportunity of writing you. I beg to say that I regret the necessity which has compelled you to seek the congenial climate of California, and do hope that you are enjoying better health and are doing well. The Executive Council would perhaps have appointed you as the organizer as provided for by the resolution of the Convention, but there were a number of things that interfered. You understand the sentiment which has been cultivated among some of our fellow workers in the West; they wanted a Western organizer permanently in the field, travelling from place to place and wanted a Western man, too. You understand that the funds of the A.F. of L. are very limited, that the contributions from organizations are very small, and that we have no other means of raising funds. They see the large number of organizers in the East, but you know that they are not under salary.

You held a commission for years from the A.F. of L. in Grand Rapids and never received a dollar for your services. The work of the entire corps of organizers is given voluntarily and gratuitously. The reason why there is not an equal number of organizers in the far West is because industry has not developed to that extent in the far West, as it has in the East and North. I hope though that soon we may witness greater development and with it a greater growth of our movement. Of course, you understand that the position of Organizer for the West is not a permanent position, and that the appointment of Brother MacArthur has been for a specific time. If opportunities present themselves, the Executive Council will avail itself of such opportunities as may come to it, and as our means may allow, to from time to time, appoint men to do special organizing work. In the meantime, I ask you to accept the enclosed commission as organizer for Los Angeles, and vicinity.

Under separate cover, I mail to your address a copy of the April issue of the American Federation[ist] in which you will find some matter that may interest you, particularly in regard to the effort to divide the movement of our country.

Wishing you the very best of health and success and hoping to hear from you at your convenience, I am,

Fraternally yours,   Saml Gompers
President   A.F. of L.

TLpS, reel 15, vol. 23, pp. 559-60, SG Letterbooks, DLC.

1. Frank H. Gill was a Los Angeles cigarmaker.
2. William M. Hawkins, a Los Angeles printer, was secretary of the Los Angeles County Council of Labor (CL) and secretary of International Typographical Union 174.
3. The Los Angeles County CL was organized in 1890 and received an AFL charter in 1894.

To Jacob Cox[1]

May 12th, [1898]

Confidential.
Mr. J. A. Cox, Organizer,
Spruce Street, New Castle, Pa.
Dear Sir and Brother:

A matter has come to my attention, which I deem it my duty to acquaint you with at once. You remember you wrote here to Secretary

Morrison in regard to a man by the name of Geo. C. Jones[2] of McKeesport, Pa. It seemed peculiar that this man Jones, a stranger to you should call upon you at New Castle in regard to organizing the men of the National Tube Works of McKeesport, and particularly peculiar that he should volunteer the statement that our organizer there, Mr. D. H. Blood, did not have the confidence of the men. The information coming to me in the most direct manner,[3] is that Mr. Jones is nothing more nor less than an employee of the Gilkison Detective Agency of Pittsburg, and I write you this information to warn you [against] having him ingratiate himself into your confidence and through that into the confidence of the working men of Mc-Keesport, and thus help him to betray the interests of the men to the corporations. In the letter which reaches me from an authoritative source, I am told that detectives report to the Agencies who in turn report to employers and "many a poor fellow is discharged and deprived of a livelihood by this system."

Have you heard anything as to what work this man is doing; where he is employed, his habits and his means of support? These should be known to you, or if not known, it would be well for you to learn them. If there is any information you can give in regard to this, I wish you would do so at your earliest convenience and in the interest of our movement, I ask you to regard this communication as confidential at least for a time.

Fraternally yours,   Saml Gompers.
President   A.F. of L.

TLpS, reel 15, vol. 23, pp. 585-86, SG Letterbooks, DLC. Typed notation: "Dic. S. G."

1. Jacob A. Cox was a foreman at the New Castle, Pa., *News.*
2. The name George C. Jones was probably an alias.
3. William Warner to SG, May 9, 1898.

To James Duncan

May 14, [1898]

Mr. James Duncan,
#2 N. Holliday St., Baltimore, Md.
Dear Friend:—
Your favor of the 13th inst. to hand, and contents noted. I regret to learn the circumstances which you mention in regard to the unpleasant controversy[1] which has arisen between the Soft Stone Cutters

and your Local Union. I had heard something of it, or rather, read something of it in one of the papers; but I did not learn that the Local Federation had expelled your Local Union.

Of course, it would be unwise and improper for me to express an opinion now. I might be called upon to express an opinion in an official way. I had hoped, however, that the matter may be adjusted before it reaches here. You may rest assured that I shall keep a sharp lookout in regard to the matter, and will not be caught into making any hasty or illy considered statements.

It is very gratifying, the unparalleled success that our people are experiencing in their conflict with Spain. Of course, she is only a seventh rate power; and before the intelligence, energy, and manliness of our people, they must inevitably be crushed. It is the old versus the new. The uninterrupted successes may have another dangerous aspect, however, not for the present, but for the future. It may so fill our jingoists with our invincibility that they may be wanting to go around the world with a chip on their shoulders, and dare any one to look at it, much less knock it off. Citizenship in a great and powerful country is something to be proud of; but, being great and powerful, it behooves us to do what we can that we may use that power with discretion and in the interests of right and humanity, and not unnecessarily pick quarrels with people of other nations.

As the result of our present war, I am afraid that there will be a tendency to depart from that wise and safe policy of the founders of our Government in the establishment of what is become to be known as the Monroe Doctrine, and also in the avoidance of foreign "entangling alliances." It seems to me that there is an effort being made to have our country enter into the struggle of European and Asiatic nations for "conquest." I hope that the great future, which it is the mission of our country to fulfill, may not be thwarted by this present contest. I love to think that the American people, being a self-governing people, may work out the highest possible civilization, and that the peoples of other countries, living under monarchical, and, in some instances, effete, institutions, may look upon the American people as their example of progress, development, intelligence, civilization, and power of self-government, and that they may struggle to attain the same principles and results, and all uniting in the cause for the establishment of true freedom and justice among men.

When I started out writing this letter, I had no idea that I would write you upon this subject, but it has been in my mind for some time. I ask your pardon for trespassing upon your attention in this way.

Fraternally yours,   Saml Gompers
President   A.F. of L.

TLpS, reel 15, vol. 23, pp. 615-17, SG Letterbooks, DLC.

1. Jurisdictional struggles between the Baltimore branch of the Granite Cutters' National Union of the United States of America (GCNU) and a local union of marble and freestone cutters early in 1898 led the Baltimore Federation of Labor (FL) to expel the GCNU local. The following year, however, the Baltimore FL reversed its decision and the granite cutters reaffiliated.

To William Thornburgh[1]

May 14, [1898]

Mr. Wm. Thornburgh,
Manager, Shelby Steel Tube Company,
Cleveland, O.
Dear Sir:

Your favor of the 5th inst. to Mr. Frank Morrison was duly received, and as per your suggestion and our practice, an investigation was undertaken in regard to the matter of dispute[2] between our Tube Workers Union[3] and your Company. I find that the statements of our members are verified that the discrimination of your Company toward organized labor was plainly manifest, when 5 men who were in your employ were discharged, and at the time of the discharge were told by your Superintendent, Mr. Avery, that the men were discharged because they were union men, and Mr. Avery further stated that he intended to discharge every union man in the Mill.

There is one thing in declaring that you "have no objection to a man belonging to any organization he sees fit," and then discharging employes because of their membership in a union, and a threat to discharge every union man in the Mill.

Our men nor our organizations have no desire to interfere with the methods of "running" your business, but we do believe that our men have a right to organize for their mutual and common protection, without punishment being [meted out?] to them in the form of an effort to deprive them of the opportunity to earn their livelihood, for this in truth, is what a discharge of the character means to workmen.

I gather from your letter that you are an intelligent man. If I do not mistake you in that regard you must know that with the concen-

tration and development of industry, with the ever-increasing pro-
ductivity of the laborer and constant introduction of new machines
and the improvement of the old, a division and sub-division of labor,
the frequent keen competition of employers for trade, all have a
tendency to compel the workman to give his labor at lower wages
and to work long hours. Unless this effort and tendency is met by
some power to check it, there is no limit to the awful conditions to
which the workers of our country would not be forced down. That
power to check is, of necessity, the organizations of labor, and far-
seeing public spirited employers who are prompted by an enlightened,
self-interest will, instead of antagonizing and seeking to crush organization of workmen, give it their encouragement.

I have often said, and I now repeat it, that the fair-minded employer,
one willing to concede fair conditions and terms of employment to
his workers has naught to fear from organization. It is the most
avaricious employer, the one who if allowed to go on uninterfered
with by organized labor, would compel the fair-minded employer to
acquire his evil course, or be forced out of business. It is the union
of labor which protects the fair-minded employer from the unfair
competition of [the] most avaricious of their contemporaries, prevents
the destruction of the business and the Chinesizing of the workmen.
It is in this sense which our Secretary wrote when he said in his letter
to you of April 28th, "the protection also of the employer."

We do not want to "run your business," nor interfere with your
methods of running your business, but we do believe that we have a
right to be heard in our organized capacity, as to the conditions under
which we shall sell our labor to you.

You can readily understand that as an individual the workman —
a workman in a concern such as yours — can have no influence in
changing or improving the conditions of his employment.

We do not pretend to say that we are faultless, that we have never
been guilty of a folly, or never fallen into an error, but we submit
that it is unjust, unfair and unintelligent to discharge workmen from
your employ because they are union men, and to declare that no
union workmen shall be employed by you. I do not think that you,
or the entire management of your Company will look back over its
history and claim that its course has been entirely infallible. So far
as the present matter in dispute is concerned, it certainly seems from
the evidence before us that the men were not guilty of wrong doing
toward your Company.

It appears that some time in March the union made a request for
"55¢ per hundred all billets under 1¾, and the largest billets they
ever had were 3⅛ x 11, and they received 1 car load 3⅛ x 11 and

3⅜ x 16." The men think that they ought to have more money for poking them. The men claim that they had not been making fair wages for some time. They ought to have "day work at 22½¢ per hour, or $2 per day for 9 hours.["] It appears that your Superintendent requested that this matter be submitted in writing. I quote the above figures from a copy of their report to you, submitted on March 29th. On March 30th, they submitted another letter making a request for an increase of 10% in wages in several departments, outside of the machine and finishing rooms.

In looking over official copies of these letters to your Company, I find that they are couched in the most respectful language; That, when the committee of the union called for an answer, your Mr. Avery replied that he had no answer to make. He then sent for a man by the name of Kessler, and asked him to take the foremanship, in place of Mr. Smiley. When the former asked Mr. Avery why he wanted to displace Smiley, he answered, "he is a union man, and we intend to break up the union." It was when this information was conveyed to the men that they took the action they did, that is, endeavored to change the course and policy of your Company toward them and their organization.

In view of all these facts, I submit that the men have acted very carefully, and with every regard to the rights of your Company, and with a great deal of restraint upon themselves, realizing that their wages were constantly on the decline, which they hoped to avert with your co-operation.

We are requested to make this state of affairs known to our fellow workers throughout the country, and the sympathetic public, with the view of exerting some influence upon you to give a greater consideration to the requests of the men. I ask you to take into consideration the reasonable requests made by the Tube Workers' organization into our union, and to accord the full right of organization to these men without let, hindrance and prejudice, and that they be re-instated by you.

Hoping for an early and favorable response, I am,

Very respectfully yours,   Saml Gompers.
President   A.F. of L.

TLpS, reel 15, vol. 23, pp. 627-30, SG Letterbooks, DLC.

1. William Thornburgh, general manager of the operating department of Shelby Steel Tube Co.

2. On July 20, 1898, the AFL Executive Council placed the Shelby Steel Tube Co. on its boycott list; it remained there at least through 1899.

3. AFL Seamless Tube Workers' Union 7033 of Elwood City, Pa., where a Shelby Steel Tube Co. plant was located, was chartered in February 1898.

To the Executive Council of the AFL

Washington, D.C., May 16, 1898.

Confidential.

To the Executive Council, American Federation of Labor.

Colleagues:

During the Salt Lake City conference I was in constant correspondence with our friend Walter Macarthur. Mr. Macarthur wired here saying that a plan had been proposed for a Western division of the movement, with Executive Officers for the West, and that as a Western organization it should be entitled to representation by delegates in the councils of the Executive Council and in the Convention of the A.F. of L. I wired that we favored State Federations, and would perhaps recognize by a law that the Western unions should be distinctively represented on the Executive Council.[1] At the conclusion of the proceedings, I received a telegram from Mr. Macarthur as follows:

"Organization completed. Title, Western Labor Union. Constitution adopted by 101 to 7. System defective. No danger. Substance, whole fear populistic hippodrome."

I received a letter written at the conclusion of the second day's proceedings, that is, on the evening of May 11th. There were 119 delegates in attendance, of this number 77 were miners as delegates from the Western Federation of Miners. The Western Federation of Miners held its regular Convention at Salt Lake City, notwithstanding the invitation to the unions that each union was to be represented by one or two delegates. 77 delegates to the miners' Convention were admitted. Before they were admitted the delegates in attendance discussed the matter, and protested against the proceeding. It was then stated that the hall where the Convention was being held was hired by the Western Federation of Miners, that the delegates to the conference were there as the guests of that organization, and that it would be a most ungracious thing not to admit all the delegates. "The miners and Montana trade unions had between them about 100 delegates, the remainder was composed of Salt Lake City delegates, with a few scattering from Ogden and Cripple Creek. The States represented were California (I think by Macarthur himself), Montana, Arizona, Colorado, North and South Dakota and Idaho." Mr. Macarthur adds that "The only fair delegates were from California and Arizona."

I presume that the information should be considered confidential, yet it is of such importance that I regard it as my duty to acquaint you with it.

Fraternally yours, Saml Gompers.
President A.F. of L.

TLpS, AFL Executive Council Vote Books, reel 8, frame 283, *AFL Records.*

1. SG to Walter MacArthur, May 11, 1898, reel 15, vol. 23, p. 579, SG Letterbooks, DLC.

To Thomas Reed

June 11, [1898]

Hon. Thomas B. Reed,
Speaker House of Representatives,
Washington, D.C.
Dear Sir:—

Inasmuch as the House of Representatives has now under consideration a bill[1] for the annexation of the Hawaiian Islands to the United States, and since there are a number of features involving principles affecting the working people of our country in the proposition to annex these islands, I beg to address you, and through you, the Honorable, the House of Representatives, as briefly as possible summarizing a few of the objections which prompted the delegates to the Convention of the American Federation of Labor, held at Nashville, Tenn., December 15-21, 1897, to protest against the annexation of Hawaii to the United States.

Of a population estimated at about 100,000, Hawaii contains about 50,000 contract slave laborers made up as follows:

About 80 per cent. Chinese and Japanese.

About 20 per cent. Portuguese from Azore Islands and South Sea Islanders.

Some of the features of the contracts under which these 50,000 laborers work in Hawaii may be briefly stated here.

1. The terms of the contract usually run for seven years.

2. That the laborers have no right to change their employers, or leave their employment.

3. That the contract to labor is specifically enforceable by the laws of Hawaii.

4. That any time a laborer may serve in prison for desertion from labor is added to the term of the life of the contract to labor.

The laborers are corralled in gangs of from twelve to sixteen, each gang having an overseer on horseback armed with a whip with which diligence to labor is enforced.

The overwhelming number of contract slave laborers in Hawaii is employed in the sugar industry, and the master-employers have always insisted that the sugar industry can not be successfully conducted without this species of slave labor in those islands.

Though this point [is] contested, yet if Hawaii should become annexed to the United States the status of the laborers may not be changed; and if the Sandwich Islands as a part of the United States are permitted to continue a species of labor repugnant to the free institutions of our country, there is no safeguard against the extension of the same species of contract slave labor to the sugar industry of Louisiana and the cotton fields of the Southern States.

It required more than twenty years of constant organization, agitation, and education to legislatively close the gates of our country to the Chinese. The wisdom of that legislation has been demonstrated until there are few, if any, who now advocate its repeal.

The annexation of Hawaii would, with one stroke of the pen, obliterate that beneficent legislation and open wide our gates, which would threaten an inundation of Mongolians to overwhelm the free laborers of our country.

The annexation of Hawaii to the United States would be the admission of a slave state side by side with the free states of America; and, in the language of the statesmen of our own and all other countries: "We can not be part free, and part slaves. We will have to be either all free, or all slaves."

Though the number in Hawaii is small in comparison to the people of the United States, yet the dangers and the possibilities are such as to make the workers apprehensive.

In the war in which the people of our country are engaged, the workers are gladly volunteering their lives and their all upon the altar of the honor and the interests of our country; but we submit that in the effort to make Cuba free and independent, we should not hazard the loss of our own liberty.

The foregoing is submitted in the name and by the authority of the American Federation of Labor.

Very respectfully,   Saml Gompers.
President.

TLpS, reel 15, vol. 23, pp. 929-31, SG Letterbooks, DLC.

1. On May 4, 1898, Francis G. Newlands of Nevada introduced a joint resolution to annex the Hawaiian Islands (H. Res. 259, 55th Cong., 2d sess.). An amended

version of the resolution passed the House on June 15 and the Senate on July 6. President William McKinley signed the measure on July 7 and Hawaii formally became a U.S. Territory on Aug. 12, 1898 (U.S. *Statutes at Large*, 30: 750).

Excerpts from Samuel Gompers' Testimony before a Subcommittee of the Education and Labor Committee of the U.S. Senate

June 16, 1898.

. . .

STATEMENT OF MR. SAMUEL GOMPERS, PRESIDENT OF THE AMERICAN FEDERATION OF LABOR.

Mr. *Chairman*[1] *and Gentlemen:* I had not any idea that there would be any opportunity for the presentation of the laborers' side of this question to-day.[2] It is very gratifying to my colleagues and to myself to at least find that we have had a bill drafted for the establishment of eight hours, which means something, and the appearance of the gentlemen[3] here to-day representing these large interests is the best testimony that we are on the right lines.

It would have been some gratification to us, too, if at the previous hearings[4] before your honorable committee we could have had the assistance of a stenographer, who might have taken down what we could have said in advocacy or what we did say in advocacy of this bill.

The *Chairman.* I will state that as we were unable to have a meeting of the full committee for this hearing to-day, it was thought best to have a meeting of this subcommittee and to have the proceedings taken down in full so that they might be reported to the full committee. . . .

. . .

Mr. *Gompers.* . . .

Let me answer some of the statements that have been made here.

We, perhaps, like other men, have our faults, and perhaps we have some virtues that others possess. We, too, may be foolish, but we have not yet been guilty of repeating the folly that has been used so long ago, that the organizations of labor say that there shall be a fixed wage paid exactly to every man, no matter whether his work be excellent or poor. It is utterly absurd for any man claiming any intelligence in our day to assert that seriously as a fact.

What the organizations of labor insist upon is that if a man is worthy of his hire he is worthy of being paid a living wage. If his work is worth anything it is worth a wage upon which he can live. The establishment of a minimum wage is what we ask, and I would say through you gentlemen to Mr. Payson[5] that we have not any objection to him or anyone he represents paying the workman as much more above the minimum as their generosity may prompt them to pay. We do object to their being paid wages below a living wage. . . .

. . .

The contentment that exists among the workingmen! Mr. Cramp[6] never heard of any discontent in his yards! If I dared, I would show him affidavits in my possession from men who have been employed in his yards who were willing and who gave me their names that I could transmit them to the Secretary of the Navy.

Mr. *Cramp*. Send them in.

Mr. *Gompers*. I did not interrupt Mr. Cramp and I will not tolerate interruption. I sat here gnawing my very lungs at the outrageous statements that were made to this committee, and refrained from saying a word, even by way of interrogation or interruption.

The men who gave me their affidavits said they knew very well it meant the loss of their jobs and the victimization of them not only in the Cramp yard, but with every other large employer of labor, to take the course which they did in regard to reporting; but they were willing to bring it into the courts, and I think the honorable chairman of this committee will remember that at the first hearing of this bill I called attention to the fact that I had sent a statement making complaint to the Assistant Secretary of the Navy, and that he then directed and called attention to the affidavits presented by me. I was directed to proceed to the courts; that the officers of the Government of the United States were not the parties that could undertake the prosecution.

Mr. *Mantle*.[7] To what did these complaints refer particularly?

Mr. *Gompers*. The violation of the eight-hour law in the Cramp shipbuilding yard. The fact that there is such peace and contentment in the Bethlehem Iron Works goes without saying. It is the peace that reigns at Warsaw.[8] Very much like it. You have heard that as soon as there was any attempt made to plant the Amalgamated Association [of Iron] and Steel Workers at the Bethlehem Works—one of the safest, one of the best, organizations of the workingmen in the country, and composed of the most honest and sincere and patriotic men in this country—that they were locked out.[9] Our friend[10] says they were locked out because they made an attempt to organize the Amalgamated Association within their plant. The attempt to organize for their own protection met with a lockout and the throwing of the men into the streets, for aught this generous concern cared, to starve.

The fact that they are working twelve and fourteen hours a day is the best evidence of that contentment that comes with slavery.

And as to the sneering and contemptuous remark, deserved perhaps, of this strike[11] that occurred in the Cramps', fomented by a Scotchman and by some one else from Baltimore, we heard from the gentleman[12] that that strike failed because the fellow scooted with the funds — $2,000. Perhaps the amount was not high enough to commend itself to the respect of some gentlemen. Perhaps, if it had been a railroad or a bank representing widows and orphans, it might have commended itself to a greater degree of respectability. Some misguided fellow who scoots with $2,000 is the subject for their contempt and ridicule.

If, as some gentlemen said, this would mean less wages, how is [it] that others say it would be more wages? Some have said we want to deprive some of these men of their liberty, and yet the men in the next breath admit that it would mean an increase in wages. One of the two claims is improper and unjust and baseless. I have in mind the fact it would involve in time the more general establishment of the eight-hour work day.

The whole history of factory legislation, both in this country and in Europe, has its basis in reaching those which can be reached within the limits of constitutional powers of Government. The first efforts made to limit the hours of labor in England have been not to limit the hours of men, but to limit the hours of the women and children in the mills, in the factories, and it was by that means that the hours of men were reached, by reason of taking the women and children out of the mills.

The history of factory legislation in our country has been from the same standpoint. We have not undertaken, except within these past few years in Utah, to regulate the hours of men; but when in our legislation which we have undertaken to restrict and limit the hours of labor, it has been to limit the hours of labor of women and children. We have reached the limitation in the hours of labor of men by that process; and there is now pending in Congress either a joint or concurrent resolution for the submission of a constitutional amendment[13] to lessen the hours of labor in the textile industries of the United States.

. . .

In the case of Utah, which has been recently admitted as a State into the Union, they have a constitutional provision empowering the legislature to limit or restrict the hours of labor in certain industries. The legislature has availed itself of that power and has passed a law limiting the hours of labor of those employed in the smelting industries of the State, and that law has been declared constitutional by the Supreme Court of the United States upon an appeal by the smelting companies of the State of Utah.

Of course it would be unwise and impracticable to omit in that question what is the feeling of the people in your employ, and we have the reply of the representatives of the Carnegie Steel Company, and you heard that reply! You heard the reply of the employees of the Carnegie Steel Company upon the banks of the Monongahela some few years ago,[14] I believe; and it was all "harmony." The men are in "thorough accord." Ask them to vote upon it, and you will see 75 or 80 per cent voting against an eight-hour law. Yes; if that vote is taken under the supervision of a Mr. Frick, or a Mr. Corey,[15] or some other representative of the companies, because voting other than as they wish means walking along the streets without work.

But notwithstanding all your attempts to lock out union men or close your establishments to the efforts to organize, men will organize, and by making plain and open organization impossible you compel men to do that in secret which you deny them the right to do openly and publicly. This not only applies to one house; it applies to everyone whom it may concern.

It was remarked here whether we have a right to speak for these men. Let me see what right we have to speak for them. First, I should say that I have the honor, in part, to represent the American Federation of Labor, an organization composed of nearly all the trades unions of the United States, the exceptions being the steam railroad brotherhoods and one or two others. If I may be permitted, I would gladly submit the roster of our organization, so that it may be made a part of your record.

The *Chairman.* Certainly; there can be no objection to that.

Mr. *Gompers.* I have them here; probably a few written additions since June 4.

Mr. *Mantle.* How many members are embraced in those organizations?

Mr. *Gompers.* About 620,000. With the exception of the organizations I have stated, representing every trade in the United States, the roster is as follows:[16]

. . .

Mr. *Perkins.*[17] And you say, Mr. Gompers, the consensus of opinion among those different organizations is that Congress should pass a law that would not permit them to make a contract whereby they shall work, no matter what their pay, more than eight hours a day?

Mr. *Gompers.* The consensus of opinion is, that it is absolute that the hours of labor should be eight per day as the maximum, except under certain emergencies in which the country or the employer may be placed.

Mr. *Perkins.* I think we all agree on that. But that no one shall be permitted to make a contract for ten hours, even if you pay him for his overtime, is not that an interference with individual liberty of action? I make this query for you to answer: Whether it is the consensus of opinion among the 620,000 men whom you represent that Congress should pass a law depriving them of the right of making a contract with another calling for more than eight hours labor per day.

Mr. *Gompers.* Let me answer that in this way: Perhaps two-thirds of the members of the organizations to which I have just referred have adopted as the law of their own organizations that the hours of labor in their particular industry shall be eight hours, and no more. Another percentage of these organizations, which I am not prepared at this moment to give, have laws in which they declare that the hours of labor shall not be more than nine per day; and in others, again, the rule is that the hours of labor shall not be more than ten per day.

They have been limited in their opportunities to carry out the idea of limiting the hours of labor to less than ten or less than nine by those who are not organized; but there is not a difference of opinion, there is no difference of opinion at all, among the organized workingmen as to what the limitation of the hours of labor mean. They understand, in spite of all attempts to befuddle the mind, that less hours of labor means more leisure and more liberty and less slavery; that less hours of labor means higher wages, better conditions, a better standard of life; that less hours of labor means all that.

In speaking of the workmen, first I want to say that—although perhaps some of our friends may question it—I want to assure them through this honorable committee that, even though they do not know it, I have the honor to represent many of their employees, many of whom would, as a safety for their own livelihood when put to the test and asked the question, be compelled to say "no"; but occasionally you find a volcano arising under your feet when you imagine yourself in a fancied security of peace and contentment in your establishment.

I want to say this in carrying out the thought that I tried to convey a little while ago. The aim is to bring the industries of the United States upon the eight-hour workday. That is our purpose, and we hope and we expect that the Congress of the United States shall help us in that effort.

This Committee on Education and Labor was created, as the Committee on Labor of the House was created, because organized labor of the country had taken no direct political action to be represented in Congress or the Senate by its own representatives; and therefore the Committee on Education, as it was then, expanded its powers and became the Committee on Education and Labor of the Senate. So this committee and the Committee on Labor of the House should be the spokesman of the hopes and aspirations, as well as the safety, of the workingmen of this country. Upon no other pretense is there an excuse for a Committee on Labor of the House or for adding the words "and Labor" to the Committee on Education of the Senate.

We insist that for all the work done for the Government, whether directly or indirectly, within certain specified limits, and you can make them or devise them and we shall agree with them, but that all the work done for the Government shall be done on an eight-hour basis. We know that if that is done it will mean the gradual assistance in the general direction to the establishment of the eight-hour workday; but I doubt the wisdom of captains of industry who stand in the way of the establishment of the eight-hour workday among the working people of our country.

To-day we are manufacturing at a ratio never dreamed of by our forefathers. We are producing the wealth of the country at such prodigious rates that the imagination stands aghast and the genius of all the ages gone by and the genius of to-day are laying their laurels at our feet. Commerce is driven so rapidly, in a way unknown before, the lightning is harnessed to do man's bidding, water is utilized to drive wheels and propel machinery, all this producing the wealth of the world; and yet, in spite of this, in spite of this progress, in spite of all this development and growth and the ability to produce the wealth of our country and of the world, we have still in this year of grace 1898 to meet the same contention, the same narrowness that the friends of labor had to meet in the early days of the century, when the effort was made to relieve the toilers of our country of an hour from their burdensome toil. To-day you are asked, you members of the Senate, How can you regulate the hours of labor; how can you limit them to eight per day?

I wonder whether the gentleman had in mind the fact that the Senators do adjourn sometimes; that the Senate has a vacation sometimes. I imagine that the gentleman who addressed you, as a representative of these large companies, has a vacation sometimes, and that he does not spend the entire year in his law shop or in a factory eight hours a day.

There is no comparison; there is no application at all. These men work not simply with muscle, but with brain and brawn, and who, with modern machinery, have their nerves wrought up to the highest possible tension for nine, ten, eleven, twelve, and in some peaceful, beneficent institutions, as we have heard from representatives here this morning, even fourteen hours a day.

Yes; we want eight hours. We want eight hours for the workingmen of our country; and as citizens of this country, with all the rights and all the responsibilities of citizenship and manhood, we want eight hours. We want the Government of the United States to stand, not simply as an employer, as every other employer stands, on this business principle of getting the very last drop of blood out of the worker at the lowest possible wage he can get the worker to work for, but as an employer of labor who realizes the great forces that are at play to-day, and that, under the exigencies which are occurring in our day and in our contemporaneous times, they may compel a departure from well-established principles—realizing, too, that in industry there are changed conditions from the conditions which existed when the Constitution of our country was first formed, and hence it needs liberal interpretation in industry as well as in politics.

We want eight hours; we want the Government of the United States, as far as it is possible, to insist that the eight-hour workday shall not be infringed upon by anyone who attempts to do work for the Government.

. . .

I feel confident that, upon grounds of public economy, upon the grounds of public weal, upon the grounds of the highest morals, upon the grounds of the best spirit of patriotism and the safest course for the gradual solution of this problem by which we are confronted in our age, the movement to reduce the hours of labor is beyond peradventure the best and easiest, doing the greatest amount of good with the least possible injury. I think it is agreed by all sorts of men that the condition of affairs as it has gone on for awhile is not satisfactory. I imagine that we all hope for something by which this great problem can be met and worked out.

The trades unions of our country and of our time approach the captains of industry in a spirit of fairness, and say: Because of this great, wonderful development of industry and commerce, this great wealth-producing force of our times, a wholesome, a proper, and reasonable reduction in the hours of labor is needed, and eight hours a day is what is fair and reasonable and should not be contended against.

We have no fear that when this question is reported to the Senate that it will concur in the judgment of the House. This bill, even going as far as some of our friends say it will, yet can be safely defended upon every ground of the highest duty to our country, to our people, and to the citizenship of our country.

Mr. *Mantle.* I would like to ask Mr. Gompers, as he is well informed on the subject, how many industrial wage earners there are in the United States?

Mr. *Gompers.* I should say about 15,000,000 or 16,000,000.

Mr. *Mantle.* That includes the farmers of the country?

Mr. *Gompers.* Yes, sir.

Mr. *Mantle.* I had reference more particularly to those engaged in the manufacturing industries.

Mr. *Gompers.* I should say about four millions and a half.

Mr. *Mantle.* And your organization represents about 620,000?

Mr. *Gompers.* Yes, sir. Pardon me for a moment. There was a thought that escaped me and I am glad you referred to that, because it recalls it. Who, pray, has the authority, who has the credentials to speak for the unorganized workmen? Certainly not the unorganized workmen themselves, because the very fact of their unorganized condition renders them incapable of intelligent, joint expression of opinion.

The organized branch of labor does not represent the majority, I am free to say.

Mr. *Mantle.* But they speak for themselves?

Mr. *Gompers.* They speak for themselves, and, inasmuch as they are the only workmen who meet for considering these problems, none but them can speak for the wage-earners, I respectfully submit.

. . .

Mr. *Mantle.* Your general contention is that the United States has adopted the general policy of an eight-hour day for all of those in its employ?

Mr. *Gompers.* Yes, sir.

Mr. *Mantle.* But owing to defects in the law, or to defects in its administration, the terms of the law are not complied with in practice. And what you now seek is to strengthen this law so it will have force and effect in every direction?

Mr. *Gompers.* That is exactly it, and better stated than I could have stated it.

Mr. *Mantle.* There have been very perplexing questions put forth in regard to the ramifications which this question must take, and the application of this law will be almost illimitable. Now, it resolves itself into the practical question of what it will do in operation, and I should like you to say a word upon this point—as to this statement made by these gentlemen here as to the complications which must result through an attempt to enforce it in its proposed shape, and its effect, as suggested here, upon kindred industries; how that is all going to work if we pass this law. I should like to have some answer to that.

Mr. *Gompers.* I do not want to appear pretentious.

Mr. *Mantle.* I want your views.

Mr. *Gompers* (continuing). But I think it is agreed that in our time industry has so shaped itself that it does not at all depend upon the continuity of thought of one worker, but in any one branch of an industry, with proper methods and machinery, and exact scientific applications or application of scientific laws governing that industry, the product does not suffer by reason of different shifts of men going to work where others have left off.

. . .

Mr. *Mantle.* One other question. This has a bearing on the question of individual liberty of the citizen. That has been referred to here. Of course, there is an impression that this is the freest country on earth; that men have the greatest latitude here as to liberty of action. That is a thing that we naturally and rightly pride ourselves upon a great deal, and I would like you to say a few words on that, the idea being that men by mutual consent may, of course, bind themselves to anything; but as to the proposition of whether Congress has a right to step in to that extent and say that a man shall not be permitted to work more than eight hours, whether he wants to or not, without any reference to his individual wishes, I want to get the point of view from the laborers' standpoint.

Mr. *Gompers.* Individual liberty is a principle that the workingmen of our country are not willing to surrender. They regard it as a something that has cost too much to be ruthlessly destroyed; but they also realize that it is the song of the siren to which they are listening when they are told that a reduction of the hours of labor, either by their own action or indirectly by the action of the Government limiting the number of hours of labor in modern industry, is the taking away of their personal liberty.

To-day the worker is a distinctive and different man and his relations to his employer are entirely different from what they were when the Constitution of the country was devised and framed. Then the man who employed one or two or three workmen was a fairly large employer in industry. Then conditions of industry were comparatively primitive. To-day the individual employer has passed away. It is not only an employer with an employer in partnership, but partnership with partnership into a company, into great corporations until, as we have heard here, in order to carry on successful industry we see from five to fifteen thousand workmen employed by one company.

Where is the freedom of contract between an individual and a company representing from $15,000,000 to $50,000,000? Where is the opportunity to enter into a free contract between an individual employee and such a company? These questions enter into modern industry and the relations of the workmen and the employer, and a declaration of political liberty which does not involve an opportunity for economic independence is a delusion.

. . .

Mr. *Mantle.* You believe that this law would be the entering wedge which would help to solve the whole question?

Mr. *Gompers.* I do. I believe that as truly as I know I am addressing you now, that there is no safer, no truer, no better way—because it is the most natural method of adjusting the relations between employer and employed, and of solving this great problem upon safe and rational grounds—than the proposition which we, as the representatives of the trades unions, make to you to-day.

Mr. *Perkins.* Your reply to Senator Mantle, of course, is all right; but, if you will excuse me, I do not think you quite get to the point. In the language of Ingersoll,[18] we believe in the liberty of man, woman, and child. I believe that in the abstract. Now, this is used in the singular number. Shall Congress pass a law containing a stipulation that no workman or mechanic in the employ of a contractor or subcontractor shall be *permitted* to work more than eight hours? You did not answer Senator Mantle so it was [not] quite clear to my mind what your reason is for saying that this individual shall not be permitted to make a contract to work more than eight hours for you, no matter what you pay him.

Mr. *Gompers.* It is the exercise of the police power of the Government in this direction. The Government in its wisdom denies the right of anyone setting fire to his house. He might argue that that would be interfering with his individual liberty, because it is his house. The Government says that he shall not do that, because it might endanger the house of someone else.

. . .

But endeavoring to answer the question Senator Perkins put to me, and concretely to answer that question which Senator Mantle put, that the bill provides no workman shall be permitted to work more than eight hours a day, I would say that this provision applies to the contractors, and says that the contractor shall not permit that workman to work on Government work for more than eight hours. That man could, without violating the law, work two or three or more hours on other work without violating the law, but on Government work he could not do that. Hence I think the Constitution or right of individual liberty would not be infringed upon. I realize, though, that it would be rather inconvenient for him to get a job at some other place, and we want to make it inconvenient for him to do two men's work when there are so many walking the streets without any work at all.

. . .

U.S. Congress, Senate Committee on Education and Labor, *Report of Hearings . . . relative to H.R. 7389 . . .* , 55th Cong., 3d sess., 1898, S. Doc. 127, pp. 4, 42, 44-47, 58-62, 64-66.

1. James H. Kyle (1854-1901), a minister, was an independent senator from South Dakota (1891-1901). He was chairman of the U.S. Industrial Commission from 1898 to 1901.

2. SG was testifying in favor of the eight-hour bill. The hearings on June 16, 1898, had been scheduled to allow opponents of the measure to present their views.

3. Those appearing against the bill included officers or attorneys representing the Bath Iron Co., Bethlehem Iron Co., Carnegie Steel Co., Harlan and Hollingsworth Co., Newport News Ship Building and Dry Dock Co., Pusey and Jones Co., and William Cramp and Sons' Ship and Engine Building Co.

4. The previous hearings were held on Mar. 1 and 8, 1898.

5. Louis E. Payson, a Washington, D.C., lawyer, represented the Newport News Ship Building and Dry Dock Co.

6. Charles H. Cramp was president of William Cramp and Sons' Ship and Engine Building Co. of Philadelphia.

7. Lee Mantle (1851-1934), a newspaper publisher and editor, was a Republican senator from Montana from 1895 to 1899.

8. On Sept. 16, 1831, when informing the French Chamber of Deputies of the fall of Warsaw to Russian troops, during the "November Insurrection" for Polish independence (Nov. 29, 1830-Oct. 5, 1831), Foreign Minister Horace François Bastien Sébastiani declared, "Peace reigns in Warsaw." Sympathy for the Polish cause was widespread in France despite the government's neutrality in the revolt, and Sébastiani's remark provoked indignation among the deputies, one of whom reportedly exclaimed, "Yes; the tranquillity of the grave" (*Times* [London], Sept. 19, 1831).

9. A reference to a strike that began in June 1883 when the Bethlehem Iron Co. fired a union employee. The local lodge of the National Amalgamated Association of Iron and Steel Workers of the United States demanded his reinstatement. The firm refused and locked out some two thousand men on June 28. It resumed production on July 20 but rehired only nonunion workers. On Aug. 14 the union members voted to disband their local and apply for their old jobs.

10. Robert P. Linderman, president of the Bethlehem Iron Co.

11. On Aug. 17, 1891, about three hundred workers struck the Cramp shipyards in Philadelphia for higher wages. The walkout ended unsuccessfully on Oct. 12.

12. Charles H. Cramp.

13. On Jan. 5, 1898, Representative William C. Lovering of Massachusetts introduced a joint resolution (H.Res. 109, 55th Cong., 2d sess.) proposing a constitutional amendment empowering Congress to establish uniform hours of labor in manufacturing. The resolution failed to move beyond the House Judiciary Committee.

14. A reference to the Homestead strike of 1892 (see *Unrest and Depression*, p. 189, n. 1).

15. William Ellis Corey was general superintendent of the Carnegie Steel Co.

16. The list included all national and international unions, state branches, city central bodies, and directly affiliated locals attached to the AFL as of June 4, 1898.

17. George C. Perkins (1839-1923), Republican governor of California from 1880 to 1883, was a senator from the state from 1893 to 1915.

18. Probably Robert Green Ingersoll, lawyer and lecturer. See *The Early Years of the AFL*, p. 184, n. 2.

To James O'Connell

June 18. [1898]

Mr. James O'Connell, G.M.M.,
330 Monon Block, Chicago, Ill.
Dear Sir and Brother—

The note containing your favor of the 15th inst. in regard to the Fauber Company[1] was duly to hand, and I beg to thank you for calling my attention to it. The official announcement was written and given to the printer, but evidently was not set up, and must have gone astray. I regret this, as of course it means the delay of a month in its official promulgation. However, I beg to assure you that the matter will receive prompt attention and publication.

We had a splendid hearing[2] before the Senate Committee on Education and Labor on our Eight Hour Bill. No doubt you saw some reference to it in the papers. The representatives of the largest shipbuilders, Armour Plate, and other Iron and Steel Manufacturers were here, among them was Mr. Cramp himself; representatives of the Carnegie Iron and Steel Company, the Bethlahem Iron Works and several others. Vice-Presidents McGuire and Duncan were present, and made excellent addresses. I assisted in the work, and I am sure that the impression of every one there was that we have completely upset every claim made, both by the attorneys for the companies, yet they had the best that money can [. . .] to the [. . .] all men of the companies. Of course I should have been delighted if you could have been present, but the notice of the meeting came too late for that purpose. The hearing started at 10:30 in the morning, and the opponents occupied until about 1:30, and they then wanted to know whether any one could defend the bill. They asserted that no one could be found who would father it. I then spoke for the bill, and apart from my argument in its favor, I attacked the Committee in a manner in which they conducted the previous hearings as compared to the one of that today, and handled the Companies, and their attorneys in such a manner that they were all compelled to allow the full hearing, which lasted until ½ past four. I assure you that our boys made these millionaires and their representatives look mighty small.

The question of argument is not that which will not have its effect in this contest for our Eight Hour Bill. If there is any doubt at all, the appearance of these men against the bill shows that we are on the right track. It will have to be by force of numbers demonstrating to the Congress that the working men of the country want that bill beyond any doubt whatsoever, and everything must be done in order to accomplish the desired result. If you and your colleagues can write letters to the Senators, you should do so, not only of your own City, but of all, even if necessary to get up a circular and have your locals do likewise. It is a sharp and a hard fight which must be made if we want to secure the Eight Hour Bill, it is so thoroughly effective in its provisions.

Our friends join me in sending you kindest wishes.

Sincerely yours,   Saml Gompers.
President   A.F. of L.

TLpS, reel 15, vol. 23, pp. 969-70, SG Letterbooks, DLC. Typed notation: "Dic. S. G."

1. The W. H. Fauber Co. of Chicago, a manufacturer of bicycle cranks, refused to deal with the International Association of Machinists and fired employees for union membership. After SG's and O'Connell's unsuccessful attempt to resolve the dispute in April 1898, the AFL Executive Council placed the firm on the AFL boycott list. Official notice of the boycott appeared in the *American Federationist* in July (5: 101).

2. See "Excerpts from Samuel Gompers' Testimony before a Subcommittee of the Education and Labor Committee of the U.S. Senate," June 16, 1898, above.

To Alexander Gompers[1]

June 25, [1898]

Mr. Alexander Gompers,
99 Harrison Ave., Brooklyn N.Y.
Dear Brother:

Your favor of the 20th inst. to hand, with Mr. Beam's[2] card. I would say that the clerks who make their sales in the retail stores to customers are organized in local unions under the jurisdiction of the Retail Clerks National Protective Association. The name and address of the general secretary are Mr. Max Morris,[3] 2307 Champa St., Denver, Colo. I am not sure however, that the business Mr. Beam follows comes under its jurisdiction, more than likely it would be more appropriate under the American Agents Association.[4] You might suggest to Mr. Beam that he could now write direct, stating fully and clearly, his purpose, and I should be pleased to answer him at the earliest possible moment.

By the way, your excuse for not writing is positively ridiculous. You say that you spell poorly, and because of this you do not care to write. I am sure that the same reason might be given for a person declaring their inability to swim, and yet never making any attempt to go near a bath tub, much less a river. It is by practice that we reach any stage of perfection in anything. I am surprised that I have not oftener heard from yourself or Lou.[5] I do hope that both of you are doing well.

Do you read the American Federationist? I sometimes believe that it contains matter of general interest, and would be so, particularly to sincere trade unionists. I am glad that the boys are at home, enjoying their vacation with you. You say that they do not remember me. Have you no picture, photograph or wood-cut of mine? I am rather surprised, for they have not been so scarce. Under another cover, I send you a copy of last September's issue of the Federationist. It contains a group picture of the Executive Council and may do as a reminder to the boys, to whom I ask you to remember me, and also to the rest of the folks.

On July 2nd., union 144 is to have its annual picnic, and inasmuch as the wife and Sadie are going to New York for a while, I propose that they shall go there in time to attend the celebration. If at all possible, and I think I can make it, I shall come down and attend the picnic too. It would be a most pleasurable occasion for me to meet all the members of the family there.

With love to you, all the folks and friends, and hoping to hear from you at your early convenience, I am,

Sincerely yours,   Saml Gompers

TLpS, reel 16, vol. 24, pp. 29-30, SG Letterbooks, DLC.

1. Alexander GOMPERS, SG's brother, was a cigarmaker.
2. Probably Andrew Beam, a New York City agent.
3. Max MORRIS was secretary-treasurer of the Retail Clerks' National Protective Association (Retail Clerks' International Protective Association from 1899) from 1896 to 1909, and an AFL vice-president from 1899 to 1909.
4. The American AGENTS' Association.
5. Louis GOMPERS, SG's brother, was a Brooklyn cigar manufacturer.

To P. J. McGuire

July 8, 1898.

Mr. P. J. McGuire,
Box 884, Philadelphia, Pa.
Dear Sir and Brother:

Your favors of the 5th and 7th insts., together with a copy of your reply to president Ratchford, of the Miners, came duly to hand. I beg to say, as I wired you, that you did not enclose Mr. Ratchford's letter, nor the copy of the letter, the original of which you say he sent me. I shall answer fully when I see Mr. Ratchford's letter. In the meantime, it would be well for you to know that not only I was traveling upon the road[1] when several of his communications reached here, but I was also engaged in our legislation, and then again the application to place West Virginia coal on our unfair list had to go the rounds of our Executive Council before being published in the American Federationist.

There have been some of our friends of the labor press, yourself included, who have published the circular[2] as sent out by the Miners. This I could not do, as President of the A.F. of L., in the American Federationist, because it was necessary to have the vote of the Executive Council approving the action. That is the reason it did not appear in the June issue, but does in the July number.

On Monday I am to be at Zanesville at the Flint Glass Workers Convention[3] and demonstration, and on Tuesday at Muncie, Ind., where the Green Glass Bottle Blowers[4] hold their Convention.[5] I am to appear before them that day for the purpose of inducing them to become affiliated with the A.F. of L. In all likelihood, I may have an hour to stop over at Indianapolis, and then shall call at the Miners' office and talk the matter over with Mr. Ratchford. I shall write him to-day,[6] calling his attention to the fact that I shall see him at his office.

I shall send you formal reply[7] in regard to Mr. Ratchford when I have the opportunity of seeing his letter to you.

Yesterday Secretary Morrison and I had two interviews with the President, one in the morning and the other in the afternoon. They were held at the suggestion of Senators who were favorable to our Eight-Hour Bill. In the morning interview we urged his aid in influencing Senators who were both openly and secretly antagonizing our measure. He promised to aid. I then took occasion to mention the action of our Executive Council[8] in regard to appointments on the Industrial Commission,[9] and I want you to feel assured that I did not use the language contained in circular #36[10] to the Executive Council. The latter was simply used for our Council for brevity's sake. As a matter of fact, the language which you suggested was practically that employed in conveying the information. The President regretted our action, and thought it unreasonable. We assured him that we were more concerned in regard to our Eight-Hour Bill than in placing two or three men in any position within the gift of the Government.

In the afternoon interview we sought to have him talk to certain Senators, whom we mentioned by name, in regard to our Eight-Hour Bill. This interview was rather prolonged, and he broached the subject of the submission of names for appointment on the Commission. I reiterated our position in respectful terms, and I think he appreciated the sincerity of our motives.

In conversation with a few Senators after our interview with the President, they congratulated us upon our attitude, and said that though it might be disadvantageous for the present, it would redound to the advantage of our movement soon. Senators and Congressmen would understand that we did not seek our own personal advancement at the expense of our fellow-workers, but that our methods and motives would hereafter be above question or suspicion. In almost direct terms it has been intimated to me from several sources that if I would assent, the President would appoint me as a member of the Commission. I conveyed to the parties my determination that no matter whether the appointment is tendered to me through the solicitation of others or from the President's own initiative, I should refuse to accept, at any rate, certainly, if our Eight-Hour Bill was not enacted into law. I feel confident that this information will be communicated to the President. (As I am dictating this portion of the letter, I am informed that Congress has adjourned and both of our bills have passed but one of the Houses.)

In regard to the Painters matter, I would say that it seems to me you should have an interview with secretary Elliott at your earliest convenience. Inasmuch as you indicate that you will be extremely busy during the coming week, I would suggest that either the latter end of the coming week or the beginning of the week, July 18th, ought to be set for that purpose. I could either come over to meet you at Baltimore and participate in the conference, or, after you have concluded it, you could come here for the same purpose. Please let me know which date you will set for the purpose indicated.

Fraternally, Saml Gompers.
President A.F. of L.

TLpS, reel 16, vol. 24, pp. 144-47, SG Letterbooks, DLC.

1. SG was traveling between May 28 and June 8, 1898, stopping in Frankton, Ind., Oshkosh and Kenosha, Wis., and Kewanee and Chicago, Ill.

2. The circular, issued by the United Mine Workers of America (UMWA) and dated June 16, 1898 (*American Federationist* 5 [July 1898]: 99), called for a boycott of West Virginia coal because that state's coal operators refused to cooperate in establishing a system of uniform wages and hours.

3. The American Flint Glass Workers' Union of North America convention met July 11-21, 1898.

4. The GLASS Bottle Blowers' Association of the United States and Canada (GBBA).

5. The GBBA convention met July 11-19, 1898.

6. SG to M. D. Ratchford, July 8, 1898, reel 16, vol. 23, p. 153, SG Letterbooks, DLC. In a subsequent meeting, SG explained his action on the UMWA's circular to Ratchford's satisfaction.

7. SG to McGuire, July 18, 1898, reel 16, vol. 24, p. 194, SG Letterbooks, DLC.

8. The AFL Executive Council had ratified SG's proposal not to submit nominations for the U.S. Industrial Commission to President William McKinley as long as the federal eight-hour bill had not been passed. To do so, Gompers argued, would imply greater concern with "the appointment of some to a position than a measure in the interests of the working people of our country" (SG to the AFL Executive Council, June 30, 1898 [circular 36], AFL Vote Books, reel 8, frame 297, *AFL Records*).

9. On June 18, 1898, President McKinley signed a law (U.S. *Statutes at Large*, 30: 476) authorizing the creation of an Industrial Commission "to collate information and to consider and recommend legislation to meet the problems presented by labor, agriculture, and capital." The commission was to comprise five senators, five congressmen, and nine "other persons" appointed by the president to "fairly represent the different industries and employments." Empowered to hold hearings and divide its work among subcommittees, the commission originally had a two-year mandate. The results of its investigations, conducted from 1898 to 1901, were published as the *Report of the Industrial Commission*, 19 vols. (Washington, D.C., 1900-1902).

10. See note 8, above.

To Ralph Easley[1]

July 18, [1898]

R. M. Easley, Esq.,
Secretary, etc., Pacific Federation of Chicago,
215 First National Bank, Chicago, Ill.
My dear Sir:—

Your circular letter of the 8th inst., enclosing a call for a national conference[2] to discuss the future foreign policy of the United States, reached here during my absence on business in connection with our movement. I regret this, as I should certainly have been pleased to give it earlier attention.

I beg to enclose the copy of the call, signed as requested. I trust that the conference may be productive of great good to all our people.

Very truly yours, Saml Gompers
President A.F. of L.

TLpS, reel 16, vol. 24, p. 198, SG Letterbooks, DLC.

1. Ralph Montgomery EASLEY was an organizer of the Chicago Civic Federation (serving as its secretary from 1893 until 1900) and, later, of the National Civic Federation.

2. The National Conference on the Foreign Policy of the United States met Aug. 19-20, 1898, at Saratoga, N.Y. SG was one of the large group of prominent business, civic, academic, and labor figures who participated. The conference focused on the question of territorial expansion in the aftermath of the victory over Spain. It adopted resolutions approving the actions of William McKinley's administration before and during the war, advocating American protectorate status for the former Spanish colonies until they were capable of self-government, establishing public schools and permanent U.S. naval bases in the protectorates, and relegating the question of annexing territories by "mutual desire" to future consideration. Other resolutions called for civil service reform of the diplomatic corps, arbitration of international disputes, and the outlawing of privateering. On Sept. 15, 1898, a committee of conference participants that included SG presented the resolutions to President McKinley.

To Robert Fisher[1]

July 22, [1898]

Inspector of Mines,
Indianapolis, Ind.
Dear Sir:—

I am in receipt of a letter under date of July 14th from Kingman, your state, complaining very bitterly that the Inspector of mines of Indiana does not visit places where his services could be of great value in protecting the lives and limbs of miners. I am told that some of the mines are very dangerous, and not safe to work in. It is said that not long since there was a man who had his leg broken in three places; another had his back hurt; and that it took six hours to get a mule out of the four slopes; that the shaft is being worked by incompetents, and that applies equally to the engineer who is "more of a farmer than anything else."

It is suggested that you or some subordinate might ask for the old Clark Bank, 4½ miles east of Kingman; that there [are] some men down there who would give full information. The writer asks that the matter be given immediate attention.

The letter was addressed to me at Zanesville, where I was on July 11th, and it was forwarded here, reaching me to-day.

I hope that you will give this matter your immediate attention, and oblige,[2]

Yours very respectfully, Saml Gompers.
President A.F. of L.

TLpS, reel 16, vol. 24, p. 301, SG Letterbooks, DLC.

1. Robert Fisher was Indiana state inspector of mines.

2. Fisher replied that the mines in Kingman employed fewer than ten men and, therefore, did not come under his jurisdiction.

To James Duncan

July 23, [1898]

Mr. James Duncan,
Drawer 118, Bal. Md.
Dear Sir and Brother:

Your favor with enclosures to hand, and contents noted. In regard to the attitude of Senator Kyle towards our eight-hour bill, let me say that if you will look at the Congressional Record you will find that Senator Cannon,[1] of Utah, sought to have the bill considered, and that Senator Platt,[2] of Conn., publicly declared that the chairman of the Senate Committee on Education and Labor (Senator Kyle) had assured him that the bill "would *not* be considered at this session of Congress."

Senator Cannon properly characterized the action of Senator Kyle by repudiating the authority for giving any such pledge or promise. As a matter of fact, you will see in Senator Kyle's letter of the 9th inst. to you that there was an understanding "that any member of the committee should be at liberty to call the bill up at any time he might see fit, and that our action in the committee room should not in any way abridge such individual action of any member of the committee after the bill had been placed on the Senate calendar."

It is true, as Senator Kyle says, that an "effort was made to have the bill taken up out of order by unanimous consent, but that it was unsuccessful."

But we are in no wise under obligations to Senator Kyle in any effort of his to make the effort other than unsuccessful. As a matter of fact, I have it upon almost the very best authority, that Senator Kyle approached Senators, telling them that "President Gompers, of the A.F. of L., is in favor of having the eight-hour bill deferred until the next session so that it can be *properly amended.*"

When this was conveyed to me, I, without mentioning this, had an interview with him that was *very warm.* That he appreciated it was evident; for, when we parted, he did not either say "good-day," or "good-bye." But before parting, however, I stated to him that we wanted the bill substantially as it stood now (omitting the two commas), the ship-builders and other interests to the contrary notwithstanding. This was said to him because of his hemming and hawing and saying that there were other industries besides railroads that wanted the bill amended. I emphatically told him that we did not want to have this bill further amended or deferred, and, as the authors and sponsors of the bill, and representing those who are interested in seeing it enacted, we wanted it to be voted upon before adjournment.

I am writing thus fully to you for your information, but I deem it unwise that it be made public at least for a time. I think the report should be made in an official way. If Senator Kyle will retrieve his steps so that we can secure the eight-hour law, I am perfectly satisfied that the incident shall be buried; but, if he does not, every means should be resorted to in order that his double dealing should be made known to the workers and people generally of our country.

I set the batteries at work (See how militant we are all becoming!) in the rear of Senator Platt, and organized labor has been sending him letters that he must have regarded as an entire fusilade from an unexpected quarter. During the session, he simply acknowledged the letters; then he tried to defend himself, and now he is urging that he voted against the bill because the workingmen "would be the greatest sufferers, and the ones who would object to its operations if enacted into law." I think with practical action we may soon have him change his attitude again, and perhaps favor the bill. At least, I hope so, and shall work to that end.

I ask your permission to retain Senator Kyle's letter, as I have all of those written by him upon the subject which have been forwarded here.

Enclosed you will find Mr. Drew's letter. In your last note you say that it is unnecessary to reply to the questions propounded by him. What Mr. Drew says is true. The Bimetallist organization[3] of Great Britian [Britain] meets annually at the places where the trade union Congresses are held; and, no doubt learning that you are to be a delegate to Bristol,[4] he has written you upon the subject. During McGuire's and my visit to the Cardiff Congress, we had a very interesting interview with a number of the men. There was a banquet, which both he and I attended, and addresses. It was a most interesting occasion.

By the way, you have not said anything in regard to your trip abroad. When will you go? You ought to make arrangements soon, so as to secure decent accommodations. I certainly would like to see you before you leave, and have a talk over matters which would be of mutual interest, and which might perhaps aid you in some of the things which will come up to you for consideration on the other side. I could also give you names and addresses of men perhaps whom it would be pleasant to meet.

Secretary Morrison joins me in sending best wishes, and expressing the hope that you can keep cool.

Sincerely yours, Saml Gompers.
President A.F. of L.

TLpS, reel 16, vol. 24, pp. 336-39, SG Letterbooks, DLC.

1. Frank Jenné Cannon (1859-1933), a Utah editor and publisher, was a Republican territorial delegate to Congress (1895-96) and a U.S. senator (1896-99).

2. Orville Hitchcock Platt (1827-1905) served as a Republican U.S. senator from Connecticut (1879-1905).

3. The Bimetallic League was founded in 1888.

4. The TUC met Aug. 29-Sept. 3, 1898, in Bristol, England.

ARCHIBALD, James Patrick (1860-1913), an Irish-born paperhanger and member of the Irish National Land League, was an officer in the New York City Central Labor Union and its successor, the Central Federated Union, from 1882 to 1904, with the exception of one year. He was prominent in the KOL in the late 1880s, representing District Assembly 49 and paperhangers' National Trade Assembly (NTA) 210 in the General Assembly and organizing for the Knights in England, Scotland, and Ireland. He served as district master workman of NTA 210 from 1888 to 1890. In 1895 he helped found the National Paper Hangers' Protective and Beneficial Association, serving for seven years as its president. This union was unable to compete with the AFL's affiliate in the trade, the Brotherhood of Painters, Decorators, and Paper Hangers of America, and merged with it in 1902. Archibald then served the Brotherhood as general organizer, local and district officer, and AFL delegate. In politics Archibald moved from leadership in the Henry George New York City mayoralty campaign in 1886 to support of Grover Cleveland and a leading place in the New York state Democratic party. He served as warden of the Ludlow Street Jail in 1895, was active after the turn of the century in the New York City Civic Federation, was president of the Democratic Association of Workingmen of Greater New York, and for several years was the city's deputy commissioner of licenses. Archibald served as a lobbyist and officer of the Workingmen's Federation of the State of New York and the New York State Federation of Labor.

ARTHUR, Peter M. (1831-1903), a Scottish immigrant, was grand chief engineer of the Brotherhood of Locomotive Engineers (BLE) from 1874 until his death. He was a charter member of BLE Division 46 in Albany, N.Y., was its chief engineer in 1868, and represented it in BLE conventions from 1866 to 1874. Arthur served as second grand assistant engineer of the BLE from 1869 to 1874. As grand chief engineer he maintained the BLE's independence from the AFL and other labor organizations.

511

ASKEW, Robert (1865-1937), a miner's son, was born in England, where he worked in a cooperative store until he was eighteen. Thereafter he became a miner, working in England and Australia before immigrating to the United States in 1893. He continued mining in Michigan and Illinois and settled in Michigan about 1894. In 1895 he was a founder of the Northern Mineral Mine Workers' Progressive Union, serving as organizer and president (1895-97) and secretary-treasurer (1897-98). He then became a clerk in the Ishpeming, Mich., Co-operative Society and was president of the Michigan Retail Clerks' Association (1898-99) and an AFL general organizer (1899-1901). Between 1904 and 1908 he was a railroad cashier and warehouse foreman. He moved to Utah about 1910 and became a rural postman, a job he held for some twenty-three years. Askew was president of the Utah branch of the National Rural Letter Carriers' Association from 1910 to 1919. In 1919 he helped found the National Federation of Rural Letter Carriers (NFRLC) and was chairman of its executive council until 1924 as well as editor of its organ, the *Message* (1921-22). He also served as president (1919-24) and secretary (1924-25) of the NFRLC Utah branch.

BARNES, John Mahlon (1866-1934), a cigarmaker born in Lancaster, Pa., was a member of the KOL in the 1880s. He joined the CMIU in 1887 and served as secretary of CMIU 100 of Philadelphia (1891-93, 1897-1900) and of CMIU 165 of Philadelphia (1903-4). In 1902 he was elected first vice-president of the Pennsylvania State Federation of Labor. He joined the SLP in 1891 and served as corresponding secretary of the Philadelphia Central Committee and as an organizer for the Philadelphia American Branch of the SLP in the 1890s. He helped form the Socialist Party of America (SPA) in 1901 and served as the secretary of its Philadelphia branch and as the Pennsylvania representative on its national committee in the early years of the decade. He was elected executive secretary of the SPA in 1905, a position he held until 1911. In 1912 and again in 1924 he was the party's campaign manager.

BARRETT, John H. (1863?-99), worked as a painter in Denver from the early 1880s to 1897. He was a member of Brotherhood of Painters and Decorators of America (BPDA) 79 of Denver and an AFL organizer. In May 1897 he was elected president of the Colorado State Federation of Labor. The same year he was elected general secretary-treasurer of the BPDA's western faction and moved to its headquarters in Lafayette, Ind., where he died before completing his term of office.

BECHTOLD, Charles F., was secretary of St. Louis local 6 of the

National Union of the United Brewery Workmen of the United States (NUUBW) from 1888 to 1892. In 1892 he was elected secretary of the NUUBW, holding the position jointly with Ernst Kurzenknabe until 1899 and with Julius Zorn from 1899 to 1901.

BLACKMAN, William (b. 1861), was born in New York and by the early 1890s worked as a locomotive engineer in Seattle. There he was master (1890-93) of Brotherhood of Locomotive Firemen 407 and secretary (1895-97) of American Railway Union 98. He helped organize the Pacific Northwest Labor Congress in 1897, which the following year became the Washington State Labor Congress (from 1902 the Washington State Federation of Labor). Blackman was president of the organization from 1898 to 1906; he also served as an AFL organizer part of this time. He was appointed the Washington State Bureau of Labor's first factory, mill, and railroad inspector when the bureau was created in 1897. He held the post until 1900; from 1901 to 1905 he was the bureau's commissioner. In 1906 he ran unsuccessfully for Congress as a Democrat. A resident of Olympia from 1897, he moved to Washington, D.C., about 1915, where he was a commissioner of conciliation for the U.S. Department of Labor (1915-18). Afterwards he worked briefly as a clerk.

BLOCK, George G. (1848-1925), secretary of the Journeymen Bakers' National Union (JBNU) from 1886 to 1888, was born in Bohemia and immigrated to New York City in 1870. Moving to Philadelphia in the 1870s, he worked as a pocketbook maker and a journalist, joined the Social Democratic Workingmen's Party of North America, and, during 1877, was organizer for the Philadelphia American section of the Workingmen's Party of the United States. Block returned to New York City in the early 1880s where he joined the staff of the *New Yorker Volkszeitung*. He helped found the New York City Central Labor Union and was secretary of the Executive Committee of Henry George's 1886 mayoralty campaign. In 1885 he established the *Deutsch-Amerikanische Bäcker-Zeitung* through which he helped generate interest in organizing the JBNU in 1886. He served as editor of the journal until 1889. Around 1889 he went into the liquor business.

BOHM, Ernest (1860-1936), secretary of the Central Labor Federation of New York City from 1889 to 1899 and of the Central Federated Union of New York City from 1899 to 1921, was born in New York. He was a compositor, clerk, and manager of a cloak operators' union early in his career, becoming secretary of the Excelsior Club of the KOL in 1881 and corresponding secretary of the New York City Central Labor Union in 1882. During the 1880s and 1890s he was active in the organization of the brewery workers, serving briefly as an editor of the *Brauer Zeitung*—official journal of the National Union of United Brewery Workmen—in 1888. He supported Henry George in his 1886 mayoralty campaign, participated in the formation of the United Labor party, and served as secretary of the Progressive Labor party in 1887. Bohm was a member of the SLP and, from 1896 to 1898, secretary of the general executive board of the Socialist Trade and Labor Alliance. During World War I he worked with the American Peace League, but then allied with SG in the prowar effort. After the war he served as secretary of the New York City Farmer-Labor party (1919-21). From 1921 he was a leader of the Bookkeepers', Stenographers', and Accountants' Union—AFL Federal Labor Union 12646—holding several positions including the presidency.

BOYCE, Edward (1862?-1941), born in Ireland, came to the United States about 1882 and worked on railroads in Wisconsin and Colorado before becoming a miner. He was a member of the Leadville (Colo.) Miners' Union, which was affiliated with the KOL, from 1884 to 1886. Moving to Idaho in 1887, he joined the newly formed Wardner Miners' Union in 1888 and was its corresponding secretary until 1892. Boyce was active in the 1892 Coeur d'Alene strike and, as a consequence, served a six-month jail term for contempt of court. After his release in 1893, he was elected president of the Coeur d'Alene Executive Miners' Union, filling that post until 1895. He was a founder in 1893 of the Western Federation of Miners (WFM), of which he was general organizer (1895) and president (1896-1902). He also served as a Populist in the Idaho state senate from 1894 to 1896. In 1898 he was a founder of the Western Labor Union. He declined renomination as WFM president in 1902 and in 1909 moved to Portland, Ore. There he engaged in the mining business and was vice-president (1920-29) and president (1930-41) of the Portland Hotel Co.

BRAMWOOD, John W. (1857?-1932), was born in England and immigrated to Fall River, Mass., at the age of four. He was apprenticed in the printing trade and at age sixteen moved to Longmount, Colo. He served as president of International Typographical Union (ITU) 49 in Denver from 1895 to 1896. In 1896 he was elected secretary-treasurer of the ITU and moved to Indianapolis. He held the position until 1908 when he resigned to purchase part interest in a printing concern.

BREMER, Alexander H. W. (b. 1850), a native of Denmark, immigrated to the United States in 1877. By 1887 he was working as a musician in New York City, an occupation he followed (except for a brief period as a clerk) until around 1902. He was president of the New York City Musical Mutual Protective Union (MMPU; National League of Musicians of the United States [NLM] 1) from 1893 to 1898, and served as an NLM vice-president (1893-95) and president (1895-98?). He was again president of the MMPU (American Federation of Musicians 310) in 1918.

BURNS, John Elliott (1858-1943), a British machinist and a leader of the 1889 London dockers' strike, joined the Amalgamated Society of Engineers in 1879. He was a member of the Social Democratic Federation from 1884 to 1889, the year he was elected to the London County Council. In 1892 he was elected to Parliament as an Independent Labour candidate, and he was reelected until 1918 (beginning in 1895 as a Liberal/Labour candidate). He was one of the fraternal delegates from the TUC to the 1894 AFL convention in Denver, and in 1895 SG helped him set up a speaking tour of American cities to promote the principles of trade unionism. In 1906 Burns became a cabinet member in the ruling Liberal government; he resigned his post in 1914, however, in protest against Britain's entry into World War I.

CAHILL, Thomas P. (b. 1862), was born in England, immigrated to the United States in 1870, and eventually settled in Lawrence, Mass., working in turn as a weaver, salesman, editor, and laborer from 1881 to the end of the decade. Active in the KOL, he was master workman of one of the city's local assemblies, probably Local Assembly 5433, in the 1880s. In 1889 he cofounded Weavers' Protective Union 1 and in 1891 ran unsuccessfully as a labor candidate for the state assembly. He was general secretary of the National Union of Textile Workers of America in 1895 and 1896 and general secretary of the United Textile Workers of America in 1898. Cahill became an insurance agent in 1900 and continued in that business after moving to Cincinnati the next year.

CARNEY, William A. (1860?-1906?), born in England, immigrated to the United States around 1884 and settled in Pittsburgh where he worked in the iron mills as a rougher. He was a member of Monongahela Valley Lodge 53 of the National Amalgamated Association of Iron and Steel Workers of the United States (NAAISW), serving as its corresponding representative in the late 1880s and as vice-president of NAAISW District 1 from 1890 to 1895. From 1891 to 1893 he was second vice-president of the AFL, and he served as an

AFL organizer through the mid-1890s. Between 1895 and 1898 Carney organized workers for the NAAISW in Pennsylvania and West Virginia and assisted in strikes.

CARRICK, Michael Patrick (1857-1904), a painter, was born in Ireland and immigrated to the United States in 1872. A member of Pittsburgh KOL Local Assembly 1397, Carrick helped organize the Brotherhood of Painters and Decorators (BPDA) in 1887. He served as secretary of BPDA 15 in Allegheny, Pa., between 1887 and 1894. When factional struggles split the BPDA in 1894, Carrick supported the western faction, headquartered in Lafayette, Ind., serving as general organizer. Although Carrick was elected general president of the western faction in 1896, he resigned this post in 1897 in favor of unity in the BPDA. Carrick was also active in the United Labor League of Western Pennsylvania, serving as secretary in 1895 and as agent in 1897, and in the National Building Trades Council, of which he was a vice-president in 1897. In 1901 Carrick was elected general secretary-treasurer of the BPDA; he held that office until his death.

CARROLL, Edward M. (b. 1866), born in Illinois, was a Chicago plasterer. A member of Operative Plasterers' International Association of the United States and Canada (OPIA) 5, he served as secretary-treasurer of the OPIA from 1894 to 1898, when he was censured for malfeasance in office; he was president of the Chicago Building Trades Council from 1896 to 1900. He was a cofounder of the National Building Trades Council of America and its first general president (1897-98). Carroll was a Chicago civil service commissioner in 1900, practiced law from 1901 to 1905, and was a contractor from 1906 to at least 1913.

CARTER, William Samuel (1859-1923), a native of Austin, Tex., worked successively as a railroad baggageman, fireman, and engineer from 1879 to 1894. He edited the *Locomotive Firemen's Magazine* (1894-1904; after 1901 the *Brotherhood of Locomotive Firemen's Magazine*) and served as general secretary and treasurer (1904-9) and president (1909-22) of the Brotherhood of Locomotive Firemen (after 1906 the Brotherhood of Locomotive Firemen and Enginemen). From 1918 to 1920, he was also director of the Division of Labor of the U.S. Railway Administration.

CHANCE, George (1843-1900), born in Staffordshire, England, immigrated to the United States in 1852 and settled in Wilmington, Del., where he published a newspaper from 1865 to 1870. Shortly afterwards he moved to Philadelphia where he joined International Typographical Union (ITU) 2 and worked as a printer for the *Record* from 1883 to 1894. He was also an active member of the KOL from the early 1880s to the early 1890s. Associated with the utopian socialist movement inspired by Edward Bellamy, after leaving the *Record* he managed the American Press Association—an enterprise established by Bellamyites. He was president of ITU 2 from 1892 to 1897, and was president of the Legislative Labor League of Pennsylvania and of the Pennsylvania Federation of Labor as well as an AFL organizer in 1897. Chance served on the AFL Legislative Committee from 1898 to 1900. In his later years he operated a job printing shop in Philadelphia.

CLARK, Edgar Erastus (1856-1930), born in Lima, N.Y., served three terms as chief conductor of Division 124 of the Order of Railway Conductors of America (ORCA) in Ogden, Utah. In 1889 he was grand senior conductor of the ORCA, and from 1890 to 1906 he was grand chief conductor—the leading officer of the union. Clark also edited the ORCA organ, the *Railway Conductor,* from 1893 to 1906. President Theodore Roosevelt named him to the arbitration commission during the anthracite coal strike of 1902. He resigned his post with the ORCA in 1906 to accept an appointment by Roosevelt to the Interstate Commerce Commission, on which he served until 1921, twice as chair (1913-14 and 1920-21). He was subsequently a member of the Washington, D.C., law firm of Clark and LaRoe.

CLIFFORD, Patrick H. (b. 1865), a Pennsylvania-born miner, was a resident of Aspen, Colo., while serving as president of the Western Federation of Miners from 1894 to 1895. By 1900 he was living in Denver where he was a mining inspector.

CONNOLLY, Thomas F. (variously Connelly; b. 1857), was born in England and immigrated to the United States in 1869. He settled in Lowell, Mass., where he was in turn a textile operative, an insurance agent, and a spinner. By 1894 he was president of the Lowell Mule Spinners' Union. In 1894 and 1895 he ran unsuccessfully for the Massachusetts senate on the ticket of the People's party, and from 1895 to 1897 he was master workman of the KOL Justice Assembly. Connolly cofounded the Lowell Textile Council in 1898 and was its secretary from 1900 to 1902. During this period he also served as financial secretary of the Lowell weavers' union (1899-1902) and the Lowell carders' union (1899), was a member of the executive council of the National Federation of Textile Operatives (1898-99), and vice-president of the American Federation of Textile Operatives (1900-1901). In 1903 he apparently moved to Boston where he worked as a clerk.

COUNAHAN, Michael J. (1863-1924?), born in New York City, was a Pittsburgh plumber active in the International Association of Journeymen Plumbers, Steam and Gas Fitters, in the late 1880s. After the founding of the United Association of Journeymen Plumbers, Gas Fitters, Steam Fitters, and Steam Fitters' Helpers of the United States and Canada (UAJP) in 1889, he was a member of UAJP 27 of Pittsburgh. In 1892 he was elected general secretary of the UAJP, and in 1893 he became secretary-treasurer, serving until 1897. He was also editor of the *United Association Journal* from 1892 to 1897. Counahan operated a plumbing contracting business from 1898 until the end of World War I and served as a clerk in the Pittsburgh city controller's office in the 1920s.

COWEY, Edward (1839-1903), was president of the West Yorkshire Miners' Association (1873-81) and the Yorkshire Miners' Association (1881-1903). He was a founder of the Miners' Federation of Great Britain in 1888 and a member of its executive committee until his death. From 1893 to 1903 he was a member of the Parliamentary Committee of the TUC.

CREAMER, James J. (1861-1918), was born in Richmond, Va., where he apprenticed as a machinist at the age of seventeen. He joined KOL Local Assembly 3157 in 1884 and subsequently served as its secretary. In 1888 he was a charter member of the Order of United Machinists and Mechanical Engineers (after 1889 the National Association of Machinists, and after 1891 the International Association of Machinists) and he served as the organization's grand foreman (1889-90), grand master machinist (1890-92), and edited the *Machinists' Monthly Journal* (1893-95). From 1895 until his death he worked as a gas inspector for the city of Richmond. In 1911 he was elected to the Virginia House of Delegates as a Democrat, serving one term.

CROWLEY, Timothy M. (b. 1857), a native of Ireland, immigrated to the United States in 1865. By the early 1880s he lived in Meriden, Conn., working first in silver plating firms and then as a grocer, an orchestra leader, and a piano and music dealer. A member of the Musical Protective Union of Meriden, he served as president of the Connecticut State Branch of the AFL (1895-96). He also served as a Democratic member of the Connecticut House of Representatives from 1893 to 1894. In 1906 he moved to Hartford, Conn., working as an inspector, musician, salesman, and, between 1916 and 1932, in the real estate business.

DAWLEY, William L. (1860-1909), was born in upstate New York and apprenticed as a machinist in Seneca Falls. After working in

Auburn, N.Y., for three years, he settled in Atlanta in the late 1880s. There he was a member of the KOL's Gibraltar Assembly and in 1888 a founder of the Order of United Machinists and Mechanical Engineers of America (after 1889 the National Association of Machinists, and after 1891 the International Association of Machinists), serving as its first secretary. Dawley moved to Richmond, Va., around 1890. There, he served as the organization's grand secretary–finance (1889-91) and general secretary-treasurer (1892-95), and worked as a grocer. About 1898 he returned to Atlanta where he was a machinist until his death.

DEBS, Eugene Victor (1855-1926), born in Terre Haute, Ind., entered railroad work as an engine-house laborer and became a locomotive fireman. He was elected first secretary of Vigo Lodge 16 — the Terre Haute local of the Brotherhood of Locomotive Firemen (BLF) — in 1875 and became grand secretary and treasurer of the BLF and editor-in-chief of its journal, the *Firemen's Magazine* (after 1886 the *Locomotive Firemen's Magazine*), in 1880. Debs resigned as an officer of the Brotherhood in September 1892 to begin building a single union for all workers employed in the industry; he resigned the editorship in 1894. He founded the American Railway Union (ARU) in 1893 and served as its president, leading it in a victorious strike against the Great Northern Railroad in 1894. The same year he was arrested and in 1895 imprisoned for defying a federal court order in connection with the refusal of ARU members to handle Pullman cars while Pullman Co. workers were on strike. The Pullman strike effectively destroyed the ARU.

After six months in prison Debs turned his energies to political activity, first supporting the People's party campaign of 1896, and the next year publicly embracing socialism. In 1897 he organized the Social Democracy of America (SDA), a socialist communitarian movement. In 1898 he followed Victor Berger's lead in leaving the SDA to establish the Social Democratic Party of the United States (SDPUS), an organization committed to socialist electoral activity. Debs served on the executive committee of the party and in 1900 polled 100,000 votes as the presidential candidate of the SDPUS and a wing of the SLP led by Morris Hillquit. In 1901 Debs participated in the creation of the Socialist Party of America (SPA). He ran for president as the party's candidate in 1904, 1908, 1912, and 1920, making his best showing in 1912 with 6 percent of the vote. Debs joined with William D. Haywood and other radicals in 1905 to form the Industrial Workers of the World, a revolutionary syndicalist industrial union that he hoped would function as the economic arm of the SPA; he resigned three years later.

During World War I, Debs was prosecuted under the Espionage Act, receiving a ten-year sentence because of a 1918 speech in which he questioned the sincerity of capitalist appeals to patriotism. SG supported the campaign for clemency that culminated in a presidential pardon in 1921. After his release, Debs attempted to rebuild the SPA, which had been devastated by government repression inspired by the party's pacifist position during World War I.

DeLeon, Daniel (1852-1914), was the leading figure in the SLP from 1891 until his death. Born in Curaçao, he was educated in Germany in the late 1860s and studied medicine in Amsterdam until 1872 without completing his course of study. Between 1872 and 1874 he immigrated to the United States, working as a school teacher in Westchester, N.Y., until he entered the Columbia College School of Law in 1876. He earned his law degree in 1878 and practiced in Brownsville, Tex., until 1882 and in New York City from 1882 until at least 1884. From 1883 to 1889 he was a lecturer at the Columbia College School of Political Science and active in reform and radical movements. He supported the mugwump campaign of 1884 against the Republican presidential candidacy of James G. Blaine, worked in Henry George's 1886 mayoralty campaign, was a member of KOL Local Assembly 1563 from 1888, and participated in the utopian socialist Nationalist movement from 1889 to 1890, when he joined the SLP. He ran for governor of New York on the SLP ticket in 1891.

DeLeon never held a major national office in the SLP, but in 1891 he became editor of the party's official organ, *People*, a position he held until shortly before his death, and this journal formed the foundation of his leadership in the SLP. In 1891 he was elected a delegate to KOL District Assembly (DA) 49 and he subsequently played a prominent role in the KOL. Working with People's party adherents in DA 49, whose slate he supported in the 1893 state elections, he helped engineer Terence Powderly's replacement by James R. Sovereign in 1893 as KOL general master workman.

The alliance with Sovereign dissolved in 1895, however, in a dispute involving Sovereign's refusal to allow the SLP to nominate the editor of the KOL's journal. The 1895 General Assembly rejected the credentials of DA 49's delegates, and DeLeon launched an alternative labor federation, the Socialist Trade and Labor Alliance (STLA), in December of that year. The *People* served as the STLA's official organ, and DeLeon was a member of its general executive board, functioning as its leader. In conformity with the principles of the "new trade unionism," the STLA accepted the affiliation of SLP branches as well as trade unions; after 1898, however, it served as a weak adjunct of the party, centered increasingly in New York City, until it merged with the Industrial Workers of the World (IWW) in 1905. DeLeon helped frame the constitution of the IWW at its 1905 founding convention in Chicago and was active until he was denied a seat at the 1908 convention, culminating a struggle with the organization's syndicalist faction. Although DeLeon's supporters withdrew and set up a second IWW in Detroit, he discouraged the establishment of the new organization and was never active in it.

DONNELLY, Michael J., was a founder in 1897 of the Amalgamated Meat Cutters and Butcher Workmen of North America (AMCBW) and its president from 1898 to 1907. In 1895 and 1896 he was secretary of AFL Sheep Butchers' Protective Union 6146 in Kansas City, Mo., and in 1899 he organized AMCBW 36 of Omaha, Nebr. Donnelly resigned the AMCBW presidency in 1907, beset by personal problems, and left the labor movement. He worked as a cigar salesman and at other jobs, and in 1916 he was a camp cook in Texas when the AFL commissioned him as an organizer for the Chicago area, but he never filled the position.

DOWER, George W. (1852-1925?), was born in Toronto. A printer, he joined International Typographical Union (ITU) 91 in 1872. He was active in the KOL and the Toronto Trades and Labor Council in the 1880s and 1890s, and appointed an ITU district organizer in 1893. Except for the 1890-91 term, Dower served as secretary-treasurer of the Dominion Trades and Labor Congress (from 1892 Trades and Labor Congress of Canada) from 1888 to 1900. In his later years he worked in Toronto as a proofreader.

DOYLE, Peter F. (b. 1859), was born in Ireland and came to the United States in 1873. A stationary engineer living in Chicago by the late 1890s, he was secretary of the National Union of Steam Engineers in 1898 and secretary-treasurer of the International Union of Steam Engineers (IUSE) from 1898 to 1899. He was also a member of the Engineers' Progressive Union of Chicago—IUSE 1. Doyle served as secretary-treasurer of the Illinois State Federation of Labor (1897-98) and the Chicago Federation of Labor (1897-98), was president of IUSE 1 (1898), and was an AFL organizer (1898).

DUGGAN, Michael (b. 1858), was born in Ireland and came to the United States around 1890. He settled in Lowell, Mass., and worked as a textile operative. A member of the Lowell cotton mule spinners' union, he served as its financial secretary (1898) and president (1904-

7), and from 1903 to 1908 was treasurer of the Lowell Textile Council. Duggan was elected president of the National Cotton Mule Spinners' Association of America (from 1898 National Spinners' Association of America) in 1892 and occupied that post, perhaps continuously, until 1904. After leaving the union's leadership, he worked as an insurance agent from 1906 to 1908, and then as a janitor until at least 1911.

DUNCAN, James (1857-1928), a granite cutter born in Scotland, immigrated to the United States in 1880. He joined the Granite Cutters' National Union (GCNU) in 1881 and in the early 1880s served as an officer of GCNU locals in New York, Philadelphia, Richmond, and Baltimore, where he settled in 1884. He subsequently served as Maryland state organizer for the GCNU, general organizer for the AFL, and president of the Baltimore Federation of Labor (1890-92, 1897). Duncan was an officer of the GCNU (after 1905 the Granite Cutters' International Association of America) from 1895 to 1923 (secretary, 1895-1905; international secretary-treasurer, 1905-12; and international president, 1912-23). He edited the *Granite Cutters' Journal* from 1895 to 1928. He served the AFL as second vice-president (1894-1900) and first vice-president (1900-1928) and was acting president of the Federation during President John McBride's illness in 1895. He represented the AFL at the meetings of the TUC in Bristol (1898) and the International Secretariat in Budapest (1911). President Wilson appointed him envoy extraordinary to Russia in 1917 and a member of the American labor mission to the peace conference in Paris in 1919.

EASLEY, Ralph Montgomery (1856-1939), was born in Browning, Pa. He founded a daily newspaper in Hutchinson, Kans., and then moved to Chicago to work as a reporter and columnist for the *Chicago Inter Ocean*. He helped organize the Chicago Civic Federation (CCF) in 1893, leaving the *Inter Ocean* to serve as the CCF's secretary. He resigned from that position in 1900 and moved to New York to organize the National Civic Federation (NCF), bringing together prominent representatives of business, labor, and the public in co-operative reform efforts and in the settlement of labor disputes. Easley served as NCF secretary (1900-1902) and as chairman of its Executive Council (1902-39) and was associated in this work with SG—the NCF's long-time vice-president. In his later years Easley increasingly devoted himself to opposing radical labor organizations and social movements.

EATON, Horace M. (b. 1865), a laster from Maine, was general secretary and treasurer of the Boot and Shoe Workers' Union from its founding in 1895 until 1902; he edited its journal, the *Union Boot and Shoe Worker,* from 1900 to 1902. Eaton resigned in 1902 to become superintendent of a shoe factory in St. Louis.

EDMONSTON, Gabriel (1839-1918), a founder and the first president of the Brotherhood of Carpenters and Joiners of America (1881-82), was born in Washington, D.C., and served in the Confederate army. He helped organize Washington carpenters in 1881 and was carpenter of the House of Representatives in the 1880s. A member of the FOTLU Legislative Committee from 1882 to 1886, he was elected its secretary in 1884. He introduced a series of resolutions at the FOTLU 1884 convention calling for the inauguration of the eight-hour movement. From 1886 to 1888 Edmonston served as treasurer of the AFL.

ELDERKIN, Thomas J. (b. 1853), a London-born sailor, came to the United States in 1869, working in Scranton, Pa., and Buffalo, N.Y., before settling in Chicago. In 1878 he helped organize the Lake Seamen's Benevolent Association (variously the Lake Seamen's Union), serving several terms as its secretary in the 1890s. In 1892 he was a founder of the National Seamen's Union of America (after 1895 the International Seamen's Union of America) and was elected its first general secretary and treasurer, serving until he resigned the office in 1899. The 1894 AFL convention elected him fourth vice-president; he served for one term. In the late 1890s Elderkin was serving as a vessel dispatcher in Chicago, and he was living there as late as 1917.

ELLIOTT, John T. (1836-1902), a founder of the Brotherhood of Painters and Decorators of America (BPDA), was born in Baltimore. Following the Civil War he moved to Philadelphia and joined the International Workingmen's Association (IWA). The IWA General Council in New York City elected him U.S. general secretary for 1871-72, and this brought him actively into socialist and reform politics and relief efforts in the city during the depression of the 1870s. He was involved in organizing the Grand Lodge of Painters of America in 1871, the first national painters' union, which lasted until 1876.

Returning to Baltimore in 1879, Elliott organized KOL Local Assembly 1466 and served as secretary of District Assembly 41. He resigned from the Knights in 1882 and in 1887 helped organize the BPDA and was elected general secretary-treasurer. Elliott presided over the BPDA (after 1899, the Brotherhood of Painters, Decorators, and Paperhangers of America) during years of factionalism, in which the painters divided into two groups, Elliott's eastern faction based in Baltimore, and a western faction headquartered in Lafayette, Ind. Poor health forced him to retire in 1900.

ELM, Johann Adolph von (1857-1916), born in Hamburg, was a cigarmaker and an active socialist and trade unionist. He immigrated to the United States in 1878 in the face of the Bismarckian anti-socialist laws and during his four years in New York became a CMIU member and a friend of SG's and Adolph Strasser's. Returning to Germany in 1882, he became secretary of the Verband der Zigar-rensortierer (Cigar Packers' Union) and was instrumental in arranging its merger with the Deutscher Tabakarbeiter-Verband (German Cigarmakers' Union). When the official ban on socialist and labor activities eased in 1890, Elm took part in the founding of the General-kommission der Gewerkschaften Deutschlands (General Commission of German Trade Unions) and from 1894 to 1907 served as a member of the Reichstag representing the Sozialdemokratische Partei Deutschlands (Social Democratic Party of Germany). Elm was also prominent in organizing and managing several cooperative ventures and an insurance plan linked with the German trade unions. When SG visited Europe in 1895, Elm served as his liaison with the German labor movement.

EMRICH, Henry (b. 1846?), a cabinetmaker born in Prussia, immigrated to New York in 1866 and joined the Cabinet Makers' Union two years later. Emrich was active in the political organization of the New York City Central Labor Union in the 1880s. He served as secretary of the International Furniture Workers' Union of America between 1882 and 1891 and was its delegate to the FOTLU and AFL conventions between 1885 and 1889. He was elected sixth vice-president of the FOTLU in 1885 and treasurer of the AFL in 1888 and 1889.

EVANS, Christopher (1841-1924), an Ohio miners' leader and AFL secretary from 1889 to 1894, was born in England and immigrated to the United States in 1869. He helped found the Ohio Miners' Amalgamated Association, serving as its president in 1889, and the National Federation of Miners and Mine Laborers (NFMML). As secretary of the NFMML from 1885 to 1888, he participated in joint conferences between miners and operators to establish annual scales of prices and wages in the Midwest coal region. After 1895 he became an organizer for the United Mine Workers of America (UMWA) and the AFL, and in 1901 he was appointed UMWA statistician.

EVANS, E. Lewis (1865-1955), born in Canada, was a tobacco worker from 1890 and a member of AFL Tobacco Pressmen's and Helpers'

Union 6046 of St. Louis. He served as secretary-treasurer (1895-1925) and president (1926-40) of the National Tobacco Workers' Union of America (after 1898 Tobacco Workers' International Union).

FISCHER, Henry (1866?-1908), a member of AFL Tobacco Factory Workers' Union 6063 of St. Louis, was president (1895-1908) of the National Tobacco Workers' Union of America (from 1898 Tobacco Workers' International Union).

FITZPATRICK, Patrick Francis (1835-99), was born in Ireland and immigrated to the United States at the age of sixteen. Apprenticed as an iron molder in Troy, N.Y., he eventually settled in Cincinnati, where he held offices in Iron Molders' Union of North America (IMUNA) 4 until 1898 and was one of the founders of the city's Building Trades Council. From 1879 to 1890 Fitzpatrick was president of the IMUNA.

FOSTER, Frank Keyes (1855-1909), was born in Massachusetts and worked as a printer in Connecticut before settling in Boston in 1880. He was active in the International Typographical Union and represented the Boston Central Trades and Labor Union at the 1883 FOTLU convention, where he was elected secretary of the Legislative Committee. A member of KOL Local Assembly 2006, he was elected secretary of District Assembly 30 and a member of the Knights' General Executive Board in 1883. In 1884 he began editing the KOL organ in Massachusetts, the *Laborer* (Haverhill). Foster ran unsuccessfully for lieutenant-governor of Massachusetts in 1886 on the Democratic ticket. In 1887 he helped found the Massachusetts State Federation of Labor and served as treasurer (1887), secretary (1889-95), and chairman of the legislative committee (1892-93, 1900-1907). He founded the *Labor Leader* (Boston) in 1887 and was its editor until 1897.

FOX, Martin (1848-1907), president of the Iron Molders' Union of North America (IMUNA) from 1890 to 1903, was born in Cincinnati, and there joined IMUNA 3 in 1864. For most of his career he belonged to IMUNA 20 of Covington, Ky. He began serving as a trustee of the IMUNA in 1878 and was a clerk in the IMUNA president's office from 1880 to 1886. In 1886 he was elected secretary of the union, holding that position until he became president. Fox represented the AFL at the Birmingham meeting of the TUC in 1897. Following his retirement from the IMUNA presidency, he was a paid consultant to the organization until 1907. Fox was also active in the National Civic Federation from its founding in 1900, serving on its administrative council and in its division of conciliation and mediation.

FURUSETH, Andrew (1854-1938), was president of the International Seamen's Union of America (ISUA) from 1897 to 1899 and from 1908 to 1938. Born in Furuseth, Norway, he went to sea in 1873 and arrived in California in 1880, making his home in San Francisco. In 1885 he joined the Coast Seamen's Union (known as the Sailors' Union of the Pacific from 1891), serving as its longtime secretary (1887-89, 1891-92, 1892-1936). The 1894 AFL convention voted to send him to Washington, D.C., to lobby for a bill to regulate the conditions of seamen. From 1895 until 1902 he was an AFL legislative representative, continuing as legislative representative of the ISUA for the remainder of his life.

GARLAND, Mahlon Morris (1856-1920), president of the National Amalgamated Association of Iron and Steel Workers of the United States (NAAISW) from 1892 to 1898 and fourth vice-president of the AFL from 1895 to 1898, was born in Pittsburgh, Pa. An iron puddler and heater, he joined the NAAISW in the late 1870s. He was fired in 1878 for union activities and found work in several midwestern cities before returning to Pittsburgh in 1880. There he joined NAAISW South Side Lodge 11 and in the mid-1880s served two terms on the city's select council. From 1890 to 1892 he was assistant president of the NAAISW, before assuming its presidency. He resigned from office in 1898 and accepted an appointment as U.S. collector of customs for Pittsburgh, retaining that post until 1915. Garland was a Republican congressman from 1915 until his death.

GELSON, James (1859-1918), a Brooklyn printer, was a member of International Printing Pressmen's Union of North America (IPPU) 51 of New York City. He was secretary-treasurer of the IPPU (after 1897 the International Printing Pressmen's and Assistants' Union of North America) from 1892 to 1898.

GOLDWATER, Samuel (1850-98), was born in Poland and immigrated to New York City in 1859, apprenticing as a cigarmaker and joining CMIU 15. He was active in the labor movement and the SLP in Chicago in the 1870s and 1880s, helping form the Chicago Trade and Labor Council (later the Trade and Labor Assembly of Chicago), serving as president of CMIU 11, and running for local offices on the SLP ticket. Moving to Detroit in 1886, he was twice elected president of the Detroit Trade and Labor Council and helped organize the Michigan Federation of Labor. He also served as a CMIU vice-president in 1895. Goldwater was elected city alderman as an independent Democrat in 1894 and 1896, and twice ran unsuccessfully for mayor, dying in the midst of his second campaign.

GOMPERS, Abraham Julian (1876-1903), was the son of SG and Sophia Gompers; he worked in New York City in the clothing industry as a cutter. In 1901, after he contracted tuberculosis, his parents sent him to convalesce at the Denver home of Max Morris, secretary and treasurer of the Retail Clerks' International Protective Association. Abraham worked briefly for the association before his death.

GOMPERS, Alexander (1857-1926), SG's brother, was born in London and immigrated with the family to the United States in 1863. He was a cigarmaker and an early member of CMIU 144. He married Rachel Bickstein, and they had six children.

GOMPERS, Alexander Julian (1878-1947), was the son of SG and Sophia Gompers. He was a cigarmaker and cigar manufacturer in New York City and in Washington, D.C. From 1914 to 1947 he served as an official of the New York State Department of Labor. He and his wife, Ella Appelbaum Gompers, had three children: Esther, Sophia, and May.

GOMPERS, Louis (1859-1920), SG's brother, was born in London and immigrated with the family to the United States in 1863. He became a Brooklyn cigar manufacturer and president of the Retail Tobacco Dealers' Association. He married Sophia Bickstein, and they had seven children.

GOMPERS, Rose. See MITCHELL, Rose Gompers.

GOMPERS, Sadie Julian (1883-1918), the younger daughter of SG and Sophia Gompers, was born in New York City. After the family's move to Washington, D.C., she studied voice for over seven years and then sang in vaudeville and on the concert stage. According to SG, she cut her career short after deciding that her long performing tours, during which her mother traveled with her, were disrupting the Gompers household (SG, *Seventy Years*, 1:477-78). Sadie Gompers died of pneumonia during the World War I influenza epidemic.

GOMPERS, Samuel Julian (1868-1946), was the son of SG and Sophia Gompers. Born in New York City, he left school at the age of fourteen to work in a New York City print shop. He moved to Washington, D.C., about 1887 and worked as a printer in the Government Printing Office, a compositor in the U.S. Department of Commerce and Labor, and a clerk in the U.S. Census Office. He was a member of the Association of Union Printers and the Columbia Typographical Union

(International Typographical Union 101). In 1913 he became chief of the Division of Publications and Supplies of the U.S. Department of Labor, and in 1918 he became chief clerk of the Department of Labor, a position he held until 1941. Gompers and his wife, Sophia Dampf Gompers, had one child, Florence.

GOMPERS, Sophia Dampf (1870?-1959), was born in New York City and moved to Washington, D.C., after her marriage to SG's son, Samuel Julian Gompers, in 1892.

GOMPERS, Sophia Julian (1850-1920), SG's first wife, was born in London and immigrated to the United States about 1858. She was living with her father and stepmother in Brooklyn and working as a tobacco stripper in a cigar factory when she married SG in 1867. Between 1868 and 1885 she and SG had at least nine children, six of whom lived past infancy: Samuel, Rose, Henry, Abraham, Alexander, and Sadie.

GREENE, Prince W. (b. 1870), born in Alabama, was a Phoenix, Ala., weaver. He served as president (1897-1900) and secretary-treasurer (1900-1901) of the National Union of Textile Workers of America (International Union of Textile Workers from about 1900). He also edited the *Phoenix-Girard News* and the *Southern Unionist,* was a special AFL organizer for the South, and was active in founding the United Textile Workers of America in 1901.

HARRIS, Daniel (1846-1915), a Civil War veteran and cigarmaker, was born in England and immigrated to the United States in the early 1860s. During the 1877-78 cigarmakers' strike the Central Organization of the Cigarmakers of New York appointed Harris to its Committee on Organization for Pennsylvania. In the late 1880s Harris was president of CMIU 144. He served as president of the New York State Workingmen's Assembly from 1892 to 1897 and of the New York Federation of Labor in 1899 and from 1906 until his death.

HART, Lee M. (1862-1916), was born in Maryland and worked as a theatrical stage employee in Chicago in the early 1890s. He was elected treasurer of the newly formed National Alliance of Theatrical Stage Employes of the United States (NATSE) in 1893 and president in 1894, serving a one-year term. In 1895 and 1896 he served as president of the Illinois Brotherhood of Theatrical Stage Employes. Elected secretary-treasurer of the NATSE in 1898, he held this position in the union of Theatrical Stage Employes until he retired in 1914.

HAYES, Max Sebastian (1866-1945), was born on a farm near Havana, Ohio, and apprenticed as a printer at the age of thirteen. He moved to Cleveland in 1883, joining International Typographical Union (ITU) 53 in 1884 and serving as an ITU general organizer for the next fifteen years. In 1891 he cofounded the *Cleveland Citizen* and subsequently worked as the paper's associate editor (1892-94) and editor (1894-1939). He was active in the labor movement of Cleveland as corresponding secretary (1896-97) and recording secretary (1898-1901) of the Cleveland Central Labor Union, recording secretary (1902-3) of the United Trades and Labor Council, and recording secretary (1910) of the Cleveland Federation of Labor.

Politically, Hayes was associated with the People's party campaign in 1896 and was active in the SLP from 1896 to 1899. He was one of a group of SLP members who broke with Daniel DeLeon's leadership in 1899 and two years later participated in launching the Socialist Party of America (SPA). A leading SPA trade unionist within the AFL, he challenged SG unsuccessfully for the Federation presidency in 1912. Hayes was an SPA candidate for Congress in 1900 and for Ohio secretary of state in 1902, losing both races. He helped organize the Consumers' League of Ohio in 1900 and wrote the state's workmen's compensation bill that was passed in 1911. He was chairman of the executive committee of the newly formed National Labor party in 1919; in 1920 he ran as the Farmer-Labor party's vice-presidential candidate. In 1933 he was a charter member of the Cleveland Metropolitan Housing Authority, and from 1933 to 1935 served on the Ohio State Adjustment Board of the National Recovery Administration.

HOLMES, David (1843-1906), was president of the Amalgamated Weavers' Association (1884-1906) and a member of the Parliamentary Committee of the TUC (1892-1900, 1902-3).

HOWARD, Robert (1845-1902), a spinner and union organizer in Lancashire, England, immigrated to the United States in 1873. In 1878 he became secretary of the Fall River Mule Spinners' Association, serving until 1897. At the same time he played a leading role in national organizations of the trade—the Amalgamated Mule Spinners' Association, of which he was principal officer from 1878 to 1887, and the National Cotton Mule Spinners' Association. Howard campaigned for shorter-hour legislation and other labor measures. A Democrat, he served in the Massachusetts House of Representatives in 1881 and the Massachusetts Senate from 1886 to 1893. He was treasurer of the FOTLU Legislative Committee in the early 1880s and was elected master workman of KOL District Assembly 30 in

1886. In the mid-1890s he conducted an organizing campaign among southern textile workers for the AFL.

HUGHES, James F. (1854-1937?), was born in Pennsylvania and worked in Pittsburgh as a tinner and also, briefly, as a bookkeeper, machinist, and laborer. He was secretary of the Tin, Sheet Iron, and Cornice Workers' International Association (TSICA) from 1895 to 1897, and secretary-treasurer of the Amalgamated Sheet Metal Workers' International Association, as the TSICA was renamed in 1897, from 1897 to about 1900.

JOHNSON, Jesse (b. 1848), born in Philadelphia, was a Nashville printing pressman. He was a member of International Typographical Union 20 from about 1887 to 1889 and president of International Printing Pressmen's Union of North America (IPPU; after 1897 the International Printing Pressmen's and Assistants' Union of North America) 37 from about 1891 to 1894. He served as an IPPU vice-president (1895-96) and president (1897-98) and was an AFL organizer in the early 1890s and again later in the decade. After leaving printing in 1900, Johnson was a solicitor until 1909 and then Nashville city weigher.

JONES, Theodore S. (1861?-1938?), was born in Wales, immigrated to the United States about 1882, and settled in Kansas City, Mo. A carpenter by trade, he was president of United Brotherhood of Carpenters and Joiners of America 160 for two terms in the 1890s and president of the Kansas City Building Trades Council in 1898. He helped found the National Building Trades Council of America in 1897, serving as its vice-president (1897-98), president (1898-99), and as vice-president again beginning in 1899. In addition to work as a carpenter and as a contractor, Jones held a variety of municipal offices including street inspector, superintendent, and clerk and deputy for the recorder of deeds.

JUNIO, John Joseph (b. 1842), born in Boston, was president of the CMIU (1867), president of the New York Cigar Makers' State Union (1875-77), and an officer of CMIU 6 of Syracuse, N.Y. He was active in labor reform, representing the Mechanical Order of the Sun at the National Labor Union Congress in 1868, running for New York secretary of state on the Workingmen's Party of the United States ticket in 1877, serving as state chairman of the Greenback-Labor party, and representing District Assembly 152 at the KOL General Assembly in 1887. He was an organizer for the CMIU in the mid-1880s. After moving to Auburn, N.Y., in the 1890s he served as president of the Central Labor Union and CMIU 311 of that city.

KELLY, James T. (1862-1930), was born in Overton, Pa. He was elected vice-president of AFL St. Louis Wiremen's and Linemen's Union 5221 in January 1891, serving in that office until he helped form the National Brotherhood of Electrical Workers of America (NBEWA) in November of the same year. He was grand secretary-treasurer (1891-95) and grand secretary (1895-97) of the NBEWA, and editor of its journal, the *Electrical Worker,* from 1893 until 1897. After 1897 Kelly remained active in NBEWA (after 1899 the International Brotherhood of Electrical Workers) 1 of St. Louis, serving as press secretary for many years. He later became a contractor.

KENEHAN, Roady (1856-1927), was born in Ireland and apprenticed as a blacksmith. He immigrated to the United States in 1873 and lived in Philadelphia. Traveling west in 1878, he prospected for gold in several western states before settling in Denver where he worked as a horseshoer. He joined Journeymen Horseshoers' National Union of the United States (after 1892 International Union of Journeymen Horseshoers of the United States and Canada [IUJH]) 29 of Denver and served as its president and delegate to the Denver Trades and Labor Assembly. Kenehan served as secretary-treasurer of the IUJH (1890-1910), third vice-president of the AFL (1895), and editor of the *International Horseshoers' Monthly Magazine* (1899-1910). He was a member of the Colorado State Labor Board of Arbitration (1897-1903?), was elected state auditor in 1908 and 1912 and state treasurer in 1910, and was appointed federal director of labor for Colorado in 1918. From 1921 until his retirement in 1923 he was a Denver tax agent.

KIDD, Thomas Inglis (1860-1941), a woodworker, immigrated to the United States from Scotland in 1884, residing in Nebraska before moving to Denver at the end of the decade. He helped organize woodworkers in Nebraska, Colorado, and Minnesota and was elected general secretary-treasurer of the newly formed Machine Wood Workers' International Union of America (MWWIU) in 1890. He held this position for the next five years and continued as general secretary of the MWWIU's successor, the Amalgamated Wood Workers' International Union of America from 1895 to 1905. In these positions he edited the union's journal, the *Machine Wood Worker* (retitled the *American Wood-Worker* and subsequently the *International Wood-Worker*). Kidd moved to Chicago in 1892 and played a prominent role in the Populist-labor alliance in Illinois. He was the AFL's sixth vice-president from 1898 to 1900 and its fifth vice-president from 1900 to 1905. In 1907 he became a New York sales representative for the Milwaukee-based

Brunswick-Balke-Collender Co. and in 1913 became its branch manager in Milwaukee.

KIRCHNER, John S. (1857-1912), a cigarmaker, was born in Maryland and became active in the labor movement in 1877 when he joined a Baltimore local assembly of the KOL. After moving to Philadelphia he was recording secretary of KOL Local Assembly 53 for several years. He helped organize CMIU 100 and filled various offices (financial secretary, president, and corresponding secretary) in that union during the 1880s. He was financial secretary of the Philadelphia Central Labor Union in 1886 but resigned that position because of his duties as CMIU organizer for Pennsylvania as well as a CMIU vice-president (1885-87). In 1886 he was appointed secretary of the FOTLU upon the death of William H. Foster.

KLAPETZKY, William E. (1867-1916), was born in Syracuse, N.Y., where he became a charter member of Journeymen Barbers' International Union of America 18 in 1889. He served the International as a vice-president (1891-93), general secretary (1893-94), and secretary-treasurer (1894-1904), and edited the *Journeyman Barber,* the union's journal, from 1905 until 1914. Klapetzky represented the AFL at the 1907 meeting of the TUC.

KURZENKNABE, Ernst (1860?-1927), was national secretary of the National Union of the United Brewery Workmen of the United States (NUUBW) from 1888 to 1899, holding this position jointly with Charles Bechtold after 1892. He was an editor of the *Brauer Zeitung,* official journal of the NUUBW, from 1888 to 1896. A former secretary of NUUBW 1 of New York City, Kurzenknabe moved to St. Louis during his tenure as national secretary. Between 1900 and 1920 he worked variously as a saloonkeeper, cashier, and bookkeeper before becoming a reporter for *Amerika,* a German-language paper, about 1921.

LABADIE, Joseph Antoine (1850-1933), born in Paw Paw, Mich., was apprenticed to a printer in South Bend, Ind., in 1866. After settling in Detroit in 1872, he joined International Typographical Union 18 and in 1878 became a KOL organizer. He was also active in politics, running unsuccessfully for mayor on the Workingmen's party ticket in 1879 and playing an active role in the SLP. In the early 1880s Labadie worked as a labor journalist for several papers and was one of the publishers of the *Labor Review* and the *Times,* a trade union paper. He played a major role in establishing the Detroit Trades and Labor Council in 1880, becoming its corresponding secretary, and was also a founder and first president (1889-90) of the

Michigan Federation of Labor. Labadie became a philosophical anarchist in 1883 and was a close associate of Benjamin Tucker, a leading anarchist thinker; he frequently wrote for Tucker's journal, *Liberty*, until its demise in 1908. In 1893 Labadie was appointed clerk of the Detroit Water Works, a post he held until about 1920.

LEGIEN, Carl (1861-1920), was born in Marienburg, Prussia, and raised at an orphanage in nearby Thorn. He apprenticed to a woodcarver at the age of fourteen. After three years of compulsory military service and two years as a traveling journeyman, Legien settled in Hamburg and joined the local union of woodcarvers in 1886. He was elected president of the Vereinigung der Drechsler Deutschlands (Union of German Woodcarvers) at its founding in 1887. In 1890 he stepped down from this office to become secretary of the newly founded Generalkommission der Gewerkschaften Deutschlands (General Commission of German Trade Unions). He led this organization (renamed Allgemeiner Deutscher Gewerkschaftsbund [General German Federation of Trade Unions] after 1919) until his death. He also edited its official organ, the *Correspondenzblatt*, from 1891 to 1900. Under his leadership the German trade union movement grew from a regionalized group of craft unions to the most powerful centralized industrial union movement in Europe. A member of the Sozialdemokratische Partei Deutschlands (SPD; Social Democratic Party of Germany), Legien served as a socialist deputy in the Reichstag from 1893 to 1898 and from 1903 until his death. As a social democrat, Legien was instrumental in integrating the concerns of the German union movement into the political program of the SPD. He helped inaugurate the annual meetings of the International Secretariat of Trade Union Centers (after 1913, the International Federation of Trade Unions) in 1900. He was secretary of this organization from 1903 to 1919.

LENNON, John Brown (1850-1923), president and subsequently general secretary of the Journeymen Tailors' National Union of the United States (JTNU; later renamed Journeymen Tailors' Union of America), was born in Wisconsin and raised in Hannibal, Mo. He moved to Denver in 1869 where he helped organize a tailor's union and the Denver Trades Assembly and held offices in both. In 1883, Lennon's local affiliated with the newly formed JTNU; Lennon subsequently served as president of the national union (1884-85), General Executive Board member (1885-87), and general secretary and editor of the *Tailor* (1887-1910). He was treasurer of the AFL from 1890 to 1917, a member of the U.S. Commission on Industrial Relations

(1913-15), and of the Board of Mediators of the U.S. Department of Labor (1917).

LITTLEWOOD, Herbert, an Olneyville, R.I., weaver, was general secretary and organizer of the National Union of Textile Workers of America in 1896.

LLOYD, Henry (b. 1855), was the general president of the United Brotherhood of Carpenters and Joiners of America (UBCJA) from 1896 to 1898. He was born in Albany, N.Y., and moved to Toronto in 1864, joining the Millwrights' Union of Toronto in 1876 and local 27 of the UBCJA in 1884. During the 1880s he was active in the Toronto Trades and Labour Council. In 1888 the UBCJA elected him a vice-president, and he held this position until 1890. He moved to Boston in that year and joined UBCJA 33, functioning as its president for two terms. He took an active role in the Boston Central Labor Union, serving as its president in 1896. In 1895 he ran unsuccessfully for the Boston School Board on the Workingmen's Political League of Boston ticket. The 1898 AFL convention elected him a delegate to the TUC. About 1900 he began to sell insurance and moved to the Boston suburb of Somerville; as late as 1915 he continued to work as an insurance agent in Boston.

LYNCH, Edward J. (1872-1920), a native of Ireland and a resident of Meriden, Conn., from the late 1880s, was secretary-treasurer of KOL National Trade Assembly (NTA) 252 (brass workers) from 1890 to 1895. After NTA 252 merged in 1895 with the United Brotherhood of Brass Workers to form the United Brotherhood of Brass and Composition Metal Workers, Polishers, and Buffers (from 1896 the Metal Polishers', Buffers', Platers', and Brass Workers' Union of North America), Lynch served the new union as a vice-president (1895-96) and president (1896-1902, 1903-5). He was secretary-treasurer of the Metal Trades Federation of North America (1902-3). Lynch lived in New York City from about 1898; after leaving office, he moved to Newark, N.J., and worked in the post office. From 1912 to 1920 he was a foreman at the Westinghouse Electrical Manufacturing Co.

MACARTHUR, Walter (1862-1944), was business manager (1891-94) and then editor (1895-1900, 1901-13) of the *Coast Seamen's Journal,* published by the Coast Seamen's Union (CSU; later the Sailors' Union of the Pacific Coast) and the National (later International) Seamen's Union. He was born in Glasgow, Scotland, where he received one year of university education before serving in the British merchant marine (1876-86). As a member of the U.S. merchant marine (1886-91), he came to San Diego in 1887 and joined the CSU in 1889. He was elected president of the San Francisco Federated Trades Council in 1892, secretary of the Council of Federated Trades of the Pacific Coast in 1893, and chaired the committee that organized the AFL's California state labor federation in 1901. MacArthur wrote numerous books and pamphlets on seamen's laws and maritime affairs, and from 1913 to 1932 was U.S. shipping commissioner for the port of San Francisco. He was also active in the National Civic Federation.

McBRIDE, John (1854-1917), the only person to defeat SG for the presidency of the AFL, presided over the formation of the United Mine Workers of America (UMWA) and was its second president. The son of an Ohio miner, he was elected president of the Ohio Miners' Protective Union in 1877 and master workman of KOL District Assembly 38 in 1880, and served as president of the Ohio Miners' Amalgamated Association from 1882 to 1889. In 1885 he was a founder and first president of the National Federation of Miners and Mine Laborers and in 1886 presided over the founding convention of the AFL, declining the Federation's nomination for president. He served as president of the National Progressive Union of Miners and Mine Laborers in 1889 and was a leader in merging that union with KOL National Trade Assembly 135 in 1890 to form the UMWA. He became president of the UMWA in 1892 and served until 1895.

McBride served as a Democrat in the Ohio legislature from 1884 to 1888, was commissioner of the Ohio Bureau of Labor Statistics from 1890 to 1891, and later became active in the populist movement. He was elected president of the AFL over SG in 1894, and narrowly lost to SG the next year. McBride purchased the *Columbus Record* in 1896, and subsequently pursued various occupations including editor, saloonkeeper, and federal labor conciliator.

McBRYDE, Patrick (1848-1902?), secretary-treasurer of the United Mine Workers of America (UMWA) from 1891 to 1896, was born in Ireland and raised in Scotland, where he became active in local miners' organizations. He came to the United States in the late 1870s, remaining for several years before returning to the Scottish mines. About 1884 he immigrated to the United States, settling in the Pittsburgh area where he joined KOL Local Assembly 151. McBryde represented KOL National Trade Assembly 135 at the founding convention of the National Progressive Union of Miners and Mine Laborers and served as its secretary-treasurer (1888-90). In 1890 he was elected to the National Executive Board of the newly founded UMWA. After retiring from the miners' union in 1896, he served as commissioner for mine operators in Ohio.

MCCRAITH, Augustine (1864?-1909), was born in Canada. He moved to Boston, where he was a member of International Typographical Union (ITU) 61, and later president (1891-92) and secretary (1892-95) of ITU 13. Between 1895 and 1896 he was secretary of the AFL. Later he moved to New York City, where he was an active member of ITU 6.

MCDONNELL, Joseph Patrick (1847-1906), born in Ireland and active in the Fenian movement, joined the International Workingmen's Association (IWA) after moving to London in 1868 and served as Irish secretary of the IWA's General Council. He immigrated to New York City in 1872 and began editing the *Labor Standard,* an organ of the Workingmen's Party of the United States (WPUS), in 1876. He later moved the paper to Boston (1877) and then (1878) to Paterson, N.J., where he helped organize the International Labor Union. In 1883 he helped organize the New Jersey Federation of Trades and Labor Unions; he served as its chairman until 1897. In 1884 he was a founder of the Paterson Trades Assembly. He became New Jersey's first factory inspector in 1884 and, in 1892, was appointed to the New Jersey Board of Arbitration. McDonnell continued to publish the *Labor Standard* until his death.

MCGREGOR, Hugh (1840-1911), was an English-born jeweler. He served as a volunteer with Garibaldi's army and immigrated to the United States in 1865. During the 1870s he was a member of the International Workingmen's Association and a founder and active organizer of the Social Democratic Workingmen's Party of North America. He served as secretary of its New York City branch in 1875 and its Philadelphia branch in 1876, returning to New York City in the spring of that year to edit the new English-language organ of the party, the *Socialist.* A participant in the Economic and Sociological Club, he apparently left the socialist movement and became active in a small circle of New York City positivists. During the late 1880s he served as SG's secretary, directing the AFL office during the president's absence. He helped organize seamen on the Atlantic coast and between 1890 and 1892 served as secretary of the International Amalgamated Sailors' and Firemen's Union. He later worked briefly in the AFL's Washington office.

MCGUIRE, Peter James (1852-1906), chief executive officer of the United Brotherhood of Carpenters and Joiners of America (UBCJA), was born in New York City. He joined a local carpenters' union there in 1872 and became a member of the International Workingmen's Association. He was involved in relief efforts in New York City during the depression of the 1870s and played a major role in organizing the Tompkins Square demonstration of January 1874. In 1874 he helped organize the Social Democratic Workingmen's Party of North America and was elected to its Executive Board; that same year he joined the KOL. During the late 1870s McGuire traveled widely, organizing and campaigning first on behalf of the Workingmen's Party of the United States and then for the SLP. After living for a time in New Haven, Conn., he moved to St. Louis in 1878 and the following year was instrumental in the establishment of the Missouri Bureau of Labor Statistics, to which he was appointed deputy commissioner. He resigned in 1880 to campaign for the SLP and for the Greenback-Labor party. In 1881 he was elected secretary of the St. Louis Trades Assembly and, as a member of the provisional committee to organize a carpenters' national union, began editing the *Carpenter*. Through that journal he generated interest in organizing the Brotherhood of Carpenters and Joiners (later the UBCJA); he was elected secretary of the union at its founding convention later that year and held the position until 1901. McGuire moved to New York City in 1882, was a founder of the New York City Central Labor Union, and became a member of KOL Spread the Light Local Assembly 1562. He subsequently moved to Philadelphia. He served as secretary of the AFL from 1886 to 1889, second vice-president from 1889 to 1890, and first vice-president from 1890 to 1900.

McGuire, Thomas B. (b. 1849), a leader of KOL District Assembly (DA) 49 and a member of the Home Club, was a marble polisher and truck driver. Born in New York City, he served in the Union army during the Civil War. He became active in the labor movement in the early 1870s and subsequently served as an officer in KOL local assemblies 2234 and 1974. McGuire was master workman of DA 49 in 1886 and a member of the Knights' General Executive Board from 1886 to 1888 and from 1892 to 1897; he lectured for the Order in the interim. In 1893 he was a member of the Advisory Committee of the People's party. During the 1890s he resided in Amsterdam, N.Y.

McHugh, Edward (1853-1915), a Scottish printer, was a cofounder in 1889 of the National Union of Dock Labourers and its general secretary from 1889 to 1893. In 1896 the International Federation of Ship, Dock, and River Workers sent him to the United States to organize longshoremen on the east coast. He founded the American Longshoremen's Union with the assistance of Henry George in October 1896 and served as its president from 1896 until 1898, when it disbanded.

McHUGH, James F. (1853-1914), was born in Wisconsin and was a member of the Minneapolis local of the Journeymen Stonecutters' Association of North America (JSANA) when he was elected secretary of the national union in 1891. He served as JSANA secretary-treasurer from 1892 until his resignation in 1912.

McKINNEY, Joseph W. (1856-1917?), was born in Chicago where he joined a local painters' union in 1873. Active in KOL Local Assembly 1940, he joined Brotherhood of Painters and Decorators of America (BPDA) 147 in 1891. He served as general president of the BPDA from 1892 to 1894 and was elected general secretary-treasurer in 1894 but, in a dispute with the incumbent, was unable to take office. He then participated in the formation of a rival faction of the painters' union, which established its headquarters in Lafayette, Ind.; he was the general secretary-treasurer of this so-called western faction from 1896 until resigning in 1897.

McNEILL, George Edwin (1837-1906), a Boston printer born in Massachusetts, was secretary of the Grand Eight-Hour League and president of the Boston Eight-Hour League. He helped lobby for the establishment of the Massachusetts Bureau of Statistics of Labor and served as its deputy director from 1869 to 1873. McNeill was an officer of the Sovereigns of Industry, president of the International Labor Union in 1878, and secretary-treasurer of KOL District Assembly 30 from 1884 to 1886. He was editor or associate editor of several papers including the *Labor Standard* in Boston, Fall River, Mass., and Paterson, N.J., and in 1887 published *The Labor Movement: The Problem of To-Day.* He helped organize the Massachusetts Mutual Accident Association in 1883 and was elected its secretary and general manager in 1892. In 1897 he served as the AFL's fraternal delegate to the TUC.

MADDEN, Stephen (b. 1855?), was a leader of the National Amalgamated Association of Iron and Steel Workers (NAAISW) from 1887 to 1899. He was born in Wales and immigrated to the United States in 1864, settling in Pittsburgh where he worked as a puddler. For most of his years in the NAAISW's leadership he was assistant secretary (1887-90, 1893-94, 1896, 1899), with intervening periods as secretary (1890-92) and secretary-treasurer (1897-98). From 1904 to 1927 he served as chief clerk of the bureau of electricity of Pittsburgh.

MAHON, William D. (1861-1949), was born in Athens, Ohio, and worked as a coal miner in the Hocking Valley district. He moved to Columbus, Ohio, in the late 1880s where he worked as a mule car driver and helped to organize street railway workers in the early

1890s. In 1893 he was elected president of the Amalgamated Association of Street Railway Employes of America (AASREA) and shortly thereafter moved to Detroit. He served as president of the AASREA (after 1903 the Amalgamated Association of Street and Electric Railway Employes of America) until retiring in 1946. Mahon was presiding judge of the Michigan State Court of Arbitration (1898-1900), a member of the Executive Committee of the National Civic Federation, and a member of the AFL's Executive Council (1917-23, 1935-49).

MANN, Thomas (1856-1941), a British machinist, was a member of the Amalgamated Society of Engineers (ASE) and, until 1889, of the Social Democratic Federation. A leader of the London dock strike of 1889, he became president of the Dock, Wharf, Riverside, and General Labourers' Union of Great Britain and Ireland at its founding in mid-September of that year, serving until 1892. In 1891 he was one of seven trade unionists on the Royal Commission on Labour, which was formed to discuss the question of industrial relations. Mann was secretary of the Independent Labour party from 1894 to 1896. In 1916 he joined the British Socialist party and in 1920 helped found the British Communist party, remaining a member until his death. From 1919 to 1921 he was secretary of the Amalgamated Engineering Union, successor to the ASE. Mann stood unsuccessfully for Parliament four times.

MAWDSLEY, James (1848-1902), was general secretary of the Amalgamated Association of Operative Cotton Spinners (1878-1902) and a member of the Parliamentary Committee of the TUC (1882-83, 1884-90, 1891-97). He served on the Royal Commission on Labour from 1891 to 1894.

MILLER, Owen (1850-1919), a musicians' leader, was born in New Jersey. He enlisted in the U.S. army at the age of twenty-one and transferred to St. Louis in 1873, serving for the next ten years in the arsenal band. He became president of the Musicians' Mutual Benefit Association (MMBA) of St. Louis in 1885, serving for thirty years. In 1886, when the MMBA joined the KOL as Local Assembly 5938, he was its master workman. The MMBA also apparently became local 8 of the National League of Musicians (NLM), which organized in 1886. NLM 8 affiliated with the AFL as MMBA 5579 in 1891, even though the NLM refused to join the Federation. Miller served as president of the NLM (1891-92, 1894-95) and in 1896 led a contingent out of the League to form a rival union, the American Federation of Musicians (AFM). He also helped organize the St. Louis Central Trades and Labor Union in 1887, serving seven times as president, and in 1888 he was elected to the Missouri senate on the Union Labor ticket. He served from 1889 to 1893. Miller served as president of the AFM between 1896 and 1900 and as its secretary from 1900 to 1918. He was editor of the *International Musician* from 1901 to 1919.

MILLS, Henry S., a former Lawrence, Mass., textile operative, was general treasurer (1896-97) and general secretary (1897-98?) of the National Union of Textile Workers of America. He also worked as an insurance agent beginning as early as 1896.

MITCHELL, Rose Gompers (1872-99), was the daughter of SG and Sophia Gompers. She married Samuel Mitchell in 1891; they lived in New York City and had two children, Henrietta and Ethel.

MITCHELL, Samuel (1867?-1932), who married SG and Sophia Gompers' daughter Rose in 1891, worked in New York City as a letter carrier and postal clerk, eventually becoming a clerk foreman. While a letter carrier, Mitchell belonged to branch 36 of the National Association of Letter Carriers.

MORGAN, Thomas John (1847-1912), a Chicago machinist and brass finisher, was born in Birmingham, England, where he married Elizabeth Chambers. They immigrated to the United States in 1869, and he worked for the Illinois Central Railroad, joining the International Machinists and Blacksmiths of North America in 1871, and serving as president of his local in 1874. Beginning in 1876, he was active in the Social Democratic Workingmen's Party of North America and its successor, the Workingmen's Party of the United States. He was an organizer and officer of the Chicago American Section of the SLP and ran unsuccessfully as its candidate for alderman in 1879 and 1881. He was a founder of the United Labor party in Chicago in 1886, and he ran unsuccessfully for mayor of the city on the SLP ticket in 1891. He helped found the Council of Trades and Labor Unions of Chicago in 1877, joined Local Assembly 522 of the KOL in 1879, helped organize the Chicago Central Labor Union in 1884, and founded the Machine Workers' Union of Chicago in 1886. In 1891 Morgan helped organize the International Machinists' Union, serving as its general secretary in 1894 and 1895. Morgan left the Illinois Central in 1893 to study law, and in 1895 was admitted to the bar. In 1894 he took a leading role in forging a Populist-labor alliance. In 1896 he edited the *Socialist Alliance*, the monthly organ of the Socialist Trade and Labor Alliance. He helped launch the Social Democratic party in 1900, serving as secretary of its national campaign committee and running unsuccessfully as its nominee for state's attorney of Cook Co., Ill. He became a leader in the Socialist

Party of America, running unsuccessfully for a variety of offices including U.S. senator in 1909. From 1909 until his death he was editor and publisher of the *Provoker.*

MORRIS, Max (1866-1909), was born in Mobile, Ala., and moved to Breckenridge, Colo., in 1880. He worked as a retail clerk in Glenwood Springs and Leadville, Colo., organized a clerks' union in Cripple Creek, Colo., and on settling in Denver around 1890, organized the Denver Retail Clerks' Union. A member of Denver Local 7 of the Retail Clerks' National Protective Association of America (RCNPA; after 1899 Retail Clerks' International Protective Association), he became RCNPA secretary-treasurer in 1896, serving until 1909. He edited the union's journal, the *Retail Clerks' National* (later *International*) *Advocate* from around 1899 to 1909. Morris was AFL fifth vice-president (1899-1900) and fourth vice-president (1901-9). He served as a member of the Colorado House of Representatives as a member of the People's party (1899-1900) and as a Democrat (1901-4), and for many years served on the board of managers of the National Jewish Hospital for Consumptives in Denver.

MORRISON, Frank (1859-1949), was born in Frankton, Ontario. His family moved to Walkerton, Ontario, in 1865, where he became a printer. Beginning about 1883 he worked at his trade in Madison, Wis. In 1886 he moved to Chicago, where he joined International Typographical Union 16. From 1893 to 1894 he studied law at Lake Forest University, becoming a member of the Illinois bar in 1895. The following year he was elected secretary of the AFL, serving in that post from 1897 to 1935, and as AFL secretary-treasurer from 1936 until his retirement in 1939. During World War I Morrison chaired the wages and hours subcommittee of the committee on labor of the Advisory Commission of the Council of National Defense.

MORRISSEY, Patrick Henry (1862-1916), began working for the railroads as a call boy and was a founding member of Brotherhood of Railroad Brakemen lodge 62 of Bloomington, Ill., in 1885. He served as an officer in his lodge and as vice-grand master (1889-95) and grand master (1895-1909) of the brotherhood (after 1890 the Brotherhood of Railroad Trainmen). After retiring from office, he was president of the Railway Employes' and Investors' Association and assistant to the vice-president in charge of operation for the Chicago, Burlington, and Quincy Railroad Co.

MUDGE, William (b. 1862), emigrated from England in 1887 and was an iron ore miner in Negaunee, Mich., becoming secretary of the Marquette Co., Mich., mine workers' union. He was secretary of the Northern Mineral Mine Workers' Progressive Union from its founding in 1895 until 1897, when he was elected president; he served in this office no later than 1900.

MULHOLLAND, John F., worked in a Toledo, Ohio, family business and then as a painter and machine hand in the 1890s. He was a founder of the International Union of Bicycle Workers (from 1898 the International Union of Bicycle Workers and Allied Mechanics, and from 1900 the International Association of Allied Metal Mechanics), serving as its president from 1896 until its absorption by the International Association of Machinists in 1904.

NEUROTH, William B. (1850-1902), was born in Germany and immigrated to the United States, joining CMIU 9 in Troy, N.Y., in 1879. After settling in Denver he joined CMIU 24. He served as a vice-president (1887, 1890, 1892-96) of the CMIU.

O'CONNELL, James (1858-1936), born in Minersville, Pa., learned his trade as a machinist's apprentice and later worked as a railroad machinist. O'Connell served as a lobbyist for the KOL in Harrisburg, Pa., in 1889 and 1891. He joined National Association of Machinists (after 1891 International Association of Machinists [IAM]) lodge 113 of Oil City, Pa., around 1890, became a member of the IAM general executive board in 1891, and served as grand master machinist of the IAM from 1893 to 1911. He moved to Chicago in 1896. O'Connell was third vice-president of the AFL from 1895 to 1913, second vice-president from 1914 to 1918, and president of the AFL Metal Trades Department from 1911 to 1934; he represented the AFL at the 1899 meeting of the TUC. He also served on the U.S. Commission on Industrial Relations from 1913 to 1915, and on the Council of National Defense committee on labor in 1917.

O'DONNELL, Thomas (b. 1852), immigrated to the United States from England in 1873. By 1880 he had settled in Fall River, Mass., working as a mule spinner. He is recorded as serving intermittently as treasurer of the National Cotton Mule Spinners' Association of America (from 1898 the National Spinners' Association of America and from 1906 the International Spinners' Union) from the early 1890s into the second decade of the twentieth century; for several years around the turn of the century he was its secretary. Between the late 1890s and 1911 he was also secretary for a number of terms of the Fall River Mule Spinners' Association, an affiliate of the national organization.

O'SULLIVAN, John F. (1857-1902), a Boston journalist and labor organizer, was born in Charlestown, Mass. He wrote on labor for the *Boston Labor Leader* and *Boston Herald* before joining the *Boston Globe* in 1890 as a reporter and labor editor. In the late 1880s he became active in organizing sailors, serving as treasurer of the Boston sailors' union. He was president of the International Amalgamated Sailors' and Firemen's Union from 1889 to 1891, and of the Atlantic Coast Seamen's Union from its founding in 1891 until his death. He was active in the Boston Central Labor Union and served two terms as its president in the early 1890s. He was also active in the Massachusetts Federation of Labor as a member of the legislative committee. In 1894 he married Mary Kenney. O'Sullivan was secretary of Newspaper Writers' Union 1 of Boston from 1896 until his death and served the International Typographical Union as an organizer and as a vice-president (1897-1902).

O'SULLIVAN, Mary Kenney (1864-1943), the first AFL national organizer for women, was born in Hannibal, Mo. She apprenticed to a dressmaker but eventually became forewoman in a printing and binding company. In the late 1880s she moved to Chicago where she worked in local binderies and became active in AFL Ladies' Federal Labor Union (FLU) 2703. She served as the FLU's delegate to the Trade and Labor Assembly of Chicago and organized women binders into the Chicago Bindery Workers' Union. In 1892 Kenney served for five months as an AFL organizer for female workers, concentrating her efforts in New York and Massachusetts. Returning to Chicago, she continued to organize women and successfully lobbied for a state factory law regulating the employment of women and children. After its passage, she became a deputy to Chief Inspector Florence Kelley.

In 1894 Kenney married John F. O'Sullivan. They lived in Boston, and over the years she wrote articles for the *Boston Globe* on women, trade unions, and labor issues. She continued to organize women workers with the support of the Women's Educational and Industrial Union and also helped found and served as executive secretary of the Union for Industrial Progress, a group studying factory conditions. At the 1903 AFL convention she was one of the founders of the National Women's Trade Union League (NWTUL), serving as its first secretary (1903) and later as its vice-president (1907-9); she resigned from the NWTUL in 1912. In 1914 she became a factory inspector for the Massachusetts Department of Labor and Industries, holding that post until her retirement in 1934.

PEARCE, William Charles (b. 1859), was born in England and began working in the coal mines at the age of eight; he was orphaned when he was thirteen. In 1880 he immigrated to Ohio, settling in Corning in 1882. He became an active member of the local miners' union and served as secretary-treasurer of United Mine Workers of America (UMWA) District 6 from 1891 to 1896. From 1896 to 1900 he was secretary-treasurer of the UMWA, which required his relocation to Columbus, Ohio, and subsequently to Indianapolis. Resigning his office in 1900 after an audit had revealed discrepancies in the accounts, Pearce went into business in Indianapolis.

PENNA, Philip H. (1857-1939), was born in England and immigrated to the United States in 1881, working in coal mines in Brazil, Ind. He was president of the Federated Association of Miners and Mine Laborers of Indiana in 1888 when that organization became District 11 of the National Progressive Union of Miners and Mine Laborers, and he continued as president of the district until 1890. He helped form the United Mine Workers of America in 1890, serving as its vice-president (1891-95) and president (1895-97). In the following decade he became secretary of the Indiana Coal Operators' Association, holding that post until his retirement in the 1920s.

PERKINS, George William (1856-1934), longtime president of the CMIU, began his career in the union by joining Albany, N.Y., local 68 in 1880. He was a vice-president of the CMIU from 1885 to 1891 and acted as president for six months in 1888 and 1889. In 1891 he was elected president, an office that he held for the next thirty-five years. In 1918 he was appointed to the AFL's Commission on Reconstruction and represented the American labor movement at the International Federation of Trade Unions conference. He became the president of the AFL Union Label Trades Department in 1926, serving until his death.

PHILLIPS, John (1850-1904), a national hatters' leader, was born in Ireland and immigrated to the United States in 1860. He settled in Brooklyn, where he was secretary of a hat finishers' local of the National Trade Association of Hat Finishers of the United States of America in 1878. Phillips served as national secretary of the association through most of the 1880s. In 1896 this organization, renamed the International Trade Association of Hat Finishers of America, merged with the National Hat Makers' Association of the United States to form the United Hatters of North America (UHNA). Phillips became secretary of the UHNA, retaining this position until his death.

POMEROY, William Curtis, born in Kentucky, worked as a waiter on riverboats between New Orleans and St. Louis before moving to Chicago in the mid-1880s. There he helped organize the catering trades into KOL Local Assembly 7475 in 1886 and was a founder of the Waiters' League of Chicago, which affiliated with the AFL in 1890. Pomeroy became active in the Trade and Labor Assembly (TLA) of Chicago as its financial secretary in 1886 and was the dominant figure in the TLA and the Illinois State Federation of Labor (FL) in the early 1890s. He was an AFL organizer from 1893 to 1894 and in 1896. In 1891 he helped found the Waiters' and Bartenders' National Union (after 1892 the Hotel and Restaurant Employees' National Alliance and after 1898 the Hotel and Restaurant Employees' International Alliance and Bartenders' International League of America). Pomeroy held official positions with the Alliance as editor of its journals, the *Purveyor* (1893-94), the *American Caterer* (1896-98), and the *National Purveyor* (1897-99), and as its vice-president (1896-99). He launched the *Labor Gazette* in 1894. He was also active in politics, fielding a Labor party ticket in the 1892 Chicago city elections and establishing his own People's party for the 1894 elections. In 1896 he worked closely with Mark Hanna in William McKinley's presidential campaign.

Throughout the 1890s Pomeroy faced repeated charges of corruption. In 1896 the AFL convention rejected his credentials as a delegate after a challenge from the Illinois State FL, and in 1897 the AFL received complaints from locals of the Alliance that culminated in formal charges before the AFL Executive Council in 1898. The following year Pomeroy attempted to form a rival organization, and in 1900 the Alliance expelled him.

PORTER, James Edward (1856-1936?), a New Orleans longshoreman and cotton screwman, was a prominent black trade unionist. He was born a slave in Mississippi and came to New Orleans in 1865 or 1866. A leader of the 1892 New Orleans general strike, he was also an AFL organizer, secretary for many years of one of the city's longshoremen's unions, and a vice-president from 1901 to 1903 of the International Longshoremen's Association (from 1902, the International Longshoremen, Marine, and Transportworkers' Association). In 1900 Porter organized a black central labor organization in New Orleans, which the AFL chartered in 1901 as the New Orleans Central Labor Union.

POWDERLY, Terence Vincent (1849-1924), general master workman of the KOL, was born in Carbondale, Pa. Apprenticed as a machinist, he moved to Scranton, Pa., and joined the International Machinists and Blacksmiths of North America in 1871, becoming president of his local and an organizer in Pennsylvania. After being dismissed and blacklisted for his labor activities, Powderly joined the KOL in Philadelphia in 1876 and shortly afterward founded a local assembly of machinists and was elected its master workman. In 1877 he helped organize District Assembly 5 (number changed to 16 in 1878) and was elected corresponding secretary. He was elected mayor of Scranton on the Greenback-Labor ticket in 1878 and served three consecutive two-year terms. At the same time he played an important role in calling the first General Assembly of the KOL in 1878, where he was chosen grand worthy foreman, the KOL's second highest office. The September 1879 General Assembly elected him grand master workman, and he continued to hold the Order's leading position (title changed to general master workman in 1883) until 1893. Active in the secret Irish nationalist society, *Clan na Gael,* Powderly was elected to the Central Council of the American Land League in 1880 and was its vice-president in 1881. He became an ardent advocate of land reform and temperance and, as master workman, favored the organization of workers into mixed locals rather than craft unions, recommended that they avoid strikes, encouraged producers' cooperatives, and espoused political reform.

In 1894 Powderly was admitted to the Pennsylvania bar, and in 1897 President William McKinley, for whom he had campaigned, appointed him commissioner general of immigration. President Theodore Roosevelt removed him from his position in 1902 but in 1906 appointed him special representative of the Department of Commerce and Labor to study European immigration problems. Powderly was chief of the Division of Information in the Bureau of Immigration and Naturalization from 1907 until his death.

POWERS, Richard (1844?-1929), an Irish-born sailor, came to New York City in 1861 and, after Civil War service, settled in Chicago and worked as a sailor on the Great Lakes. He helped organize a lumber vessel unloaders' union in 1877 and a sailors' union (known both as the Lake Seamen's Benevolent Association of Chicago and the Lake Seamen's Union) in 1878, serving as president of the latter organization from its founding into the 1890s. He was a member of the Legislative Committee of the FOTLU from 1881 to 1885, and that body sent him to Washington, D.C., to lobby for seamen's measures. He was also active in the KOL, representing District Assembly 136 at the 1886 General Assembly, and in the *Clan na Gael,* a secret Irish nationalist society. From the late 1880s Powers worked variously as inspector of drains, clerk, vessel dispatcher, saloonkeeper, deputy collector of internal revenue, and real estate salesman.

PRESCOTT, William Blair (1863-1916), was born in Ontario, Canada, and in 1883 joined International Typographical Union (ITU) 91 of Toronto. He served as president of the ITU from 1891 to 1898 and then worked as a proofreader for newspapers in Indianapolis and Baltimore.

RATCHFORD, Michael D. (1860-1927), was born in Ireland and in 1872 came to the United States and began work as a miner in Ohio. He served as president (1890-92) of the United Mine Workers of America (UMWA) local at Massillon, Ohio, was a UMWA organizer (1893-94), president of UMWA District 6 (1895-96), and president of the UMWA (1897-98). He resigned the UMWA presidency to serve on the U.S. Industrial Commission (1898-1900); he was subsequently appointed Ohio commissioner of labor statistics, a post he held until 1908. Ratchford left public office to work for the mining industry as commissioner for the Ohio Coal Operators (1909-12), secretary of the Pitts Vein Operators (1911-12), and from 1913 as commissioner for the Illinois Coal Operators' Association.

RAUSCH, William E. (b. 1866), was born in Indiana and worked as a general contractor, machinist, and carpenter in Toledo in the 1890s. He was a cofounder in 1896 of the International Union of Bicycle Workers (from 1898 International Union of Bicycle Workers and Allied Mechanics); he was elected temporary secretary at its founding meeting and then served as its secretary-treasurer (1897-99). After leaving the union, Rausch worked as a county clerk in 1900; he was later the manager of a collection agency.

REICHERS, Charles F. (1850?-1929), a New York City garment worker and one of the founders in 1891 of the United Garment Workers of America (UGWA), served as that organization's general secretary (1891-95) and president (1895-96). Reichers was born in New York and was an active member of UGWA 5 of Brooklyn throughout the 1890s. He left the union in 1896 to start a children's clothing business but returned to the UGWA as an organizer when his venture failed shortly thereafter. With a group of UGWA members he launched a cooperative clothing company in 1898, heading the company until 1921 when he retired to California.

REID, James P., was an Olneyville, R.I., weaver who served as president (1896) and subsequently general secretary (early 1897) of the National Union of Textile Workers of America. He later became a dentist.

ROGERS, Louis William (1859-1953), was born in Iowa and taught for five years during the 1870s in Iowa and Kansas public schools; by the mid-1880s he was a free-thought lecturer. He subsequently began working as a railroad brakeman and editor. He founded and edited the *Railroad Patriot* in St. Joseph, Mo. (1888-89), then in 1889 moved briefly to Colorado, where he became a member of Snowy Range 30 (Denver) of the Brotherhood of Railroad Brakemen (BRB; from 1890, the Brotherhood of Railroad Trainmen) and edited the *Denver Patriot* and the *Vona Herald*. Named editor (1889-92) of the BRB organ, the *Railroad Brakemen's Journal* (from 1890, the *Railroad Trainmen's Journal*), he moved to Galesburg, Ill.; then, in Chicago (1892) and Oshkosh, Wis. (1892-93), he published and edited the *Age of Labor* (merged with the *Labor Advocate* in 1893 to become the *Labor Advocate and Age of Labor*). In 1893 Rogers helped organize the Wisconsin State Federation of Labor and became active in the American Railway Union (ARU), serving on its executive board and, in 1894, editing the ARU organ *Railway Times*. He was also Cook Co., Ill., chairman for the People's party in 1894. After serving a jail term in 1895 along with other ARU leaders for his role in the Pullman strike, Rogers moved to Pueblo, Colo., working as an AFL organizer and publishing and editing the *Industrial Advocate* (1896). He was editor in 1897 of the *Social Democrat*, organ of Eugene Debs's Social Democracy movement, and managed Debs's lecture tours for two years at the end of the decade. He also served as president of the Michigan State Federation of Labor from 1898 to 1899. After the turn of the century Rogers became active in the mystical theosophist movement, becoming a lecturer, vice-president (1918-20), and president (1920-31) for the Theosophical Society in America (TSA), traveling extensively, writing many books and pamphlets, and editing the TSA journals *Ancient Wisdom* (1935-36) and *The Voice* (1951-52).

Ross, Samuel (1865-1948?), was born in Stalybridge, Cheshire, England, and began working in a textile mill at the age of seven. He immigrated to the United States in 1880, settling in New Bedford, Mass., where he worked as a mule spinner. In 1886 he was elected secretary of the New Bedford Mule Spinners' Association, and the next year helped found the National Cotton Mule Spinners' Association of America (NCMSA; from 1898 the National Spinners' Association of America, and from 1906 the International Spinners' Union), serving as president (1889), secretary for much of the period between 1891 and 1911, and vice-president (1919-20). From about 1892 to 1928 and in 1932 he was secretary of the New Bedford Mule Spinners' Association, an affiliate of the NCMSA and later of the United Textile Workers of America (UTWA); he served as a vice-president of the UTWA from 1902 to 1903. He also served a term as president of the New Bedford Central Labor Union (1900-1901). Ross was a Republican member of the Massachusetts house (1892-

99, 1902-8) and senate (1909-14) and ran unsuccessfully for the U.S. Congress in 1914. He engaged in the clothing business from 1910 to 1914.

RUHE, C. H. William (1851-1941?), born in Pennsylvania, worked in Pittsburgh as a bookkeeper, foreman, and a musician. He was president of National League of Musicians of the United States (NLM) 15 of Pittsburgh in the late 1880s and 1890s and president of the NLM from 1892 to 1894. From 1930 to 1940 he was superintendent of the Allegheny County Soldiers' and Sailors' Memorial Hall.

SANIAL, Lucien Delabarre (1836-1927), a French-born journalist, came to the United States in 1863 as a war correspondent for *Le Temps*. A prominent leader of the SLP, he drafted the party's platform in 1889, edited its organs the *Workmen's Advocate* (1889-91) and the *People* (1891), and ran for mayor of New York on the SLP ticket in 1894. Around 1902 Sanial left the SLP; he later joined the Socialist Party of America, remaining an active member until breaking with the party in 1917 over its opposition to World War I. Sanial spoke at the founding convention of the American Alliance for Labor and Democracy in 1917.

SARGENT, Frank Pierce (1854-1908), grand master of the Brotherhood of Locomotive Firemen (BLF) from 1885 to 1902, was born in Vermont and was a textile operative, farm laborer, and a U.S. cavalryman before becoming a railroad worker. He joined BLF Lodge 94 of Tucson, Ariz., in 1881 and in 1883 was elected vice grand master of the Brotherhood. He was named to the U.S. Industrial Commission in 1898, and Theodore Roosevelt appointed him U.S. commissioner general of immigration in 1902. Sargent was active in the National Civic Federation and was one of the labor representatives to its Division of Conciliation and Mediation.

SCHILLING, George Adam (1850-1938), a German-born cooper, emigrated with his parents and settled in Ohio in 1852. He worked as an itinerant cooper before moving to Chicago in 1875. There he was associated with the anarchist movement. He helped establish the Chicago English-speaking section of the Workingmen's Party of the United States in 1876, and with Thomas Morgan and Albert Parsons led the English-speaking branch of the SLP in the late 1870s, publishing the *Socialist* between 1878 and 1879. In 1878 he was a member of the provisional committee that drew up the program of the International Labor Union. He ran unsuccessfully for alderman of Chicago in 1879 and 1880 and for mayor in 1881. After 1886 Schilling was an advocate of Henry George's single-tax movement, serving as president of the Chicago Single Tax Club. He helped organize a committee favoring amnesty for the Haymarket anarchists and led their defense before Governor Richard J. Oglesby of Illinois in 1887. A member of the executive board and master workman of KOL District Assembly 24 in the late 1880s, he led its secession from the KOL in 1889 in reaction to Terence Powderly's condemnation of the Haymarket defendants and failure to support the eight-hour movement. Between 1893 and 1897 he served as commissioner of the Illinois Bureau of Labor Statistics under Governor John P. Altgeld. In the late 1890s he was a member of the Chicago Civic Federation, and subsequently he served as a member (1903-5) and president (1905-7, 1911-15) of the Chicago Board of Local Improvements.

SCHLÜTER, Hermann (1851-1919), was editor-in-chief of the *New Yorker Volkszeitung* from 1891 to 1919. Born in Germany, he was apparently active in the Chicago labor movement during his youth. Returning to Germany, his activities there resulted in his expulsion in the early 1880s. After living for a time in England, where he collaborated with Karl Marx and Friedrich Engels, he went to Switzerland to help edit the banned organ of the Sozialdemokratische Partei Deutschlands (Social Democratic Party of Germany), *Der Sozialdemokrat.* When Swiss authorities forced members of the paper's editorial board to leave the country in 1888, Schlüter immigrated to the United States, joining the staff of the *New Yorker Volkszeitung.* In addition to his work on that paper, he wrote several books on labor and socialism.

SHEVITCH, Sergius E. (variously Sergei E. Schewitsch; 1848-1911), was born in Russia and worked there as a government clerk (1870-76) before coming to the United States in 1877. Because of his facility in three languages, he was an important figure in the SLP in New York City during the 1880s. He was a member of the *New Yorker Volkszeitung* editorial board after 1878 and edited the paper in 1890. In 1887 he edited the *Leader* and ran unsuccessfully for mayor of New York City on the Progressive Labor party ticket. Shevitch left the United States in 1890 and, after living for a time in the Baltic provinces, took up residence in Munich.

SMITH, William J. (1853-1906), of Pittsburgh, served as president of the American Flint Glass Workers' Union of North America (AFGWU) from 1885 to 1900 and held concurrent positions as secretary in 1885 and as treasurer from 1887 to 1900. As a lamp chimney blower in Pittsburgh in the 1870s, Smith joined KOL Local Assembly 320. He was a delegate to the convention establishing the AFGWU in 1878. After leaving the union, he served as an agent and later as an auditor for the Macbeth-Evans Glass Co. of Pittsburgh.

SORGE, Friedrich Adolph (1828-1906), a leading American socialist, was born in Saxony. He participated in the Revolution of 1848 and the Baden uprising in 1849, and, after a brief period of imprisonment in 1849, settled in Geneva. Swiss authorities forced him to leave the country in 1851, and he immigrated to New York City in 1852, living there for about two years before moving to Hoboken, N.J.

In 1857 Sorge helped found the Communist Club in New York. He embraced the idea that trade unions had to play a central role in the emancipation of the workers and rejected the emphasis placed by followers of Ferdinand Lassalle on the primacy of political action. In 1868 he became the leader of the Social Party of New York and Vicinity and the designated U.S. spokesman for the General Council of the Marx-led International Workingmen's Association (IWA). He became secretary of Section 1 of the IWA in the United States in 1869 and first corresponding secretary of the IWA's Central Committee for North America at its establishment in 1870. He also served as the delegate of his section to the National Labor Union between 1869 and 1871. When the 1872 Hague Congress of the IWA moved the organization's General Council from London to New York City, Marx supported Sorge's appointment as IWA general secretary, a position Sorge held until resigning in 1874.

In 1876 Sorge participated in the founding of the Workingmen's Party of the United States, but he withdrew in 1877 after the political faction gained control. He helped form the International Labor Union (ILU) in 1878. In 1883, after the ILU had dwindled to a single branch in Hoboken, he reorganized that body as the International Labor Union of Hoboken; it dissolved in 1887. For the remaining years of his life, Sorge supported himself as a music teacher and wrote articles for labor publications including, on SG's request, a serialized history of the U.S. labor movement that appeared in *Die Neue Zeit* (Stuttgart) between 1891 and 1896.

SOVEREIGN, James R. (b. 1854), was born in Grant Co., Wis., and grew up on a farm in Illinois. After working in the Midwest as a cattle driver and a bridge and tunnel construction worker, he became a marble carver in 1874. He joined the KOL in 1881 and in the 1880s was active in the Knights as a labor journalist and lecturer. He was appointed commissioner of labor statistics for Iowa in 1890 and reappointed in 1892. A representative of the Iowa state assembly to the KOL General Assembly in the early 1890s, he was elected general master workman in 1893 and served until 1897. He took an active part in the populist movement, serving on the national executive committee of the People's party in 1896 and helping run the party's Chicago branch headquarters during the 1896 presidential campaign. In 1898 Sovereign was living in Wallace, Idaho.

STEINBISS, Herman W. (d. 1923), worked variously as a clerk, chipper, bartender, and painter in St. Louis from 1886 to 1895. A member of Brotherhood of Painters and Decorators 46, he was secretary of the St. Louis Building Trades Council (1896-97) and, from 1897 to about 1912, general secretary and general secretary-treasurer of the National (after 1904, International) Building Trades Council of America (IBTCA). He also edited and published the council's organ, the *Labor Compendium* (1904-12?). Steinbiss was a cofounder in 1907 of the Joint Legislative Board of the State of Missouri—a labor lobbying group—and at the same time served on the Executive Committee of the Children's Protective Alliance of Missouri. After leaving the IBTCA, he worked as a clerk from 1913 to 1921.

STEPHENS, Uriah Smith (1821-82), born near Cape May, N.J., trained for the Baptist ministry, apprenticed as a tailor, and taught school in New Jersey before moving to Philadelphia in 1845. He worked there as a tailor until 1853 when he embarked on travels through the Caribbean, Central America, Mexico, and California. Returning to Philadelphia in 1858, he became a member of the Garment Cutters' Association in 1863 and, after its dissolution in 1869, joined with several cutters to launch the KOL. He became the first master workman of KOL District Assembly 1 in 1873 and the first grand master workman of the KOL in 1878. In 1878 he ran unsuccessfully for Congress on the Greenback ticket. Stephens resigned his KOL post in 1879.

STRASSER, Adolph (1843-1939), was born in Hungary and immigrated to the United States about 1872. He became a cigarmaker, helped organize New York City cigar workers excluded from membership in the CMIU, and played a leading role in the United Cigarmakers. Strasser was a member of the International Workingmen's Association and, in 1874, helped organize the Social Democratic Workingmen's Party of North America, serving as its executive secretary. He was also a founder of the Economic and Sociological Club. In 1876 he was a delegate to the unity congress that organized the Workingmen's Party of the United States, and he aligned with the trade unionist faction of the party. During 1876 and 1877 he worked to establish a central organization of New York City trade unions, and his efforts culminated in the founding of the Amalgamated Trades and Labor Union of New York and Vicinity in the summer of 1877. Strasser was elected vice-president of the CMIU in 1876 and president in 1877 and successfully promoted the reorganization of the union in the late 1870s and early 1880s. After retiring as president in 1891, he continued to work for the CMIU as an organizer, auditor, and troubleshooter. In addition he served as an AFL lecturer, member of the Federation's legislative committee, and AFL arbitrator of jurisdictional disputes. He ended his labor career in 1914, becoming a real estate agent in Buffalo, and in 1919 he moved to Florida.

STRONG, Philip (b. 1852), born in New York, worked as a cooper in Chicago where he became a member of Coopers' International Union of North America (CIUNA) 2, serving as its secretary in 1895. He was general secretary of the CIUNA from 1892 to about 1897. He was still working as a cooper in Chicago as late as 1900.

SULLIVAN, James Henry (b. 1861), was born in Lenox, Mass., attended school in Westfield, Mass., and lived in England for a period before settling in Holyoke, Mass. There he was a textile worker and then a painter. He joined KOL Local Assembly 5005 in 1882 and served on the city council in 1886. About 1892 he moved to Springfield, Mass., where he helped organize Brotherhood of Painters and Decorators of America (BPDA) 257, serving as its secretary in 1894. Beginning in the late 1880s Sullivan also lived and worked intermittently in Baltimore, joining BPDA 1 there in 1893. In 1894 he was elected general president of the eastern faction of the divided BPDA, an office he held until 1898. By the end of the decade he had taken up residence in Baltimore where he was business agent for the Baltimore Federation of Building Trades and an AFL organizer. He also continued to be active in the painters' union in Baltimore at least until World War I, and he manufactured emblem buttons and badges there between 1917 and 1921.

SULLIVAN, James William (1848-1938), a printer from Carlisle, Pa., moved to New York City in 1882 after serving his apprenticeship in Philadelphia. He worked for the *New York Times* and the *New York World* and joined International Typographical Union (ITU) 6, becoming a leading figure in the ITU. He was a strong supporter of land reform and edited the *Standard* with Henry George from 1887 to 1889. From 1889 to 1892 he was managing editor of the *Twentieth Century.* A close associate of SG, he participated in the Social Reform Club and the People's Institute of the Ethical Culture Society. He became a leading advocate of the initiative and referendum, traveling to Switzerland in 1888 to gather information for his *Direct Legislation by the Citizenship through the Initiative and Referendum* (New York, 1892), which appeared in several subsequent editions through the mid-1890s. Sullivan served with SG in the National Civic Federation, accompanied him to Europe in 1909, helped to edit the *American Federationist,* and served with SG on the Advisory Commission of the Council of National Defense during World War I. He opposed labor movement involvement in socialist political activities, publishing *Socialism as an Incubus on the American Labor Movement* (New York, 1909) and a report critical of English socialism (in Commission on Foreign Inquiry, National Civic Federation, *The Labor Situation in Great Britain and France* [New York, 1919]).

TAKANO, Fusataro (1868-1904), was born in Nagasaki and attended lower school in Tokyo before moving to Yokohama where he worked in his uncle's store and attended commercial school. In 1886 he came to San Francisco and in 1890 he helped organize the Shokkō Giyū-kai (Fraternal Society of Workers) to study American trade union methods with an eye to labor problems attending Japan's industrialization. He returned to Japan in 1896 and became editor of the English-language *Japan Advertiser.* In 1897 he helped reconstitute the Shokkō Giyū-kai in Japan and in the same year was appointed secretary of the new Rōdō Kumiai Kisei-kai (Society for the Promotion of Trade Unions). He founded Kyōeisha, a consumers' cooperative, in 1899. In 1900, discouraged by the Japanese government's opposition to trade unions, he traveled to North China as a correspondent for the *Japan Advertiser.* He died there four years later.

THOMAS, Llewelyn R. (1859-1935), born in Catasauqua, Pa., worked as a patternmaker and draftsman in Pittsburgh, where by 1894 he was a member of the local union of the Pattern Makers' National League of North America (from 1898, the Pattern Makers' League of North America). He served as president of the national union (1894-1902), secretary-treasurer of the Metal Trades Federation of North America (1901-6), and editor of the *Iron City Trade Journal* (1908). Thomas was a commissioner of conciliation with the U.S. Department of Labor from 1917 into the 1930s.

TILLETT, Benjamin (1860-1943), a British seaman and dock worker, helped organize the Tea Operatives' and General Labourers' Association in 1887 and was a leader of the London dock strike of 1889. In its aftermath he was a founder of the Dock, Wharf, Riverside, and General Labourers' Union of Great Britain and Ireland and its general secretary until 1922. In 1910 he helped organize the National Transport Workers' Federation. He was a member of the Parliamentary

Committee of the TUC (1892-95) and a founder of the Independent Labour party in 1893, serving on its executive council during its first year. In 1900 he helped establish the Labour Representation Committee, direct predecessor to the Labour party. Tillett stood unsuccessfully for Parliament four times before serving as a Labour Member from 1917 to 1924 and 1929 to 1931.

TOBIN, John F. (1855-1919), was born in Guelph, Ont., where he attended school and apprenticed in the shoe trade at the age of fourteen. He worked in various Canadian cities before moving to the United States in 1881, where he worked chiefly in Buffalo and Rochester, N.Y. He first joined the Knights of St. Crispin when he was sixteen and joined the KOL in 1884 and the Boot and Shoe Workers' International Union of America (BSWIU) in 1890. Blacklisted because of his union activities, he was a self-employed cobbler in Rochester for a time, and later moved to Quincy, Mass. When the BSWIU and the Lasters' Protective Union of America amalgamated to form the Boot and Shoe Workers' Union in 1895, Tobin was elected general president, holding the office until his death.

TRACY, Thomas F. (1861-1916), was born in Massachusetts and worked as a cigarmaker in Boston. President of CMIU 97 in 1894, he also served as a member of the Massachusetts State Federation of Labor's Legislative Committee. He was a vice-president of the CMIU from 1896 until his death. In 1910 Tracy moved to Washington, D.C., to serve as secretary-treasurer of the AFL's Union Label Trades Department, a position he also held until his death.

TURNER, Frederick (b. 1846), general secretary-treasurer of the KOL from 1883 to 1886, was born in England and immigrated to the United States in 1856, settling in Philadelphia. A Civil War veteran, he became a goldbeater and helped organize local assemblies of the KOL in that trade in Philadelphia, New York, and Boston in 1873 and 1874. As a result of his organizing activities, he was blacklisted in 1877 and became a grocer. He served as financial secretary and recording secretary of Pennsylvania District Assembly 1 and from 1880 was a member of the Knights' General Executive Board. After the Order divided the secretary-treasurer's position in 1886, Turner served as general treasurer until 1888.

TURNER, John (b. 1864), was a British labor leader. A grocery worker from Essex, he joined the Shop Hours League in 1884 and became financial secretary and a member of the executive board of the Socialist League in 1886, serving as its delegate to the 1889 Paris socialist congress. In 1889 he founded the United Shop Assistants'

Union (merged with the National Union of Shop Assistants, Warehousemen, and Clerks in 1898) and served as its president. After the 1898 merger, Turner was the new union's first organizer and, from 1912 through at least 1924, its general secretary. He lectured in the United States in 1896 under the auspices of state and local labor organizations.

VALESH, Eva McDonald (1866-1956), a printer, journalist, and labor organizer, was born in Maine and moved to Minneapolis in 1877. She worked for the *Spectator,* had become a member of the International Typographical Union (ITU) and the KOL by the 1880s, and headed the labor department of the *St. Paul Globe,* writing a series on working women for that paper in 1887 and 1888. She became the manager of the industrial department of the *Minneapolis Tribune* and in 1891 was a state lecturer and treasurer for the Minnesota Farmers' Alliance and a lecturer for the National Farmers' Alliance. In 1891 she married Frank Valesh, a state deputy commissioner of labor. About 1898, she moved to New York City where she worked for the *New York Journal,* became a member of ITU 6, and served as an AFL organizer. From 1900 to 1909 she was managing editor of the *American Federationist,* and she served in the women's section of the National Civic Federation in 1909. She subsequently edited the *American Club Woman* magazine and for about twenty-seven years was a proofreader for the *New York Times* prior to her retirement in 1952.

WARD, William E., Jr., (1862-1925?), born in New Jersey, was a member of Brotherhood of Painters and Decorators of America (BPDA) 169 of Jersey City, N.J. He served as a general vice-president of the western faction of the BPDA from 1896 until 1897 and as an organizer for the brotherhood in New Jersey.

WATCHORN, Robert (1858-1944), an English-born miner, immigrated to the United States in 1880, settling in Ohio. He worked as a miner in Pennsylvania and New York, became a member of the KOL, and in 1888 was elected president of the Pittsburgh division of KOL National Trades Assembly 135. He was elected secretary-treasurer of the newly formed United Mine Workers of America in 1890, but resigned in 1891 to become chief clerk to Pennsylvania Governor Robert Pattison. He helped secure passage of the 1893 amendments to the Pennsylvania factory inspection law and was appointed that year as the first chief factory inspector of the state. In 1895 he accepted a position as an inspector with the U.S. Bureau of Immigration. He became commissioner of immigration at Ellis Island in 1905, retaining that office until 1909. In 1910 Watchorn moved to California where he became treasurer and a director of the Union Oil Co. Moving to Oklahoma in 1913, he purchased substantial holdings in several oil companies, forming his own company in the 1930s, and engaged in extensive philanthropic activities.

WEBER, Frank Joseph (1849-1943), was born in Milwaukee and became a sailor on the Great Lakes at an early age, joining a seamen's union in 1868 and subsequently becoming a member of the KOL. He helped organize the Milwaukee Federated Trades Council (FTC) in 1887 and the following year organized local unions of cargo handlers and carpenters. He was the FTC's chief officer as president in 1893 and as general secretary from 1902 to 1934. In 1893 he was instrumental in the formation of the Wisconsin State Federation of Labor, serving until 1917 as its chief officer (president, 1893; state organizer, 1894-1917). He also worked as an AFL organizer for several years beginning in the mid-1890s. Weber was active in the People's party and served as a socialist assemblyman in the Wisconsin legislature for six terms betweeen 1907 and 1925.

WEISMANN, Henry (1863-1935), was born in Bavaria and immigrated to the United States, settling in San Francisco at the age of eighteen. He became a member of Burnette Haskell's anarchist International Workingmen's Association (known as the Red International) and worked with Haskell in publishing the *Truth* from 1882 to 1884. Weismann joined KOL Progressive Assembly 2999 in 1884 and helped found the Representative Council of the Federated Trades and Labor Organizations of the Pacific Coast. While serving as president of the Anti-Coolie League, Weismann was imprisoned for several months on charges of possessing explosives. Following his release he organized San Francisco locals for the Journeymen Bakers' National Union of the United States and helped organize coast seamen and brewers as well. He moved to New York City in 1890 and the following year became editor of the official organs of the Journeymen Bakers' and Confectioners' International Union (JBCIU), the *Bakers' Journal* and the *Deutsch-Amerikanische Bäcker-Zeitung;* the union merged the two publications in 1895. The JBCIU combined the offices of editor and international secretary in 1895 and selected Weismann to fill the joint position. He remained the chief executive officer until resigning in 1897 and leaving the labor movement. He subsequently became active in Republican politics in King's Co. (Brooklyn) and Suffolk Co., N.Y. In 1903 he graduated from the Brooklyn Law School and acted as a lawyer for the Boss Bakers' Association. From 1915 to 1918 he was president of the New York State and Brooklyn branches of the

German-American Alliance. After 1918 he continued to practice law as the senior member of the firm of Weismann and Holland.

WHITE, Henry (1866-1927), general secretary of the United Garment Workers of America (UGWA) from 1895 to 1904, was born in Baltimore and lived in Rochester, N.Y., before moving to New York City about 1886. In 1891 he helped form the UGWA, and he was a leader in the New York City clothing cutters' union that became UGWA 4. During the early 1890s White was active in the New York City labor movement as secretary (1891-92) of the short-lived New York (City) Federation of Labor; in 1893 he was secretary of his local union, a member of the executive board of UGWA locals 4, 5, and 28 (clothing cutters' unions), a member of the General Executive Board of the UGWA, and the UGWA's general auditor. He became the editor of the UGWA's official organ, the *Garment Worker*, in 1893, retaining that position until 1903 and continuing as the editor of the journal's successor, the *Weekly Bulletin of the Clothing Trades*, until 1904. In 1904 he resigned as general secretary in a dispute over his intervention to end a general strike against the open shop. He subsequently continued his career as an editor and writer on economic and labor issues, particularly for the garment trade publication the *Clothing Designer and Manufacturer* and its successor, the *Clothing Trade Journal*.

WILSON, Duncan Douglas (1858-1915), a machinist from Birmingham, Ala., was born in Scotland where he apprenticed in his trade and joined the Amalgamated Society of Engineers. He worked as a machinist on British merchant ships for nine years before settling in Alabama in 1885. There he became active in the Birmingham Trades Council, was elected to the General Executive Board of the International Association of Machinists (IAM) in 1891, and was elected to the state legislature on an independent labor ticket, serving from 1894 to 1895. In 1895 he was elected IAM grand foreman (title changed to vice-president in 1899) and remained in this office until 1901. He was editor of the IAM's organ, the *Monthly Journal of the International Association of Machinists* (after 1902 the *Machinists' Monthly Journal*), from 1891 until his death.

WINES, Abner G. (1850-1917?), an Ohio native, was a St. Louis printer and a member of International Typographical Union (ITU) 8. From 1893 to 1896 he was secretary-treasurer of the ITU and editor of the *Typographical Journal*. In 1898 he became a salesman for a St. Louis type foundry.

WOOD, James, was born in Australia. He immigrated to the United States and resided for many years in Binghamton, N.Y., where he was a member of CMIU 218. He moved to Cincinnati in 1897. He served as a CMIU vice-president (1893-1905) and as one of its organizers.

WOODS, Samuel (1846-1915), a British miners' leader, was president of the Lancashire and Cheshire Miners' Federation (1881-1915) and vice-president of the Miners' Federation of Great Britain (1889-1909). He served as secretary of the Parliamentary Committee of the TUC from 1894 to 1904, and as a Liberal/Labour Member of Parliament (1892-95, 1897-1900).

WRIGHT, Carroll Davidson (1840-1909), born in New Hampshire, studied law in Vermont and moved to Boston in 1871 after service in the Civil War. He was elected to the Massachusetts Senate as a Republican in 1871 and served as chief of the Massachusetts Bureau of Statistics of Labor from 1873 to 1888 and as commissioner of the U.S. Bureau of Labor (after 1888, the Department of Labor) from 1885 to 1905. During the last four years of his life he was president of Clark College.

ORGANIZATIONS

The American AGENTS' Association, a union of traveling salesmen and other canvassing agents, organized and affiliated with the AFL in 1895. It succeeded the American Agents Union, founded in 1893. Its charter was revoked in 1900.

The Journeymen Bakers' National Union of the United States was organized in 1886, participated in the formation of the AFL that year, and was chartered by the AFL in 1887. In 1890 it adopted the name Journeymen BAKERS' and Confectioners' International Union of America and, in 1903, it became the Bakery and Confectionery Workers' International Union of America.

The Journeymen Barbers' National Union, founded in 1887 by unions formerly affiliated with the KOL, affiliated with the AFL in 1888 as the Journeymen BARBERS' International Union of America.

Responding to an AFL invitation, delegates from local bicycle workers' unions met in December 1896 in Cincinnati to organize the International Union of BICYCLE Workers; it received an AFL charter before the end of the year. The union was renamed the International Union of Bicycle Workers and Allied Mechanics in 1898, and the International Association of Allied Metal Mechanics in 1900. It merged with the International Association of Machinists in 1904.

The National Boilermakers' and Helpers' Protective and Benevolent Union organized in 1881 and in 1884 changed its name to the International Brotherhood of Boiler Makers and Iron Ship Builders' Protective and Benevolent Union of the United States and Canada. In 1887 it affiliated with the AFL as the International Brotherhood of Boiler Makers. It withdrew in 1893 and merged with the National Brotherhood of Boiler Makers to form the Brotherhood of BOILER Makers and Iron Ship Builders of America, which affiliated with the AFL in 1896. In 1906 the boiler makers adopted the name International Brotherhood of Boiler Makers, Iron Ship Builders and Helpers of America.

The Boot and Shoe Workers' International Union of America (BSWIU) was organized in 1889 by seceding locals of shoemakers' National Trade Assembly (NTA) 216 of the KOL; it affiliated that year with the AFL. In 1895 the BSWIU merged with another AFL affiliate, the Lasters' Protective Union of America, and with the remnant of NTA 216 to form the BOOT and Shoe Workers' Union.

The National Union of Brewers of the United States organized in 1886 and affiliated with the AFL as the Brewers' National Union in March 1887. Later that year it changed its name to the National Union of the United BREWERY Workmen of the United States, and it became the International Union of the United Brewery Workmen of America in 1903. After a prolonged series of jurisdictional disputes the AFL revoked the union's charter in 1907; it reinstated the Brewers in 1908. In 1917 the union became the International Union of United Brewery and Soft Drink Workers of America, and in 1918, the International Union of United Brewery, Flour, Cereal, and Soft Drink Workers of America.

Delegates to the AFL's 1896 convention from directly affiliated local unions of butcher workmen agreed to establish a national organization in the retail and meat packing branches of their industry. The Amalgamated Meat Cutters and BUTCHER Workmen of North America was organized and chartered by the AFL in 1897.

The Brotherhood of Carpenters and Joiners of America was organized in 1881 and was chartered by the AFL in 1887. In 1888 the Brotherhood and the United Order of American Carpenters and Joiners merged, forming the United Brotherhood of CARPENTERS and Joiners of America.

The Cigar Makers' National Union of America was organized in 1864 and changed its name to the CIGAR Makers' International Union of America in 1867. It participated in the formation of the FOTLU in 1881. The following year, seceding New York City locals formed the Cigarmakers' Progressive Union of America; the Progressives rejoined the International in 1886. The AFL chartered the CMIU in 1887.

The Retail CLERKS' National Protective Association of America was organized in 1890 as an AFL affiliate. It changed its name to the Retail Clerks' International Protective Association in 1899.

The Coopers' International Union organized in 1870 and in 1881 participated in the formation of the FOTLU. After a period of dormancy in the 1880s, it reorganized as the COOPERS' International Union of North America in 1890 and the following year affiliated with the AFL.

The National Brotherhood of ELECTRICAL Workers of America was organized in 1891 and affiliated with the AFL in the same year. In 1899 it became the International Brotherhood of Electrical Workers.

The American FLINT Glass Workers' Union of North America was organized in 1878 by locals formerly affiliated with the KOL. It affiliated with the AFL in 1887.

The Gewerkschafts Union der Möbel-Arbeiter von Nord Amerika (Furniture Workers' Union of North America) was organized in 1873, and in 1882 it changed its name to the International FURNITURE Workers' Union of America. It affiliated with the AFL in 1887 and in 1895 merged with the Machine Wood Workers' International Union of America to form the Amalgamated Wood Workers' International Union of America.

The Tailors' National Protective Union joined with members of KOL Garment Cutters' National Trade Assembly 231 in 1891 to form the United GARMENT Workers of America. The new union affiliated with the AFL the same year.

The Independent Druggist Ware Glass Blowers' League (founded in 1867) divided in 1884 into the eastern or Green Bottle Blowers' League, and the western or Green Glass Workers' League, and the two organizations affiliated with the KOL in 1886 as district assemblies 149 and 143, respectively. They merged as National Trade Assembly 143 in 1889. In 1891 the organization withdrew from the KOL and formed the United Green Glass Workers' Association of the United States and Canada. It changed its name to the GLASS Bottle Blowers' Association of the United States and Canada in 1895, and affiliated with the AFL in 1899.

The United HATTERS of North America was created in January 1896 by the merger of the International Trade Association of Hat Finishers of America and the National Hat Makers' Association of the United States; it received its AFL charter in September 1896.

The Journeymen Horseshoers' National Union of the United States was organized in 1874. It changed its name to the International Union of Journeymen HORSESHOERS of the United States and Canada in 1892 and affiliated with the AFL in 1893.

The Waiters' and Bartenders' National Union organized and affiliated with the AFL in 1891. The following year it changed its name to the HOTEL and Restaurant Employees' National Alliance and in 1898 to the Hotel and Restaurant Employees' International Alliance and Bartenders' International League of America.

The National Amalgamated Association of IRON and Steel Workers of the United States was organized in 1876 and in 1887 was chartered by the AFL. In 1897 it changed its name to the National Amalgamated Association of Iron, Steel, and Tin Workers and in 1908 dropped "National" from its name.

The National Union of Iron Molders (after 1874 the IRON Molders' Union of North America) was organized in 1859 and in 1881 participated in the formation of the FOTLU. It was chartered by the AFL in 1887. In 1907 it changed its name to the International Molders' Union of North America.

The Building LABORERS' International Protective Union of America was founded in 1887 and affiliated with the AFL in 1898; it was suspended in 1900 for non-payment of its per capita tax and dropped from the AFL rolls in 1901. In 1907 it joined with a small number of seceding locals of the International Hod Carriers and Building Laborers' Union of America to form the Building Laborers' Union of New England.

The locomotive engineers organized the Brotherhood of the Footboard in 1863. In 1864 the organization became the Brotherhood of LOCOMOTIVE Engineers.

The Brotherhood of LOCOMOTIVE Firemen organized in 1873, and in 1878 merged under its name with the International Firemen's Union. In 1906 it adopted the name Brotherhood of Locomotive Firemen and Enginemen.

The Lumber Handlers of the Great Lakes was founded in 1892 and received its AFL charter in 1893 as the National Longshoremen's

Association of the United States. In 1895 it was renamed the International LONGSHOREMEN'S Association. It became the International Longshoremen, Marine, and Transport Workers' Association in 1901, and the International Longshoremen's Association again in 1908.

The International MACHINISTS' Union of America (IMUA) was established in 1891 and chartered that year by the AFL. The AFL's 1895 convention revoked the IMUA's charter because the International Association of Machinists had affiliated with the Federation earlier in the year.

The Order of United Machinists and Mechanical Engineers of America organized in 1888 and the following year changed its name to the National Association of Machinists. It changed its name to the International Association of MACHINISTS in 1891 and in 1895 affiliated with the AFL.

The METAL Polishers', Buffers', and Platers' International Union of North America was organized in 1892 and chartered by the AFL the same year. In 1896 it merged with the United Brotherhood of Brass and Composition Metal Workers, Polishers, and Buffers to form the Metal Polishers', Buffers', Platers', and Brass Workers' Union of North America.

The Western Federation of MINERS, a regional, industrial union that claimed jurisdiction over mine, mill, and smelter workers in the hard rock mining industry, was founded in 1893 and affiliated with the AFL in July 1896. It paid no dues to the AFL after December 1896, however, and in 1898 it disaffiliated; it subsequently helped organize the Western Labor Union (renamed American Labor Union in 1902). In 1905 it participated in the formation of the Industrial Workers of the World, but it withdrew three years later and reaffiliated with the AFL in 1911. In 1916 it changed its name to the International Union of Mine, Mill, and Smelter Workers.

The National Progressive Union of Miners and Mine Laborers and KOL National Trade Assembly (NTA) 135 united in 1890 to form the United MINE Workers of America (UMWA), which affiliated with both the AFL and the KOL. The merger recognized the Progressives and NTA 135 as equal partners in the UMWA. NTA 135 retained its name, structure, and practice of secrecy, and officers' titles such as president and master workman were often used interchangeably. Gradually the UMWA outgrew these residual divisions, and in 1894 the Knights' General Assembly excluded NTA 135 on the grounds that it was dominated and controlled by the UMWA.

Several northern Michigan iron miners' locals combined in 1895 to form the Northern Mineral MINE Workers' Progressive Union (NMMWPU), which received an AFL charter in 1895. The NMMWPU was absorbed by the Western Federation of Miners in 1904.

Though the National League of Musicians of the United States repeatedly rejected affiliation with the AFL, many of its locals, along with independent musicians' unions, affiliated directly with the AFL. In 1896 these founded the American Federation of MUSICIANS; the union affiliated with the AFL the same year.

The National League of MUSICIANS of the United States was founded in 1886. It held its last convention in 1902.

The Brotherhood of PAINTERS and Decorators of America (BPDA) was organized in 1887, affiliating with the AFL the same year. In 1891 the union withdrew from the Federation, but it reaffiliated the following year. In 1894 the BPDA split between western and eastern factions headquartered, respectively, in Lafayette, Ind., and Baltimore. The eastern faction adopted the name Brotherhood of Painters, Decorators, and Paperhangers of America in 1899, and the two factions merged under that name in 1900.

In 1887 members of nine KOL local assemblies organized the PATTERN Makers' National League of North America (renamed Pattern Makers' League of North America in 1898), which received an AFL charter in 1894.

In 1889 representatives of KOL District Assembly 85 and the moribund International Association of Journeymen Plumbers, Steam, and Gas Fitters founded the United Association of Journeymen PLUMBERS, Gas Fitters, Steam Fitters, and Steam Fitters' Helpers of the United States and Canada (UAJP). The UAJP affiliated with the AFL in 1897. In 1913 the AFL required that the International Association of Steam and Hot Water Fitters and Helpers, also an AFL affiliate, surrender its charter and join the UAJP. The merged organization was known as the United Association of Plumbers and Steam Fitters of the United States and Canada; it was renamed the United Association of Journeymen Plumbers and Steam Fitters of the United States and Canada in 1921.

The International Printing Pressmen's Union of North America was founded in 1889. It affiliated with the AFL in 1895 and in 1897 changed its name to the International Printing PRESSMEN'S and Assistants' Union of North America.

The Order of Railway Telegraphers of North America was founded in 1886, reorganized as the Order of RAILROAD Telegraphers of North America in 1891, and chartered by the AFL in 1900.

The Brotherhood of Railroad Brakemen of the Western Hemisphere organized in 1883. In 1886 it changed its name to the Brotherhood of Railroad Brakemen and in 1890 to the Brotherhood of RAILROAD Trainmen.

The Conductors' Union, organized in 1868, changed its name to the Conductors' Brotherhood at its first annual convention in 1869. In 1878 the union became the Order of RAILWAY Conductors of America.

The Brotherhood of RAILWAY Trackmen of America was formed in 1896 when the Brotherhood of Railway Track Foremen of America (founded 1891) reorganized itself to include white laborers. Granted an AFL charter in 1900, the union was subsequently renamed the International Brotherhood of Maintenance of Way Employes in 1902 and the United Brotherhood of Maintenance of Way Employes and Railway Shop Laborers in 1918. The union was suspended from the AFL between 1919 and 1922.

Eugene Debs played a leading role in creating the American RAILWAY Union in early 1893; the organization was formally launched in Chicago later that year. The ARU's defeat in the Pullman strike in the summer of 1894 brought on its decline, and it disbanded in June 1897.

The National Seamen's Union of America organized in 1892 as a federation of several regional sailors' unions including the Sailors' Union of the Pacific, the Lake Seamen's Union, the Gulf Coast Seamen's and Firemen's Union, and the Atlantic Coast Seamen's Union. The following year it affiliated with the AFL and in 1895 changed its name to the International SEAMEN'S Union of America.

The National Cotton Mule SPINNERS' Association of America was established in 1887, affiliating with the AFL in 1889. It became the National Spinners' Association of America (NSAA) in 1898 and in 1901 merged with the United Textile Workers of America (UTWA), though retaining autonomy within this organization. The NSAA became the International Spinners' Union in 1906; in 1914 it withdrew from the UTWA and, after fruitless efforts at reconciliation, lost its AFL charter in 1919.

The Journeymen STONECUTTERS' Association of North America organized in 1887 and was chartered by the AFL in 1907.

The STOVE Mounters' International Union was organized in 1892 and received an AFL charter in 1894.

The Amalgamated Association of STREET Railway Employes of America was established in 1892 and affiliated with the AFL in 1893. It absorbed the Brotherhood of Surface Car Employes in 1894. In 1903 it changed its name to the Amalgamated Association of Street and Electric Railway Employes of America.

The Journeymen Tailors' National Union of the United States, composed of custom tailors, was organized in 1883 and was chartered by the AFL in 1887. It changed its name in 1889 to the Journeymen TAILORS' Union of America and in 1913 to the Tailors' Industrial Union. The following year it merged with the Amalgamated Clothing Workers of America (ACWA) but in 1915 seceded from the ACWA and reassumed the name Journeymen Tailors' Union of America.

The National Union of TEXTILE Workers of America was organized in 1891, affiliated with the AFL in 1896, and changed its name to International Union of Textile Workers in 1900. The following year it merged with the American Federation of Textile Operatives and several AFL federal labor unions to form the United Textile Workers of America.

The National Alliance of THEATRICAL Stage Employes of the United States was organized in 1893 and affiliated with the AFL in 1894. It became the National Alliance of Theatrical Stage Employes of the United States and Canada in 1899, the International Alliance of Theatrical Stage Employes of the United States and Canada in 1902, and the International Alliance of Theatrical Stage Employes and Moving Picture Machine Operators of the United States and Canada in 1915.

The National TOBACCO Workers' Union of America was organized in St. Louis in 1895, and chartered by the AFL in the same year. It became the Tobacco Workers' International Union in 1898.

The TRADES Union Congress of Great Britain, the central organization of that country's trade union movement, was founded in 1868.

The National Typographical Union was organized in 1852 by a group of locals that had held national conventions in 1850 and 1851 under the name Journeymen Printers of the United States. In 1869 it adopted the name International TYPOGRAPHICAL Union (ITU). Although ITU members participated in the formation of the FOTLU in 1881 and in the organizing of the AFL in 1886, the union did not affiliate with the Federation until 1888.

The Machine Wood Workers' International Union of America organized in 1890 and affiliated with the AFL the same year. It merged with the International Furniture Workers' Union of America in 1895 to form the Amalgamated WOOD Workers' International Union of America, which merged with the United Brotherhood of Carpenters and Joiners of America in 1912.

INDEX

Names of persons or organizations for whom there are glossary entries are followed by an asterisk.

Italics indicate the location of detailed information. While this index is not cumulative, it does include references to substantive annotations in earlier volumes that are relevant to this one but that are not repeated here; these appear first in the index entry. The reference to Alva Adams's annotation in volume two, for example, appears in this index as *2:88n.*